AN ENTERTAINING TALE OF QUADRUPEDS

AN ENTERTAINING TALE OF QUADRUPEDS

Translation and Commentary

Nick Nicholas / George Baloglou

COLUMBIA UNIVERSITY PRESS NEW YORK

Columbia University Press
Publishers Since 1893
New York Chichester, West Sussex

Library of Congress Cataloging-in-Publication Data
Diåegåesis paidiophrastos peri tåon tetrapodåon zåoåon. English
An Entertaining tale of quadrapeds / translation and commentary, Nick Nicholas, George Baloglou.
p. cm. — (Records of Western civilization)
Translation of a late Byzantine Greek poem.
Includes bibliographical references (p.) and index.
ISBN 0-231-12760-X — ISBN 0-231-12761-8 (pbk.)
1. Animals—Poetry. I. Nicholas, Nick. II. Baloglou, George. III. Title. IV. Series.
PA5310.D47E5313 2003
881′.02—dc21 2003004917

♾

Columbia University Press books are printed on permanent and durable acid-free paper.
Printed in the United States of America
c 10 9 8 7 6 5 4 3 2 1
p 10 9 8 7 6 5 4 3 2 1

In memory of
Phaedon Koukoules
(1881–1956),
a twentieth-century Byzantine

CONTENTS

FOREWORD

> The sun had climbed halfway up the eastern sky. It was still early in the day, but a group of elephants had already gathered by the river and were drawing up water in long drafts in their trunks to quench their thirst. Then they ambled one by one over to an enormous tree whose foliage formed so vast a roof that all twenty-eight giants could rest in the shade beneath. A tribe of green monkeys frolicked in the sweeping branches, swinging down from their tails and ranting and raving at the uninvited guests below. They barked and twanged and hollered in every possible pitch, according to their size. Suddenly, the pachyderms, too, were growling and trumpeting. The squad got up, circled furiously around the tree, then calmed down again. What had disturbed them was a second group of elephants passing by, a short distance away, on their way to the water. The monkeys kept railing, but without the slightest effect on the elephants.
>
> —R. Künkel, *Elephants*

Elephants normally pay no attention to what monkeys say, yet this is what happens in the poem before you. Some six centuries ago, the story goes, a monkey's calculated attack insulted a proud elephant and brought an end to an unusual gathering of animals—a tumultuous peace conference, most memorable for its "revolutionary" ending. The herbivores, unwilling to attend the implausible conference at first, ended up slaughtering and chasing off their carnivore oppressors.

The poem is written in Greek: neither the lively tongue of present-day Greece nor the lapidary language of classical Greece but rather a hectic mixture of the two. It was penned by someone who placed his trust in God rather than nation or reason. Not that the poet was a preacher—just someone for whom religion, and Orthodox Christianity in particular, was the only immutable truth in a transitory world. His world was rapidly changing, with the Byzantine Empire increasingly squeezed between East and West: Constantinople, where the poem was likely composed, was a shadow of its former self in the fourteenth century, and its "Roman" residents had learned to live with the Turks and the Latins at their doorstep.

Did the poet hold any hope for a change for the better, despite these rather unfavorable conditions? Even if he did, he has failed to tell us. More likely he was disappointed about his circumstances, for reasons we can only guess. An indignant dissident rather than an inspired visionary, he bequeathed us this vibrant call piercing through the decline around him, to be discerned to our day through the animals' rambunctious debates and testimonies on life's sweet and fleeting nature.

If very few people know of this *Entertaining Tale of Quadrupeds* today—let alone have much time for it—could the situation have been any different at the time the poem was written? Could this poem have been a best-seller (or rather, "best-reciter") of its day? Did monks, courtiers, or youngsters spend pleasant evenings debating its meaning and praising its humor over a few goblets of wine, as relief from those bleak times? We cannot expect answers to such questions from authors who have not even given us their names, or from scribes who copied them liberally, emending them to their taste. But works such as these were not taken seriously, and the majority of them that failed to make the transition to print were consigned to oblivion.

As a result, the *Tale* and many other medieval Greek works had been forgotten by the time the modern Greek state was established in 1830. And as the new state was more interested in promoting past glories than recent disappointments, the first scholars who bothered to look at those obscure manuscripts written in "Barbarous Greek" were not citizens of the new kingdom but two Western Europeans, Émile Legrand and Wilhelm Wagner, in the 1870s (not withstanding the pioneering work of scholars such as Dimitrios Mavrofrydis and Konstantinos Sathas). Their work has gradually borne fruit, and in the last few decades there has been an explosion of research on medieval vernacular Greek language and literature. Still, this has been mostly confined to the academic sphere; even in Greece such works were until recently absent from the school curriculum. And many specialists would dispute their interest, particularly as literature, for a lay audience.

Our book, offering the *Tale*'s first translation into English, began as a challenge to this concept: we felt that the sarcastic animal speeches remain entertaining six centuries after they were composed, transporting the reader to an era where people's lives and animals' lives were more closely intertwined than they are today. We also believe that the author wrote his narrative with a lot more finesse than has usually been assumed. At a deeper level, we have found on the long way to publication that the poem reveals to us a lot about the structure of the society that produced it, its relation to other works of Greek literature, and the arduous journey of the Greek language through the centuries. Such issues are examined in the introduction, the appendices, and the Commentary and should be of interest, we hope, to both the specialist and the general reader.

This work includes an extensive introduction, intended to orient the nonspecialist reader into the social, literary, and linguistic environment that gave rise to the *Tale*. We also address some issues that have not been adequately covered until now in the literature: where and when the work was written, what influences it displays from other sources, what its literary characteristics are, and how it fits in with the long-standing debate on the orality of medieval vernacular works. Then we give our translation, in parallel with Papathomopoulos's edition (2002) of the text. We follow this with a Commentary, mostly dealing with the realia and allusions in the text, and some notes on textual issues. We conclude with three major appendices: the relationship between the *Tale* and the work to which it is most closely related, the *Book of Birds*; the evidence for historical allusion in the text; and issues involving the authenticity of various sections of the text.

As neither of us is a professional Byzantinist or philologist, a few words are due on the origins of this work. It all started with a trip that Baloglou took in the summer of 1990 around western Crete, where, inspired perhaps by his late evening walks around Chania's medieval Old Town, he purchased an anthology of medieval Greek poetry from a local bookstore (Koutsompogeras 1979). Being an animal lover and moved by a colorful form of Greek he did not even know existed, he fell in love with the poem, to the extent of posting a rough translation on the Internet during the 1993–94 academic year and recording it on tape in January 1997. Still, his greatest contribution to the future of the *Quadrupeds* was recruiting Nicholas to the project, thanks to the miracle of the Internet, in the summer of 1995: Nicholas added meter to a radically reworked translation (April 1996); gave a decidedly more scholarly flavor to the project; and, most importantly, dared to envision and insist on a book as the outcome. The project was largely set aside in 1997, as Nicholas undertook his doctoral dissertation on modern Greek dialectology at the University of Melbourne. On its completion, the project was resumed in 1999 and benefited greatly from Nicholas's access to the resources of the *Thesaurus Linguae Graecae* at the University of California, Irvine, where he was employed as a research associate.

Each of us inevitably approaches the poem from different directions. For Baloglou, who grew up in Greece reading newspapers in *katharevousa* and learning ancient Greek in high school, the poem's comfortably archaic language was almost a return to his youth and to a youthful dream of studying philology. More to the point, the *Tale* was for him a gateway to medieval Greek literature and its mixed, "adventurous" language. Nicholas, who was brought up in Australia and heard Cretan Greek at home, viewed those archaisms with some distaste; he was much more interested in the *Tale*'s modernisms, particularly as it tied in with his linguistic research on medieval and modern Greek.

Although not a single page has not been debated between us, it would be appropriate to mention that Nicholas did most of the writing and Baloglou most of the scrutinizing. We are pleasantly surprised at how the different perspectives (and ideologies) just mentioned have enriched, rather than undermined, our collaboration. This book has not ended up as either of us envisioned it—and is probably all the better for it. We learned a good deal from each other, as well as from several other researchers, to whom we would like to express our gratitude.

We are particularly indebted to **Manolis Papathomopoulos**, who had been preparing his new critical edition (Papathomopoulos 2002) of the *Tale* independently of us and with whom we got in touch only after completing the first draft of our work. Professor Papathomopoulos was generous enough to offer us his text for inclusion in our book and has offered us appreciable encouragement and constructive criticism when it was most welcome. We are privileged to have worked with him and to have offered him our own input on his critical edition.

We also owe a significant debt to **Vasiliki Tsiouni-Fatsi**, who gave us the first modern critical edition of the work (Tsiouni 1972), at a time when comparatively few resources were available. Though we have accepted Papathomopoulos's text as our base text, most of our work was done using Tsiouni's. In a curious twist of fate, Nicholas was doing research in Athens for three months before realizing that Tsiouni-Fatsi worked in the office one story above him. We fortunately realized this in time to engage in fruitful discussions with her.

Tassos Karanastassis, who has been a longtime collaborator of the *Dictionary of Vernacular Medieval Greek Literature* (*Λεξικό της Μεσαιωνικής Ελληνικής Δημώδους Γραμματείας*; Kriaras 1968–97), advised us on the translation and guided us in our first steps through his unparalleled knowledge of medieval Greek. He has repeatedly come to our aid on specific lexical issues, both within and beyond the scope of the currently published dictionary, and has been to us an exemplar of dedication to the study of language. We are also obligated to **Hans Eideneier**, who has published extensively on the *Tale* and other medieval Greek works, and to **Valentina Šandrovskaja**, whose translation of the poem into Russian (Šandrovskaja 1956a) has been a useful point of reference. Finally, we are deeply indebted to the scholarship of **Phaedon Koukoules**, whose monumental treatise, *Byzantines' Life and Civilization* (Koukoules 1947–55) has been an invaluable guide into the lives of people and beasts alike.

Additional thanks are due to **Eleftheria Giakoumaki**, acting director of the Center for the Compilation of the *Historical Dictionary of Modern Greek* (*Κέντρον Συντάξεως Ιστορικού Λεξικού της Νέας Ελληνικής*), who allowed us access to the center's archives in January 1996. We are grateful to **Judith Herrin**, who included a portion of our translation (the elephant's monologue) in her recently published *Medieval Miscellany* (Herrin 1999:90–91). **Antonia Giannouli** has been helpful far beyond the call of collegiality, particularly with regard to bibliographic matters. And a number of experts have helped or encouraged us in one way or another: Panagiotis Agapitos, Alexander Alexakis, Theodora Antonopoulou, †Robert Browning, Marie-Helene Congourdeau, Florin Curta, Mohamed el-Fers, Sysse Engberg, Theodoros Kaltsas, Neile Kirk,

George Kolias, Taxiarches Kolias, Elizabeth Kosmetatou, Nike Koutrakou, Julia Krivoruchko, Leonid Kulikov, Angeliki Laiou, Maria Pantelia, Marios Philippides, Andreas Rhoby, Nikos Sarantakos, Liliana Simeonova, Astrid Steiner-Weber, Notis Toufexis, Panos Vasiliou, and Diana Wright. Likewise, we acknowledge the interest and assistance of other friends, such as Dorina and Apostolos Doxiadis, Emily Farranto, Aleka Graikou and Agis Zamanis, Loukas Kanakis, Katia Margolis, Rachel Mines, John Morris, and Patrick Murphy.

In addition to the many scholars whose works are cited in our bibliography, we are grateful to the many individuals, amateur and professional alike, who have contributed, through the information treasury of the Internet, data that have proved useful in our study. For their promptness in making available to us references not online, we thank the **Interlibrary Loan staff** of the University of Melbourne; the University of California, Irvine; and the State University of New York, Oswego, where Baloglou has been teaching mathematics since 1988.

Finally, we thank the city of **Thessalonica**, the new "Queen of Cities," which provided a fitting backdrop to our collaboration.

Nick Nicholas (University of Melbourne)
George Baloglou (SUNY Oswego)

Publication of this work was supported through funding from the Australian Academy of the Humanities, the Office of Research and Sponsored Programs at SUNY Oswego, and the Kalypso and Grigorios Grigoriadis Foundation in memory of Byzantinist Iordanis Grigoriadis (1956–1999).

CONVENTIONS

We have gone against what seems to be the current mainstream in Anglophone Byzantine studies in using a Latinate rather than Hellenized transliteration. This may be at least partly attributed to our extensive use of the *Thesaurus Linguae Graecae*—which, being a classical corpus that has only latterly ventured into Byzantine territory, has stuck with Latin for its bibliographical information.

Parenthetical references to centuries are abbreviated with Roman numerals; for example, (vi A.D.) = (sixth century A.D.).

Greek texts are given with the orthography and punctuation with which they were published and have not been normalized. The reader should not be surprised to see some eccentricities, particularly in nineteenth-century accentuation (overuse of the grave) but also in the late twentieth century (abandonment of the grave). On rare occasions, we have not been able to view the primary source of a quotation; the orthography and punctuation used is then that of the secondary source (Kriaras 1968–97).

Alternative manuscript readings are denoted by { }; our clarifying interpolations are denoted by ⟨ ⟩.

Translations of both scholarly citations and source texts are our own unless otherwise indicated.

AN ENTERTAINING TALE OF QUADRUPEDS

INTRODUCTION

The Late Byzantine World

> I am very moved by one detail
> in the coronation at Vlachernai of John Kantakuzinos
> and Irini, daughter of Andronikos Asan.
> Because they had only a few precious stones
> (our afflicted empire was extremely poor)
> they wore artificial ones: numerous pieces of glass,
> red, green, or blue. I find
> nothing humiliating or undignified
> in those little pieces of colored glass.
> On the contrary, they seem
> a sad protest against
> the unjust misfortune of the couple being crowned,
> symbols of what they deserved to have,
> of what surely it was right that they should have
> at their coronation—a Lord John Kantakuzinos,
> a Lady Irini, daughter of Andronikos Asan.
>
> —Constantine Cavafy, "Of Colored Glass"

The Holy and Apostolic Roman Empire—restored by the grace of God and His Holy Mother to Michael VIII Palaeologus in the Year of Our Lord 1261, after fifty-seven years of captivity under the plundering Latins, when Constantinople, the Queen of Cities, became once more the capital of the One True Empire in the temporal world—had seen better decades than the 1340s. In the previous seventy years, a steadily shrinking Byzantine Empire—as history records its name—had been at war with Bulgaria, Serbia, several Turkish emirates, the mercenaries of the Catalan Company, the French Principality of Achaea, the Kingdom of Sicily, the Golden Horde, and the breakaway Greek Despotates of Epirus and Thessaly. The empire's hold on Asia Minor, its heartland, was tenuous and soon to be extinguished. Huge Greek-speaking erstwhile sections of the empire—such as Crete, Cyprus, the Ionian islands, and most of the Aegean—remained under Latin dominion, never to be restored to imperial rule. The empire had lost all economic self-sufficiency and become the battleground for the great trading republics of Italy, Venice and Genoa, whose blockades often held the citizens of the Queen of Cities at ransom. Its people had to endure Michael VIII's attempts to bully them into submission to the Vatican, the squandering of the empire's funds to pay off mercenaries and bribe allies, and the depredations of the imperial tax collectors. Its emperors endured challenges from the rival imperial family of the Lascarids, as well as from their own kin, culminating in the civil war between Andronicus II and his grandson Andronicus III (1321–1328). During the former's reign, the Byzantine navy was dissolved (Nicol 1993:108; Ostrogorsky 1968:483, 491), with the empire henceforth surrendering its maritime suzerainty to Venice and Genoa.[1]

When Andronicus III died in 1341, Byzantium seemed to be rallying somewhat, with northern Greece finally reintegrated into the empire. Within four months, however, it was once more embroiled in civil war. On one side stood John Cantacuzene, Andronicus's trusted advisor, who had assumed the role of regent. On the other stood Empress Anne of Savoy and Patriarch John Calecas. The real power behind the throne, though, was Grand Duke Alexius Apocaucus: a nouveau riche protégé of Cantacuzene, who turned against him when he saw that Cantacuzene would not further his advancement. The second civil war was devastating to the empire, not least because it divided Byzantine society to an unprecedented extent. Cantacuzene represented the rich landowning nobility, and it proved easy for Apocaucus in Constantinople to incite the mob against them. There was revolt against the aristocracy in Adrianople and other cities of Thrace and Macedonia. In 1342 Thessalonica was declared a republic—a development without precedent in Byzantine history—and was run for seven years as a commune by the Zealot party. Apocaucus, in his assumed role as champion of the people, lent his support to all these uprisings. The war between Cantacuzene and Apocaucus, however, was in the main fought on their behalf (hardly with altruistic motives in mind) by the Serbs and the Turks.[2]

By the time Cantacuzene won the first round of the war in 1347, the empire was devastated and spent—so much so that the Black Death, which visited it that year, seems to have made little impression on contemporary Byzantine historians (Nicol 1993:216–17). And neither was Cantacuzene's coronation in that same year an auspicious occasion. The imperial crown jewels had been pawned off by Anne of Savoy to Venice in 1343, never to be redeemed (Nicol 1993:199; Ostrogorsky 1968:526); it was for this reason that John Cantacuzene had to be crowned with colored glass. To add to the empire's humiliation, the coronation took place in the chapel of Vlachernae, as the cathedral of St. Sophia had not yet been fully repaired from the portentous earthquake of the previous year (Nicol 1993:215).

By 1364, the time *An Entertaining Tale of Quadrupeds* is set, the region's political picture had become much clearer. Only one state that mattered remained in the vicinity: the emirate founded by Osman (Othman) in Bithynia, across the Propontis from Constantinople and already developing into the Ottoman Empire. John VI Cantacuzene had abdicated in 1354, and John V Palaeologus, for whom Cantacuzene had acted as regent, was not equal to the task of rebuilding Byzantium.[3] John V resumed attempts—always against the strenuous opposition of his people—to submit the Orthodox Church to the Holy See, hoping to ensure in return a Western crusade against the Turks. In the process, he became the first emperor forced to travel to the courts of lesser, Western kings to solicit their help (Nicol 1993:264; Ostrogorsky 1968:537–38)—a far cry from the days when the Byzantine court would barely deign to marry off the niece of a usurper to the western Holy Roman Emperor.[4]

But the efforts of the mendicant emperor came to naught, just like each such effort before and after—most notably the nominal proclamation of church union at the 1439 Council of Florence (Nicol 1993:355–59). The defeat in 1371 of the Serbs on the Maritsa River meant the Ottomans were now unimpeded in Europe (Nicol 1993:275; Ostrogorsky 1968:541). By 1372, the Byzantine Empire, already constituting little more than the outer suburbs of Constantinople, was a vassal state of the Ottomans (Nicol 1993:277; Ostrogorsky 1968:541–42).[5] The emperors continued to beg, and the empire continued to shrink; it remained a political entity only at the mercy of the sultan. There were some lucky escapes for Byzantium, such as Sultan Bayezid's crushing defeat at the hands of Timur (Tamerlane) in 1402 and his successor Süleyman's generous amity to the emperor. Fifty-one years later, in 1453, the amity ran out, and Constantinople—the city the world knows today as Istanbul—fell to the twenty-one-year-old Mehmet II the Conqueror.

Vernacular Medieval Greek Literature

> The cultural debt of the East to the West was of a more unexpected order. The thirteenth-century Frankish conquerors of Constantinople and the Morea rendered to their Greek victims the same unintentional but signal literary service that the contemporary Mongol conquerors of China likewise inadvertently performed for the Chinese. . . . In a barbarian-ridden

> Orthodox Christendom the same cause produced the same effect on a minor scale, in the flowering of a popular lyric and epic poetry.
>
> —A. J. Toynbee, *A Study of History*

Simultaneously with this decline in Greek fortunes—and, it might be said, as a response to it (Browning 1980:189, 1983:72)—this same era, the Byzantine dynasty of the Palaeologi, saw a prodigious amount of writing; one may fairly speak of a Palaeologan literary renaissance (Runciman 1970).

Of course, the output of this renaissance was rather different from that of its Western counterpart a century or so later—or, for that matter, from what was being done in the West at the time. Byzantine literature in general enjoys a very low reputation, and despite the recent explosion in scholarly attention to Byzantium, the modern reader is still hard put to find any that appeals to modern tastes. Byzantine intellectual society was not structured in such a way as to encourage literary freedom and spontaneity. Literature was thus undertaken differently in Byzantium, and comparisons between the West and East are beside the point. To explore the reasons for this would take us far afield, but it is worth mentioning how keenly the weight of the classical tradition was felt by Theodore Metochites, a writer and statesman active in the fourteenth century:

> Πάντα ὡς εἰπεῖν φθάσαντ' ἄλλοις εἴληπται καὶ οὐδὲν ὅ τι λείπεται μεθύστερον νῦν ἡμῖν μοιρίδιον εἰς χρῆσιν τῇ φωνῇ.
>
> [Practically every topic has been taken by others already; nothing is now left as our share at this late date.][6]

The Christian East in general was a civilization that cherished stability over progress and tradition over innovation. The eminent Byzantinist Alexander Kazhdan has offered an epigrammatic statement of this difference: "The west, so it seems, was groping feverishly and painfully for the Kingdom of Heaven, whereas Byzantium nurtured the illusion of having attained it" (1984:285). So what Byzantines were writing could not resemble what Westerners were writing: the way its literature developed could not, by its very nature, find a counterpart in Dante or Chaucer.[7]

The Palaeologan literary renaissance employed the archaic Greek of the learned. But some literature undertaken during this time was written in a language much closer to the vernacular. Since the first century A.D., writing in vernacular Greek had been discouraged by the literary establishment, who felt that the quality of classical writing could only be emulated by imitating its language. From then on, anyone who thought they had something of consequence to say—including the Christian theologians, once they became part of the establishment—said it either in Attic Greek proper or in the only slightly more modern Koine (common) of the state, which was also pretty much the language of the Greek Bible. Whoever used a more humble language, such as writers of less high-brow religious literature, was rarely assured posterity; much of this literature was suppressed in the tenth century, with Symeon Metaphrastes ("The Translator") substituting linguistically acceptable versions.[8]

The first break in this pattern occurred in the late twelfth century, in the last years of the Comnenan dynasty of Byzantium. It is a timid break: Michael Glycas's *Prison Verses,* written to beg pardon from the emperor who had imprisoned him and containing a smattering of vernacular proverbs; the satirical *Ptochoprodromos* poems; the "How to Survive in Byzantine Society" precepts of *Spaneas* (whose manuscript tradition is too complex to disentangle whether it was even written originally in the vernacular); and probably the first redaction of the epic poem of *Digenes Akrites,* "Basil, the Twyborn Borderer," which may have been based on earlier oral versions.[9] None of these poems were written in a consistently vernacular idiom, and none of them would have any pretense of upstaging the more prestigious writing being done in Atticist Greek by the great scholars of Constantinople.

It was, however, a start, and by the 1300s a sizable number of vernacular works had been written. Many of these reflect the changed circumstances of the Greek-speaking world. With most of that world ruled by Westerners, the traditional institutions upholding classical learning held less sway over the literate (Browning 1983:72). The Byzantine romance, for example, modeled on novels of late antiquity and written in a more conservative idiom, had to compete with romances following Western prototypes. Indeed, the medieval Greek "best-seller" *The War of Troy* (preserved in seven manuscripts) is a translation of the Old French romance *Le Roman de Troie.* Gradually, people with something of consequence to say started saying it in a more vernacular tongue—be it laws, chronicles, diplomatic letters, wills, or sermons. In a reversal of Symeon Metaphrastes' endeavor, Byzantine scientific and pseudoscientific works, including veterinary, astrological, and medical texts, began appearing in vernacular paraphrases.[10] And a homespun vernacular literature, uneasily straddling the divide between the old and the new, started to emerge.

The burden of classical heritage, however, condemned this literature: it was never taken up by the best Greek literary minds in any seriousness—even though, as Hans-Georg Beck (1971:8) has argued, it was probably written by the learned and thus not truly folk literature (see "Orality"). Although the vernaculars of Western Europe emerged as respectable literary idioms, the stigma associated with the Greek vernacular persisted throughout Byzantium and beyond. Palaeologan commentators on classical works are consistently apologetic when glossing an obscure archaic word with a more modern term ("as some say vulgarly"),[11] and the term *Graecobarbara* to denote modern Greek remained in use in scholarly Latin even in the nineteenth century.[12] And neither was much ambition displayed by the practitioners of the time: vernacular medieval Greek literature is almost always anonymous and has no great poets to boast to the world. Still, vernacular Greek literature has been unfairly maligned by most commentators: some of these poems are not without their charm, and they have a lot to tell us about life in Byzantium. The *Entertaining Tale of Quadrupeds* is such a poem.

As already mentioned, Byzantine vernacular poetry comes in several distinct genres. The romances form a major group, with eleven instances extant. Some of these were translated or adapted from Western prototypes. Others, composed originally in Greek, still display influences from either the Western chivalric novel or the Hellenistic Greek romances—reprised in Byzantium by learned authors such as Theodore Prodromus. (See Beaton 1996 for a comprehensive treatment of the genre.) A distant relative to these works is the "epic" of *Digenes Akrites,* which pays much attention to the hero's courtship. (See Beaton and Ricks 1993.)

There are also epic poems dealing with historical personages: the *Belisariad,* lauding Justinian's brilliant general Belisarius; the various versions of the *Alexander Romance*; the *Achilleid*; the *Byzantine Iliad*; and others. These works take considerable liberties with the established accounts; they were intended as light reading rather than scholarship. In this, they differ little from the Western romances of the time, remaking Achilles and Alexander in the troubadours' own image—or for that matter, the contemporary pop culture phenomenon of *Xena*. The estrangement of medieval Greeks from their own classical heritage is nonetheless startling to the modern observer—who actually has better access to the original narratives. Byzantium may have had Homeric scholars of the caliber of Eustathius of Thessalonica (the definitive scholiast on Homer), but the narratives in question are typically drawn rather from thirdhand sources, like Dictys the Cretan (sixth century A.D.).[13] In general, vernacular medieval literature has only a superficial dependence on older literature and typically relies on lower, postclassical sources. There is much more Aesop and Hellenistic romance to be found in these works than anything of Homer, the tragedians, or Aristophanes.[14] The emphasis in these poems on a glorious past—at a far cultural and ideological remove from the Byzantine present—was probably not unrelated to an emergent feeling of the decline and fall of the society they knew.

Other vernacular poems have a historiographical or descriptive focus; these include several laments on fifteenth-century battles, including those on the fall of Constantinople itself, and verse chronicles of Western-held Greece. The best known of the latter is the *Chronicle of Morea,* a work written from the anti-Byzantine point of view, consciously repudiating both classical and Greek Orthodox tradition. There are also moralizing verses, such as *Spaneas* and the Eastern-inspired *Story of Ptocholeon.* Toward the end of the period, love poetry from Rhodes and the Aegean also appears, as well as the beginnings of the Cretan Renaissance.

Vernacular Greek Byzantine literature is conventionally taken as ranging from Glycas's *Prison Verses* to the laments following the fall of Constantinople in 1453, but even before that date, it overlaps with the literature of the Cretan

Renaissance. The dividing line between Byzantine and Modern Greek literature is rather tricky to set, and obviously Greek culture did not change overnight in 1453. As good a date as any has been proposed by Savvidis (1993): 1509, when the first vernacular Greek book, the *Apokopos* by the Cretan Bergadis (Bregadin), was printed. An account of a journey to hell reminiscent of Dante rather than Odysseus, the *Apokopos* marked the beginning of a new type of literature, in prose, mass-produced in the form of chapbooks from Venice. With very few exceptions, Byzantine vernacular literature was not perpetuated in this form.[15]

From its inception in the late fourteenth century, Cretan literature was already more forward-looking than its Byzantine counterpart. In its full flowering, the Cretan Renaissance owed much to Italy and little to Byzantium: it was at such a remove from Greek prototypes that classical figures were routinely referred to with Italian names, and the surviving autograph manuscripts of Cretan plays are in the Latin alphabet.[16] Cretan literature belongs to a different culture and thus does not properly fall under our purview.

Humor and Dissent in Late Byzantium

> Since these times do not allow for rational action nor what befits prudence—the more so when a plague sent by God is about to strike.
>
> —Nicephorus Gregoras

Humor and dissent are two sides of the same coin. Both are employed to articulate resistance against an oppressive social order. Indeed, the distinction between the two can often blur. Though Byzantium was by general admission a more static society than its counterparts in the West, instances of this general human tendency can still be observed within it. As a vehicle for both humor and dissent, the *Entertaining Tale of Quadrupeds* is a significant text for our understanding of Byzantine society. In order to situate its testimony properly, it should be compared with other late Byzantine manifestations of both traits.

Humor

It has been easy to regard Byzantium as humorless—a rigid theocracy where monks dwelled on the eternal verities, the peasantry toiled without relief, and the soldiers fretted about one invader after enough. Easy though it may be, this assumption is also quite unfair: the Byzantines may have wished to commit to paper only what passed muster with God or Homer, but wit could certainly peep through in their learned tradition. One need only consider Leontius of Neapolis's *Vita of Symeon the Fool,* the Lucianic satire *Timarion,* or Theodore Prodromus's *Battle of Cats and Mice.* Even in the deadly serious tradition of

Byzantine historiography, one can discern an occasional flash of humor: for example, Anna Comnena reports in the *Alexiad* (3.3–8) that her grandmother Anna Dalassina appointed a hanger-on, Eustratius Garidas, as patriarch—not knowing what else to do with him. And just as humor in the medieval West passed from Latin bookishness to vernacular outspokenness, so, too, did vernacular Greek open the door to a more forthright kind of humor, the best-known instance of which is the earliest, the *Ptochoprodromos* poems.

The anonymous author of the four poems, known to us as Ptochoprodromos ("Poor Prodromus," who may or may not represent Theodore Prodromus), bemoans to the emperor his sundry hardships as henpecked husband, impoverished scholar, and put-upon monk. No plea for specific action is ever made, and the social order is never questioned. Still, the author's society is harshly, if indirectly, criticized, and both sarcasm and farce are employed to that effect. Perhaps the most effective sarcasm from a modern viewpoint is to be found in *Ptochoprodromos* 3.401–19: the same abbot who sends for the best doctors when he falls ill "treats" his sick monks with a three-day fast. The poet concludes that his abbot is a doctor worth recommending to the emperor, who will then be as safe as one never in fear of drowning in a dry riverbed or of being bitten by a dead dog!

The fourth *Ptochoprodromos* poem contains farce to rival an animated cartoon, especially verses 163–202: the undernourished scholar, who also happens to be a priest, is denied access to a tempting cured tenderloin on his relatives' dinner table until a mysterious noise in the basement takes everybody downstairs. Then our priest quickly consumes the fillet and joins everybody else in their investigations—but only after placing the innocent family cat on the table. In all, *Ptochoprodromos* is an inventive, vivid picture of everyday life in Byzantium, with the hero in his various guises ambling from one disaster to another.

A more benign farce, focused on thirst rather than hunger, is the theme of *Father Wine* (Κρασοπατέρας), a whimsical poem detailing a drunken monk's view of the world in his stupor. The monk emerges from his drunken haze (seeing butterflies in a yellow sky) and muses how fine it would be if the sun were a barrel of wine; how foolish the Jews in the desert were to ask Moses for water instead of wine; what a shame it is the vine does not grow as tall as Mount Ararat; and that, if the four rivers of Paradise all ran with wine, they'd be fine for his four meals a day—as long as no houseguests turn up. The poem muses and amuses; it belongs to a long line of songs in praise of drink, and there is little scope for offense in its comical exaggerations.

The opprobrium gathered around the *Mass of the Beardless Man* (Σπανός) is perhaps more understandable but ultimately misplaced. The *Mass,* widely circulated in its time, is an ingenious, relentless, and quite filthy parody of some of the highlights of the Greek Orthodox Mass, reformulated as an agglomeration of insults heaped upon an unnamed beardless victim. The inventive genius of the author is so overwhelming that it flows over into parodies of popular remedies, wills, and prenuptial agreements. The *Mass* circulated in repeated editions as a chapbook from Venice and seems to have garnered a better reception among the readers of the time than among Byzantinists. Indeed, Karl Krumbacher (1897:2.810), the first historian of Byzantine literature, went so far as to consider the work a Satanist Black Mass.

Krumbacher's reaction is the rule rather than the exception: humor, unlike tragedy, is notorious for being incapable of traveling far in time or space. As anyone who has worked on Aristophanes—or, indeed, Shakespeare's comedies—can attest, it is difficult for the contemporary scholar (let alone reader) to understand the subtleties, and therefore the sense of humor, of a society so different from our own. Parodies may be too obvious to be appreciated, and allegories too subtle to be noticed. In her groundbreaking work on the *Ptochoprodromos* poems, Margaret Alexiou (1986:31) wondered whether "it is Byzantinists, rather than Byzantines themselves, who lack a sense of humor." Her work has launched a reversal in this trend, and far from not seeing the humor in *Ptochoprodromos,* she has in fact observed more there than any previous researchers: she hints, indirectly yet persistently, at the presence of sexual allegory, often referring to ancient sources such as Aristophanes. (See also Alexiou 1999.)

The sex in the poetry of Stephen Sachlikis, by contrast, is scarcely concealed by any allegory. Sachlikis was a dandy in fourteenth-century Crete whose excesses had landed him in jail by the time the *Entertaining Tale of Quadrupeds* is set; while there, he wrote a virulent attack on the prostitutes of Candia. He has little more time for the villagers or lawyers into whose company he is forced. Sachlikis is mostly a poet of indignation, but as a ne'er-do-well he takes obvious delight in using the Cretan Greek equivalents of four-letter words in describing the local working girls' proclivities. The poem even incorporates a Parliament of Whores, assembled to petition the authorities for working space.[17]

Sachlikis's work is something rather different from the other instances of humor considered. It comes from Crete, it is eponymous, it rhymes, and its language is already a fairly mature modern Cretan dialect rather than the teetering macaronic idiom of most vernacular medieval Greek poetry. Indeed, his work challenges the reader to class it as modern rather than medieval. It is not only the outward form of the poetry that leads to this conclusion or even its profanity, which after all is exuberantly topped by the *Mass*. His poetry takes place in a world where God and emperor are irrelevant: divine order no longer obscures personal quest. The Byzantine theocracy, prominent even in the clerical buffoonery of the *Mass* and *Father Wine,* has nothing to do with Sachlikis—though it still has much to do with his contemporary, the Cretan diplomat Linardo Della Porta.[18] The split between Sachlikis and Della Porta is emblematic of the split between Byzantine and modern Greek culture, and the *Tale,* as we shall see, is still decidedly on the former side of the split.

Dissent

Very few late Byzantine works show any favor toward the lower classes. The norm in that era's learned writing was for writers to appeal for patronage, often exaggerating their own poverty and entertaining their aristocratic readers with displays of mendicant erudition. This trait also appears in vernacular Byzantine literature, both in the authoring of Michael Glycas's *Prison Verses* and the *Ptochoprodromos* poems. The writer thus places himself in a client relation with the rich and cannot afford himself the independence to engage in class criticism. Within Byzantine learned literature, Alexius Makrembolites' *Dialogue between the Rich and the Poor* (Ševčenko 1960), written around 1343, is therefore unique. Makrembolites castigates the upper classes from a theological viewpoint for their greed and lack of compassion toward the poor. In fact, his minimal, superficial references to classical literature have led Ševčenko, the work's editor, to suggest that he belonged to the lower echelons of the Byzantine literate, a class from which we otherwise have very little eponymous testimony.

But the *Dialogue* is not a conventional piece of church moralizing. The times during which it was written were desperate: right in the middle of the disastrous civil war of the 1340s and just as the Ottoman Empire had started whittling away at what was left of Byzantium. And although the *Dialogue* is hardly *The Communist Manifesto* (as Ševčenko [1960:202] put it, "The *Dialogue* will be disappointing to those who examine late Byzantine texts for traces of *articulate* revolutionary thinking—a thing which in my opinion did not exist"), the desperation of the times makes itself felt in Makrembolites' condemnation of the rich, along with the nagging doubt that perhaps the Turks' successes were owed to a superior morality:

> Ἢ οὐκ αἰδεῖσθε ἀκούοντες ὅσα οἱ ἐξ ἐθνῶν εἰς τοὺς ὁμοφύλους ποιοῦσι πένητας καὶ εἰς τοὺς ἡμῶν αἰχμαλώτους [οὗτοι γὰρ ἀπαξιοῦσι σύνδειπνον ποιῆσαί ποτε τὸν μὴ συνδιαιτώμενον πένησι, καὶ οὐδ᾿ εὐχῆς κοινωνοῦσιν αὐτῷ, ἀλλ᾿ ἐξωθοῦσι καὶ τοῦτον ἐκεῖθεν εὐθύς...], πῶς οὐδένα τούτων τῆς προσηκούσης προνοίας ἀπαξιοῦσιν; ὅσον δὲ καὶ τὸ ἄτοπον, Ἑβραίους μὲν καὶ τοὺς τοῦ Μωάμεθ φιλανθρώπους εἶναι καὶ ἐλεήμονας, τοὺς δὲ Χριστοῦ μαθητάς, τοῦ φύσει φιλανθρώπου καὶ ἐλεήμονος, ἀσυμπαθεῖς εἶναι καὶ γλίσχρους πρὸς τὸ ὁμόφυλον. καὶ γὰρ δι᾿ ἡμᾶς καὶ τὰ τοῦ παρόντος αἰῶνος εἰλήφατε ἀγαθὰ καὶ τὰ τοῦ μέλλοντος λήψεσθε, ὅσοι τὸν ἔλεον ἔχετε. (205)
>
> [Are you not shamed to hear how the gentiles treat the poor ones of their kin or their prisoners of war from among us? (For they deem it unworthy ever to have meals with such a one who disdains to eat together with the poor, and they exclude him from the communion of prayer, casting him out immediately from there. . . .) Why do they not

consider any one of them unworthy of due care? It is the height of unreasonableness that Jews and Mohammedans should be humane and merciful, while the disciples of Christ, Who was by nature humane and merciful, should be heartless and niggardly towards their kin. Indeed it is to us ⟨the Poor⟩ that you owe the goods of this world, and only those amongst you who have mercy towards us will partake in the rewards of the future life.] (218)

The poor in Makrembolites' *Dialogue* (who do just about all the talking, with the rich reduced to strawman arguments) know how indispensable they are to the running of the economy and that they are no less deserving of its rewards. The place of the rich in society, on the other hand, is openly disputed, even though the authority of the emperor himself is never doubted:

Πλὴν εἰ καὶ δυσγενεῖς διὰ τὴν ἀϋλίαν δοκοῦμεν ὑμῖν, ἀλλὰ καὶ χρήσιμοι ἐσθ' ὅτε πεφύκαμεν· τῇ ὕλῃ γὰρ ἀλλ' οὐ τῇ φύσει ὑμῶν διϊστάμεθα, καὶ τῆς παρ' ἡμῶν ἀναγκαίως καὶ αὐτοὶ βοηθείας δεῖσθε. ἐξ ἡμῶν γὰρ οἱ τὴν γῆν ἐργαζόμενοι, οἱ τὰς οἰκίας, οἱ τὰς ὁλκάδας, οἱ χειρεπιστήμονες, δι' ὧν αἱ πόλεις πᾶσαι συνίστανται· ἐξ ὑμῶν δ' αὐτῶν τίνες;—ῥητέον γὰρ καὶ τοῦτο, εἰ καὶ ὑμῖν ἐπαχθές—κυβευταὶ καὶ τρυφηταὶ καὶ οἱ τὰς κοινὰς συμφορὰς ἐξ ἀπληστίας πραγματευόμενοι καὶ οἱ τὰς πόλεις συγχέοντες καὶ τὴν πενίαν αὐξάνοντες· κεχαρισμένα γὰρ ἂν ἔδοξε τῷ θεῷ δράσας καὶ ὁ τοῦ κοινοῦ προστάτης, τοὺς μηδὲ τῶν οἰκείων προνοουμένους εἰ τοῦ ἀρχείου ἐξώθησεν, ἵνα μὴ ἐκ τῆς σφῶν κακίαν καὶ αὐτὸς ἂν μολύνοιτο. (210)

[However, although we may seem to you of contemptible extraction because of our lack of substance, still how often we prove to be useful. For we differ from you in substance, not nature, and you are necessarily in need of our aid. Indeed it is among us that the tillers of the soil, the builders of houses and merchant ships and the craftsmen are drawn, through whose endeavors all cities subsist. And who comes from among you? For this too must be stated though it be offensive to you—gamblers, voluptuaries, people bringing public calamities with their greediness, disrupters of civic order, spreading poverty. The ruler of the state would perform an act pleasing to God should he expel from the palace those who neglect even their own dependents so as not himself to be contaminated by their evil.] (222)

The dialogue is unique among the works in learned Greek in its protest of social inequality. It is hardly surprising then that Makrembolites should have belonged to the lower rungs of the Byzantine intelligentsia. But even in the predominantly anonymous vernacular literature of the time, voices of dissent are rarely heard. The times, after all, did not encourage such dissent; when the very future of Christendom seemed to be at stake and when the rich themselves could legitimately start to cry poor (as Makrembolites' rich in fact do: see appendix 2), it would have seemed impious—not to mention utterly impractical—to raise such matters in literature.

This makes the vernacular instances of dissent all the more valuable, even though most of them are compromised as independent testimonies.[19] The alternative ending of the *Book of Birds,* for instance, as discussed in appendix 1, appears to be a direct transposition of the ending of the *Entertaining Tale of Quadrupeds. The Vita of the Esteemed Donkey* has the learned classes, represented by the fox, ultimately beaten by the "unlettered" donkey. But the *Vita* and its rhyming counterpart, the *Fair Tale of the Donkey the Wolf and the Fox,* belong to the very end of the period, are clearly meant as entertainment rather than political comment, and probably owe a greater debt to the West than to anything in Byzantium.[20] The vernacular romances are largely devoid of any political content, other than their reveling in bygone (usually Greek) glories; they do not comment overtly on the sad state of the contemporary Greeks.

The only other vernacular text that could be considered to articulate social dissent is the *Belisariad.* In that work, the envy of noble families is responsible for the blinding of Justinian's general. The families are named and anachronistically include the Palaeologi, the Cantacuzeni, the Lascares, and the Ducae—the imperial families of late Byzantium. The common folk, on the other hand, are portrayed as a significant political force, giving prudent advice to the emperor—who does well to hearken to it. The story of Belisarius's blinding related in the *Belisariad* is founded in history, but the "democratic" spirit of the *Belisariad,* and the conclusions it draws about Belisarius's disgrace, originate with the author (Bakker and van Gemert 1988:41). They therefore point explicitly to his political attitudes. Yet, though it concludes with a Byzantine victory, the *Belisariad* does not display the envious nobles defeated in battle, unlike the *Entertaining Tale of Quadrupeds*; it inhabits a world of Realpolitik rather than fable. And according to Bakker and van Gemert, the conclusion of the *Belisariad,* striking as it may be, is a response to the strife not of the mid-fourteenth century but of the 1390s—when the doom of the Eastern Roman Empire was already certain:

> Θεέ, οὐράνιε βασιλεῦ, ψεύστην νὰ μὲ ποιήσῃς,
> τὸ γένος τῶν ᾿Αγαρηνῶν τὸν κόσμον θέλει φάγει,
> Ρωμαίους καὶ Σέρβους, Βλάχους τε Οὔγγρους τε καὶ Λατίνους!
> ᾿Αμέλειαν ἔχουν οἱ Ρωμαῖοι, φθόνον πολὺν καὶ μέγαν,
> μονάφεντον καὶ ὁρμητικὸν ᾿Αγαρηνῶν τὸ γένος,
> ἕναν θεὸν λατρεύουσιν, ἕναν αὐθέντην τρέμουν,
> σπουδήν, ὁμόνοιαν θαυμαστὴν ἔχουν εἰς τὸν δεσπόζων,

ποτὲ ὁμόνοιαν οἱ Ρωμαῖοι, ποτὲ μοναυθεντία,
ποτὲ καλῶν ἀνάκλησιν οὐκ ἠμποροῦν νὰ ἰδοῦσιν.

[God, Lord in Heaven, make a liar of me:
the Sons of Hagar[21] will consume the world,
Romans, Serbs, Vlachs, Hungarians and Latins!
The Romans grow indifferent; they've much envy.
The Sons of Hagar have a single master
and are a race that cannot be held back.
One God they worship; one lord do they fear,
with zeal and wondrous concord to their master.
But ne'er the Romans concord; ne'er one master;
ne'er a return to good times will they see.] (χ 572–79)

This means that if the *Tale* turns out to articulate social dissent, it is a document of great importance in investigating the attitudes of the Byzantines to the world. What political allusions are in fact made in the *Tale* is an issue we defer to the section "Characteristics of the *Tale*" and to appendix 2.

Literary Parallels

There Hector was in strife; I'll say no more;
no war more horrible was ever seen
by Darius or Dictys to retell.

—*War of Troy*

The *Entertaining Tale of Quadrupeds* belongs to a distinct group of humorous and satirical medieval Greek poems about animals, of which there are two types. Verse fables, the first type, are essentially fairy tales about animals and are represented in late medieval vernacular literature by three poems: the *Vita of the Esteemed Donkey* (Συναξάριον τοῦ Τιμημένου Γαδάρου) and its rhymed variant *A Fair Tale of the Donkey the Wolf and the Fox* (Γαδάρου Λύκου καὶ Ἀλουποῦς Διήγησις Ὡραία), mentioned earlier (we refer to the two collectively as the *Donkey Tale*), and the Cretan *The Cat and the Mice.* These poems have a well-defined story consisting of a single episode, and each one has a straightforward moral. The fox and wolf in a sea voyage conspire to eat the donkey through a mock confession of sins, only to be outwitted in the end; the cat befriends the mice and plays dead, only to eat them at his funeral. The second type, to which the *Tale* belongs, has been called animal epics (*Tierepen* in Krumbacher 1897:2.873, continued in Kazhdan 1991 s.v. ANIMAL EPICS). Given that there is more description than plot in these works, however, we prefer to call them epic bestiaries. The other poem in this group is the *Book of Birds* (Πουλολόγος). Unlike the verse fable, the epic bestiary does not tell a single story; it is essentially episodic, involving the presentation of a sequence of animals disputing in pairs (in well-ordered sequence in the *Book*, more fluidly in the *Tale*). The poems are framed within a narrative event: the lion's conference in the *Tale*, the eagle's son's wedding in the *Book*. But most of the story proceeds oblivious to this, and the poem is propelled by enumeration rather than plot. Neither is there much narrative continuity in evidence between any of the paired episodes.

Traditionally, two other poems are classed with the *Tale* and the *Book of Birds*: the *Book of Fruit* (Πωρικολόγος) and its variant, the *Book of Fish* ('Οψαρολόγος). However, all that these share with the *Tale* and the *Book of Birds* is a propensity toward enumeration. Otherwise, these are quite different in intent, being brief prose parodies of Byzantine protocol (substituting fruit or fish for potentates of the court) and probably written one or two centuries earlier.

Although verse fables about animals are quite common in the world's literature, the epic bestiary is a conflation of genres unique to Byzantium, with several different types of poems feeding into it.

The first genre contributing to poems like the *Tale* is the bestiary: a listing of various animals and their idiosyncrasies, of a religious nature, intended to provide illustrations to the faithful of the precepts of Christianity. Bestiaries were very popular both in the West and the East; their prototype, and the only instance to have circulated in the East, is the *Physiologus*, probably first written around Alexandria between the second and fourth centuries A.D. Poems like it were a major source of medieval notions about animals, particularly the more exotic sorts with which Europeans had limited contact. The following excerpt from the *Physiologus* on elephants, which was worked into the *Tale*, is fairly typical of the just-so stories featured in bestiaries:

> Ἡ δὲ φύσις τοῦ ἐλέφαντος τοιαύτη ἐστίν· ἐὰν πέσῃ, οὐ δύναται ἀναστῆναι· οὐκ ἔχει γὰρ ἁρμογὰς εἰς τὰ γόνατα αὐτοῦ [ὡς καὶ τῶν λοιπῶν ζῴων]. πῶς δὲ καὶ πίπτει; ἐὰν θέλῃ ὑπνῶσαι, ἐπὶ δένδρου ἑαυτὸν ἀνακλίνει καὶ κοιμᾶται· οἱ οὖν κυνηγοί, εἰδότες τὴν τοῦ ἐλέφαντος φύσιν, ὑπάγουσι καὶ πρίζουσι τὸ δένδρον παρολίγον, ἔρχεται οὖν ἀνακλῖναι ἑαυτὸν ὁ ἐλέφας, καὶ ἅμα τῷ δένδρῳ συμπίπτει, καὶ ἄρχεται βοᾶν κλαίων, καὶ ἀκούει ἄλλος ἐλέφας, καὶ ἔρχεται βοηθῆσαι αὐτῷ, καὶ οὐ δύναται ἐγεῖραι αὐτόν· βοῶσι δὲ οἱ δύο, καὶ ἔρχονται δώδεκα ἐλέφαντες, καὶ οὐδὲ αὐτοὶ δύνανται τὸν πεπτωκότα ἐγεῖραι· εἶτα οἱ πάντες βοῶσιν· ὕστερον δὲ πάντων ἔρχεται μικρὸς ἐλέφας, καὶ ὑποτίθησι τὴν προμοσχίδα αὐτοῦ ὑποκάτω τοῦ ἐλέφαντος, καὶ ἐγείρει αὐτόν.
>
> Εἰς πρόσωπον οὖν τοῦ 'Αδὰμ καὶ τῆς Εὔας λαμβάνονται ὁ ἐλέφας καὶ ἡ γυνὴ αὐτοῦ· [...] ἦλθεν οὖν ὁ μέγας ἐλέφας, τουτέστιν ὁ Νόμος, καὶ οὐκ ἠδυνήθη αὐτὸν ἐγεῖραι· εἶτα ἦλθον οἱ δώδεκα ἐλέφαντες, τουτέστιν ὁ χορὸς τῶν προφητῶν, καὶ οὐδὲ αὐτοὶ

ἠδυνήθησαν ἐγεῖραι τὸν πεπτωκότα· ὕστερον δὲ πάντων ἦλθεν ὁ νοερὸς καὶ ἅγιος ἐλέφας, [ὁ Κύριος ἡμῶν Ἰησοῦς Χριστός], καὶ ἤγειρε τὸν ἄνθρωπον ἀπὸ τῆς γῆς. ὁ ὢν μειζότερος πάντων, [ἤτοι ὁ Χριστὸς καὶ νέος Ἀδάμ], ἐγένετο πάντων δοῦλος· ἐταπείνωσε γὰρ ἑαυτόν, μορφὴν δούλου λαβών, [γενόμενος ὅμοιος αὐτῶν], ἵνα πάντας σώσῃ.

Καλῶς ὁ Φυσιολόγος ἔλεξε περὶ τοῦ ἐλέφαντος.

[And the nature of the elephant is as follows: if he falls down, he cannot rise up again, for he has no joints in his knees {as do other beasts}. And how does he fall? If he would sleep, he reclines himself against a tree and falls asleep. So the hunters, knowing the nature of the elephant, go and saw the tree close to falling. The elephant thus goes to lie back and falls down together with the tree, and he starts to cry out and weep. And another elephant hears him and comes to help him and cannot raise him. Then the two of them cry out together and twelve elephants arrive, and they, too, cannot raise the fallen one. Then all of them cry out together; and last of all the small elephant comes and places his trunk underneath the elephant and raises him.

Now the elephant and his wife represent Adam and Eve. . . . So the great elephant came, that is to say, the Law, and he could not raise ⟨fallen Adam⟩. Then the twelve elephants came, that is to say, the choir of the prophets, and they could not raise the fallen one either. Then last of all came the Virtual and Holy Elephant, {our Lord Jesus Christ,} and raised Man up from the earth: He who is the greatest of all, {namely, Christ the New Adam,} became "the slave of all" (Mark 10:44) for He "made Himself of no reputation, and took upon Him the form of a servant," (Philippians 2:7) {becoming like unto them,} for He "will have all men to be saved." (1 Timothy 2:4)

The Physiologus has spoken well on the Elephant.] (*Physiologus* 1.43)

Related to the bestiary is the fable—particularly the Aesopic fable, which was hugely popular in the Middle Ages (see Koukoules 1947–55:6.330–32 for the popularity of Aesop in Byzantium). Whereas the bestiary is more of a catalog interspersed with occasionally fantastical scenes of the life of beasts, the fable is a discrete narrative with anthropomorphized animals. As we shall see, the *Tale* treats its animals more like a bestiary, but it also exploits Aesopic fable. Unlike the versions of Aesop that have circulated in contemporary mass culture, the fables with which the Byzantines were familiar were pithy and moralized explicitly. The following fable, which also appears in the *Tale* (771–75), illustrates what Aesopic fables sound like in the original. Though it is succinct by modern standards, it is in fact the longest of the three extant versions:

κάμηλος θεασαμένη ταῦρον ἐπὶ τοῖς κέρασιν ἀγαλλόμενον φθονήσασα αὐτῷ ἠβουλήθη καὶ αὐτὴ τῶν ἴσων ἐφικέσθαι. διόπερ παραγενομένη πρὸς τὸν Δία τούτου ἐδέετο, ὅπως αὐτῇ κέρατα προσνείμῃ. καὶ ὁ Ζεὺς ἀγανακτήσας κατ' αὐτῆς, εἴγε μὴ ἀρκεῖται τῷ μεγέθει τοῦ σώματος καὶ τῇ ἰσχύι, ἀλλὰ καὶ περισσοτέρων ἐπιθυμεῖ, οὐ μόνον αὐτῇ κέρατα οὐ προσέθηκεν, ἀλλὰ καὶ μέρος τι τῶν ὤτων ἀφείλετο. οὕτω πολλοὶ διὰ πλεονεξίαν τοῖς ἄλλοις ἐποφθαλμιῶντες λανθάνουσι καὶ τῶν ἰδίων στερούμενοι.

[A camel, seeing a bull proud to have horns, grew jealous and wished to gain as much. So she went to Zeus and begged him to grant her horns. And Zeus, fed up with her (for she was not satisfied with the size of her body and her strength but wanted ever more), not only did not put horns on her but also took off part of her ears. Thus, many looking on others with envy end up losing even what they have.] (*Aesop: Fables* 119)

The third genre contributing to the epic bestiary is that of the conference of animals. This motif recurs in the folklore of many nations and formed part of the literatures of both Western Europe and the Middle East. Perhaps the most famous instance of this genre is Chaucer's *Parlement of Fowles*:

The highest perches went to birds of prey
As rightfully they should, without dissension;
Then smaller birds, who under Nature's sway
Eat worms or things that I don't care to mention.
The lowest in the ranks at this convention
Were waterfowl; but seed-birds on the green
Sat in such numbers as were never seen.
. . . .

What should I say? All birds of every kind
That in this world have feathers, men could see
Assembled there as Nature had designed.
Before the Goddess each in his degree
Was going about his business eagerly,
Seeking to choose, according to his state,
With her consent, his partner and his mate. (Chaucer 1975:586–88)

The Arabic *Island of Animals* (Johnson-Davies 1994), written in the tenth century, is also worth noting as a parallel. Although its tenor is rather different to the *Tale*'s (it is a theologically motivated fable arguing for the humane treatment of animals), it has some aspects familiar from the *Tale*: an irascible lion, king of the predators (p. 21) (though his domain is reduced to a seventh of the animal kingdom [p. 19] and he has no dominion over herbivores); the leopard as the lion's minister (p. 25); cats and dogs regarded as far too friendly to humans (pp. 25–27); donkeys overly burdened (p. 10); and both the camel and the elephant—as well as the rabbit—derided as misshapen (pp. 18–20).

The fourth genre is that of the didactic poem. In an age when verse was too widely used to be confined to "poetic" subject matter, it was not unusual for instructional material to be set to verse for learning by schoolchildren. Didactic poetry is a venerable institution, with many classical instances. Indeed, the first examples we have of the *dekapentasyllabos* or *politikos*[22] meter (the iambic heptameter that has become the meter par excellence of modern Greek verse) are verse mnemonics of academic subject matter (Jeffreys 1974). Jeffreys and Jeffreys (1986:511–13) have argued that the very catchiness of the vernacular meter promoted this mnemonic use. The following example, attributed to the eleventh-century renaissance man Michael Psellus, is atypical only in its brevity:

Στίχοι τοῦ Ψελλοῦ εἰς τοὺς ιβ' ἀποστόλους, περιέχει δὲ εἷς ἕκαστος αὐτῶν τὸ τέλος, τὸ ὄνομα, τὸν φονεύσαντα καὶ τὸν τόπον

Σταυροῖ Πέτρον κύμβαχον ἐν Ῥώμῃ Νέρων.
Ῥώμη ξίφει θνῄσκοντα τὸν Παῦλον βλέπει.
εἰρηνικῷ τέθνηκε Λουκᾶς ἐν τέλει.
ζωῆς ὕπνον πρύτανιν ὑπνοῖ Ματθαῖος.
Μάρκον θανατοῖ δῆμος Ἀλεξανδρέων.
καὶ μὴ θανὼν ζῇ καὶ θανὼν Ἰωάννης.
σταυροῦσι Πατρεῖς ἄνδρες ὠμῶς Ἀνδρέαν.
νεκροῦσι λόγχαι τὸν Θωμᾶν ἐν Ἰνδίᾳ.
Βαρθολομαῖος σταυρικῷ θνῄσκει πάθει.
καὶ τὸν Σίμωνα σταῦρος ἐξάγει βίου.
μάχαιρα τέμνει τοὺς Ἰακώβου δρόμους.
ἴσον Πέτρῳ δίδωσι Φίλιππος μόρον.

[Verses by Psellus on the XII Apostles,
containing the death of each, the name, the murderer, and the place.

Nero had Peter crucified in Rome,
head down, and Rome saw Paul die by the sword.
Luke made a peaceful end, and Matthew sleeps
the sleep that is the lord of life forever.
An Alexandrian mob put Mark to death.
John lived in life and lives yet having died.
Cruelly the Patrans Andrew crucified.
Lances in India were Thomas's doom.
Bartholomew suffered his death by cross.
And crucifixion took the life of Simon.

The dagger did cut short the path of James.
And Philip shared the selfsame fate as Peter.] (*Psellus: Poems* 90)

The fifth genre is that of satirical allegory. This, too, is a venerable institution, being an old and widespread means of exercising social criticism while escaping retribution. The reader need go no further to find a modern instance of this form than George Orwell's *Animal Farm*. The best-known such medieval allegory is the *Romance of Renard the Fox,* which circulated in most of Western Europe. In the various forms of *Renard,* the animals are clearly depicted in terms of a feudal court, and the poems are not particularly subtle in lashing out at the excesses and greed of barons or clergymen. Renard, for example, asks a "kiss" of the titmouse, relaying King Lion's declaration of a truce to his own, rather selfish ends:

Lady, by the baptismal vow
That made me godfather to your son,
I swear I've never said or done
Anything that could cause you harm.
And do you know why your alarm
Is now a foolishness indeed?
King Noble the lion has decreed
That there shall be peace in all his lands,
And every vassal he commands
Has sworn that he will do his part
So no new argument can start—
God willing, they will keep the truce.
So now you see why there's no use
In being afraid. At last the poor
Will have a chance to feel secure;
They're overjoyed—they need no longer
Fear lest the quarrels of the stronger
Bring them the suffering of war—
That will not happen anymore. (Terry 1983:39–40; *Renard* 2.486–508)

There is an element of this kind of satire in the *Donkey Tale:* the story is framed as a saint's life, the animals parody the sacrament of confession, and pedants are mocked in the form of the fox. But the targets of the *Donkey Tale* are fairly generic. Similarly, satire is present in the *Book of Fruit* and the *Book of Fish,* but this is intended as parody rather than critique, and there seems to be little combative intent to them. By contrast, the style of the *Book of Birds,* and possibly also the *Tale,* suggests veiled references to specific individuals and circumstances.

Elements of all five genres are present in both the *Tale* and the work to which it is most closely related, the *Book of Birds,* a combination that seems to be unique to Byzantine literature. Although the raw materials came from the classical and Hellenistic past, Western Europe, Asia, and contemporary folklore, there would appear to be no precedent for the combination of all these elements into the epic bestiary. The mixture is quite different, too, between the two works, so it is helpful to take a closer book at the *Book of Birds* to determine how each work is conceived; this we undertake in appendix 1.

Fact and Fiction in the *Tale's* Zoology

> Nature's great masterpiece, an elephant,
> The only harmless great thing; the giant
> Of beasts; who thought, no more had gone, to make one wise
> But to be just, and thankful, loth to offend,
> (Yet nature hath given him no knees to bend)
> Himself he up-props, on himself relies,
> And foe to none, suspects no enemies,
> Still sleeping stood; vexed not his fantasy
> Black dreams, like an unbent bow, carelessly
> His sinewy proboscis did remissly lie
>
> —John Donne, *Progress of the Soul* 39

To a large extent, the scenes in the *Tale* are grounded in observation. It is simple to trace to natural history the origin of such episodes as the horse put out to pasture, the omnivorous boar, or the famished fox. In fact, that with which the author is not familiar tends to be passed over; this explains why his description of the leopard is so succinct, for example. In a few instances, however, the author is clearly not exploiting personal observation but has made use of elements from the culture around him—either written or oral. We have already seen two instances of this at work. One, from the *Physiologus,* is the story of the fallen elephant, depicting a fictional hunting method, and the elephant's associated lack of joints. The other is the brief allusion to the Aesopic camel. These references to written sources indicate that the author is no naïf but is part, however humbly, of the literary culture of his time; they confirm that the *Tale* was not created in a purely oral, preliterary context. We now examine the other instances where the *Tale*'s content may have been drawn from cultural rather than natural knowledge.

The *Physiologus*

The *Physiologus,* the moralizing and fantastical compendium of animal lore already mentioned in "Literary Parallels," was one of a number of "low" middle Byzantine texts that did not fulfill the intellectual or linguistic demands associated with normal Byzantine learned writing. (These texts—the era's "undercurrent of fictional narrative"—also included Aesop, the *Life of Aesop,* the *Alexander Romance,* and the translations from Arabic and Syriac of *Kalilah and Dimnah [Stephanites and Ichnelates], Barlaam and Joasaph,* and *Sinbad [Syntipas]*: Beaton 1996:31.) Because the *Physiologus* was the most readily accessible reference on animals in Byzantium and the primary compendium on exotic beasts for most Europeans of the time, it was likely the first source to which the author would have recourse for his description of exotic fauna. The author has been careful not to be too expansive about the lion, the elephant, and the leopard (animals not indigenous in his times to the Balkans or Asia Minor—unlike the camel, for instance),[23] but anything said about them should be traced to literary sources akin to the *Physiologus.*

In addition, there were learned compendia of animal lore continuing on from antiquity: Aristotle's *Historia Animalium* (*iii* B.C.); Aristophanes of Byzantium's commentary on Aristotle (*iii* B.C. but surviving only in a *x* A.D. abridgement by Constantine VII Porphyrogennetus); Claudius Aelian's collection of animal lore (*ii* A.D.); Oppian's didactic poem on hunting (*ii–iii* A.D.); and Timothy of Gaza's collection of information on exotic animals (*v–vi* A.D. but surviving only in Porphyrogennetus's abridgement of Aristophanes and in an *xi* A.D. summary).[24] But time and again, it appears that the author of the *Tale* did not turn to these sources (even though they were frequently more accurate—particularly Aristotle and Aristophanes) but limited himself to what he could glean from the *Physiologus.*

The fierce-eyed lion, with his twisting tail (18)

Not much is said about the lion as an animal in the *Tale*: he is more a king than a feline. But two adjectives do slip in: ἀγριόφθαλμος, "fierce-eyed," and γαγκλαδοραδάτος, "twisting-tailed." Both of these might be attributed to the *Physiologus,* which is all the likelier as the description of the elephant, two verses later, is unambiguously Physiologan. "Twisting-tailed" is a plausible supposition for the author to have made in response to the following:

> πρώτη αὐτοῦ φύσις ἐστὶν αὕτη· ὅταν περιπατῇ ἐν τῷ ὄρει καὶ ἔρχηται αὐτῷ ὀσμὴ τῶν κυνηγῶν, τῇ οὐρᾷ αὐτοῦ συγκαλύπτει αὐτοῦ τὰ ἴχνη, ἵνα μὴ ἀκολουθοῦντες τοῖς ἴχνεσιν αὐτοῦ οἱ κυνηγοὶ εὕρωσιν αὐτοῦ τὴν μάνδραν καὶ κρατήσωσιν αὐτόν.
>
> [The first nature of the lion is the following: when he walks in the mountains and the smell of the hunters comes to him, he covers his tracks with his tail so that the hunters do not follow his tracks to find his den and capture him.] (*Physiologus* 1.1)

The story is attested in Claudius Aelian, the second-century compiler of animal gossip:

> Λέων ὅταν βαδίζῃ, οὐκ εὐθύωρον πρόεισιν, οὐδὲ ἐᾷ τῶν ἰχνῶν ἑαυτοῦ ἁπλᾶ εἶναι τὰ ἰνδάλματα, ἀλλὰ πῇ μὲν πρόεισι, πῇ δὲ ἐπάνεισι, καὶ αὖ πάλιν τοῦ πρόσω ἔχεται, καὶ μέντοι καὶ ἵεται ἐς τοὔμπαλιν. εἶτα προφορεῖται τὴν ὁδόν, καὶ ἀφανίζει τοῖς θηραταῖς ἰέναι κατὰ στίβον τὸν ἑαυτοῦ καὶ ῥᾳδίως τὴν κοίτην ἔνθα ἀναπαύεται καὶ οἰκεῖ σὺν τοῖς σκύμνοις εὑρίσκειν. καὶ ταῦτα μὲν λεόντων ἐστὶν ἴδια δῶρα φύσεως.
>
> [The Lion when walking does not move straight forward, nor does he allow his footprints to appear plain and simple, but at one point he moves forward, at another he goes back, then he holds on his course, and then again starts in the opposite direction. Next he goes to and fro, effacing his tracks so as to prevent hunters from following his path and easily discovering the lair where he takes his rest and lives with his cubs. These habits of the Lion are Nature's special gifts.] (*Aelian* 9.30)

This does not quite mean that the lion uses his tail to efface his tracks; that claim seems to have been the *Physiologus*'s innovation, presumably inspired by the lion's distinctive tail. Aristotle (*Historia Animalium* 9.630a) mentions that fleeing lions stretch their tails like dogs, but this does not account for what the *Physiologus* asserts. However, though the circumstantial evidence suggests a Physiologan allusion, the medieval depiction of lions usually involved a twist in the tail; the illustrations of the lion in the manuscripts of the *Tale*'s Constantinopolitan manuscript confirm this (see "Manuscript C Illustrations"). So the author could have derived the notion himself from pictorial depictions of the lion.

"Fierce-eyed," although perfectly plausible for the lion, might have originated in a misreading of the following:

> Δευτέρα φύσις τοῦ λέοντος. ὅταν καθεύδῃ ὁ λέων ἐν τῷ σπηλαίῳ, ἀγρυπνοῦσιν αὐτοῦ οἱ ὀφθαλμοί· ἀνεῳγμένοι γάρ εἰσι. καὶ ἐν τοῖς Ἄισμασιν ὁ Σολομὼν μαρτυρεῖ λέγων· «ἐγὼ καθεύδω, καὶ ἡ καρδία μου ἀγρυπνεῖ».
>
> [The second nature of the lion: when the lion sleeps in the cave, his eyes are awake, for they are open. And in the Song of Songs, Solomon witnesses: "I sleep, but my hearth waketh" (Song of Songs 5:2).] (*Physiologus* 1.1)

Although most manuscripts have ἀγρυπνοῦσιν, "keep awake," manuscript M of the first redaction[25] has ἀγριαίνουσιν, "grow wild."[26] Whether through a manuscript like M or through his own misreading, the author may well have understood the lion to be fierce eyed rather than waking eyed.

The story of the waking-eyed lion is attested in Aelian (5.39, 12.7) and Plutarch (*Quaestiones conviviales* 4.5.2). Aelian attributes it to Democritus, and Wellmann (1930:78, 82) concludes that the notion that the lion sleeps with his eyes open was first promulgated in Bolus/Pseudo-Democritus, in the third century B.C., and is ultimately Egyptian in origin. Of course, it is unlikely that the author had direct access to any of these sources, and it is far likelier that he based himself only on a reading of the *Physiologus*. Still, it is always possible that the author, independently even of the *Physiologus,* is referring to the lion simply as an animal horrible to behold: see discussion in Commentary, verse 18.

A beast with neither joints, nor knees, nor ankles (20)

The elephant was an animal with which Byzantium had had little direct contact since the early seventh century and their final battles with the Sassanid Persians (Scullard 1974:198–207). What the elephant looked like, at least, could still be gleaned by a Constantinopolitan who looked in the right places; sculptures of elephants were still to be seen in the city in the early eighth century. The *Parastaseis Syntomoi Chronikai,* a somewhat confused account of the sights of Constantinople compiled at that time, record the collapse of one such statue in living memory (§17); another still stood, complete with an imaginative story (typical of the collection) on what it was doing there—although as its description shows, the compilers of the *Parastaseis* needed to seek out expert opinion on how big an elephant was:

> Ἐν οἷς ἐλέφας ἵσταται παμμεγέθης· ὡς οἱ θηριοδεῖκται ἡμῖν ἐβεβαίωσαν, μὴ γίνεσθαι ἐπάνω αὐτοῦ τὸ μέγεθος τῶν ἐλεφάντων, τῶν δὲ μεγάλων ἕως οὕτως. Οὗτος ὁ ἐλέφας ὑπὸ Σευήρου τοῦ Κάρου Ἕλληνος ἐτυπώθη θέαμά τι κατὰ τὴν παράδοσιν. Ἐν γὰρ τῇ αὐτῇ χρυσορόφῳ Βασιλικῇ τὸν ἐλέφαντα παραμένειν εἰς θέαμα ἐξαίσιον· [...]. Ἐν αὐτῷ δέ φασι τῷ ἐλέφαντι παραμένειν τῷ τόπῳ ἐκείνῳ Καρκινήλον ἀργυροκόπον ἐν πλαστοῖς ζυγοῖς· ὥστε ‹τῷ› διατρέφοντι τὸν ἐλέφαντα, φασίν, ‹θάνατον› ἀπειλεῖν, ὅτι κατεπορθεῖτο τούτου τὸ οἴκημα· καὶ πολλάκις διαβεβαιωσαμένου θάνατον τῷ θηριοτρόφῳ, εἰ μὴ τοῦτον κρατήσει· αὐτὸς δὲ διὰ † τὰς βαγύλας ἐλαιοφόρους κρατῆσαι οὐκ ἐνεδίδου· ὃν καὶ φονεύσας ὁ αὐτὸς ζυγοπλάστης τῷ ἐλέφαντι εἰς βρῶσιν προέθηκε· τοῦ δὲ θηρίου ἀτιθάσου ὄντος, καὶ αὐτὸν ἐξανήλωσεν. Ὃ καὶ Σευῆρος ἀκούσας θυσίας τῷ θηρίῳ οὐκ ὀλίγας προσήνεγκεν. [...] ὃ καὶ ἕως τῆς σήμερον τοῖς φιλοσοφοῦσιν ἐν πείρᾳ προτέθειται θέαμα.
>
> [With these stands a huge elephant; as the exhibitors of animals have assured us, elephants do not come greater in size than this, the big ones being as big as this. This elephant was set up by Severus the son of Carus the pagan as a spectacle, according to tradition. For in the same golden-roofed Basilica they say the elephant lived, an extraordinary

> spectacle. . . . And they say that in the same place as the elephant lived Carcinelus, a silversmith who used rigged scales. They say he threatened the elephant's keeper because his house was being damaged, and he frequently vowed that he would kill the keeper if he did not keep the animal in check. But the keeper would not consent to control the elephant with reins. The user of rigged scales killed him and offered him to the elephant as fodder, but the elephant, being wild, killed him too. And when Severus heard this he offered many sacrifices to the beast, and they were at once commemorated in statues in that place. . . . And this spectacle is accessible until the present day for philosophers to test.] (*Parastaseis* 37)[27]

In addition, there are Byzantine mosaics of elephants surviving to this day in the Great Palace in Istanbul (Cutler 1985), and two elephants can still be clearly seen today (and, it follows, in the fourteenth century) on the Kamara in Thessalonica, the triumphal arch built by Emperor Galerius in the third century. Nevertheless, the elephant that Emperor Constantine Monomachus (1042–55) brought with him to Constantinople was unusual enough to prompt Michael Attaleiates to record the event:

> καὶ ζώων ἀσυνήθεις ἰδέας τοῖς ὑπηκόοις ἐξ ἀλλοδαπῆς παρεστήσατο γῆς, μεθ᾽ ὧν καὶ τὸν μέγιστον ἐν τετραπόδοις ἐλέφαντα, ὃς θαῦμα τοῖς Βυζαντίοις καὶ τοῖς ἄλλοις Ῥωμαίοις, ὧν εἰς ὄψιν ἐλήλυθε διερχόμενος, ἐχρημάτισεν.
>
> [He presented to his subjects certain beasts from foreign lands of unusual appearance, among them the largest of all quadrupeds, the elephant, who was a marvel as he passed by to the citizens of Constantinople and the other Romans, for whom his image had long faded from memory.] (*Attaleiates: History* 48)

The *Oneirocriticon of Achmet,* a dream interpretation manual written two centuries earlier, makes reference to elephants bound with "bonds" (κούρκουμον) (§269); however, the Byzantine compiler of the manual includes the elephant in the material drawn from Persian and "Egyptian" sources. The other references to elephants that Koukoules (1947–55:3.251) identifies are all early Byzantine: St. Gregory the Theologian, John Malalas, Patriarch Nicephorus (referring to Emperor Heraclius). After Constantine Monomachus, there is no reason to believe an elephant was ever again brought to Byzantium. In the early fifteenth century, Demetrius Raoul Cabaces, a landowner in the Peloponnese, had to ask the visiting Italian antiquarian Ciriaco of Ancona to draw an elephant in his scrapbook (Ševčenko 1960:174–75)—the irony being that by that stage in history, an Italian was far likelier to have seen an elephant than a Byzantine was.[28]

It is consistent with this fading from memory that the image of the elephant presented is more fabulous than accurate. Anyone who vividly remembers a visit to a circus will have a hard time believing the author's claim about the elephant having neither joints nor knees nor ankles (20): elephants can very much kneel. Likewise, anyone familiar with Indian traditions will know that elephant trappers hardly have to wait for the animal to fall asleep leaning on partially chopped tree trunks (960–68): pits or nooses are rather more effective (Carrington [1959:143–51, 163–72] describes killing and trapping methods, respectively), whereas the elephant's ability to sleep standing up does not at all imply that he can never "have a lie-down" (945–46) or that he cannot get up once he falls (951–54). Even without the benefit of zoo trips or safaris, readers need not be misled by the author's elephant stories, given his reliance on as suspect a source of lore as the *Physiologus*.

As one would expect, the *Physiologus*'s curious notions have a classical pedigree. The belief that the elephant has no knees is old enough that Aristotle felt compelled to refute it:

> ὁ δ' ἐλέφας οὐχ ὥσπερ ἔλεγόν τινες, ἀλλὰ συγκαθίζει καὶ κάμπτει τὰ σκέλη, πλὴν οὐ δύναται διὰ τὸ βάρος ἐπ' ἀμφότερα ἅμα, ἀλλ' ἀνακλίνεται ἢ ἐπὶ τὰ εὐώνυμα ἢ ἐπὶ τὰ δεξιά, καὶ καθεύδει ἐν τούτῳ τῷ σχήματι, κάμπτει δὲ τὰ ὀπίσθια σκέλη ὥσπερ ἄνθρωπος.
>
> [The elephant does not behave as some used to allege, but settles down and bends its legs, though it cannot on account of its weight settle down on both sides simultaneously, but reclines either on the left or on the right, and in that posture goes to sleep. Its hind legs it bends just as a human being does.] (*Aristotle: Historia Animalium* 498a)

Wellmann (1930:30) attributes this old notion to Ctesias, the Greek doctor in the court of Artaxerxes in the fourth century B.C. who wrote a fabulous account of India. The notion was a long time dying. Both the unbending knees and the recliner-tree first turn up in Agatharchides' second-century B.C. account of the Red Sea:[29]

> οὐκ ἐπὶ γῆς δὲ ἀναπεσόντες ὑπνοῦσιν, ἀλλὰ τοῖς παχυτάτοις καὶ μεγίστοις δένδρεσι προσανακλίνοντες ἑαυτοὺς, ὥστε τοὺς μὲν δύο πόδας τοὺς πλησίον τοῦ στελέχους πρὸς τὴν γῆν ἐλαφρῶς ὑπερείδεσθαι, τὴν δὲ πλευρὰν τὸ πᾶν σῶμα ἐκδεχομένην ὀχεῖσθαι πρὸς τῇ φύσει τοῦ ξύλου, καὶ τοῦτον τὸν τρόπον τῆς καταφορᾶς τυγχάνειν οὐκ εἰλικρινοῦς, ἀλλὰ παρεψευσμένης [. . .] ἐκ τῶν ὄπισθεν τοῦ δένδρου τόπων πρίουσιν, ἕως ἂν μήτε κλίνῃ τὸ πᾶν μήτε ἰσχύον ἄγαν (καὶ ἰσχυρὸν) ἀπολείποιτο, μένῃ δὲ ἑστηκὸς ἐπὶ βραχείας ῥοπῆς. Τὸ δὲ ζῷον ἀπὸ τῆς νομῆς ἐπὶ τὸν συνήθη τῆς κοίτης τόπον ἀνακλινόμενον αἰφνίδιόν τε πίπτει, τοῦ ξύλου

κλασθέντος, καὶ πρόκειται τοῖς θηράσασι δεῖπνον ἕτοιμον· τὰς γὰρ ὀπισθίας κόψαντες οὗτοι σάρκας, καὶ ποιήσαντες ἔξαιμον τὸ ζῷον, εἶτα νεκρὸν, πρὸς τὴν ἑαυτοῦ χρείαν ἕκαστος τὰ μέλη διαιροῦσιν.

[For they do not sleep by lying on the earth, but they recline against the thickest and largest trees so that the two legs closest to the trunk hold it up gently against the ground, while the one side, taking up the weight of the entire body, is supported by the tree. And they are brought down in the following way—not honestly, but by deceit. . . . ⟨The hunters⟩ saw the tree from behind, until it neither falls over nor would take too much to fall; it stays upright on a tenuous balance. And when the animal comes back from feeding to its usual sleeping place, it reclines and suddenly falls, as the tree breaks. And the hunters have a ready meal; they chop off its hind flesh and bleed the beast to death. Then they split the meat up among themselves according to their need.] (*Agatharchides* 55)

Agatharchides' account in turn was recycled by later authors of geographical compendia:

εἴωθε γὰρ τοῦτο τὸ ζῷον, ἐπειδὰν ἀπὸ τῆς νομῆς πληρωθῇ, πρὸς ὕπνον καταφέρεσθαι, διαφορὰν ἐχούσης τῆς περὶ αὐτὸ διαθέσεως πρὸς τὰ λοιπὰ τῶν τετραπόδων· οὐ γὰρ δύναται τοῖς γόνασι πρὸς τὴν γῆν συγκαθιέναι τὸν ὅλον ὄγκον, ἀλλὰ πρὸς δένδρον ἀνακλιθὲν ποιεῖται τὴν διὰ τῶν ὕπνων ἀνάπαυσιν. διόπερ τὸ δένδρον διὰ τὴν γινομένην πρὸς αὐτὸ πλεονάκις πρόσκλισιν τοῦ ζῴου τετριμμένον τέ ἐστι καὶ ῥύπου πλῆρες, πρὸς δὲ τούτοις ὁ περὶ αὐτὸ τόπος ἴχνη τε ἔχει καὶ σημεῖα πολλά, δι' ὧν οἱ τὰ τοιαῦτα ἐρευνῶντες Αἰθίοπες γνωρίζουσι τὰς τῶν ἐλεφάντων κοίτας. ὅταν οὖν ἐπιτύχωσι τοιούτῳ δένδρῳ, πρίζουσιν αὐτὸ παρὰ τὴν γῆν, μέχρι ἂν ὀλίγην ἔτι τὴν ῥοπὴν ἔχῃ πρὸς τὴν πτῶσιν· εἶθ' οὗτοι μὲν τὰ σημεῖα τῆς ἰδίας παρουσίας ἀφανίσαντες ταχέως ἀπαλλάττονται, φθάνοντες τὴν ἔφοδον τοῦ ζῴου, ὁ δ' ἐλέφας πρὸς τὴν ἑσπέραν ἐμπλησθεὶς τῆς τροφῆς ἐπὶ τὴν συνήθη καταντᾷ κοίτην. κατακλιθεὶς δὲ ἀθρόῳ τῷ βάρει παραχρῆμα μετὰ τῆς τοῦ δένδρου φορᾶς ἐπὶ τὴν γῆν καταφέρεται, πεσὼν δ' ὕπτιος μένει τὴν νύκτα κείμενος διὰ τὸ τὴν τοῦ σώματος φύσιν ἀδημιούργητον εἶναι πρὸς ἀνάστασιν. οἱ δὲ πρίσαντες τὸ δένδρον Αἰθίοπες ἅμ' ἡμέρᾳ καταντῶσι, καὶ χωρὶς κινδύνων ἀποκτείναντες τὸ ζῷον σκηνοποιοῦνται περὶ τὸν τόπον καὶ παραμένουσι μέχρι ἂν τὸ πεπτωκὸς ἀναλώσωσι.

[This animal is accustomed to going to sleep when it is finished feeding, but the way it does so is different from other quadrupeds. For it cannot bring its whole bulk to the ground with its knees, but it rather rests and sleeps leaning against a tree. For that reason the tree, reclined

> against by the beast so often, is worn and full of dirt. Furthermore, the surroundings have many signs and tracks, through which the Ethiopians, searching these matters, find the elephants' sleeping places. So when they find such a tree, they saw it near the ground, until it is about to fall. Then they cover their tracks and quickly leave before the beast arrives. When the beast is full of food in the evening, it comes to its usual sleeping place. Lying with all its weight, it is immediately toppled to the ground by the tree. It falls on its back and lies there through the night, as its body has not been made for getting back up. And the Ethiopians who sawed the tree come in the daytime and kill the beast without danger, make their tents in the area, and stay until they have consumed the fallen beast.] (*Diodorus Siculus* 3.27.2, quoting Agatharchides)
>
> ἄλλοι δὲ σημειωσάμενοι τὰ δένδρα οἷς εἰώθασι προσαναπαύεσθαι, προσιόντες ἐκ θατέρου μέρους τὸ στέλεχος ὑποκόπτουσιν· ἐπὰν οὖν προσιὸν τὸ θηρίον ἀποκλίνῃ πρὸς αὐτό, πεσόντος τοῦ δένδρου πίπτει καὶ αὐτό, ἀναστῆναι δὲ μὴ δυναμένου διὰ τὸ τὰ σκέλη διηνεκὲς ὀστοῦν ἔχειν καὶ ἀκαμπές.
>
> [And others, noting the trees on which it is accustomed to reclining, go to it from the other side and cut its trunk. So when the beast reclines on it, the tree falls and it falls, too. It cannot get up because its legs have a long unbending bone.] (*Strabo* 16.4.10, quoting Agatharchides)

The story, unfounded though it was[30] and refuted even by Aelian in the second century (6.37), continued on its way regardless, passing to Basil of Caesarea (*iv* A.D.; *Hexaemeron* 9.5), Nonnus (*v/vi* A.D.; *Dionysiaca* 43.29), Timothy of Gaza (*vi* A.D.; §25), Constantine VII Porphyrogennetus's redaction of Aristophanes of Byzantium (*x* A.D.; 2.131, citing Basil—though 2.80 preserves Aristophanes' own agreement with Aristotle against the belief), Michael of Ephesus (*xi–xii* A.D.; *In librum de animalium incessu commentarium* 154)—and ultimately the *Mass of the Beardless Man* (see Textual Notes, verse 942). The notion was inevitably transmitted to Western Europe and was accepted by both Shakespeare (*Troilus and Cressida* 2.3.113) and Donne (*The Progress of the Soul* 39; see epigram) (Carrington 1959:225).

So pervasive was the *Physiologus*'s version of how to trap an elephant that it turns up even in unrelated stories of modern Greek folklore: a folk tale from Zante (Minotos 1953, cited in Veloudis 1977:lxxi) uses the sawed tree to dispatch not an elephant but Alexander the Great himself. The very implausibility of the account makes it likelier that the Physiologan account passed into popular culture, where it was manipulated and distorted. As will be seen below in "Folklore against the *Physiologus,*" modern Greek folklore also shares with the *Physiologus* notions about the enmity of deer and snakes, and of the effects of burning deer horn—although in the latter case, at least, the direction of transmission seems to have been from folklore to the *Physiologus,* rather than vice versa.

The mimic monkey, mockery of the world (37)

The *Tale* refers to "the mimic monkey, mockery of the world" (37), who is "more cunning than the fox by far" (933a); he is addressed by the elephant as "you louse-munching, nit-nibbling, disgusting dirt-face" (972). Three manuscripts of the *Physiologus* contain a chapter on the monkey (πίθηκος), which they describe as μιμηλότατον καὶ πονηρότατον, καὶ ὅσα θεωρεῖ τὸν ἄνθρωπον ποιοῦντα, ταῦτα καὶ αὐτὸ ὁμοίως ποιεῖ, "most mimicking and most cunning, and whatever it sees Man doing, it does the same" (Sbordone 1936:318). A vernacular version of the Pseudo-Epiphanian strand of Physiologan stories, including the monkey's, repeats the claim that the monkey (now going by its vernacular, Arabic appellation, μαϊμοῦ,[31] also used in the *Tale*) is πονηρώτατον, καὶ μιμεῖται πολλὰ τὸν ἄνθρωπον, καὶ ὅσα ἐβλέπει καὶ κάμνη, τὰ κάμνη καὶ αὐτὰ ὁμοίως, "most cunning, and mimics Man a lot, and whatever it sees him doing, it does the same" (305).

These notions of the monkey were old. Aelian describes the monkey as μιμηλότατον ζῷον, "a most imitative beast" (5.26), whereas the sixth-century zoologist Timothy of Gaza describes it as ἀσελγέστατον καὶ πανοῦργον, "most licentious and wily" (§51). Moreover, the association of mimicry with the monkey, in the form of the performing macaque, was a commonplace in Europe, especially from the twelfth century on (Rowland 1973:11). The propensity of the monkey to eating lice is not mentioned by the ancient zoologists or the *Physiologus* and must likewise have originated in observation—or at least common sense, given the plausibility of small animals eating insects.

The references that Koukoules (1947–55:3.248–49) finds to performing monkeys in Byzantium are mostly early (especially Libanius, *iv* A.D.), and the instances in the *Oneirocriticon of Achmet* (§136, §280) are identified with "Persian and Egyptian" (i.e., Muslim) source material. But Manuel Philes, in the early fourteenth century, refers to "mimic monkeys" in a poem praising the emperor:

> Τοὺς γὰρ βασιλεύσαντας ἐκ πλείστου χρόνου,
> Καὶ τὴν τύχην δείξαντας ἐκ τῶν πρακτέων,
> Ἡ σὴ φύσις τίθησι πιθήκους μίμους,
> Λέον πρὸς αὐτούς, εἰ παραβάλλοιντό σοι
> Κατὰ τὸν ἁρμόζοντα τοῖς κρότοις νόμον.

> [For those who reigned in times of yore and proved
> favored, in carrying their duties out—
> your nature makes of them mere mimic monkeys,
> and you a lion, if compared to you
> according to the rule that fits applause.] (*Poems* 2.95.176–81)

And the *Assizes of Cyprus,* a thirteenth-century legal text, state that

> Τὸ δικαίωμαν τῶν ***μαμούνων*** τὰς φέρνουν ἀπαὶ τὴν Σαρακηνίαν, ὁρίζει τὸ δίκαιον νὰ λάβουν τέλος εἰς τὰ μάρκα ρ', μάρκα ιβ' ἥμισον
>
> [For the privilege to ⟨import⟩ ***monkeys*** brought from Saracenia ⟨Muslim lands⟩, the law determines that they should be taxed at twelve and a half marks from every hundred marks.] (241)

Koukoules (1947–55:3.248–49) also mentions that performing monkeys were led about by Gypsies, who arrived late to Byzantium, though without providing justification for the claim. So the author of the *Tale* would not have lacked opportunities to observe monkeys.

The deer, who sucks down snakes (52)

Shortly after the appearance of the jointless elephant, the snake-sucking deer is mentioned in passing. The snake-sucking deer legend had made it into the *Physiologus,* and the allusion in the *Tale* can readily be explained by reference to it:

> ***Original redaction***
>
> Ὁ μὲν Δαυὶδ λέγει· «ὃν τρόπον ἐπιποθεῖ ἡ ἔλαφος ἐπὶ τὰς πηγὰς τῶν ὑδάτων, οὕτως ἐπιποθεῖ ἡ ψυχή μου πρὸς σὲ ὁ Θεός». ὁ Φυσιολόγος ἔλεξε περὶ τῆς ἐλάφου ὅτι ἐχθρὰ τοῦ δράκοντός ἐστι πάνυ. ἐὰν φύγῃ ὁ δράκων ἀπὸ τῆς ἐλάφου εἰς τὰς ῥαγάδας τῆς γῆς, πορεύεται ἡ ἔλαφος καὶ ἐμπιπλᾷ τὰ ἀγγεῖα αὐτῆς πηγαίου ὕδατος, καὶ ἐξεμεῖ ἐπὶ τὰς ῥαγάδας τῆς γῆς, καὶ ἀναφέρει τὸν δράκοντα καὶ κατακόπτει αὐτὸν καὶ ἀποκτείνει.
>
> Οὕτω καὶ ὁ Κύριος ἡμῶν ἀπέκτεινε τὸν δράκοντα τὸν μέγαν [τὸν διάβολον] ἐκ τῶν οὐρανίων ὑδάτων [...] οὐ δύναται γὰρ ὁ δράκων βαστάζειν ὕδωρ, οὐδὲ ὁ διάβολος λόγον οὐράνιον.
>
> Ἐοίκασι τοίνυν ἐλάφῳ κατ' ἄλλον τρόπον οἱ ἀσκηταί, οἱ τὸν ἐνάρετον καὶ ἐπίπονον βίον διὰ σκληραγωγίας πολλῆς ἄγοντες, ὡς δεδιψηκότες ἐπὶ τὰς πηγὰς τῆς σωτηρίου μετανοίας τρέχοντες, διὰ τῶν τῆς ἐξομολογήσεως δακρύων κατασβεννύουσι τὰ βέλη τοῦ πονηροῦ τὰ πεπυρωμένα, καὶ καταπατοῦντες τὸν μέγαν δράκοντα, ἤτοι τὸν διάβολον, ἀποκτένουσιν αὐτόν.
>
> [David says: "As the hart panteth after the water brooks, so panteth my soul after thee, O God" (Psalms 42:1). The Physiologus has said about the deer that he is the dragon's great enemy. Whenever the dragon flees, the deer departs ⟨to the sources of water⟩ and fills his body with spring water; he pours the water into the earth's cracks and floods the dragon out, promptly killing him.

This is how our Savior pumped out the great dragon, {the devil,} out of the heavenly water. . . . For the dragon is not capable of suffering water, nor can the devil bear the heavens' speech.

The ascetics, who lead a virtuous and toilsome life with great hardship, resemble the deer in another way. Thirsting for the springs of saving repentance they run; with the tears of confession they extinguish the fiery arrows of the Enemy; and trampling on the great dragon (namely, the devil), they kill him.] (*Physiologus* 1.30)

Alternate version

Ἔλεξε καὶ τοῦτο ὁ Φυσιολόγος· οἱ ἔλαφοι ὅπου ἐὰν καταντήσωσιν ὄφιν, καταπίνουσιν αὐτόν, καὶ τρέχει καὶ ἐλαύνεται σφοδρῶς. ἐλαυνόμενος δὲ καὶ τρέχων, μὴ ἱστάμενος ἐπὶ δύο καὶ τρεῖς ἡμέρας, ‹ὁ ὄφις› χωνεύεται ὑπ᾽ αὐτοῦ· χωνευθέντος δὲ τοῦ θηρίου, οὐρεῖ ‹ὁ ἔλαφος› αὐτὸ κάτω διὰ τῆς οὐρήθρας, καὶ ὅπου ἂν πέσῃ τὸ οὖρος ἐκεῖνο, γίνεται μόσχος ἄκρατος.

Οὕτω καὶ σύ, νοητὲ ἄνθρωπε, πολλὰ κοπιάσας καὶ δραμών, δυνήσει ἀπορρῖψαι τὴν δυσωδίαν τοῦ διαβόλου.

Καλῶς ὁ Φυσιολόγος ἔλεξε περὶ τῆς ἐλάφου.

[The Physiologus has said this, too: a deer, wherever it meets a snake, swallows it and runs off, driven urgently. And as it is driven to run, not standing still for two or three days, the snake is digested by it. When the beast is digested, the deer urinates it through its urethra, and wherever that urine falls, the purest musk is generated.

Thus, too, you, O intelligent man, after much effort and a long race, will be able to be rid of the stench of the devil.

The Physiologus has spoken well about the deer.] (*Physiologus* 1.30 bis)

Byzantine redaction

Ἔστι γὰρ ὁ ἔλαφος μόρφωσιν ἔχων δορκάδος [ἀγρίας], τὸ δὲ κέρας αὐτοῦ τρίαρχον κατὰ τὰς τρεῖς ἀνακαινίσεις αὐτοῦ. οὗτος μὲν ζῇ ἔτη πεντήκοντα, καὶ μετὰ ταῦτα ἐκτρέχει ὡς καλὸς δρομεὺς τὰς νάπας καὶ τὰς ὕλας [καὶ τοὺς φραγμοὺς] τῶν ὀρέων, καὶ ὀσφραίνεται τὰς ὀπὰς τῶν ἑρπετῶν, καὶ ὅπου ἐστὶν ὄφις τρισέκδυτος, διὰ τῆς αὐτοῦ ὀσφραινότητος γινώσκει αὐτόν, καὶ εὐθέως ἀποφθέγγεται τρεῖς φωνὰς μεγίστας ἀγρίας, καὶ τίθησι τὸ ῥάνθος αὐτοῦ ἐπὶ τὴν θύραν τῆς ὀπῆς, καὶ ἀναφέρει τὴν πνοὴν αὐτοῦ ἔσω, καὶ εἰς οἷον βάθος κεῖται ὁ ὄφις, ἀνέρχεται ἐν τῷ λάρυγγι τοῦ ἐλάφου, καὶ οὕτω καταπίνει αὐτόν· διὰ τοῦτο ἔλαφος ὀνομάζεται, διὰ τὸ ἑλεῖν τοὺς ὄφεις ἐκ βάθους. λαβὼν δὲ τὸν ὄφιν, τρέχει εἰς τὰς πηγὰς τῶν ὑδάτων· ἐὰν γὰρ διὰ τριῶν ὡρῶν ἀφ᾽ οὗ τὸν ὄφιν λάβῃ οὐ πίῃ ὕδωρ, τελευτᾷ, εἰ δὲ πίῃ ὕδωρ, ζήσεται ἄλλα πεντήκοντα ἔτη. διὰ τοῦτο εἶπεν ὁ προφήτης Δαυίδ· «ὃν τρόπον ἐπιποθεῖ ἡ ἔλαφος ἐπὶ τὰς πηγὰς τῶν ὑδάτων, οὕτως ἐπιποθεῖ ἡ ψυχή μου πρὸς σὲ ὁ Θεός».

Καὶ σὺ οὖν, νοητὲ ἄνθρωπε, τρεῖς ἀνακαινίσεις ἔχεις ἐν ἑαυτῷ, [τουτέστι] βάπτισμα ἀφθαρσίας, χάρισμα υἱοθεσίας καὶ τὴν μετάνοιαν, καὶ ὅταν ἕλῃς τὸν ὄφιν ἐν τῇ καρδίᾳ σου, τουτέστι τὴν ἁμαρτίαν, δράμε εὐθέως ἐπὶ τὰς πηγὰς τῶν ὑδάτων, τουτέστιν ἐπὶ τὰς φλέβας τῶν θείων Γραφῶν, καὶ τὰ τῆς προφητείας ἑρμηνεύματα, καὶ πίε ὕδωρ ζῶν, τουτέστι τῶν ἁγίων δώρων κοινωνῶν ἐν μετανοίᾳ, ἀνακαίνιζε λοιπὸν σεαυτὸν τῇ μετανοίᾳ, καὶ μὴ νεκροῦ τῇ ἁμαρτίᾳ.

Καλῶς ὁ Φυσιολόγος ἔλεξε περὶ τοῦ ἐλάφου.

[The deer looks like a {wild} roebuck, and his horn is three-branched, in accordance with his three revivals. He lives fifty years. And after those fifty years he runs out like a good runner through the ravines and the gorges {and the troughs} of the mountains, and he smells out the reptiles' holes; wherever the snake is that has changed his skin three times, he recognizes him through smell and immediately cries ferociously three times. And he places his mouth on the hole's entrance and sucks his own breath in; however deep the snake may lie, he comes out all the way up and into the deer's throat, who swallows him; that is why he is called ἔλ-αφος ⟨deer⟩ because of his ἑλεῖν ⟨pulling⟩ ὄφεις ⟨snakes⟩ from the depths. And after catching the snake, he runs to the springs; unless he drinks water within three hours, he dies; but if he finds water, then he lives for another fifty years. That is why David says: "As the hart panteth after the water brooks, so panteth my soul after thee, O God."

And you, O intelligent man, you have three revivals: {namely} baptism into incorruptibility, the gift of adoption ⟨into the communion of God⟩, and penitence. And whenever you pull the snake, namely, sin, into your heart, run fast to the spring, namely, the veins of the holy scriptures and the interpretations of the prophecies, and drink fresh water, namely, partake in penitence of the communion of the holy gifts. And so renew yourself through penitence and die not in sin.

The Physiologus has spoken well on the deer.] (*Physiologus* 2.4)

Wellmann (1930:32, 84) finds the snake-sucking legend must have come to Greece very early on, as it is quite widespread (*Plutarch: De Sollertia Animalium* 976d; *Aelian* 2.9; *Origen: Scholia in Canticum Canticorum* 268; *Basil of Caesarea: Homilies on the Psalms* 300). Wellmann (1930) further believes it is based on a Democritan tradition of the enmity between the snake and the crab.

Your mouth is one place and your trunk is elsewhere (940)

In one aspect the *Tale* may break ranks with the tradition of the *Physiologus*. The *Tale* has the monkey claim that

> your mouth is one place and your trunk is elsewhere;
> you pick your food up here and move it there
> to eat it. (940–42)

The first redaction of the *Physiologus* is strangely silent about the elephant's most distinctive trait. However, the second redaction, which Sbordone (1936) terms "Byzantine" and dates to the fifth or sixth century, is explicit:

> Ἔστι γὰρ ὁ ἐλέφας μεγέθη ζῷον, προμυκίδα ἔχον ἐν ἑαυτῷ τοῦ διαφθεῖραι πάντα τὰ ζῷα, [ὁμοίως δὲ τὴν βρῶσιν καὶ τὴν πόσιν διὰ τῆς προμυχίδος αὐτοῦ κυβερνᾶται]
>
> [For the elephant is a large beast, having a trunk such that he can destroy any beast. {Likewise its food and drink are handled by its trunk.}] (2.3)

The phrasing of the Byzantine *Physiologus* is vague enough to be misunderstood. This misunderstanding turns up in other authors, for example, Basil of Caesarea (*Hexaemeron* 9.5: ἔχει δὲ τὴν προνομαίαν, τὴν τοῦ τραχήλου χρείαν ἀποπληροῦσαν, δι' ἧς καὶ τὴν τροφὴν προσάγεται, καὶ τὸ ποτὸν ἀνιμᾶται, "And it has a trunk, which acts as its throat, through which it brings in food and draws up drink"). The ancient zoologists, on the other hand, knew precisely what the function of the trunk is (Aristotle, *Historia Animalium* 497b: ἔχει δὲ μυκτῆρα τοιοῦτον καὶ τηλικοῦτον ὥστε ἀντὶ χειρῶν ἔχειν αὐτόν· πίνει γὰρ καὶ ἐσθίει ὀρέγων τούτῳ εἰς τὸ στόμα, "Its nose, however, is of such a kind and of such a size that it can be used instead of hands: its method of eating and drinking is to reach with this organ into its mouth"; *Aelian* 4.31: μυκτῆρα δὲ κέκτηται χειρὸς παγχρηστότερον, "It has a proboscis which is far more serviceable than a hand"), and so does the *Tale*.

It is noteworthy that the *Tale* is accurate on a point where its most readily accessible sources are either inaccurate, silent, or hopelessly vague. Given how unlikely it was for the author to have ever seen an elephant in the flesh as well as his clear unfamiliarity with Aristotle and (as far as we can tell) Aelian, we are at something of a loss to explain this accuracy. If the author did sneak a peek at a zoology text and got a more truthful description of the elephant's trunk, then it is peculiar he didn't get more information out of it and instead repeats the vagaries of the *Physiologus* elsewhere. Zoology was not dead in late Byzantium, however (see "Manuel Philes," following), and there were still intellectuals in Byzantium who knew a thing or two about elephants; the author may have obtained the information from them at first or second hand. Alternatively, the author may have made use of a realistic depiction of the elephant eating, with a mouth distinct from its trunk, in mosaic or sculpture—such as are known to have been extant in Constantinople.[32]

If the author did in fact consult a zoology text or talked to someone who did, that text might well have been the eleventh-century abridgement of *Timothy of Gaza,* which was used precisely as a zoology textbook. The abridgement—and in all likelihood, the original itself—were written in Koine and were thus more accessible to moderately educated Byzantines than were the authoritative texts like Aristotle. *Timothy* is the source that matches the *Tale*'s description of the elephant the closest: he repeats the claim about its knees (§25.1, ὅτι ὁ ἐλέφας γόνατα οὐκ ἔχει, "that the elephant has no knees"); he knows what the function of the trunk is (§25.2, ὅτι προβοσκίδα ἔχει, δι' ἧς πάντα ποιεῖ ὡς διὰ χειρός, "that it has a trunk with which it does everything as with a hand"); he is vague about its tusks (§25.3, ὅτι ὀδόντας ἔχει μεγάλους ἢ κέρατα, "that it has big teeth or horns"); he knows that it is captured through deceit—though not in the same way as in the *Physiologus* (§25.5, ὅτι παρὰ τοῖς Μαύροις δόλῳ καὶ τάφροις ἀγρεύονται, "that they are caught among the Moors with trick(s) and in ditches"); and that it bears towers in battle (§25.11, ὅτι πύργους οἱ ἐλέφαντες ἔχουσι ξυλίνους ἐπὶ τῶν νώτων πεπληρωμένους ὁπλιτῶν καὶ μάχονται, "that the elephants have on their backs wooden towers filled with soldiers, and fight").

Incidentally, though Aristotle (*Historia Animalium* 595a) states explicitly that the elephant eats fruits and grass and Porphyrogennetus's redaction of Aristophanes of Byzantium repeats this fact (2.78),[33] there is no reason to suppose the author of the *Tale* knew whether the elephant was a carnivore or a herbivore. There is no mention of the elephant's diet in the main version of the *Physiologus* apart from mandrake, and that for aphrodisiac purposes—although the Byzantine redaction (*Physiologus* 2.3) does refer to the elephants "grazing" (νεμόμενοι) when they come across the mandrake. In fact, the vernacular verse version of the *Physiologus* (roughly contemporary with the *Tale*) draws the quite reasonable conclusion from the Byzantine redaction that because the elephant destroys animals with its trunk, it must be a carnivore:

μεγεθεστάτος πέφυκεν, καὶ προμηχίαν ἔχων
μακρὰν ἔξω τῆς φύσεως παρὰ τῶν ζώων ὅλων·
καὶ μὲ τὴν προμηκίδαν του πᾶν ζῶον διαφθείρει,
ἔναι μακρὰ, καμαρωτὴ ὡσὰν δρεπάνου τάξιν,
καὶ πάντα ζῶον καταλῦ καὶ πάντα τρῷ κ' ἐσθίει

[He's born enormous, and he has a trunk
far from what's natural to any beast.
And with his trunk all beasts can he destroy;
it's long and curved and rather like a sickle.
All beasts he kills; all he consumes and eats.] (*Vernacular Physiologus* 3–7)

The legend reported in the *Parastaseis* (see "A beast with neither joints...") likewise suggests the elephant was believed able to eat humans.

Folklore Against the *Physiologus*: The Deer Horn

Those who would hail the deer as a hero in the fight against snakes (52) will be delighted to find out that the odor of his burning horn forces snakes away from their nests (347–350):

> And should snakes happen to infest a house
> and people set my horn's insides alight,
> then its strong odor drives them out at once:
> no longer can they make their nests therein.

This is an old belief, and the combination of the deer's reputed snake-snuffing and snake-sniffing is reported at least as early as Aelian:

> Ἔλαφος ὄφιν νικᾷ, κατά τινα φύσεως δωρεὰν θαυμαστήν· καὶ οὐκ ἂν αὐτὸν διαλάθοι ἐν τῷ φωλέῳ ὢν ὁ ἔχθιστος, ἀλλὰ προσερείσας τῇ καταδρομῇ τοῦ δακέτου τοὺς ἑαυτοῦ μυκτῆρας βιαιότατα ἐσπνεῖ, καὶ ἕλκει ὡς ἴυγγι τῷ πνεύματι, καὶ ἄκοντα προάγει, καὶ προκύπτοντα αὐτὸν ἐσθίειν ἄρχεται· καὶ μάλιστα γε διὰ χειμῶνος δρᾷ τοῦτο. ἤδη μέντοι τις καὶ κέρας ἐλάφου ξέσας, εἶτα τὸ ξέσμα ἐς πῦρ ἐνέβαλε, καὶ ὁ καπνὸς ἀνιὼν διώκει τοὺς ὄφεις πανταχόθεν, μηδὲ τὴν ὀσμὴν ὑπομένοντας.
>
> [A Deer defeats a snake by an extraordinary gift that Nature has bestowed. And the fiercest snake lying in its den cannot escape, but the Deer applies its nostrils to the spot where the venomous creature lurks, breathes into it with the utmost force, attracts it by the spell, as it were, of its breath, draws it forth against its will, and when it peeps out, begins to eat it. Especially in the winter does it do this. Indeed it has even happened that a man has ground a Deer's horn to powder and then has thrown the powder into the fire, and that the mounting smoke has driven the snakes from all the neighbourhood; even the smell is to them unbearable.] (2.9)

Although the combination of two such formidable snake-repellent features in one animal is too good to be true, at least some sources had worked out a causal connection between them:

> ἔλαφος δὲ ‹εἴρηται› παρὰ τὸ ἑλεῖν τοὺς ὄφεις· αἱ γὰρ ἔλαφοι, ὅτε ἀφανεῖς ὦσιν οἱ ὄφεις, τὸ κέρας αὐτῶν προστρίβουσι τῇ πέτρᾳ, ὃ θερμαινόμενον ποιεῖ ἀναθυμίασιν, ἧς μεταλαμβανόμενοι οἱ ὄφεις τῶν φωλεῶν ἐξίασιν.
>
> [It is called "deer" by virtue of pulling snakes ⟨see *Physiologus*⟩. For when snakes are nowhere to be seen, deer rub their horns against a

stone. This being heated gives forth fumes, and when the snakes sense them, they flee their nests.] (*Scholia in Iliadem e cod. Genevensi gr. 44* 3.22)[34]

The legend of burning deer horn as incense is also present in the *Physiologus,* but only in a single manuscript (the *xi* A.D. *Mosquensis graecus* 432 Matthaei = 317 Vladimir, Sbordone's Π):

> Τρίχες γὰρ ἐλάφου ἐὰν φανῶσιν εἰς οἰκίαν, ἢ ὀστέον αὐτοῦ ἐὰν θυμιάσῃ τις, οὐδέποτε ὀσμὴν δράκοντος θεωρήσεις ἢ ἴχνος. ὅπου γὰρ φόβος Χριστοῦ ἐὰν εὑρεθῇ εἰς τὴν καρδίαν σου, οὐδέποτε πονηρὸν φάρμακον ἀναβαίνει εἰς τὴν καρδίαν σου.
> Ὁ Φυσιολόγος οὖν οὐκ ἀργῶς ἐλάλησε περὶ τῆς ἐλάφου.
>
> [For if deer hair appears in a house or if someone burns a deer bone, you will never see either the odor or the trace of a dragon.[35] And whenever there is fear of Christ found in your heart, the poison of evil never rises to your heart.
> So the Physiologus has not spoken idly about the deer.] (*Physiologus* 1.30)

As discussed by Wellmann (1930:19) and Sbordone (1936:100), the version of the legend involving the deer is commonplace in late antiquity (*Aelian* 9.20; *Basil of Caesarea: Homilies on the Psalms* 28.122A; *Eustathius of Antioch: Commentary on the Hexaemeron* 741A; *Timothy of Gaza* §131, §132). All other manuscripts of the first redaction of the *Physiologus,* however, attribute this quality to the elephant instead:

> Ἡ δὲ φύσις τοῦ μικροῦ ἐλέφαντος τοιαύτη ἐστίν· ἐὰν θυμιάσῃς αὐτοῦ τρίχας ἢ ὀστέα ἔν τινι τόπῳ, οὔτε δαίμων, οὔτε δράκων, οὔτε τίποτε κακὸν ἐκεῖ εἰσέρχεται.
>
> [And the nature of the small elephant is as follows: if you burn its hair or bones in a place, neither demon, nor dragon, nor anything evil shall enter therein.] (*Physiologus* 1.43)[36]

Although the deer version is widely known, the elephant version is found outside the *Physiologus* only in a late Arabic source.[37] Wellmann (1930) suspects there has been confusion between ἔλαφος, "deer," and ἐλέφας, "elephant," and gives precedent for this in Pliny (*Natural History* 11.279)—who has the *elephant* sucking up snakes.[38]

At any rate, the *Tale* has not taken up the majority Physiologan version of the incense legend, involving the elephant. This could be because the author realized the elephant version, sounding suspiciously like an afterthought in the *Physiologus,* was in error. It would also be rhetorically weak to have the elephant in the poem repeat a claim already made by the deer. All the same, it is unlikely that the *Tale* has adopted the story involving the deer from the single, Muscovian manuscript of the *Physiologus* that relates it. This raises a problem in that the readiest source of such beliefs is indeed the *Physiologus*. A corpus of early Byzantine texts outside the *Physiologus* attests the belief that the *Tale* reports. But as we establish with regard to the *Tale*'s language, style, and natural history, the *Tale*'s author does not seem to have had direct access to anything as learned as St. Basil's homilies or Eustathius of Antioch's commentaries; thus, the author must have derived the notion from another source.

It is true that the notion of deer incense and snakes turns up in several places, including Byzantine dictionaries, to which we know the author had access.[39] But the nature of the source that the author is likely to have used instead may be surprising. Unlike the elephant story, the deer story has been preserved in contemporary folklore. In the modern Greek *Ilios* encyclopedia (Passas 1961:6.569) we find that the deer legends are alive and well in Greece: some Greeks believe that a deer cannot get pregnant without eating a snake, whereas the odor of the burning deer horn is held to force away not only the snakes of a single house (as stated in the *Tale*) but those of an entire neighborhood or region as well.[40] Loukopoulos (1940:51–52) cites one version of this modern legend, from Aetolia:

> Ἔτσι λένε πὼς τὸ ἐλάφι καὶ τὸ γάμο του ἂν κάμη, δὲ γκαστρώνεται, ἂν μὴ πρῶτα βρῇ καὶ φάη φίδι. Κι αὐτὸς εἶναι ὁ λόγος ποὺ τὰ λάφια κυνηγᾶνε τὰ φίδια· ὅπου κι ἂν τὰ βροῦνε, ὅπου κι ἂν τὰ συντύχουν, χυμοῦν γιὰ νὰ τὰ φᾶνε.
>
> Μὰ καὶ τὰ φίδια ξέρουν τί τὰ περιμένει, γι᾿ αὐτὸ καὶ σὰν ἰδοῦν ἐλάφι, τὸ κόβουν λάσπη. Φεύγουν κι ὅλο φεύγουν, σαράντα ράχες μπορεῖ νὰ προσδιαβοῦν στὸ φευγιό τους, καὶ πάλι νὰ μὴ σταθοῦνε.
>
> Τὰ φίδια τὰ φοβοῦνται τὰ λάφια, γι᾿ αὐτὸ καὶ τὸ ἐλαφοκέρατο εἶναι σκιάχτρο τους. Ἔτυχε νάχης πάνω σου ἐλαφοκέρατο, ξῦσε λιγάκι μὲ ἕνα κοφτερὸ μαχαίρι νὰ πέσουν ξέσματα στὴ φωτιά, καὶ φίδι γιὰ φίδι δὲ μένει πουθενά· ἀπὸ τὴ μυρουδιά τους ξολοθρεύονται.
>
> [So they say that even after her wedding, the deer will not fall pregnant unless she first finds and eats a snake. And that is the reason why deer hunt snakes; wherever they find them, wherever they meet them, they rush to eat them.
>
> But snakes, too, know what awaits them, so they are off like a shot the instant they see a deer. They just flee and flee; they may go past forty mountain ridges on their way, without stopping.
>
> Snakes do fear deer; that's why deer horn is a talisman against them. If you happen to have some deer horn on you, scrape a bit with a sharp knife so that the shavings fall in the fire, and there will not be a trace of a snake left; they are exterminated by the smell alone.]

So the simplest explanation is that the deer legend was already extant in late ancient folklore—whence it was reported by Aelian, Basil of Caesarea, Eustathius of Antioch, and Timothy of Gaza, and misconstrued by the *Physiologus*. The legend survived into late Byzantium, to be reported by the *Tale*, and into modern times. In this case, the *Tale* is no longer appealing to the *Physiologus* but directly to the *Physiologus*'s folk origins.[41]

Manuel Philes

There are, of course, other witnesses of Byzantine animal lore. In particular, Manuel Philes' early-fourteenth-century poem *On the Features of Animals* (Μανουήλου τοῦ Φίλη Στίχοι Ἰαμβικοὶ περὶ Ζῴων Ἰδιότητος), dedicated to Co-Emperor Michael IX Palaeologus, is a valuable reference point for comparing the *Physiologus* with other traditions, including contemporary folk notions.

On the Features of Animals states, as does the *Tale*, that the burning of deer horn scrapings on burning coal generates odors that force snakes away:

> Πρὸς τοῖς γε φασὶ, κεἴτις τοῦδ᾽ ἐκ τοῦ κέρως
> ξέσειε λεπτῶς, εἶτα τὸ ξύσμα τόδε
> αὔοι, κράτιστε, ἐμβαλὼν ἐπ᾽ ἀνθράκων
> ὁ καπνὸς εὐθὺς ἐξελάσσει τοὺς ὄφεις,
> ὀσμὴν ἐκείνην μὴ δυναμένους φέρειν.
>
> [They further say that if one scrapes the horn
> but thinly of that beast, and after that,
> Your Highness, burns the shavings up on coal,
> the smoke will drive out all the snakes at once,
> for they cannot withstand the smell it gives.] (1245–49)

In this instance, Philes is staying faithful to the version of the story promulgated by Aelian.[42] Philes also expounds on snake sucking, devoting most of his section on the deer to its courageous battle against snakes (1230–44). But, unlike the *Physiologus,* he says nothing about the deer drinking spring water.

Indeed, a close comparison between the two works shows that Manuel Philes does not rely on the *Physiologus*. When it comes to the elephant, for example, on which Philes writes both in *On the Features of Animals* (923–71) and *Exposition on the Elephant* (1–381), he knows that, as amply attested by Aristotle (*Historia Animalium* 595a) and Aelian (10.12), the elephant is an easily domesticated herbivore (partial to sweet melons, among other foods) and that the Indians capture it using not falling trees but pit traps, from which the elephant is capable of escaping. The way the elephant escapes, however, is a scene typical of the *Physiologus*: the largest member of the herd lies down so that everybody else climbs out of the pit stepping on it, and then they in turn help it out by throwing into the pit tree trunks that it uses as a staircase (299–315).

Philes has an overall decent knowledge of the exotic animal: he gives a fairly good description of the animal's physiology and is aware of such details as that it does not eat or drink through its trunk (42), that its trunk is used "instead of a hand" (ἀντὶ χειρὸς εὑρέθη) (52),[43] that its skin is wrinkly (60), and that its trunk is composed of "broken sections" (εἰς τομὰς κεκλασμένας) (96). Yet he still shares the *Physiologus*'s belief that the elephant has no joints (106–13) and states that its front legs are unequivocally shorter than the back ones (122–23). Philes also duplicates Aelian's fantastical enmity between the elephant and the serpent (244–61).[44] So despite his secular topics, Manuel Philes does not avoid the excesses of the *Physiologus,* common after all to medieval works on animals and indicating his thorough dependence on ancient written sources—particularly Oppian. (It would hardly occur to a Byzantine scholar to verify an antique claim through actual observation.)[45]

In most of what he wrote about the elephant, we may presume that the author of the *Tale* either was unfamiliar with Manuel Philes or trusted him no more than the *Physiologus*: there is no reference to pits in the *Tale* or the elephant's spectacular escape. The *Tale* does make indirect reference to the elephant's handlike trunk as well as the deer horn's snake-repelling powers; neither of these is directly Physiologan. Both are mentioned by Philes, although we can by no means be certain that is where the author got his information: the deer horn seems to be folkloric, and the author might even have worked out the comparison between the trunk and a hand himself through the depictions available to him.

At any rate, it is unlikely that the animal lore of the *Tale* needs be explained by appeal to any source other than personal observation, oral tradition, or low sources such as the *Physiologus.* The classical and Byzantine zoologists—Aristotle, Aristophanes of Byzantium, Aelian, Oppian, Manuel Philes—are conspicuous by their absence in the *Tale,* though it is possible that the author picked up information from them at third hand as previously discussed (with Timothy of Gaza particularly suspicious in this regard). This is hardly surprising: the moralizing *Physiologus* was humble reading, and Timothy of Gaza was little better, whereas Aristotle and Philes were out of the author's reach.

For all that, it is worth noting that the *Tale* barely even scratches the surface of what is available in the *Physiologus.* There is nothing about the perfumed breath of the panther, friend of all beasts but the dragon;[46] of how humans hunt the monkey; the elephant's reluctance toward coitus; or even the fox playing dead to trap birds. The author seems to have dipped into the *Physiologus* only when he needed to, and his dependence on it is ultimately superficial; his dependence on Philes is, if anything, even more so. Not that the author needed to depend on them that much: everyday animals are accurately described and discussed in the *Tale,* which makes it a work far more reliable in its natural history than the *Physiologus* or even Philes. The author was under no compulsion to reproduce their fantastical menageries.

The *Alexander Romance*

The military use of the elephant, so famous in antiquity, is not mentioned either in the *Physiologus* or by Philes. And though the ancients made ample mention of it, it seems no more plausible that the author of the *Tale* had recourse to ancient historians than ancient zoologists. And neither would the author have had much opportunity to hear of elephants in battle firsthand: the Turkish emirates had no need of elephants to make headway in Asia Minor.

So we need to identify a written source for the author's familiarity with the elephant's use in battle ("Just like a tower, safe and fortified," 906); this needs to be a source to which the author could plausibly have had access. We have seen one zoological text that does mention this use and that might just have been accessed by the author: *Timothy of Gaza,* as preserved in its eleventh-century abridgement. But the way the author describes that use makes us believe the source could instead be sought in the *Alexander Romance,* a proto-novel first written around the second century B.C. that tells of Alexander of Macedon's fabulous conquests and exploits. It was hugely popular in Byzantium and appeared in a number of versions, in an increasingly colloquial linguistic idiom. Indeed, by the sixteenth century the *Romance* was extant in several versions in vernacular modern Greek. It is thus a text that, like the *Physiologus,* Aesop, and the Psalms—and unlike Aristotle or Aelian—the author would have found accessible without a thorough classical education.

Though the very earliest version of the *Romance* mentions elephants fighting alongside the Indians against Alexander (α 3.3.1, 3.4.11), it does not mention men riding elephants. If anything, elephants are pictured as fighting Macedonians of their own accord:

> Πῶρος δὲ ὠτρύνθη ἀναγνοὺς τὰ γράμματα ‹καὶ› συνάγει τὰ πλήθη καὶ πλείστους ἐλέφαντας καὶ ἕτερα γενναῖα θηρία, ἅτινα συνεμάχοντο τοῖς Ἰνδοῖς. ὡς δὲ ἦλθον ἐγγὺς οἱ Μακεδόνες καὶ Πέρσαι καὶ ἑώρων τὴν παράταξιν τοῦ πολέμου, ἐφοβήθησαν οὐ τοὺς ὄχλους, ἀλλὰ τοὺς θῆρας. ἐκεῖ μὲν οὖν ἐδειλάνθη καὶ ὁ Ἀλέξανδρος ὁρῶν τὸ ξένον τῶν θηρίων· ἀνθρώποις γὰρ ἔθος εἶχε μάχεσθαι.
>
> [Porus was incensed on reading the letters, and he assembled his host and many elephants and other brave beasts, which fought alongside the Indians. So when the Macedonians and the Persians approached and saw the battle array, they feared not the host but the wild beasts. And even Alexander recoiled, seeing the strange sight of the beasts, for he was used to fighting humans.] (*Alexander Romance* α 3.3.1)

The first mention in the *Romance* of towers built on top of elephants (cf. verses 909–13) comes in version ε, dated to the sixth century:[47]

> ἐπὶ τούτοις ἄφνω ἐλέφαντες ἐμφαίνονται τῇ Ἰνδῶν παρατάξει ξύλινα ***τείχη*** ἐπιφερόμενοι, καὶ ἐπ᾽ αὐτῶν ἄνδρες ἔνοπλοι ἦσαν [Κγ: ἵσταντο] λίθους καὶ δόρατα ταῖς χερσὶν ἔχοντες. ὡς δὲ ταῦτα ἐθεάσαντο Μακεδόνες ἀπέκαμον καὶ τῇ προγονικῇ περιπίπτουσι δειλανδρίᾳ. [...] Καὶ δὴ ἡμέρας καταλαβούσης τὸ Ἰνδικὸν εἰς μάχην ἐξῄει στρατόπεδον. ἐλέφαντας δὲ, ὡς προεῖπον, ἐπιβεβηκότες δίκην περιπατοῦσαι πόλεις ἐφαίνοντο ***τοῖς τείχεσι κατωχυρωμέναι.***
>
> [Then suddenly elephants emerged in the Indian army bearing wooden ***fortifications***; and on these there were {*manuscript K and recension* γ: there stood} armed men, with spears and stones in their hands. When the Macedonians saw this, they flinched, and they fell into their ancestral cowardice. . . . And when day came, the Indian camp went to war; riding on elephants, as I said above, they appeared like walking cities, ***with fortified walls***.] (*Alexander Romance* ε 36.4, 6)

Alexander goes on to scare off the elephants in a way that deals their majesty a blow far more severe than anything the *Tale*'s monkey could deliver:

> κελεύει δὲ τοῖς ὁπλίταις ποιῆσαι τοῦτο· ὁπόταν πλησίον γένωνται ἐλεφάντων, κατεχόμενα ἔμπροσθεν ἀκοντίσαι σμικρότατα χοίρων βρέφη μεγάλα γρυλίζοντα. ὡς οὖν ἐλέφαντες εἶδον, εὐθέως ἄνω καὶ κάτω ἐκτιναγέντες τὰ ***καστρίδια*** ἔρριψαν καὶ ἀνυποστρεπτὶ φεύγουσιν.
>
> [He ordered his infantry to do the following: whenever they got near the elephants, they should prod forward small piglets, which would squeal loudly. When the elephants saw them, they immediately tossed themselves up and down, casting down the ***forts***, and fled without turning back.] (*Alexander Romance* ε 36.6)[48]

Though the *Tale* has mercifully passed over the piglets (hardly an incident to which the elephant would wish to own up), its wording is reminiscent of ε. The *Tale*'s account uses the same word for "fortified" (κατωχυρωμένους) and "forts" (κάστρη; in *Alexander Romance* ε, the diminutive καστρίδια). It makes the comparison to walls in one manuscript tradition of the *Tale,* verse 906.[49] And the *Tale* refers explicitly to combatants standing inside towers made of wood. The comparable passage in Timothy, on the other hand, does not sound as close to the *Tale*: it uses the same word for "towers" (πύργους) as the other manuscript tradition of the *Tale,* but its towers are simply "filled" with soldiers, and otherwise are not described at all. We thus think it likely that the

Tale's description of the elephant in battle is drawn directly from the *Alexander Romance,* in a Byzantine version akin to version ε, if not ε itself.

Aesop and Folk Tale

Normally, the *Tale* avoids the storytelling so characteristic of animal narratives. In one instance, however, a full-fledged story is elaborated within the *Tale*: the horse's account of the embassy of donkeys (689–739). The following story, from the village of Pera in Cyprus, is quite close to the story in the *Tale* and probably represents its immediate folk origin:

> Ὁ γάρος ἀγκάλεσεν τὸν μάστρον του̣ πῶς (δ)ὲν κανεῖ ποὺ τὸν βαρυφορτώννει, ἔβαλλέν του̣ πέντε τζ̌οιλὰ σιτάριν, καβαλ̣λ̣ικᾶ̣ τον χέμι, τζ̌ι̯ ἔδ̌ει τον τζ̌αὶ τζ̌εῖνον πουπανωγόμαρ̣ον, τζ̌ι̯ οὖλ̌λον κακοστραδκι̯άν. «Στὸ ἔβκα φορτωμένον καλλιτζ̌εύκει μου τζ̌αὶ ποστέκω πολλά. Στὸ κατέβα, ποὺ πονοῦν τὰ πόδκι̯α̣ μου̣, πάλε ἔν᾽ καβαλλάρη̣ς, στὸ ἰσ̌ι̯οτόπιν τὰ ἴδια. (Δ)ὲν πρέπει τζ̌αὶ τζ̌εῖνος νὰ παρπατᾶ̣ τζ̌αὶ νὰ̣ μὲ καλλιτζ̌εύκη̣ ἅμα εἶμαι ξηφόρτωτος;» «Πρέπει», ἐσυμφώνησεν τζ̌ι̯ ὁ δικαστής. «Νὰ χαρῇς, νὰ μοῦ (δ)ῴκη̣ς ἕναν χαρτίν̣, ποὺ νὰ τὸ γράφη̣ τοῦτον, ἀφοῦτις ηὗρές το δίτζ̌ι̯ον, νὰ τὸ δοῦν τζ̌ι̯ οἱ ἄλλοι, τζ̌αὶ νὰ σταματήση̣ τοῦτον τὸ κακόν.» Ἔ(δ)ωκέν του τὸ χαρτὶν ὁ̣ δικαστής. Ἁρπάσσει το τζ̌ι̯ ὁ γάρος στὸ στόμαν του τζ̌ι̯ ἀγκάνισε τζ̌αὶ κλάσε, κλάσε τζ̌ι̯ ἀγκάνισε, ἐπῆεν τσιννητὸς νά ᾽βρη τοὺς ἄλλους γάρους, νὰ τοὺς τὸ πῇ, μὰ ᾽ποὺ τὴν πολλὴν ἀγκανι̯ὰν τζ̌αὶ τ᾽ ἀ̣νασύρματα, ἐκατάπκι̯εν τὸ χ̣αρτίν. Βρίσκει τοὺς ἄλλους γάρους τζ̌ι̯ ἐλάλεν τους τὴν ἀπόφασιν τζ̌αὶ πῶς ἐγλυτῶσαν ᾽ποὺ τὸ πουπανωγόμαρον. «Ποῦ ᾽ν᾽ το, ρέ, τὸ χ̣αρτίν», λαλεῖ του ἕνας τους. «Ἴντα νὰ σᾶς πῶ», λαλεῖ τους τζ̌αὶ τζ̌εῖνος, «᾽ποὺ τὴν χαράν μου τζ̌αὶ τὴν ἀγκανι̯ὰν ἐκατάπκι̯α το. Τώρα, πὸννά κοπρίσω, νὰ̣ μυριστοῦμεν τζ̌αὶ ν᾽ ἀσκοπήσουμεν τὰ κόρκα μου, πέρκιμον τζ̌ι̯ εὕρουμέν το.» Ἔδει ᾽ποὺ τότες, ποὺ οἱ γαδάροι γυρεύκουν τὸ χαρτὶν τζ̌αὶ μυρίζουνται τὰ κοτσιρογάουρα τζ̌αὶ τὰ δικά τους τζ̌αὶ ᾽νοῦ ᾽ς τ᾽ ἄλλου.
>
> [The donkey complained against his master that, as if it weren't enough being loaded up heavily by him, his master had put five *koila* of wheat on him and rode him on top of that, so he had his master as a top load and always on rough paths. "On the way up, he rides me while I'm loaded up, and I get really tired. On the way down, when my legs ache, he still rides me; on a level path, it's the same story. Shouldn't he walk, too, and ride me only when I'm unloaded?" "He should," the judge agreed. "Do me a favor: give me a paper saying so. Because you've found what's fair, the others should see it in writing, too, and put an end to this evil." The judge gave him the paper. So the donkey grabbed

it in his mouth and, braying and a-farting, farting and a-braying, he went running to find the other donkeys to tell them; but what with the great braying and gulping, he swallowed the paper. He found the other donkeys and told them the decision and how they'd been saved from overloading. "Where's the paper, then?" one of them said to him. "What can I tell you?" he answered. "I was so happy and braying so hard that I swallowed it. Now that I'm going to have a shit, let's sniff and look through my dung, in case we find it there." And from then on, donkeys have been looking for the paper and sniffing both their own dung and each other's.] (Hioutas 1978:60–61)

Note that in this telling the excretory denouement is not confused as it is in the *Tale*: the donkeys plausibly wait for the letter to appear in dung rather than urine.

The *Tale*'s version of the story is reminiscent of a fable in Aesop ("a free and expanded treatment of the Aesopic fable," as Vasiliou [1996:79] puts it), which goes somewhat differently:

ὄνοι ποτὲ ἀχθόμενοι ἐπὶ τῷ συνεχῶς ἀχθοφορεῖν καὶ ταλαιπωρεῖν πρέσβεις ἔπεμψαν πρὸς τὸν Δία λύσιν τινὰ αἰτούμενοι τῶν πόνων. ὁ δὲ αὐτοῖς ἐπιδεῖξαι βουλόμενος, ὅτι τοῦτο ἀδύνατόν ἐστιν, ἔφη τότε αὐτοὺς ἀπαλλαγήσεσθαι τῆς κακοπαθείας, ὅταν οὐροῦντες ποταμὸν ποιήσωσι. κἀκεῖνοι αὐτὸν ἀληθεύειν ὑπολαβόντες ἀπ᾽ ἐκείνου καὶ μέχρι νῦν, ἔνθα ἂν ἀλλήλων οὖρον ἴδωσιν, ἐνταῦθα καὶ αὐτοὶ περιιστάμενοι οὐροῦσιν.

ὁ λόγος δηλοῖ, ὅτι τὸ ἑκάστῳ πεπρωμένον ἀθεράπευτόν ἐστι.

[Once some load-bearing donkeys, because they continuously bore loads and were vexed, sent envoys to Zeus seeking some relief to their pains. And wishing to show to them that this was impossible, he told them that they would be rid of their misfortune only when they made a river by urinating. And they believed him to have told the truth, so from then on to this day, wherever they see each other's urine, they stand there and urinate, too.

The myth means that each person's fate is inescapable.] (*Aesop: Fables* 196)

It seems that the *Tale* has conflated two closely related fables, using the urine of Aesop but the farting and judge's letter of the folktale. The two fables may ultimately be related, yet as an independent story, the *Tale*'s version does not make much sense. And neither is it plausible that the author of the *Tale* had bowdlerized references to defecation: the verb χέζω, "to shit," occurs no fewer than six times in the poem. So it would seem that beyond quoting Aesop with regard to the camel, the author also attempted to rehabilitate a contemporary folk tale by giving it an Aesopic flavoring. The attempt has proven unsuccessful, but it does indicate once again that the author has not turned his back on book learning (even if it is as humble as Aesop), and in this instance he has been influenced enough to essay some "correction" of his material.[50]

It has already been noted that the *Tale* also mentions a fable involving the camel requesting horns. The allusion to the camel dancing (86, 1068) is likewise Aesopic; beyond the proverb Ἡ κάμηλος ἔλεγε τῇ μητρὶ "ὀρχήσομαι," κἀκείνη "τέκνον," φησί, "καὶ ὁ περίπατός σου καλός ἐστιν" (The camel said to her mother, "I will dance," and she replied, "Child, it's alright if you just walk") attributed to Aesop (*Proverbs* 86), fables 85 and 142 speak of a camel dancing.

Pantechnes

In the mid-twelfth century, the metropolitan of Philippoupolis (Plovdiv), Constantine Pantechnes, wrote a rhetorical description in the learned idiom of a hunt using pards (παρδάλεις)—which can be clearly identified as cheetahs in his detailed description. The evidence (considered in Nicholas 1999:266–68) suggests that by the time the *Tale* was presumably written, hunting pards were known in Byzantium by reputation rather than observation, but "pards" themselves could still be sighted on occasion in Constantinople.

Still, precisely because cheetahs would no longer have been as common a sight, one might expect that the author, in mentioning pards, had recourse to written sources. We have seen the author exploit written sources already and make very eclectic use of them—the *Physiologus* on the elephant in particular. We have also seen that he does not have any demonstrable familiarity with the classical zoologists. In this regard, the *Tale* may display influence from an unexpected source. The phrasing of Pantechnes, who unambiguously describes a cheetah hunting a hare, is almost identical to the *Tale*'s:

> Ἡ δὲ πάρδαλις μόνη τοῦ λαγὼ κατατρέχει ***καὶ ἅλμασιν ὀξυῤῥόποις μὴ πλείοσι δυεῖν ἢ καὶ τριῶν φθάσασα*** ξυμποδίζει καὶ τοῖς ἔμπροσθεν ποσὶ καταπαίουσα, ὀξυπραγέσι παλάμαις αἱρεῖ, καὶ τάχιον ἢ λόγος ὑπ᾽ ὀδόντα τοῦ θηρὸς ὁ πτὼξ ἐν ἀτόμῳ γίνεται.
>
> [And the cheetah pursues the hare alone, ***and reaching it with swift-turning bounds not more than two or three in number***, it entangles it, and striking it with its front feet, it lifts it up with swift-acting palms; and faster than speech the hare ends up under the teeth of the beast, within an indivisible moment.] (*Pantechnes* 51)

> In just two bounds, or three at times, I reach
> (Εἰς δύο μου πηδήματα ἢ καὶ πολλάκις τρία [. . .] φθάνω το)
> and pin down any animal I chase.

I clench it with my claws to stop it fleeing,
and then I eat it to my heart's content. (*Tale* 872–74)

A cheetah's strides might be considered leap-like, if one is charitable enough: the cheetah's gallop is composed of seven phases, two of which have all four of its legs off the ground. The first has the cheetah's limbs fully extended, and the second flexed, with the cheetah's limbs bunched together (Wrogemann 1975:26–27). The cheetah can thus look like it is bounding forward. In fact, the description of the capture in the *Tale* is strongly reminiscent of Pantechnes as well.

The problem with positing Pantechnes as a source for the *Tale* is that it is not the kind of text to which we would expect the author to refer. Although the syntax of Pantechnes' essay is not especially difficult, it is a rhetorical exercise (an *ekphrasis*) and as such has Atticist vocabulary far beyond that of the *Tale*. Hunting with cheetahs is never mentioned in the *Tale,* and neither are the elaborate tricks the cheetah trainer had to employ to extract the cheetah's quarry from the cheetah, as detailed by Pantechnes.

So there are two alternatives. If the *Tale*'s author used Pantechnes, he ignored everything but the immediately relevant description of how the pard's prey is captured. There is precedent for such selectivity in his use of *Physiologus*; but the author is at pains to say anything at all about the great cats, so his ignoring the rich detail Pantechnes has to offer, as well as the very fact that hunting is involved, is perplexing.[51] We would also have to accept that the author had access to a kind of text we would not expect, given the linguistic level of the books we suspect him to have read. The influence of Pantechnes is not out of the question here, but it is problematic.

The other alternative is that the similarity is coincidental. This could be either because the author is not in fact describing a cheetah but a smaller cat, that can plausibly use multiple pounces to down its prey, or because he independently witnessed a cheetah hunt and came up with the same description as Pantechnes. The evidence for the former possibility is considered in "A Conundrum of Cats." The latter is not impossible; the reference to two or three bounds could have been independently derived from observation. The verb for "catch up," φθάνω/φθάσασα, likewise stands out as a similarity between the two texts, but is just about the only way the notion could be expressed in the Greek of the time. The cheetah was released at close quarters to the sighted hare, so it would presumably reach its prey very quickly. We would have to posit that the author could still witness a cheetah hunt; we have no firm evidence that he could, but it cannot be ruled out, particularly if the author had spent time in the Muslim East. Whether a cheetah or a different feline is intended, in any case, coincidence is still likelier than that the author had access to as obscure a text as Pantechnes'.

Of Mice and Timothy

One more passage in the *Tale* (138–40) echoes a literary source:

῎Αν εὕρῃς δὲ ἀβούλλωτον ῥογὶν νὰ γέμῃ λάδιν,
χαλᾷς κάτω τὴν οὔρην σου καὶ σύρνεις τὸ ἐλάδιν
καὶ τὴν οὐράν σου ***λείχοντα*** χορταίνεις τὴν κοιλίαν σου.

[And should you find a pitcher of oil unsealed,
you ***dip*** your tail and draw the oil back out,
and ***licking*** at your tail, you fill your belly.]

περὶ μυῶν. [...] ὅτι εἰς τοὺς λύχνους τὰς οὐρὰς ***χαλῶντες*** τὸ ἔλαιον ἀνιμῶσι καὶ ***λείχουσιν*** ὅτε τὰς κεφαλὰς οὐ δύνανται ἐμβαλεῖν.

[On Mice.... That they ***dip*** their tails into lamps and draw out the oil and ***lick*** it when they cannot put their heads in.] (*Timothy of Gaza* [abridgement] §38)

ἐν μέντοι τοῖς λύχνοις τοῖς στενόχωρον τὸ στόμα ἔχουσιν ἀποροῦντες πολλάκις οἱ μύες καθιέναι τὴν κεφαλήν, τὴν οὐρὰν ***ἐγχαλῶντες*** ἀνιμῶσι τὸ ἔλαιον, καὶ οὕτως αὐτὸ τῷ στόματι ***περιλείχουσιν***.

[Often mice, being unable to fit their head into lamps with a narrow mouth, ***dip*** their tails and draw out the oil and thereby ***lick*** it ***up*** with their mouths.] (Constantine VII Porphyrogennetus's redaction of *Aristophanes of Byzantium* 2.368; after *Timothy of Gaza*)

There are, as with Alexander's elephant and Pantechnes' cheetah, similar words used in the two texts: the *Tale* has χαλᾷς for "dip, let fall" and λείχοντα for "lick," whereas the wording in the abridgement of *Timothy* is χαλῶντες and λείχουσιν, the selfsame verbs. The notion mentioned is at least as old as the *Batrachomyomachia* (*ii–i* B.C.), in which Athena complains of the mice that στέμματα βλάπτοντες καὶ λύχνους εἵνεκ᾽ ἐλαίου, "My flowery wreaths they petulantly spoil, / And rob my crystal lamps of feeding oil" (180). This is, however, commonplace behavior in rodents and turns up in quite unrelated texts:

"You little witch!" cries grandmama,
"You're like the naughty rat
I found within the cellar once,
Who on a barrel sat,
Filled with molasses, which he reached
By dipping in the hole
His great long tail from which he licked
The sweets he thus had stole." (Anonymous 1999 [1880–1900?])

> The mouse king stood as close to it as he dared, then he stuck out his tail, in the same manner as mice do when they take the cream off the top of the milk with their tails. (Andersen 1974:527)

The similarity is remarkable, and we have already seen reason to suspect the author had access to *Timothy of Gaza* in its abridgement. But the author could have readily made this observation personally, so it is not necessary to appeal to a written source for this information. In the case of "lick," in fact, the λειχ- stem is the only classical stem on offer, and as discussed in the Commentary, verse 139, the verb χαλῶ in the archaic sense "loosen" also turns up in the *Book of Birds*.[52]

Untraced Beliefs

There are two beliefs about animals for which we have not been able to find a direct antecedent in Greek literature.

And you're a beast that's born in sin and brought up out of wedlock (867)

The word for "leopard," λεόπαρδος or λεοντόπαρδος, is a compound of "lion" and "pard" (on the identity of which, see discussion in "A Conundrum of Cats.") The mixed parentage of the leo-pard is explicitly described in postclassical sources—in a rather vivid domestic drama by *Timothy of Gaza*:

> κεφ. ιβ. περὶ λεοπάρδου. ὅτι ἐκ συνουσίας λέοντος καὶ παρδάλεως τίκτεται.
> ὅτι ἡνίκα λέαινα τίκτει ἐκ παρδάλεως, κρύπτει τὸ τεχθὲν καὶ ἑαυτὴν ἵνα μὴ ὁ λέων εὑρὼν διασπαράξῃ.
> ὅτι ἐν πολλοῖς λούεται ποταμοῖς ἵνα ἀπορρύψηται τὴν ὀσμήν· ἐὰν γὰρ αἴσθηται ὁ λέων, ἀναιρεῖ καὶ οὐκέτι οὐδὲ ἄλλῃ συγγίνεται.
>
> [Chapter XII. ON THE LEOPARD
> 1. That it is born from the intercourse of a lion and a pard.
> 2. That the lioness when she cubs (having conceived) from a pard, hides the (new) born (cub) and herself lest the lion may find her and rend her in pieces.
> 3. That she washes herself in many rivers to wash off the smell; for if the lion perceives (anything) he kills her and never again mates even with another (lioness).] (*Timothy of Gaza* [abridgement] §12)
>
> Λεόπαρδος μέντοι τὸ ζῷον καὶ αὐτὸ διαφόρους ἔχει τοὺς γειναμένους· τίκτεται γὰρ λέοντός τε καὶ παρδάλεως κοινὸν ἐς

ἔρωτα ξυνελθόντων. σῴζει δὲ μητρὸς μὲν τὸ χρῶμα καὶ στίγματα καὶ ὁρμήν, πατρὸς δὲ μέγεθος καὶ θυμοειδὲς αὐτὸ καὶ ἄτρεστον.

[Of course, the leopard also has different parents, for it is born of the lion and the pard coming together for sex. And it preserves its mother's color, spots, and vigor and its father's size, temper, and fearlessness.] (Constantine VII Porphyrogennetus' redaction of *Aristophanes of Byzantium* 2.274; after Timothy of Gaza)[53]

The *locus classicus* for the libidinousness of great cats is not Greek but Latin—in Pliny:

magna his libido coitus et ob hoc maribus ira. Africa haec maxime spectat, inopia aquarum ad paucos amnes congregantibus se feris. ideo multiformes ibi animalium partus, varie feminis cuiusque generis mares aut vi aut voluptate miscente: unde etiam vulgare Graeciae dictum semper aliquid novi Africam adferre. odore ***pardi*** coitum sentit in adulteria leo totaque vi consurgit in peonam; idcirco ea culpa flumine abluitur aut longius comitatur.

[Sexual passion is strong in this species, with its consequence of quarrelsomeness in the males; this is most observed in Africa, where the shortage of water makes the animals flock to the few rivers. There are consequently many varieties of hybrids in that country, either violence or lust mating the males with the females of each species indiscriminately. This is indeed the origin of the common saying of Greece that Africa is always producing some novelty ⟨*Aristotle: Historia Animalium* 606b⟩. A lion detects intercourse with a ***leopard*** in the case of an adulterous mate by scent, and concentrates his entire strength on her chastisement; consequently this guilty stain is washed away in a stream, or else she keeps her distance when accompanying him.] (*Pliny: Natural History* 8.43–44)

The leopard does not feature in the *Physiologus,* but the author did not need to read Timothy or Aristophanes to work things out from the name of the animal alone, in whatever compendium of animals to which he had access. The word "leopard" was hardly unknown to Byzantines; Nicholas (1999:278–83) discusses several instances of its use.

The speculation on the extramarital relations of the lion and the pard sounds custom-made for Byzantine religious allegory or for some of the wilder flights of fancy of the Byzantine etymologists. Indeed, we know that in the West the connection between great cats, lust, and miscegenation (already explicit in Pliny 8.17) was made emblematic of the leopard in the Middle Ages. In the fourth century, St. Ambrose had already identified the leopard's spots with the impulses of the soul, and the leopard is a commonplace in the bestiaries—and thence in authors such as Dante—as a symbol of sin or lust (Rowland 1973:116–17).

Although the leopard is present in Byzantine literature, we have not been able to identify an explicit expression of this belief. But we have no reason to doubt the notion would have been current there also. A passage in George Monachus's *Chronicon* alludes to it in an unflattering description of Emperor Leo V (see Koutrakou 1991):

> Ἐκ τῆς Ἀσσυρίων γοῦν λεαίνης καὶ τῆς Ἀρμενίας παρδάλεως ἑτεροθαλὲς σύνθετόν τε καὶ ἀλλόκοτον τίγριδος εἶδος ἐκ νόθου καὶ κιβδήλου ἐξέφυ γονῆς, Ἀρμένιον ἢ Ἀσσύριον εἰδεχθὲς τέρας, καὶ Λέων μὲν τὴν προσηγορίαν, λέοντος δὲ τὸ μὲν ἁρπακτικὸν εἰς τὸ ἀσφαλὲς κεκτημένος, τὸ δὲ ἐλευθέριον οὐδαμῶς προιέμενος
>
> [So he was begotten from a Syrian lioness and an Armenian pard as a miscegenated, mixed, and peculiar species of tiger, of illegitimate and base parentage, an Armenian (rather than Syrian) repulsive monster. He was Leo by name, and he had acquired the lion's habit of seizing ⟨its prey⟩ away to safety—though by no means taking on the lion's nobility.] (*George Monachus* 781)

In any case, the miscegenation apparent in the word's etymology would easily have led the author autonomously to such a conclusion—especially when, as is obvious from the poem, he is hard put to say anything at all about the leopard.[54] Still, the absence of a Byzantine demonology of the leopard comparable to the West's suggests that this is the author's extrapolation from a dictionary, possibly etymologizing on the adulterous origin of the leopard—although it should be said that none of the surviving Byzantine dictionaries or *Etymologica* to which we have had access mention the leopard.[55]

For anywhere it lies, no flea will land (882)

The final exotic tradition about animals is that the pelt of the pard (which, as discussed in the following section, might be either the leopard, the cheetah, or the lynx) is resistant to fleas. We have not found anything suggesting such a belief in Greek literature, and the context in which the line is uttered makes us suspect this is a Middle Eastern tradition that had reached Byzantium orally—but remained associated with sultans and emirs.[56] This statement is consistent with the *Tale*'s overall preference toward oral rather than literary sources. Koukoules (1947–55:2.273) sanguinely says that "as a bedspread, instead of carpets, they [Byzantines] also used wild animal skins, particularly pards', which had the property, so they believed, of repelling fleas from the sheets." But Koukoules' unique source on this is the *Tale,* which suggests that what is being described there is a foreign, not a native Byzantine belief.[57]

Leopard-skin couches must have been a Byzantine institution: Emperor Nicephorus II Phocas, on the eve of his assassination in 969,

> πρὸ τῶν σεπτῶν εἰκόνων τῆς τε θεανδρικῆς τοῦ Χριστοῦ μορφῆς, καὶ τῆς Θεομήτορος, καὶ τοῦ θείου προδρόμου καὶ κήρυκος, παρὰ τὸ παρδάλειον δέῤῥος καὶ τὸν κοκκοβαφῆ πῖλον, ἐπ᾽ ἐδάφους διανεπαύετο.
>
> [rested on the ground, before the venerable images of the both divine and human form of Christ, and the Mother of God, and the Divine Forerunner and Preacher ⟨John the Baptist⟩, by the leopard skin and the scarlet-dyed felt-cloth.] (*Leo the Deacon* 86)

But by the time of the *Tale*, the leopards were where the Muslims were. Cantacuzene (1.447) reports the Ottoman Emir Orhan sending him presents, including leopard skins:

> ἔπειτα ἀλλήλους ἠμείβοντο δώροις, Ὀρχάνης μὲν ἵππους πέμψας καὶ κύνας θηρευτικὰς τάπητάς τε καὶ ***παρδάλεων δοράς***· βασιλεὺς δὲ ἐκπώματά τε ἀργυρᾶ καὶ ὑφάσματα οὐκ ἐξ ἐρίων μόνον, ἀλλὰ καὶ Σηρικὰ, καὶ τῶν βασιλικῶν ἐπιβλημάτων ἓν, ὃ περὶ πλείστου παρὰ τοῖς βαρβάρων σατράπαις ἄγεται ἀεὶ καὶ τιμῆς εἶναι δοκεῖ τεκμήριον καὶ εὐμενείας·
>
> [Then they gave each other presents; Orchanes sent horses and hunting hounds, carpets and ***leopard skins***, whereas the emperor sent silver goblets and textiles not only woolen but silk as well, and one of the imperial tapestries, which is always held in high esteem by the satraps of the barbarians and is considered a token of honor and favor.]

And even if leopards or cheetahs were still brought over to Byzantium, either for show or for the hunt (Nicholas 1999:267–68), the *Tale* strongly suggests that the use of leopard skins had by then become associated with Muslims, either Turkish (emirs) or Arabic (sultans).[58] Indeed, the use of leopard skins was so endemic among the Turks that it was decreed that in the Ottoman procession of guilds, leopard keepers and lion keepers should parade in the company of fur merchants instead of shepherds, as reported by Evliyâ Çelebi (von Hammer 1968:1.2.205).[59]

A Conundrum of Cats

The relation between fleas and pard is not the only puzzling thing about the cats in the poem. The identity of the lion and of the domestic cat is not in question, but that of the three other cats mentioned—the πάρδος, "pard," the λεοντόπαρδος, "leo-pard," and the γατόπαρδος, "cat-pard"—is far from straightforward and requires clarification. The following conclusions, based on Nicholas (1999), may be drawn as to the identities of the three felines.

Though πάρδος is typically glossed as "panther" or "leopard" (the two being the same species), Comnenan sources refer extensively to hunting with pards. Because there is no tradition of taming leopards, the cheetah is clearly meant instead. But though the Comnenans and the Ottomans had a tradition of cheetah coursing, it is not as apparent that the Palaeologans did. There is no incontrovertible evidence that the practice continued after the Fourth Crusade, and the references to the pard in Palaeologan vernacular Greek almost all characterize the pard as a proverbially brave beast—a characteristic that better fits the leopard than the rather docile cheetah.[60] It seems that the cheetah had by that stage become as exotic in Byzantium as the leopard of ancient lore. Word of both would have come through from the East, and we can discern no attempt to differentiate between the two in Byzantium or, for that matter, in antiquity.

Matters are even more complicated for the *Tale,* in which the "leopard" clearly refers to the "pard" as "short-tailed" (884). It is risky to make too much of a single word. But in seeking to make sense of the fabulous pard, the author had little material with which to work. As seen, his phrasing of the manner in which the pard catches its prey is quite similar to how Pantechnes describes the cheetah, but it is not so similar as to prove that the author of the *Tale* had read Pantechnes. After all, the author does not even mention that the pard is used in hunting, as Pantechnes made explicit—though the same author does not hesitate to describe the dog's use in hunting. Unless the author is deliberately passing such knowledge over, he may well simply have been unaware of the fact. In that case, in a scramble to find some characteristic with which to describe the pard, he may have used the only feline that can be fairly characterized as short tailed and the only wild feline indigenous to the Balkans: the lynx.[61]

The illustrator of the Constantinopolitan manuscript of the *Tale* (see "Illustrations") clearly portrays the pard as a cheetah, complete with collar. This does not mean that the author also knew the pard to be a cheetah, particularly as the manuscript is known to have been copied and illustrated in Venetian Negroponte (Euboea) rather than Constantinople (Reinsch 1998; see "Manuscript C Illustrations"). The Italians were familiar with cheetahs, which had made their West European debut as hunters in thirteenth-century Sicily, in the court of Frederick II (Miller 1872:35–37). Given this, the Venetian-influenced illustrator would have been in a much better position to identify the pard with the cheetah than the Byzantine author had been.[62] And the pard's tail in the illustration is certainly not noticeably shorter than the leopard's—though it is pointing down, unlike the leopard's proud appendage. So the illustrator and the author have not been working from the same script.

"Leopard" seems to have been a name for the cheetah in Roman times—as distinct from the "pard," the animal *now* known as the leopard. However, the term gradually became a purely literary term (as Byzantine usage shows), and the only salient characteristic of this feline that survived was the supposition that it was a hybrid of the lion and the pard. Timothy of Gaza still knew the leopard to be spotted, as seen in "Untraced Beliefs." The *Tale* is distant enough from this remembrance that its leopard castigates the *pard* for being "motley" (884).[63] And the illustrator of the Constantinopolitan manuscript draws the leopard as nothing so much as a scraggy version of the lion—with not a spot in sight (contrary to the practice in Western bestiaries).

The cat-pard is likely a borrowing from the Italian *gattopardo,* which appears to have originally referred to the cheetah. The *Tale* does not display any awareness of the curious happenstance that, at one stage or other, all three cats in question have been identified with the cheetah—the leopard (λεόπαρδος) in Roman antiquity, the pard (πάρδαλις/πάρδος) in Comnenan Byzantium, and the cat-pard (κατόπαρδος) in Renaissance Italy. In fact, the *Tale* doesn't display much awareness of what exactly the cat-pard was at all, apart from a feline comparable to the pard, the leopard, and the lion (887–88).

It should be clear from the foregoing that any rendering of the *Tale*'s words for the great cats in modern translation will be purely conventional. In addition, terms for one cat are routinely shifted to another in European languages, as felines have become better understood and differentiated. Thus, the Italian *gattopardo* has shifted from "cheetah" to "serval"; the French *once,* English *ounce,* and Spanish *onza* from "lynx" to "snow leopard" to "cheetah"; and the Russian барс from "leopard" to "snow leopard" (Heptner and Sludskii 1992:48, 203).

The hybrid name of the λεοντόπαρδος was certainly a conventional allusion to ancient lore rather than a concrete reference to an extant animal. Because so much is made of its compound name, however, we follow the practice of translations of the Western bestiaries and refer to it as "leopard."

The description given of the πάρδος in the *Tale* is not internally consistent. The leopard's epithet "short-tailed" suggests the lynx. The pard walking away from its quarry (876) is likewise consistent with a lynx rather than a cheetah. The talk of the pard's bravery in the *Tale,* and through much of Byzantine vernacular literature, is probably a reminiscence of the leopard. But the description of the beast "reaching" (i.e., catching up) with its quarry and, more important, the pattern of usage elsewhere in Byzantine Greek—the parallels with Pantechnes and the use of πάρδος as a hunting animal in the vernacular texts of *Digenes* and the *Alexander Romance* (see Nicholas 1999:262–65)—suggest the cheetah. The cheetah, moreover, makes a more fitting match to the leopard than the lynx, and the illustrator of the Constantinopolitan manuscript clearly understood the pard to be a cheetah. That is the rendering we choose for πάρδος, although we are inclined to think that the author had only heard of cheetahs, and had the concrete image of a lynx in mind instead.

The κατόπαρδος, finally, could be any wild feline other than a "pard" and native to North Africa, the Middle East, or southern Europe—for instance, a European wild cat (*Felis silvestris*), a sand cat (*Felis margarita*), a jungle cat (*Felis chaus*), a caracal (*Felis caracal*), or a lynx (*Felis lynx*). In fact, the word may have at some stage encompassed all of these. There are only two proposals on the table, however: Kriaras's (1968–97) identification with the modern Greek γατόπαρδος, "cheetah," echoed by Alexiou (1980) in his edition of *Erotokritos,* and Šandrovskaja's (1956a) tentative дикая кошка, "wild cat."[64] If the word was a loan into Greek from Italian, it almost certainly meant "cheetah." If the word was coined locally, it would have denoted something considered a hybrid between the pard (cheetah) and the cat: a lynx, for example. But we suspect the κατόπαρδος is indeed a cheetah (Nicholas 1999:286–89). The problem for the translation is that the pard has already been identified as the cheetah. It is likely that the author was simply unable to identify the Byzantine pard as being the same as the Italian cat-pard. The least speculative thing to do with this cat, which is only a marginal participant in the *Tale* in any case, is to leave it uninterpreted as "cat-pard."

Foreign Influences

> They [the inhabitants of Asia Minor] had not as yet received the beef-eating Latins into their homes, and thus did not know that they pour out their wine both unmixed and pure in the same way that they pour out their unmitigated gall.
>
> —Nicetas Choniates, cited in T. M. Kolbaba, *The Byzantine Lists*

We have already considered in "Literary Parallels" a few works from outside Byzantium that display some thematic kinship with the *Tale*. In most cases, any direct influence can be safely ruled out. There is little chance, for example, that the *Tale*'s author had heard of his contemporary Geoffrey Chaucer—though Chaucer, ironically, does seem to have heard of *Digenes Akrites,* making reference to an *Arcite* in *The Knight's Tale*. Nonetheless, the similarity in general outline between the Byzantine epic bestiaries and similar poems in the West has made an impression on scholars (see, for instance, Kazhdan 1991 s.v. Animal Epic, Diegesis ton Tetrapodon Zoon, Poulologos). We discuss here the two likeliest candidates to have exerted influence on the *Tale*. Though we do not find any evidence of such influence, the differences between the *Tale* and these two animal poems, the originally French *Renard* cycle and the Arabic (ultimately Indian) *Kalilah and Dimnah,* are illuminating.

Renard

The first literary evaluation of the *Tale,* written before the *Tale* was even published, was by André Gidel in 1864 (published in 1866).[65] Gidel's study concerned the influence of Western models on medieval Greek literature; it is subtitled *Imitations in Greek of Our* [French] *Chivalric Romances from the Twelfth Century on.* After a pioneering though not always well-informed[66] study of the chivalric romances proper—several of which were indeed closely based on French and Italian models—Gidel turned to the *Tale* and posited a Western model for it in *Renard the Fox*. It is worthwhile to present his arguments here and see how well they now bear out.

It should be said at the outset that Gidel (1866) does not—and indeed cannot—postulate direct imitation of the French *Renard* cycle. He instead sees a pervasive cultural influence at work:

> The author of this Greek work has no intention other than profiting from the memory of reading the French poem and exploiting it to his own ends in a more or less original manner. We dare see in this a proof—if not more striking, at least just as precise—of our influence in the East. The literal translation of a French romance is testimony to the conquest at its onset; we see it imposed onto the vanquished, and in the form that must have been most agreeable to the conquerors. Being freer, and indeed more removed, imitation attests that our victory was long-lasting. (311)

As becomes obvious, Gidel's belief that the *Tale* draws on the West is largely based on begging the question: Gidel starts from the presumption that the *Tale* must have been based on Western prototypes, rather than proceeding from autonomous evidence for this, and couches his presumption in language that nowadays would be characterized as little short of colonialist:

> In the [impoverished] state of imagination the Greeks lived in the Middle Ages, could they have invented a form of narrative so novel and daring? Wouldn't the path have been easier to follow after a great given example than to open it up for the first time? (324)

The "reflections" of the French work that he finds in the Greek are far from convincing—the more so as the author already admits that indigenous traditions, such as ancient Greek and Middle Eastern tales of animals, could just as easily have given rise to "such a minor Iliad." In each instance, Gidel contends that the parallels between *Renard* and the *Tale* are too close to be attributed to coincidence. To us, it seems rather that given their common subject matter, these traits are an inevitable component of any parliament of animals.

For example, the parallels between the lion's court in *Renard* and the *Tale* are hardly surprising: given the contention that the lion is a king (which surely predates even Aesop), it would be surprising if the lion were not described with all the trappings of human royalty—including a court. Furthermore, because lions were no longer familiar to medieval Europeans, Orthodox or Catholic, it is to be expected that the lions are idealized figures in both poems and that "one would search in vain for the animal beneath the mask" (325): all either author would have known about the lion, outside the garbled traditions of the *Physiologus* and the bestiaries, would be that he was a testy king figure.

The lack of names of animals in the *Tale* is a strong argument against any influence from *Renard*. In that text, the beasts are fully anthropomorphized and readily identifiable satirical types—as distinct from the *Tale,* where the participants are in a curious limbo between humanity and farm produce. The *Vita of the Esteemed Donkey,* by contrast, where Western influence is more apparent,[67] does give its protagonist the name Νίκος, "Nick," even if only as a reward for his victory (νίκη). So the few parallels between the names in *Renard* and the epithets in the *Tale* cannot mean much; they are, as Gidel (1866:328) admits for the fox, part of natural history—which is the same in France and Greece. The cat is called Moustache in *Renard* and (Gidel claims) μουστάκατα in the *Tale* ("[long-]whiskered");[68] the similar sound of the two words proves little—particularly as it is not the cat at all that the *Tale* calls long-whiskered, as Gidel thought, but the rat! Accusing the dog of being mangy ("you get the itch") need hardly be an allusion to the name Roonel in *Renard*; the Greek author would have already seen his fair share of mangy mutts without needing to refer to a French poem. As for the bear, Gidel finds it implausible that the author could have come up with the epithet μελισσοφάγε ("honey-munching"), which to him seems not to describe the actual behavior of bears; instead, he attributes it to a trick Renard plays on the story's bear Gros-brun/Bruin. Yet the notion that the bear was a honey eater was widespread enough that the name of the animal is derived from "honey eater" in the Slavonic languages (Old Church Slavonic медвѣдь).

Neither are the incidents that Gidel adduces from the *Tale* any more convincing. For instance, he admits there would be plenty of native precedent for characterizing the fox as cunning and learned as well as a threat to barnyard animals. It is all the more surprising, then, that he goes on to see an echo of Chanteclere the Rooster's complaints of being tricked by Renard in the hare complaining to the fox. Poultry and rabbit were the staple of the fox's diet around the farm, and the fox was proverbially renowned for cunning.[69] It is hardly unexpected to find the victims complaining in a bestiary of her trickery—the more so because it is a different animal complaining in each poem!

Finally, medieval French fabliaux feature the wolf learning letters from a priest: "A," says the priest, to which the wolf replies, "A." "B" ("beh"), says the priest, to which the wolf replies, "lamb."[70] This anecdote mocks the wolf's ineptitude as a scholar, and Gidel sees it reflected in the boar's retort to the sheep: "where did you get this learning? / Was it your friend, that Old Man Wolf, who taught you?" (431–32). But the *Tale* does not give any specifics of the wolf's learning and grants him colleagues in the dog, the nanny, and the billy goat. This is a conceit the author of the *Tale* could easily have devised on his own, and it is not particularly reminiscent of the fabliau.

In fact, it is difficult to see anything at all of *Renard* in the *Tale*. The *Renard* cycle was based since its inception, in the Latin *Ysengrimus,* on the enmity between the fox and the wolf; the two animals do not even acknowledge each other's existence in the *Tale*. While sniffing and skulking about like animals should, the French *Renard*'s animals are also anthropomorphized enough to be depicted on horseback; nothing could be further from the *Tale*. The participants of *Renard* have complex social interactions; the animals are married (the foxes Renard and Hermeline, the wolves Ysengrin and Hersent, the lions Noble and Fiere, the chickens Chanteclere and Pinte), and indeed much of the dramatic impetus of *Renard* lies in the consequences of Renard's adultery with and/or rape of Hersent. Again, other than the billy goat as silent partner to the nanny, nothing of the sort is to be seen in the *Tale*. And *Renard* is full of stories of encounters between beasts—usually involving Renard tricking his victim into ignominy. Other than the horse's fable, there are no stories as such in the *Tale*. When humans act against animals in *Renard*, they do so as instruments of Renard's cunning. The *Tale* has vignettes of human cruelty to animals, which the animals' adversaries are all too glad to relate—but for which they can hardly take credit.

There is one incident in *Renard* reminiscent of the *Tale*: in the early *Branches* 2 and 1 a universal truce has been proclaimed by King Noble, and it is Renard's violation of the truce in killing the hen Copee, rather than Renard's rape of Hersent, that enrages the lion into action (*Renard* 1.355ff.)—just as it is the lion's violation of the truce in the *Tale* that leads to the final battle. The accusers are hardly the same, but King Noble's outburst against Renard could have been spoken by the *Tale*'s ox against his King Lion:

> "Vengeance I'll have on anyone
> For breaking the peace and murdering!" (1.376–77; Terry 1983:104)

But tempting though it is to see *Renard*'s influence in the universal peace in the *Tale*, this seems unlikely. The truce is a narrative necessity in the *Tale*: it would be impossible otherwise to bring the animals together. The assembly of animals in *Branche* 1 is convened under rather different terms: the assembly is for Renard's trial, not as an end in itself, and the truce was an already established fact—though ignored by the feuding Renard and Ysengrin. And King Noble's court has a well-defined feudal setup, which one could be rather more confident would forestall "all unforeseen disorder or confusion" (*Tale* 118). So the truces in the two poems are not particularly similar, and their presence may safely be presumed a coincidence.

The connections that Gidel (1866) draws with *Renard* are tenuous and do not substantially shed light on our understanding of the work. They have accordingly been abandoned in modern scholarship.[71] Gidel, it should be noted, was unaware of the *Book of Birds*, which clearly constitutes a much more promising prototype for the *Tale* than *Renard* (see discussion, appendix 1) and which is if anything even more distant from the world of the humorous French fabliaux.

We do not know of any other Western work for which a parallel with the Byzantine epic bestiaries might be claimed. Bird conventions are not a frequent topic of poetry, and the *Book of Birds* is an easy target for comparison with Chaucer's *Parlement of Fowles*. But Chaucer was at most an infant at the time the *Book* was presumably written. Moreover, Chaucer's *Parlement,* with its courtly celebration of love, has no subject matter in common with the *Book* and its vicious, underhanded arguments—much less the burlesque and politicking of the *Tale*.

Kalilah and Dimnah

Byzantine literature was influenced by Eastern as well as Western literature. A number of Byzantine works, both learned and vernacular, are derived from Arabic or Persian narratives or are outright translations: *Barlaam and Joasaph, Syntipas, Ptocholeon,* and so on. But things don't look any more promising for identifying Eastern influences on the *Tale*. The problem is that whenever animals appear in literature, they are almost always put to use in fables or fablelike narratives, and this is not a characteristic of the *Tale*. We may reject influence from the Islamic moral tractate *Island of Animals,* for instance; the *Island* debates whether humans are entitled to be overlords of the animals, whereas the *Tale* blithely assumes it. The *Island* has a much broader repertoire of animals and a very different agenda; there is nothing humorous or trivial about it, and neither does its didacticism extend to catalogs or enumerations.

Furthermore, the parallels we have noted in our discussion of the *Island* do not amount to much for all their suggestiveness: they constitute commonplaces. The one explicit structural similarity, a great cat acting as minister, is an inevitable choice in a leonine court emulating human courts. In fact, it recurs in versions of the *Renard* cycle. The leopard reappears as the lion's advisor (named Firapeel) in the conclusion of the Flemish *Van den Vos Reynaerde* (Best 1983:98) and is paired with the lynx as umpire of the duel between Renard the Fox and Isegrijn the Wolf in the later *Reinaerts Historie* (128).[72]

The rather more famous cycle *Kalilah and Dimnah,* as disseminated in Arabic, was hugely influential on animal storytelling in both East and West, yet even less of a case can be made for its influence on the *Tale*. *Kalilah and Dimnah* did not lack for opportunity to do so: it had already been translated twice into Byzantine Greek by the twelfth century, where it came to be known as *Stephanites and Ichnelates* (Beck 1971:41–42). The work proved hugely popular, as proven by its survival in over forty manuscripts. But just as the scandalous merrymaking of *Renard* is alien to the worldview of the *Tale,* so, too, is the narrative exuberance of *Kalilah and Dimnah*. Where the *Tale* is at pains to give one fable and allude to a second, *Kalilah and Dimnah* illustrates its moral teachings by piling stories upon stories; whenever any character within a fable wishes to make a point, he launches another fable.[73]

King Lion inevitably shows up in the Arabic narrative and is as testy as one has come to expect: "The lion was conceited and obstinate in his opinions, while these were anything but perfect" (Irving 1980:3)—though the lion goes on to be scared out of his wits by the roaring of an abandoned bull. It is ironic that *Kalilah and Dimnah*'s lion turns out to have nothing to fear from the bull—but plenty from the jackal Dimnah, whereas in the *Tale* it is the ox that dispatches King Lion. The lion is attended by "a leopard who was one of his noblest companions. He had very special rank, and lingered night and day in his privacy" (Irving 1980:48). This is the same as in the *Island of Animals* and indicates merely the plausibility of a lion king being attended by other great cats. Even if the *Tale* drew this notion from a source like *Kalilah and Dimnah,* it is hardly a noteworthy step.

Other than the conventional figures of the feline court, the two narratives do not share identifiable characters: the eponymous jackals of *Kalilah and Dimnah* are nowhere in sight in the *Tale*. Needless to say, none of the profusion of stories in *Kalilah and Dimnah* is even slightly reminiscent of any events in the *Tale*. Neither is the sententiousness of *Kalilah and Dimnah* to be found in our text: the *Tale* makes do with two proverbs (424, 610a), of which the first hardly suggests proverbial wisdom, whereas the second is hopelessly glib in context. The *Tale* does contain a story within a story, the horse's tale of the donkeys.[74] But this is a far cry from the narrative ebullience of *Kalilah and Dimnah*'s multiply nested stories.

There are only two incidents reminiscent of episodes of the *Tale*—the mouse thieving from the monk (Irving 1980:78–84) and the uneasy truce of the cat and the mouse (149–54). In both cases the differences are far more striking than the similarities. The mouse in *Kalilah and Dimnah* thieves from a basket of food in full view of the monk, rather than inconspicuously in the cellar. Its eventual solace in a Hindu withdrawal from the world would not likely have crossed the mind of the *Tale*'s arrogant rat. The cat and mouse in *Kalilah and Dimnah* find themselves in a temporary alliance begotten of need—the mouse helps the snared wildcat out to avoid being eaten by her, the weasel, or the owl, yet the mouse does not let his guard down against his new ally even when delivered from his other foes. Whatever the underlying intent of the strange embassy in the *Tale,* binding the cat and rat together, its lesson is certainly not as straightforward as *Kalilah and Dimnah*'s—and the *Tale*'s rat does not seem to know much about wariness. Once again, one cannot make a case for the author of the *Tale* being influenced by *Kalilah and Dimnah* in any way.

Survivals of the *Tale*

> If someone, after inquiry and scrutiny, writes down my story in detail, even though he cannot tell everything, he will compose an account of most of what I say. But if perchance some lover wishes to describe it, he will refashion it according to his wish and fancy. —*Libistros and Rhodamne*

The theme of a convention of animals has captured the imaginations of many peoples and been manifested in many forms. So the existence of three versions (all from Cyprus) of a modern Greek folk song with similar content to the *Tale* (appendix 4) leads to an obvious question: are these songs a direct continuation of the *Tale,* as argued by several researchers? Or are they independent developments of the same prevalent theme?

The perpetuation of the *Tale* in folk song is not in principle impossible. The hero of Cappadocian heroic lays, immortalized in *Digenes Akrites,* is sung of to this day in various parts of the Greek-speaking world. This is an instance of cultural continuity that proved pivotal to the political coloring of folklore studies in Greece (Herzfeld 1986 [1982]:119–21), although it would be an exaggeration to claim that the modern folk songs preserve the story of the medieval romance: all that recurs are the names of Digenes and a couple of his opponents together with the premise that he is a warlord. This does nonetheless establish precedent for the oral transmission of text from late Byzantium into modern Greece. And it has also proven possible in Greek for extensive texts to pass from written provenance (to which the *Tale* no doubt belongs: see "Orality") to oral: there are many recorded instances in living memory of people able to recite all ten thousand verses of the seventeenth-century Cretan romance *Erotokritos,*[75] and smaller excerpts of the romance are still frequently sung.

But a couple of crucial elements are missing. First, the medium for the transmission of written poems to oral was not the manuscript but the mass dissemination of cheap popular editions—the chapbook, the Renaissance equivalent of the paperback. These editions were popular well into the nineteenth century and provided the route for *Erotokritos,* a product of the Veneto-Cretan nobility, into the readership of the common folk throughout the Greek-speaking world. But Byzantine vernacular poems rarely made any inroads into these editions. The poems that did circulate are rhymed versions of their narratives, conceived outside Byzantium and, indeed, after the Byzantine state ceased to exist. An unrhymed poem would not survive in the new, print world; people would have to go out of their way to rhyme the *Tale* in order to bring it to a new market.[76]

We are aware of two exceptions to this claim; both, we would contend, are exceptions that prove the rule. Karanastassis (1991) discusses a survival from the *Mass of the Beardless Man* in a song sung by a monk in a short story by Alexandros Papadiamantis, written in the nineteenth century. The passage in question appears in a manuscript version of the *Mass* (A 343–45) but not in the printed version; Karanastassis concludes that the song, which is reminiscent of *Ptochoprodromos* 4, was commonly sung before the *Mass* was written (early sixteenth century). It was interpolated into its manuscript, Karanastassis believes, as a popular monastic song, despite having little to do with the Beardless Man. The song continued in its popularity to be reported by Papadiamantis in the nineteenth century in a linguistically normalized form. The fate of the song is a counterexample to what we claim: a text fragment possibly derived from a

Byzantine vernacular poem and written down in a text not consigned to printing survived in recognizable form through six centuries of oral transmission. But the closed society of the cloister, with its mandatory literacy and relishing of underground parody like the *Mass,* is a special case. In the absence of printing, it is possible for monks to have passed down through the centuries a six-verse stanza of special interest to them, sung to the tune of a well-known hymn. But no community, even a monastic one, could pass down a text as loosely structured as the *Tale* in recognizable form, even under the best circumstances, and even if the *Tale* held much more interest to that community than we think plausible.

The same objection, we feel, holds for the other such instance: the religious alphabet poems collected by Kakoulidi (1964). These poems display a strong influence from church language and date from the fifteenth through the eighteenth centuries. Versions of the same poems have also been recorded in oral form in the twentieth century. It is hard to believe that religious acrostics could have any origin but written (Kakoulidi 1964:70), and the poems have frequently borrowed from eponymous church poetry (72). Yet the manuscripts themselves are frequently clearly written from memory rather than copied (14, 71), so they arguably passed into the oral domain as soon as they were composed. But we believe this is merely Karanastassis's phenomenon on a larger scale: the poems have a mnemonic device (the alphabetic acrostic) and are associated with the church (a literate domain). So these acrostics were passed down through the same mechanism as Karanastassis's song, by churchmen in the first instance. Indeed, this transmission would have been reinforced by the frequent manuscript transcriptions made of the poems, and often enough the acrostics made it into print anyway (29, 36, 43, 46). Once again, this is not at all comparable to the case of the *Tale*.

It has been claimed that there was a concerted effort to preserve vernacular medieval literature in the fifteenth and sixteenth centuries (as reflected in its manuscript history, including that of the *Tale*).[77] Yet most such poems were never afforded a pathway into the mass distribution through print that took place during that period: the *Tale* thus gained no means of becoming orally transmitted. This is proven, if anything, by the Cypriot song version of the *Donkey Tale*—a work that did circulate in print from Venice and was thereby available to posterity. Unlike the *Tale*-like songs, the Cypriot donkey song "is very close to the Byzantine work, and thus admits of direct comparison" (Eideneier 1987:417). Such comparison includes the mention of Καβάκα, the name of the hen that the fox steals, as well as its elderly owner (*Vita* 162; *Fair Tale* 162); both are mentioned in the Hatzioannou *Quadrupeds*-like song (song 3 in appendix 4)—the end of which also refers to the *Donkey Tale*.[78]

Moreover, the nature of the *Tale* itself would have impeded such transmission. It is for the most part a meticulous laundry list of utilitarian concerns, with only sparse flashes of plot—a far cry from the usual concerns of ballad or romance and ill poised to guarantee popular reception. The songs that have been adduced as echoes of the *Tale* are considerably shorter, as is the list of their participants. And though they share the *Tale*'s instrumentalist treatment of animals, comical in-fighting, and the framing premise of a convention, nothing here can be pinpointed as a direct reminiscence of the *Tale*. Frying pork pies and cats wallowing in ash are commonplaces of the barnyard. The rat creeping into the cellar is as close as the *Tale* and the songs get in specifics.[79] If the songs' animals say the same things as the *Tale*'s, that is simply because they only have that much to say about themselves in terms of human exploitation in the first place. Neither does the correspondence between the songs' and the *Tale*'s formulas on animals' entrances seem as clear to us as it does to Eideneier (1987:419).

On the other hand, the songs contain a lot of material quite foreign to the *Tale*: the sheep eating an artichoke to replenish her wool, the pots filled with pork or pig fat, the trapped fox (absent also from the *Donkey Tale*). We might postulate that the Cypriot singers interpolated these episodes into the *Tale*; but the songs seem to be all interpolation and no *Tale*. The only narrative continuity between the *Tale* and the songs is the episode that Eideneier (1987:416) points out: the rat challenges the cat, in pairwise disputation. The rat's venture is foolhardy enough to draw attention; it may point to an underlying oral tradition of the old enmity starting off with the rat's challenge. But the *Tale,* in the form we have it, is an essentially written work (see "Orality"). Even if it shares a common origin with the songs—something very hard to prove at this remove—its own relation with them is at best tenuous.

So we should reject the presumptions by Hatzioannou (1934–37:631), Papaharalambous (1945–46:262), and Eideneier (1987) that the songs belong to the *Tale.* (Papaharalambous goes so far as to speak of the "surviving" portion of the *Tale,* from which the other animals and the lion's judgment are "missing.") These songs, one must conclude, are nonce comical inventions, sharing a common origin with the *Tale* in a widespread premise; they are not its direct continuations.

The songs, it should be noted, are from Cyprus, which had been severed from the Byzantine Empire even before the Fourth Crusade and until the fifteenth century was still under French rather than Venetian suzerainty. The possibility of direct transmission is thus even further reduced, as there would have been limited channels of communications between Cyprus and the rest of the Greek-speaking world. It is again far likelier that these songs represent an older notion of a convention of "useful" animals, independent of the *Tale*: it features none of the *Tale*'s exotic creatures.

This leads us to suspect that the *Tale* bears some similarity to *Digenes* in its textual history. The two poems were constructed on the basis of an extant folkloric tradition—*Digenes* chaining Cappadocian lays into a narrative, the *Tale* perhaps getting at least the idea of an animal convention from folk songs.[80] As a result, both poems have modern parallels in song. Yet neither poem was able to feed back into that tradition, the way the *Donkey Tale* or *Erotokritos* did, because they did not make the transition into print. That *Digenes* failed to do so is something of a surprise (Kechagioglou 1993:129–30)—enough of a surprise that around 1770 Caesarius Dapontes, on finding two now lost manuscripts of the work in Mount Athos, promised to do something about it:

> Καὶ ὅλα δὲ χειρίσια, δὲν εἶδα τυπωμένον·
> ’ς τὸν τύπον, καθὼς φαίνεται, δὲν βρίσκεται βαλμένον.
> Τύπωσαν Ἐρωτόκριτον, Σωσάνναν, Ἐρωφίλη
> καὶ ἄλλα καὶ δὲν τύπωσαν, κρίμα, καὶ τὸν Βασίλη.
> Ζωὴν ἂν ἔχω ἐκ Θεοῦ, θέλω μὲ στιχουργίαν
> νὰ τὸν συνθέσω καὶ αὐτὸν κ’ εὐθὺς ’ς τὴν Βενετίαν
> χαρὰ ’ς τὸν σταμπαδοῦρον δέ, ὁποῦ τονε σταμπάρῃ,
> ὅτι πολὺ διάφορο κ’ ὄνομα θέλει πάρει.

> [It’s all handwritten; I haven’t seen it printed;
> it hasn’t gone to press, it seems. They’ve done
> Erotokritos, Susanna, Erophile,
> and others; yet, for shame, they’ve not done Basil.
> If God but grants me life, I shall compose him
> with art of verse as well; then, off to Venice.
> Lucky the printer there who will produce him!
> For he shall gain much fame and profit, too.] (Lambros 1880:c; Trapp 1971:15)[81]

With much less romantic heroics than the poem of *Basil Digenes Akrites,* it is much less surprising that the *Entertaining Tale of Quadrupeds* did not make a permanent impression on either peasants or intellectuals.

Composition of the *Tale*

> Come, gather, Reason, Thou my finest Knowledge.
> Speak prudently, my Tongue. Establish, Mind.
> Now let the Three join forces, write this nobly,
> speak truthfully, or tell this prudently.
> Watch, lest we stumble and become undone!
>
> —*Account of Famed Venice* 1–5

Date of Composition

Obviously the poem was written before its first surviving manuscript, dating from 1461. The existence of two families of manuscripts (see “Manuscripts”) pushes the date of composition further back. The poem itself mentions the date of 1364. This does not necessarily mean the poem was written in that year: even if the poem had a political intent behind it, there could have been obvious motivation for the poet to use an arbitrary, fictional date rather than a contemporary one. Compare George Orwell’s use of 1984 or the instance at the conclusion of *The Mass of the Beardless Man* (D 1820): Ἐτελειώθη ὁ μιαρὸς σπανὸς ἔτει ͵αψρθʹ μηνὶ Μπαμπούλα λεʹ, "The filthy beardless man died in the year seventeen hundred and ten-ty nine ⟨sic⟩, on the thirty-fifth day of the month Bogeyman."

All the same, there are several indications that the composition of the poem cannot be far removed from the latter half of the fourteenth century. First of all, the date in the *Mass* is truly arbitrary, whereas the *Tale* gives a date that must reasonably have been close to when it was actually written. The poem seems to have been composed at a time when the Byzantine Empire was still a going concern with which foreign nations could draw "false peace" (as stated in the poem's prologue) and that could still hope to vanquish those nations. That description fits pre-1372 Byzantium better than Byzantium in vassalage to the Ottoman Empire—though Byzantines clung to hope of divine intervention until the very end and would have taken some time to realize that no worldly power could restore Byzantium any longer. If the prologue to the poem, expressing those sentiments, is in fact a subsequent addition as has been claimed (see appendix 3), the poem itself must have been written even earlier. The contents of the poem proper also reflect life in a prosperous Byzantium; this becomes more plausible the earlier one looks in the fourteenth century and could hardly have reflected the life experience of an author to whom Byzantine affluence was a distant memory.

On the other hand, it is widely accepted, as discussed in appendix 1, that the *Tale* was written after the *Book of Birds*. Tsavare (1987:102–12) has argued that the *Book* was written after 1274 and before 1331, whereas Makris (1993:408) has suggested that it be dated shortly before 1345. The strong presence of Italian loanwords, and the poet's familiarity with Western mores, places the *Tale* at least a generation after 1204, though one cannot be any more precise than that.

The Middle Eastern references and loanwords (e.g., παπούτζιν, "shoe, slipper," 515; τζοχοϋφανδωμένα, "woven with serge," 504) would suggest a fourteenth- or fifteenth-century date. However, most of the loanwords are Persian or Arabic rather than specifically Turkish: they could thus be referring to Saracen realia as easily as Turkish realia—which could push the date back to the fourteenth or even the thirteenth century. In addition, the Middle Eastern terms used in the poem were either already in use in Byzantium (and ultimately of Persian or Arabic origin) or were concerned with the Muslim military and leadership[82] and not the common Turkish or Arabic folk or Muslim religious practice (Tassos Karanastassis, personal communication.) In particular, the ζαρκούλιν, "gold-embroidered cap," as an expressly military hat illustrates the latter tendency, although the status of the σαρπούζιν, "fur hat," is more ambiguous (see Commentary, verse 512.) This also suggests an earlier date, before the routine coexistence of Turks and Greeks. The author would have seen Muslim soldiers and officers wearing *zerqulās* and *sharbūshs* and would have worked out that they were made of felt, but although the sheep talks at length about the garments of Christian clergy (503–8), no mention is ever made of Muslim religious leaders.

The *Tale*'s political terms associated with the Muslim world had different interpretations in the fourteenth and the fifteenth century. In the fifteenth, the Ottoman leader had been accorded the title of *sultan,* and *emir* referred to lesser authorities within the Ottoman state (Kazhdan 1991, s.v. EMIR: "In early Islamic times only commanders of armies used the title, but later persons exercising administrative and financial authority adopted it."). The Ottoman use of these terms led Ševčenko (1974:78) to consider a fifteenth-century date plausible for the *Tale*. However, although both Orhan (1326–1362) and his son Murad I (1362–1389) claimed for themselves the title of sultan, Murad's son Bayezid I was the first Ottoman ruler to be officially granted the title by a caliph, in 1395, and to be called *imperator,* "emperor," by contemporary Westerners (Inalcik 1973:55–56). Despite the claims of Bayezid's predecessors, the Turks in the fourteenth century were still ruled by several distinct emirs, and the title of sultan was associated not with the Turks but with North Africa: the three Berber states of the Maghreb and the Mameluk dynasty in Cairo.[83]

Three independent Greek testimonies bear this out. In Cantacuzene's *History,* Σουλτάν refers only to the erstwhile Seljuk sultan of Iconium (1.83), whose state had dissolved into the Turkish emirates by the fourteenth century, and the current sultan of Cairo (3.90ff.)[84] The romance of *Imperios and Margarona* (admittedly an adaptation from the Italian) has the verse Σουλτάνος τὸν ἀγόρασεν, τοῦ Καϊριοῦ αὐθέντης, "The sultan purchased him, the ruler of Cairo" (624). And Linardo Della Porta, in diplomatic service to Venice, refers to his 1389 visit to the Σαρεκηνὸν σουλτάνον Βαρβαρίας / καὶ ρήγαν εἰς τὴν Τύνιστον καὶ αὐθέντην Ἀραβίας, "Saracen sultan of Barbary, king of Tunis and master of Arabia" (the sultan of Tunis, Abu Al 'Abbas Ahmad; 1.1252–53). On the other hand, he speaks of the Ottoman Murad I, whom he visited around 1385, as an emir (1.1241: τὸν ἀμιρᾶν, τὸν μέγαν Ἀμουράτην, "the emir, the great Amouratis"; cf. 1.1307; 1.1348, etc.).

So if the *Tale* was written in the fourteenth century and the author used the term correctly (as Westerners, Byzantine historians, and other Muslims did), then the reference to the sultan and emirs no longer concerns an Ottoman sultan and his underlings but an Arab sultan or sultans and their lesser Turkish colleagues. This would make "sultan(s) and emirs" (493–94, 757, 878–79) parallel to emperors and kings (250, 297) rather than emperors and magnates (400–401, 500)—certainly a plausible comparison to draw. Although verse 494 refers to the rugs "on which the sultan and emirs repose," suggesting perhaps a single Muslim overlord, this could have just as easily referred to the Mameluk sultan in the fourteenth century as to the Ottoman sultan in the fifteenth; and verse 878 speaks of sultans in the plural ("Also my skin is valued by the sultans").

An Egyptian identification of the *Tale*'s sultan is reinforced by the fact that we have identified the σαρπούζιν in verse 512 with the Egyptian *sharbūsh* rather than the vaguer Turco-Persian *serpuş* (see Commentary.) In fact, although the other Muslim references in the poem are not concrete enough to date it to either the fourteenth or the fifteenth century, the σαρπούζιν does offer a *terminus ante quem,* if our identification with the *sharbūsh* is correct. The *sharbūsh* was abolished after 1382, and it appears to have been forgotten thereafter (see Commentary, verse 512). It would be unreasonable to expect an author, writing as far away as Byzantium, to mention in the fifteenth century a long-obsolete foreign military cap—especially in the matter-of-fact way verse 512 does. The *sharbūsh* must likely still have been in use, or at least in recent memory, when the poem was written. This places the *terminus ante quem* not long after 1382.

Although we have no definite conclusion, the overall evidence strongly suggests that we need not move very far from 1364 as the date of the poem's composition. The date itself was not a landmark of any significant event in Byzantium. The main event of that decade, addressed in histories of the period, was John V Palaeologus's attempts to woo the West into military support in exchange for church union (see appendix 2). If the "false peace" of the nations had a contemporary referent, rather than being an all-too-familiar commonplace for the Byzantine Empire, it would have either been fear of the papacy or wariness at the Ottoman emirs' increasing overlordship against their state—although the memory of the strife with Serbia and Bulgaria (both of which took their signed treaties lightly) was yet green.

Place of Composition

Robert Browning (1980:196) had no doubt that the *Tale* was written in the "mother city" of the empire: "And several vernacular poems, such as the Belisarius poem and a curious allegorical poem on the four-footed beasts, were clearly the work of metropolitan circles."[85] This assumption is echoed by Tsiouni (1972:30), who edited the *Tale* under Browning's supervision—although Tsiouni also allows for another major Byzantine city, such as Thessalonica. The author displays knowledge of the activities of an industrious middle class (including arrow makers and bow makers, goldsmiths, scribes, and doctors) as well as details of the dress, habits, and diet of an affluent upper class. This would place the poet in a city, and indeed likely in a major city such as Thessalonica or Constantinople. (We are of necessity dealing with the author's life experiences; where he physically penned the *Tale,* of course, we cannot know.)

Tsiouni (1972:28–30) has argued that the derogatory reference to Jews (424) is a further argument pointing toward one of the "twin capitals" of Byzantium.[86] But because Jews lived throughout the Greek-speaking world, with anti-Semitism following close behind them, the mere mention of a proverb (lacking even the blunt immediacy of the *Book of Birds*'s (55) ἀποθηκάριν τοῦ Μωσὲ γεμάτον σκυλινέαν, "satchel of Moshe's full of dog turds") cannot be relied on too much. In any case, an anti-Semitic proverb like the *Tale*'s could have spread to regions in the empire without Jewish communities,[87] so this cannot be used as conclusive evidence of the poet's location.

Does any internal evidence suggest this city was in Byzantium itself, as opposed to Western- or Ottoman-held territory? For different reasons, a Western-occupied region has been argued for by both Xanthoudidis (1927–28:350–53, 359), always on the lookout for evidence to claim medieval vernacular Greek works for Crete, and Gidel (1866:311), always on the lookout to claim medieval vernacular Greek imitation of French works. Xanthoudidis's linguistic adventurism has since been dispensed with (Koukoules 1936; Eideneier 1976:454–55 with specific reference to the *Tale*); the archaisms of Cretan Greek are shared throughout the Aegean and need not point to anywhere specific in medieval Greece. Moreover, as Šandrovskaja (1956b:193) has pointed out in reference to the *Asperges* episode (384–88) (against Xanthoudidis 1927–28:359), familiarity with Western mores does not necessitate composition in a Western-occupied region: Italian trading colonies were widespread in the territory of the empire itself, notably in Thessalonica and Constantinople. And as Eideneier (1976:455) has argued, nothing about the Italian loanwords in the text requires extended contact with the West as anything but trading partners: "If the given Venetian loanwords were assembled, they would prove the opposite: the text has a series of Western words, which seem to have belonged to common Medieval Greek as a whole."

The *Asperges* episode shows the poet to be no admirer of the Catholic rite (see "Faith and Country"). Furthermore, the poet portrays an Orthodox church hierarchy in full prosperity, with the chain of command from patriarch to monk intact (503–8, 915–19). This makes composition under Western dominion less likely: the Orthodox kept their priests and monks in those regions, but the upper echelons of church administration were Catholic.[88] Although contemporary Catholic bishops had elaborate crosiers corresponding to the Orthodox staffs (Herbermann 2000, s.v. CROSIER) so that δοκανίκια in verse 917 could refer to either, a poet in Western territory would be unlikely to single out petticoats (505) or ivory seats (915) made for patriarchs rather than popes. Neither would he mention Catholic bishops in the same breath as "head abbots with their beards so long" (919)—beards having been proscribed for the Catholic clergy since the sixth century (Herbermann 2000, s.v. BEARDS).

Further proof of a Byzantine context for the poem is given by the maintenance of the Byzantine distinction between emperor (βασιλεύς—*basileus*) and king (ῥῆξ—*rex*).[89] *Rex* appears four times in the text. Three of those times, *rex* co-occurs with *basileus*—twice as a synonym of *basileus,* because the two occur in idempotent half-verses (a pervasive feature of Greek vernacular verse): 250, "in royal courts, imperial palaces," and 297, "it is the kings and emperors who eat me" (literally: "the *basileis* consume me, the *reges* eat me"), and once with *rex* and *basileus* next to sultans and nobles in a listing: 757, "emperors, noblemen, and kings and sultans." But the remaining instance clearly places the *rex* and his queen the *regina* (ῥήγαινα) in a Western context: 491–92 "and these are owned by queens ⟨ῥήγαινες⟩, and kings ⟨ῥηγάδες⟩ as well, / and counts ⟨κόντες—the term is Italian⟩ and knights ⟨καβαλάριοι⟩ and others of their rank." The evidence for the persistence of the distinction is not as strong as one would like but still points to a Byzantine outlook in the poem.

An alternative not brought up until Ševčenko (1974) is that the poem was composed under Turkish dominion. Ottoman religious tolerance meant that the Orthodox church hierarchy stayed intact in their regions. However, there is no mention in the *Tale* of the habits of the common Islamic folk, who were quite numerous and long established in Asia Minor at the time, but only of their leadership (493–94, 756–63, 878–82) (and their military, if the ζαρκοῦλιν and σαρπούζιν in verse 512 are indeed military caps.) The references in the *Tale* to Middle Eastern clothing prove little: many such items mentioned in the *Tale* had been taken up as fashionable in the Byzantine court, as a perusal of Pseudo-Codinus's *De Officiis* shows. Likewise, it is entirely possible that Ottoman headgear had passed into usage in Byzantium, as Scarce (1987:31) holds. The example she brings up, the daughter of the emperor of Trebizond in 1432, is not from Byzantium but from the Pontus, but it would be difficult to argue that by that stage Constantinople was under any less cultural pressure from the Turks than Trebizond. So the Turkish hats mentioned in the *Tale* might be either a result of exchanges with Ottoman officialdom, the practice of the omnipresent Turkish mercenaries, or an otherwise unattested fad among the Byzantine nobility. There is no reason to read into these references any more extensive contact with the Turks than would normally be expected in late Byzantium. In fact, there is a case to be made (as argued under "Date of Composition") that at least some of the Muslim references are not Turkish at all but Arabic.

As time went on, the Ottomans assumed increasing overlordship of Byzantium; the stronger the Ottomans grew, the less Byzantines might be inclined to raising their ire in literature. But the extent to which the Turks held the literate Byzantines in thrall should not be overstated. Makrembolites (see "Subversion and Politics") suspects the Turks of being morally superior to the Byzantines, but he does so in a "noble savage" argument, and he does not flatter the Turks or hail their victories. And despite the close personal relationship that Cantacuzene enjoyed with the emirs of both Bithynia and Aydin, in his writings the Turks remained infidels and Mohammed, the arch-heretic. But the *Tale* is unlikely to have been the kind of text that would attract Ottoman authorities' attention and thus require circumspection. So the absence of any overt anti-Islamic sentiment in the *Tale* is not much of an argument for composition under the Ottomans.

More compelling is the fact that whenever mentioned in the poem, Muslims appear not in the guise of commoners but are represented only by their sultans and emirs. This is in contrast to the Westerners, who appear not only as knights, counts, and kings (ῥηγάδες) but also as priests and church congregations. Tales of sultans' thick carpets (493), gold-wrought saddles (759), and leopard-skin covers (880) could belong to the eleventh century as easily as the fourteenth; they display Muslims as a force to be reckoned with internationally but not as a people with whom the *Tale*'s denizens had everyday dealings. Knowledge of the material of which Muslim military caps are made (512) likewise does not establish extensive familiarity with Muslim civilians.

And because the *Tale* lacks the rogues' gallery of hostile nations featured in the *Book of Birds,* the preponderance of Westerners over Muslims in the text lends itself to a very simple explanation: although there were Turkish communities in Thessalonica and Constantinople of long standing—enough to have their own mosques (Kazhdan 1991, s.v. MOSQUE; TURKS)—they were relatively small compared with the Italian trading communities established there. The references of the *Tale* reflect the demography of the major cities of Byzantium and not the ethnic mix on its battlefields. We also note that the *Tale* displays more familiarity with Muslim officialdom than one might expect of the average Byzantine writer. Though it is unlikely the poem was written under Ottoman dominion, it is not impossible that the poet had spent some time in a region under Muslim rule, either as an emissary or a hostage. (A prisoner, we suspect, would have had opportunity to observe more of the common Muslim folk, and less Muslim luxury, than the *Tale* evinces.)

The most clear-cut evidence for a Byzantine origin of the poem is given by its prologue, which shows that the poet, or at least someone along the line of the poem's textual transmission, identified himself explicitly with Byzantium: "when all the nations draw with us false peace, / hoping audaciously, by force of might, / to lead us into absolute perdition, / yet are we saved by just, inviolate oaths."[90] These verses make no sense spoken outside Byzantium, and Xanthoudidis (1927–28:354) is clearly grasping at straws when he posits that the putative Cretan author of the poem identified himself with Byzantium, over 150 years after Crete had become a Venetian colony.[91] The Byzantine provenance of the poem thus remains by far the likeliest option.

The Author of the *Tale*

Ševčenko (1974) has surveyed the eponymous intellectuals active in the fourteenth century in Byzantium. He has found them to number over a hundred, sixty of whom lived in Constantinople, and estimates that there was a ratio of one writer to between 2,500 and 4,450 inhabitants of the city. This means both that "literature was fairly rigorously pursued in the fourteenth century" and that Byzantine intelligentsia was a quite small and close-knit coterie, in which everyone knew everyone else: "The criss-crossing of the lines of correspondence shows that everybody was in touch with everybody else at some time, either directly or through a potential intermediary" (70).

Over half of the authors in Ševčenko's survey were churchmen, and half of those were monks. (Monasticism was a mobile state: monks could eventually become patriarchs, and statesmen could equally retire to the monastery.) Of the remaining authors, most belonged to the court in some function, either as officials or friends of the various emperors; twelve were freelance teachers, mostly of grammar and rhetoric. Although it was a commonplace for Byzantine intellectuals to bemoan their poverty, Ševčenko concludes that

> the distance between the social depths from which they cried and the top could not have been too great. . . . Intellectuals of late Byzantium either belonged to the top levels of the society of their time, or were associated with men who did belong to these levels. If they were poor, it was either because times were bad even for people near the top, or because the impoverished Byzantine ruling class had little to spare for its following. (1974:75–76)

Was the author of the *Tale* part of this coterie, or did he stand outside it? At first sight, the poem seems to have arisen from a subliterary class: it is consciously humble, both in language and content, compared to the products of the Byzantine intelligentsia. But Hans-Georg Beck (1971:8–9) has advanced the thesis, now generally accepted, that in Byzantium vernacular literature is not true folk literature and popular literature did not arise spontaneously from the underclasses but rather moved "from above to below," written by the learned classes experimenting with the vernacular as a literary tool. The movement from below to above is associated only with the periphery and the later literature written under Western rule—the *Chronicle of Morea* being perhaps the best example.

Indeed, for all its low repute, authors writing in the vernacular do not seem to have been at all ignorant of learned culture. Vernacular writing displays many of the rhetorical devices favored by the learned Byzantines (particularly the romances, in their use of the *ekphrasis,* the rhetorical description, and other standard devices such as parallelism: Beaton 1996:147–50; Ševčenko 1974:77–78). Ševčenko (1974) finds evidence for a learned background in the text of the *Tale* itself:

> The Story of the Quadrupeds, ostensibly dating from the late fourteenth century, shows familiarity with scribal practices and with a grammarian's classroom. Its author knows that a boar's fang is used to shine up paper or parchment. He knows that bookmen bind books in sheep's skin, black, red, or of another color. He knows that inkpots are made of bull's horn. He knows that πτώξ is the high-class name for a hare (it's Homeric), because πτήσσω means "to be afraid"; in other words, he had handled a lexicon. At the same time, he is familiar with the various garments worn by the Patriarch, the Metropolitan, and monks. He is as likely to have been a scribe in an office of some prelate, per-

> haps even the Patriarch, in the early period of the Turcocracy as to have been an unlearned "bourgeois" writing in the year 1364. (78)

One might add, as we have already argued, that the poet had likely read the humbler examples of middle Byzantine prose—Aesop, the *Romance of Alexander,* and the *Physiologus;*[92] that his direct quotation of texts extends only to the Psalms, the first text any Byzantine read at school (Koukoules 1947–55:1.1.55–56); and that a lexicon may also have supplied him with an etymology of the modern Greek word for "dog" (see Commentary, verse 201).

The most plausible conclusion is that the author of the *Tale* belongs to the lower echelons of the Byzantine literati (men like Makrembolites, according to Ševčenko [1960:194–95]), who knew works like Aesop, *Physiologus,* sundry saints' *Lives,* and standard lexicons and grammars but were at a remove from classical literature. He would thus be comparable to the contemporary translator of the *Roman de Troie* into the vernacular Greek *War of Troy,* who knew Constantine Manasses' paraphrase of the *Iliad,* and probably Tzetzes' paraphrase, but had no demonstrable firsthand knowledge of the *Iliad* itself (Papathomopoulos and Jeffreys 1996:lxii–lxv). Even the level of occasional classical allusion that Alexiou (1986, 1999) hints might be present in the *Ptochoprodromos* poems—though she does not definitively establish it—is untenable when it comes to the *Tale.*

One further instance of the author's marginal acculturation into classical norms is the reference to "padres" in 386. The diminutive φραγκοπαπαδούρια, referring to Catholic priests, is clearly dismissive, yet Vasiliou (1996:66) has argued that this cannot constitute an insult because it occurs midway through a passage of (self-)praise. The consistency that would be required here—that one may not side-swipingly denigrate in the middle of a positive passage—is a convention of classical rhetoric, to which Byzantine learned writers adhered.[93] Because we are convinced that φραγκοπαπαδούρια is in fact negative (see "Faith and Country"), this indicates to us instead that the author of the *Tale* did not pay much attention to either classical literary conventions or Byzantine rhetorical conventions. The devices and wordplay that Beaton (1996:149–50) finds in the vernacular romances are conspicuous by their absence in the *Tale,* and although the *Tale*'s descriptions share with the *ekphrasis* a predilection for craft over nature, its rapid-fire cataloging owes little to the leisurely products of the Byzantine rhetorical curriculum.[94]

Krumbacher (1897:2.878–79) had associated the etymology of πτώξ in the *Tale* with its professed didacticism: "Like in the *Physiologus,* the Byzantine schoolmaster gives himself away in the *Tale* with a learned *etymology,* verse 335 concerning the Hare." Likewise, Dölger (1964:205–6) sees the use of the proverbial expression about Jews (424) as a "typical trait of late Greek rhetoric, and may have been crammed in school"—which is why the boar responds to the sheep by calling her "a new sophist, greater than the fox" (429), just as the dog responds to the fox's etymologizing by claiming her to "play the sophist"

(204). The hypothesis is plausible, though not the only explanation of the text: proverbs were used in rhetoric precisely because they were used by commoners, and it seems odd to associate a mere proverb with learning. There is little else in the sheep's six-line speech on which to pin the accusation of learning, so the boar probably does think of the proverb (explicitly announced as such) as a display of erudition. But compared with what appears in the romances, it is not a particularly impressive display.

Makris (1993:411 n.3) has recently claimed that the *Tale* was written in a monastic environment. Although the claim itself is plausible (as seen, half the authors of Constantinople at the time were churchmen, and half of those were monks), the verses that Makris cites as evidence do not bear scrutiny. Thus, Makris assumes the rat's σταςίδιον (180) is a choir stall or pew, which is the meaning of the word surviving in modern Greek. But we know that the word retained its original meaning of "spot" (it is a diminutive of *stasis,* equivalent to "station") into the seventeenth century and was used to refer to the fishing spots so lucrative for monasteries. Monks may have used the word σταςίδιον, but that does not make a monk of the rat (see Commentary, verse 180).

Although certain phrases may have had a religious origin, in a theocracy like Byzantium it is to be expected that such expressions would end up in the common parlance of any halfway-educated Byzantine. Of the verses Makris adduces:

> Verse 197 uses an expression that could be taken as monkish: ἐν ταπεινῷ τῷ σχήματι, which we have rendered as "low-profile" but which literally means "in humble form."[95] There is nothing to say, though, that the expression was restricted to descriptions of monks.[96]
>
> Verse 330 ("you only walk at night, which renders you / the equal, in your ways, of ghouls and demons!", literally, δαιμόνων τάξιν ἔχεις, "you have the behavior of demons") shows only that the deer (and the author) are familiar with Christianity and popular superstition.
>
> The word γέροντας in verse 690 may refer to monks as well as "elders"; it hardly proves the author to be one of those monks, telling old tales in the persona of a horse.
>
> Verses 392–401 show that the author knows how icons are painted; 503–8, that he knows how clerics dress; and 597–600, that he knows what kind of cheese goes into an abbot's casserole. The author may thus have been affiliated with a monastery but may just as easily have been working at the patriarchate in Constantinople or at a major archdiocese, and he is certainly no less aware of the cobblers', bookbinders', scribes', and cheese makers' art.
>
> Finally, even if in verses 914–19 the author refers to the uses of ivory in making patriarchs' seats and senior clerics' staffs, he says in the same breath (920–29a) that they are used to make chesspieces, knife handles, and mirrors for fair maidens.

All one can draw from the verses that Makris has adduced, then, is a vague suspicion that the author is somehow affiliated with the church, but nothing has been conclusively established.

The oddest contention that Makris makes is that the obscenity of the work displays a "lack of worldliness" on the part of the poet and therefore demonstrates a monastic origin for the work. It is true enough that Greek clerics (when no one was looking) enjoyed scatology: *The Mass of the Beardless Man* was a best-seller widely circulated among clerics (Eideneier 1977:14–16) and could have been composed only by someone who knew the text of the Greek Orthodox mass deeply. But to conclude from this that monks were the only Byzantines capable of peddling smut or alluding freely to prurient matters simply does not follow—not that there is all that much smut in the *Tale* anyway. The quadrupeds' insults to each other are delivered with scatological gusto, but they say nothing that was not part of common lore. The hare is known to be a "hornball" (327).[97] The ox's penis was used to make whips to flog transgressors and this usage persisted up to the twentieth century (see Commentary, verse 635). And mention of the ox's penis inevitably brings on mention of the donkey's genitalia, whose prominence (86) was proverbial. (The English expression "hung like a horse" has prevailed only by accident of alliteration.)

To contend, then, that verse 86 displays lack of worldliness is to project a later age's sensibilities onto the poem. It is likelier that the *Tale*'s prurience (such as it was) was associated with its relatively narrow audience, close-knit enough to take the obscenities in the spirit intended. Yet the mass audience *The Mass of the Beardless Man* found as a chapbook belies even that much. And that the author was no aberration in his time when it came to animal pornography is shown by the illustration of the donkey in the *Tale*'s Constantinopolitan manuscript (C)—executed by someone obviously other than the author and featuring a rather prominent "fifth leg."[98] (See "Manuscript C Illustrations.")

All the same, the absence of any mention of παπᾶδες (parish priests, the clergy with whom laypeople had the most contact),[99] as well as the omission of episodes of family life, is consistent with the cloister. There is no reference at all to issues and practices pertinent to family life. Animal genitalia—especially male genitalia—are freely mentioned, but courtship and marriage are topics avoided by the author. Neither is there any notion of eroticism or romance (as distinct from vulgarity) for all the poem's liberality. (The one exception [767] proves the rule: the author claims horsemen love their horses as much as their own wives.)

The author could thus easily have been a monk or a church official.[100] There is something detached about the descriptions in the *Tale,* particularly in view of all its plush images of royal and noble life, certainly not restricted to a rapidly declining Byzantium but incorporating other lands ruled by kings and sultans. This sounds like someone recalling past journeys and glories rather than the present impoverished and doomed polity. It is an indulgence that a prominent Byzantine retired to the monastery—as happened frequently in those times, including no less a figure than the monk Joasaph, formerly known as Emperor John VI Cantacuzene—would allow himself fondly.

The Purpose of the *Tale*

The *Tale* creates at first the surreal impression that it was intended primarily for posterity rather than its contemporaries. The bulk of its 1,082 verses (122–978) is devoted to how animals participated in medieval daily life. The description of their uses is quite informative for twenty-first-century readers but hardly detailed enough to educate those animals' fourteenth-century owners or hunters: Byzantines would be hard put to use the *Tale* as a textbook. Yet precisely because the real-life references of the *Tale* were familiar to its contemporary audience, they would have been less distracted than the modern reader by its profusion of details—and better equipped, as a result, to follow the *Tale*'s humor, drama, and whatever underlying message it might bear. It is not inconceivable that those endless catalogs served a narrative purpose themselves, allowing for many entertaining moments based on how animals viewed each other's uses and fate and building up to the drama of the battle at the end of a lengthy reading or recitation.

That said, animal life was certainly well known to medieval adults but not necessarily to their offspring. Therefore, the *Tale* could have been a tool facilitating the education of Byzantine children—just as its (admittedly suspect) prologue states. Gidel (1866:322), for example, adopts this viewpoint: "We would not be inaccurate in identifying the root idea of this work as the intention the poet had of teaching children to discern the characteristics of different animals and to recognize the services humans derive from each as well as the intention of demonstrating to them the contradictory development and discussion of a single subject considered under different points of view."

The obvious counterobservation (made first by Krumbacher [1897:2.878] and repeated in Koukoules 1947–55:1.1.117, among others) is that the *Tale*'s considerable profanity would outweigh its educational content. Again, we should be careful not to define profanity and inappropriateness by modern standards. Even in a society much more theocratic than ours, there was room for license in expression: one may compare the sexual frankness of Elizabethan England with the censorious repression of their Victorian descendants. Indeed, an erotic novel like Heliodorus's *Aethiopica* (*iii* A.D.) could even form part of the late Byzantine school curriculum:

> John Eugenikos, brother of Mark, the metropolitan of Ephesus who played so important a part at the Council of Florence in opposition to the proposed union of the churches, is the author of a very short introduction to the novel of Heliodorus. It includes a hint that the novel may have been adopted for reading in school, because there is an assertion that it contains nothing dangerous for young readers. Eugenikos defends Heliodorus for the contents as much as the style, and ob-

serves that the alleged potential danger is no more real than that arising from the Song of Solomon. (Wilson 1996:272)

All the same, it is highly unlikely that a text like the *Tale* would have entered any curriculum, especially because the point of schooling in Byzantium (and for a long time after Byzantium) was to ground students in good Atticist Greek—not to make a study of vernacular idioms such as "fart like walnuts rattling" (171) or "tongue sharp as a host of scissors" (585). Arts and crafts were certainly nothing for which literacy was required, nor likely to be a special object of study in an educational system geared toward expressing the everyday and the commonplace as floridly and vaguely as possible. As for Gidel's surmise that the *Tale* was a demonstration of the art of rhetoric, one need only point out that the horse is no Libanius, and there were plenty more reputable models of rhetoric available to a Byzantine schoolmaster (see also discussion in "The Author of the *Tale*").

If we dispense with education, we are left with entertainment, and we should consider the possibility of the *Tale* being enjoyed during the lighter moments of social gatherings. Recitations of literary works were routine in the Middle Ages, both in the West and the East. (The evidence for recitations of the vernacular Greek romances and chronicles is discussed in Jeffreys and Jeffreys 1986:5–7, Beaton 1989:184–89, and Cupane 1994–95.) Reading was thus regarded as a social event as much as an individual pastime. Beaton (1989) in particular stresses that the use of vernacular poetry as court light entertainment in the twelfth century could easily have continued in the fourteenth century with the vernacular romances. So there was a precedent for audiences gathering to hear the *Tale*'s entertaining stories.

Against this, one must weigh the fact that the *Tale* speaks in terms of reading (ἀναγινώσκωνται) rather than hearing (verse 2) and is one of the first vernacular Greek poems, along with the *Chronicle of Morea,* to single out a "friend" as its unique addressee (φίλε μου: 10a). Indeed, the solitary reader was a late innovation, and the literate in the Middle Ages thought of reading in oral rather than visual terms (Clanchy 1979:214–20). Though the verses in question belong to the suspect prologue of the *Tale* (see appendix 3), they indicate, as Beaton (1990:178) argues, a turn from public performance toward silent reading—a turn certainly in place by 1461 and the first extant manuscript of the *Tale.* But it is impossible to tell at this remove whether the *Tale* was originally intended for declamation or individual reading.

At any rate, despite the folksy content and (at times) diction of the *Tale,* it would be risky to assume that it was meant for a broad audience.[101] Beck's hypothesis (1971) that vernacular Byzantine literature was produced by intellectuals for their own entertainment has by now gained universal acceptance, and it accounts very well for the Byzantine romances authored in Greek, with their rhetoric and classical allusions. The *Tale* and the *Book of Birds* need not count as exceptions to this trend, especially given how differently they read to Sachlikis's poetry (one of the first instances of vernacular Greek that Beck would consider as written "from below" rather than "from above"). The author of the *Tale* had some learning, and it is reasonable to assume that its intended audience was not dissimilar in education to the author. Beaton (1990:179) sees in the prologue of the *Tale* the beginning of a trend for writers explicitly addressing a public of a rather different sort than the nobility for which the romances were intended. But given the question over the authenticity of the *Tale*'s prologue and its confusingly articulated "pedagogical" intent, definitive instances of an educational or popularizing program should be sought elsewhere. The first such instance that Beaton identifies is the epilogue of the *Belisariad*, which originates in the archetype of the extant manuscripts and thus dates from the 1390s (Bakker and van Gemert 1988:41):

> καὶ ἐμετάφερον αὐτὴν λόγου παιδείας χάριν,
> ὅπως γνωρίζουν οἱ πολλοὶ τὸν φθόνον τῶν Ρωμαίων,
> τὸ πῶς ἐχάσαν παντελῶς τὰ κάστρη καὶ τὰς χώρας
>
> [I have transposed it for the sake of learning
> so that the many know the Romans' envy,
> how they have lost their forts and towns completely] (χ 562–64)

The case for a subversive rather than entertaining purpose is reinforced if the *Tale* contains a concealed political message (see appendix 2). The *Tale* could have been enjoyed during underground readings of dissident intellectuals during one of the several crises of the fourteenth century, fostering some kind of ideological camaraderie (if revolutionary solidarity was, as discussed in "Dissent," unlikely). It may seem far-fetched to postulate Byzantine samizdats, but conditions were harsh enough for the intellectual Gregory Acindynus to die in hiding "in the underground," as Ševčenko (1974:87) puts it, in 1348; the letters he sent to his followers in Constantinople (one of which Ševčenko cites) could have been read only in clandestine meetings. The *Tale* admittedly reads as pure entertainment and may well have been intended as such, yet the temper of the times would have encouraged readers to search it for hidden meanings, whether they were intended or not.

Characteristics of the *Tale*

> The elements of satire, which incidentally give insights into contemporary culinary practice, arise generally out of the implied contrast between animal and human behavior.
>
> —Elizabeth Jeffreys, in A. Kazhdan, ed., *The Oxford Dictionary of Byzantium*

Class Struggle in a Byzantine Farmyard

Although the *Tale* concentrates on a struggle between carnivores and herbivores, culminating in the victory of the latter (see "Subversion and Politics"), there are open questions as to who belongs where: one of the carnivores' ambassadors, the monkey (36–37), could barely be counted a meat eater by virtue of eating fleas and lice (973; see also Tsiouni 1972:40); and another, the rat, is more of an omnivore. We know that King Lion's coregent, the elephant, is definitely not a carnivore—though he is classified as such by association, and the author's command of zoology may have been deficient on this point (see "Fact and Fiction in the *Tale*'s Zoology"). And the boar that shamelessly consumes its own kind's flesh (440–45) would have a great deal of difficulty passing as a herbivore (53), whereas the bear is indirectly accused by the wolf of being a herbivore (847).

These questions might be resolved if one looks at the two camps as consisting not of herbivores and carnivores but of domestic and wild animals. This classification has internal evidence to recommend it: verse 15 talks of clean and useful (καθαρὰ καὶ εὔχρηστα) animals gathered at one place, whereas verse 16 informs us of bloodthirsty and loathsome (αἱμόβορα καὶ βδελυκτά) animals gathered at another. Under this classification, it is easy to accept the boar/pig as a useful animal (363–404), while the monkey and even the elephant may be regarded as wild: people use the elephant as a tank (906–13) and turn his tusks into ivory (914–29), but this happens in remote places such as India or Africa, and even there he is not quite a farm animal.[102]

But this alternative classification runs into problems when it comes to the most typical pets, the cat and the dog: they are carnivores but domestic as well. The distinction may lie in them not being "useful": people keep cats and dogs at home, but they do not eat their meat, they do not drink their milk, and they do not use their body parts to make any products. Moreover, the rat (159–78) and the fox (220–34) have drawn some rather unflattering portraits of our pets: they view them as pests, if anything. Conversely, the deer is not domestic but is as useful as human hunting skills and folk magic allow (340–50). Still, though the bear's fat (851–54) and the cheetah's skin (878–82) make those animals just as useful, that is not the camp to which they are assigned. Perhaps the useful animals are precisely those that contribute to people's diet. But then what do we make of the hard-working animals absent from the Greek dining table, such as the horse, the donkey, and the camel (the members of the useful animals' embassy)? Clearly none of this can be pushed too far; the author has made a rough-and-ready division of the animals, mainly based on whether they are meat eaters or not. The exceptions to the scheme we have discussed are probably just a matter of convenience.

More important, the *Tale* describes not just a struggle between two groups of animals but the closest possible analogue to a class struggle of which a fourteenth-century author could have conceived. The carnivores routinely prey on the herbivores and are explicitly depicted as a ruling class; both camps are deeply aware of that (71–72, 989–91). Given the confusion in the animals' groupings, might the *Tale* also contain allusions to class betrayal, whatever class may have meant in the poem's context? Might the elephant, the natural leader of the herbivores, be a traitor to his class, with our author perfectly aware that elephants are not meat eaters? Notice that the elephant plays absolutely no role in the final battle, after which his whereabouts remain unknown. And—if perhaps less likely—could the boar be a traitor to the carnivores? That would be particularly interesting in view of the boar's decisive role in the herbivores' victory.

And what to make of the fox? Her case deserves particular attention, as she belongs to a class of her own: she had come to be associated in vernacular literature not only with cunning but also with the worst qualities of the learned classes. The two variants of the *Donkey Tale* explicitly contrast the learned fox with the unlettered donkey who is the hero of the story, and the association is no less explicit in the *Tale:* she is called "most scholarly and intellectual" (272) and is said to engage in "high philosophizing" (213) (see Dölger 1964:204–6, who counts these as instances of negative attitudes toward the Byzantine intelligentsia). The fox may simply be acting out her traditional duplicity when—according to the dog—she swaps sides in the battle (1060–63). But just as the Byzantine intelligentsia was often in a kind of limbo between their mendicancy and their rich patrons, the fox manifests conflicting loyalties.

Whatever the definition of the two camps and whether the class struggle is between predators and prey or loafers and workers or inedible and edible animals or whatever, the concept of class betrayal is undeniably there. The poem is enriched by it, whether or not such developments allude to contemporary political events. The dog is certainly domestic and is accordingly permitted to praise himself (249–59), but he has initially been placed in the carnivores' camp (25–26) and is still fighting beside them toward the middle of the battle (1036). Yet he appears to have switched sides before its conclusion, encouraging the herbivores' attack while simultaneously accusing the fox of high treason (1058–65). Moreover, the rat, initially appointed as the carnivores' representative (34), has also switched sides, beating the kettledrums carried by the camel to boost the herbivores' morale (1044, 1069). The fox's reported betrayal may come as no surprise, but its effect is reinforced by the parallels with the rat and the dog. Our author definitely had treason and betrayal in mind, and it is interesting that in all three cases the defections (real or imagined) are to the lowly herbivores from the powerful carnivores. (The elephant may be a counterexample but is too exotic to be of much use.) The quadrupeds are in any case not bound to an established camp but are mobile and alert to the changes of fortune in their conflict. They are very much "political animals."[103]

Irony and Contradiction

One of the most characteristic features of the *Tale* is the recurring use of irony in an understated yet powerful fashion. Almost from the beginning of the *Tale* (33–37), for instance, the reader senses that something is amiss: the carnivores' embassy to the herbivores consists of three small animals, two of which have been at bad terms with each other since time immemorial (cat and rat),[104] the third well known as a laughingstock among animals (monkey). Two out of the three "do not even belong to the party," as Tsiouni (1972:41) puts it, their carnivore status being questionable. This is an inauspicious embassy. And toward the end of the *Tale* (1058–65), the dog accuses the fox of duplicity—displaying no little duplicity himself in informing his putative enemies, though he fought on the side of the carnivores twenty-two verses before.[105]

This "do as I do, not as I say" attitude is a persistent theme through the *Tale*: the ewe criticizes the nanny for having large breasts (and worse) (468); the deer accuses the hare of cowardice (331–35); the boar, no long-tail himself, makes fun of the deer's short tail (353–56); the horse commiserates the donkey for being eaten by the wolf (803–6)—only to hear the terrible truth from the wolf himself right afterward (818–19); and so on. Most interestingly, the monkey blames the elephant for using his trunk to pick up food in one spot and eat it elsewhere (938–41): a questionable habit characteristic not only of large-clawed crabs, as the monkey points out, but also of monkeys themselves![106]

These insincere protestations are an obvious device, yet the use of irony pervades the poem at a deeper level also. For example, the long-eared yet voiceless hare is appointed crier of the herbivores (44): is this an ill omen suggesting that the herbivores will ultimately not heed King Lion's call, or is the crier's speed and swiftness (45) meant to compensate for his lack of voice? And right after King Lion's stern warning against any disorder (119–21), the cat immediately begins to insult the rat without any provocation (127). Later on we see that despite his wallowing in mires (388), the boar's hair contributes to Christian piety in several ways (392–401)—the poet now glad to turn a blind eye to the boar's ill repute. Conversely, large animals such as the ox (628–30) and the cheetah (878–82) meet a more ignominious end, baiting tiny fish and repelling fleas, respectively. And near the end, the badly beaten cheetah's call to his bloodthirsty brothers for help (1033–34) is nothing if not ludicrous.

A recurring device in the poem is to have an animal ridiculed right after a self-exalting monologue. We have already mentioned the monkey's thorough ridicule of the elephant (936–68). The boar retorts to the hare and deer that the meats they have so fulsomely praised in fact taste so poorly that some of his own meat needs to be added whenever they are cooked to make them bearable (381–83). As soon as the ewe provides an extensive list of her services to humanity, the nanny rebukes her by pointing out that only large animals are entitled to bragging (541–44)—a self-defeating move, as it turns out (578). And right after the donkey waxes lyrical on his sexual organ and challenges the horse to come up with a response (649–57), the latter delivers a devastating torrent of insults to him (665ff.)

A more subtle device is the swift change of tone within a single animal's discourse. It takes only twelve verses for the hare to switch from a cordial, joyful greeting (270) through a cloyingly hesitant reservation (275) to a full-blast rebuke of the fox as a hare strangler (282)—culminating with a call for retribution through birds of prey (295). Likewise, the wolf starts off defending the offended honor of the camel and donkey (813) and then immediately switches to a savage attack against the horse, exulting in consuming him along with the donkey (817–19). It is worth noting that the two most savage retorts in the *Tale* are also the most effective; the interventions of the hare and the wolf switch the camps involved in the disputes from carnivore to herbivore and back. So these volatile episodes play a structural role in the poem (see "Structure").

Likewise, the author uses protestations of humility as a rhetorical device: the boar begins a fairly lengthy bragging session by begging to be allowed to "state a few, succinct, brief facts" (357–58), and the buffalo ends his self-praise declaring that he "is not one to talk" and adding solemnly that "verbosity betokens foolishness" (610–10a). Whether we can take the animals at their word is, of course, another question; the buffalo's "many other graces" (609) that he chooses to omit seems a rather calculated ploy. But the very question gives the poem a depth that one might not expect on a cursory reading. The notion that the boar sets off to be succinct yet ends up overcome by his own rhetoric is one that may provoke the reader's empathy.

One has to look very hard to find other examples of Byzantine works where positive and negative valuation alternate so consistently and where sarcasm is employed so deliberately to bring down the puffed-up protagonists. Though similar to the *Tale,* the *Book of Birds,* as discussed in appendix 1, features rhetorical pairs of accusation and defense rather than vaunting and deflation, so it does not match the *Tale* in this regard. This delight in dressing down conveys a spirit of dissent out of tune with the prevalent view of Byzantium as stuffy and regimented. It also makes the *Tale* sound surprisingly modern.

Comedy

Two kinds of humor are at work in the *Tale*. One has been covered by the foregoing section: the *Tale* can work quite subtly in bringing down the mighty and deflating their aspirations. The other is more readily apparent to the *Tale*'s readers. The animals' exchanges have a coarse and decidedly unsubtle tone: no curse is too distasteful, no depiction too unflattering to make the quarrelsome animals' point. To a significant extent, this is accomplished by the stentorian compound epithets the animals come up with, of which there is a full listing in appendix 5. Though they do not owe anything to Homer (as Šandrovskaja [1956b] suggested) and were associated in Byzantium with romances rather than comedy (see "Imagery" and "Compound Epithets"), their pomp is just right for the poem. And the epithets never occur alone; they are always piled up, with cumulative effect, and more often than not with conscious exploitation of syntactic parallelism and meter (see "Meter" for examples).

The coarseness of the animals' exchanges is tied up with a startling vigor in their diction, particularly when the animals are on the attack rather than lauding themselves (and getting sidetracked into catalogs). The vignettes the animals draw of their opponents in disgrace are vivid and remorseless. They are consistently in the present tense and second person so that they come across as accusation as much as description: "this is what you do!" (This makes the horse's tale-within-the-*Tale* [691–739] stand out all the more.) The dog's rhapsody on the fox's torments in the wilderness (240–48) and the monkey's learned analysis of the elephant's lack of sleep (942–54) are perhaps the most spectacular such instances.

To add to their impact, the vignettes are described directly and straightforwardly, usually without the digressions characteristic of the self-praises but with loving attention to unflattering detail. There is little delicacy about this side of the humor of the *Tale*; when it does not involve bodily violence or suffering, it is as replete with toilet humor as any British comedy. (Witness, for example, the combination of violence and farting in 171, of thirst and farting in 246, or of coprophagy and cannibalism in 438–43.)

Yet even in these straightforward exchanges, the author still sets up surprising juxtapositions that elevate the level of his humor. For example, the sheep likens the boar's "most pernicious" cannibalism to the consumption of "the finest flour" (440–45), whereas the buffalo describes the ox's verbosity with a level of articulatory detail of which a phoneticist would be proud (583–86).

Not all the humor of this more obvious kind is combative. Though the narrator for the most part plays the straight man to the animals' antics, sometimes he seems to be having fun at their expense. The donkey's flatulent arrival on scene (646–47) is hardly decorous, but it is the narrator, not the horse, making the joke here. And the rat beating the drums carried by the camel (1044), or the malformed boar sidling up to the graceful deer (320), again make the beasts look ludicrous and would not be out of place in a modern-day cartoon.

There is also something droll for the modern reader in the cat's reference to his "humble teeth" (τὰ ταπεινά μου δόντια [146]) or the hare's praising of his foot, "a limb of slight renown" (τὸ εὐτελές μου μέλος [310]). One may see in these passages a refreshing dose of self-deprecation—or the narrator's sentiments intruding into the beasts' speeches. We have already seen protestations of humility used as a rhetorical device; it is possible that these passages are part of the author's occasional strategy of understatement, particularly when the animals make threats of physical violence: the cat will make a "teensy jump" (143) to gnash the rat with his "humble teeth" (146), the dog will jolt the cat "oh-so-gently" (187), and the lion will stretch out his palm "just a smidgeon" to strike the leopard "a tiny bit" (893–94). This strategy displays a rhetorical flair that makes the threats, sly rather than impetuous reactions, all the more effective.

But contemporary readers should be wary of second-guessing a Byzantine audience's sensitivities. What may sound ironic or humorous to us may very well have been straightforward and ordinary to them. A case in point is the horse's claim that his rider loves him as much as his wife (767). This sounds like the horse having an inflated opinion of himself, but that is a cultural judgment, and in a society valuing martial over romantic values the claim might not be far from the truth.

The interplay in linguistic levels within the *Tale* makes it even more difficult to tell when the author is being serious and when he is being facetiously macaronic, exploiting the poem's roller-coaster alternation between Atticist and vernacular Greek. For example, the juxtaposition of the colloquial diminutive ποδάριν, "foot," and the learned εὐτελές μου μέλος, "limb of slight renown," in verse 310 looks to a contemporary Greek reader as a joke, comparable to the linguistic satires of the humorists Souris and Bostantzoglou on modern Greek diglossia and pomposity. This is an easy trap for a modern Greek speaker to fall into, but it is a trap nonetheless, and we cannot surmise that the author set out to make fun of either learned or colloquial Greek—let alone the hare himself.

Subversion and Politics

Perhaps the most striking feature of the *Tale* is the way it questions authority, from beginning (when the herbivores are reluctant to accept King Lion's invitation) to end (when the cheetah admits that there is no way for King Lion and his nobles to survive without preying on the herbivores). And there are numerous instances where privileged animals are ridiculed by lesser ones. Perennial thieves such as the rat and the fox expose the indiscretions of our trusted guards, the cat and the dog (159–78; 220–36). The hard-working ox is revealed to be no more industrious or productive than his semidomesticated cousin, the buffalo (583–608). A beast of burden such as the lowly camel points out how brutally the proud horse, "the seat and throne of men" (81), is exploited in old age (784–94). The name and rank of the powerful is taken in vain by the goat (543) and even the leopard (888), himself a member of the ruling class. Much more audaciously, the elephant, coregent of the animal kingdom, is insulted by the cowardly monkey (936–68). There are some curious reversals at work here; this does not escape the king's notice (981–83), and he is not amused.

Neither do the reversals end there. The most surprising feature of the plot of the *Tale*—which seems to have escaped many scholars who have worked on it—is that the final victory in the ensuing battle is not the carnivores', as would seem inevitable, but the herbivores'. Though this was noticed by Sathas in his political study in 1894 (Sathas 1972 [1872–94]:7.xxxvii; see appendix 2), it was first remarked on in a literary study of the *Tale* only as late as Tsiouni 1972:54.[107] The poem nowhere states this outcome explicitly, but the turn of events is clear enough. Of the ten carnivores mentioned in the poem, one is at the least much the worse for wear (cheetah), three have been killed (lion, bear, leopard), one deserts (rat), another is an informant to the enemy (dog), and four (the monkey, who is a carnivore by political association; the cat; the wolf; and the fox) are shown fleeing in 1072–74. The herbivores, by contrast, are depicted confident and rallying, with only one of them killed (deer). A herbivore victory is the last thing one would expect in such a battle, and the author has invested some meaning in it.

So in the *Tale* we see the mighty constantly brought down, ridiculed, and in the end defeated. This is characteristic of fable in general, but the consistency with which it is pursued, and the explicit framing allusions to human royal courts and diplomacy, display a deliberately programmatic use of the device. Note that there is never any direct criticism of human nobles in the *Tale*: most animals are eager to stress how useful they are to the upper classes, whose way of life is implicitly held up to admiration. The picture of nobles painted by the dog and the hare is nothing if not glowing; and no mention of a noble is ever far from the adjective μεγάλος, "great." The talk of "large-cloaked noble ladies, / who have long tails to drag behind their dresses" (304–5) may at first glance seem to be poking fun. In the context of the poem as a whole, however, it is unlikely to constitute anything more than a whimsical observation.

At the same time, the author keeps the common folk in mind: the dog feels sorry for the "infinite injustice" caused to poor people by the fox's barn incursions (192–93), and various animals discuss extensively how artisans and craftsmen use their body parts to make their products. Its unhappy ending notwithstanding, the donkey story, the only one explicitly embedded in the *Tale* (691–739), can be viewed as a deliberate though not necessarily supportive reference to the plight of laborers. And the rat defends his right to steal on the grounds of not being associated with the ruling (human) class ("never have I been cajoled by Man," 155–58).

Moreover, even if no criticism of human nobles is made, it is clear that the *Tale* takes a dim view of the animals' ruling class. Bloodthirsty great cats are styled as the imperial court of the animals, explicitly using the terms used to describe the Byzantine court. Whether by premeditation or necessity, they violate their solemn oaths and pay for it with their lives. Courtiers are characterized as "maligners" (ἀποφουμιστάδες, 22), and the first presentation of the other carnivores (but for the dog, who ultimately defects) is no more complimentary. The cheetah, in the heat of battle, overtly proclaims the amorality of the strong toward the weak (1025–26). Just as explicitly, the conclusion of the poem quotes Psalms to refute the cheetah and uphold justice for the weak (1078–79). And even within the narrative of the *Tale,* the carnivores are not allowed to speak for as long as the herbivores (seven carnivores have 206 verses against 575 verses for thirteen herbivores). In fact, although the carnivores struggle to find instances of their usefulness to humans, known instances of such—the cheetah's employment in hunting (Nicholas 1999:259–68; see "Pantechnes") or the use of the fox in the treatment of arthritis[108] (Koukoules 1947–55:5.414)—are passed over in the poem.[109]

These expressions of dissent, compounded with the deflation to which the mighty have been subjected, constitute a deliberate strategy of the author and come as a surprise to the present-day reader. Such disrespect, not only for the self-important (as discussed previously) but also for the "important," is a modern, even democratic trait—not at all typical of a worldview where God was in His heaven and all was right with the world. The anonymous author, reluctant to criticize the powerful of his day directly, could well have resorted instead to an extended animal-centered parable.

Faith and Country

Once the poem proper begins, the author makes no effort to present himself as either pious or patriotic, despite the pronouncements of the prologue.[110] One should bear in mind that at the time the concept of the nation-state did not exist and the author lived in a multi-ethnic empire. Admittedly, this empire was rapidly shrinking so that by his time it had become Greek-speaking for the most part, but its subjects still called themselves "Romans" rather than "Greeks" or "Hellenes." And the most important defining characteristic of Byzantium's subjects was never their ethnicity but their Christian Orthodox faith.

Still, not everyone in the Eastern Roman Empire was an Orthodox Christian: there were "Franks" (Westerners), Jews, and other religious groups living there, and the author has not neglected to offer brief comments on them. The Jews are mentioned only once, and by way of proverb at that, but in the most negative tone: "The Jew stinks, and his satchel's just as smelly" (424; see the Commentary).[111] Likewise, the Gypsies, relative newcomers to the empire, are quickly dismissed as either "foolish" bear trainers (846) or (if we accept the reading in manuscript L) a matter-of-fact addition to the catalog of invective directed against the fox: "lying, thieving, loathsome, / innards-devouring, swindling goddamn [gypsy/sorceress]" (285–86).[112]

Far more complex is the issue of the Franks—in Constantinople, Venetians and Genoese; in Greece, also Florentines, Catalans, and French. These were known to the Byzantines not only as foreigners residing among them but also as de facto representatives of powerful, reviled states, occupying large chunks of former Byzantine territory. No animals have been allowed to address direct insults toward such influential people, who are in fact mentioned as equal to the Romans in the sheep's words (495). Yet the boar refers to their priests with the belittling diminutive φραγκοπαπαδούρια ("Frankish priestlings," *padres* in our translation), mocking them for sprinkling the congregation during *Asperges* with a brush made out of his mire-wallowed hair (384–88). Because Orthodox priests sprinkle the faithful using a sprig of basil instead of boar hair, one is inclined to see a backhanded insult here (so already Xanthoudidis 1927–28:359)—all the more because the diminutives used elsewhere by the author, such as βοδάκιν ("little ox," 591) and ἀλογάκιν ("little horse," 782), are definitely of a mocking nature.

Only a few verses later, the boar boasts about brushes again, but here the poet neutralizes any negative associations of the boar through his fulsome praise of the holy icons and frescoes painted with his hair and decorating mansions (392–401). The contemporary reader may see some irony in the juxtaposition;

the author might not have. Note that icons ("images") were at the time still a universal feature of Christianity ("Christian folk, wherever they may be," 398); unlike the Protestants, the Catholics never repudiated religious imagery.[113] So icons would not have singled out the Orthodox for validation: the quality of painting honors both, and the unclean origin of the paintbrushes besmirches both. The poem is thus not necessarily contrasting pious Orthodox with ludicrous Catholics in this instance. And the effect of boar hair here is underemphasized compared with that in the hands of the padres, for whom the author certainly does not show the same respect he does toward the Orthodox clerics throughout the poem.

Consistent with what is known about that period, one concludes that faith mattered much more than country to the author: the only sarcasm addressed toward the Franks—but for a passing noncommittal association of asinine anatomy with Western crockery (655)—refers to their Catholicism, not their imperialistic policies toward Byzantium.[114] Likewise, the Jews and Gypsies (easy targets throughout Europe) are held to ridicule (see Commentary, verse 285) because of their different beliefs or customs, not any threat they might pose to the empire, whereas avowed enemies of the empire sharing its creed, the Bulgarians and the Serbs, go unmentioned.

This impression is reinforced by the author's attitude toward Muslims, whose leaders, despite their religion, are never depicted negatively in the *Tale*: they were perhaps too alien to Orthodox Christianity for the author to be concerned with their religion, whereas their steady advances against Byzantium apparently did not concern our quadrupeds at all. Muslims are, if anything, still exotic and held in some awe; the sheep lauds the use of her wool in the sultan's rugs (493–94); and the cheetah, the use of his skin on the sultan's bedding (878–82). Likewise, Western kings (ῥηγᾶδες) are held in esteem. In fact, the author's equal treatment of Byzantine emperors (βασιλεῖς) and foreign rulers is one more testimony to his apparent lack of patriotic fervor. The anti-Semitism or anti-Catholicism of the *Tale,* by contrast, is contempt for the familiar and is probably not even all that conscious. The author mocks the Other within while ignoring the Other knocking at the door.

The poem's heavy orientation toward religion, underlined by indirect references to the *Physiologus* and the quotation of Psalms at the end of the battle and combined with an apparent indifference (save for the disputed prologue) toward contemporary historical events, gives the impression of an author withdrawn from society. The author is not so godly as to turn preacher, of course, and his use of the *Physiologus*'s allegories is decidedly secular. Still, the emperor by that time had been demoted from the near-divinity he held in the Byzantine theocracy: imperial institutions had loosened the thrall they held over their subjects near the end of the empire.[115] Tsiouni (1972:39) sees confirmation of this attitude in the slaughter of the central authority figure at the end of the *Tale*. To an author placing his faith in God rather than empire, this would no longer come as the end of the world.

Rise and Fall

Another feature that sets the *Tale* apart is its preoccupation with mundane topics of day-to-day existence, such as the joys and perils of daily life, the pitfalls of old age, and death. Hunting and hiding scenes, cooking and killing methods, farm and workshop life are all described vividly. In fact, some details of daily life given in the *Tale* are not easy to find in other sources, which makes it an important reference work, more often cited for the information it provides than for any literary merit. (See "The *Tale* as a Source.")

In the circle of humans, two animals and their masters are shown enjoying life and work as peers. The hunting dog is proud of his good life and choice food and the fancy musical collar his master puts around his neck. The horse, from the comfort of the stable he occupies all year long, knows that his rider loves him both in war and peace as much as his wife, and treats him accordingly. Both descriptions, which would not be out of place in a learned Byzantine rhetorical exercise, are suffused with an irrepressible vitality and joy: the animals have risen as far in standing as humans will allow.

And yet these pampered animals are shown to fall from grace and meet a terrible death: the dog is stoned on a dunghill, the horse is literally put out to pasture. This is part of the author's general strategy of pulling down the vanity of the self-important. The decline and fall of beasts is a recurring theme, even beyond the realm of humankind. The donkey is subject to harsh treatment, but his predator the fearsome wolf is himself depicted in hiding, terrorized by insects. And the wolf's genetic relative the fox, notorious as the executor of countless hens and hares, enjoys no better a lifestyle, anxiously seeking out water in the wilderness.

But death is not always painted in dark colors. Most animals speak proudly of their posthumous contributions: exquisite meat dishes, fine clothes and mattresses, strong ropes, and many other products in an era when humans not only lived closer to animals but depended heavily on them as well. In some cases, the description of such services turns quite poetic: the hare describes how he is "preserved in golden bowls with grains of pepper" (300), and the elephant knows that his "bones" will eventually frame mirrors "in which young lasses gaze upon their image" (929). In fact, the animals take pride in the use to which their parts are put; the elephant, having spoken of ivory mirrors, exults of his "merits and advantages" (933a);[116] the hare is consoled that even when eaten, "it is the kings and emperors who eat me" (297); whereas the sheep's catalog of "native merits" starts with the sheep eaten (474) and ends with the sheep skinned (513).

The animals' doom strikes a different chord from the Byzantine notions of human death, recurringly greeted as the "haven of salvation":[117] whether in decline or regeneration, the animals' death is viewed in entirely materialistic terms. This preoccupation with postmortem functionality is rather an inevitable consequence of the way the poem has been conceived. Whether the author additionally intended some kind of allusion to posterity or the cyclicity of life is a question we leave to the appropriately inclined reader.

Animals by a Human Yardstick

The utilitarian emphasis of the *Tale* makes it uniquely anthropocentric among bestiaries: the poet primarily treats the animals as animals, exploited by humans for their produce and by-products. When the manners of preparing boar meat are being enumerated, the boar is not standing in for a Byzantine personality or even engaging in fable-like debate as an anthropomorphized disputant. In this, the *Tale* far exceeds the *Book of Birds*: the wild birds in the latter do not value themselves against humans, as the wild animals still do in the *Tale.* And the *Book* spends much less time on such valuation than the *Tale*: 47 out of 668 verses of the *Book* (7 percent) value birds by human standards, detailing what people do with the animals or what the animals do for people, as opposed to 334 out of 1,095 verses in the *Tale* (30 percent).

The *Tale* also has no parallel in the *Physiologus* or, for that matter, in the Western bestiaries. These frequently deal with exotic animals and refer to their salient properties, typically with an ulterior moral motive. In confining himself for the most part to the barnyard, the poet has ruled out this avenue for himself. To reduce an animal to an exemplar or a moral vehicle becomes much easier when that animal is out of the sight of humans, and it does not hurt if the animal is known only through hearsay or is entirely fictional. Witness the use to which elephants and unicorns are put in normal bestiaries.

When by contrast the animal is part of everyday life, it is difficult to relate to it as an entity in and of itself—particularly in a culture like that of the Greek countryside, in which the notion of the household pet has been marginal. The unicorn is virtuous and the elephant is steadfast, yet the only thing a medieval poet could say about a rat is that it is a pest to humans (129–40). The only thing to say about a sheep is that it produces food, clothing, and covers—for humans (483–520). This purview pervades the poem; the valuation in which the animals engage is, whether directly or indirectly, consistently instrumentalist. It even leads to absurdities such as the ox having both a penis (635) and teats ("your own [milk]," 597): being a spokesperson for Byzantine animal husbandry, the ox cannot afford to have a gender (though the distinction is made for the billy goat, 453–56, and the ram, 479–82). This is a world in which animals conceive of themselves primarily in relation to humans. In this, the *Tale* is unlike its forebears. This is not the world of Aesop or the fabliaux, where the animals engage in truly dramatic episodes as individuals; the animals' individualism here is reserved for their episodes of invective.

Still less is this the moralistic world of the *Physiologus* or the Western bestiary. The elephant in the *Physiologus* falls and cannot get up, a failing exploited by hunters. This much is antique lore; the *Physiologus* then enlists a procession of other elephants coming to its aid, ending with a baby elephant so implausible that the analogy with Christ actually comes as a relief. The elephant in the *Physiologus* is a metaphor, reminiscent of T. S. Eliot's hippopotamus. No such sentimentality or allusion is to be found in the *Tale*: as the monkey reports with glee, when the *Tale*'s elephant is down, he stays down and is promptly harvested for ivory (951–57).

Although instrumentalism gives the author something to say about oxen and camels, this anthropocentrism even extends to those exotic animals in the *Tale* that, in other bestiaries, would be exemplars autonomous of humanity. King Lion's "seat-mate" actively colludes in this instrumentalism: the majesty of the elephant is not that of the largest of land beasts but that of the ancient equivalent of the tank (906–13). The elephant's majesty is thus appraised only where he finds use: in human warfare. And for all that, the poet still spends two to three times as long talking about what humans make with his tusk once he is dead as he does about the elephant when living.

This instrumentalism extends to animals from which one would least expect it. After the cheetah's boasting on his rapaciousness, the reader is shocked to hear the afterthought that his skin is also a flea repellent known to sultans (878–82): even after defining himself so strongly against other animals ("able to overpower any beast"), the cheetah is compelled to define himself against humans as well. This need is made explicit when the wolf and the bear each exclaim about the other that they are worthless precisely in that they are useless to humans (837, 848—a claim the bear, at least, manages to refute: 851–54). This shows that, though the instrumentalism of the poem is an inevitable side effect of talking about the barnyard, it is not an accidental result; it is integral to the conception of the poem.

The only animals to escape human valuation are the monkey, the leopard, and the lion.[118] The lion, of course, lies outside the discourse of the disputation and is there not as a feline (notwithstanding the threat of his claw in 893–95) but as a king. As for the exotic pair of the leopard and the monkey, they seem not to have engaged the author's instrumentalist imagination at all. They both function as more of a dramatic device, accelerating the lion's fateful intervention, than anything else.

Because the way the poet relates to barnyard animals is the way most people relate to them in real life, this unsentimental approach could arise easily; the Cypriot songs considered in "Survivals of the *Tale*" are also manifestations of this trait. It would be rash to count this instrumentalism as a literary coup of the poet: it is a businesslike rather than imaginative move. Neither would we contend that it makes for a better poem: the catalogs are historically quite useful but only intermittently make for entertaining reading, and the failure to fully anthropomorphize the disputants seems to reflect a lack of dramatic ambition more than anything else. The tension between anthropomorphism and instrumentalism exhibited in the poem is an immediate result of the conflation of genres so characteristic of it.[119]

"No purebred"

Having investigated several aspects of the *Tale,* we can now turn to an issue that strikes the modern reader immediately: the *Tale* is a mixed bag. It starts off with a bold statement of political intent and then embarks on an account of a convention of beasts. One expects the convention to provide some illustration of the *Tale*'s program, particularly as it has all the trappings of statecraft: the lion is accompanied by a coregent, councilors, emissaries, and no less than three parliaments; the two parties conduct diplomacy and conclude treaties; the meeting takes place under the penalty of decapitation for any disruption of the peace. But the lion says explicitly that the convention is intended to "trade a couple of friendly jests" (100), and all thoughts of politics are discarded once the convention is underway, to be brought up only on the three occasions when the lion is compelled to intervene. The *Tale* instead ends up constantly switching between satire, humor, and didacticism.

The most plausible explanation for the multiplicity of genres in the *Tale* is that the poet had nowhere near as strict an agenda about his work as modern readers might expect. The basis of the argument for different authorship of the prologue and conclusion (see appendix 3) is precisely that they belong to a different genre than the poem itself. But even if we exclude them and only look at the poem proper, we still have to reconcile the convention, with its political trappings, the vignettes of animals arguing, and the extensive catalogs of their uses, into a single poem. And we must conclude that the author set off to write about a convention of animals—whether politically motivated or not and whether in imitation of the *Book of Birds* or not (see appendices 1 and 2)—and on the way added in whatever seemed appropriate. The catalogs of uses for animals are not put in because they serve some didactic function. Many of those functions would have been undeniably common knowledge—we hardly need to be told that clothes are made out of wool. Rather, they are there because, as noted in "Animals by a Human Yardstick," they are what a *human* would find interesting for an animal to say.

The same goes for the fable of the donkeys, the sundry vignettes, and the scatological insults. If the author is to write up a convention of animals, he will have the animals sound off on how useful they are (because that will keep the text going) and have them give extensive catalogs (because that will allow the poet to display his wide practical knowledge of Byzantine industry) as well as tell stories and vignettes (which fit the convention theme more naturally). The author would not have been fussed about the poem alternating between two or three genres: this is what animals at a convention will talk about, as far as he is concerned, and the author was certainly eager to find topics for other animals to take offense at and keep the flow of disputation going.

Corroboration for all this is given by the fact that the much more overtly political *Book of Birds* is also inconsistent in its genre. For all that it contains very specific allusions, the *Book* is not constant political invective from start to finish. It has a mix of didacticism, fable (and, in addition, biblical story), and invective for its own sake, reminiscent of the *Tale*—although in the instance of the *Book* the allusive just-so stories are much more prominent and the didactic element is underemphasized.

The *Book* is a more allusive work than the *Tale,* which leads to speculation on whether the digressions in both works might not merely be a case of a rambling narrator. The issue has been discussed to date only with regard to the *Book*: Makris (1993:410–11) has attributed the mixture in the *Book*'s genres to a rewrite of the *Book,* in which the political sections of the poem (whose point would have been lost on the next generation of readers) were dropped and the text was padded out with such material as would please what Makris believes was its predominantly monastic audience. This cannot be ruled out in the case of the *Book,* as its "extraneous" material is limited in extent and clearly mismatched with the just-so stories.[120] But such a hypothesis cannot be entertained in the case of the *Tale;* with the digressive material left out, there would not be much left of the *Tale*. So filler will not explain its inconsistencies.

A related possibility is that the long catalogs and utilitarian digressions are inserted in the narrative not as filler but in an attempt to conceal an unpalatable story still present in the text—either on the part of the original author or a later adaptor. Although this is in principle possible for the *Tale,* there is little internal corroboration for such concealment. With the (unlikely) exception of the "bearded" hare (326; see Commentary), nothing in the dialogues of the *Tale* is cryptic or allusive the way the *Book* frequently is. So if the digressions have been inserted to conceal something in the *Tale,* it is hard to see what they are concealing.

Finally, it has been suggested to us by a prominent Byzantinist that the scribes of the *Tale* may not have inserted the digressions but instead removed original, politically allusive verses. This is possible as an explanation but not particularly economical: the verses would have had to be removed without leaving a discernible trace, from a large number of places in the text, yet with the political thrust of the conclusion remaining in place. Furthermore, such an account posits one more level of transmission between the original text and the text(s) we now have. In the absence of any evidence to the contrary, we reject this possibility as well.

The *Book* gives one reason to suspect that its digressions do not originate with the author; the *Tale* digresses, we conclude, because the author intended it to digress.

Literary Evaluation

The style of this poem deserves little praise.

—A. C. Gidel, *Études sur la Litterature Grecque Moderne*

Plot

The author had a relatively simple story in mind, which he succeeds in communicating to the reader, despite minor problems here and there. The framework of the story itself, a convention of worthies, is a commonplace of narrative poetry, which the poet expands on with details reminiscent of contemporary politics. The description of the characters involved in the beginning is very brief, followed by preliminary events (extensively described diplomatic missions and negotiations) that foretell in part what is to happen in the end.

The negotiations themselves are recounted with keen verisimilitude. For example, the envoys are chosen with sensitivity, even if the king's embassy is (deliberately?) mismatched: the powerful send their weakest representatives, belittling their addressees, and the weak send their most imposing, to make the best impression from their disadvantaged position. The herbivores express understandable concern at what the carnivores' embassy might portend and muster their own forces (40–54). And the language the animals use in their politicking would not sound out of place in a modern press conference.

The setup of the transition in the *Tale* from one dialogue to the next tends to be both smooth and episodic: whenever an animal hears its name being mentioned, it is a matter of order and honor for it to step forward and provide an appropriate response (or monologue). As already seen, the most vehement responses, the hare's and the wolf's, are precisely those that trigger a change in the camp from which the disputants are drawn. And when a pair of animals steps up to speak (deer and boar, ox and buffalo), the second animal takes offense at something the first has presumed to say: the animals are mercurial and their alliances fleeting.[121] (As a deft counterweight to this mercuriality, and to the treacheries and desertions in the battle, it is worth noting that the boar—who blew up at his partner the deer in the debate [353ff.]—avenges the deer's death in the battle [1051–54].)[122]

So the altercations follow each other smoothly. Particularly adroit is the staging of the withdrawal of the small animals in favor of the larger ones, triggered by the smaller animals' own words (544–45) and constituting a major turning point in the *Tale*. There are other instances of inventiveness: the cat's lightning-fast response to the rat's overhasty challenge (125–26); the dog's foreshadowing of the next three debaters (255); the goats preempted by the sheep's retort even as they were halfway to the podium (453–57—see appendix 3); or the donkey's weak and pleading response to the avalanche of rhetoric from the horse (740–44).

For most of the *Tale,* however, the dramatic component is limited to the initial and final exchanges between the animals as each arrives on the scene. In fact, one has to make a special argument for the author's sense of drama: in the deluge of catalogs and invective, it is easy to miss. Plot development of the framing story, the convention, comes to a halt—the animals spend most of their time enumerating their functions and painting unflattering vignettes of their opponents. This is often amusing but does not advance the plot significantly—although the contrast of this building up with the ensuing dressing down is an effective dramatic device. And the enumerations go on too long for modern taste: although they can paint some vivid pictures, their expression is at times mechanical, and they come across to the modern reader as pedantic and unwelcome digressions. One might contend, though, that the leisurely pace of the main poem lulls the reader into a sense of complacency, which makes the final battle, with its abruptly quicker pace, all the more surprising and attention grabbing.

Indeed, toward the end of the *Tale,* something changes. The author would seem at first glance to have gotten about as tired as the reader, and switches into summary mode. After the expansive tale-within-a-tale the horse offers (691–739), the passages grow increasingly shorter, and more emphasis is given to altercation than description. The exchange of the bear and wolf is rushed, as is that of the cheetah and leopard. The leopard and monkey get away with saying hardly anything about themselves at all. The cheetah and the leopard enter rather abruptly: rather than setting the ground subtly to introduce them, as occurred for the ox and buffalo, the author has the bear quite mechanically yield the floor to them (855–58), with a deference uncharacteristic of the quadrupeds. And the final battle scene is described perfunctorily, particularly given the level of detail of the initial embassies or the extensive dialogues. There is an abundance of tactics but not of strategy, the animals are dispatched without much ceremony or lead-up, and the rapid-fire parrying of the animals sits awkwardly with the surrounding commentary.

In all, the rhythm of the last third of the *Tale* is much faster than the leisurely pace it has followed until this point. There are several explanations for this, all of which are probably at work. First, the exotic animals left to the end of the *Tale* are those least familiar to the author, and despite some use of the *Physiologus,* the poet finds he has the least to say about them. (This view was first supported by Gidel 1866:329; see also Eideneier 1983:227.) Second, the poet could not sustain an expansive narrative; this is particularly obvious in the battle, a scene that the poet seems to us uncomfortable in handling. Third—by surprising contrast—the poet is actually quite successful in building up tension to the final outcome by accelerating the plot: the lion's interventions and the events bringing them about are well thought out and lead inexorably to the battle. Finally, if the poet had an ulterior motive for his digressions—either to distract from his political contentions or to serve some didactic purpose—the need for such digressions evaporates once the fulfilment of those motives, the battle, is arrived at, so the pace of the narrative can pick up again.

There is one point of respite in the hasty last third of the *Tale:* the elephant's stately monologue (906–29a). This is followed by a marvelous dramatic move: the monkey's expansive insults toward the elephant right after his oration makes the reader about as indignant as King Lion (981–91), almost crying out for a violent ending. Yet the end catches everybody by surprise, involving as it does the defeat of the carnivores: it took such pains to bring these animals on stage, only to see them being killed and dispersed shortly afterward.

Imagery

In contrast to other works of the time (the romances in particular), imagery is a weak point of the *Tale,* which by its very nature limits the potential for poetic images and metaphors. The whole story essentially takes place at one and the same place, rather summarily described (107), and to escape from the confines of that dull environment would require an exceptionally talented narrator indeed. The author has made things even more difficult for himself than necessary because he uses the same phrase, μέσον τοῦ συνεδρίου, "middle of the conference," to describe both the center stage, where animals make their speeches (e.g., 829–31), and the throng of animals to which they return afterward (e.g., 933). By conflating both foreground and background in the same phrase, the author hardly displays a keen sense of space for the poem's setting.

The author has certainly made an effort to work around these confines: the deer (316–20) and the horse (659–64) arrive on stage accompanied by a halfway poetic description. The graphic way certain animals find death at the hands of humans and rivals (or escape it through hiding) may generate some compassion—or disgust—on the reader's part. And the description of culinary, household, and armory items can at times make one feel sorry for having been born six centuries too late. But, on the whole, the *Tale* fails to move the contemporary reader by the strength of its images. There are only a couple of remarkable metaphors: in a poem where animals are routinely likened to humans, noble ladies wearing long ball dresses are conversely said to drag long tails behind them (305); and even though the exact meaning of θρόνος in verse 81 remains ambiguous (as our translation concedes), to call the horse the "throne of men" certainly indicates that the author had a sense of the poetic.

Compounds

Vernacular medieval Greek often relies on lengthy compound words for the creation of powerful images—although not with the surprising juxtapositions of, say, Anglo-Saxon kennings. The ψωμοκαταλύτης rat who squanders bread (130); the ἀλευροκαταχέστης cat who shits thoroughly through flour (159); the κλαδοτρυπολόγος hare who deals with holes through branches (327); and the πετροφαγωμένη goat who is worn down by boulders (468) are all examples of this. Compound words are occasionally put to positive use, too: the dog exults that his precious collar (254) is χαντρατοκουδουνᾶτον, "bedecked with beads and bells," and the donkey praises his mighty organ (651) for being ῥουθωνοκεφαλᾶτον, "headed with a nostril."

Such compounds are also characteristic of the *Book of Birds* and are anticipated in *Ptochoprodromos* (παραγεμιστοτράχηλος, μεταξοσφικτουράτος, "with a stuffed nape, with a silk apron" [3.69]). But the genre they are most characteristic of is the Byzantine romance:

> Characteristic of this "common" language is an extravagance, that must surely be self-conscious, in the coining of new compound words. . . . In vernacular verse texts of the fourteenth and fifteenth century this resource . . . is exploited with a reckless exuberance unparalleled at any other period and in any other kind of writing. To what extent this "piling up" was characteristic of spoken usage or was a peculiarity of the art-language of vernacular poetry, is difficult to tell. But a glance at some of the more recondite compounds thrown up in the romances assures us that these can only have been the proud creations of poets writing on this particular theme, to whatever degree they may have based themselves on a resource available in common parlance. (Beaton 1996:93–94)

One could argue that the author is familiar with the compound words that paint such fittingly imposing verbal pictures of the protagonists' charms in the Byzantine romances and that he creates words of similar texture to fortify the animals' insults. But as Beaton (1996) points out, it is unlikely that these compounds were a regular feature of the spoken vernacular of the time. If anything, they may represent a connection between vernacular and learned Byzantine literature, which also features expansive compound words (themselves, presumably, in imitation of Aristophanes.) For instance, John Tzetzes (*xii* A.D.) comes up with κομπορηματοχρηματομετεωροφέναξ, "braggart cheat buoyed by his words and his money" (*Tzetzes: Epistulae* 4.6), and Constantine of Rhodes (*ix–x* A.D.) is spectacular in the invective he strings together in his epigrams—each twelve-syllable verse a single word (pausing only for the occasional *and*), going on in the case of his poem against Leo Choerosphactes for twenty-four verses:

> λαρρυγγοφλασκοξεστοχανδοεκπότα·
> κασαλβοπορωομαχλοπροικτεπεμβάτα·
> ὀλεθροβιβλιοφαλσογραμματοφθόρε·
> σολοικοβαττοβαρβαροσκυτογράφε·
> καὶ ψευδομυθοσαθροπλασματοπλόκε·
> Ἑλληνοθρησκοχριστοβλασφημοτρόπε·
> καὶ παντοτολμοψευδομηχανοῤῥάφε·
> καὶ τρωκτοφερνοπροικοχρηματοφθόρε·
> ἀῤῥητοποιονυκτεροσκοτεργάτα·
> καὶ νεκροτυμβοκλεπτολωποεκδύτα·
>
> [You flask-in-gullet–pint–mouth-gaping–gulper!
> You harlot-whore–lewd-beggar–shirt-lifter!
> Disastrous-book–false-letter–ruiner!

Solecist-babbling–barbarous-hide–writer!
Fake-fairytale–and–cracked-creation–monger!
You pagan-creed–and–Christ-blaspheming-type!
All-daring–and–mendacious–mal-intriguer!
You bride-gift-gnawing–dowry-money–waster!
Acts-unspeakable–nightly-darkness–worker!
You gravesite-corpses-robbing–clothes-despoiler!] (*Constantine of Rhodes,* 624)

So compound epithets were part of the cultural milieu of Byzantium, and the author of the *Tale* coined words that would have been intelligible to an unlearned audience but stylistically distinctive, even at their most vulgar.

One might compare with profit the informal Greek language electronic mailing list Hellas, extant since 1988.[123] Some of its subscribers frequently form similarly extravagant and vulgar compounds, which, although intelligible to its readership, are hardly a normal part of either spoken or written modern Greek.[124] The mailing list forms a special intermediate zone between written and spoken language (cf. December 1993), which allows these nonce forms into being; they would be unlikely to arise in either spoken conversation between those subscribers or their formal written discourse. Vernacular Byzantine literature may have occupied a similar niche for its practitioners between the spoken vernacular and written literary Attic—using words too intricate for the spoken language and too coarse for the written. (There is a parallel in scribes emulating oral formulas in written literary works; see discussion in "Orality.") If Beck's (1971) surmise is correct and Byzantine vernacular literature was written by the learned—and typically for the learned—then the original readership of these works would have formed a self-selected coterie not dissimilar to a contemporary electronic mailing list.

For the reader's convenience, we have collected all compound words (including Greek original and literal meaning) in appendix 5.

Structure

The structure of the *Tale* is best considered by comparison to the poem often regarded as its companion piece, the *Book of Birds*. As Eideneier (1982:303) has pointed out:

> Both works [the *Tale* and the *Book of Birds*] are structured in detail. Their structure is correlated not only with the external framework of sequencing speech and response but within each individual speech—which may range from a simple insult, aided by polysyllabic compound adjectives and nouns in a climaxing effect, to entire narratives as proof of a negative image of the opponent. After this (in the *Book of Birds*

only in the response) follows the corresponding animal's self-praise, again ordered in its entirety by a strict structural scheme.

The *Book* is indeed suffused with structure; so much so, it almost becomes mannered. The birds speak in strict alternation: the wild bird speaks first, making its accusations against the domestic; then the domestic responds, defending itself and counterattacking the wild bird. (What the domestic bird says in self-defense is often utilitarian in nature, so the author is reluctant to have the wild birds present such arguments.) Each time a new pair is introduced, the same verse is used: ἐκεῖνα οὐκ ἐσίγησαν τὴν ὄχλησιν τὴν εἶχαν, "they did not cease the tumult that possessed them." The first verse of each speech, and the verses connecting successive speeches, are also strongly predictable. And even in the speeches themselves, the accumulation of insults appears poised rather than spontaneous.

The *Tale* is much more chatty than this. Vasiliou (1996) has argued that it, too, has a structure in place of (double) accusation and rebuttal, but even if this is accepted (and the *Tale* seems too fluid to admit it), rebuttals merge into each other and vary widely in length. The quadrupeds do not fall into sequences of different pairs (Eideneier 1983:227): an animal can hold the floor as long as it successfully rebuts its challengers. (The horse endures the challenge of both the donkey and the camel and is expelled only by the wolf; likewise, the boar has to confront the deer, the hare, and the sheep.) There are formulas linking speeches in the *Tale,* too, but they vary much more than in the *Book* and consist of smaller compositional units: "right in center stage" (μέσον τοῦ συνεδρίου), "spoke such words as these" (τοιούτους λόγους λέγει), "get out of center stage" (ἔβγα/ἐβγᾶτε/φεύγα ἀπὸ τὴν μέσην), "he withdrew and stood" (ἀπῆλθεν/ἐξῆλθεν καὶ ἐστάθηκεν) (Eideneier 1983:231), and so on. Neither is what each animal has to say well ordered: once the animals embark on utilitarian catalogues there is no stopping them, but they slot in their boasts and insults before or after the catalogs, and barely even wait for an insult to be uttered before responding to it (appendix 3).

Nonetheless, though the *Tale* is not as consciously neat as the *Book,* there are some clear structural trends in place. Many of these have been pointed out by Eideneier (1983:228–29). The accumulation of polysyllabic insulting epithets so characteristic of the *Tale* tends to occur at the start of a speech—twenty-five of the forty speeches in the convention (124–991) contain compound epithets directed at the addressee, and twenty-three have the compounds in the first five verses, eighteen in the first two verses. The expression ἀκόμη/ἀκμὴν καὶ τό, "even the," at the start of a verse introduces a new feature of self-praise seventeen times in the poem.[125]

The use of synonyms is also a characteristic of the *Tale* and of much medieval and modern Greek folk poetry; it is an instance of poetic parallelism at the lexical level. In "Language" and "Comedy" we mention instances where the *Tale* adjoins learned and vernacular words for the same notion. But there are also several instances where the synonyms are not noticeably distinct in linguistic register—καὶ ὑπερφυσιώθηκες καὶ ὑπερεκαυχίσθης, "you have over-puffed and over-boasted," (542); πῶς ἐπολυλογήσασιν, πῶς ἐμακρυλογῆσαν, "how they have spoken much, how they have spoken at length," (552); γομάρια ἀβάστακτα, φορτώματα μεγάλα, "unbearable burdens, great loads," (770); and so on. (See also "Meter.")

There is also clear structuring of the narrative of the *Tale* at the episodic level. The framing episodes to the debate have a narrative symmetry absent from their counterparts in the *Book:* the embassy of the carnivores (17–39) is matched by that of the herbivores (40–54); the attack of the carnivores (1035–37) likewise matches the attack of the herbivores (1066–70); and the start of the battle (992–94) echoes the start of the assembly (103–7) with the repetition of the expressions "you should have seen" (τότε νὰ εἶδες) and "uproar and havoc" (ἡ ὄχλησις, ἡ ταραχή)—the latter formula also turning up ominously in the lion's rebuke (892).

Cleverly, and unlike the *Book of Birds,* most debates in the *Tale* take place within rather than across the two camps of the carnivores and herbivores: it is the animals with the most in common that have the most to argue about. This is a deliberate structural move on the part of the author: the *Tale* uses contrasts between similar animals as the impetus for its utilitarian narrative. What is enumerated about the buffalo depends on what is enumerated about the ox. The *Book,* on the other hand, does not actually compare its disputants with each other. It instead consistently formulates their disputes in autonomously adversarial terms—what the swan says to the stork has little to do with what the stork had said to the swan. In maintaining the disputes within the camps until the final battle, the *Tale* emphasizes the cohesion of the camps; we come to associate the carnivores with each other, rather than pairing off each carnivore with a corresponding herbivore. This makes the final battle, in a sense, inevitable: the camps, kept apart for so long, need to explode against each other. By contrast, the wild and tame birds in the *Book* expend their combativeness through disputation in pairs. Nothing in that poem allows for a climactic battle between those two groups, and the war threatened at the end of the poem (and realized in some manuscripts; see appendix 1) involves two completely different groups—the eagle and his entourage versus all his subjects, tame and wild.

There is such cohesion in the camps debating among themselves in the *Tale* that there are only two interactions between a carnivore and a herbivore, and both are one-sided: the hare forces out the fox (270–313), bringing in the herbivores, and the wolf expels the horse (812–27), bringing back the carnivores. These shifts are major structural breaks in the poem, which the author has taken care to mark out explicitly, both by metrical devices (see "Meter") and by an abrupt shift in tone (see "Irony and Contradiction"); they are two of the three major shifts in the plot of the poem before the battle. The third such shift, namely the ox and buffalo taking the floor (546–77), is unrelated to the alternation of camps. Rather, it occurs as part of an overall structure of escalation in size and ferocity of the participants, from rat up to elephant, which the lion explicitly points out to the pair (564–67). The ox and the buffalo are the first large animals to speak, and the lion's intervention marks this as a turning point just as do the effects used in the other two major shifts. The escalation propels the plot of the *Tale* (such as it is) on to its bloody resolution. The author of the *Tale* has thus crafted the episodic development of his narrative with care.[126]

The Hero

> In real tragedy it is not the hero who gets killed, but the chorus.
>
> —Joseph Brodsky, Nobel lecture

As most animals get only one chance to talk and their speeches are often centered on themselves rather than interaction with the other animals, there is little room to imbue the characters with detail; the *Tale* is much closer to an elementary school pageant, made up of a succession of skits, than a fourteenth-century emulation of classical Greek comedy. There are a couple of dramatically appropriate episodes in the vignettes painted by the animals—the pathos of the hare's plight, the wolf's menace, the monkey's impudence—but nothing like an extended characterization.

Yet one figure in the *Tale* may be regarded as tragic, and that is none other than King Lion. With his imperial appearance and his long pedigree of nobility and regality, the reader has reason to have high expectations of the lion.[127] These expectations will be frustrated. The king makes four active appearances in the *Tale*. The first two appearances (112–21, 556–68) portray an enlightened king, eager to maintain peace and justice in his kingdom. His last intervention (981–91) destroys any such hopes: it shows the lion to be a violator of his oath and of the trust placed in him by his subjects. The transition is shocking and tragic: the lion's ostensive best intentions are frustrated, and the promise of a new order is annulled. The reader is left to ponder how this could have come about: did the lion have an honorable intent, defeated by circumstance, or did he scheme those circumstances into being from the outset?

The crucial episode to resolving this is the lion's third intervention (891–903), where it is still not clear whether he had already made his mind in favor of war as usual or whether he simply concedes that peace might be unattainable. Particularly puzzling is verse 892 and the lion's reference to impending havoc (ἡ ὄχλησις, ἡ ταραχή, ἡ μέλλουσα γενέσθαι). As our translation indicates, this is open to either interpretation. The lion is speaking in barely restrained rage and proceeds to make a rather nasty threat to the leopard; this would make sense either if the whole event was planned or if the lion had snapped in anger. Yet μέλλουσα, "impending," properly refers to something fated to happen and seems a weighty choice of verb as opposed to, say, "could happen" (δύναται) or "will happen" (θέλει); it seems to emphasize the inevitability of the outcome rather than the lion's capricious decision. (This ambiguity is of course related to the possible political interpretations of the poem discussed in appendix 2.)

If King Lion had simply set a trap for the herbivores and planned everything ahead of time, then he becomes just another politician. If he yielded to a momentary frustration instead of an inexorable fate, he becomes merely pitiable rather than tragic. But the tragic element in the *Tale* remains, and the author has skillfully laid the groundwork for the lion's critical third intervention through the leopard's unexpected—and ill-considered—lack of respect, preparing the reader for what is about to happen (884–88).

The Misfit

> And of all the wild beasts, the tamest and easiest to domesticate is the elephant; for they both learn and understand much, and can even be taught to kneel before the king.
>
> —*Aristotle: Historia Animalium*

A problem that comes up frequently in our analysis of the poem is what to make of the elephant. This is an exotic animal, granted an important role in the court. Moreover, through his dramatic exchange with the monkey, he is pivotal to the development of the *Tale*'s plot: the narrative calls for a radical reversal in order to bring about its catastrophic ending, and an otherwise detached figure like the elephant, explicitly favored and invited by the king, is a convenient target.

Yet the elephant vanishes from the scene just before the final battle, which his appearance was instrumental in provoking. And in several regards the elephant fails to fit in with the scheme set up in the poem for the other animals. We consider elsewhere (particularly appendix 2) the possible political motivations for the author introducing such a troublesome beast into the *Tale*. But the political interpretation of the poem is not a given, and the author may have intended the elephant as a dramatic follow-on to the other exotic beasts, the leopard and the cheetah, introduced in turn as the lion's courtiers. For whatever reason the elephant is there, he poses a structural problem for the author, which can be viewed independently of any "meaning . . . and depth" (5).

The elephant is a fabulous and huge creature about which the author knows little, save what the *Physiologus* relates about elephant hunting, its use in battle from the *Alexander Romance,* and the fact that ivory is a luxury commodity. The author may well not even realize that the elephant is a herbivore and thereby unsuited to the lion's court: as seen, the author of the vernacular *Physiologus* presumed the elephant to be a carnivore, and the abridgement of *Timothy of Gaza* does not discuss the beast's diet. Even if the *Tale*'s author did know that the elephant was a herbivore, he could not very well place him in the company of the ox and the horse. Their camp is characterized not only as καθαρά, "clean"—i.e., herbivorous—but also εὔχρηστα, "useful"—i.e., domestic. The author seems unaware of the agricultural uses to which the elephant is put by humans in India and would plausibly regard the elephant as a wild animal, undominated by humans. His use as a tank, documented in the *Alexander Romance* and by Timothy of Gaza, was presumably too far removed from the author's experience to place the elephant on the same footing as the horse. The elephant could not be integrated into the barnyard, so the author could place him only outside the barnyard, in the court, in the company of the other wild and exotic beasts—the lion, the leopard, and the cheetah.

Even in the battle, the author would have trouble fitting the elephant into the order of things. We have speculated that there is a political allusion being made through the elephant's absence (see "Class Struggle in a Byzantine Farmyard"), but there may be a more mundane reason for it. Though the monkey points out the vulnerability of the elephant, he would still have been assumed formidable in battle. With the image of the elephant so overwhelming, an elephant squashing the cheetah instead of the buffalo trampling him would hardly be considered fair play; it would be, instead, a reprise of *Bambi Versus Godzilla*. Furthermore, the victory of the herbivores needs to be a dramatic surprise; with the elephant on their side, it would be a foregone conclusion. Likewise, if the elephant were to be counted as a carnivore, it would be hard to see any horse or ox making a dent in him in order to bring about their unexpected victory. And, of course, the author would have had no exposure to how the elephant battles his way in the jungle; he would not even be sure whether the elephant uses his tusks (assuming he knew elephants have tusks—see Commentary, verse 914), his teeth, his feet, or as the vernacular *Physiologus* surmised, his trunk. In the end, the simplest way out for the author was to pretend he'd never even mentioned that troublesome "disaster in the realm of animals"—and, we might add, in his own narrative.

The Text of the *Tale*

> And so I found it to be contrary
> to all we'd spoken of—I'll tell you how:
> full of mistakes, ill-written, uncorrected;
> and it was quite decrepit through old age.
>
> —*Alexander Romance* ρ

Manuscripts

The *Tale* is attested in five manuscripts: the Constantinopolitan (C; *Graecus Seraglio* 35), the Parisian (P; *Graecus* 2911), the Viennese (V; *Vindobonensis*

Theol. Gr. 244), the Lesbian (L; formerly *Lesbiacus* 92, now *Petropolitanus* 721), and the St. Petersburgian (A; *Petropolitanus* 202). A sixth manuscript, 29 of Cardinal Sirlet's[128] library, was reported in 1848; it has since been lost (Tsiouni 1972:45).

C

The Constantinopolitan manuscript (described in Bouboulidis 1964, Tsavare 1987:39–43, and Reinsch 1998) is one of the most important manuscripts for vernacular Greek literature. It contains, alongside the *Tale,* the *Book of Birds,* two *Ptochoprodromos* poems, the *Book of Fruit,* the *Lay of Armoures,* and five other vernacular poems. An anthology of vernacular poetry, it was written in 1461, and exceptionally for a vernacular manuscript, we know who the scribe was:

> Ἐγράφι σὺν θ(ε)ῶ ἁγίω τὸ παρὸν ἐν μ(η)ν(ὶ) ιουνί(ω) κα αυξα· διά χιρὸς ἑμοῦ ἀμαθοῦ καὶ ἐλαχίστου παρὰ πάντων· νικολ(άου) υἱοὺ π(α)π(ὰ) μηχαήλ: ὁ τοῦ ἁγιόμνήτι: εὐχεστέ μοι φίλτατοι ἔρρωσθαι: καὶ μὶ καταραστε διὰ τον κ(ύριο)ν:
> διὰ συνδρωμεῖς και ἐξόδους κυρ(οῦ) πρικοῦ ἥψιλα:
>
> [This was written with the aid of Holy God on the twenty-first of the month of June, 1461, by the hand of myself, the unlettered and most humble of all Nicholas, son of Father Michael Agiomnitis ⟨Hagiomnetes⟩; wish me good health, dear friends, and curse not, for the sake of the Lord.
> Under the commission and expenses of Sir Prikos Ipsila.] (f. 179r. Bouboulidis 1964:109–10; Reinsch 1998:249)

As Reinsch (1998) has found, Nicholas Agiomnitis was from Venetian Negroponte (Euboea), whereas his father was from Athens. Negroponte fell to the Ottomans in 1470; sometime between 1474 and 1478, Nicholas left Negroponte for Mount Athos, becoming a monk and taking the name Nicephorus. He continued work as a scribe there, copying ecclesiastical, liturgical, and medical learned texts. His attested scribal career ranged from 1461 to 1502.

Agiomnitis, as the son of a married priest and an Athonite monk himself, was clearly Greek Orthodox, but a number of things about his manuscript of the *Tale* relate it to the West. One such link is the use of anno Domini dating, uncharacteristic of Byzantium (Reinsch 1998:253); when Agiomnitis was copying manuscripts in Mount Athos as the monk Nicephorus, by contrast, he used Byzantine-style dating from the creation of the world (e.g., Reinsch 1998:254–55 fn. 34.) Another is the Western look of the illustrations of the beasts (see "Illustrations"). Yet another is the fact that the formulas Agiomnitis uses, "Wish me good health . . . and curse not, for the sake of the Lord" (εὔχεσθέ μοι ... ἔρρωσθαι καὶ μὴ καταρᾶσθε διὰ τὸν Κύριον), and "under the commission and expenses" (διὰ συνδρομῆς καὶ ἐξόδου), were both characteristic of Greek manuscripts copied under Western rather than Byzantine or Ottoman dominion (Reinsch 1998:253). It comes as no surprise then that though the manuscript subsequently ended up in the sultan's palace library, the copying of the manuscript took place in Negroponte, which was still in 1461 a Western dominion. So there is no reason to think that it was written at the behest of Mehmet II (Reinsch 1998:252–55).

The scribe's patron, who would seem to be a Pierre (Π[ιε]ρίκος is a Greek diminutive of Πιέρ[ος]), might also be a link to the West. We know of a fifteenth-century scribe called Pierios Ypsilas from Aegina who copied a manuscript in Milan in 1497 and lectured on Aristotle in Bologna from 1507 on. Tsavare (1987:40) tentatively identifies Prikos Ipsila with this Pierios Ypsilas. However, the date of 1461 may be too early for this to work, and Reinsch (1998:250) suspects *Prikos* is instead an abbreviation of the honorific *Patrician* (πατρίκιος, *patrikios*), used in another manuscript written by Agiomnitis to describe his patron.

V

The Viennese manuscript (Wagner 1874:v–xiv; Tsavare 1987:46–48; Papathomopoulos and Jeffreys 1996:c–ciii) is another renowned anthology of vernacular Greek, famous from Wagner's pioneering edition (1874) of its contents. It contains much of the vernacular medieval Greek corpus as well as astrological and theological works. The manuscript has been written by various hands and in various formats of paper, though most of it (including the *Tale*) is by a scribe signing himself as Demetrius; it appears to have been put together out of various quires of Greek texts circulating independently. The manuscript was purchased in Constantinople by the Austrian ambassador Ogier de Busbecq around 1550 and brought to Vienna. At least part of it dates from the 1510s, though the individual quires could have been written independently. V contains the *Tale* written as prose, without line breaks, and is among the works Demetrius wrote in a very compressed and abbreviated script (Papathomopoulos and Jeffreys 1996:ci)—unlike the parts of V written by him that can be dated to the 1510s. The latter parts of V may have been written as late as the late 1540s (Papathomopoulos and Jeffreys 1996:ciii).

P

The Parisian manuscript dates from the late fifteenth century. Unlike the other manuscripts in which the *Tale* has appeared, this is not an anthology of vernacular Greek texts; the *Tale* is in fact the only text it contains. As a result, the only information we have on the manuscript is in Tsiouni 1972:13–15, 27, and Omont 1888–98:2.58. We know that the manuscript belonged to Cardinal Jules Mazarin, in his time the most powerful man in France, who donated his library to what was to become the French National Library in 1661.

P features linguistic idioms that Xanthoudidis (1927–28:353) identified as Cretan. However, Xanthoudidis is notorious for claiming Byzantine vernacular works as Cretan, and his thesis has not stood the test of time. Nevertheless, P may well have been written by a scribe from the broader Aegean area.

A

The St. Petersburg manuscript (Hesseling 1924:306–8; Šandrovskaja 1956a:212; Šandrovskaja 1960:10–20; Tsavare 1987:43–45) dates from the latter half of the sixteenth century and ended up in St. Petersburg in 1875; its origins are unknown. It contains eight vernacular poems, including the *Book of Birds,* the *Book of Fruit, Spaneas,* and the *Lay of Armoures*. Unlike C, it is hardly a luxury manuscript; it contains doodles, snippets of popular remedies and hagiographies, and several random blank spaces. A preserves the text of the *Tale* in its worst state: it has serious gaps in the text (1–64, 168–97, 557, 570, 575–605, 657a, 795, 817–18, 882–1082), mostly because of leaves falling out; little care for its meter; frequent garblings of words (leading scholars to suspect the scribe's command of Greek: Šandrovskaja 1956a:218); and many spelling mistakes.

L

Finally, the Lesbian manuscript (Šandrovskaja 1960:10–20; Tsavare 1987:49–50) was written in 1625. The manuscript was held in a monastic library in Lesbos, where it was sighted in 1884; afterward it went missing until it was identified with a manuscript brought to St. Petersburg in 1915 (Šandrovskaja 1956a:212). Most of the manuscript is dedicated to religious works, but at the end it contains three vernacular works: the *Tale,* the *Book of Birds,* and a hitherto unpublished vernacular version of the *Physiologus*. L displays a text distorted in another way: its language is consciously and consistently modernized, as was typical for the later manuscripts of vernacular Byzantine works; for example, κατζικόπουλα instead of ἐρίφια, "kids," 190; τζηκουροκόπτουν instead of ἀξινογλύφουν, "axe," 963.[129]

Relation Among the Manuscripts

Like all medieval vernacular texts, there are many differences in the *Tale*'s manuscripts. These originate in the scribes' feeling that they were entitled to take liberties with the texts they were copying; the background against which this took place, and the nature of those liberties, is discussed extensively in "Orality." Scribes also deviated from the original text because of practical exigencies. For instance, Nicholas Agiomnitis interpolated verse 291a into the Constantinopolitan manuscript of the *Book of Birds* in order to avoid a blank line before the illustration on the next page (Notis Toufexis, personal communication).

Many of the manuscript deviations in the *Tale* are immaterial to the standing of the text; there are several cases where a scribe is carried away repeating himself rather than preserving the text in the source manuscript. In addition, it is obvious that manuscripts L and A linguistically modernize the text. In fact, notwithstanding the theoretical reasons against ignoring any manuscript's reading ("*recentiores non deteriores*"), we have not found any instances where these manuscripts have decided a textual issue raised in the three older manuscripts. In our opinion, Tsiouni's edition relies too much on L, with the effect of forcing modern Greek readings into the text. Thus, cases such as verse 663, where the older verb forms ἐχιλιμήντρισεν (P) and ἐχρημάτησεν (CVA) are rejected by Tsiouni in favor of L's standard modern Greek ἐχλιμίντρισεν, "neighed," or verse 1053, where the active χύνει, "spills" = "rushes," (PCV) is rejected in favor of L's medial χύνεται (which happens to be how modern Greek expresses the concept), give a distorted image of the text's language. By treating L and A with suspicion, Papathomopoulos's edition has avoided that particular pitfall.[130]

Still, the instances where the different versions of the text are equally plausible, both linguistically and pragmatically, become quite frequent in texts where the scribe is at liberty to adapt. As discussed in "Orality," this makes the enterprise of editing medieval texts much murkier than editing classical texts. In the frequent instances in the *Tale* where one or more manuscripts include a verse absent in the others, the issue of whether to regard the reading as original becomes primarily one of literary taste and is often arbitrary. Neither is it safe to assume that scribes only added material: we have clear instances where a single manuscript takes it upon itself to edit out verses that may be redundant in context but are nonetheless widely enough attested to be original (e.g., V 221 and 226.)

It is clear from the critical apparatus of the text that the manuscripts fall into two families; P comprises one, and the other four, the other. The procedure of free variation followed by the scribes makes it difficult to formulate a stemma (family tree) for the four manuscripts, as required by the classical practice of textual criticism in order to identify deviations. The errors that would allow such a stemma to be constructed do not all fall into a consistent pattern. All the same, the fact that both V and L omit verses 545–81, suggesting a dropped folio in a common prototype (*Tale* manuscripts tend to contain 15–20 verses per page; cf. the similarly sized lacuna for 865–95 in L) makes it obvious that they have a common antecedent. And inspection of the critical apparatus leads one to conclude that V and L group together, as do C and A.

There remain instances in which V and L pattern with P rather than C and A. Papathomopoulos in his edition explains this as contamination (i.e., cross-copying) of VL from P—though, because at times it is V following P, at times L, and at times both, the mechanics of such a contamination are not obvious. In order to account for the similarly complicated textual history of the *Book of Birds* while still adhering to a classical stemmatic analysis, Tsavare (1987) has also postulated contamination between the prototypes of her two manuscript groups. Contamination is a recognized fact of life for the copying of classical manuscripts: scribes would check classical texts against more than one source manuscript, or alternative readings would be frequently given within the same source—so errors in a given manuscript could originate in more than one source. Tsavare's painstaking stemmatic approach, and its appropriateness for vernacular works, has occasioned a lively debate (Eideneier 1988b; Tsavare 1993), and we have no doubt that Papathomopoulos's approach will as well.

We admit to some disquiet about postulating contamination for medieval texts; the scribal meticulousness inherent in postulating it—scribes seeking out multiple versions of the text and copying from them selectively—seems inconsistent with the scribes' creative free-variation attitude toward vernacular texts.[131] As a result of this free variation, some instances where V or L match P will be accidental. (To give a trivial example, ἐμέ, 153 CLA; ἐμέν, 153 PV.) On the other hand, contamination is the simplest explanation of cases like the presence or absence of verses 61 and 612a, and although there are several good examples of the groupings PL, PV, and PVL, the instances of groupings that would contradict it, PC and PA, are rare (though the case of verse 151, missing in PC, is puzzling).[132] And cross-copying is not the only possible explanation for contamination; particularly in a close-knit literary society (such as the society we believe brought the *Tale* into being), scribes could easily have sighted more than one version of the *Tale* in their career. Although we remain agnostic as to whether there has been contamination in the text, we have accepted as our base text Papathomopoulos's edition, which assumes there has been.[133]

At the same time, it is intractable to choose one family of manuscripts over the other as a more reliable witness of the text: both families have presented untenable readings. For example, in verse 377, CVLA all have the reading μὲ τὴν γῆν, "Indeed, they salt and store me all year round, / and place me inside jugs, and jars as well, / laboring ***with the earth*** and all the like"; P has the reading μὲ πτικήν, which though garbled easily allows the reconstruction (first proposed by Koukoules 1911–12:372) με πηκτήν, turning ***me into brawn*** and all the like," fitting the context much better. On the other hand, in verse 477, where VCLA have εὐστόμαχα, "digestible" (of lamb meat), P has εὔστοχα, "well-aimed, sagacious."[134] The same goes with structural elements of the poem. For example, CVLA omit connecting passages like 858–59, but the passage does not contribute much to the text, and one could just as easily posit that P had added it. The same can be said for the connecting passage 961a–b, present only in C (see Textual Notes).

In a few instances, however, individual scribes have intervened in the text in a significant way. The greatest deviations are in P, which constitutes a separate family of manuscripts. In most cases, the initiative for the deviations seems to us to belong to the scribe of P rather than the scribe of the archetype of CVLA. The herbivores' call (40–54) is present only in P, and we argue in appendix 3 that it is an interpolation by that scribe, as is the case for 76–78. P has also clearly interpolated 309, which reiterates 307, and possibly also 661, whose syntax (four unconnected verbs) is uncharacteristic of the poem. Conversely, P omits 838–42, the bear's mockery of the wolf, substituting it with 837, a restatement of 836. Only P contains the episode of the donkey by the brook (685–88), although it is difficult to tell whether it is original or not. And P has taken the initiative in censoring out any mention of Zeus from the *Tale* (see Commentary, verse 771). Finally, P swaps verse 916 with 917; the only other manuscript to disturb the order of verses is L, swapping 693 with 694.

The other manuscripts do not seem to present as much initiative individually in manipulating the text—not deliberately, at least, because A's lacunae are legion. Still, the prototype of CVLA displays its own share of intervention; we do not find its omission of 795 justified, for example (see Textual Notes). The episode of "elephants prefer blondes" (927a–g) is clearly an interpolation in C, as is the horse's peroration in 664a–c and the reiteration in 1048a–b. As seen, Agiomnitis was not above tampering with text to fit a rubric for the *Book of Birds*. The interpolation of 664a–c in the *Tale* might have a similar motive, as it is followed immediately by a picture of the donkey and the ox—although as it stands, the picture is in the middle of the page and 664a–c is on the top, so Agiomnitis did not solve a serious page-formatting problem this way. L effaces any mention of sultans and emirs (*emperor, magnates,* 494; *magnates,* 757, page missing, 878–79). What purpose this might have served in 1625, when organized Greek resistance to Ottoman rule was still a long way off, is hard to say; perhaps the distinction between emperor and sultan had been by then forgotten (see also "Language"). And V has cut out any mention of the boar's cannibalism (see Textual Notes, verse 439), just as C passes over the death of the deer—the only herbivore killed (1052).

Tallying the instances in which each manuscript inserted or deleted verses, or merged two verses into one ("contracted"), we can gain some notion of which scribes were more "interventionist." The results are given in Table 1.[135]

Table 1 tells us several things. First, it confirms that P is very different from the other manuscripts; it is at variance two and a half times as often as its closest rival, C. Second, the other two oldest witnesses, C and V, take a very different approach to the text: Nicholas Agiomnitis almost always expands it, whereas Demetrius always cuts it down. Both scribes actively interfere with the text and so cannot be relied on unquestioningly. The other two manuscripts, L and A, are not as adventurous with the text—consistent perhaps with their lateness, when scribes had the model of the printed book in mind and no longer felt at ease intervening with their copy. (Modernizing the grammar of the text is not at the same level of intervention as inserting new connective passages.) There is also evidence in the table for the groupings CA and VL.

The first edition of the *Tale* by Wagner in 1874 relied on the two manuscripts then known, V and P, with Wagner using P as his basis.[136] Šandrovskaja's translation also frequently appeals to P, even though it is meant to be based on VLA. Although Tsiouni's edition does not show a uniform bias (cf. 377, where she follows CVLA instead), overall it remains close to P and has been reproached for this by Eideneier (1976, 1995). Eideneier favors C, the oldest manuscript, as the best witness of the text or at least equal in value to P and

Table 1. Verse Discrepancies Among Manuscripts

	Instances	*Verses*
Present only in P	16	6, 40–54, 76–78, 309, 343a, 557, 570, 661, 685–88, 837, 858–59, 894, 924, 968, 1075a
Absent only in P	11	10a, 124, 241a, 255a, 344, 372, 610a, 673a, 838–42, 959a, 1001
Contracted only by P	2	471–72, 1060–61
Contracted by all but P	2	177–78, 486–87
Total deviations in P	**31**	
Present only in C	11	480a, 576a, 664a–64c, 747a, 831a, 919a, 927a–27g, 929a, 933a, 961a–61b, 1048a–48b
Absent only in C	2	717–18, 1052
Total deviations in C	**13**	
Absent only in V	6	134–35, 221, 226, 274, 439–43, 897
Contracted only by V	4	139–40, 619–20, 760–61, 1022–23
Total deviations in V	**10**	
Present only in L	2	542a–42b, 1024a
Contracted only by L	2	502–3, 938–39
Total deviations in L	**4**	
Present only in A	1	344a
Absent only in A	1	817–18
Contracted only in A	2	791–92, 868–69
Total deviations in A	**4**	
Present only in VL	2	657a, 1070a
Absent only in VL	3	4, 191, 254
Total deviations in VL	**5**	
Present only in CA	2	269a, 729a
Total deviations in CA	**2**	
Absent only in PC	1	151
Present only in PV	1	61
Contracted only in PV	1	612a
Present only in PL	1	(795)[1]

[1]The content of P 795 and L 795 is independent: they do not originate in a common prototype.

V. Hesseling (1924:315)—who had not sighted manuscripts C and L—expresses a preference for V over P as a linguistically more conservative text, a trait he attributes to greater antiquity rather than scribal pedantry. Beck (1971:174), conversely, argues that P has the linguistically more conservative text. Mitsakis (1976:409) questions Tsiouni's use of P when it had been established to be Cretan by Xanthoudidis, whereas she argued the *Tale* was composed in Constantinople or Thessalonica. But the alleged Creticisms of P are not at all as obvious as has been claimed, and an edition using P would be no more heterogeneous linguistically than is typical of the time. Besides, rejecting P on the basis of the tentative geographical origin of the *Tale* seems especially foolhardy, particularly as scribes moved around.

We do not feel we can weigh in on one side or another or even that we should. P certainly retains a lot of demonstrably good readings, and its modernisms are minimal compared with those of L. And we have just seen that C has a marked tendency toward interpolation, so treating it as the *codex optimus* (as Eideneier has suggested) would be a problematic venture. The discrepancies between the two families of manuscripts are at any rate minor, concerning for the most part choice of wording rather than substantial difference in content. An edition based primarily on C or V rather than P would not result in any essential change to the translation.

The edition we have adopted, Papathomopoulos's, is rigorously stemmatic, yet it, too, is frequently confronted with a choice (*selectio*) between the two families' readings that cannot be resolved through the stemma alone. In collaborating with Papathomopoulos, we have followed the usual ways to attempt to resolve this: the author's usage (*usus*), plausibility, meter, formulas, and so on. We do not believe Papathomopoulos's edition is discernibly biased toward one or the other family of manuscripts.

Illustrations

Of the manuscripts containing the *Tale*, three are illustrated. The illustrations in A are few and "very simple and unartistic" (Tsiouni 1972:21), and Tsavare (1987:45) concurs for the illustrations it gives for the *Book of Birds* ("totally artless"); samples are shown in Šandrovskaja (1956a:213–15). Those in L "are not of any importance and bear no connection to the text of the poem" (Tsiouni 1972:18); as Tsavare (1987:50) notes, the scribe left room for pictures, but these were never drawn in, so the blanks were later filled in with doodles by the manuscript's owners.

By contrast, the illustrations in C are extensive and appropriate to the subject matter, as is in fact the case throughout the manuscript: compare, for example, the illustrations of the Calendar poem immediately following the *Tale* (Eideneier 1979) or the *Book of Birds* (Tsavare 1987:42). The drawings are "beautifully naive" (Tsiouni 1972:16) and reminiscent of the Western medieval, heraldic depiction of animals. The quadrupeds usually have their tongues hanging out, and the lion, leopard, and dog have their tails upright in heraldic flourish.

It was common for the illustrator to be distinct from the scribe (Tsavare 1987:42), so our illustrator is presumably not Nicholas Agiomnitis himself—although he clearly would have been a denizen of Euboea, like Agiomnitis. As already mentioned, the scribe often left blank spaces for the illustrator/rubricator to fill in with illustrations and headings. As discussed in "Manuscripts," this responsibility led Agiomnitis to tamper with the text of the *Book of Birds*. The interpolation of 664a–c is an uncertain instance of this in the *Tale,* but the rubrics that Agiomnitis added are much more extensive than in P, the only other manuscript of the *Tale* with rubrics (though without illustrations): nineteen rubrics in P, thirty-six illustrations (most with rubrics) in C. Agiomnitis has realized the dramatic importance of the battle and supplies its almost one hundred verses—a tenth of the poem—with no fewer than fourteen illustrations. P, by contrast, gives the battle scene the single rubric "Beginning of the War."

We have already referred to some peculiarities in depictions of specific animals: the elephant was clearly drawn by someone with little idea of what elephants actually looked like and the leopard is a purely conventional figure, whereas the cheetah, by contrast, is depicted realistically. The donkey's priapism in the illustrations reflects the popular jocular preoccupation with the donkey's penis (reflected in the *Donkey Tale* as well as the *Entertaining Tale of Quadrupeds*). The horse is the only other animal that (as one might expect) is depicted priapically. But compared to the extravagant donkey, the horse seems to have been hard done by.

Orality

Cultures throughout the world have produced traditional, often quite extensive narrative poems, sung by bards or their equivalents without recourse to written texts. Keeping such a poem going for a long time necessitates some shortcuts, and several common traits have been identified in these songs. Their singers have a common stock of formulas, fitting the meter of the song; this metrical requirement distinguishes them from commonplace expressions of normal speech. These formulas are repeated throughout the poem, either verbatim or as templates, and allow the singer to keep the song going in the right meter by inserting them on the fly. Oral narrative poems are also characterized by recurrent themes: standard episodes such as assemblies and missives recur within a song and between songs so that the singer need not make up the episode from whole cloth each time it is performed. Finally, when different singers sing what they consider the same song, they are committed only to repeating the storyline and not the exact words (despite their protestations to the contrary): each singing is a retelling, though the commonality of formulas and themes ensures that the songs sound rather similar.

A breakthrough was made when Milman Parry and Albert Lord realized that Homeric poetry displayed the characteristics of Bosnian (Christian and Muslim) narrative folk poetry and that this could be accounted for by their having originally been oral poems written down rather than intrinsically written conceptions (Lord 1960). Orality explains a lot in Homer, and attempts have been made since to apply the concept in other domains. As has been established through extensive research, primarily by Elizabeth and Michael Jeffreys (Jeffreys 1973, 1974; Jeffreys and Jeffreys 1983, 1986), vernacular Byzantine literature abounds in formulaic expressions, recurring within and across works. There has thus been a long-lasting debate among scholars on whether the vernacular poems are in fact originally oral.

Three hypotheses have been formulated to answer why the same formulas recur in work after work.[137] Giuseppe Spadaro (1987) has held that the formulas have been plagiarized by the authors of the works from each other, whereas Arnold van Gemert and Wim Bakker (1987) have investigated scribal interference between works copied out in the same manuscript. Although there are confirmed instances of each in Byzantine literature, however, the most satisfactory theory has been that of Elizabeth and Michael Jeffreys (1971, 1979, 1983, 1986), who hold that the formulas reflect orality in transmission of the texts, though not necessarily an oral origin of the texts themselves. The formulas, they argue, draw on a wellspring of a contemporary corpus of oral poetry. This theory has since been refined by Roderick Beaton (1990, 1996), who points out that the formulas do not appear to be those of folk song.[138] Rather than postulate a now lost medieval oral corpus as a source for them, Beaton (1996:179) (following Bäuml 1984) believes the formulas to be artificial, as indicated by their linguistic archaism, and devised so that the written vernacular poems would sound like, and have the authority of, contemporary oral ballads—and other written vernacular poems, which were doing likewise (Beaton 1996:181–82). Medieval literary taste preferred adherence to tradition, in this case a nascent tradition of vernacular writing, over originality as an end in itself (cf. Bäuml 1984:43). An excellent illustration of how formulas were exploited to lend authority to a text lies in the recently published *War of Troy,* a translation from the Old French *Roman de Troie,* which introduces many of the standard formulas of medieval Greek into the text independently of the original (Papathomopoulos and Jeffreys 1996:lxxxi–lxxxvi; Jeffreys and Jeffreys 1979).

Transmission

There are two issues to be considered: first, whether the poems were originally written or oral, and second, whether the poems underwent oral transmission—that is, whether the divergences between the manuscripts of a poem may be explained not as different copies of a written archetype but as different tellings of the story by distinct bards.

Medieval vernacular works seem to be almost all written poems in origin, with a well-defined archetype for the manuscript versions, although possibly in some cases with a period of oral transmission. There seems to be no other way to explain the chaos in the manuscripts of Sachlikis, for example—though we can be sure he wrote down his poetry:

> ἐπιάσα τὸ κονδύλι μου χαρτὶν καὶ καλαμάριν,
> νὰ γράψω διὰ τὴν θλῖψίν μου, τὸ δολερὸν γομάριν
>
> [I've picked my pen up, ink and paper, too,
> to write about my woe, that painful burden] (*Strange Narrative* 23–24)
>
> καὶ τἄγραψα εἰς τὴν φυλακὴν διὰ τὲς ἀρχιμαυλίστριες...
> καὶ τὰ παιδία τοῦ σκολειοῦ, πολλὰ τὰ τραγουδοῦσαν
>
> [I wrote in jail about the major whores . . .
> and schoolkids often sang my verses out] (*Strange Narrative* 111–12)

There is much deviation between the different versions of a given poem surviving in manuscript but almost never so great as in the different versions of an oral poem, which are in essence complete retellings. For the most part, medieval poems were simply copied none too closely by the manuscripts' scribes, who felt entitled to introduce slight variations in a manner consistent with the variations in oral performance. In that respect, they behaved rather differently than they did with classical texts, which were copied faithfully. In effect, the scribes put themselves in the position of oral bardic performers of the poems (see Jeffreys 1973:194; Eideneier 1982–83; Beaton 1996:182–84) and treated the texts with the embellishment and variation that bards would employ.[139]

The tendency of the scribes copying vernacular works not to adhere strictly to notions of textual accuracy is at odds with the respect with which scribes (often the same scribes: see Agapitos and Smith 1994; Beaton 1996:268; Toufexis 2001) treated classical works.[140] This makes it particularly difficult to apply traditional textual criticism to vernacular works. Developed to enable the restoration of the original classical texts from their extant manuscripts, textual criticism works by drawing up a stemma of manuscripts and relies on identifying clear-cut errors in transmission; when one family of manuscripts makes sense and the other does not, then the first family gives the original reading in that instance. When the scribes are consciously working to preserve the text, inadvertent deviations are easily identified: they bring about inconsistencies, they echo previous passages in inopportune places, or they fail to match what we know of the literary conventions of the original.

As a result of the scribal liberties taken with the vernacular texts, by contrast, there is great textual heterogeneity in the works preserved in more than one manuscript. It is typical to have most verses differ in some small way from manuscript to manuscript, in a way usually irreconcilable with the stemmatic analysis of manuscripts of classical texts. Furthermore, because the concern for literal copying was absent, it is much more difficult to identify one reading as an erroneous distortion of another than for classical texts: the variations introduced are typically much of a muchness. Our problem is that medieval scribes were worse poets than Homer—so we can easily tell if they tampered with his text—but not necessarily any worse than the authors of works such as the *Tale*. At times, we are lucky enough to have a readily identifiable prototype derivable from the entire manuscript tradition of a work; although there may be deviations on every line, they are relatively minor, and most of them can be eliminated as aberrations. At other times, the manuscript readings deviate so wildly from each other that one should properly speak of adaptations of the text, rather than versions, and one cannot derive a unique prototype at all.

Presented with this kind of difficulty, the business of textual criticism becomes inherently more difficult than for classical texts: "Thus there must have been one single original version to which we may aspire to attain. Unfortunately, again through the intervention of memory, that single version has been lost beyond all recovery. In the attempt to find the correct original version, the editor is forced to make numerous impossible decisions between forms of equal validity" (Jeffreys and Jeffreys 1971:159).

Medievalists and Byzantinists have come to question the very applicability of classical textual criticism to such texts (e.g., Robinson 1996; Jeffreys 1996), or its usefulness (Beaton 1996:218; Robinson 1997). It appears that restoration is still possible for many works, however, particularly as we are still dealing for the most part not with retellings but with identifiable variants of a single written prototype: the manuscripts of the *Tale,* for instance, are nowhere near as heterogeneous as those of the *Belisariad,* let alone *Digenes*. This makes it possible for editions of single manuscript versions to be condemned as bad form.[141]

The difficulties in identifying the right reading mean that different editors will make different decisions. This also takes place in classical texts, but the differences between readings here are much more noticeable. According to classical textual criticism, each manuscript should be considered equally as a valid witness of the original text (unless it has been ruled out as a copy of another surviving manuscript). Tsavare's *Book of Birds,* for example—as Jeffreys (1996:44) finds, the only medieval vernacular Greek edition between 1987 and 1996 to attempt a fully stemmatic treatment of its text—picks and chooses between its manuscripts (*selectio*) without any overt bias other than avoiding the two latest manuscripts. However, there is a perceived intractability of composing a full-fledged stemma and the risk of stemmatic reconstruction leading to a linguistically anachronistic text, as readings from manuscripts of different dates are combined. This has led to a tendency for editions of Byzantine vernacular texts to revisit the old-fashioned practice of treating some manuscripts more equally than others and to pick one manuscript as the basis for an edition (*codex optimus*). Though this has been in the past a matter of convenience, it is advocated explicitly by Jeffreys (1996:44) as a way out of the stemmatic impasse for cases where a single such "best" manuscript is identifiable. It is also not at all unusual for editors to admit their inability to formulate a single critical text and to give different redactions in parallel in their edition instead; for example, Bakker and van Gemert's four-way edition of the *Belisariad* (1988), or Trapp's synoptic edition of *Digenes* (1971). Because the individual manuscript deviations can be appreciable, it is often preferable to publish them all than to suppress them in favor of a single text; the retellings of the story are often no less interesting than the putative original telling of the story.[142]

It seems, however, that the manuscripts of the *Tale* do allow a single critical text to be derived. There are deviations between the two families of manuscripts—P on the one hand and the other four manuscripts on the other—but they are relatively small. With the exception of the "elephants prefer blondes" interpolation in C (927a–g), the donkey by the brook (685–88), and the herbivores' call to assembly in P (40–54; see appendix 3), they do not extend any further than the insertion here and there of a redundant verse. Indeed, Jeffreys and Jeffreys (1983:316) are inclined to believe that the epic bestiaries are unlikely to display traits of oral transmission because their episodic structure has been so well preserved in the surviving manuscripts—without any of the jumbling and lacunae characteristic of, for example, the manuscripts of Sachlikis. (So also Eideneier 1983:227.) Indeed, they note that "it is interesting that Eideneier (1982) finds so much oral influence in such unpromising material."

The manuscripts of both the *Book of Birds* and the *Tale* are consistent in the sequence of monologues they contain. This is all the more remarkable for the *Book of Birds,* because its structure of fourteen accusation–counteraccusation pairs is so modular: a pair could have easily fallen out in transmission without being missed. As discussed in appendix 3, it has been argued that a disruption in the exchange between the fox and the dog is observable in the *Tale.* But this putative disruption is present in all the manuscripts and is (for lack of better evidence) authorial. The obvious conclusion is that the *Tale* and the *Book* were transmitted in written form, whatever other manifestation orality may have had in their history. The scribes may have felt free to modernize a word here or improvise a cussword there, but the confusion of the text evident in other vernacular works is absent in this case. (All significant textual variations have been remarked on in the Textual Notes.)

Eideneier (1982:302–5), in his study (a significant contribution to our knowledge of how the *Tale* and *Book* are built up), also points out the frequent variation between manuscripts, where words are replaced by synonymous expressions. This leads him to the conclusion that the manuscripts are "transcriptions of works devised for oral delivery"—namely, that such replacements as πᾶσα ἑνός for τοῦ καθενός in verse 66, where both mean "of each one," or ἄτυχε, "unfortunate," by ἄθλιε, "miserable," in 588, necessitate distinct oral performances where the bard remembered and reconstructed the verse differently. As Beaton (1996:179–82) has showed, that is not necessarily the case: the scribes could easily have been bards, or at least in contact with the bardic tradition, and have taken it on themselves to make such variations on paper rather than orally.[143] Indeed, the relatively minor scope of divergences strongly suggests it all did happen on paper; oral transmission lasting over two centuries, from around 1364 to around 1625, could be reasonably expected to have wreaked much more havoc on the overall structure of the text than can be observed. And as Eideneier (1982:304) acknowledges for the hapax legomena compound invectives, their consistent preservation in the poem in almost all cases displays a conscious "attempt to retain a stable text."

Somewhat more problematic for a theory of written transmission are errors where a word is replaced not by a synonym but by a soundalike. For example, although manuscripts C, L, and P give in verse 6 the reading μεθ' ἡμῶν, "with us" ("when all the nations draw *with us* false peace"), V interprets this as μὲ θυμόν, "with anger," an exact soundalike—which also happens to fit the context logically. But many of these instances can be dismissed: vernacular scribes' command of historical Greek orthography was often shaky, especially when they had to deal with the vernacular language's grammatical innovations, and knowing themselves all too well the kind of liberties scribes took with texts, they would have felt perfectly entitled to emend the text before them.

In addition, soundalikes are a typical error in the transmission of classical as well as vernacular works. The scribes may be presumed to be internally dictating to themselves, rather than necessarily having the text dictated to them.[144] The potential for error thus introduced would be magnified in an idiom without an established written norm or orthography, so soundalikes are immaterial to deciding whether transmission was oral or written.[145] In this case, for example, it is as likely that the scribe of the Viennese manuscript misread μεθ' ἡμῶν to himself as it is that he misheard it from another, and it is as likely that he misheard it dictated as that he misheard it recited. Similarly, where CVL have ἰσχύν, "power," in verse 10 ("For God shares *power* out"), P has εὐχήν, "prayer, blessing"; the two words sound alike, but it is likelier that the scribe of the Parisian manuscript, none too perspicaciously, emended the text to make God give out something more stereotypically associated with Him.

And there are times when the text becomes hopelessly garbled, in a way difficult to associate with oral transmission. For example, Eideneier (1993) and Papathomopoulos (2002) believe that the original reading for verse 186 was something like V's ν' ἁλίσκωσα, "seized." This obscure verb proved too much for the work's copyists. P gives it as ναχήσβωσα, which is meaningless; C has ν' ἀλήσβωσα, which is little better. And the modernizing manuscript L gives up entirely and replaces it with νὰ πήδησα, "jumped" (the reading that Tsiouni adopted in her edition). Gibberish like ναχήσβωσα is far likelier to originate in faulty copying than in any transcription of an oral performance; it is even less likely to have survived from mouth to mouth.

Formulas

The *Tale* as it stands contains a number of formulas; these have been analyzed by both Šandrovskaja (1956b) and Eideneier (1982). The most characteristic such cliché in the *Tale* is the expression μικροί τε καὶ μεγάλοι, "both great and small," which occurs nine times in the poem in its various permutations of case and gender. This particular formulaic expression, especially useful in that it constitutes a heptameter hemistich (half-verse), is prevalent in all early modern Greek vernacular literature.[146]

Other formulas particular to the *Tale* are "stood in center stage" (ἐστάθην εἰς τὸ μέσον) (nine times), "clean and useful" (καθαρὰ καὶ εὔχρηστα) to refer to herbivores (four times), and "my/your merits and advantages" (καλὰ καὶ τ' ἀγαθὰ τὰ ἔχω/ἔχεις) (three times). The formulas are noticeable on reading the poem, but as our following statistical investigation establishes, they are nowhere near as dense as is characteristic of oral poetry or, for that matter, Homer. Neither are they as distinctive or poetical; indeed, just as μικροί τε καὶ μεγάλοι is little more than a conventional medieval Greek way of saying "all" in a hemistich,[147] so, too, ἐστάθην εἰς τὸ μέσον is clearly a conventional way in the *Tale* of marking the entry of a new quadruped. There is not even the formula τί νὰ σὲ λέγω τὰ πολλά, "why should I tell you much = to make a long story short," characteristic of the *Chronicle of Morea* (Jeffreys 1973:179) and the *War of Troy* (Papathomopoulos and Jeffreys 1996:lxxxv).[148] The use of ἐστάθην εἰς τὸ μέσον is an instance of the episodic use of formulas—though nowhere near as extensive as in the *Book of Birds*—but there is no evidence of formulaic composition comparable to the way the *Chronicle of Morea* may be said to be formulaic.

The *Tale* also features expressions used as formulas elsewhere in Byzantine literature, though they do not occur repeatedly in it. For example, μετὰ χαρᾶς μεγάλης, "with great joy," (704) is one of the main formulas of the *War of Troy* (Jeffreys and Jeffreys 1979:119; Papathomopoulos and Jeffreys 1996:lxxxiv), and καὶ παλαμέα κρούει τον, "and he struck him with his palm," (1052) is reminiscent of the chivalric formula καὶ κονταρεὰν τοῦ ἔδωκεν, "and he struck him with the lance" (Jeffreys and Jeffreys 1979:132). And as Eideneier (1991:47) points out, the repeated [τότε] νὰ εἶδες, "[then] you should have seen," of the *Tale,* which also turns up in *Ptochoprodromos* (1.212, 4.224), might "belong to the toolkit of any bard."[149] All this establishes, however, is that the *Tale* was conceived in the same milieu as the other vernacular texts.

This is an inevitable consequence of the fact that formulas traveled from work to work. In fact, the version of *Father Wine* contained in manuscript V of the *Tale* interpolates as its first verse "My lords, you should all know, both great and small" (Ἄρχοντες, νὰ ἠξεύρετε, μικροί τε καὶ μεγάλοι)—a verse absent in the other manuscripts of *Father Wine* and somewhat out of place in context. This means that the scribe of V may well have transported it from works like the *Tale* into his text of *Father Wine.* And as Jeffreys and Jeffreys (1983:334) report, μικροί τε καὶ μεγάλοι frequently appears in the Greek translation of the *War of Troy,* whereas the French original merely has "all." So such formulas were available to scribes and to translators for their own modification of the texts they transmitted. Because a formula such as μικροί τε καὶ μεγάλοι could travel from text to text, there is no guarantee that all its occurrences are authorial; they could easily have been multiplied by the text's scribes. (The extraneous intrusion of the "center stage" formula by CVLA in 281 is good evidence of this: see Textual Notes.)

Likewise, Eideneier's detailed studies (1982, 1983) of the language of both the *Book* and the *Tale* have found that verbatim repetition of formulas in the texts is almost nonexistent—in contrast to highly formulaic texts such as the *Chronicle of Morea.* Moreover, Eideneier finds that the phrases that are repeated verbatim are more akin to archaistic clichés than authentically oral verse formulas. The formula μικροί τε καὶ μεγάλοι, "both great and small," is in fact an excellent illustration of this (Eideneier 1982:302): τε, "and," had died out in spoken Greek centuries before—according to Jannaris (1897:§1708), by A.D. 600. Such expressions are thus not in themselves sufficient evidence of oral composition. (This has been a criticism on the part of both Eideneier and Beaton of the most prevalent formulas pointed to in Jeffreys and Jeffreys' research.)

A statistical study of the *Tale* confirms these findings. This is done here after the methodology prescribed in Jeffreys' study (1973) of the Copenhagen *Chronicle of Morea* and the Byzantine learned poetical version of the *Alexander Romance.*[150] Jeffreys finds the strongly formulaic *Chronicle of Morea* to be 32 to 38 percent formulas (peaking at 53 percent in the span of verses 8801–8900), whereas the learned *Alexander Romance* is only 9 to 13 percent formulas. He also finds (Papathomopoulos and Jeffreys 1996:lxxxi) a density of around 35 percent characteristic of most of the *War of Troy.* The corresponding counts for the *Tale* are given in Table 2.

It is typical in studies of formulaic usage in texts to give a sample of text with the formulas highlighted. We do this in appendix 6 for verses 601–700 of the *Tale,* where the formulas are present in a density closest to that for the poem overall.[151]

The *Tale* is clearly on the low end of formula density. Although any threshold is necessarily arbitrary, Jeffreys (1973:191) reports that Lord sets the limit for a genuine oral composition as distinct from a literary imitation at 25 percent, whereas Duggan (whose work on French romances Jeffreys emulated) sets it at 20 percent; Duggan's (1973:23) least repetitious romance, *Buevon de Conmarchis,* was 15 percent formulas, and his most formulaic, the *Prise d'Orange,* was 39 percent formulas. The *Tale* aligns not with the *Prise* but with *Buevon*: its use of formula is likely not the usage of an oral text or even the *Chronicle of Morea* (for which an oral origin is highly unlikely) or the *War of Troy* (for which it can be definitely ruled out). Of course, one should not overvalue the statistic; thematic coherence in a text increases the likeliness of repetition (as Jeffreys [1973:182], in fact, found likelier for the *Alexander Romance* than for the *Chronicle of Morea*), and a poem like the *Chronicle* has far more narrative

Table 2. Formula Density in the *Tale*.

Verses	*No. of Hemistichs*	*Certain Repetitions*	*Possible Repetitions*	*% Certain*	*% Overall*
1–100	202	51	10	25	30
101–200	200	37	10	18	23
201–300	204	25	6	12	15
301–400	200	25	16	12	20
401–500	200	20	11	10	15
501–600	202	55	8	27	31
601–700	208	30	11	14	20
701–800	202	50	8	25	27
801–900	202	48	6	24	27
901–1000	206	34	4	17	18
1001–82	164	21	3	13	15
All	**2,190**	**396**	**93**	**18**	**22**

coherence than the *Tale,* which owes much of its formulaic repetition to physiological resemblances between animals. Nonetheless, the result is consistent with what we argue in the next section: the *Tale* is not oral in origin.

Origin

There are only two Byzantine poems whose oral origin is not in doubt: the *Lay of Armoures* and the *Sons of Andronicus,* which are almost certainly transcriptions of ballads from the Akrites cycle. The remainder, it is typically assumed, are of written origin, whether they were transmitted in written or oral form. Thus, Mohay (1974–75:177) appeals to verse 2 of the *Tale*'s explicit mention of reading ("for youngsters, students, and young men to read [ἀναγινώσκωνται]") and verse 4's mention of writing ("as written [γέγραπται] to draw out and stir up learning") as counterevidence to orality. However, the authenticity of the prologue has been questioned, so this evidence needs to be set aside. Verse 2 certainly speaks for written *transmission*—but for that matter, so does the very existence of five manuscripts of the *Tale.* And it is counterbalanced within the prologue by verse 10a, "let me set forth this tale"—in the Greek λέξω, "I will speak." Verse 4 makes the written origin of the poem explicit and is attested in the *Tale*'s two oldest manuscripts, C and P. Even if the prologue is inauthentic, it would still indicate that someone not far removed from the origin of the poem, either in time or in social environment, considered it to have been initially written rather than spoken.

The structure of the *Tale* is repetitive in a way reminiscent of oral poems. For example, the structural similarity of the carnivores' and the herbivores' assembly shows the poet reusing his material, and the two embassies are similarly formulated, down to each having a member for odd jobs and ridicule (the monkey and the camel, respectively.) The rat in his announcement anticipates the lion's order to assembly (59–66, 93–102). The wording of the transition between dialogues is formulaic, and there are recurring phrases in the descriptions and catalog. However, although an oral poem cannot resemble a written poem, a written poem can easily emulate an oral poem, particularly if there is no other model available to a poet for writing in the vernacular.[152] And we have already seen, in "Fact and Fiction in the *Tale*'s Zoology"and "The Author of the *Tale,*" ample evidence for the author's literacy.

By contrast, formulas actually identifiable from modern folk song, though extant in the vernacular romances, are much less frequent than the types of formula that Jeffreys and Jeffreys have identified (Beaton 1996:178–79). As mentioned earlier, Beaton concludes that such formulas thus represent not archaic grammatical survivals in extant oral use ("real" oral formulas being infrequent) but instead artificial emulations of oral verse formulas. Indeed, the kind of expressions used in the *Tale* are hardly impressive as formulas and are more akin to literary clichés; again, this suggests written rather than oral origin (see "Formulas"). Such a case may also be made for the *Tale*'s compounds (see "Compounds"), although it must be said that these are not as obviously literary as their counterparts in the romances. And as shown, the frequency of formulas in the *Tale* is not enough to characterize it as oral.

An oral prototype, finally, is highly unlikely as a motivation for the conflation of genres in the *Tale*. There are ample folk precedents for both the convention of animals and the burlesque treatment of barnyard happenings. Indeed, in the Cypriot songs discussed in "Survivals of the *Tale,*" we even see animals succinctly praising their meat and wool. But nothing in oral literature matches the avalanche of functions detailed by the poet, and there would be no clear motivation for an oral poet to devise such a compendium. The *Tale* may have drawn extensively on folklore, but it is itself, in structure and intent, a product of the scriptorium.

Language

Just as Latin was the language that intellectuals used in the medieval West, medieval Greek scholars studiously avoided the vernacular of their time and used an idiom emulating any one of three prestige dialects: Homeric Greek, the Attic Greek of the classics, or the Koine Greek of the New Testament and the Roman state. The vernacular was considered beneath contempt and was not used for any scholarly endeavor until the nineteenth century. As seen, the first timid attempts at a vernacular written literature in Greek were made only in the twelfth century, with the works of Glycas and *Ptochoprodromos*.

By the fourteenth century, when the *Tale* is presumed to have been written, a strong corpus of vernacular literature had formed. Yet the language used was not a pure vernacular and did not become so until the seventeenth century—

by which time the last copyists of medieval works were themselves modernizing the language they used. (Witness the Lesbian manuscript of the *Tale,* described in "Manuscripts.") The language used is mixed, with persisting elements of archaic Greek known to have died out in the vernacular (such as old noun declensions and the use of the dative). It has been frequently pointed out (e.g., Beck 1971:7; Browning 1983:8; Beaton 1996:93; Horrocks 1997:276) that such a mixture was inevitable at a time when whoever was literate was literate in classical Greek. With no models of vernacular writing to follow and a deep conviction in the merit of classical Greek over the vernacular, the temptation to at least sprinkle the text with shibboleths of a more "correct" idiom was irresistible.

This occurred even though authors frequently did not know enough classical Greek to do the job successfully. The *Chronicle of Morea,* for instance, is notorious for its misdeclined archaic nouns and its clumsy overuse of classical discourse particles. Although this is not as endemic a characteristic of the *Tale,* there are occasional hypercorrections: μεγαλάπτην for μεγαλαύτην, "big-eared" (44, 327), or the accusative use of the nominative form in τὸν λέων, (1008—although the correct τὸν λέοντα occurs in 866). And among the discourse particles, γάρ, "because," (occurring 33 times in the text) is used hypercorrectly as a filler—for example, in verses 614 and 968.

The admixture of archaic elements pervades both the vocabulary and morphology of the *Tale.* The provenance of archaic influence varied with the level of education and aspirations of the Byzantine writer: the heavy guns of Homer and Attic would be brought out by self-conscious intellectuals, whereas a humbler author would be satisfied with Koine.

The *Tale* appears to draw its higher diction from Koine alone. The word νευρώνω, "fasten a sinew to a bow," (625) can be explained by the Homeric use of νεῦρον to mean "string fastening the head of the arrow to the shaft" (*Iliad* 4.151). But the use of νεῦρον as "sinew" had survived in Greek (see Commentary, verse 624), and with sinews remaining a ready source of cord, the verb would be formed autonomously. The Homeric word πτώξ, "hare," (335) (*Iliad* 17.676) is cited as "literary" (γραφικῶς); it is unintegrated into the poem.

The potential for classical diction is no more promising. For example, the use of ἀστεῖον (65) (<ἄστυ, "city") to mean "civil, urbane" has an impeccable Attic pedigree, having been used in that way by Plato (*Phaedo* 116d), but in the *Tale* it seems likelier to bear its later meaning of "amusing" (see Commentary). The word used for "fishing," ἄγραν τῶν ἰχθύων (629), occurs in Homer for hunting (*Odyssey* 22.306) and in Sophocles for fishing (*Ajax* 880). But though the word is absent from the standard modern vernacular, it seems to have been part of the medieval vernacular after all, because Koukoules (1947–55:5.389) reports the word surviving in the island of Nisyros as ἄγρη. And the word is used in Aesop (e.g., in fables 13 and 21) and in Luke 5:4, in both cases with reference to fishing. The word for "boast" in 422, ἐμεγαλαύχησας, is Aeschylan (*Persians* 533, *Agamemnon* 1528)—but also turns up in Psalms 9:39.

And although εὐωχία, "good cheer, feast," in 71 is used by Aristophanes (*Acharnians* 1009; *Frogs* 85) and gave most copyists of the *Tale* trouble, it also turns up in Aesop (fables 47 and 80) and the Septuagint.[153] So in all these cases, the author could have learned these words in his humbler, Koine reading.

Koine antecedents for the archaisms of the *Tale,* on the other hand, are plentiful, and Attic words turning up in the *Tale* are best explained as reflecting rather Koine sources, as already seen with ἄγραν and ἐμεγαλαύχησας. The formulaic use of (ἀπο/προσ)φθέγξατο, "he uttered," for example (thirteen instances in the *Tale*), is matched by the use of the verb in the New Testament and the Septuagint (twenty-seven instances). And in some cases, the word used in the *Tale* bears only the meaning it acquired in Koine and not its original, classical meaning. For example, the use of the passive ὑπεραίρομαι to mean "exalt oneself" (152), as opposed to its classical meanings "to be lifted over" or "to excel," is no earlier than St. Paul (2 Corinthians 12:7).[154] And as we establish in our Commentary to verse 681, the poem's use of κάθαρμα as "freak" rather than "villain" is likewise better explained by appeal to Koine rather than classical Greek—in particular, the *Life of Aesop*.[155]

Only three words might be considered bona fide learned, other than the cited πτώξ. The Attic ἀγχίνοια, "sagacity," (114) is absent from both the Septuagint and the New Testament. The word is present in Aesop (*Fables* 39b) and the earlier versions of the *Alexander Romance* (α 1.24.4, 3.23.8, 3.27.9; β 3.23, 3.27)—but not the vernacular versions and not version ε, which is the version it seems the author had read to get his information on the elephant (see "The *Alexander Romance*"). The word was obscure enough to be glossed in Byzantine dictionaries (*Lexicon in orationes Gregorii Nazianzeni; Pseudo-Zonaras; Lexica Segueriana: Glossae rhetoricae, Collectio verborum utilium*), and its use once by Aesop (who also uses the adjective ἀγχινούστερος, "more sagacious," in fable 143) may not be enough to make it a truly Koine word. Still, the author could easily have learned the word from Aesop and would have readily been able to look it up in the same dictionaries where he found πτώξ. By itself, ἀγχίνοια is not sufficient to prove any real familiarity with Attic on the part of the author.

The second such word is νέμω, "to share out" (10). This verb was used in ancient Greek to mean both "share" (Liddell–Scott–Jones 1940, s. v., A) and "graze" (Liddell–Scott–Jones 1940, s. v., B). In Koine, it seems only the latter sense survived: "graze" and the related sense "dwell" are the only meanings with which the verb is used in the main corpus of Aesop's fables[156] and in the Septuagint (e.g., Exodus 34:3: καὶ τὰ πρόβατα καὶ αἱ βόες μὴ ***νεμέσθωσαν*** πλησίον τοῦ ὄρους ἐκείνου, "neither let the flocks nor herds ***feed*** before that mount"), whereas the verb is not used at all in the New Testament. The word is glossed in this sense in Byzantine dictionaries (*Etymologicum Gudianum, Etymologicum Magnum, Lexicon Artis Grammaticae, Suda, Thomas Magister: Ecloga nominum et verborum Atticorum, George Choeroboscus: Epimerismi in Psalmos, Pseudo-Zonaras*), and although it is used elsewhere in vernacular medieval Greek, the only other instance of "share" given in Kriaras 1968–97 is from Ducas (e.g., 24.6: εἰ τίνι ***νέμει*** τὸ κράτος ἡ τύχη, "if Fortune ***grants*** someone power")—a work only somewhat vernacular. The vernacular instances of the word mean instead "dwell," "destroy," and "enjoy." This word is somewhat less easy to explain away, but it is worth noting that it occurs in the prologue, whose authenticity has been called into question (see appendix 3), so it may have been interpolated by someone else. At any rate, the expression Θεός νέμει, "God gives out," (a modification of τύχη νέμει, "Fortune gives out," as seen in Ducas) was used by Byzantine scholars,[157] and the verb is also used in the church (e.g., the Pentecost hymn: Πνοῇ βιαίᾳ γλωσσοπυρσεύτως ***νέμει*** Χριστὸς τὸ θεῖον Πνεῦμα τοῖς Ἀποστόλοις, "With a violent breath Christ ***shares out*** the Holy Spirit in tongues of fire to the Apostles"; or the Good Tuesday *aposticho*n: Δεῦτε, πιστοί, ἐπεργασώμεθα προθύμως τῷ Δεσπότῃ· ***νέμει*** γὰρ τοῖς δούλοις τὸν πλοῦτον, "Come, ye faithful, let us labor willingly for the Lord; for he ***shares out*** riches to His servants"). So one could learn the word in Byzantium without being exposed to classical learning directly.

The third such word is καρυκεία, "casserole" (370). The word is not Attic, being first attested in Plutarch (*Quaestiones conviviales* 644b), but like the sauce from which it is derived, καρύκη, its reference is classical. (The original καρύκη was a Lydian sauce made of blood and spices.) Koukoules (1947–55:5.43–47) does not adduce any contemporary attestation of καρύκη or καρυκεία after the seventh century, and the stem is glossed in Byzantine dictionaries: the *Suda,* the *Etymologicum Gudianum,* and *Lexica Segueriana: Collectio verborum utilium.* It is also glossed in the Scholia on Lucian (17.11, 25.54). Because the word needed to be glossed, it was probably no longer in use in late Byzantium—whereas by contrast, early scholia (*Scholia in Aelium Aristidem* Tett, 187.12) use the word itself as a gloss. This is also the only instance of the stem in vernacular medieval Greek recorded in Kriaras 1968–97. It should be pointed out that P has instead the commonplace word μαγειρείαν, "cookery"; καρυκείαν is the *lectio difficilior,* but one cannot rule out the scribe of the prototype of CVLA, eager to show off his learning, plugging in a word still current in learned writing (it was used by Constantine VII Porphyrogennetus, Michael Psellus, Anna Comnena, and Nicetas Choniates). In fact, Papathomopoulos in his edition (which we have used) has chosen not to adopt καρυκεία as a reading.

Still, even this much antique diction in the *Tale* is restricted to abstractions and verbs: when the author needs to name something concrete (with the possibly inauthentic exception of καρυκεία), he is consistently vernacular. This clearly differentiates the vernacular texts from the intellectual mainstream of Byzantium, which uniformly called a spade *ye olde scoevel.* For example, the *Tale* and other vernacular texts have no compunction in referring to sultans and emirs with Asiatic words (Σουλτάνοι, Ἀμιράδες). By contrast Cantacuzene, anxious not to deviate from the lexicon of Thucydides, referred to Emir Orhan, son of Osman the founder of the Ottoman Empire, as Ὀρχάνης δὲ ὁ τῶν αὐτόθι [= κατὰ τὴν Βιθυνίαν] Περσῶν σατράπης, "Orchanes the satrap of the Persians in Bithynia" (*Historiae* 1.342). And although Cantacuzene at least makes the concession of calling the sultan of Egypt Σουλτᾶν, *Soultan* (e.g., *Historiae* 3.90), the pro-Ottoman Michael Critobulus and the detached Laonicus Chalcocondyles not only refuse to use the Arabic word in their histories of the fall of Constantinople but go so far as to speak of the *Basileus* Mehmet II (*Critobulus: Historiae* 4.4.3, etc.; *Chalcocondyles: Historiae* 2.295.13, etc.).[158]

Similarly, none of the many household or military objects arrayed in the *Tale* is given a classical name when a distinct vernacular word is available. Unlike learned Byzantines, the author has no compunction in using loanwords from outside Greek. By way of illustration, the description of the horse's array in battle (759–63) includes alongside the Greek (χρυσο)πετάλιν, "(golden) horseshoe" (from a word that in classical Greek meant "leaf"), three loans from Latin (ἐντελιμπροστέλινα < *antellina* + *postilena,* "front and rear straps"; σέλας < *sella,* "saddle"; χαλιναροκαπίστελα < χαλινάριν + *capistrum,* "bridle and halter") and one from Arabic (χριμιζίν < *qirmisi,* "crimson"). Even the one noun in the passage to have survived with its meaning intact from classical Greek, (βροντο)κούδουνα, "thunderous bells," has had its vowels change from the classical form κώδων. Likewise, the sheep's description of nobles' and clerics' clothing (500–509) contains three loans from Venetian (τζαλούνια < *zalo,* "yellow"; σκαρλάτα < *scarlato,* "scarlet"; γρίζα < *griso,* "gray"), one from Latin (ῥάσα < *rasum,* "cassock"), and three compounds where part of the word is foreign: one from Latin (ὑποκάμισα < ὑπό, "under" + *camisia,* "shirt"), one from Turkish (τζοχοϋφανδωμένα, "woven with serge" < *çuha* + ὑφαίνω, "woven"), and one from Celtic or Slavonic (γουνοεσωφόρια, "fur petticoat" < *gun(n)a* + ἐσωφόριν, "petticoat").

The language of the narrative of the *Tale*—both in vocabulary and grammar—is differentiated from that of the dialogues. The motivation for this is clear: the narrative voice needs to be distanced from the invective and vulgarity of the animals and to be framed as more conventional discourse. The fact that the narrative links between the dialogues are rife with stereotypical expressions goes a long way toward establishing this differentiation. For example, though 785 of the 1,095 verses of Papathomopoulos's edition are dialogue, the classical absolute genitive construction occurs four times in the narrative (29, 50, 314, 1075), and zero times in the dialogue; for instance, καθίσαντων οὖν τοῦ βοὸς ἅμα μὲ τὸ βουβάλιν, "And so the ox sat by the buffalo" (50). Similarly, there are eight datives in the narrative (11, 12, 197, 320, 352, 935, 1078, 1079) but only three in dialogue (the cliché κοινῷ τῷ λόγῳ, "it's common knowledge" [756] and two instances of μοι, "to me," in 539 and 610). And of the forms of adjectival participles obsolete in modern Greek (active and passive aorist), thirty-six occur in narrative (e.g., Συναθροισθέντων δὲ ὁμοῦ καὶ προκαθεζομένων, "So having all assembled and sat down" [29]) but only fourteen in dialogue (e.g., καὶ ψεύδεσθε, κομπώνετε τοὺς ἀκούοντας πάντας, "In this you lie, deceiving all who hear you" [362]). In general, the syntax of the animals' speeches is much simpler, too: the seemly conjunctions and participles of the narrative are replaced by highly colloquial parataxis (clauses joined by *and*) and quite simple subordinations and relativizations. This is counterbalanced with more archaic vocabulary in the prologue and formulaic transitions—particularly the words for *say*.

Though the battle is told by the narrator, the action-packed struggle there, too, demands language as straightforward as in the disputations—whose natural continuation the battle is; thus the battle is likewise in the vernacular. Indeed, the linguistic switch back to a formal register takes place only at verse 1075—the genitive absolute in Ἡλίου βασιλεύοντος, "as the sun crowned the horizon"; the participle in 1077 (τὸ ῥηθὲν διὰ τοῦ ὑμνογράφου, "that said by the Psalmist"); the dative and simple future in the biblical citation immediately following (ἐν τῇ πολλῇ δυνάμει, "in much strength," and σωθήσεται, "will be saved"). This signals a resumption of the authorial distancing, right at the conclusion of the work; order is restored linguistically, just as it is in the animal kingdom.

Notwithstanding the tendency of different levels of language to be used in different contexts, the language of the *Tale,* like the language of vernacular medieval poetry in general, is mixed. The differentiation between the two levels cannot be overstated in any case, as there is archaism still going on in the dialogues. For example, the ancient discourse connective γάρ is very much at home in the animals' discourse (thirty of the thirty-three instances), and the dialogues also include archaic futures (φθέγξομαι [359]) and perfects (τετιμημένον [301], μεμιγμένον [853], κέκτησαι [939]).[159] The contrast can be abrupt within a single segment; for example, the stately language of the introduction, with its participles and postmodifying adjectives, is interrupted by modernisms such as ἀποφουμιστάδας (22), φουντοουραδάτη (27), and μεγαλομουστακᾶτον (34). Similarly, the boar's outburst to the deer (353–59) is thoroughly vernacular but includes archaisms such as ἀείποτε (355) and, in a characteristic formula, the old future φθέγξομαι and the old demonstrative τούσδε (359). And there are several instances where the old and new words are conjoined as synonyms; for example, the parallel use of ἐσθίω and τρώγω, "eat," in 297 and 475; ἀνεντήρητος and ἄφοβος, "fearless," in 319; βρώματα and ταγισερά, "food," in 673a; or μεμονωμένον and μοναχόν for "alone" in 831. This admixture can come across as macaronic: the *Tale* in some instances moves toward sounding classical and in others toward sounding colloquial but never quite actually sounds like either. The *Tale* has a sound all of its own, and its very inconsistency—echoed in later times by Greek writers such as Papadiamantis, Cavafy, and Embirikos—forms an integral part of its charm.

Meter

The *Tale* is written in iambic heptameter, known in Byzantium as *politikos* and in modern Greece as *dekapentasyllabos,* the verse form par excellence of vernacular Greek poetry from the tenth to the twentieth centuries (Jeffreys 1974). The verse features a strong caesura (midverse break) between the eighth and ninth syllables; the break is always lexical as well as metrical and usually also syntactic and semantic. As a result, the hemistich (half-verse) is prominent in Greek verse-building: the formulaic building blocks of Byzantine vernacular verse typically span a hemistich, and indeed there are frequently two variants of the same formula, one to fit into the first hemistich and one to fit into the second. Greek verse is also structured around repetition between hemistichs, with the second hemistich frequently echoing the first. Examples from the *Tale* include the following:

εἰς κάμπον ὡραιότατον, εἰς ὁμαλίαν μεγάλην 64
a fairest plain, a large and spacious valley

ἐσθίουν με οἱ βασιλεῖς, τρώγουν με οἱ ῥηγάδες 297
it is the kings and emperors who eat me
("the emperors consume me, the kings eat me")

πῶς ἐπολυλογήσασιν, πῶς ἐμακρυλογῆσαν 552
have babbled at great length and greater verbiage
("how they have spoken a lot, how they have spoken at length")

The caesura is also a structuring element in the poem's use of epithets. For example, the caesura is used to balance instances of parallelism:

ὁ πάντα τρώγων βρώματα καὶ πάντα κατεσθίων 26
consuming and devouring any foodstuff
("eating all foods and consuming all")

εἰπέ με, μαυροπείσματε, εἰπέ, ψωλογομάριν 665
Tell me, you bloody-spited Dick-O-Matic,
("tell me, black-spited one, tell, dick-burden")
πῶς σὲ φορτώνουν, ἄτυχε, πῶς σὲ ῥαβδοκοποῦσι
tell me how people burden you, poor fool! Tell me how people flog away at you!
("how they burden you, unfortunate, how they keep flogging you")

There are typically three epithets in a verse, of which the first two occupy the first half of the verse and the third, the second half:

Μακρύουρε, μακρόμυτε, μεγαλομουστακᾶτε 127
You long-tailed, long-nosed, and long-whiskered fool!

τζυκαλογλεῖφε, τυροφᾶ καὶ ψωμοκαταλύτη 130
pot-licking cheese-munching bread-squanderer!

Σὺ δὲ αἰσχρέ, παμμίαρε, *But you, you shameful, filthy*	ἀλευροκαταχέστη *flour-shitter,*	159
μαγγαναρέα, μιαρή, *swindling . . . loathsome . . .*	κοιλιοχορδοφᾶσα *innards-devouring*	286

This configuration is typical of the modern Greek folk song "rule of three" in its use of the heptameter: three related notions are presented, often with syntactic parallelism and the repetition of a key word, of which the third is greater than the first two and constitutes the rhetorical focus. Accordingly, the first two are crammed into a hemistich each, and the third gets a verse of its own, or the first two are crammed into one hemistich and the third into the second:

Γυναίκεια φόρεια φόρεσε, *It wore a woman's clothes,*	γυναίκεια πασουμάκια, *a woman's slippers,*	9
γυναίκεια ἐβγῆκε κ᾽ ἔκατσε νὄξω ᾽ς τὸ πεζοδρόμι. *and in a woman's form sat by the footpath.*		
καὶ ποιὸς νὰ μπῇ, καὶ ποιὸς νὰ βγῇ, *Who'll go in? Who'll come out?*	καὶ ποιὸς νὰ μοῦ τὸ βγάλῃ; *Who'll bring it to me?*	19
—Ἐγὼ νὰ μπῶ, κ᾽ ἐγὼ νὰ βγῶ *—I'll go in, I'll come out,*	κ᾽ ἐγὼ νὰ σοῦ τὸ βγάλω. *I'll bring it to you.* (Politis 1914, §90b)	

The rule of three can also be seen at work in the *Tale* in its larger, hemistich scope:

Χαρά στην τὴν κυρᾶ ᾽λωποῦ, *Well done, my Lady Fox!*	χαρά στην τὴν κορδῶναν, *Well done, my toff!*	270
χαρά στην τὴν μαστόρισσαν καὶ τὴν σοφίστριάν μου *Well done, dear master and philosopher*		

The English meter par excellence used in our translation, the iambic pentameter, does not have an equivalently strong caesura, so this particular structural element is not as prominent in translation.

The Byzantine heptameter was different from its modern Greek equivalent. In particular, it admitted anapestic hemistich beginnings (˘ ˘ ¯), disallowed in the modern meter—usually in the second hemistich. It also had a much greater tolerance of hiatus—adjoining vowels not being glided together into one syllable. And it allowed elision across a caesura (Garantoudis 1993). As a result, Byzantine verse sounds clumsy to modern Greek ears. This compounds the problem that already exists, of the scribes themselves not being too careful in transmitting the meter. The combination of the two has encouraged modern scholars to intervene drastically in their editions of Byzantine texts, often being biased toward manuscript readings that follow the modern Greek model of the meter.

In its meter, the *Tale* shows itself as archaic. Although the *Tale* is one of the texts that do not elide across the caesura (Garantoudis 1993:215), hiatus is frequent. And although anapests vanish from the Greek heptameter after the fifteenth century (Beaton 1996:42) and are absent in the verse of the Cretan Renaissance, they are still quite healthy in the *Tale*. Out of the 1,094 verses of Tsiouni's edition of the *Tale,* 32 are anapestic (i.e., have either the first or second of both hemistichs start with an anapest).[160] In Papathomopoulos's edition, 55 verses out of 1,095 are anapestic.[161] There are 47 more verses with anapests in the manuscripts rejected by Papathomopoulos as readings.[162] This means between 2.9 percent and 9.3 percent of the *Tale*'s verses are anapestic, with the edition we use having 5.0 percent. This is a far cry from the obsessively anapestic Grottaferrata *Digenes.* (Tiftixoglu [1974:43] finds 23 percent of its verses having an anapestic first hemistich; the *Tale* has no more than 3.6 percent anapestic first hemistichs, Tsiouni's edition has 1.3 percent, and Papathomopoulos's edition, 1.8 percent.) Nonetheless, its meter is arguably typical of the time: the vernacular Escorial *Digenes*—depending on how one defines an anapest and to what extent Alexiou's editorial intervention is justified—has between 4 percent and 7 percent of its verses anapestic (Garantoudis 1993:202).[163]

Nine of the anapestic readings in the *Tale* rejected by Papathomopoulos, we should note, were formulated only by the scribe of L, an extremely late manuscript (1625)—subsequent, in fact, to much of the Cretan Renaissance. This suggests that the anapest survived much longer among the scribes of vernacular works than may have been thought—though there are frequent instances, particularly in L (!) and A, when the scribes deliberately mis-stress words in order to avoid anapests (e.g., οὔδε, ALP 412; οὐδέ, CV 412).[164]

Although some of the anapestic verses deserve to be rejected as original—and L's innovations are among them—the anapest is nonetheless clearly part of the conception of the poem and should not be dispensed with. This is a problem with Tsiouni's edition (e.g., her emendation of verses 810 and 831a and her preference for an extrametrical over an anapestic reading in 680), which we believe Papathomopoulos's edition has avoided.

˘ – ˘ ˘ ˘ ˘ ˘ – ˘ – ˘ ˘ ˘ –˘
ὠνείδισες δέ καὶ ἐμὲν τοὺς ὄνους πῶς ἐσθίω 814 Tsiouni

˘ – ˘ ˘ ˘ ˘ ˘ – ˘ ˘ –˘ ˘ – ˘
ὠνείδισας δέ καὶ ἐμὲν πῶς ἐσθίω τοὺς ὄνους
814 Papathomopoulos

and blaming me as one who preys on donkeys
("and you have blamed me, that I eat donkeys")

The past bias against the anapestic heptameter is only one of the instances where medieval Greek verse has suffered from attempts to assimilate it to modern Greek meter (Garantoudis 1993:190–98). This bias has far-reaching effects. For example, Tiftixoglu's survey (1974) of the anapestic heptameter is prompted by the question of whether Theodore Meletiniotes' romance parody *To Chastity* (early *xiv* A.D.) quoted from *Digenes* or vice versa. The Grottaferrata *Digenes* has abundant anapests, whereas *To Chastity* has virtually none; Tiftixoglu (1974:14) concludes that *Digenes* must have come first, because otherwise "we would have to presume an unjustifiable metrical 'worsening,' which . . . besides is unthinkable for the second half of the fourteenth century anyway."[165]

As Koder (1969:87–93, 1972:217–18) and Tiftixoglu (1974:47–58) show, the anapest is an archaic feature of the Greek iambic heptameter, and its heyday was the tenth through the twelfth century. In fact, Jeffreys (1974:182–85), in his history of the heptameter, believes the anapest corresponds to the original form of the verse, deriving from the Roman trochaic *versus quadratus*.[166] Using Tiftixoglu's counts (which involve only anapests in the first hemistich), works written before 1100 tend to have between 3 percent and 5 percent initial anapestic hemistichs, with occasional instances of up to 20 percent. In the late twelfth century, by contrast, initial anapests are absent except in John Camaterus's *Introduction to Astronomy,* which has 7 percent; neither Glycas nor *Ptochoprodromos* (or for that matter Theodore Prodromus) use them. In the fourteenth century, poems vary between 0 percent (*Spaneas, Callimachus and Chrysorrhoe, Book of Birds*) and 2.2 percent (*Belthandros and Chrysantza*).

The anapest was clearly on the way out by the fourteenth century: "It is difficult to avoid the conclusion that a fifteenth-century reader or hearer of this text [the *War of Troy,* which has around 16 percent anapestic first hemistichs and 10 percent anapestic second hemistichs] would have found a noticeable degree of archaism in its meter" (Papathomopoulos and Jeffreys 1996:lxxxviii). But it would be an exaggeration to say that the anapest had died by 1364. For starters, Tiftixoglu and Koder count only initial anapests; by Tiftixoglu's reckoning, the *Tale* has only 1 percent anapestic verses, and our counts corroborate this (Papathomopoulos's edition, as seen, has 1.8 percent). But 1.8 percent is still not 0 percent, which is the proportion of anapests the modern form of the meter allows. And the *Tale* clearly prefers second anapestic hemistichs—presumably as less disruptive to the iambic meter than first hemistich anapests: the iambic beat is established in the first before being suspended in the second. So the anapests are moved into a less prominent position; they have not yet been abolished.[167] The presence of anapests in other contemporary vernacular poems, even at the 1 percent or 2 percent level, means the anapest was still a mechanism available to versifiers.

It is significant that the *Tale*'s original meter be respected, not only because this leads us back to the original wording of the text but also because there is evidence that the author consciously used metrical effects. For instance, most of the anapests (initial or final) found in the *Tale* are scattered, turning up once every thirty or so verses. In two instances in the CV manuscript tradition, however, they are densely packed in—two instances in five verses and three instances in three verses, respectively. These passages are the entry of the wolf (810–14) and the rally of the carnivores to the aid of the fallen cheetah (1037–39). The passages are thematically linked. The wolf has the most brutal words to say in the *Tale*: no other carnivore exudes such unadulterated bloodlust, and his words serve to reintroduce the carnivores to the stage. And the rally of the carnivores is the one instance in the battle where they look like they might win—"bloody and loathsome" as they are. We do not think this is an accident: the author has consciously used an unsettled meter to convey unsettling turns in the *Tale*.[168]

Other such concentrations of anapests occur at the beginning of the poem proper (five to six instances, verses 10–15); the cat caught stealing (three instances, 165–78); the dog beaten to death (two or three instances, 229–36); the boar boasting of his meats (four to nine instances, 360–83); the lion's announcement of battle and the first narration of the battle (one to five instances, 990–99). But for the boar's episode, all of the episodes are either notably violent or (in the case of the beginning of the poem) momentous. In the instance of the battle, it is likely that individual scribes (particularly V and L) took the initiative to augment the number of anapests already there.

Similarly, choriambs (trochaic beginnings of an iambic hemistich: a commonplace metrical license throughout Europe) are packed in to the beginning of the elephant's monologue: five instances in the four verses 906–9, consistently in all the manuscripts. Once again, the subject matter—the stately confidence of the elephant in battle—is mirrored effectively in the choice of meter.

The *Tale* in Modern Times

> Allegory, gnomic declarations of wisdom, parody of affairs important at the time, derisory description—these are some of the components of medieval poetry for which our education has minimally prepared us. After all, such literary categories were destined to retreat gradually in the ensuing centuries, to the point that they were expelled for good from the domain of what constitutes literature.
>
> —M. Vitti, *Ἱστορία τῆς Νεοελληνικῆς Λογοτεχνίας*

The *Tale* as a Source

It has been the fate of vernacular medieval Greek literature to serve during most of its modern career as little more than a quarry for linguistic and historical research. The romances have recovered from this marginalization; it would be premature to say the same for the epic bestiaries.

Accordingly, the *Tale* shows up routinely, along with the remainder of the vernacular corpus, in linguistic surveys of medieval Greek, from Jannaris 1897 to Joseph 1983. But in view of its unusual emphasis on Byzantine everyday life and the strong testimony it yields, the *Tale* has found particularly frequent use as a primary source on Byzantine realia. We need not provide a comprehensive list of the authors who have referred to it in one way or another—although they come up routinely in the secondary literature we have consulted (e.g., Greenfield 1988; Kolias 1988), and even Elizabeth Jeffreys's 200-word description of the *Tale* (Kazhdan 1991, s.v. DIEGESIS TON TETRAPODON ZOON) speaks of "the elements of SATIRE, which incidentally give insights into contemporary culinary practice." We prefer to focus instead on the way it has been mined by the Byzantinist Phaedon Koukoules in his compendium *Βυζαντινῶν Βίος καὶ Πολιτισμός* (*Byzantine Life and Culture*) (1947–55), a source on which we have in turn relied heavily in the present work.

Koukoules' work is a monumental survey of Byzantine realia through the full extant learned and vernacular corpus. Though it falls somewhat short on analysis, its breadth and its reliance—often through personal experience—on folklore now disappearing makes it unlikely to be superseded. As one would expect, the work casts wide for its evidence—including Byzantine legislation, glossaries, sermons, and far from least, narratives like the *Tale*.

In most cases, as the reader will see in our Commentary, Koukoules does not use the *Tale* exclusively but supports its testimony with additional sources, ranging from ancient authors to contemporary personal observation. For example, the *Tale*'s πασπαλᾶς is explicated with reference to contemporary dishes of the same name in Greece (see Commentary, verse 380), whereas the *Tale*'s report of ox hair used in fishing is confirmed from the poetry of Sachlikis (see Commentary, verse 630). In some cases, however, the *Tale* is the unique source adduced. Examples include the use of bear fat to alleviate the pains of "arthritis" (Koukoules 1947–55:5.418) (853; as we discuss in our Commentary, Koukoules misunderstands the disease involved); the otherwise unattested placement of bells on the hunting dog's collar (5.395; not to be confused with the commonplace hawking bells) (254); the casting of taboo meats to the dogs (5.60) (252; see Commentary for questions on this passage); and the use of leopard skin to repel fleas (2.273) (882; Koukoules fails to mention that the belief is indirectly attributed in the *Tale* to Muslims, not Byzantines).

For the most part, Koukoules repeats evidence from the *Tale* without any criticism. But there are a few cases where it seems that he had doubts and the *Tale*'s testimony has been passed over. For example, he states that "the Byzantines used the deer's horns in numerous ways" (5.415) without giving any further details. He thereby fails to mention the legend of its snake-repellent properties. And even a few less controversial testimonies, such as the buffalo's use as a farm animal or the fox's fate in the hands of the tanner and the furrier, have been passed over.

In all, the *Tale* supplies a rich source of information on everyday life at the time, and its descriptions are largely borne out by other sources, as we discuss at various instances in our Commentary. However, Koukoules' exploitation of it has not been as critical as it might have been, and some caution is warranted regarding his conclusions.

Previous Editions and Translations

The last manuscript copy of the *Tale* was made in 1625. We know that manuscripts containing the *Tale* ended up in the libraries of the sultan (C), the sixteenth-century scholar Cardinal William Sirlet (S, now lost), and the seventeenth-century politician Cardinal Jules Mazarin (P), but we cannot be sure that their recipients actually read them. The *Tale* is not included in the corpus that Charles Fresne Du Cange (1958 [1688]) used for his dictionary, although the *Book of Birds* and *Ptochoprodromos* are, and manuscript P had by then been donated to the Royal French library. In all, the *Tale* was ignored until the resurgence of vernacular medieval Greek studies in the nineteenth century.[169]

Though André Gidel published a study on medieval texts including the *Tale* in 1866 (working from the Parisian manuscript), the text of the *Tale* was first published by Wilhelm Wagner in his *Carmina Graeca Medii Aevi* in 1874—the publication that spearheaded this resurgence. Wagner was familiar only with the Parisian and Viennese manuscripts of the work and gave preference to the former as the basis of his edition. Like all the nineteenth-century editions of medieval vernacular works, there are misreadings, bad editorial and metrical choices, and inconsistencies in Wagner's text. But these were inevitable under the circumstances, and Wagner is owed a significant debt as a pioneer in the field. The years following saw editorial and lexical commentaries on the *Tale* by scholars such as Phaedon Koukoules (1911–12), Dirk Hesseling (1924), and Stefanos Xanthoudidis (1911–12, 1927–28); these concentrated on clarifying obscure words, although Xanthoudidis also conscripted the *Tale* into his program of claiming the majority of medieval Greek literature for Crete.

Although Bouboulidis (1964:107) announced a "forthcoming" edition of the *Tale* by G. Protopapa-Bouboulidou[170] and Šandrovskaja (1956a) also promised an edition, nothing further appeared until the edition done by Vasiliki Tsiouni(-Fatsi). This was her 1969 doctoral dissertation at Birbeck College, University of London, under the supervision of Robert Browning; it was nominally published in 1972 by the University of Munich but released in 1975. It is the first treatment of the work to incorporate all five extant manuscripts. Tsiouni's edition incorporates an introduction discussing the manuscripts of the *Tale* and its possible interpretations as well as a grammatical commentary. Though Tsiouni's edition does not incorporate a translation, it has an extensive glossary into English of all postclassical words. Our interpretation of several of these deviates from hers, and we point out these instances in our Commentary.

Although we have relied on Tsiouni's edition for most of the time we have worked on the *Tale,* the edition we use as our base text is Manolis Papathomopoulos's (2002). This edition attempts to tackle the text of the *Tale* on strictly stemmatic terms. In some instances where establishing the text is a matter of *selectio* between the two extant manuscript families, Papathomopoulos and we have profited from discussion with each other; we regard our work as complementary to his. As a result of this discussion, we have no disagreement as to the text serious enough to compel us to deviate from his text in our translation.

Sections of the *Tale* have also been reprinted in Zoras's anthology (1956) of Byzantine poetry and Politis's (1966–67) anthology—in the latter with a few emendations.

There have been three renderings of the *Tale* into other languages. One is Tsiouni's brief summary in English at the beginning of her edition (1972:48–54). This is a succinct rendering, in straightforward prose: the hare is reproached for "exceeding sexuality" (327), for example, and the cheetah "holds the opinion" that the natural order of things is for the nobles to eat the herbivores (1025–26). Little detail of the exchanges is given, but even at this level one may note some differences in interpretation between Tsiouni and us. For instance, Tsiouni depicts the lion appealing to the carnivores and herbivores as distinct parties (28–37); we regard the lion as leader of the carnivores as well as of all animals, so we see no reason to see the lion as sending an embassy to the other carnivores. Tsiouni considers the πάρδος, "pard," a male *panthera* (17–27); we have identified it with the cheetah. Finally, Tsiouni contends the he-buffalo and she-buffalo are distinct animals in the battle (1003–40), a notion we reject as uneconomical (see discussion in appendix 3).

The other two translations predate Tsiouni's edition and rely on specific manuscripts. The first was by André Gidel and involves a more extensive prose summary, in French, of the Parisian manuscript (Gidel 1866:311–22). The summary preserves much of the wording of the text, although not consistently: for instance, it states that "the monarch has conceived of a political project to bring concord amongst the subjects of his empire." And (unsurprisingly at a time when studies in medieval Greek were still nascent) Gidel makes some erroneous surmises in his translation: σκουφᾶδες are rendered as "wearers of hats" rather than "bookbinders," whereas ἀξούγγιν is not the name of the particular ointment made of bear fat ("Do they not make of my fat an ointment called *axonge*?"), as Gidel puts it, but the postclassical Greek word, Latin in origin, for "fat" in general. And the donkey's "mighty dick" is rendered as "longer, thicker, and tougher nerves." Notwithstanding the puritanism of the time, it is easiest to attribute this to an inattentive literal rendering of νεῦρον.

In fact, Gidel's inattentiveness ranges beyond the purely linguistic. Nothing in the text justifies his assertion that the cat, the rat, and the monkey arrive "at a kind of viceroyal territory ruled by the ox and the heifer"; for all the noise the ox and buffalo make later, the world of the herbivores comes across as a republic and not a tightly organized monarchy like the lion's. And in the horse's fable, the donkeys send their request to a king in the text; despite the obvious similarity to the Aesopic fable discussed in "Literary Parallels," there is no mention in the *Tale*'s version of the story of either Mount Olympus or Zeus, which Gidel interpolates into his rendering. Likewise, Gidel (1866:329) says of the *Tale* that "its knowledge of natural history does not go much further; it soon exhausts the few traditions of Aelian on the camel." Aelian, in fact, has a fair few traditions about the camel—for instance, that Bactrian camels live to be a hundred, that the Persians bred camels and horses together, and that camels seek out muddy water to drink.[171] None of these are reflected in the *Tale,* though the last trait, at least, would seem custom-made for the *Tale*'s invective.

The only other instance we know of a complete translation of the *Tale* was undertaken in Russian by V. S. Šandrovskaja (1956a), a complete translation based on the Lesbian, St. Petersburgian, and Viennese manuscripts, though with frequent reference to the Parisian. (Šandrovskaja worked fairly closely with Wagner's edition, as she did not have direct access to the Viennese and Parisian manuscripts, and was unaware of the Constantinopolitan [1956a:221].) But for Šandrovskaja's occasional refusal to render an obscenity, we have been pleasantly surprised by how accurate her rendering is—the more so given its relatively early date within vernacular Byzantine philology. We have appealed to her renderings frequently in the Commentary to our translation. Šandrovskaja also contributed a study of realia referred to in the *Tale* and lexical problems encountered as well as a brief literary analysis (Šandrovskaja 1956b)—which pays more attention to the text as literature than has been usual in the field. Šandrovskaja's work predates contemporary work on the orality of Byzantine texts and thus makes too much of the supposedly Homeric nature of the compounds and epithets in the *Tale* and the epic nature of the bestiary: the beasts do vituperate each other, but it is far-fetched to attribute a Homeric character to their accusations. Nevertheless, Šandrovskaja picks up on the formulaic nature of the text, the mixed nature of the text's language, the political circumstances surrounding its composition, and the stylistic freshness of the work. In all, Šandrovskaja is one of the few researchers who have been well disposed toward the text.

The Reception of the *Tale*

The truth is, this text has occasioned more than its fair share of censure. These started with Gidel himself:

> The style of this poem deserves little praise; it will be found only to have quite mediocre qualities; the language lacks elegance and color. One seeks in vain either depth or the picturesque. The author instills little variety in the manner in which he introduces each person on the stage. The movement is always the same and results in monotony. In the enumeration of the services humans derive from each animal, he

> aims more toward exactitude than grace and occasionally offends against common sense. The poet does not use much discrimination in the details he offers his readers; he prefers to speak all than to speak well. He is humble in his views, familiar in his expression. He is far from giving his actors a speaking voice and expressive attitudes. He has no notion of scenery, and in the entire poem one does not find the least hint of description of where the action unfolds. (1866:329)

All the same, Gidel recognizes the originality in genre of the work within Byzantium, to the point of postulating that the *Tale* must have been inspired by *Renard* (see "Foreign Influences")—being unaware of the *Book of Birds*. Krumbacher is only slightly more positive:

> Its chief merits are coarse spontaneity and a burlesque, often boorish humor. However, the exchanges of the animals suffer from immoderate length, and the introduction of speakers is dominated by a repetitiousness presumably imitating folk song (if not ancient epic), which, however, is tiring in this instance. The scenic background is neglected, and the composition is faulty. (1897:2.878)

Though not literary, Sathas's reading of the *Tale* in 1894 is interesting as an early response (see also appendix 2).

> The satire on the Quadrupeds, related to the *Book of Birds,* depicts wild and tame beasts assembling on the invitation of King Lion, in order to consider the means of mutual assistance and defense against their common enemies. But though they revile one another on their superiority and usefulness, as do the birds in the *Book of Birds,* the perfidious king gives the signal to the other carnivorous beasts to massacre and devour the tame beasts, which have imprudently fallen into their claws. The common danger expels cowardice from the tame beasts, and the victims, assembling strategically for battle, repel the hostile members of their race. (1972 [1872–94]:7.xxxvii)

Knös is somewhat more favorable and remarks on the use of irony in the animals' descriptions:

> If the author in composing his book did not have a properly pedagogical intention for the young, it is not impossible that he had in mind an informative mission, explaining to adults the characteristics of each animal. This he does with some irony, better appreciated by the more adult, and he has the animals deliver speeches full of imagination and folk psychology and not without a certain wit. We encounter the same phenomenon in the numerous Western animal tales that refer to con-

> ventions of animals. But this poem is purely Greek, marked with a somewhat harsh and crude simplicity and naïveté, and a burlesque humor.
>
> From a literary point of view the style is quite mediocre, abounding in detail and lacking in the gift of imagination, but the composition does not lack a certain value. Although the dialogues of the animals are somewhat long and monotonous, the language is expressive and lively, even if it at times makes use of a few learned elements. (1962:152)

More recent appraisals have been more positive. Given how little of value Dimaras finds in most Byzantine vernacular poetry, his appraisal of the *Tale* is positively glowing:

> The unknown author is spirited in his descriptions and his remarks are judicious.. . . Not lacking from the work is a certain quality of folk humor.. . . A sarcastic tone, moreover, which characterizes the recriminations among the animals, becomes witty, and there is great freedom of language. Also, the different parts of the work are more artistically unified. We see a narrative that is linked in a perfectly coherent manner. (1972:45–46)

("These latter qualities," Dimaras goes on to say in the next paragraph, "are lacking from the *Book of Fowl* [Birds].") So, too, Politis, less expansively: "A meeting of all the animals, harmless and bloodthirsty, at the invitation of their king, the lion, is related with much humor.. . . It has vigor and genuine humor, and sometimes is piquant and very free. Humor and wit dominate the descriptive and didactic elements" (1973:36).

The Present Translation

> For example, one wonders how the enraged yet wounded response of James II to the conspirators, "Α, βρε, τούτον είναι αποὺ σας ετίμησα," could possibly have been rendered any better by the phlegmatic British translator ("Oh, fellow, and is this for the honour I did you?") than by the Bulgarian, equivalent in his Oriental frenzy: "А бре, това е, задето ви почетох!"
>
> —G. Kechagioglou, *Τζώρτζης (Μ)πουστρούς (Γεώργιος Βο(σ)τρ(υ)νός ή Βουστρώνιος)*, referring to the translations of the *Chronicle of Bustron* by Richard Dawkins and Petăr Tivčev

Textual Issues

The current translation is a translation of Papathomopoulos's text. As noted, we have no major disagreements with him on the text such as would affect the translation, although there are some matters we raise in the Textual Notes. Because our intent was not to produce a new critical edition of the text and we have not inspected the manuscripts, we have not gone into much detail on these disagreements. We likewise have not intervened in Papathomopoulos's selection of verses to include from the source manuscripts, although we argue in some detail in our Commentary and Textual Notes which verses we think are plausibly original.

On a few occasions, we have added text from C that does not appear in the critical edition to give the reader a flavor of the source manuscript. In particular, we have inserted into the text C's digression on elephants in the boudoir (927a–g), as a significant textual discrepancy, though without any claim as to its authenticity; we have also inserted C's concluding verses and CV's title. These interpolations are in square brackets and italics. There are some other interpolations C makes that Papathomopoulos doubts are authorial but that he has hesitated to actually excise from the text. In both his edition and our translation, such verses are indicated in square brackets, without italics.

Our Textual Notes discuss only the more salient issues that arise in the text and are not intended as a substitute for the critical apparatus in Papathomopoulos 2002 or Tsiouni 1972.

Versification and Lineation

In our translation, we have used iambic pentameter, the dominant English meter just as iambic heptameter is the dominant vernacular Greek meter. The tension between form and content is a familiar preoccupation of poetic translation, and in giving a verse translation we acknowledge that we are running counter to the present-day trend in English, which is to subordinate form wholly to content, particularly in scholarly translation. Betts's prose translation (1995) of the romances represents the rule rather than the exception in contemporary work. Mavrogordato's metrical *Digenes* (1956) is, if anything, looked upon as odd.[172]

In this context, a verse translation needs to be defended. For one, the trend away from verse translation is not a contemporary universal but is largely restricted to English language scholarship—in line with the greater prevalence of free verse in contemporary poetry in English over many other languages. Eideneier (1991), for instance, has recently provided verse translations into German (in heptameter) of the *Ptochoprodromos* cycle, without occasioning condemnation.

More importantly, our primary aim has been to make the poem readable for a contemporary English language audience while at the same time giving it the feeling of the narrative poetry with which the reader would be familiar. This is a move toward cultural translation, and it has dictated our choice of the pentameter. A narrative poem is quite a different experience than running prose. This difference does not inhere only in its different typographical aspect, although that does create its own semiotic (as recently entertainingly exploited in *Poetry Under Oath* [Simon 1998], free-verse renderings of Clinton and Lewinsky testimony). The difference also resides in the verse as a structural unit absent in prose and in the use of meter as a cohesive or contrastive device. These formal aspects are unmistakably part of what a poem communicates.

It is an impossible task for the translator to match the original foot for foot and caesura for caesura. The degree to which there is such a match will always be relative. We readily admit that our pentameter translation is not as close to our original as Eideneier's heptameter is to his—even if at the cost of some filler words. And we acknowledge that the hemistich cannot be a structural unit in our chosen meter the same way it is in heptameter. But the very presence of meter and verse conveys a stylistic and structural message to the reader; any verse, in effect, is better than no verse. (This is a principle followed by free-verse translations of metrical verse originals.)

All the same, introducing such constraints into a translation increases the likelihood of it being unfaithful to the original. We have been aware of this danger and have tried to minimize it, aiming to have our translation read as an autonomous piece of verse storytelling while not going astray from the content of the original. Managing this, of course, has involved some compromises. The scansion of the translation is at times pragmatic in its looseness, in order to allow a more literal translation. Particularly in series of invectives like "pot-licking cheese-munching bread-squanderer!" (130), further liberty is taken with stress placement than is usual with English pentameter, and at times an additional weak syllable is added, as in "and give you such a kick, it'll split your head" (748). These are occasional deviations, however, and do not compromise the overall integrity of the meter.

Our insistence on verse but not on rhyme was undertaken with this aim in mind. Rhyme was already in use in England in the 1360s, whereas its first certain use in Greek dates from Sachlikis, only a decade later. If we were to undertake a thorough cultural translation, writing the poem as a contemporary Englishman would have, we would be bound to use rhyme. And the stylistic connotations of English rhyme would have been entirely appropriate for many medieval and modern Greek poems. But we have considered the constraints this would have imposed on our rendering too great a price to pay. And although there is precedent in rhyming translation of older Greek texts in the form of Stephanides' *Erotokritos* (Kornaros 1984), among others, such a venture would have been too greatly out of step with contemporary practice.

In all, whether a translation is rendered in free verse, metered verse, or rhymed metered verse is simply a matter of degree, with the translator taking on the responsibility that the form and content of the original are judiciously matched in the output. We have chosen a different degree to what is prevalent in contemporary English language scholarship, and we ask for our readers' indulgence in this.

The lineation of the original Greek according to Papathomopoulos's lineation (which is consistent with Tsiouni's and Wagner's) is given in the right margin. At times, because of syntactic and metrical constraints, words in the translation are displaced from the verse in which they appear in the original. As an aid to the reader gaining something of the experience of the original manuscripts, we have added cross-references to the illustration rubrics in the Constantinopolitan manuscript, as boldface numbers in brackets in the margins of the verses before which they appear. We have also added the rubrics accompanying the Parisian manuscript (frequently in the manuscript's margins) as right-marginal notes. The illustrations of the Constantinopolitan manuscript are reproduced separately, along with their legends in Greek and English.

We have not consistently respected the order of paratactic expressions in our translation of the *Tale*'s catalog. Neither have we felt bound to preserve the number of verses of the original. These deviations are of little interest to an English language reader, and a reader who knows Greek can easily enough recover these changes by inspection of the original text, so we have not made a special note of them.

Register

The language and register of the original vacillates (see "Language"). The author clearly tries to use his "Sunday best" Greek, and there is much in the formulaic poem that cannot have been the vernacular of time. Yet often enough the quadrupeds come up with turns of phrase that are nothing if not colloquial. This inconsistency is reflected to some extent in our rendering. It is nowhere near as prominent as in the original; although English does have recourse to different registers of language, these have never been as grammatically distinct as in Greek. Besides, to exaggerate the discrepancies in register would be stylistically inappropriate for a contemporary audience.

Still, it would be irresponsible to the poem not to render its prologue in something of a stately tone ("to lead us into absolute perdition") and its disputation in a much coarser tenor ("You've chattered quite enough, you babbling shithead!") The result has not, we hope, come out as unduly anachronistic.

Our ventures in both stylistic directions have been cautious. We have lightly embellished the translation's language with old-fashioned expressions and syntax where appropriate though we have not shied away up-to-date cusswords or obscenities. In some instances, the register we have chosen is at odds with the original. For example, the rat starts his speech reviling the cat (152) with St. Paul's ὑπεραίρεσαι, "you exalt yourself"; in accordance with what the rat goes on to say, we have evened it out to the broader "you think too big." Such deviation is, we believe, legitimate in making a translation readable in contemporary English.

Inasmuch as the English used in this translation has a regional provenance, that provenance is Australian—in line with the background of Nicholas, the native English speaker of the two translators. We have not allowed ourselves undue extravagances in this regard, but the reader will note in general a tendency to Commonwealth rather than American colloquialisms: *arse, toff, loon, hornball, bloody-spited, fit to burst, donkey, hullo, lasses, thrash,* and so on. (There have been exceptions: *prairie, croak, goddamn, padres, jackass, squash.*)

Wording

As our concern has been to make the poem approachable to a contemporary nonspecialist English-speaking audience, some of our choices in wording have been liberal. For instance, we have used *Greeks* where the original has *Romans* (Ῥωμαῖοι). The Byzantines always resented being identified with a particular ethnicity instead of Imperial Rome and (outside a small intellectual elite) would not under any circumstances have named themselves *Hellenes (Greeks),* a term they associated with paganism. But to an uninitiated reader, who would associate Romans with Italy rather than Constantinople, a more faithful rendering would only serve to confuse matters. *Byzantines,* on the other hand, is a label for the Eastern Roman Empire first used in the sixteenth century; until then it only meant "Constantinopolitans." It would not only be anachronistic in translation but pedantic as well. And by the time the *Tale* was written, Byzantine dominion was largely limited to ethnic Greeks anyway. Likewise, we have referred to *Westerners* where the original has *Franks* (Φράγκοι)—a term most readers would associate with Merovingians rather than Crusaders, though its use persists to this day throughout the Arabic cultural sphere and has only recently receded in Greece. *Latins* or *Catholics* would have been more familiar terms, yet we have felt that they, too, would have ultimately been confusing.[173]

Among other wording choices that the reader familiar with the original may find surprising, we have chosen "cheetah" for πάρδος, based on internal evidence in the poem (as discussed in "A Conundrum of Cats"), rather than the classical (but obscure) *pard* or the more frequent but vague rendering *panther,* used by both Šandrovskaja and Gidel. Although συγκάθεδρος, "seat mate," (19) denotes a definite position of honor in the Byzantine court, we have chosen to translate it elsewhere as "peer" (109) and "who sits beside me" (899). Although μοχθηρόν primarily means "noxious" and seems apt invective to direct to the boar, it was in fact a normal medieval Greek term for the animal.[174] The original uses εὔχρηστον, "useful," to characterize farm animals, which we have rendered, in the interest of clarity, as "domestic."[175] And in accordance with contemporary taste, the amount of literal repetition in the original has been reduced, with some use of synonyms. This applies in particular to verbs of speaking, for example, in verse 214, where the original has ταῦτα λέγει, "says this," echoing verse 203 (τοὺς λόγους τούτους λέγει, "says these words"), whereas our rendering has "answered thus" and "spoke like this," respectively. We have cut down overall on the number of formulaic expressions in our rendering as less acceptable to modern readers.

Occasionally, we have allowed ourselves a colorful rendering absent in the original to compensate for an expression or nuance impossible to render literally. For example, we have used "fart early, and fart often" where the original has the weighty three-part compound συχνοπυκνοκλάνης, "often-and-densely–fart" (246), and "heralded by blasts of breaking wind, in he ran" where the original has the compound πορδοκοπῶν, "fart-laboring," in emphatic position before the main verb εἰσέδραμε, "ran in" (647). And we have the horse call the donkey a "Dick-O-Matic" where the original has ψωλογομάρι, "dick-donkey"/"dick-burden" (665). These liberties, all accounted for in our Commentary, are in keeping with the spirit of the *Tale* and necessary to make it communicate to a contemporary English language reader as vigorously as it did to a medieval Greek reader.

The profusion of compound words in the *Tale* has been discussed in "Compounds." Some of these words have been rendered as compounds in the translation (e.g., βορβοροπηλοκύλιστε, "mud-and-quagmire–weltering" [612]), but the constraints of English grammar and style have meant it has not been possible to do so for all of them (e.g., τορνοεμφωλευμένα, "with jewel settings lathed," literally "lathe-nested" [917]). This is unavoidable but regrettable nonetheless, as much of the literariness of Byzantine poetry lies in the compound rather than the phrase.

The gender of the animals in the translation, and in our references to them in this discussion, follows the grammatical gender of the animals in Greek (or at least, the majority of such instances, because some animals display variable gender; see appendix 3 on the "he-buffalo" and "she-buffalo"). Thus, the translation speaks of "Lady Fox" (270) but "Old Man Wolf" (432).

The punctuation and paragraphing of the translation, finally, is ours, although we have largely followed Papathomopoulos. The original manuscripts had minimal punctuation, and thus there is always some arbitrariness involved in punctuating such a text.

Further Reading

In this bibliography, we have concentrated on works available in English that can serve as an introduction to the field for interested readers. Much of the important work on vernacular Byzantine literature is in German and modern Greek. Still, this bibliography can serve to introduce readers further afield.

Late Byzantine History

Ostrogorsky 1968 remains the authoritative overall survey of Byzantine history. Nicol 1993 is a comprehensive and detailed history of late Byzantium, which provides much background information to the social setting of the poem. Nicol 1996 is a valuable supplement to Nicol 1993, giving the biography of that pivotal (and tragic) figure of late Byzantium, John VI Cantacuzene. A less pedantic but highly readable account of the period is given in Norwich 1995. The circumstances of John V Palaeologus's mission to Rome (considered in appendix 2 as a possible background for the *Tale*) are discussed in Halecki 1930. Ševčenko (1961) gives a summary of how contemporary Byzantine intellectuals commented on the decline of Byzantium in the fourteenth century. Vryonis (1971) examines the immediate cause of that decline—the displacement of Christianity by Islam in Asia Minor.

Byzantine Culture

The definitive reference on Byzantine realia, and a work that relies in no negligible part on the *Tale,* is Koukoules (1947–55), in Greek. *The Oxford Dictionary of Byzantium* (Kazhdan 1991) is an extremely useful English language reference. A good all-around introduction to Byzantine culture is given by Beck 1978. Kazhdan and Constable 1982 give a valuable counterpoint to the old kings-and-battles approach to Byzantine history, emphasizing the social forces at work in the empire. The bleak agrarian circumstances of late Byzantium—the feudal social context of the "Byzantine farmyard"—are outlined in Laiou 1977. A comprehensive account of the Byzantine intellectual milieu of the fourteenth century is given in Ševčenko 1974.

Byzantine Literature

The old standard of Krumbacher 1897 has now been superseded as an overall survey of Byzantine literature by Hunger 1978 for learned literature and Beck 1971 for vernacular literature. Summary histories of Byzantine vernacular literature are not hard to come by in histories of modern Greek literature; one may consult Knös 1962, Dimaras 1972, Politis 1973, Vitti 1978, and Trypanis 1981.

The vernacular genre most thoroughly studied is that of the romances; Beaton 1996 is a comprehensive introduction. Considerable attention has been devoted to *Digenes*; current issues in *Digenes* research are outlined in Beaton and Ricks 1993. Among the humorous poems, the most comprehensive analysis to date is Alexiou's (1986) on *Ptochoprodromos,* a paper that triggered a renewal in the appreciation of the genre.

The history of the verse form used in the *Tale* (and the overwhelming bulk of medieval and modern Greek poetry) is given in Jeffreys 1974; see also Jeffreys and Jeffreys 1979.

The issue of the orality of medieval Greek literature remains tangled; Jeffreys and Jeffreys 1983, 1986 are summaries of the debate by its most prominent participants. The best introduction to modern thinking on orality remains the pioneering text, Lord 1960.

Few Byzantine vernacular works are available in English translation. One may mention the three romances translated by Betts (1995); the several renderings of *Digenes*—including, most recently, Ricks 1990 and Jeffreys 1997; and the Chronicles of Makhairas (Dawkins 1932), Morea (Lurier 1962), and the Sultans (Philippides 1990).

Byzantine Language

There are several good references on the history of Greek. Browning 1983 is the standard text on medieval and modern Greek, but Horrocks 1997 is more comprehensive and goes into considerable linguistic detail. The language of the various forms of Byzantine literature is outlined in Browning 1978.

The Entertaining Tale of Quadrupeds

The first edition of the *Tale* is Wagner 1874; the modern critical editions are Tsiouni 1972 and Papathomopoulos 2002. Other than discussion of the meaning of παιδιόφραστος (rendered here as "entertaining"; see Commentary, verse 1) and proposals of variant readings (Koukoules 1911–12; Hesseling 1924; Xanthoudidis 1911–12, 1927–28), there has been little secondary literature on the *Tale*. The reviews of Tsiouni's edition (Eideneier 1976; Mitsakis 1976; Trapp 1976) contain valuable information, as does Šandrovskaja's (1956a, 1956b) translation and commentary. Eideneier (1982, 1982–83, 1983, 1985) has dedicated considerable attention to the use of formulas in the epic bestiaries; he also considers the survival of Cypriot songs similar to the *Tale* (Eideneier 1987—see appendix 4). Tsavare (1987) compares the structure of the *Tale* to that of the *Book of Birds*. Reinsch (1998) and Toufexis (2001) discuss the scribe of the Constantinopolitan manuscript of the work, Nicholas Agiomnitis. Vasiliou (1996) has dedicated an extensive study to the structural integrity of the *Tale*, which is considered in some detail in appendix 3. Makris's study (1993) of the *Book of Birds* describes in its concluding remarks the milieu in which the *Tale* was authored, and Sofianos (1996) comments on the initial acrostic of the *Tale* (see discussion in appendix 3). Eideneier 1995, finally, is a charming paper on what the *Tale* reveals about how Greek donkeys bray.

Notes

1. For the history of Byzantium in the late thirteenth and early fourteenth centuries, see Nicol 1993:41–184; Ostrogorsky 1968:450–509.
2. On the Second Civil War (1341–1347 and 1351–1354), see Nicol 1993:185–208; Ostrogorsky 1968:509–27.
3. For the long but unremarkable reign of John V, see Nicol 1993:253–95; Ostrogorsky 1968:531–49.
4. Otto II, married to Theophano, niece of John I Tzimiskes, in 972.
5. As far as the Emir Umur of Aydin was concerned, in fact, Andronicus III and John VI Cantacuzene, who had paid him generously for his support, had already been his vassals decades before (Zachariadou 1989:220–21).

6. Theodore Metochites, *Miscellanea* 14; cited in Wilson 1996:259.
7. See also discussion in Beck 1971:12.
8. See Browning 1978, 1983 for extensive discussion of the language of postclassical literature.
9. For all that *Digenes* may well have had an oral prototype, its earliest redaction (Grottaferrata) is in Byzantine Koine. The "popular" *Digenes* is represented by a late and textually perturbed manuscript (Escorial). There has been a long-running controversy over whether the Escorial or the Grottaferrata reflects the original text better. At issue is whether *Digenes* was first written down as a learned poem inspired by Cappadocian folk songs or in a language directly emulating those folk songs. For further discussion, see Ricks 1990; Jeffreys 1997.
10. Examples of vernacular scholarly works include the vernacular *Hippiatrica* (horse medicine) (*Excerpta Lugdunensia*); John Staphidas's practical medical manual, dated 1384 (*Staphidas*); the vernacular version of the *Physiologus* (Gidel and Legrand 1873); and any number of astrological texts published in the *Catalogus Codicum Astrologorum Graecorum* series.
11. For instance, in the Arethan scholia to Lucian (24.12), λημᾶν*] ὀφθαλμιᾶν: λήμη γὰρ ὁ συναγόμενος ἐν τῷ ὀφθαλμῷ ῥύπος, "*λημᾶν: ὀφθαλμιᾶν.* λήμη is the filth that gathers in the eye"—to which manuscript Δ adds ὃν καὶ τζίμπλαν φασὶν οἱ ἀγροικώτεροι, "which the more uncouth call τζίμπλαν [sleep-crust]."
12. See, for example, Dindorf's foreword in Dübner 1877.
13. For Dictys, see Papathomopoulos and Jeffreys 1996:xlv–xlvi.
14. In fact, the direct influence of the *Iliad* itself on Hermoniacus's vernacular paraphrase of the *Iliad* needs to be explicitly argued for (Jeffreys 1975). And Alexiou's association (1986, 1999) of *Ptochoprodromos* with Aristophanean humor is by no means settled—though Ptochoprodromos is arguably one of the cleverer vernacular authors.
15. See, for example, Angelou's listing of chapbooks (*Ἀναγνώσματα τοῦ Νέου Ἑλληνισμοῦ,* "Readings of Modern Hellenism," or *Λαϊκὰ Λογοτεχνικὰ Ἔντυπα,* "Popular Literary Editions") in Dalla Croce (1988:114*–115*). The list contains forty-two works; eight may be characterized as originally Byzantine vernacular, though mostly in modernized or rhymed versions—the *Chapbook of Alexander the Great, Apollonius of Tyre, The Fair Tale of the Donkey the Wolf and the Fox,* the *Belisariad,* the *Rime of Imperios,* the *Mass of the Beardless Man, Spaneas* (as the *Consolatory Teachings*), and the *Life of Aesop*. (To these one should add the *Book of Fruit,* printed as an appendix to the *Life of Aesop*.) As Kechagioglou (1982:19) says,

> Research has also been slow to describe and analyze the mechanisms that permit or impede popular narratives becoming popular readings: why did works like *Alexander, Belisarius,* or *Apollonius* become written and, later on, printed texts, but not stories like St George's, etc.? There is a similar problem with the conditions for the conversion or not of a popular reading into a printed text: why did works like Loukanis's *Iliad, Belisarius, Apollonius,* and, later on, *Sinbad* enter into the corpus of editions from Venice, but not works like Hermoniacus's *Iliad, Digenes Akrites,* the *Story of Ptocholeon, Barlaam and Joasaph,* or *Stephanites and Ichnelates*?

One might suggest that the sixteenth century had no time for stories from the fourteenth. But the sixteenth-century chapbooks persisted in chapbook form with little alteration into the nineteenth, so antiquity alone does not explain the break in transmission—and the break was far from total, after all.

16. For example, the autograph of Foskolos's *Fortounatos* (Vincent 1980).
17. Unfortunately, Sachlikis's work is not well preserved in the extant manuscripts, which went through enough popular transmission to distort the text beyond repair; it appears impossible to yoke them together in a single critical edition.
18. Christ turns up in a bona fide prayer when Sachlikis recalls his ills and begs to be delivered from prison. Otherwise, he turns up only as an interjection, a target of gamblers' oaths, an accurser of jailers, and as proclaiming a nighttime curfew in the Gospel(!). (Prison prayer: *Counsels* 2.381, 384; interjection: *Strange Narrative* 37, 246; *Counsels* 2.404, 667; target of gamblers' oaths: *Counsels* 1.130; accurser of jailers: *Strange Narrative* 541; curfew: *Counsels* 1.110, 115.) The figure of the emperor, so prominent in the *Ptochoprodromos* poems, is nowhere to be seen in Sachlikis's poems and is not replaced by the distant doge, the ruler of Venice. And although Glycas in a similar predicament begged the emperor for clemency in his poetry and Della Porta in prison wrote a biblically flavored dialogue with Truth, Sachlikis does not waste his breath on authorities or abstractions; his words are directly addressed only to his son Francis.
19. Of course, just because there is attestation of dissent in the vernacular, we should not assume that this is the "voice of the people." As both Beck (1971) and Beaton (1996) repeatedly stress, there is no reason to doubt that the vernacular literature of Byzantium was written by the literary elite. However, the low prestige of the vernacular, and the anonymity that accompanied it, may have given authors opportunity to express dissatisfaction, something they could not normally declare within the bonds of patronage and centralized authority. (On the extent of those bonds, see Ševčenko 1974:81–87.)
20. On the *Vita of the Esteemed Donkey* and the *Fair Tale of the Donkey the Wolf and the Fox,* see "Literary Parallels" and "Foreign Influences" in this volume.
21. The "sons of Hagar" (Ἀγαρηνοί) are the Muslims, by conflation with the Arabs, who traditionally traced their ancestry to Abraham through Hagar and Ishmael rather than Sarah and Isaac.
22. The former name, δεκαπεντασύλλαβος, "fifteen-syllable," is modern; the latter, πολιτικός, "urban/commonplace," is Byzantine. We use *iambic heptameter* to refer to the verse form (see "Meter").
23. The leopard is in fact indigenous to southern Anatolia, though rare (Turnbull-Kemp 1967:4). But southern Anatolia was largely off limits to the Byzantines in the late fourteenth century, and as discussed in "A Conundrum of Cats," the *Tale*'s leopard is not necessarily the same animal as the modern leopard.
24. On Timothy of Gaza, see Bodenheimer and Rabinowitz 1949.
25. *Codex Ambrosianus graecus* A 45 sup. (Sbordone 1936:xiii).
26. The confusion is understandable, although the two words are not ultimately related: ἀγρυπνῶ literally means "to hunt after sleep" (< ἄγρα, "hunt"), whereas ἀγριαίνουσιν < ἄγριος, "wild," is derived not from "hunt" but from ἀγρός, "field" (see Frisk 1970 s.v.)

27. The story is repeated in *Anonymus Treu,* p. 13, *Patria Constantinopoleos* 2.41 and in the *Suda* (s.v. βασιλική).
28. Still, as Carrington (1959:200–201) and Bedini (2000 [1997]:30) report, from A.D. 500 to 1500 elephants are recorded as having been brought to (Western) Europe extremely infrequently: in 797 (Charlemagne), "1214" (Frederick II of Sicily; likelier 1228, at the end of his crusade), 1254 (Louis IX of France: "little more than a decade later" than Frederick II's), 1477 (René d'Anjou of Naples), and 1497 (Ercole d'Este). It is only after 1500 that elephants started routinely being brought to Europe again.

    Ciriaco of Ancona was to serve as one of Mehmet II's translators (Lambros 1908:65) but was presumably already well-traveled enough as a merchant before Mehmet's accession to have caught sight of an elephant.
29. There was an ancient confusion between the Ethiopians and the Indians, the two dark-skinned peoples with whom the Greeks had contact. Stories about Indian elephants would thus have been transferred readily to their "Ethiopian" (= African) counterparts.
30. Scullard (1974:130) comments on Agatharchides' tree account: "This of course is nonsense . . . but it could easily have arisen from the fact that elephants often do rub, rest and even sleep against trees; thus hunters would know where to locate their prey." Moreover, lying down would make elephants vulnerable to predators such as lions (George Kolias, personal communication).
31. The word μαϊμοῦ has in fact also been derived from μιμῶ, "mimic" (so Koraës; see Andriotis 1983 s.v.) Although that derivation is no longer accepted, the association would have been irresistible ever since the word was introduced into Greek.
32. This precision in identifying the elephant's trunk is certainly not displayed by the illustrator of the Constantinopolitan manuscript of the *Tale,* incidentally, whose elephant looks like nothing so much as an aardvark, with no discernible mouth and which in two out of its three depictions is even missing its tusks. See also Commentary, verse 914.
33. Aelian (10.10) likewise lists the elephant's diet—at least during the process of taming—as ἄρτοι οἱ μέγιστοι καὶ κριθαὶ καὶ ἰσχάδες καὶ ἀσταφίδες καὶ κρόμμυα καὶ σκόροδα καὶ μέλι χύδην σχίνου τε καὶ φοίνικος καὶ κιττοῦ φάκελοι καὶ πᾶν ὅσον ἐδωδίμου ὕλης καὶ ἐκείνοις συντρόφου καὶ ἐκ τούτου τοι καὶ φίλης, "very large loafs of bread, barley, dried figs, raisins, onions, garlic, honey in large quantities, bundles of mastic branches and of palm-leaves and of ivy and any edible and familiar substance which is for this reason welcome to them."
34. So also *Etymologicum Gudianum* and *Etymologicum Magnum,* s.v. ἔλαφος; *George Choeroboscus: Epimerismi in Psalmos* 129; *Scholia in Iliadem (D Scholia)* 3.22. If the attribution of the *D Scholia* to Didymus is accurate, then the belief is as early as first century B.C.–first century A.D.—even before Aelian. But scholia tended to accumulate from manuscript to manuscript, so it is impossible to know who exactly came up with the notion. The other references are middle to late Byzantine.
35. Snakes and dragons are interchangeable in Greek lore.
36. The second (Byzantine) and third (Pseudo-Basilian) redactions do not mention the legend under either animal.

37. *The Miracles of the Arab Ibn Zohr,* as cited in the "Treatise on Simples" by the thirteenth-century Andalusian botanist and pharmacist Ibn al-Baitar (Leclerc 1883:52).
38. However Wellmann (1930:85) also points out that elephant fat was held to be a remedy against poisonous animals (*Aelian* 1.37, 10.12: στέαρ δὲ ἐλέφαντος ἦν ἄρα τοῖς ἰοβόλοις ἔχθιστον· εἰ γάρ τις χρίσαιτο ἢ ἐπιθυμιάσειεν αὐτοῦ, τὰ δὲ ἀποδιδράσκει πορρωτάτω, "But it seems that the fat of an elephant is detested by poisonous creatures, for if a man rubs himself with it or burns some, they flee away to a great distance").
39. *Pseudo-Zonaras, Etymologicum Genuinum, Etymologicum Gudianum, Etymologicum Magnum,* all s.v. ἄνθος.
40. In contrast, the *Physiologus* elephant legends do not seem to have survived in Greek folklore—hardly surprising, given the animal's absence from the vicinity of Greece.
41. The legend also turns up in Western bestiaries; for example, "The one of the horns which is on the right of the head is the more useful one for healing things. To keep snakes away, you can burn either of them" (White 1954:39). As the bestiaries used a variety of sources besides the *Physiologus,* including Aelian and Pliny, this is not surprising; the West would likelier have gotten the account from Aelian than from Greek peasants.
42. To make things more complicated, Philes claims that another way to repel snakes is to burn vulture feathers (132–33).
43. Philes' claim that elephants pick arrows from their skin using their trunks (278–79) is not beyond the bound of reason but nonetheless probably reflects an active imagination.
44. The enmity between the elephant and the serpent is recapitulated in the Pseudo-Basilian *Physiologus* (3.29), ending in the death of both combatants.
45. Such inaccuracies are not surprising in view of what we read about other animals in Philes. When it comes to the swan (222–34), for example, one is delighted by a poetic, if unrealistic, elaboration on the swan song: as the swan approaches death, his feathers become so sparse that the wind blowing through them produces exquisite music!
46. "By medieval standards, dragons were unpopular. In some mysterious way they always seemed to be coming into possession of beautiful maidens, although how a dragon would know that they were beautiful—let alone maiden—has never been explained. Perhaps they employed panders to maintain their stocks, perhaps they ate the maidens on certain dragon feast days. Unfortunately the natural history of dragons seems to have been sadly neglected. One real point does emerge. Dragons were *bad.* Conversely, the imaginative bestiaries considered the equally imaginary Panther to be better than good. The next step was obvious, and good Panthers were attributed with the power of killing bad dragons" (Turnbull-Kemp 1967:149–50).
47. Whichever of the many sources on elephant warfare version ε drew on, it had little to do with Alexander himself. Scullard (1974:240–41) concludes that the use of towers mounted on elephants is no earlier than Pyrrhus, King of Epirus, a century later, and coins show Alexander on horseback fighting Porus and a mahout (driver) bareback on an elephant.

The late vernacular prose versions keep building on the notion of walking fortresses; the *Chapbook of Alexander the Great* (*Alexander Romance* Φ 202) goes so far as to claim that up to twenty men could stand in such a tower.

48. The late vernacular prose versions, rather less spectacularly, have Alexander's soldiers use bells to scare the elephants (E 94.1; Φ 202–3). The historical Alexander had to make do with mere spears, pikes, scimitars, and axes to contain Porus's elephants (Scullard 1974:70–71). The pig story was first recounted of Pyrrhus's invasion of Italy (e.g., *Aelian* 1.38) and Scullard (1974:113–16) regards it as plausible.
49. Manuscripts CLV use τοῖχος, as against manuscript P's πύργος, "tower," used in our edition of the text. The neuter noun τεῖχος, the word used in *Alexander Romance* ε, can mean either a city wall or a fortification in classical Greek. The *Tale*'s homonymous masculine noun τοῖχος is the wall of a building instead in classical Greek, but it is hard to believe that the distinction would have survived in the vernacular, and only a city wall would make sense in context anyway.
50. Alternatively, the author might have himself adapted the Aesopic fable to make it more colorful, and his version in return was made more realistic by Cypriot readers of the *Tale,* giving rise to the modern fable. But as we discuss at some length in "Survivals of the *Tale*" in relation to a comparable instance, that direction of traffic is unlikely.
51. This would at least be strong confirmation of a suspicion we express in "Subversion and Politics," however, that the author is biased against the carnivores, and passes over their usefulness.
52. The vernacular would have offered γλείφοντα instead of λείχοντα; this vernacular form is indeed what the most recent manuscript of the *Tale* (L) uses. On the other hand, we currently have no evidence that modern Greek χαλαρώνεις, "loosen, slacken," was extant at the time to substitute χαλᾷς.
53. Note that, in citing Timothy of Gaza, Constantine VII Porphyrogennetus gets the lion's and pard's genders the other way round. Although Porphyrogennetus's quotations are frequently verbatim, he should not always be trusted as faithfully relaying the now lost authors he cites.
54. To be fair, as discussed in Nicholas 1999:257–59, the very existence of a leopard distinct from the pard, as understood by the ancients, is questionable. The author is hard put to say much about the classical leopard because it barely corresponds to a living cat at all.
55. There is no lack of Byzantine etymologies of the learned word for pards, however (see Commentary, verse 869). Because the word for leopard was not classical, it was probably ignored by the etymologists.
56. We are assuming that the nobles and grandees (οἱ ἄρχοντες, οἱ εὐγενεῖς) mentioned between the sultans and emirs in verse 879 are likewise Muslim.
57. Cyranides (2.1.24), a magical text from around the first century A.D., reports this belief for bear skins: τὸ δὲ δέρμα αὐτοῦ ἐπιτεθὲν ὅπου ἂν εἰσι ψύλλοι, φεύξονται καὶ οὐδόλως παραμένουσιν, "With its skin placed wherever fleas are, they flee and do not remain at all." The shift from one wild beast's skin to another could have been made readily within Byzantium, but we would need more explicit evidence than this to claim so.

58. On the distinction in the fourteenth century between Turkish emirs and Arabic sultans, see "Date of Composition."
59. There is also attested Turkish use of lynx skins: "After him rode several trumpeters, blowing their trumpets without intermission, who were followed by about 300 Turkish hussars, ornamentally dressed in pelisses of spotted lynxskin, who sometimes shouted, sometimes sprang from their horses, and exhibited tokens of great exultation" (Wratislaw 1862:17—account from the 1590s). So the reference to the use of pelts does not decide the question considered in "A Conundrum of Cats," namely, which animal is represented by the pard.
60. "The cheetah differs from other wild cats in its mild disposition and is trained comparatively easily, becoming strongly attached to the person who trained it. It will not bite even during vigorous play, and goes well on a leash" (Heptner and Sludskii 1992:725).
61. There is some circumstantial evidence for such a shift downward in the denotation of πάρδος at the time, as discussed in Nicholas 1999:272–73. Two suggestive instances are πάρδος coming to mean "tomcat" in modern Pontic Greek and the use of Παρδίτζη as a nickname for a domestic cat in the *Vita of the Esteemed Donkey* (179, 189).
62. On the reasons for considering the author a subject of Byzantium, see "Place of Composition."
63. There is a good chance that as so often occurs in the *Tale* (see "Irony and Contradiction"), the leopard is being hypocritical in accusing the cheetah of traits it also carries. But the author's ignorance is a plausible enough alternative.
64. Tsiouni's edition of the *Tale* (1972:143) glosses κατόπαρδος as "a kind of small leopard."
65. Gidel's study was based on the Parisian manuscript of the *Tale,* to which he had access.
66. For instance, Gidel (1866:134ff.) adduces as an argument for a French origin of *Belthandros and Chrysantza* its mention of falconry. But as Krumbacher (1897:2.859) pointed out, falconry was already popular in the Comnenan court ("ebensowenig is die Sitte der *Falkenjagd* eine fränkische Erfindung") and could easily be brought up by a native Byzantine.
67. Krumbacher (1897:2.882) regards the *Vita of the Esteemed Donkey* as "clearly an offshoot of the famous story of *Renard the Fox.* The most important features of the narrative are also found in Western Renard stories, but in the Greek story they are unified in a whole, for which no direct precedent can be found."
68. Though Gidel's wording suggests otherwise, both the Greek μουστακάτα and the French *Moustache* are clearly epithets rather than actual names: Tibert is the cat's proper name in *Renard,* whereas μεγαλομουστακάτος is a description in the *Tale* (34, 127).
69. The fox's cunning was prominent enough in Aesop but continued to be mentioned in Byzantium; Koukoules (1947–55:6.318) cites Cosmas of Jerusalem (*viii* A.D.; Migne 1857–87:38.413):

    Διὸ καὶ πολλοῖς τοῖς μυθεύμασι γελωτοποιοῖς θρυλλοῦσι τοῦτο πολλοί· καὶ γὰρ λέοντα τὸν βασιλικώτατον ἠπάτησε καὶ πετεινὰ καὶ κτήνη καὶ θήρας φασί· καὶ ὅτι φυσικὸν ἔχει τὸ πανοῦργον λέγουσι σχηματίζεσθαι θάνατον καὶ ἐξογκοῦσθαι πρὸς ἀπάτην τῶν πετεινῶν, ἡνίκα δὲ καθήκοντα ὡς ἐπὶ πτώματι διασπᾶν αὐτὰ καὶ κατεσθίειν.

[Hence many tell this story in laughter-inducing fables, for they say she has deceived the most royal lion and fowl and tame beasts and wild beasts. And they say that it is her nature to undertake the deceit of pretending to be dead and swelling up, to trick fowl, so that when they perch on her like a corpse, she savages and devours them.]

70. Pope Urban II used a similar anecdote in 1096: "I spoke in seriousness a certain proverb that ought to have shamed them, if they wanted to heed it, about the wolf set to learn the alphabet: when the teacher said A, he would say 'lamb,' and when the teacher said B, he would say 'pig'" (Ziolkowski 1993:207).
71. So already in Krumbacher (1897:2.878): "The *Western epics,* in which animal assemblies are described, are comparable; but there is no Frankish model known for the *Tale*—it is likelier to be in its entirety an *independently Greek work*" (emphases in the original).
72. Even if the *Reinaerts Historie* leopard and lynx are reminiscent of the *Tale*'s leopard and "pard" (which, as we have seen, is in some respects identifiable with the lynx), one can safely dismiss any possible influence on the *Tale*: this Dutch version of the *Renard* story was produced around 1380.
73. The tale of the Greedy Wolf in chapter 3 of *Kalilah and Dimnah* (Irving 1980:79) represents a quadruple nesting of stories.
74. The second Aesopic passage in the *Tale,* the horse's mention of Aesop's fable on camels (771–75), should be considered an allusion rather than a distinct narrative.
75. An example of someone who had memorized *Erotokritos* in its entirety is the "Cretan Runner" George Psychoundakis's father, Nicolas (Psychoundakis 1955:13).
76. There are five Byzantine poems that were "rhymed" into print: the rhyming *Fair Tale of the Donkey the Wolf and the Fox,* the *Rime of Belisarius,* the *Rime of Apollonius of Tyre,* the rhymed version of the romance of *Imperios,* and the *Rime of Alexander* (*Alexander Romance* ρ, which also circulated more widely in prose two centuries later as *Alexander Romance* Φ: the *Chapbook of Alexander the Great*). Of the remaining chapbooks of Byzantine provenance (see note in "Vernacular Medieval Greek Literature"), the *Life of Aesop* and the *Book of Fruit* were in prose, and the *Mass of the Beardless Man,* being a close parody of the Mass, could not be rendered in rhyme and remain effective. The only texts to make it to print as unrhymed poems were *Spaneas,* Loukanis's *Iliad,* and the *Theseid* (Kechagioglou 1982:19). Of these, only the moralizing *Spaneas* was a text composed before 1450, and the other two works are translations (the *Theseid* being a translation of Boccaccio and Loukanis's *Iliad* an adaptation of Hermoniacus's earlier retelling, though more faithful to the actual text of the *Iliad*). As Kechagioglou (1993:128) points out, prose chapbooks, supplanting rhymed poems, did not start to sell well until the 1640s.
77. Hatzigiakoumis (1977:37, 81) has been much cited for his observation that most vernacular medieval Greek manuscripts date from the late fifteenth or early sixteenth centuries and are to be found in Western European libraries.

Hatzigiakoumis concludes that the copying of these texts (or at least the romances, which were his topic of research) was undertaken as a conscious act of preservation of Byzantine low culture by the exiled Greek scribes, working for the benefit of the Renaissance in the West—and inspired by the Renaissance embrace of vernacular literature. (See also Eideneier 1985:46–47.)

78. The fact that καβάκα now means in Cypriot Greek "a large fat hen" (Hatzioannou 1934–37:631) does not diminish the similarity. Another song based on the *Donkey Tale* is given by Hatzioannou (1934–37:628–29), and Papaharalambous (1945–46:263–66) follows the *Tale* song with an oral retelling of the *Donkey Tale* very close to the original.
79. The λλιοβουτήματα in the Hatzioannou version (song 3, appendix 4) are "dippings of the sun," that is, sundowns, and have nothing to do with the *Tale*'s rat dipping his tail in oil (139). It would be fanciful to interpret it as ἐλαιοβουτήματα, "dips in olive [oil]." Whereas the *Tale* speaks of the cat being beaten in the cellar (170), the Papaharalambous version (song 1, appendix 4) has the rat placed in this predicament; this makes one suspect something has become garbled in transmission.
80. However, the precedent of the *Book of Birds,* which seems to have no direct Greek folk antecedent, is more compelling as a model for the *Tale.*
81. The rhymed adaptation of *Digenes* one century before Dapontes, in its Oxford manuscript, never made it to print. Dapontes would also have rhymed *Digenes,* but God did not "grant him life" to do so; his discovery was promptly forgotten, and the work into which he jotted down his summary of its plot remains unpublished. It would be another century before *Digenes* was rediscovered in Trebizond, causing much more of a sensation.
82. Arabic/Persian terms found in the *Tale* in wide use in Byzantium: βαμβάκι < Pers. *pambak,* "cotton" (536: already in *Suda, x* A.D.); γάδαρος "donkey" < Arab. *gadar, gaidar* (644: first attested *vi* A.D., according to most sources, although Karapotosoglou [1979] claims an Indic origin and points to an *ii* A.D. attestation); ζατρίκιν < Pers. *šaxrats,* "chess" (922: already in *Anna Comnena, xi* A.D.); κοπροζάγαρος < Arab. *sakar,* Turk. *zagar,* "hound dog" (415: in Sachlikis in non-Ottoman Crete, *Strange Narrative* 128); μαϊμοῦ < Arab. *maymun,* "monkey" (37; as μαμούνα in the *Assizes of Cyprus, xiii* A.D.); παπούτζιν < Turk. *pabuç* < Pers. *babuč,* "shoe" (515: already in the *xiii* A.D. *Assizes* [where it refers to "Saracens'" footwear] and Sachlikis—see Commentary, verse 515); χριμιζίν < Arab. *qirmisi,* "crimson" (762: the *Tale* seems to be the first instance it is used in Greek—it turns up in Pseudo-Sphrantzes, Chalcocondyles, and the *Byzantine Reckoning Book* in *xv* A.D.—but it was known as a trade item also in the West; Triandafyllidis [1963:444] speculates the word may have come into Greek via the Italian *cremisi*). (Etymologies from Andriotis 1983.)

    Arabic/Ottoman military terms in the *Tale*: ἀμιρᾶς, "emir" < Arab. *amīr* (494); ἀνακαράς, "kettledrum" < Arab. *naqqāra* (1043); ζαρκούλιν, "gold-emboidered cap" < Turk. *zerqulā* (512); σουλτάνος, "sultan" < Arab. *sulṭān* (494); ταβλαμπάσιν, "drum" < Turk. *tablbaz* < Arab. *ṭabl.* (1069).

    Ottoman generic or Egyptian military terms: σαρπούζιν, "fur cap" < Arab. *sharbūsh* (512).

Ottoman civilian terms: τζοχοΰφανδωμένα, "woven with serge" < Turk. *çuha* (504).

83. The rulers of North Africa—both Egypt and the Maghreb—were also still sultans in the fifteenth century. Most of their lands were conquered by the Ottomans in the sixteenth, although the ruler of Morocco remained a sultan into modern times (Abun-Nasr 1975:220, 254).
84. The word ἀμηρᾶς, "emir," is still too vernacular for Cantacuzene, however; it occurs only in his quotation of a vernacular Greek letter from the sultan of Cairo, with reference to the overlord of Jerusalem under his authority (3.96). His normal term was σατράπης, "satrap," as seen in the excerpt cited in "Untraced Beliefs."
85. In conversation with the late Robert Browning (August 1996) we were not able to establish a firm rationale for his claim of Constantinopolitan authorship as regards the *Tale*. The claim for the *Belisariad* is established in its edition (Bakker and van Gemert 1988:34–42) and is obvious from the poem's topographical and contemporary detail.
86. The Jewish community of Constantinople had been razed in the 1204 fall of the city and was reestablished late in the thirteenth century, with Andronicus II actively encouraging Jews into Byzantium to stimulate its economy (Sharf 1995a:271–72).
87. Or at least without Jewish tanners: see Commentary, verse 424.
88. A Greek bishop in Venetian Crete was very much the exception rather than the rule (Jacoby 1989:24). The Orthodox flock of Crete was instead served by the bishop of Venetian Coron in the Peloponnese (Angold 1989:81).
89. The picture is complicated by the fact that the lion is referred to as *basileus* in the text: see Commentary, verse 17.
90. Given the doubts that have been expressed about its authenticity, the prologue needs to be considered separately from the main poem in any discussion of the poem's origins; if the prologue is subsequent to the main poem, of course, then it attests only the Byzantine identity of its adaptor. (See discussion in appendix 3.)
91. Xanthoudidis himself admits that it "seems strange." That the Greeks of Crete continued to identify the emperor of Constantinople as their rightful sovereign is not in dispute: "More indicative perhaps of the permanent mood within the Greek community in this period are two dedicatory inscriptions painted in 1436 and 1445 respectively, and displayed in two small Cretan churches commissioned by priests. Both inscriptions mention Emperor John VIII Palaeologus in their dating and thus clearly proclaim the Byzantine allegiance of the Greek clergy, undoubtedly shared by the majority of Greek laymen" (Jacoby 1989:25). Cf. also Volan's account (2000) of a dedication to Andronicus II in a Venetian-era Cretan Orthodox church, accompanied by a painting of the Last Judgment, which she reads as a reference to the belief that the Last Judgment could not take place until the emperor had restored Orthodox Christianity to the entire world. Nonetheless, the prologue of the *Tale* very much sounds like someone looking on from the inside at the depredations of the empire's enemies, not someone sympathetic to the empire but living in territory held by those enemies.

92. These texts were of relatively low prestige, but it would be an exaggeration to characterize them as outright "popular." Indeed, as Beaton (1996:31) says: "It is not until the fourteenth and fifteenth centuries that some of this narrative tradition [the *Physiologus*] takes on a relatively 'popular' form and at the same time transcends the bounds of moral didacticism to take its place in an emergent fictional literature." The works Beaton (1996:232) names as popularizing middle Byzantine low prose are in fact the late Byzantine vernacular animal narratives: the *Tale,* the *Book of Birds,* the *Book of Fruit,* and the *Donkey Tale.* But that these works were actually intended as popularizations of the *Physiologus* is rather doubtful.
93. We have not found an explicit statement of this principle in the main texts on epideictic (praising) rhetoric, by Aristotle and Menander Rhetor, or in the standard Byzantine textbooks on composition (*progymnasmata*), by Hermogenes and Aphthonius. But because the rhetorical modes were so strongly distinguished from each other by occasion (a funerary oration would hardly be conflated with a forensic oration) and the rhetoricians gave strong emphasis to their taxonomies, it would be expected that they could not co-occur in the same speech.
94. So noted by Vasiliou (1996:81) himself, who contrasts the *Tale*'s formal looseness to the *Book of Birds*'s adherence to the norms set by the late ancient formulators of the *ekphrasis,* Hermogenes and Aphthonius.
95. Ammonius uses it to refer to Christ after the resurrection (*Fragmenta in Joannem* 618); it also turns up in Leontius of Neapolis's *Life of John the Almsgiver.*
96. George Pachymeres' *History* (*xiii–xiv* A.D.) uses it to refer to both soldiers (429) and the condemned kin of Mouzalon (543) begging for mercy. See also Commentary, verse 197.
97. γαμησᾶς, "fucker"—a term that can hardly have literal force in contemporary English; glossed more decorously as *fututor* by Tsiouni.
98. Personal communication, Vasiliki Tsiouni-Fatsi (1996); attributed to her thesis advisor, †Robert Browning.
99. The only possible exception to the *Tale*'s omission of low-ranking clergy is a single reference in manuscript C (919a) to πρωτοπαπάδες, "chief priests, protopopes" (for definition, see Textual Notes). But this occurs in the same verse as ἀρχιμανδρίτες, "prelates," and though the protopope was the most senior rank a married Orthodox priest could attain, he is clearly mentioned in the *Tale* not as a link to the world of the parish but as yet another in the *Tale*'s list of church administrators.
100. Refer also to our observations in "Faith and Country."
101. The assumption that the *Tale* was intended for a broad audience has been made by Šandrovskaja (1960:12): "The popular material of the fables [the *Book of Birds* and the *Tale*] and the character of the language, which gives indications of its popular origin, make us suspect that the fables did not belong to a narrow literary circle but had spread to the broadest audience within the Byzantine population."
102. In fact, Aristotle (*Historia Animalium* 488a) distinguishes among tame animals (like the donkey and the mule), wild animals (like the panther and the wolf), and animals τὰ δὲ καὶ ἡμεροῦσθαι δύναται ταχύ, οἷον ἐλέφας, "that can be tamed readily, like the elephant."

103. The questions on possible historical interpretations of all this, the author's intent and the textual authenticity of the battle, are addressed in appendices 2 and 3.
104. The enmity between cat and rat had not passed unnoticed by the Byzantines. We have attested the proverbs Κάτης καὶ ποντικὸς ἐμάχουνταν καὶ ὁ βλέπων ἐγέλα, "The cat and mouse fought, and the onlooker laughed" (Krumbacher 1969 [1894]:84), and Ποντικοῦ βουλὰς κόψει κάτης, "The cat will cut off the mouse's plans," (Krumbacher 1969 [1894]:87)—not to mention Theodore Prodromus's *Battle of Cats and Mice* and *Studies on the Mouse*.
105. Of course, because the dog scares off the (herbivorous) boar with his barking (1059), he might not be addressing anyone in particular. But it would be odd, in that case, that his call to arms in 1064–65 is responded to by the herbivores, not the carnivores. Moreover, the dog does not flee along with the surviving carnivores (including the fox) at the end of the battle (1072–74).
106. Indeed, humans have that habit no less than elephants and monkeys and would be equally subject to the monkey's censure. The contemporary reader is reminded of the way Gary Larson makes fun of humans from an animal point of view.
107. Krumbacher (1897:2.877), for instance, says simply that "there follows a bloody battle, until the two camps are finally exhausted and nightfall puts an end to the massacre." Similar comments pervade the literature on the *Tale,* though E. Jeffreys's description of the plot in Kazhdan (1991, s.v. DIEGESIS TON TETRAPODON ZOON) concurs that "the herbivorous animals emerge victorious."
108. Theodore Prodromus asked Emperor Manuel to send him a live fox to relieve his gout:

    Ἀμηχανοῦσιν ἰατροὶ, ζητοῦσι θεραπείαν,
    Καὶ, «Δεῖ ζητεῖν ἀλώπεκα», σύμπαντες λέγουσί μοι·
    «Ἀλώπηξ μέγα φάρμακον εἰς τὴν ἀρθρῖτιν νόσον,
    Ἀλώπηξ εὑρεθήτω σοι, ζῶσα δεθήτω ξύλῳ,
    Καὶ πρὸς παφλάζον ἔλαιον ἀπορριφήτω ζῶσα,
    Καὶ τούτῳ χρῶ πρὸς ἴασιν ποδῶν σεσαθρωμένων.»

    [The doctors, at a loss, look for a cure,
    and tell me all "You must request a fox;
    fox is a mighty cure against arthritis.
    Get hold of one, then bind it live to a stake,
    and cast it live into some boiling oil.
    Use this for curing your decrepit feet."] (*Prodromus: For a Live Fox* 56–61)

109. It seems true, however, that the author would have found no use for the wolf, just as the bear exclaims (836–37). The claim made at times in the literature that wolf hides were used in antiquity in making parchment is not borne out by the extant evidence (Ryder 1964:393–94). We have not sighted any claim of it being so used in Byzantium, and it could never have constituted a regular practice in any case. Oppian's claim (*Cynegetica* 3.282ff.), repeated by Eutecnius (*Paraphrasis in Oppiani Cynegetica* 34) and Timothy of Gaza (§7), that wolf hides were used in making drums, need not detain us: Oppian and his epigones go on to claim that normal drums fall silent when such drums are near, as lambskins are afraid of wolfskins.

110. The authenticity of the prologue has been questioned in any case and is discussed in appendix 3.
111. L had originally substituted Jews for the donkeys of the story in 722—but is clearly doing so on its own initiative, rather than reflecting anything the author had to say. V does something similar with Bogdans (Moldavians) standing in for the donkeys in 691.
112. On the textual difficulties of the word used here, ματζιγγάνα (which might be a corruption of "gypsy" in the other manuscripts as well), see Commentary.
113. The accusation that the Latins did not venerate images was part of the panoply of anti-Catholic rhetoric (Kolbaba 2000:51–52), but verse 398 shows this was not the direction the author was taking.
114. The lack of concern with state enemies has already been pointed out by Vasiliou (1996) as evidence against a political interpretation of the poem; see appendix 3.
115. See, for example, Ševčenko (1974:80–81) on the low prestige of the Palaeologi as literary patrons.
116. Admittedly the elephant boasts of his merits in a textually contentious passage; see Textual Notes.
117. Λιμὴν Σωτηρίας, "Haven of salvation": sighted for instance as an inscription in the Monastery of Preveli, in southern Crete.
118. The fox is not valued instrumentally, but it is condemned for causing harm to humans (193)—and the dog does mention her hide is fit for the (human) tanner and furrier (210–12); see also Commentary, verse 306.
119. This tension between anthropomorphism and instrumentalism is consistent, however, with a class-driven interpretation of the poem (see appendix 2): the domestic animals are productive, if indeed not exploited, whereas the carnivores—as the wolf exclaims to the bear (837), in a self-defeating move—are parasitic.
120. The hen's transition from praising the imperial bodyguards she brings up to praising how fine her meat is (see appendix 1) is only one such case in point.
121. The exceptions to the latter tendency are the billy goat and nanny goat (which are of the same species and count as a single animal; at any rate, "crazy billy" [459] is hardly respectful) and the cheetah and leopard, which have been at odds from the moment they appear (861).
122. Or, as manuscript C has it, saves the deer from the leopard.
123. hellas@lists.psu.edu; also on Usenet, bit.listserv.hellas.
124. A particularly striking instance of this is the seven-part (!) epithet *polima-0oyfoxristianopeokroystopaido* (πολυμαθουφοχριστιανοπεοκρουστόπαιδο, "polymath UFO [= 'clueless' in Greek slang] Christian penis-stroking lad") (Constantine Thomas; Re: Mallia Skebouln!! Htav RE: Kale o . . . Pipis, bit.listserv.hellas, July 23, 2000).
125. Eideneier (1983:232–36) also identifies in the *Tale* and the *Book* (as well as *Ptochoprodromos*: Eideneier 1991:48–50) a tendency for particular words to occur at only certain syllables within the heptameter—just like ἀκόμη/ἀκμήν occurring at the first syllable in this case. However, it is not clear to what extent this reflects a deliberate practice sought out by poets rather than an unavoidable consequence of metrical constraints on word choice. As Eideneier (1983:232) himself admits, "This is to be expected, incidentally, when the heptameter regulates where words go."

That said, Eideneier's tracing of the history of the metrical location of πάντοτε, "always," as found in the manuscripts of *Ptochoprodromos* (Eideneier 1991:50), strongly supports the contention that poetic syntax—coupled with the tendency toward increasingly formulaic expression in later manuscript copies—did indeed affect the location of certain words in medieval verse. See Textual Notes, 926, for an instance where this affects the manuscript reading chosen.

126. The three structural breaks in the *Tale* neatly divide it up into quarters:

  Beginning—Entrance of hare (herbivores): 1–266 (268 verses)
  Hare—Entrance of ox and buffalo (large animals): 267–545 (279 verses)
  Ox and buffalo—Entrance of wolf (carnivores): 546–808 (269 verses)
  Wolf–End: 809–1082 (278 verses)

127. However, to be called a lion in Byzantium was not always meant as a compliment. Koutrakou (1991) discusses the rhetoric surrounding the names of the iconoclast emperors Leo III and Leo V (see also discussion in "Untraced Beliefs"). On the one hand the future Leo V, then a general under Michael I, set the scene for his coup by challenging his soldiers, putting his name to good use:

  ὁ δὲ καιροῦ λαβόμενος ἐπιτηδείου τὸν στρατιώτην ὄχλον ἠρέθιζέ τε καὶ βλάσφημά τινα ῥιπτεῖν κατὰ τοῦ βασιλέως ἠνάγκαζε, καὶ μὴ ἂν ἔλαφον, ἐκεῖνο δὴ τοῦ μύθου, ἡγεῖσθαι λεόντων καλὸν ἔλεγεν εἶναι

  [Seizing the moment, he started inciting the mob of soldiers and urged them to cast blasphemous aspersions against the emperor, asking them whether it was good that a deer (as the fable puts it) should be the master of lions.] (*Theophanes Continuator* 16)

  On the other hand, as Koutrakou goes on to say, Leo V's opponents took a rather different view of lions. One such reference has already been given in "Untraced Beliefs." His predecessor Leo III was similarly castigated in the *Vita of St. Stephen the Younger* §9:

  καὶ τὸν ὑπ' αὐτοῦ λαὸν ἐκκλησιάσας, μέσον πάντων λεοντοειδῶς βρύξας ὁ ἀνήμερος θὴρ καὶ λεοντώνυμος ἐκ τῆς ὀργίλου αὐτοῦ καρδίας ὡς ἐξ ὄρους Αἰτναίου πῦρ καὶ τέαφον ἠρεύξατο τὴν ἐλεεινὴν ἐκείνην φωνὴν καὶ εἶπεν· «Εἰδωλικῆς τεχνουργίας ὑπαρχούσης τῆς τῶν εἰκόνων ἀνατυπώσεως, οὐ δεῖ ταύτας προσκυνεῖν.»

  [And assembling the people under his rule, the wild beast bearing the name of a lion roared in their midst like a lion indeed, and out of his enraged heart he belched forth his miserable voice like Mount Etna belches fire and sulfur, and said: "Because the drawing of images constitutes an idolatrous practice, it is not proper that they be worshipped."]

128. Cardinal William Sirlet was a scholar active in the mid-sixteenth century. Among other achievements, he was involved in revising the Catholic catechism and missal after the Council of Trent (1566, 1570) (http://www.fordham.edu/halsall/mod/romancat.html; http://www.newadvent.org/cathen/10354c.htm; accessed September 2, 2002). He also chaired the commission that formulated the Gregorian calendar in 1582 (http://www.fusl.ac.be/Files/General/BCS/ENC4/03.html; http://dsa.netliberte.org/reforme.html; accessed September 2, 2002).

129. For description of the manuscripts of the *Tale,* see also Tsiouni 1972:13–22.
130. Papathomopoulos is in general more inclined than Tsiouni to select nonvernacular readings in his edition: for example, learned *crases* (vowel mergers across words) such as κἀμοῦ CA in 567, where Tsiouni selected P's more modern-looking καὶ ἐμοῦ. Verse 123 (see Textual Notes, 124) seems to be the only instance where Papathomopoulos follows L rather than PCVA, and even there it is as a matter only of spelling (οὕτως/οὗτος).
131. The case of Eustathius, the fifteenth-century redactor who merged the two traditions of the *Digenes* narrative into *Digenes* Z (Beaton 1993:55–56), is unique in medieval vernacular Greek literature.
132. See also verses 477, 705, 709, 748, where VLA agree against PC.
133. The consequence of accepting such contamination for the editor's stemmatic methodology is that instances where V or L match P do not represent independent traditions of the poem and cannot be considered to outweigh C's reading in particular.
134. We should note, all the same, that P is overall the work of a conscientious scribe: he may insert and delete verses, but within the verse most of his outright errors appear to be limited to anagrams and missing letters.
135. Ignoring the clear lacunae in the text, which are not intentional: VL 545–81; L 865–95; A 1–65, 168–97, 575–605, 882–1082.
136. Tsiouni and Papathomopoulos both retain Wagner's lineation; because they choose different verses than Wagner, this results in several suffixed verse numbers (e.g., 10a).
137. On the hypotheses on Byzantine vernacular formulas, see summary in Beaton 1996:164–81.
138. Beaton (1996:178–79) finds only the epic of *Digenes Akrites* has a direct oral substrate, possibly composed of songs like the extant *Lay of Armoures*. The formulas in the remainder of the vernacular works for the most part do not resemble either those in the Akritic lays or those of modern folk song.
139. Regrettably, we have minimal information on Byzantine bards. What little we do have is discussed in Jeffreys and Jeffreys 1986. Beaton (1996:177, 186) disputes that there was a well-developed bardic tradition at all in Byzantium and believes the poets simply forged a new literary style based on extant short ballads (already attested from the sixteenth century), rather than otherwise unattested extended oral narratives. Of course, whether a scribe emulates a bard or a balladeer is moot.
140. In fact, there are cases where a scribe committed orthographic barbarisms in a vernacular text but wrote out a basically correct learned text in the same manuscript (Agapitos and Smith 1994:62–63). It follows that scribes were perfectly capable of varying their degree of faithfulness to the text prototype, as well as their spelling, when switching from learned to vernacular works. So just because a scribe of learned works copied a vernacular work does not mean that he copied it verbatim.

     We know, in fact, that Nicholas Agiomnitis, who copied the first attested manuscript of the *Tale,* was such a scribe. Toufexis (2001) compares his spelling in the *Book of Birds* and in the learned texts he copied. He finds that, as expected, his learned orthography is quite good, whereas his vernacular orthography is chaotic. As already noted, Toufexis (personal communication) has also found that Agiomnitis tampered with the text of the *Book of Birds* to fit the illustrations better—something he would not dare do with the learned medical texts he copied later in his career. All the same, the lack of standardization of the vernacular could easily mean that some orthographic barbarisms were meticulously copied from their sources by scribes like Agiomnitis.

141. See, for example, the comments in Tsavare 1987:7—but note that Tsavare, like Papathomopoulos, is an exception among contemporary vernacular Byzantine philologists in advocating classical textual criticism.
142. For a survey of recent thinking on how to edit Byzantine texts (with no danger of consensus arising), see Eideneier, Moennig, and Toufexis (2001).
143. The bardic pretensions of the scribes, incidentally, would have given them added license to tamper with the original's meter as well as its wording, as becomes clear through comparison of the different manuscripts (see "Meter").
144. Thus Renehan (1969:44), referring to the transmission of classical texts: "Errors of sound are more frequent than errors of sight. (This does not necessarily imply that dictation was the normal, or even a widespread practice. Whenever a person thinks, he pronounces, if only slightly, to himself; scientists can measure such movements of the vocal organs. When one is reading, this 'silent' pronunciation is more marked, and it will be recalled that the Greeks and Romans regularly read aloud.)"
145. See Beaton (1990:181) for an argument along these lines. This was all the more so at a time when literacy was not yet as thoroughly integrated into people's lives as it is nowadays: "Just as reading was linked . . . with hearing rather than seeing, writing . . . was associated with dictating rather than manipulating a pen" (Clanchy 1979:218). Alexiou (1986:6) claims dictation was already proposed as a cause of soundalike errors in *Digenes* by Fletcher (1976)—although we have not been able to find any such claim in that paper.
146. Representative instances are given in Jeffreys and Jeffreys (1971:147) and Mohay (1974–75:177).
147. Beaton (1996:177), among others, protests that the formulas identified in medieval Greek are not "sufficiently memorable or distinctive enough to have played a significant part in a fully functioning system of oral-formulaic composition." The formulas that Jeffreys and Jeffreys (1971:143–48) identify for the romance *Imperios and Margarona* (e.g., ἐστρώσασίν του τὸ φαρίν, "they readied his steed"; λαμπροαρματωμένος, "in bright armor"; σιγά, κρυφὰ καὶ ἀνόητα, "silently, secretly, and imperceptibly"; νὰ δώσουν κονταρέας, "and strike with the lance"; μέσον χαρᾶς καὶ θλίψεως ἐκείτετον ὁ νοῦς του, "his heart was lying between joy and sorrow") are rather more promising *qua* formulas—because of the genre in which they appear.
148. The last thing the *Tale* does, of course, is make a long story short.
149. But there is nothing to say this was not merely the normal way of saying "you should have seen." One would not make a similar claim for its modern equivalent και πού να δεις, for instance.

    The other echo of *Ptochoprodromos* that Eideneier (1991:47) sees in the *Tale* looks to us as a coincidence. The verse καὶ φαίνουνται αἱ σάρκαι μου καὶ ὁμοιάζω νυκτοκλέπτην, "my flesh shows through ⟨my rags⟩; I look just like a night-thief" (4.555) starts like καὶ φαίνεται ὁ κῶλος σου, "uncovering your arse" (literally, "your arse appears") in *Tale* 356 and ends with the νυκτοκλέπτη, "night-thief," of *Tale* 833. But neither phrase looks promising as a poetic commonplace, and they arise where they are in the *Tale* quite naturally, without any need to appeal to allusion or a stock of formulas.

150. In that study, a formula is defined as a hemistich (and only a hemistich) repeating a hemistich elsewhere in the poem and is allowed to vary only in spelling, declension or conjugation, and changes of pronoun or conjunction. (We have also included formulas substituting synonyms: e.g., κάμνω and ποιῶ, "do.") The listing enumerates separately hemistichs that do not match those criteria (e.g., involving reordering of words—although Duggan [1973:11], on whose work Jeffreys' is modeled, counts these as literal repetitions) but that are still felt to be repetitions in essence.
151. Unlike the case for other such poems, no section of the *Tale* seems inherently more formulaic than any other. The drop in formulas for verses 200–500 does not seem to us to correspond to any obvious feature of the narrative.
152. So Jeffreys and Jeffreys (1983:334) on the formulas inserted into the translated *War of Troy*: "It was left an open question how many of the formulaic phrases were drawn directly from an oral tradition, and how many were made by the Greek translator because formulas were an essential part of the style he was using—probably the only style he knew for vernacular narrative." See also Papathomopoulos and Jeffreys 1996:lxxxvi.
153. Instances in the Septuagint include Esther 4:17h (=Rest of Esther 13:17) ἐπάκουσον τῆς δεήσεώς μου καὶ ἱλάσθητι τῷ κλήρῳ σου καὶ στρέψον τὸ πένθος ἡμῶν εἰς ***εὐωχίαν***, ἵνα ζῶντες ὑμνῶμέν σου τὸ ὄνομα, κύριε, καὶ μὴ ἀφανίσῃς στόμα αἰνούντων σοι, "Hear my prayer, and be merciful unto thine inheritance: turn our sorrow into ***joy***, that we may live, O Lord, and praise thy name: and destroy not the mouths of them that praise thee, O Lord"; Esther 8:12u (= Rest of Esther 16:22) καὶ ὑμεῖς οὖν ἐν ταῖς ἐπωνύμοις ὑμῶν ἑορταῖς ἐπίσημον ἡμέραν μετὰ πάσης ***εὐωχίας*** ἄγετε, "Ye shall therefore among your solemn feasts keep it an high day with all ***feasting***." Interestingly, the word turns up only in Greek-language additions to the Jewish Scriptures: 3 Maccabees (4:1, 4:8, 5:3, 5:17, 6:30, 6:35), 1 Ezra (3:20), and the Greek expansions on Esther.

    That εὐωχία was not regarded as obscure is borne out by the frequency with which it was used as a gloss in dictionaries, grammar textbooks, and scholia for more obscure Attic or Homeric words. The *Thesaurus Linguae Graecae* (2002) includes no fewer than fifty-two works in which εὐωχία is so used. By contrast, εὐωχία itself is glossed only in *Hesychius, Suda,* the *Etymologicum Gudianum,* and (in two instances of obscure classical use) in *Scholia in Aristophanis ranas (scholia vetera)* and *Scholia in Aelium Aristidem (scholia vetera).* In *Additamenta in Etymologicum Gudianum, Etymologicum Magnum,* and *Pseudo-Zonaras* the etymology for the word is given without the word itself even being glossed. This contrasts with the frequency with which ἀγχίνοια was glossed in Byzantine dictionaries (see discussion following), and shows that εὐωχία cannot have been truly obscure.
154. The only other comparable usage that Liddell–Scott–Jones 1940 gives is "give oneself airs, be coy," by Aristaenetus—who dates from the fifth century A.D.
155. See also Commentary, verses 177, 571, 654, 1013, for other Koine cases. The use of "eyebrow" to refer to arrogance (177) may be literary, but as we explain in our Commentary it cannot be classical.

156. An exception should be made for the fables preserved by Aphthonius and the Aesopic Proverbs, which are in a more learned language: *Fabulae Aphtonii* 33 γέρας αἱ τέχναι τοῖς προσήκουσι πράγμασι ***νέμουσιν***, "the arts ***dispense*** honor in the matters pertinent to them"; *Aesop: Proverbs* 21 Μενέτω κοινά, ἅπερ ἡ Τύχη ***νέμει***, "Let what Fortune ***deals out*** remain in common"; *Proverbs* 67, 118.
157. νέμω in Byzantine writers: Christopher Mytilenaeus, *Poems* 95; John Damascene, *Sacra parallela,* 1057; Manuel Gabalas, *Letters* B36.
158. Of course, Critobulus is writing as Mehmet's apologist, so he has his own reasons for using the loaded classical word *basileus* to refer to the sultan. Ducas, by contrast, who is hostile to the sultan, uses no such vocabulary.
159. Archaisms in the lion's speeches or the diplomatic exchanges cannot be counted as exceptional, because those speeches are more formal (cf. ἴδωμεν [66], στείλωμεν [73], γεγονυῖα [556]). The use of the infinitive in the text, on the other hand, is not especially archaic: it follows Joseph's description (1983) of medieval vernacular Greek infinitives as being restricted to use after modal verbs (Tsiouni 1972:128).
160. Anapests in Tsiouni's edition: First hemistich: 14, 50 (misread, according to Papathomopoulos), 128, 166, 169, 177, 240, 281, 483, 554, 568, 613, 838, 998. Second hemistich: 10, 10a, 14, 32, 61, 76, 113, 200, 230, 257, 354, 362, 412, 539, 702, 737, 990, 1039, 1046.
161. Anapests in Papathomopoulos's edition: First hemistich: 11, 14, 128, 166, 169, 177, 240, 281, 347, 365, 366, 375, 429, 445, 517, 554, 568, 613, 795, 838. Second hemistich: 10, 10a, 14, 32, 61, 76, 113, 200, 230, 234, 257, 263, 310, 354, 362, 412, 477, 576a, 598, 604, 622, 680, 702, 737, 788, 801, 810, 814, 831a, 990, 1026, 1037, 1038, 1039, 1046, 1078.
162. Anapests in verses rejected in Papathomopoulos's edition: First hemistich: 15 CLV, 20 P, 175 C, 307 P, 352 A, 373 P, 378 L, 410 P, 483 P, 542b L, 553 P, 619 L, 628 P, 638 P, 798 A, 841 L, 854 L, 998 CVL, 1057 CVL. Second hemistich: 31 P, 38 CLV, 162 V, 192 VCL, 225 A, 236 P, 345 P, 367 P, 374 V, 383 C, 474 V, 493 V, 539 CL, 576 P, 618 V, 632 LA, 670 C, 709 VLA, 719 L, 743 P, 778 CVA, 819 CVLA, 826 A, 935 L, 989 VL, 998 P, 999 L, 1021 L.
163. It should be said that the Grottaferrata manuscript of *Digenes* is extremely early for a manuscript transmitting a work associated in any way with the vernacular: late thirteenth–early fourteenth cenutury. This might explain the survival of anapests but not the extent to which they are used, which is unique in Byzantine literature. The Escorial manuscript, on the other hand, dates from the late fifteenth century—the time frame in which most Palaeologan vernacular texts are first attested.
164. On the other hand, A does not display much of an ear for meter, and it may be safely presumed that the four times it produces its own anapests (225, 352, 758, 826) are purely accidental.
165. The aesthetic judgment that a "worsening" is involved is irrelevant, of course: if anapests remained in use in 1300, then anapests were obviously acceptable to the Greek-speaking audience of the time, however grating they may be to Greek-speakers in 2000. The only oddity of the Grottaferrata (notwithstanding Alexiou's comment [1993:22] on "strange rhythms in the *politikos* verse" of the redaction) is the extent of its anapests, not the fact that they are there. As Garantoudis (1993:203–4) puts it, commenting on Alexiou's edition of the Es-

corial *Digenes,* "Ultimately, Alexiou's editorial conduct in the correction of certain anapestic hemistichs seems to be pervaded by a prescriptive attitude and is based on aesthetics (preference for iambic accentuation.) Anapestic accentuation may be considered a deviation from a norm (to the extent that study of the texts reveals that anapestic accentuation really does constitute a deviation), but as a metrical phenomenon in and of itself, it cannot be considered an instance of 'versifying clumsiness' because in this instance the notions of 'dexterity' or 'clumsiness' are purely subjective."

Papathomopoulos and Jeffreys (1996:lxxxviii) have faced similar issues in their edition of the *War of Troy*—their first inclination being to use the variant following the modern norm, their second to use the anapestic as likely more archaic. They ultimately decided to ignore meter as a deciding factor in picking their manuscript readings; there is a lot to be said for such metrical agnosticism.

166. For this reason Jeffreys prefers to analyze the aberrant meter as trochaic, following Koder, rather than anapestic, like Tiftixoglu. But because the first foot in the hemistichs involved is rarely stressed, the anapest is more accurate as a synchronic description, and does not risk confusion with the choriambus—an initial trochee (¯˘˘¯), which has always been allowed as a variant in iambic meters.

167. Compare, for example, the vernacular calendar poem *Τὰ εἰδέα τῶν δώδεκα μηνῶν* appearing in the Constantinopolitan manuscript containing the *Tale*; of its 144 verses, 2 are anapestic in the first hemistich (1 percent) and 11 in the second (8 percent) (Eideneier 1979:412)—cf. 3.3 percent anapestic second hemistichs in Papathomopoulos's edition of the *Tale*.

168. It has already been claimed elsewhere that the anapest is used for special emphasis (Bakker and van Gemert 1988:107; Alexiou 1985:lxxxv). So also Tiftixoglu (1974:46): "The *politikos* verse with an accented third syllable, not least because of the smaller number of accents compared to the 'normal' fifteen-syllable verse, has associated with it a notion of urgency and finality."

The author seems to compound the stylistic effect of the anapests in the wolf's speech with another effect, that of a repetitiveness uncharacteristic of the *Tale* as a whole: ὕβρισας, "you have insulted," twice in 813; ἐσθίω, "I eat," in 814, 816, and twice in 820; and μικρά, "small," in 822 and 823. (P attempts to neutralize this feature by substituting ὁμοίως, "similarly," through the passage.) See Textual Notes, 813.

169. There is an intriguing possibility that the *Tale* may have influenced the early eighteenth-century *Istoria ieroglifica* by the Romanian prince Demetrius Cantemir. This is a narrative using animals as veiled references to contemporary Romanian noble families; the work includes the "Greek" animal πάρδος and comes complete with alliances, truces, and a final battle. Romania was under profound Greek cultural influence during Ottoman rule (Constantinopolitan Greek nobles acted as regents there), and Cantemir himself was well versed in Greek. We are not able to pursue the issue, being deficient in Romanian, but would welcome any research in this area. (Our thanks to Florin Curta, University of Florida, for bringing this to our attention.)

170. Niki Eideneier ceased work on her own edition of the *Tale* when informed in writing by Protopapa-Bouboulidou that her edition was already in press (Ei-

deneier 1979:381)—although there has been no sign of Protopapa-Boubouli-dou's edition since.

171. *Aelian*: Bactrian longevity, 4.55; Persian breeding, 10.36; Mud drinking, 17.7.
172. For instance, Beaton (1996:233) refers to it as "scholarly and generally accurate, if often quaint," whereas Jeffreys (1993:26) reports that her students "regularly lament the eccentricities of Mavrogordato."
173. In the translated excerpts from other works given in this introduction, Commentary, and appendices, where precision was more important than readability, *Romans* and *Latins* (Λατίνοι) have been retained, but Φράγκοι are still translated as "Westerners."
174. This is reminiscent of English *swine,* but, of course, in English the word went from being the name of an animal to being an insult, whereas the path the Greek word followed, from "noxious" to "pig/boar" (and elsewhere "donkey"), was the reverse. See Commentary, verses 54, 419.
175. On the difficulty in determining how the animals were divided up by the author, see "Class Struggle in a Byzantine Farmyard."

THE TEXT

The Greek text is that of Manolis Papathomopoulos's (2002) edition of the poem; we gratefully acknowledge his permission to include it here.

The English translation was done by George Baloglou and Nick Nicholas, in collaboration with Tassos Karanastassis, of the Center for Byzantine Studies, Aristotle University, Thessalonica.

Παιδιόφραστος διήγησις τῶν ζῴων τῶν τετραπόδων

[*Στίχοι ἀστεῖοι πρὸς τὸ περίχαρον γενέσθαι τὸν ἄνθρωπον*
Καὶ οἱ μῦθοι ἔνι περιχαρεῖς πάνυ]

Διήγησις παιδιόφραστος περὶ τῶν τετραπόδων 1
Ἵνα ἀναγινώσκωνται καὶ χρῶνται ταῦτα παῖδες,
Οἱ φοιτηταὶ καὶ νεαροὶ διὰ τὴν εὐγνωστίαν·
Γέγραπται γὰρ εἰς ἕλκυσιν μαθήσεως καὶ πόθον,
Ἔχουσιν δ᾿ ὅμως ἔννοιαν καὶ βάθος τὰ τοιαῦτα,
Νόησε μόνον ἀκριβῶς τὴν ἔννοιαν τὴν ἔχουν.
Ὅταν τὰ ἔθνη μεθ᾿ ἡμῶν ποιοῦσιν ψευδαγάπην,
Ὑπερθαρροῦντες εἰς ἰσχὺν ἄρδην ἡμᾶς ὀλέσαι,
Σῴζει δ᾿ ἡμᾶς τὸ δίκαιον, τὸ ἀψευδὲς τοῦ ὅρκου.
Θεὸς γὰρ νέμει τὴν ἰσχὺν ὡς κριτὴς τῶν ἁπάντων. 10
Ἐντεῦθεν λέξω, φίλε μου, τὴν διήγησιν ταύτην. 10a

Τῷ ἑξάκις χιλιοστῷ ὀκτακοσιοστῷ τε
καὶ πρὸς τὰ ἑβδομήκοντα καὶ ἄλλῳ τρίτῳ ἔτει,
μηνὸς τοῦ Σεπτεμβρίου τε τῆς πέντε καὶ δεκάτης
ὁμοῦ πάντα συνήχθησαν τὰ τετράποδα ζῷα,
τὰ καθαρὰ καὶ εὔχρηστα ὁμοῦ εἰς ἕναν τόπον,
αἱμόβορα καὶ βδελυκτὰ εἰς ἄλλην πεδιάδα.
Ἐκάθισεν ὁ βασιλεὺς πάντων τῶν τετραπόδων
λέων ὁ ἀγριόφθαλμος καὶ γαγκλαδοραδάτος·
εἶχε δὲ καὶ συγκάθεδρον ἐλέφαντα τὸν μέγαν,
τὸν μήτε ἁρμούς, μὴ γόνατα, μηδὲ ἀστραγγάλους ἔχων. 20
Πλησίον εἶχεν μετ᾿ αὐτὸν δύο πρωτοσυμβούλους,
πάρδον καὶ λεοντόπαρδον τοὺς ἀποφουμιστάδας.
Ἦσαν δὲ ἐκεῖ καὶ ἕτερα ὠμόβορα θηρία,
λύκος ὁ νυκτοβαδιστὴς καὶ ὁ αἱματοπότης,
κύων ὁ ὑποτακτικὸς καὶ ποθεινὸς ἀνθρώποις,
ὁ πάντα τρώγων βρώματα καὶ πάντα κατεσθίων,
ἀλλὰ καὶ ἡ ἀλώπεκα ἡ φουντοουραδάτη
καὶ ἡ ὀρνιθοπνίκτρια, ἡ παμπονηροτάτη.

Συναθροισθέντων δὲ ὁμοῦ καὶ προκαθεζομένων,
τοῦ λέοντος καὶ τῶν λοιπῶν, βουλὴν τοιαύτην δίδουν 30
καὶ πρέσβεις ἀποστέλλουσιν εἰς ἅπαντα τὰ ζῷα,
τὰ καθαρὰ καὶ εὔχρηστα καὶ τετράποδα πάντα.

Πρῶτον τὸν κάτη στέλλουσιν, διότι νυκτοβλέπει,
καὶ μετ᾿ αὐτὸν τὸν ποντικόν, μεγαλομουστακᾶτον,
μακρύουρον, μακρύμυτον, εἰς συντροφίαν τοῦ κάτου.

ἔστειλαν τὸν κάτ
καὶ τὸν ποντικὸν
καὶ τὴν μιαμοῦ
ἀμπασαδόρους

An Entertaining Tale Of Quadrupeds

[*Amusing verses for one's merriment.*
And all its stories are most comical.]

An entertaining tale of quadrupeds, 1
for youngsters, students, and young men to read
and to employ for all of its good knowledge,
as written to draw out and stir up learning.
Yet note that it has meaning, too, and depth.
So understand exactly what it means:
when all the nations draw with us false peace,
hoping audaciously, by force of might, 8
to lead us into absolute perdition, 8
yet are we saved by just, inviolate oaths.
For God shares power out, as Judge of all. 10
So here, my friend, let me set forth this tale. 10a

It was in thirteen hundred sixty-four, 11/12
and on the fifteenth of the month September,
that all the animals did make assembly:
in one place all the clean, domestic beasts,
the bloody and loathsome in another plain.
There sat the king of all the animals,
the fierce-eyed lion, with his twisting tail.
His seat mate was the mighty elephant,
a beast with neither joints, nor knees, nor ankles; 20
and close to him he had two chief advisors—
the cheetah and the leopard, those maligners.
Other bloodthirsty beasts were also there:
the wolf, who stalks by night and drinks fresh blood;
the dog, obedient and dear to men,
consuming and devouring any foodstuff;
and furthermore the fox, of bushy tail,
who strangles hens and who excels in cunning.

So having all assembled and sat down,
the lion and the rest, they made decision 30
to send out envoys to all other beasts—
to all the clean, domestic animals.

They sent the cat and the rat and the monkey as ambassadors

First did they send the cat, who sees at night,
and as the cat's companion they sent
the long-tailed, long-nosed, and long-whiskered rat.

Εἴχασιν δὲ καὶ μετ᾽ αὐτοὺς ὁποὺ νὰ τοὺς δουλεύῃ
τὴν μαϊμούν, τὸ μίμηστρον, τὸ παίγνιον τοῦ κόσμου.
Ἀπῆλθαν, ἀπεσώθησαν κατὰ τὸ ὡρισμένον
εἰς τἄλλα τὰ τετράποδα τὰ καθαρὰ τὰ ζῷα.
Ταῦτα ὡς εἶδον τὸ φρικτὸν καὶ τοὺς ἐξαίφνης πρέσβεις, 40
ἐδόθη λόγος καὶ ὁρισμὸς καὶ ἐδιαλαλήθη
νὰ συναχθοῦν, νὰ μαδευθοῦν πάντα εἰς ἕναν τόπον,
εἰς πεδιάδαν ὁμαλήν, μικρά τε καὶ μεγάλα·
Ἔβαλαν οὖν διαλαλητὴν λαγὸν τὸν μεγαλάπτην,
ὡς γοργοπόδαρον, ταχύν, ἵνα συνάξῃ πάντας
καὶ νὰ ἴδωσιν τοὺς ἄρχοντας τοὺς ἀποκρισιάρους,
νὰ τοὺς φιλοφρονήσουσιν, νὰ τοὺς ἀποδεχθοῦσιν
καὶ τὰ χαρτία νὰ ἰδοῦν καὶ λόγους νὰ ἀκούσουν.

Ἦλθασιν καὶ συνάχθησαν δι᾽ ὅλης τῆς ἡμέρας.
Καθίσαντων οὖν τοῦ βοὸς ἅμα μὲ τὸ βουβάλιν 50
καὶ ἄλογον τὸ θαυμαστόν, ὄνος ὁ πολυρράβδης,
ὁ φιδοροῦφος ἔλαφος ὁμοῦ σὺν τὸ ἀγρίμι,
ἡ αἶγα καὶ τὸ πρόβατον, ὁ πολυφάγος χοῖρος
ἀπέστειλαν καὶ ἔκραξαν τοὺς ἀποκρισιάρους,
κάτην τε καὶ τὸν ποντικόν, καὶ ἅμα ἐκαθίσαν
καὶ τὰ χαρτία εἴδασιν καὶ λόγους ἐσυνῆραν·
«Τί θέλετε, τί χρήζετε, τί ἔναι τὸ λαλεῖτε;»

Ἀπιλογεῖται ὁ ποντικός, ὁ γερομουστακᾶτος·
«Ὁρίζει λέων ὁ βασιλεὺς πάντων τῶν τετραπόδων
μὲ συμβουλὴν τῶν μετ᾽ αὐτοῦ φρονίμων καὶ κριτάδων, 60
ἵνα συνέλθωσιν ὁμοῦ τὰ τετράποδα ζῷα,
τὰ καθαρὰ καὶ εὔχρηστα ὁμοῦ εἰς ἕναν τόπον,
καὶ πάντα τὰ μὴ καθαρὰ ἀλλὰ καὶ τὰ ᾽μοβόρα
εἰς κάμπον ὡραιότατον, εἰς ὁμαλίαν μεγάλην,
καὶ λόγους νὰ συνάρωμεν τινὰς ἐκ τῶν ἀστείων
καὶ ἴδωμεν τοῦ πᾶσα ἑνὸς τὸν ἔπαινον καὶ ψόγον.
Τοῦτο ἐστὶ τὸ μήνυμα λέοντος βασιλέως
καὶ τοῦτο λέγουν αἱ γραφαὶ αἱ πρὸς ὑμᾶς σταλεῖσαι.»

Τότε ἀπιλογήθησαν τὰ καθαρὰ τὰ ζῷα:
«Ἀνάρμοστοι, ἀσυντελεῖς ὑπάρχουσιν οἱ λόγοι. 70
Ἡμεῖς ἐκείνων βρώματα ἐσμὲν εἰς εὐωχίαν,
καὶ πῶς γὰρ ἔνι δυνατὸν ὁμοῦ νὰ μαδευθοῦμεν;
Στείλωμεν οὖν γε καὶ ἡμεῖς τοὺς ἡμετέρους πρέσβεις,
νὰ ἔλθουν νὰ συντύχουσιν καὶ πάτους νὰ ποιήσουν,
νὰ στερεώσουν δυνατὴν ἀγάπην καὶ φιλίαν,
καὶ τότε νὰ συνέλθωμεν τὰ τετράποδα πάντα

And by their side, attending both of them,
the mimic monkey, mockery of the world.
They left, and they arrived as was arranged
at all the other, clean beasts' meeting place.
Seeing this horrid, sudden embassy, 40
they gave out word and law, to make it known
that all of them—the great and small alike—
should gather in one place, a smooth, flat plain.
They sent the long-eared hare to be their crier,
as swift of foot and quick, to gather all,
and bid them see the noble delegates,
to pay them compliments, to make them welcome,
and see their documents and hear their words.

They came and gathered there all through the day.
And so the ox sat by the buffalo, 50
the much-flogged donkey and the wondrous horse,
the deer, who sucks down snakes, the goat as well,
the wild goat and the sheep, the glutton boar—
and then they sent to call the delegates,
the cat and rat. Together they sat down
and saw their documents and questioned them:
"What do you want? What say you? What's your will?"

The old, bewhiskered rat then made reply:
"The lion, king of all the animals,
in council with his wise and just companions, 60
orders that all the animals assemble,
together both the clean, domestic beasts
and the unclean and bloody in one place,
a fairest plain, a large and spacious valley;
and there trade witty words and come to see
the merits and the faults of each apart.
This is the message of our King the Lion,
and this is what is written down for you."

The clean beasts answered back to them as follows:
"These words are inappropriate and pointless. 70
We are as food to them in all their feasts;
how is it possible for us to join them?
No, rather let us, too, send out our envoys,
to go, negotiate with them, sign pacts,
and thus secure a lasting peace and friendship.
And only then should all we beasts assemble

εἰς κάμπον μέγαν, ὁμαλόν, εἰς μίαν πεδιάδαν,
καθὼς φησιν ὁ βασιλεὺς λέων καὶ ἡ βουλή του.»

Τότε ἐστράφησαν κενοὶ ὁ ποντικὸς καὶ ὁ κάτης.
Αὐτοὶ δὲ ἀποστέλλουσιν ἄλλους ἑτέρους πρέσβεις, 80
τὸ ἄλογον τὸ φοβερόν, τὸν θρόνον τῶν ἀνθρώπων,
καὶ ὄνον μεγαλόψωλον καὶ μεγαλορχιδᾶτον.
Εἴχασι δὲ καὶ μετ᾿ αὐτοὺς ὁποὺ νὰ τοὺς δουλεύῃ
καμήλαν τὴν κυμπόρραχην καὶ μακροσφονδυλάτην
διὰ νὰ τοὺς παίζῃ νὰ γελοῦν, νὰ τοὺς παραμυθίζῃ,
καὶ νὰ ὀρχᾶται νωτιδὰ ὡς κακογυρισμένη.

᾿Απήγασιν, ἀπέσωσαν οἱ ἀποκρισιάροι *ὅταν ἦλθαν οἱ ἀποκρισιάροι*
εἰς βασιλέα λέοντα καὶ τοὺς πρωτοσυμβούλους· *τῶν καθαρῶν ζώων*
ἀπέδωκαν καὶ τὰς γραφάς, ἐσύντυχαν καὶ λόγους, **(1)**
ἐποίησαν στοιχήματα καὶ δυνατὴν ἀγάπην 90
καὶ συνεφιλιώθησαν ὁμοῦ τὰ δύο μέρη,
μεθ᾿ ὅρκου βεβαιώσαντες καθολικὴν φιλίαν.
Καὶ εἶπαν καὶ ἐσυνέταξαν καὶ ἐδιαλαλῆσαν
νὰ μαδευθοῦν, νὰ συναχθοῦν ὁμοῦ εἰς ἕναν τόπον
τὰ ζῷα τὰ τετράποδα, μικρά τε καὶ μεγάλα,
τὰ καθαρὰ καὶ εὔχρηστα ἀλλὰ καὶ αἱμοβόρα,
καὶ ἔχθραν νὰ μὴ ἔχουσιν ἢ μάχην ἢ κακίαν,
ἀλλὰ ἀγάπην στερεὰν καὶ δυνατὴν φιλίαν,
ἀλλήλως νὰ συντύχωσιν λόγους ἐκ τῶν ἀστείων
καὶ ὀλιγούτσικα τινὰ τῶν μετεωρισμάτων, 100
ἑνὸς ἑκάστου ἔπαινον καὶ καθενὸς τὸν ψόγον
καὶ ὅσα ἔχουσιν καλὰ ἀλλὰ καὶ τὰ κακά των.

Τότε νὰ εἶδες τὰ βουνά, νὰ εἶδες καὶ τοὺς κάμπους,
νὰ εἶδες καὶ τὰ δάσητα, νὰ εἶδες τὰς λαγκάδας,
τὴν ὄχλησιν, τὴν ταραχήν, τὴν μάδευσιν τῶν ζῴων,
πῶς ἐσυνάχθησαν ὁμοῦ ὅλα εἰς ἕνα μῆνα
εἰς κάμπον μέγαν ὁμαλόν, εἰς μίαν πεδιάδα.
᾿Εκάθισεν ὁ βασιλεὺς λέων ἐπὶ τοῦ θρόνου,
πλησίον οἱ συγκάθεδροι καὶ πᾶσα ἡ βουλή του,
ὁμοῦ καὶ οἱ προάγοντες καὶ οἱ ἀκολουθοῦντες 110
καὶ ὅλον τὸ συνέδριον καὶ πᾶσα γερουσία.
Λέων εὐθὺς ὁ βασιλεὺς ἐλάλησε μεγάλως
καὶ λόγους ἐναπέτεινεν εἰς ἐπήκοον πάντων,
πολλὰ καλοὺς καὶ θαυμαστοὺς καὶ πλήρεις ἀγχινοίας·
καὶ μετὰ τοῦτο ὥρισεν νὰ μετεωρισθοῦσιν,
νὰ συντυχαίνῃ μόνος εἷς, ν᾿ ἀπιλογῆται ἄλλος

within a single plain, a great flat prairie,
as bidden by King Lion and his council."

The cat and rat went back, thus, empty-handed.
The others then sent envoys of their own: 80
the awesome horse, the seat and throne of men;
the donkey, too, of giant dick and balls;
and by their side, attending both of them,
the hunchbacked camel, with her neck so long,
to tease and make them laugh, to cheer them on,
to dance her rump out, awkward as she was.

When the delegates of the clean beasts arrived

The delegates went off and soon arrived
to see King Lion and his chief advisors.
They gave their papers in and held discussions; **(1)**
then they made pledges for a lasting peace, 90
so that both parties reconciled together,
confirming total amity by oath.
So they agreed, enacted and proclaimed
that all the animals, both great and small,
the clean, domestic ones beside the bloody,
should gather and assemble at one place,
holding no enmity, dispute, or malice
but steadfast peace and everlasting friendship—
in order to engage in witty discourse,
and trade a couple of friendly jests as well: 100
each beast discussing one another's merits, 101
and everybody's faults; what good there lies 101
in each of them, but also what is bad.

You should have seen the mountains and the prairies!
You should have seen the forests and ravines!
Uproar and turmoil as the beasts assembled!
How they all congregated in a month
within a single plain, a great flat prairie!
King Lion sat himself upon his throne,
and by his side, his peers, all of his council,
his vanguard and his retinue together, 110
and the assembly, too, and all the senate.
At once, King Lion spoke with mighty voice,
addressing words for all the beasts to hear—
words fair and marvelous and most sagacious.
And then he bade them all begin to jest:
when each one spoke, another should reply,

καὶ πάλιν ἄλλος εἷς πρὸς εἷς διὰ τὴν εὐταξίαν,
ἵνα μὴ γένῃ σύγχυσις ἢ ταραχὴ τυχοῦσα,
ἀλλὰ καὶ διελάλησεν ἀπάνω εἰς ἐτοῦτο,
νὰ χάνῃ τὸ κεφάλιν του καὶ ὅλον του τὸ γένος, 120
εἴ τις ποιήσει ταραχὴν μέσον τοῦ συνεδρίου.

Πρῶτον εὐθὺς ὁ ποντικὸς ἐστάθη εἰς τὸ μέσον
καὶ οὕτως ἀπεφθέγξατο μέσον τοῦ συνεδρίου:

«Εἴ τις καλὸς καὶ ἀπόκοτος, ἂς ἔλθῃ εἰς τὸ μέσον.» **(2)** *ὁ κάτης*
Ἀψός, γοργὸς ἐπήδησεν ὁ ταπεινὸς ὁ κάτης **(3)** *καὶ ὁ ποντικός*
καὶ ἐλοιδόρησεν αὐτὸν λέγων τοιούτους λόγους:

«Μακρύουρε, μακρόμυτε, μεγαλομουστακᾶτε,
τί μοῦ σεῖς τὸ μουστάκιν σου ἀπάνω τε καὶ κάτω;
Ἔνθεν κἀκεῖθεν θεωρεῖς νὰ εὕρῃς τρύπα νά 'μπῃς,
τζυκαλογλεῖφε, τυροφᾶ καὶ ψωμοκαταλύτη, 130
μαγαρισμένε ποντικέ, ὁποὺ μιαίνεις πάντα,
τὰ σῦκα, τὰ σταφίδια, τ' ὀξύγαλον, τὸ γάλα,
κρέας, ὀψάριν καὶ ἀγνὰ καὶ ὅσα τὰ τοιαῦτα,
σιτάριν καὶ τὰ ὄσπρια καὶ ὅσα τούτων εἴδη
καὶ ἄλλα πάμπολλα καλὰ τὰ τρώγουν οἱ ἀνθρῶποι·
τὰ μὲν ἐσθίεις, μυσαρέ, τὰ δὲ οὐρεῖς καὶ χέζεις,
τὰ δ' ἄλλα μὲ τοὺς πόδας σου σκορπᾷς καὶ καταχύνεις.
Ἂν εὕρῃς δὲ ἀβούλλωτον ῥογὶν νὰ γέμῃ λάδιν,
χαλᾷς κάτω τὴν οὔρην σου καὶ σύρνεις τὸ ἐλάδιν
καὶ τὴν οὐράν σου λείχοντα χορταίνεις τὴν κοιλίαν σου. 140
Ἐδὰ κρατεῖ με ὁ βασιλεύς, ἐδὰ κρατεῖ με ὁ ὅρκος,
ἀλλὰ καὶ τὰ στοιχήματα ὅλης τῆς συντροφίας.
Ἀμὴ νὰ πήδησα δαμίν, μικρὸν πηδηματίτζιν,
νὰ εἶδες, σκατοποντικέ, γυρίσματα τοῦ κάτη,
πῶς νὰ σὲ ἥρπαξα γοργόν, πῶς νὰ σὲ ἐμασήστην,
τὰ ταπεινά μου δόντια πῶς νὰ σὲ τραγανίσαν
καὶ πῶς νὰ ἐρρουκάνισα σφικτὰ τὴν κεφαλήν σου,
νὰ πήδησεν ὁ κῶλος σου, ἔξω νὰ ἐκρεμάστη,
καὶ οἱ κόρες τῶν ὀμμάτων σου, τὰ ἔντερά σου ὅλα.»

Τότε πάλιν ὁ ποντικὸς εὐθὺς ἀπιλογεῖται: 150
[καὶ λόγους ἐπεχείρησεν τοιούτους νὰ τοῦ λέγῃ]

«Μεγάλως ὑπεραίρεσαι, μεγάλως καὶ καυχᾶσαι.
Λέγεις ἐμὲ καὶ λοιδορεῖς ὅτι μιαίνω πάντα,

and then another, always taking turns, 117
to keep things orderly and to preclude 117
all unforeseen disorder or confusion.
Upon that point, moreover, he announced:
"If anyone disrupts the conference, 121
both he and all his breed forfeit their heads." 120

Straight off, the rat took center stage, declaring
right in the middle of the conference:

"If any of you is bold enough and decent, 124 **(2)** *The Cat and the Rat*
let him come forth and step into the center." 124
Then, brisk and swift, the humble cat jumped in, **(3)**
vituperating him with words like these:

"You long-tailed, long-nosed, and long-whiskered fool!
What's all this shaking to-and-fro your whiskers?
You seek a hole to sneak in, here and there,
pot-licking cheese-munching bread-squanderer! 130
Foul rat, there's nothing that you don't defile:
figs, raisins, buttermilk, milk, meat, and fish,
mollusks and foods like that, and grain and pulses, 133/134
and countless other goods consumed by people,
you either eat, you filth, or piss and shit on—
what you don't spill and scatter with your feet!
And should you find a pitcher of oil unsealed,
you dip your tail and draw the oil back out,
and licking at your tail, you fill your belly. 140
The king restrains me now; my oath restrains me,
as do the pledges of this whole assemblage.
Yet if I could but make a teensy jump,
you shitty rat, you'd see how cats can move!
How swiftly I would grab you; how I'd chew you;
how these my humble teeth would crunch you up;
and how I'd clench your head and gnaw at it,
until your arse popped out, to hang there limply,
along with both your eyeballs and your guts."

The rat, then, made response to this at once, 150
[trying to argue back at him as follows:]

"You think too big, cat, and you talk too big.
You have reviled me, claiming I defile things,

τὰ βρώματα καὶ πόματα καὶ εἴδη τῶν ἀνθρώπων.
Καὶ ἂν τρώγω, κάτη κάκιστε καὶ στακτοκυλισμένε,
δίκαιον ἔχω, μυσαρέ, καὶ εὔλογον νὰ τρώγω·
ζῷον γὰρ ἄγριόν εἰμι, ἀνήμερον παντάπαν,
ἀκμὴν καὶ ἀκολάκευτον ἀπὸ παντὸς ἀνθρώπου.

Σὺ δὲ αἰσχρέ, παμμίαρε, ἀλευροκαταχέστη,
ἐκεῖ ὁποὺ σὲ ταγίζουσιν, ἐκεῖ ὁποὺ σὲ ποτίζουν 160
καὶ ἀγαποῦν καὶ ἔχουν σε καὶ ὁμαλίζουσίν σε,
διατί τὰ κλέπτεις, ἄτυχε, κρυφὰ καὶ καταλεῖς τα
καὶ ἄλλα τρώγεις ἄτζαλα καὶ ἄλλα μαγαρίζεις;
Καὶ ἐκεῖνα τὰ ποιεῖς ἐσὺ λέγεις τα πρὸς ἐμένα;
Ἀλὶ καὶ ἂν σὲ εὕρουσιν, ἀλὶ καὶ ἂν σὲ πιάσουν,
ὅταν σκάπτῃς εἰς τὰ ἄλευρα καὶ χέζῃς καὶ μιαίνῃς
καὶ εἰς τὸ κεχρὶν καὶ εἰς τὰ κουκία καὶ εἰς ἅπαντα τὰ εἴδη,
χέζεις καὶ τὴν παραγωνίαν καὶ χώνεις μὲ τὴν στάκτην·

ὅταν ταῦτα σὲ εὕρωσιν ποιοῦντα οἱ ἀνθρῶποι,
νὰ εἶδες ῥαβδὲς καὶ ματζουκιὲς ἀπάνω στὰ πλευρά σου, 170
καὶ νὰ σὲ κροῦν καὶ νὰ τζιλᾷς, νὰ κλάνῃς καρυδᾶτα.
Πολλάκις εἰς τὴν κεφαλὴν νὰ τύχῃ νὰ σὲ δώσουν
καὶ νὰ ψοφήσῃς, ἄθλιε, καὶ νὰ σὲ ῥίψουν ἔξω
εἰς τὴν κοπρέαν, ἄτυχε, καὶ νὰ σὲ φᾶν οἱ χοῖροι.
Εἰ δὲ καὶ ζῇς καὶ περπατῇς καὶ εἶσαι εἰς τὸν κόσμον
καὶ εὕρῃ σε σκύλος κυνηγὸς καὶ νὰ σὲ κυνηγήσῃ,
νὰ τινάξῃ τὴν γοῦναν σου, νὰ κόψῃ τὴν ὀφρύν σου
καὶ τὴν ἀλαζονείαν σου καὶ ὅλην τὴν ἔπαρσίν σου.»

Πληρώνοντα ὁ ποντικὸς ὅλους τοὺς λόγους τούτους
ἀπῆλθεν καὶ ἐστάθηκεν εἰς τὸ στασίδιόν του. 180
Ὁ κύων δὲ ὡς ἤκουσεν τοῦ ποντικοῦ λαλοῦντος
τὸ ὄνομα, τὸν ἔπαινον καὶ τὴν τοιαύτην φήμην,
ἀψός, γοργὸς ἐπήδησεν, ἐστάθη εἰς τὸ μέσον
καὶ πρὸς τὸν κάτην ἔτεινεν λόγους τινὰς ὀλίγους:

«Ἐδὰ κρατεῖ με ἡ ἐντροπὴ καὶ ἡ ὑποταγή μου·
ἀμὴ ν᾽ ἁλίσκωσα δαμίν, νά ᾽χαψα τὴν οὐράν σου
καὶ νὰ σὲ ἀκροτίναξα μέσον τοῦ συνεδρίου,
ἐσένα καὶ τὴν ἀλουποὺν τὴν μακροουραδάτην,
τὴν πνίγουσαν τὰς ὄρνιθας καὶ τὰ μικρὰ πουλία,

all food and drink, and people's goods as well.
But even if I do, you loathsome, evil,
ash-wallowing cat, it is both right and proper 156
that I should get my food in such a way, 156
for I am wild and thoroughly untamed,
and never have I been cajoled by Man.

But you, you shameful, filthy flour-shitter,
even as people feed and water you, 160
and love you, keep you by their side, and pet you—
why do you steal things furtively, poor scoundrel, 162
and waste them, messily devouring some, 162
while some you just befoul? And why blame me
for all you do yourself? O, woe to you
if ever you're found out and ever caught
digging into the flour and shitting in it,
defiling millet, broad beans, and the like,
or shitting in the hearth and covering up 168
by throwing ash down there. When people find 168
that you have been committing these misdeeds,
then you'll see sticks and clubs fall on your ribs! 170
And when they beat you, then you'll get the squirts, 171
and you'll start farting farts like walnuts rattling! 171
They'll hit you many times around the head;
and when you've croaked it, miserable bastard,
they'll throw you out onto the dung, poor dear, 174
where pigs will eat you. If, despite it all, 174
you live, to walk and wander in the world,
and then a hunting dog should find and chase you,
he'll jolt your fur and slash your haughty eyebrow—
as well as your conceit and arrogance."

Now, when the rat had finished saying this,
he walked away and stood back at his place. 180
The dog, however, having heard the rat
mention his name, repute, and great renown,
jumped in then, brisk and swift, stood in the center,
and spelled out to the cat a few choice words:

"Right now propriety and obedience
restrain me. If I seized you just a moment,
I'd chomp your tail and jolt you oh-so-gently,
right in the middle of this conference—
you and that long-tailed fox, who strangles hens

ποὺ πνίγει τὰ ἐρίφια καὶ τὰ μικρὰ ἀρνία· 190
καὶ τὰ μὲν τρώγει ἡ κάκιστος, τὰ δ᾽ ἄλλα πίνει αἷμα
καὶ πολεμεῖ μέγαν κακὸν καὶ πλεῖον τε ζημίαν
καὶ ἀδικίαν ἄπληστον εἰς τοὺς πτωχοὺς ἀνθρώπους.»

Ὁ κάτης ἐφοβήθηκεν, φεύγει ἀπὸ τὴν μέσην·
ἐξῆλθε καὶ ἐστάθηκε μετὰ τοῦ συνεδρίου.
Ἀκούσασα ἡ ἀλωποὺ τὰς ὕβριτας τοῦ σκύλου *ἡ ἀλωποῦ*
ἐν ταπεινῷ τῷ σχήματι εἰσῆλθεν εἰς τὸ μέσον *τοῦ κύων*
καὶ πονηρὰ καὶ τροπικὰ ἐφθέγξατο τοιαῦτα:

«Τί ἔναι, σκύλε, τὸ λαλεῖς, τί ἓν τὸ τζαμπουνίζεις; **(4)**
Σκύλον σὲ λέγουν ὄνομα, ἀληθῶς σκύλος εἶσαι· 200
κατὰ γὰρ τὸ σὸν ὄνομα ἔχεις τὴν πολιτείαν.»
Καὶ ταῦτα μὲν ὡς ἤκουσεν τῆς ἀλωποῦς λεγούσης,
προσμειδιάσας ὕστερον τοὺς λόγους τούτους λέγει:

«Ἐξέβης, ἡ κυρ᾽ ἀλωπού, νὰ μᾶς φιλοσοφήσῃς;
Ποῦ ἔμαθες τὰ γράμματα, ποῦ ἔμαθες τὴν τέχνην,
γραμματικήν, ῥητορικήν, οὕτως νὰ συντυχαίνῃς;
Ἀπάνω εἰς τὴν δύναμιν καὶ φόβον βασιλέως
καὶ τῶν λοιπῶν τὴν ἐντροπὴν πολλὰ μοῦ συντυχαίνεις.

Λέγω ν᾽ ἀφήσω τὰ πολλά, νὰ παραβλέψω πάντας,
νὰ σύρω τὸ δερμάτιν σου, νὰ ᾽κδάρω τὴν οὐράν σου, 210
καὶ νὰ τὸ δώσω τὸν γναφέα, τὸν δερματογουνάρην,
νὰ σὲ δαμάσῃ ἡ ἄσβεστος καὶ νὰ σὲ κάψῃ ἡ στῦψις,
νὰ ἐξεχάσῃς τὴν πολλήν, ᾽ψηλὴν φιλοσοφίαν.»

Στραφεῖσα ἡ ἀλώπεκα τὸν κύων ταῦτα λέγει:
«Πολλὰ πολλὰ ὑπεραίρεσαι, σκύλε μαγαρισμένε,
πολλὰ καυχᾶσαι, φλύαρε, σαλιαρομυξιάρη.
Καυχᾶσαι ὅτι κυνηγᾷς λαγοὺς καὶ ἄλλα ζῷα,
πέρδικας καὶ χηνάρια καὶ ἄλλα τῶν ὀρνέων,
καὶ ἀγαποῦν σε καὶ πολλὰ καὶ ὁμαλίζουσίν σε.
Ἀλλ᾽ ὅτε σὲ εὕρουν εἰς μικρὸν πταίσιμον εἰς τὸ σπίτι 220
καὶ κλέψῃς τίποτε νὰ φᾷς ἢ τίποτε νὰ ἐγγίσῃς,
ῥαβδέας ἀποπατητὰς μεγάλας σὲ φορτώνουν.
Εἰ δὲ πολλάκις, μιαρέ, συμβῇ καὶ ψωριάσῃς,
εἰς σπίτιν ἄλλον οὐ χωρεῖς οὐδ᾽ εἰς αὐλὴν ἐμβαίνεις,

and chokes young chicks, who strangles kids and lambkins; 190
and some she eats, most evil she of beasts, 191
while others' blood she does not shirk from drinking, 191
causing thereby great harm and major damage
and infinite injustice to the poor."

The cat got scared and left from center stage,
going away to stand among the others.
The fox, then, having heard the dog insult her,
made a low-profile entrance to the stage,
while saying cunningly and tropically:

The Fox to the Hound

"Hey, dog, what are you crapping on about? **(4)**
You're dog by name, and truly dog by nature— 200
because your name and conduct go together."
And as he heard these words the fox had uttered,
the dog smiled back at her and spoke like this:

"Has Madam Fox come out to play the sophist?
Wherever did you get the education? 205
Where did you learn the skill, the rhetoric, 205
the *Ars Grammatica,* to speak like that?
Relying on the power our king exerts, 207
the fear that he inspires, and my regard 207
for all here present, fox, you've said a lot.
I think I'll cut things short, ignore them all,
pull off your hide, and skin your tail right off 210
and give it to the tanner and the furrier:
alum will burn you, quicklime will torment you.
Then you'll forget your high philosophizing."

The fox turned to the dog and answered thus:
"My, don't we brag a lot! You foulest hound,
you boast a lot, you blathering, snotty dribbler!
You boast of hunting hares and other beasts,
goslings and partridges and other birds;
that people love you greatly and they pet you.
But when they find you guilty of an offence, 220
however small, committed in the house, 220
whether you've stolen food or pawed at something,
they load you with resounding, vicious floggings!
And if—as often happens, filthy beast— 223
you get the itch, there's no indoors for you! 223
Nor will they even let you in the yard.

οὐδὲ καλὸν λόγον ἀκοῦς οὐδὲ ἐπωνυμίαν,
ἀλλ᾽ ὅπου πᾷς, ὅπου σταθῇς, ἄλλον οὐδὲν ἀκούεις,
εἰ μὴ τὸ "ὅλοι δότε τον, ὅλοι λιθάζετέ τον,
διότι μαγαρίζει μας σκύλος ὁ ψωριάρης"
καὶ κροῦν σε ἄλλοι ἀπ᾽ ἐδῶ καὶ ἄλλοι ἀπ᾽ ἐκεῖθεν
καὶ τυμπανίζουν σε καλά, ἕως οὗ νὰ ψοφήσῃς, 230
καὶ δένουν σε μὲ τὸ σκοινὶν ὡς καταδικασμένον
καὶ σύρνουν σε ἐκ τὸν σφόνδυλον, ὑπᾶν σε εἰς τὴν κοπρέαν·
οἱ μὲν λιθοβολοῦσι σε, οἱ δὲ ῥαβδοκοποῦν σε,
σκοτώνουν καὶ ἀφανίζου σε καὶ τὰ ὄρνεα τρῶ σε.
Ταῦτα εἰσὶ τὰ ἀγαθὰ καὶ τὰ καλὰ τὰ ἔχεις
καὶ ὑπεραίρεσαι πολλά, καυχᾶσαι τὰ μεγάλα.»

Ὁ κύων δ᾽ ἐντραπεὶς μικρὸν τῆς ἀλωποῦς τὰς ὕβρεις,
παράμερα ἐστάθηκεν πικροχολιασμένος
καὶ λόγους ἐπεφθέγξατο καὶ ῥήματα τοιαῦτα:

«᾽Αλωποὺ τρυπολόγισσα, βουνοαναθρεμμένη, 240
οὔποτε ἥλιον θεωρεῖς οὔτε ἡμέραν βλέπεις,
ἀλλὰ τὴν ὅλην σου ζωὴν ἔχεις την εἰς τὴν τρύπαν, 241a
εἰς βάθη σκοτεινότατα, εἰς χάσματα ὀρέων,
ἐπεθυμεῖς καὶ τὸ νερὸν δι᾽ ὅλης τῆς ἡμέρας,
τότε τὴν νύκτα νὰ ἐκβῇς καμένη ἀπὸ τὴν δίψαν,
νὰ εὕρῃς πούπετε νερὸν καὶ νὰ τὸ ἀποφρύξῃς
καὶ νὰ πρησθῇς, νὰ ὀγκωθῇς, νὰ συχνοπυκνοκλάνῃς.
Καὶ εἴ τι φᾷς καὶ εἴ τι πῇς καὶ ὅσα καὶ ἂν κοιμᾶσαι,
οὐδὲν σὲ λείπει πώποτε ὁ φόβος καὶ ὁ τρόμος.

᾽Εγὼ δὲ ἀνατρέφομαι μέσα εἰς τοὺς ἀνθρώπους,
εἰς οἴκους τοὺς βασιλικοὺς καὶ εἰς αὐλὰς ῥηγάδων 250
καὶ εἰς ἀρχόντων κυνηγῶν, μεγάλων καβαλάρων.
Ταγίζουν με χλωρά, πνικτὰ καὶ ἐψημένα κρέη·
κρατοῦν καὶ ὁμαλίζουν με καὶ βαγιλίζουσί με
καὶ βάνουν με τραχηλικὸν χανδρατοκουδουνᾶτον
καὶ κυνηγῶ ἐλάφια, λαγούδια καὶ χοίρους,
ἀγρίμια, αἰγίδια καὶ ὅσα τὰ τοιαῦτα. 255a

᾽Ακόμη καὶ τὰ δυνατὰ τὰ ζῷα τὰ μεγάλα,
ἅπερ οὐ δύναμαι κρατεῖν ἀλλ᾽ οὐδὲ καταβάλλειν,
μὲ τὰς φωνάς μου ἐξυπῶ καὶ τρέχουσιν καὶ φεύγουν
καὶ πάλιν τὰ περδίκια καὶ ἕτερα πουλία.»

No more good words for you, nor any pet names!
No, everywhere you go, wherever you stand,
you hear no words but 'Get him, everybody!
Stone him! This scabby dog fouls up the place.'
They strike you, some from here, and some from there,
making you quite a drum to beat upon, 230
until you croak. And then they string you up, 230
and drag you by the neck out to the dunghill,
just like an executed felon's corpse.
Some stone you, then, and others flog you soundly;
they kill you—wipe you out. Then vultures eat you.
Such are your merits and advantages!
Yet you're so haughty, and you brag so grandly!"

Slightly embarrassed at the fox's insults,
the dog, now feeling bilious and embittered,
stood to one side and spoke such words as these:

"You burrow-dwelling, highlands-native fox, 240
you never glimpse the sun nor see the day;
you just spend all your life inside a hole, 241a
down in the darkest depths, in mountain gorges.
You long for water there, throughout the day,
so out you come at night, all parched with thirst,
looking for water somewhere to drain out.
So you swell up, fart early, and fart often!
However much you eat, or drink, or sleep,
you never are estranged from dread and fear.

Now me, I'm raised within the midst of men:
in royal courts, imperial palaces, 250
and homes of noble huntsmen and great knights.
They feed me raw and cooked and strangled meats.
They keep me, cuddle me, and pamper me.
They even put a collar round my neck, 254
bedecked with beads and bells. And then I hunt 254
for deer and boars, for goats both wild and tame,
hares, and whatever else you'd care to mention. 255a
Why, even when it comes to large, strong beasts,
which I'm not strong enough to catch or beat,
I frighten them by barking, and they flee,
as do the partridges and other birds."

Ὡς ἤκουσεν ἡ ἀλωποὺ τοιαῦτα φθεγγομένου, 260
πάλιν τοῦ σκύλου λέγοντος καὶ ὑπερφυσιοῦντος,
ἔφησεν πάλιν καὶ αὐτὴ καὶ πρὸς τὸν σκύλον λέγει:
«Ἀρκεῖ σε, σκύλε φλύαρε, μιαρέ, ψεματάρη,
αἰσχύνθητι, ἐντράπηθι, ἄφες νὰ εἰπῇ καὶ ἄλλος.»

Τότε λοιπὸν ἐξέβηκεν ὁ σκύλος ἐκ τὴν μέσην
καὶ ἡ ἀλώπηξ ἔστεκεν μέσον τοῦ συνεδρίου.
Ὁ λαγωὸς ὡς ἤκουσεν ἐκεῖ τὸ ὄνομάν του, *ὁ λαγὸς*
ἐπήδησεν, ἐστάθηκεν τῆς ἀλωποῦς πλησίον *καὶ ἡ ἀλουπού*
καὶ ἐπεβόα πρὸς αὐτὴν χαροποιοὺς τοὺς λόγους:

«Χαρά στην τὴν κυρὰ ᾿λωπού, χαρά στην τὴν κορδῶναν, 270 **(5)**
χαρά στην τὴν μαστόρισσαν καὶ τὴν σοφίστριάν μου
καὶ τὴν λογιωτάτην μου καὶ φιλοσοφωτάτην,
ὁποὺ ἐκαταδίκασεν σκύλον τὸν μαγαρίτην
καὶ ἐκατέβαλεν αὐτόν, κόψας τὴν ἔπαρσίν του.

Ἀλλ᾿ ἔχεις καὶ ἐσὺ δαμὶν μικρὸν ὀκάτι ψέγος·
καὶ νὰ σὲ τὸ εἰπῶ ἐδῶ, μέσον τοῦ συνεδρίου.
Πολλάκις μὲ φιλεύεσαι καὶ παίζεις μετ᾿ ἐμένα.
Ἐγὼ θαρρῶ ὡς ἄκακον, μὴ ἔχων πονηρίαν,
μέσα εἰς τὴν ἀγάπην μας κατεμπιστεύομαί σε
καὶ δίδω σε ἁπλότητα καὶ ἀνεξικακίαν· 280
σὺ δὲ δράσσεις καὶ σφίγγεις με μέσον ἐκ τοῦ τραχήλου
καὶ πνίγεις με καὶ τρώγεις με μὲ τὴν ἐπιβουλίαν.
Καὶ οὔτε ἡ ἀγάπη σου ἔναι στερεωμένη,
ἀλλ᾿ οὔτε ἡ φιλία σου κρατεῖται ᾿μπιστεμένη,
ἀλλ᾿ εἶσαι ψεματάρισσα, κλέπτρια, ματζιγγάνα,
μαγγαναρέα, μιαρή, κοιλιοχορδοφᾶσα.

Καὶ ὅταν ἐξαπορηθῇς, ἐσθίεις τὰς ἀκρίδας
καὶ κλέπτεις τὰ σταφύλια καὶ τρώγεις τὰς σταπίδας.
Ἐὰν δὲ στήσουν μάγγανον πολλάκις νὰ σὲ πιάσουν,
ὥστε νὰ ζῇς, νὰ ἀναπνῇς, θέλουν σε κοπανίζει, 290
νὰ χέζῃς τὰ σταφύλια καὶ νὰ τζιλᾷς τὰς ῥῶγας,
νὰ μπαινοεβγαίνῃ ὁ κῶλος σου, νὰ χέζῃς τὰς σταπίδας,
νὰ γδάρουν τὸ δερμάτιν σου καὶ νὰ τὸ πάσσουν στάκτην,
νὰ ῥίψουσιν τὰ κρέη σου ἀπάνω εἰς τὰς πέτρας
νὰ μαδευθοῦσιν ὄρνεα καὶ νὰ σὲ καταφάγουν.

Ἀμὴ ἐγώ, κακότυχη, καὶ ἂν μὲ κυνηγήσουν,
ἐσθίουν με οἱ βασιλεῖς, τρώγουν με οἱ ῥηγάδες,

The fox, however, having heard the dog 260
bragging once more and uttering these words,
herself spoke out once more and told the dog:
"Enough, you stinking, blathering, lying hound!
Give someone else a chance—and have some shame!"

And so the dog departed from the scene,
the fox now standing right in center stage.
The hare, who'd heard his name brought up down there, *The Hare and the Fox*
jumped up and stood beside the fox and shouted
such merry-making words as these to her:

"Well done, my Lady Fox! Well done, my toff! 270 **(5)**
Well done, dear master and philosopher,
most scholarly and intellectual,
who has rebuked in force that stinking dog
and brought him down, his arrogance all broken.

You've got a tiny, teensy flaw as well, though,
which I'll bring up before the conference.
Quite often you befriend and play with me.
Harmless and guileless, I pluck up my courage.
I give you all my trust within our friendship,
showing you innocence and utter meekness. 280
And then! You grab and squeeze me by the neck,
strangle and eat me up, all through your cunning.
Neither is your affection ever constant,
nor is your friendship held reliable.
You're nothing but a lying, thieving, loathsome,
innards-devouring, swindling goddamn sorceress!

And when you're down and out, you nibble branch tips,
steal grapes, and eat the raisins hanging there.
But should they set a trap and capture you— 289
as usual—then as long as you still breathe 289
and still have life, they'll keep on beating you. 290
And then you'll shit the grapes and shoot the berries,
arse popping in and out and dropping raisins.
They'll rip your hide off, sprinkling it with ash;
they'll throw your flesh outside onto the rocks,
where birds of prey will gather and devour you.

But me, poor lady, even when they hunt me,
it is the kings and emperors who eat me;

οἱ ἄρχοντες, οἱ εὐγενεῖς καὶ πᾶσα ἀνθρωπότης,
καὶ θέτουν με εἰς τὰ χρυσᾶ καὶ ἀργυρᾶ σκουτέλια
καὶ βάνουν με εἰς τὰς χρυσᾶς κούπας μὲ πιπεράδας. 300

Ἀλλὰ καὶ τὸ δερμάτιν μου ἔναι τετιμημένον·
φορεῖ το εἰς τὴν κεφαλὴν πᾶς μέγας τῶν ἀρχόντων
καὶ ἅπας μέγας ἰατρὸς καὶ μέγας μαρκατάντος,
ἀλλὰ καὶ οἱ ἀρχόντισσες οἱ μεγαλομανδοῦσες,
ὁπού 'χουν τὰς μακρὰς οὐρὰς καὶ σύρνουν τας ὀπίσω·
ἔχουν τὰ μέσα ἐνδύματα διὰ τὴν πρεποσύνην,
εἰ καὶ πολλάκις ἔχουν τα διὰ πολλὴν ψυχρότην·
ὁμοίως καὶ οἱ ἄρχοντες ἐνδύματα εἰς ῥοῦχα
τὰ ἔχουσιν κατὰ καιρὸν διὰ πολλὴν ψυχρότην.

Ἀκμὴν καὶ τὸ ποδάριν μου, τὸ εὐτελές μου μέλος, 310
κἀκεῖνον χρείαν ἐκτελεῖ καὶ αὐτὴν τιμημένην.
Ἔχει το γὰρ ὁ χρυσοχός, συνάγει τὸ χρυσάφιν
καὶ τὸ ἀσήμιν τὸ ψιλὸν τὸ ἀπὸ ῥινισμάτων.»

Ταῦτα εἰπόντος τοῦ λαγοῦ ἐντράπη ἡ ἀλώπηξ,
ἐξέβη καὶ ἐστάθηκεν μέσον τοῦ συνεδρίου.
Ἀκούσασα ἡ ἔλαφος λαγοῦ τὴν καυχησίαν,
πηδηματίτζιν ἔποικεν εὔμορφον παρὰ πάντας
καὶ εἰς τὸ μέσον συνελθὼν ἐστάθη παρρησίᾳ,
ἄφοβος, ἀνεντήρητος, μὴ ἔχουσα δειλίαν, *ἡ ἔλαφος*
ἀλλὰ καὶ χοῖρος ὁ κυμπὸς ἅμα σὺν τῇ ἐλάφῳ. 320 *καὶ ὁ χοῖρος*
Ἡ ἔλαφος ἀπήρξατο, τοιούτους λόγους εἶπεν:

«Φλυαροκόπε λαγωέ, τί ἒν τὸ τζαμπουνίζεις; **(6)**
Καυχᾶσαι εἰς τὰ κρέη σου καὶ εἰς τὰ δέρματά σου;
Νὰ σὲ εἰπῶ λοιπὸν κι' ἐγὼ ὅσα καὶ ἂν θυμοῦμαι,
τὰ δ' ἄλλα τ' ἀπομένοντα νὰ σὲ τὰ εἰπῇ ὁ χοῖρος.

Δυόδοντε, κακόδοντε, σαλέ, σπιθαμογένη
καὶ μεγαλάπτη, γαμησᾶ καὶ κλαδοτρυπολόγε,
τ' ἀπτία σου καὶ ὁ κῶλος σου πάντα τζιμπούρια γέμουν.
Καίει σε καὶ ὁ ἥλιος δι' ὅλης τῆς ἡμέρας·
τὴν νύκταν μόνον περπατεῖς, δαιμόνων τάξιν ἔχεις· 330
καὶ ἂν ἀκούσῃς τίποτε κτύπον μικρὸν ὀμπρός σου,
κλαδὶν ἢ χόρτον νὰ σειστῇ ἢ μύγα νὰ πετάσῃ,
φεύγεις ὥσπερ διάβολος ἐκ τοῦ θυμιαμάτου.
Οὕτως γὰρ ἑρμηνεύεται ἡ σὴ ἐπωνυμία:
Πτὼξ γραφικῶς ὁ λαγωός, ὡς πτήσσω τὸ φοβοῦμαι.

lords, nobles, and all humankind consume me.
They serve me up in gold and silver platters,
preserved in golden bowls with grains of pepper. 300

My skin is also well esteemed, however.
Every grand noble wears it on his head,
and each great doctor and each major merchant,
but also all the large-cloaked noble ladies,
who have long tails to drag behind their dresses.
They put on undergarments for decorum,
while also warding off the brutal cold;
noblemen likewise wear them in their clothes,
seasonably, against the brutal cold.

Even my foot, a limb of slight renown, 310
will also serve a purpose well esteemed:
the goldsmith uses it to pick the gold
and finely grated silver from his filings."

The fox, embarrassed by the hare's remarks,
departed and stood back in the assembly.
The deer, meanwhile, who'd heard the hare's big talk,
leapt gracefully in front of everybody
and came onto the stage. She stood there boldly,
fearless and uninhibited, unblinking, *The Deer and the Boar*
joined by none other than the hunchbacked boar. 320
The deer commenced her speech with words as follows:

"Long-winded hare, what are you on about? **(6)**
You brag about your meat and skin, then, do you?
Well let me tell you what I can remember;
the boar can fill you in on all the rest.

You two-toothed, crook-toothed loon with foot-long whiskers!
You big-eared hornball sneaking round in branches!
Your ear and arse are always full of ticks.
And all day long the sun burns down on you:
you only walk at night, which renders you 330
the equal, in your ways, of ghouls and demons! 330
And if you hear the slightest sound before you,
a rustling branch or leaf, a fly go past,
you flee just like the devil does from incense.
So that explains the name you've come to have:
ptōx. Literary. Hare. From *ptēssō,* 'fear.'

Σὺ ἐπαινεῖς τὰ κρέη σου καὶ σὺ ὑπερυψώνεις;
Ἡ μαρτυρία γὰρ ἡ σὴ οὐδόλως ἀληθεύει·
καὶ γὰρ τὰ κρέατα τὰ σὰ κακόψητα ὑπάρχουν
καὶ μᾶλλον κακοστόμαχα, ἀργὰ εἰς τὸ χωνεῦσαι.
Τὸ δὲ ἐμὸν τοῦ ἐλαφίου ἀσύγκριτον ὑπάρχει· 340
ἀπάνω εἰς τὰ κρέατα τῶν τετραπόδων ζῴων,
ὅπερ ἐσθίουν ἄνθρωποι, ἔνι τὸ ἐδικόν μου·
ἀλλὰ καὶ τὸ δερμάτιν μου ἔχουν εἰς πᾶσαν χρείαν,
εἰς κόρδας καὶ ζωνάρια καὶ ἄλλα τούτων ὅσα
καὶ ἀσκοπούγγια μικρά, ἔχουν τὴν ἴσχαν μέσα·
οἱ ἄνθρωποι βαστάζουν τα, ἅπτουσιν τὴν ἱστίαν.
Εἰ δὲ τύχῃ ὀφίδια νὰ ἔναι εἰς τὸ σπίτιν
καὶ ἅψουσιν μετὰ πυρὸς τὸ κέρας μου ἀπέσω,
ἐκ τῆς ὀσμῆς τοῦ κέρατος φεύγουσιν παραυτίκα
καὶ πλέον οὐδὲν δύνονται ἐκεῖ νὰ ἐμφωλεύσουν.» 350

Ὁ χοῖρος δὲ ὡς ἔστεκεν καὶ ἡ ἔλαφος ἐλάλει,
ἀγανακτήσας ἔφησεν καὶ τῇ ἐλάφῳ λέγει:

«Ἀνέντροπε, κοψόουρε, ἔκβα ἀπὸ τὴν μέσην·
καμμίαν οὐκ ἔχεις ἐντροπὴν ἀλλ᾽ οὐδὲ σωφροσύνην·
τὴν κολοβήν σου τὴν οὐρὰν ἀείποτε σηκώνεις
καὶ φαίνεται ὁ κῶλος σου καὶ πάντες σὲ γελοῦσιν.
Ἀρκεῖ σε λέγειν τὰ πολλά, ἄφες κἀμὲ νὰ εἴπω
μικρὰ καὶ ὀλιγούτζικα καὶ κοντολογημένα·
καὶ πρὸς τὴν γνῶσιν τὴν ἐμὴν φθέγξομαι λόγους τούσδε:

Καυχᾶσθε καὶ ὑπεραίρεσθε ἔξω ἀπὸ τὸ δέον 360
ἡ ἔλαφος καὶ ὁ λαγὸς διὰ τὰ κρέατά σας
καὶ ψεύδεσθε, κομπώνετε τοὺς ἀκούοντας πάντας.
Οἱ πάντες γὰρ ἠξεύρουσιν, μικροί τε καὶ μεγάλοι,
τὸ κρέας τὸ ἡμέτερον τί νοστιμάδαν ἔχει.
Ὡς οὐδὲ ὁ ἥλιος ποτὲ ἰσάζει μὲ τὰ ἄστρα,
ὡς οὐδὲ τὸ καλὸν ψωμὶν τὸ σεμιδαλαφράτον
ἰσάζει μὲ τὸ κιβαρὸν ἢ μὲ τὴν κριθινάδαν,
οὕτως τὸ κρέας τὸ ἐμὸν μετὰ τοῦ ἐδικοῦ σας.
Ὥσπερ τὸ ἅλας γὰρ ἀρτεῖ τὰ φαντὰ τοῦ κόσμου,
οὕτως ἀρτύζει τὸ ἐμὸν εἰς πᾶσαν μαγειρίαν 370
καὶ μὲ τὰ λάχανα καλὸν καὶ μὲ τὸ κολοκύνθιν
καὶ ἐκζεστὸν καὶ μοναχόν, δίχως κανένα εἶδος,
ἀκόμη καὶ ὀπτούτζικον εὔμορφον, μυρωδᾶτον,
θέλει χλωρόν, θέλει παστόν, ὅπου νὰ μὲ γυρεύσῃ·
παστώνουν καὶ φυλάσσουν με διὰ ὅλου τοῦ χρόνου
καὶ βάνουν με εἰς τὸ σταμνὶν καὶ μέσα εἰς τὸ πιθάριν

You praise your meat? And you exalt it so?
But your account is totally invalid:
your meat is truly difficult to cook,
slow to digest, and painful to the stomach.
But my meat, venison, remains unequalled. 340
The pinnacle of meats of animals
that people like to eat is mine. Moreover,
people will put my skin to every purpose:
in strings and belts and everything like that,
and in small pouches, too, containing tinder—
by holding these up, people light their hearths.
And should snakes happen to infest a house
and people set my horn's insides alight,
then its strong odor drives them out at once:
no longer can they make their nests therein." 350

The boar stood by there, while the deer kept talking,
until he got fed up and said to her:

"You shameless, dock-tailed pest, get out of here!
You know no shame nor any common sense.
You never fail to lift your docked tail up,
uncovering your arse, for all to laugh at.
Enough with all your going on at length;
let me, too, state a few, succinct, brief facts.
Based just on what I know, I'll say these words:

You boast and brag beyond all decent measure, 360
both deer and hare, about how good your meat is.
In this you lie, deceiving all who hear you.
For everyone, both great and small, knows well
how tasty and how succulent my meat is.
Just as the stars are no match for the sun,
just as fine, fluffy semolina loaves
cannot be matched by rusks or barley bread,
so, too, your meat cannot compare with mine.
Just as salt seasons all plates in the world,
my meat will season any cookery: 370
it's good with cabbage and with squash as well;
it's fine when boiled alone, with nothing else;
it tastes and smells delicious when it's roasted;
fresh, salted, any way you can devise.
Indeed, they salt and store me all year round
and place me inside jugs, and jars as well,

καὶ πολεμοῦσιν με πηκτὴν μὲ ἄλλα τὰ τοιαῦτα,
καταμαγοῦλαν σύγλωσσην μετὰ χοιρομερίων,
λουκάνικα, ἀπάκια, πλευρὰς παχυλαρδάτας
καὶ πασπαλάδας λιπαροὺς καὶ παραμεμιγμένους. 380
Καὶ ὅταν ψήνουσιν ποτὲ τὰ ἰδικά σας κρέη,
προσβάλλουσιν ἐκ τὸ ἐμὸν ὅπως νὰ τὰ ἀρτύσῃ·
χωρὶς ἐμοῦ οὐδεμιὰν ἔχουσι μυρωδίαν.

Ἀκόμη καὶ αἱ τρίχες μου χρείαν ἀποπληροῦσιν
μεγάλην, ἀξιόλογον εἰς Φράγκων ἐκκλησίαν·
καὶ γὰρ εἰς τὸ ἁγίασμα τὰ φραγκοπαπαδούρια
μετὰ τῆς τρίχας τῆς ἐμῆς τοὺς πάντας ἁγιάζουν
καὶ τὴν βορβοροκύλισιν ποσῶς οὐδὲν θυμοῦνται.
Καὶ οὔτε τζαγγάρης ἢ σελᾶς ἢ ῥαπτοδερματάρης
νὰ ῥάψῃ δύναται ποσῶς ἄχρι κεντέαν μίαν, 390
χωρὶς νὰ βάλῃ ἀπ᾽ ἐμοῦ τρίχαν εἰς τὴν ὀργυίαν.

Οὔτε ζωγράφος δύναται ποσῶς νὰ ἱστορίσῃ,
ἐὰν μὴ βάλῃ ἀπ᾽ ἐμοῦ τρίχαν εἰς τὸ κονδύλιν,
καὶ κάμνει ἄλλα ὑψηλὰ καὶ δεύτερα καὶ τρίτα
καὶ ὅσα βούλεται ποιεῖν, ὅλα διὰ τὴν τέχνην.
Καὶ ἱστορίζει θαυμαστοὺς ναοὺς ἐξῃρημένους
καὶ τὰς εἰκόνας τὰς σεπτὰς τὰς σεβοπροσκυνοῦσιν
τὰ γένη τῶν Χριστιανῶν εἰς ἅπαντα τὸν κόσμον
καὶ ἱστορογραφίζουσιν καὶ χρωματοπλουμίζουν
σπίτια καὶ παλάτια μεγάλων βασιλέων 400
καὶ ἄλλους οἴκους φοβεροὺς μεγάλων μεγιστάνων.

Ἀκόμη καὶ τὸ δόντι μου ποιεῖ καὶ τοῦτο χρεία·
ἔχουν το οἱ γραμματικοὶ καὶ πάντες οἱ σκουφάδες,
στιλβώνουν καὶ τὰς σκούφιας, στιλβώνουν τὰ χαρτία.
Πολλάκις ἔχω το καὶ ἐγὼ εἰς χρείαν ἐδικήν μου·
ἔχω το ὡς ἅρμα δυνατὸν εἰς τὸν καιρὸν τῆς μάχης·
ὅταν ἐχθρὸς μὲ πολεμῇ ἀδίκως νὰ μὲ φάγῃ,
μετὰ τοῦ ὀδόντος κρούω τον καὶ σχίζω τον αὐτίκα
καὶ χύνω τὴν κοιλίαν του καὶ ὅλα τὰ ἐντός του.

Σὺ δέ, ἐλάφιν καὶ λαγέ, τί ψῆφος ἓν δικός σας; 410
Μίαν φωνὴν ἢ λαλιὰν ν᾽ ἀκούσητε πολλάκις,
ὁ ἥλιος οὐ βλέπει σας ἀλλ᾽ οὐδὲ ἡ σελήνη,

turning me into brawn and all the like:
hams, cheek-and-tongue meats, also sausages,
cured tenderloins and thickly larded ribs,
and fatty meats mixed and preserved in casks. 380
And even when they do cook meat of yours,
they must add some of mine to season it:
without my meat yours has no scent at all.

Even my hair fulfils a major mission
within the Western church, deserving mention:
the padres bless the folk during *Asperges*
using a sprinkler made from hair of mine—
while paying no attention whatsoever 388
to how I am wont to wallow in the mires. 388
Neither can any cobbler, saddle maker,
or leather worker sew a single stitch 390
unless my hair is first tied to the thread.
Nor can a painter ever make a painting
without my hair fixed to the paintbrushes,
some thick, some second-grade, some third-grade fine—
whatever type he wishes, for his art.
And then he illustrates with pious tales 396
the walls of marvelous and much-praised churches, 396
and paints the sacred icons, venerated
by generation after generation 398
of Christian folk, wherever they may be; 398
they illustrate and decorate in color
great emperors' houses and palaces 400
and also mighty magnates' splendid homes.

Even my tooth will serve a purpose, though,
for it is used by bookbinders and scribes
to polish both the pages and the covers.
And often I make use of it myself—
a fearsome weapon in the heat of battle.
For when the foe attacks me to devour me, 407
with no regard for justice, I employ it 407
to strike him, tearing him apart at once
and gouging out his belly and his innards.

But you! You, deer and hare! Who cares for you? 410
So often, if you hear a single sound
or but a single voice, the sun thereafter 412
sees you no more, and neither does the moon! 412

καθὼς καὶ ἡ πλησίον σας ἡ βρωμομυξαρέα,
ἡ σκατοβορβορόκοιλη αὐτὴ ἡ προβατίνα·
καὶ γὰρ εἷς κοπροζάγαρος χίλιας νὰ διώκῃ.»

Αἰσχύνθη γοῦν ἡ ἔλαφος καὶ ὁ λαγὸς ἐντράπη
τὸ ψέγος καὶ τὰς ὕβριτας καὶ λοιδορίας τοῦ χοίρου,
καὶ ὑποχώρησαν μικρὸν ὅλως καταισχυμένοι.
Τὸ πρόβατον ὡς ἤκουσεν τοῦ μοχθηροῦ τὰς ὕβρεις, *τὸ πρόβατο*
ἐξέβη τότε καὶ αὐτὸ καὶ ἔστη εἰς τὸ μέσον 420
καὶ ἥμερα καὶ ταπεινὰ ἐφθέγξατο τοιαῦτα:

«Πολλὰ ἐμεγαλαύχησας, φλυαροκόπε χοῖρε. (7)
Φησὶν ὁ ἐπιχώριος λόγος καὶ παροιμία·
Ἑβραῖος ὄζει καὶ βρωμεῖ καὶ ὅλη του ἡ θήκη·
οὕτως καὶ ἐσύ, κακόδοντε, κοπροαναθρεμμένε·
ὅσα κἂν φᾷς καὶ ὅσα πῇς καὶ ὅσα σπαταλήσῃς,
ἐὰν μὴ φάγῃς κόπρια, οὐδὲν σὲ νοστιμίζουν.»

Τότε ὁ χοῖρος ἔφησεν γελῶν καὶ χολιάζων:
«Ἦλθεν καὶ ἄλλη φιλόσοφος μείζων τῆς ἀλωπούτζας
καὶ ἔχανε τὸ στόμαν της καὶ ἔχεσαν οἱ πάντες. 430
Ποῦ ἔμαθες τὰ γράμματα, προβατομυξαρέα;
Ὁ λύκος σοῦ τὰ ἔμαθεν, ὁ φίλος σου ὁ γέρων,
ὁ κύων ὁ παγκάκιστος, ὁ ἀδελφοποιτός σου,
ἡ αἶγα μὲ τὰ γένεια, ὁ τράγος μὲ τὴν κοῦτλαν;»

Τότε εὐθὺς τὸ πρόβατον ταῦτα ἀπιλογήθη:
«Ὦ μιαρὲ σκατόχοιρε, βορβοροκυλισμένε,
ποὺ τρώγεις πάντα τὰ κακὰ καὶ ἄχρηστα τοῦ κόσμου,
σκωλήκια καὶ κόπρια, κρέατα ψοφισμένα,
ὀφίδια καὶ ἑρπετὰ καὶ σαπημένα κρέη·
ἀκόμη καὶ τὸ ὀλέθριον καὶ τὸ κακὸν τὸ κάμνεις· 440
κανένα ζῷον ἢ πτηνὸν ἢ ὄφις ἢ θηρίον
οὐκ εἰσηκούστηκε ποτὲ τὸ κρέας του νὰ φάγῃ·
καὶ σὺ ἂν εὕρῃς μοχθηρὸν καὶ ἔνι ψοφισμένον,
πολλάκις δὲ καὶ ἂν βρωμῇ καὶ ἔνι σαπημένον,
ἐκεῖ στέκεις καὶ τρώγεις το ὡς καθαρὸν ἀλεύριν·
καὶ πάντοτε ἡ μύτη σου ὀσμᾶται τὴν κοπρέαν
καὶ ἀνασκάπτει τὰ πηλὰ διόλου καὶ τὰ βοῦρκα.
Καὶ σὺ ποιεῖς τὴν ψῆφον σου καὶ τὴν ὑπόληψίν σου
μὲ ζῷα καθαρώτατα, ἀμίαντα παντάπαν.»

Just like your filthy snotty neighbor there,
the ewe, who dips her belly in mires and shit:
one mangy mutt can scare a thousand like her."

The deer was crushed then, and the hare ashamed,
with all the accusations and the insults 417
and ridicule the boar had hurled at them. 417
So they stepped back a bit, steeped in disgrace.
On hearing how the boar insulted them, *The Sheep*
the sheep, in turn, stepped up and took the stage, 420
gently and meekly saying what here follows:

"You've bragged and bragged too much, you babbling boar. **(7)**
It's just like how the local proverb goes:
'The Jew stinks, and his satchel's just as smelly.'
So, too, you gross-toothed beast brought up in dung,
no matter what you eat and drink and waste,
nothing delights you till you feast on feces."

The boar then laughed and said acerbically:
"Here's a new sophist, greater than the fox!
Her mouth's agape, and everybody shits! 430
You snot-nosed sheep, where did you get this learning?
Was it your friend, that Old Man Wolf, who taught you?
Was it the wicked dog, who's your blood-brother?
Was it the bearded nanny? Or perhaps 434
it was the billy goat, of butting brow!" 434

The sheep was quick to make reply as follows:
"O filthy shitty boar, mire wallower,
who eats all waste and foul things in the world:
dead meat, both worms and dung, and snakes and reptiles
and rotten flesh. You even dare commit
the worst and most pernicious act there is. 440
No animal or bird or snake or beast
has even once been heard of as consuming
its own kind's flesh. But you! If, on your way, 443
you come across a boar—not only dead, 443
but often stinking, too, and fully putrid—
you stop and eat it like the finest flour.
Your nose is always on alert for dung,
digging up mud and swamps from top to bottom.
Yet you compare your name and reputation
with that of purest, spotless animals!"

Ὁ χοῖρος δὲ ὡς ἤκουσεν τὰς ὕβρεις τοῦ προβάτου — 450
καταισχυνθεὶς καὶ ἐντραπεὶς ἀπέφυγεν μακρόθεν,
τὸ πρόβατον δ' ἀπόμεινεν στέκοντα εἰς τὸ μέσον.
Ἡ αἶγα δὲ ὡς ἤκουσεν, ὁμοίως καὶ ὁ τράγος, — *ἡ αἶγα, ὁ τράγος*
τοῦ χοίρου πρὸς τὸ πρόβατον τοιαῦτα φθεγγομένου,
ἐξῆλθον καὶ ἐστάθησαν μέσον τοῦ συνεδρίου,
οἱ δύο ὁμοθυμαδὸν νὰ ποῦν καὶ νὰ λαλήσουν.
Ὅμως ἡ αἶγα προπετῶς ἀπέτεινε τοὺς λόγους:

«Ἔπρεπε σέ, τὸ πρόβατον, νὰ μὴ μᾶς λοιδορήσῃς, — **(8)**
ἐμὲν καὶ τὸν λωλότραγον, τὸν συνανάστροφόν μου,
μᾶλλον δὲ ὡς ἡμεῖς τὰ σοῦ νὰ ἔχῃς συντροφίαν. — 460
Ἡμεῖς νὰ εἴπωμεν δαμὶν χοίρου τοῦ κοπροφάγου
καὶ τοῦ πλατυνορρούθουνου καὶ τοῦ κονιδιάρη.»

Τὸ πρόβατον δὲ παρευθὺς ἔφησεν πρὸς τὴν αἶγαν:
«Ἐκεῖ ὅπου ἐκατέβαλα καὶ κατεσόφισά τον,
τὸν χοῖρον τὸν κακότυχον καὶ τὸν μαγαρισμένον,
ἐσένα τί σὲ ἤθελα νὰ εἶσαι εἰς ἐντροπήν μου,
διὰ νὰ σηκώνῃς τὴν οὐράν, νὰ δείχνῃς τὸ μουνίν σου,
στραβοκερέα καὶ βυζοῦ καὶ πετροφαγωμένη,
ἁπλῶς νὰ στέκῃς ὡς λωλὴ καὶ νὰ ἀναχαράσσῃς
καὶ νὰ κουνῇς τὸ γένιν σου ἀπάνω τε καὶ κάτω; — 470
Ἐγὼ τὰς πλέω καὶ τὰς καλὰς τὰς χάριτας τὰς ἔχω
ἀκμὴν οὐδόλως εἶπον τα οὐδὲ καυχίστηκά τα·
ὅμως νὰ τὰ εἰπῶ καὶ ἐγὼ τὰ φυσικὰ τὰ ἔχω.

Περὶ τοῦ ἐμοῦ κρέατος οὐ λέγω οὐδὲ φάσκω·
οἴδασι γὰρ οἱ τρώγοντες καὶ οἱ ἐσθίοντές με
παχύτητα καὶ ἡδονὴν καὶ καλοστομαχίαν·
εὔνοστα καὶ εὐστόμαχα ἅπαντά μου τὰ μέλη.
Ἀμὴ νὰ εἴπω τὰ λοιπά, ὅσα καὶ ἂν θυμοῦμαι.

Πρῶτον τὸ κέρας τοῦ κριοῦ τοῦ ἡμετέρου γένους
καὶ κατὰ σάρκα ἀδελφοῦ χρῶνται αὐτὸ τεχνῖτες, — 480
σπαθαρομαχαιράδες τε καὶ σουβλομανικάδες·
ἔχουν το εἰς μανίκια καὶ εἰς ἑτέρας χρείας.

Περὶ δὲ τοῦ μαλλίου μου πολλὰ ἔχω νὰ λέγω·
βουρτζίζουσιν, κτενίζουσιν καὶ νήθουσι τὸ νῆμα
καὶ ἔκτοτε τὰ βάφουσιν πᾶσαν λογὴν καὶ χρόαν·
κόκκινα, μαῦρα, κίτρινα, ὀξέα, γερανᾶτα,
καὶ ἄλλα τούτων πλείονα, χρειώδη πρὸς τὴν τέχνην.

The boar, on hearing all the sheep's harsh words, 450
went far away, ashamed and in disgrace.
The sheep remained there, standing in the middle.
The nanny and the billy goat, however, *The Nanny,*
hearing the boar address the sheep like that, *The Billy Goat*
had come and stood in front of everybody,
the two of them to speak and talk as one.
But then the nanny spoke these saucy words:

"Now, sheep, you ought not to offend us thus, **(8)**
me and this crazy billy I've been raised with.
Stick to your own kind, rather, like we do. 460
It's us that should have the odd word with him,
that louse-bitten, wide-nostriled, dung-fed boar."

The sheep, however, talked right back to her:
"Just when I'd vanquished and outwitted him,
that foul, ill-fated boar, what need had I
of services like yours, to embarrass me?
You're here to lift your tail and show your cunt off,
aren't you, you queer-horned, boulder-tumbled titter!
To stand there like a fool and chew the cud
and merely shake your goatee up and down! 470
It's me that has the most and greatest gifts,
yet I have neither mentioned them nor boasted.
But let me, too, describe my native merits.

As for my meat, I need not say a thing;
for those who eat and feast on me know well
how fat, delicious, and digestible
all of my parts are, and how succulent.
So let me tell the rest, what I recall.

First off, the ram—he who is of my breed,
who is my brother and my flesh and blood— 480
has horns which are employed by many craftsmen, 480
makers of swords and knives, and skewers, too;
they're used in hilts and other necessaries.

And there's a lot to say about my wool.
First, people brush and comb and spin the thread,
and then they dye it any kind of color:
red, black or yellow, violet or blue,
and many others, needed in their trade.

Ποιοῦν κουρτίνας εὔμορφας, ὡραιοπλουμισμένας,
καὶ σχηματίζουν καὶ ποιοῦν εἴδη καὶ θεωρίας,
ἀνθρώπους, ζῷα καὶ πετεινὰ καὶ πάντα τὰ τοῦ κόσμου. 490
Καὶ ἔχουν τα οἱ ῥήγαινες ἀλλὰ καὶ οἱ ῥηγάδες,
κόντοι καβαλαρίοι τε καὶ ἄλλοι μετ' ἐκείνους.
Ποιοῦσιν σάκτια 'ψηλὰ καὶ μεγαλοπλουμᾶτα
καὶ ὁ σουλτάνος κάθεται καὶ ὅλοι οἱ ἀμιράδες·
ἁπλῶς καὶ πᾶσα γενεά, Ῥωμαῖοι τε καὶ Φράγκοι,
χρῶνται τα εἰς κλινάρια καὶ εἰς στρωμνὰς ἑτέρας.

'Ακόμη τὸ μειζότερον τὸ κάμνει τὸ μαλλίν μου·
εἶναι τὰ ῥοῦχα τὰ φοροῦν ὅλη ἡ ἀνθρωπότης
εἰς ἅπαντα τὰ πέρατα, μικροί τε καὶ μεγάλοι·
οἱ βασιλεῖς, οἱ ἄρχοντες καὶ πάντες μεγιστᾶνοι 500
φοροῦσιν τὰ τζαλούνια ὁμοῦ καὶ τὰ σκαρλᾶτα,
οἱ δ' ἄλλοι πάλιν μετ' αὐτοὺς πᾶσαν βαφὴν καὶ χρόαν.
'Ακμὴν μὲ τὸ χοντρὸν μαλλὶν κάμνουσιν καὶ τὰ γρίζα,
κάμνουσιν ῥάσα ὑψηλά, τζοχοϋφανδωμένα,
καὶ γουνοεσωφόρια πατριαρχῶν μεγάλων,
μανδία, παραμάνδια μητροπολεπισκόπων
καὶ ἐσωφόρια διπλὰ μεγάλων ἡγουμένων
καὶ ἄσπρα ὑποκάμισα τῶν νέων καλογραίων.
Τὰ δ' ἄλλα πάντα τὰ χοντρά, λέγω τὰ ἀπομονάρια,
ποιοῦν βαρέα στρώματα καὶ παραπιλωμένα, 510
κέντουκλα καὶ 'δρομάχια, 'φέλεθρα εἰς τὰς σέλας,
καπάσια, σαρπούζια, ζαρκούλια καὶ τἄλλα.

'Ακμὴν καὶ τὸ δερμάτιν μου κάμνει μεγάλας χρείας
καὶ ὁ τζαγγάρης χρᾶται το εἰς πᾶσαν του δουλείαν,
παπούτζια, ὑποδήματα, φελλάρια καὶ κλώστρας·
ἀλλὰ καὶ οἱ γραμματικοὶ ἐνδύουν τὰ βιβλία
μαῦρον εἴτε καὶ κόκκινον εἴτε βαφὴν ἑτέραν·
πολλάκις δὲ καὶ ὁ σελᾶς χρᾶται το καὶ ἐκεῖνος
εἰς σέλας, εἰς ῥαψίματα ἐντεληνομπροστέλων,
εἰς χαλινοκαπίστελα καὶ ὅσα τὰ τοιαῦτα.» 520

Ὡς πάντα ταῦτα ἤκουσαν λαλοῦντος τοῦ προβάτου,
ὑπερεθαύμασαν πολλὰ ἡ αἶγα καὶ ὁ τράγος
καὶ ἀπεκρίθησαν ὁμοῦ οἱ δύο ἕνα στόμα:

«Ἐσύ, προβάτιν ταπεινὸν ποὺ βλέπεις πάντα κάτω,
μωρόλαλον, κακόστομον, ποῦ εὗρες τόσους λόγους,

They make fair curtains, finely decorated,
with sundry pretty forms designed on them:
people, birds, beasts, and all things of this world, 490
and these are owned by queens, and kings as well,
and counts and knights and others of their rank.
They make thick carpets, richly decorated,
on which both sultan and emirs are seated,
and all folk, Greeks and Westerners alike,
use them for beds and for their mattresses.

The most important thing made from my wool,
however, are the clothes all people wear,
both great and small and unto every realm.
The emperors, the nobles, and all magnates 500
wear both the saffron and the scarlet cloth,
and those with them use any dye and hue.
And out of coarser wool are gray clothes made,
all the thick cassocks, with their woven serge:
fur petticoats for mighty patriarchs,
mantles and stoles for metropolitans,
and heavy undergarments for head abbots
and white shirts for the younger nuns to wear.
The other coarse stuff—I mean leftovers—
makes all the heavy, felt-filled mattresses 510
and covers, saddle cloths, and saddle felts;
also the wide-brimmed hats of state, the fur caps, 512
the gold-embroidered caps, and all the like. 512

Even my skin finds worthy applications.
The cobbler uses it in all his tasks,
for loafers, sandals, boots, and corkwood slippers.
But scholars use it, too, to cover books,
whether in black or red or other colors.
Often enough the saddle maker also
uses my skin for saddles, horse-strap sewing,
bridles and halters, and for all such things." 520

Hearing the sheep go on about all this,
the billy goat and nanny were amazed,
and they responded to her with one voice:

"You! Humble sheep who never dares look up,
you foul-mouthed talker of mere stuff and nonsense, 525
where did you get so many words and praises, 526

ἐπαίνους καὶ καυχήματα καὶ τὴν μακρολογίαν,
νὰ ἐπαινῇς τὰ κρέη σου καὶ τὰ δερμάτιά σου,
ἀλλὰ καὶ τὰ μαλλία σου εἰς ποικιλοβαφίαν;
Νὰ τὸ ἠξεύρῃς, ἄτυχη καὶ λωλοπροβατίνα,
ἔναι τὸ δέρμα τὸ ἐμὸν μεῖζον τοῦ ἐδικοῦ σου, 530
μεγάλον καὶ παχύτερον εἰς πάσας τὰς δουλείας.
Ἀλλά γε καὶ αἱ τρίχες μου πληροῦσιν ἄλλην χρείαν·
πλέκουν σκοινία δυνατά, δεσμεύουσιν τὰ ζῷα,
ἅπαντα τὰ τετράποδα, μικρά τε καὶ μεγάλα.
Ἀκμὴν τὰ ἔντερα ἡμῶν ποιοῦσιν καὶ τὰς κόρδας
ὁποὺ στοιβάζουν τὸ μαλλίν, μᾶλλον καὶ τὸ βαμπάκιν.
Περὶ δὲ καὶ τοῦ γάλακτος οὐκ ἔχω τί νὰ λέγω,
καθὼς ἐσὺ οὕτως κἀγὼ ἢ μᾶλλον δὲ καὶ πλέον,
καὶ ἄλλας χάριτας πολλάς, ἃς οὐκ ἐξόν μοι λέγειν·
καὶ οὐ καυχῶμαι τὰ πολλά, ὡς σὺ λωλοπροβάτιν. 540
Πόσα ἐβαττολόγησας, ληρήματα καὶ λόγους,
καὶ ὑπερφυσιώθηκες καὶ ὑπερεκαυχίσθης,
οὐχὶ νὰ ἔλεγεν ὁ βοῦς καὶ τὸ παχὺν βουβάλιν
ἢ ἄλλον ζῷον φοβερόν, λέγω ἐκ τῶν μεγάλων.»

Καὶ τότε ἀνεχώρησεν ἡ ταπεινὴ προβάτα·
ὁ βοῦς δὲ καὶ ὁ βούβαλος ὡς ἤκουσαν τοὺς λόγους
καὶ τὰ δικολογήματα αἰγὸς καὶ τοῦ προβάτου
ἐξῆλθον καὶ ἐστάθησαν οἱ δύο εἰς τὸ μέσον
καὶ ἤρξαντο προσφθέγγεσθαι πρὸς τὴν κοινότην ὅλην:

«Ἀκούεις, λέων βασιλεῦ, ἀκούετε, μεγιστᾶνοι, 550 **(9, 10)**
τὰ ζῷα τὰ μικρούτζικα, τὰ οὐδετιποτένια, *τὸ βούδι,*
πῶς ἐπολυλογήσασιν, πῶς ἐμακρολογῆσαν *τὸ βουβάλι*
καὶ ὑπερεκαυχίσθησαν καὶ πέραν τοῦ μετρίου;»

Εἶτα λέων ὁ βασιλεὺς καὶ πᾶσα ἡ βουλή του
τούτους τοὺς λόγους εἴπασιν πρὸς βοῦν καὶ τὸ βουβάλιν:

«Ἡ σύναξις, ἡ μάδευσις ἡ ὧδε γεγονυῖα
οὕτως ἐστὶ καὶ ὁ μικρὸς καθάπερ καὶ ὁ μέγας,
οὕτως δὲ καὶ ὁ ἄτιμος ὥσπερ καὶ ὁ τιμημένος,
οὕτως δὲ καὶ ὁ ἄνανδρος ὥσπερ καὶ ὁ ἀνδρειωμένος,
πάντες δὲ νὰ συντύχουσιν καὶ πάντες νὰ λαλήσουν, 560
εἷς πρὸς τὸν ἄλλον νὰ εἰπῇ καὶ ἔπαινον καὶ ψόγον,
καθὼς ἐσυνετάξαμεν μεθ᾽ ὅρκου καὶ ἀγάπης
τὰ μέρη τὰ ἀμφότερα ἡμέρων καὶ ἀγρίων.
Καὶ γὰρ ἀπὸ τὸ εὐτελές, τὸν ποντικὸν καὶ κάτην,

so many boasts and such prolixity, 526
so you can here extol your meat and skin
and laud your wool of sundry dyes as well?
You should know this, unfortunate dumb ewe:
my skin outclasses yours, being much thicker 530
and marvelous for any application.
What's more, my hair fulfils another need:
they braid strong ropes to tie down animals—
all the four-legged beasts, both great and small.
Also our guts are made into the cords
with which they fluff their wool and cotton, too.
About my milk, I don't know what to say:
it's just as good as yours, if not much better.
I've many other gifts, which I can't speak of,
for I am no dumb ewe, to brag at length! 540
How many more inanities and bunkum
could you still prattle? How you've puffed yourself!
It's not as if it was the ox who spoke, 543
the bulky buffalo, or some such other 543
formidable large animal, I'd say!"

So at that point the humble ewe departed.
The ox, though, and the buffalo, on hearing
the words and arguments of sheep and goat,
both stepped right up, took center stage, and started
addressing the entire assembly thus:

"Hear you, King Lion, hear you, noble magnates 550 **(9, 10)** *The Ox, The Buffalo*
how these small animals, these nobodies
have babbled at great length and greater verbiage,
their boasts exceeding any normal measure?"

King Lion, at that point, and his whole council
pointed out to the ox and buffalo:

"The gathering and assembly taking place here
is such that both the great and small alike,
together both the honored and obscure,
the brave and cowardly, may all converse,
and all may speak, both praising one another 560
and finding faults, just as we have agreed,
through oaths and peace—both parties, tame and wild. 562/563
Indeed, it was the lowly rat and cat
who opened our debate, which has gone on 565

ἤρξατο ἡ διάλεξις καὶ ἦλθεν μέχρις ὧδε
καὶ ἔνι χρεία νὰ ἐλθοῦν οἱ ἔριδες καὶ λόγοι
ἕως τῶν μεγιστάνων μου κἀμοῦ τοῦ βασιλέως.
Λοιπόν, λέγετε τίποτε, ἂν ἔχετέ τι λέγειν.»

Τότε ὁ βοῦς καὶ βούβαλος ἤρξαντο ταῦτα λέγειν.
Προέλαβεν δὲ ὡς προπετῶς ὁ βοῦς, τοιαῦτα λέγει: 570

«Φεύγετε, παραπτώματα, ἀποσκορακισθῆτε,
ἐκβᾶτε ἀπὸ τὴν μέσην μας, ἐμαγαρίσετέ μας,
νὰ λάμψῃ πρῶτον ἥλιος, εἶτα καὶ ἡ σελήνη,
καὶ ἄστρα τὰ μικρούτζικα νὰ σκοτισθοῦν παντάπαν.
Ἐγὼ γὰρ εἶμαι ἥλιος, τὸ φέγγος ἡ βουβάλα, **(11)**
ἐσεῖς δὲ κακορρίζικα ὡς νύκτα καὶ ὡς ἄστρα,
κακόχειρα καὶ ἄνανδρα πρὸς τὰ ἄλλα τὰ ζῷα, 576a
κακότυχα, μικρούτζικα καὶ καταφρονημένα.»

Τότε ἐκατεντράπησαν ἡ αἶγα καὶ ὁ τράγος
καὶ τἆλλα ζῷα τὰ μικρὰ καὶ ἡ λωλοπροβάτα·
ἀπῆλθον καὶ ἐστάθησαν μὲ πάντας εἰς τὴν τάξιν, 580
οἱ δύο δὲ ἀπέμειναν ὁ βοῦς καὶ τὸ βουβάλιν.
Καὶ πρὸς τὸν βοῦν ἐλάλησεν ὁ βούβαλος τοιαῦτα:

«Πῶς ἔχανες τὸ στόμα σου αὐτὸ τὸ βρωμισμένον,
πῶς ἤνοιξας τὰς χείλας σου τὰς παχυλοπετζάτας,
καὶ ἔφησεν ἡ γλῶσσα σου ἡ πολυψαλιδάτη
ληρήματα καὶ λόγια καὶ ψεματολογίας;
Ἐσὺ μὲν εἶσαι ἥλιος, ἐγὼ δὲ ἡ σελήνη;
Καὶ οὐκ ἐντράπης, ἄθλιε, νὰ τὸ ἐξεχειλίσῃς;
Οὐκ οἶδα τί 'ν' τὸ κάλλιον τὸ ἔχεις ἀπὸ μένα·
οὕτως γὰρ κάμνω καὶ ἐγὼ εἰς ἅπασαν δουλείαν 590
ὡσὰν ἐσέν, κακότυχον, μωρόλαλον βοδάκιν.
Εἰ δὲ καὶ θέλῃς νὰ εἰπῶ, νὰ καυχισθῶ ὀλίγον
καὶ νὰ λαλήσω ῥήματα καὶ λόγους ἀληθείας,
κάλλιον εἶμαι παρὰ σὲν εἰς ἅπασαν δουλείαν,
καὶ δυνατὸν καὶ μέγιστον, ὅπου καὶ ἂν μὲ γυρεύσουν,
εἰς ἅμαξαν, εἰς ἅλωναν καὶ εἰς τὴν ἀροτρίαν·

ἀκόμη καὶ τὸ γάλα μου μεῖζον τοῦ ἐδικοῦ σου,
ἀκμὴν καὶ παρὰ τῆς αἰγὸς καὶ παρὰ τοῦ προβάτου.
Κάμνει τυρὶν ἐξαίρετον, πολλὰ λιπαρωμένον,

up to this point, and it is mandatory 565
that our disputes and speeches keep on going,
up to my magnates and myself, the king.
So speak, if you have anything to say."

The ox and buffalo then started speaking,
the ox impertinently setting forth: 570

"Get lost, you offscourings! The hell with you!
You've sullied us enough; out of our way!
The time has come now for the sun to shine, 573
and then the moon. As for the tiny stars, 573
it's time for them to be snuffed out completely!
For I'm the sun; the buffalo's the moon, **(11)**
and you're as doomed as nighttime and the stars,
weak limbed and powerless to other beasts— 576a
ill fated as you are, despised and puny."

The billy goat, the nanny, the dumb ewe,
and all the other smaller animals 579
were flushed with shame then. So they stepped aside, 579
and stood with all the others orderly, 580
leaving the ox and buffalo alone.
And then the buffalo turned to the ox:

"How dared you let your filthy mouth run loose?
How dared you spread your thick-skinned lips wide open,
to let your tongue, sharp as a host of scissors,
utter such lies, frivolities, and nonsense?
So you're the sun, and I'm the moon, then! Well!
Had you no shame, you miserable beast, 588
to let such an affront get past your lips? 588
Where you outdo me, I have no idea;
for I'm as fit as you for any task, 590
you poor, ill-fated, nonsense-talking oxling.
And if you want me to speak out right here,
to brag a bit and say things as they are,
I outperform you, ox, in all assignments,
strong and excelling in whatever I'm used for,
be it for carting, threshing, or for plowing.

Even my milk is better than your own,
as well as milk from nannies and from ewes.
Its cheese is excellent and very creamy;

τὸ χρῶνται οἱ ἡγούμενοι εἰς τὰ μονόκυθρά των. 600
Ἔχουν το εἰς τὰ λάχανα, τὰ λέγουσιν φρυγία,
καὶ εἰς τὰς γούλας τὰς χοντράς, ἀλλὰ καὶ εἰς τὰ σεῦτλα.
Τρώγουν το καὶ οἱ ἄρχοντες ὕστερον εἰς τὸ γεῦμα,
ὀλιγοστόν, δαμίτζικον, ὡς διὰ νὰ χωνεύσουν.

Ἀκόμη καὶ τὸ κέρας μου μεγάλην χρείαν κάμνει·
ποιοῦν κερατοβούκινα, βαστάζουν τα στρατιῶτες
καὶ εἰς τὰ κυνηγέσια ἀλλὰ καὶ εἰς φουσσᾶτον.
Καὶ κροῦν τα καὶ φωνάζουσιν καὶ κράζει εἷς τὸν ἄλλον.
Ἔχω καὶ ἄλλα πλείονα χαρίσματα νὰ εἴπω,
ἀλλὰ ἀφήνω τα λοιπόν, οὐκ ἔξεστίν μοι λέγειν· 610
πολυλογία γὰρ ἐστὶν τεκμήριον ζαβίας.» 610a

Τότε ὁ βοῦς ἐφθέγξατο εὐθὺς πρὸς τὴν βουβάλαν:
«Βορβοροπηλοκύλιστε, λιμνοαναθρεμμένη,
πολλὰ μοῦ ἐτζαμπούνισες, φλυαροκοπρολόγε. 612a
Ὅσα εἶπες διὰ λόγου σου καὶ ὑπερεκαυχίσθης,
ταῦτα γὰρ ἔχω καὶ ἐγὼ καὶ ἄλλα πλεῖον τούτων.

Πρῶτον ἐμὲν τὸ κέρας μου χρῶνται καλαμαράδες,
ποιοῦν τὰ καλαμάρια, ποιοῦν κονδυλοθήκας,
ἀλλὰ καὶ οἱ τορνάρηδες εἰς ἅπασάν των χρείαν,
εἰς θρόνους, εἰς σελία τε, εἰς σκάκους, εἰς ταβλία,
εἰς ἠλακάτας τορνευτάς, σφονδυλοτορνεμένας,
εἰς ἄκρας κονταρίων τε, εἰς ἄκρας λαντζονίων 620
καὶ εἰς ἑτέρας πλείονας δουλείας ἀναγκαίας.

Δεύτερον πάλιν νὰ εἰπῶ καὶ περὶ τῶν νευρῶν μου·
ἔχουν τα οἱ μαΐστορες, τζαγκράδες, δοξαράδες.
Νευρώνουν τὰ δοξάρια, νευρώνουν καὶ τὰς τζάγκρας.
Ἀκόμη καὶ ὁ σαγιτᾶς νευρώνει τὰς σαγίτας
καὶ ὁ σελᾶς καὶ σαμαρᾶς χρῶνται καὶ οὗτοι ταῦτα,
καὶ ὅπου δ᾽ ἂν καὶ χρειαστοῦν, εὑρίσκουν με εἰς δέμαν.

Ἀκόμη καὶ τὸ εὐτελὲς τὸ ἄκρον τῆς οὐρᾶς μου,
χρῶνται αὐτὸ οἱ ἁλιεῖς εἰς ἄγραν τῶν ἰχθύων,
τὰς λέγουσιν ἀθερινάς, τὰς μικροτάτας πάνυ. 630

Ἀκόμη ἔχω νὰ εἰπῶ καὶ νὰ λαλήσω ἄλλον·
πολλάκις γὰρ ἂν εὑρεθοῦν καὶ γύναια ἐκεῖσε
καὶ νὰ ἀκούσουν τὸ παρὸν ἀπόφθεγμα καὶ ῥῆμα,
ἂν τύχῃ νὰ γελάσουσιν καὶ νὰ ἐμνοστευθοῦσιν.

it's used by abbots in their casseroles. 600
It's also mixed with cabbage, known as "Phrygian,"
and fat kohlrabi, and with beetroot, too.
And nobles eat it after their main courses,
a tiny, teensy bit, for the digestion.

Even my horn has an important function:
people make bugles of it, used by soldiers
both in the hunt and in the battlefield;
they sound them, call each other out, and clamor.
There's many other graces I could mention,
but I'll omit them. I'm not one to talk: 610
verbosity betokens foolishness." 610a

At once, the ox said to the buffalo:
"You mud-and-quagmire–weltering spawn of lakes!
You've chattered quite enough, you babbling shithead! 612a
What you have said about yourself, and bragged of,
I also have, along with much, much more.

My horn, first off, is put to use by scribes:
they make their pen cases, and inkhorns, too;
also by turners, for their every use:
armchairs and seats, chess sets, backgammon boards,
lathed distaffs, with their necks so finely shaped,
and spearheads, too, and on the tips of lances, 620
and many other necessary products.

Secondly, let me talk about my sinews.
They're used by craftsmen—crossbowmen and archers—
who fix them to their bows, and crossbows also;
and arrow makers, to fasten arrowheads.
But saddle makers and packsaddle makers 626
use them as well, and when there is a need 626/627
for binding any place, you'll find me there. 627

Even the mere tip of my tail is used
by fishermen in their pursuit of fish,
the so-called white bait, smallest fish of all. 630

I still have something more to state and say, though;
indeed, if women happen to be present
and hear the following remark and statement,
they tend to giggle and to be amused:

Ἔχω καὶ νεῦρον δυνατόν, μακρὺν καὶ πυρωδᾶτον,
ὁποὺ τὸ ἔχουν οἱ κριταὶ καὶ μαγκλαβοκοποῦσιν
τοὺς κλέπτας καὶ τοὺς ὑβριστὰς καὶ πάντας κακεργάτας.

Περὶ δὲ τοῦ πετζίου μου οὐκ ἔχω τί νὰ λέγω·
ὥσπερ ὑπάρχει γὰρ τὸ σόν, οὕτως τὸ ἐδικόν μου
καὶ ὡς ὠμὸν καὶ ὡς γναπτὸν εἰς ἄλλας πάσας χρείας. 640
Κάμνει λουρία εὔμορφα,γναμμένα μὲ τὴν στῦψιν,
χαλιναροκαπίστελα, ὀπισωμπροστελήνας
καὶ ἄλλα τούτων ὅμοια ἃ χρῶνται οἱ σελάδες.»

Ὡς ἤκουσεν ὁ γάδαρος βοὸς τὴν καυχησίαν, *ὁ γάδαρος, τὸ βώδι*
πῶς ἓν τὸ νεῦρον του μακρὸν καὶ ἐξεπυρωμένον,
δαμὶν ἐτζιληπούρδισεν, ἐγκάρισεν ὀλίγον,
πορδοκοπῶν εἰσέδραμεν, ἐστάθη εἰς τὸ μέσον,
ὀμπρὸς τ᾽ ἀπτία του ἔστησεν καὶ πρὸς τὸν βοῦν ἐλάλει:

«Ψέματα λέγεις, φλύαρε, καὶ περισσὰ καυχᾶσαι· **(12)**
ἐγὼ ἔχω νεῦρον τὸ παχύν, μεγαλοματζουκᾶτον, 650
μακρύν, παχὺν καὶ στιβαρόν, ῥουθωνοκεφαλᾶτον,
μὴ μόνον μεγαλώτερον παρὰ τὸ ἐδικόν σου,
ἀλλὰ ᾽περβαῖνον ἅπαντα τῶν τετραπόδων ζῴων.
Καὶ ὅταν εἰς οἶστρον κινηθῇ καὶ πυρωθῇ ὀλίγον,
ὁμοιάζει τὸ κεφάλιν του φράγκικον σαλτζαρόλιν.
Ὅμως ἐκβᾶτε τὸ λοιπόν, ὁ βοῦς καὶ τὸ βουβάλιν·
ἐγὼ δὲ καὶ τὸ ἄλογον νὰ δικολογηθοῦμεν.»

Τότε ὁ βοῦς καὶ ὁ βούβαλος ἐξέβησαν ἐκεῖθεν, 657a
ἀπῆγαν καὶ ἐστάθησαν μετὰ τοῦ συνεδρίου.
Τὸ φοβερὸν δὲ ἄλογον ὡς ἤκουσεν τοὺς λόγους,
πηδηματίτζιν ἔποικεν, ἐφόβισε τοὺς πάντας. 660
᾽Ανέβην, ἐκατέβηκεν, ἐσείσθην, ἐλυγίσθην,
τράχηλον ἐκαμάρωσεν, ἐτίναξε τὴν χήτην.
Μεγάλως ἐχρημάτισεν, ἐστάθη εἰς τὸ μέσον, *τὸ ἄλογον*
καὶ πρὸς τὸν ὄνον ἔφησεν ῥήματα τὰ τοιαῦτα:

«Εἰπέ με, μαυροπείσματε, εἰπέ, ψωλογομάριν, **(13)**
πῶς σὲ φορτώνουν, ἄτυχε, πῶς σὲ ῥαβδοκοποῦσι.

Φορτώνουν σε τ᾽ ἀλεύρια, σιτάριν καὶ κριθάριν,
τὰ ὄσπρια, τὰ φάβατα καὶ ὅσα τούτων εἴδη·
φορτώνουν σε καὶ τὸ κρασίν, ὀξίδιν καὶ ἐλάδι,
καὶ κουβαλεῖς καὶ τὸ νερόν, τ᾽ ἄχερα καὶ τὰ ξύλα, 670

I have a mighty dick, both long and fiery,
which judges use in order to thrash soundly
thieves and blasphemers and all sorts of felons.

As for my skin, I don't know what to say;
for mine is just as good as your skin is,
both raw and tanned, fulfilling many needs: 640
it makes nice straps, which are all tanned in alum,
bridles and halters, horse straps front and rear,
and others such which saddle makers use."

The donkey, having heard the ox's boast *The Donkey, The Ox*
of how his dick is long and fiery hot,
let fly a little fart and brayed a bit.
Then, heralded by blasts of breaking wind, 647
in he ran. As he stood on center stage, 647
he pricked his ears up and addressed the ox:

"You lie, long-winded fool, and boast too much: **(12)**
it's me that has a dick thick as a cudgel, 650
long, robust, plump, and headed with a nostril!
Not only is it bigger than your own,
but it surpasses any animal's.
And when it's stirred by lust and kindled somewhat,
its head becomes just like a Western saucer!
So, then, both ox and buffalo, get out!
I want to have a word now with the horse."

The ox and buffalo departed then, 657a
going to join the rest of the assembly.
But when the fearsome horse heard what was spoken,
he bucked a bit and frightened everyone; 660
he ran both up and down; he shook and posed;
he proudly raised his neck and tossed his mane.
He gave a mighty neigh, took center stage, *The Horse*
and then addressed the donkey along these lines:

"Tell me, you bloody-spited Dick-O-Matic, **(13)**
tell me how people burden you, poor fool! 666
Tell me how people flog away at you! 666
They load you up with flour and grain and barley,
pulses and fava beans and all the like,
as well as wine and vinegar and oil;
you also carry water, straw and sticks, 670

τὰ χόρτα καὶ τὰ φρύγανα, κορμοὺς καὶ εἴ τι ἄλλον,
τὰς πέτρας, τὰ χαλίκια, τὰ βήσσαλα, τὸ χῶμα
καὶ ὅσα χρῶνται οἱ ἄνθρωποι εἰς ἅπασαν δουλείαν·
ταγισερὰ καὶ βρώματα ἀπάνω σου τὰ θέτουν. 673a

Ῥαβδοκοποῦν, σκοτώνουν σε καὶ ματζουκοκοποῦν σε,
σουβλοκοποῦν τὸν κῶλον σου μὲ σίδερα καὶ ξύλα.

Πολλάκις ἂν σὲ εὕρουσιν καὶ νὰ ποιήσῃς πραῗδαν,
ὀκάπου εἰς ἀμπέλια καὶ εἰς σπαρμένας χώρας,
κόπτουσιν τὰ ἀφτία σου, χαράσσουν τὴν οὐράν σου
καὶ βάνουν καὶ χαβώνουν σε μὲ τὴν χλωρὴν τὴν βέργαν,
καὶ οὔτε πίνεις οὔτε τρῴς οὔτε σεῖς τὴν οὐράν σου, 680
καὶ εἶσαι κάθαρμα, πομπὴ καὶ γέλοιον τῶν ζῴων.

Καὶ ἂν τύχῃ νά ᾽ναι καὶ κακὸν σαμάριν τὸ σὲ στρώνουν,
ἐγδέρνει καὶ τὴν ῥάχιν σου, πληγώνει τὰς πλευράς σου,
καὶ τρώγουν σε συζώντανον κόρακες καὶ κουροῦνες.
Καὶ ἂν ἓν καὶ εὕρῃς καὶ νερὸν καὶ νά ᾽σαι φορτωμένος,
γυρίζεις καὶ τὸν κῶλον σου καὶ βρέχεσαι καὶ στέκεις
καὶ κάμνεις νοικοκύρην σου καὶ σκᾷ ἀπὸ τὸ κακόν του
καὶ δούδει σου καὶ ῥαβδακές, καῖνε καὶ ἀποδαγκάνεις.

᾽Ακόμη, πομπογάδαρε, νὰ σὲ εἰπῶ καὶ ἄλλον,
τὸ ἤκουσα ἀπ᾽ τοὺς γέροντας καὶ τοὺς προπάτοράς μου. 690
Ἐσεῖς ἐβάλετε βουλὴν τοιαύτην οἱ γαδάροι
καὶ ἕναν ἐξελέξατε τὸν εἴχετε φρονέα
νὰ ἀποστείλετε αὐτὸν ἕως τὸν βασιλέα,
νὰ δεηθῇ καὶ νὰ εἰπῇ καὶ νὰ παρακαλέσῃ
διὰ τὰ ἀπανωγόμια τὰ βάνουν εἰς τὴν μέσην
καὶ βαρεοφορτώνουν σας ὥστε νὰ ἀναπνῆτε,
μὲ ὁρισμὸν προστάγματος νὰ ὁρίσῃ νὰ τὸ κόψουν.
Ὁ βασιλεὺς δ᾽ ἐπήκουσεν τὴν δέησιν τοῦ ὄνου·
κατὰ τὴν ὥραν ὥρισεν καὶ πρόσταγμαν ἐποῖκεν
καὶ ἔγραφε καὶ ὥριζε πάντας γαδουρολάτας, 700
τοὺς ἔχοντας τὰ ὀνικὰ εἰς ἅπαντα τὸν κόσμον,
μηδὲν τολμήσειεν κανεὶς ἢ μικρὸς ἢ μεγάλος
νὰ βάλῃ εἰς τὸν γάδαρον ἄλλον ἀπανωγόμιν.

Ἐστράφη δὲ ὁ γάδαρος μετὰ χαρᾶς μεγάλης
βαστάζων εἰς τὸ στόμαν του καὶ εἰς τὰ δόντιά του
τὸ πρόσταγμαν καὶ ὁρισμὸν τοῦ βασιλέως ἐκείνου.

greens, brushwood, trunks and all things of the sort,
stones, gravel, bricks and dirt—and, in a word,
whatever people use in any work,
and any kind of edible or food, 673a
it's on your back that they will pile it up. 673a
They flog you, club you, clobber you to death;
they prod your arse with irons and with sticks.

It often happens—should they find you looting
a vineyard somewhere or some field they've sown—
that they will cut your ears and slash your tail
and rein you in by force of a green switch.
Then you won't eat, or drink, or shake your tail. 680
No, you become an outcast then, a freak, 681
a laughingstock for all the animals. 681

And if it's just your luck they've made you wear
a faulty packsaddle, it skins your back, 683
cutting your ribs wide open, and right there 683
the crows and ravens eat at you alive.
And if you come across a spring while loaded,
you turn your arse to it and get all wet,
just standing there. Your boss, then, fit to burst,
flogs you such stingers that you bite your lips.

Moreover, outcast donkey, let me add
this tale my ancestors and elders told me. 690
It's said you donkeys made a resolution,
electing one of you you held as prudent,
and sent him all the way up to the king
to plead and argue and request of him
that all the extra loads piled on your back,
which overload you as long as you still breathe,
should be abolished by him by decree.
The king considered then the donkey's plea,
and right there he decided to make law,
writing an order to all donkey owners, 700
masters of donkeys all throughout the world,
that henceforth no one, great or small, may dare
place any extra load onto the donkey.

And so the donkey, full of joy, turned back,
holding between his teeth and in his mouth
the order and decree that king had made.

῾Ως ἦλθεν, ὡς ἀπέσωσεν ὁ ὄνος ἐκ μακρόθεν,
κοπιασμένος τὰ πολλά, κοντὰ εἰς ἕνα μίλιν,
καὶ εἶδεν ὁμοθυμαδὸν ὁμοῦ τοὺς ὄνους ὅλους,
ἐγκάριξεν ἐκ τὴν χαρὰν τὴν ἄπληστον τὴν εἶχεν 710
φωνάζοντα καὶ τρέχοντα τζιλοπορδοκοπῶντα.
"Καλὴν καρδίαν ἔχετε, τὸ γένος τῶν γαδάρων·
ἤφερα γὰρ τὸν ὁρισμὸν ἀπὸ τὸν βασιλέα,
νὰ μᾶς φορτώνουσι ᾽λαφρὰ εἰς τὴν ἀνάπαυσίν μας,
νὰ κόψουσιν παντάπασιν καὶ τὸ ἀπανωγόμιν."

᾽Απάνω δὲ εἰς τὸ γκάρισμα καὶ εἰς τοὺς λόγους τούτους
καὶ εἰς τὸ τζιληπούρδημαν καὶ εἰς τὴν χαρὰν ἐκείνην
καὶ εἰς τὸ ἀναρρούφισμαν τῆς ἐγκαρισματίας,
ὁ ὄνος ἐκατέπιεν γραφὴν τοῦ βασιλέως
καὶ ἦλθεν εὔκαιρος, κενὸς εἰς τοὺς ἑτέρους ὄνους, 720
καὶ ἠρωτήσασιν αὐτὸν τὸ τί καλὰ μαντᾶτα·
καὶ εἶπε: "Νὰ ἠξεύρετε, τὸ γένος τῶν γαδάρων,
ὅτι ἐβάστουν πρόσταγμαν ἀπὸ τὸν βασιλέα
καὶ ἔγραφε καὶ ὥριζεν εἰς ἅπαντα τὸν κόσμον,
ἵνα κοπῇ παντάπασιν καὶ τὸ ἀπανωγόμιν·
ἐγὼ δὲ ἀπὸ τὴν χαρὰν τὴν εἶχα τὴν μεγάλην,
ὡς εἶδον καὶ τὴν σύναξιν ὁμοῦ τὴν ὑμετέραν,
ἐγκάρισα, ἐφώναξα τζιλοπορδοκοπῶντα,
κατέδραμα δαμίτζικον νὰ δώσω συχαρίκιν
[καὶ εἰς τὸ τζιληπούρδισμα, εἰς τὴν χαρὰν ἐκείνη] 729a
καὶ εἰς τὸ ἀναρρούφισμα τῆς ἐγκαρισματέας 730
τὸ πρόσταγμαν ἐσέβηκεν εἰς τὰ ἐντός μου μέσα.
Λοιπόν, βαστάξετε δαμὶν ἕως νὰ κατουρήσω
καὶ θέλει ἔβγη τὸ χαρτὶν καὶ θέλω σάς το δώσει."
Καὶ ἀπ᾽ ἐκείνου τοῦ καιροῦ κἀκείνης τῆς ἡμέρας
ἕως ἐδὰ καὶ πάντοτε γυρεύετε, γαδάροι,
καὶ ὅταν κατουρήσετε, σκύπτεσθε καὶ ὀσμᾶσθε
καὶ τίποτε οὐχ εὕρετε, ἀλλ᾽ οὐδὲ νὰ εὑρῆτε
καὶ τὸ ἀπανωγόμιον πάντοτε θέτουν σάς το,
νὰ σᾶς βαρυφορτώνουσι, νὰ σᾶς ῥαβδοκοποῦσιν.»

Τότε καὶ ὁ γαΐδαρος μικρὸν ἀπιλογεῖται: 740
«Πολλὰ μὲ ἐλοιδόρησες, πολλὰ μὲ ἐκατεῖπες,
ἄλογον ἀλαζονικόν, ἀλλὰ καὶ ἐπηρμένον.
Οὕτως γὰρ ἔχουν καὶ ἐμὲν ὡς ἔχουν καὶ ἐσένα,
ταγίζουν καὶ ποτίζουν με, βάνουν με εἰς τὸν στάβλον.»

Now, as the donkey was returning home,
arriving from afar, he was exhausted. 708
And when, with just a mile to go, he saw 708
the donkeys waiting for him all together,
he brayed with boundless joy and called them out, 710
running and farting merrily on the way:
'Rejoice, O donkeys! Be ye of good cheer!
For I have brought the mandate of the king
that they should load us lightly to relieve us,
forbidding extra loading altogether.'
And just as he was braying out these words,
letting fly farts and overcome with joy,
as he was gulping down amidst his braying,
the donkey swallowed down the royal mandate,
reaching the other donkeys empty-handed. 720
And when they asked him what the good news was,
he said: 'O donkeys! I must let you know
that I was carrying the king's own mandate,
in which he wrote and gave the world an order,
forbidding extra loading altogether.
And out of the delight that overwhelmed me,
especially when I saw you assembled,
I brayed, I cried, I let fly farts aplenty,
and sped somewhat to bring you this good news.
[Letting fly farts, and overcome with joy,] 729a
as I was gulping down amidst my braying, 730
the mandate passed within me to my innards.
So hold on just a minute till I piss:
the paper will come out, then, and you'll have it.'
And since that time, and since that very day,
right up to now, and for all time henceforth, 735
you donkeys keep on looking for that mandate, 735
and anywhere you piss, you stoop and sniff
but haven't found it yet; nor will you ever.
And they keep placing extra loads on you,
flogging and burdening you heavily."

And then the donkey made a brief response: 740
"You've mocked me and have spoken out against me
too much, you arrogant, conceited horse.
After all, people treat me just like you:
they feed me, water me, house me in stables."

Τὸ ἄλογον ὡς ἤκουσεν μεγάλως ἐθυμώθη
καὶ πρὸς τὸν ὄνον ἔφησεν ὑβριστικοὺς τοὺς λόγους:

«Γοργόν, ὦ σκατογάδαρε, φύγε ἀπὸ μπροστά μου,
μὴ ἁπλώσω τὸ ποδάριν μου καὶ δώσω σε κλοτζέαν
καὶ σχίσω τὸ κεφάλιν σου, τζακίσω τὰς πλευράς σου,
ὥστε νὰ ζῇς, νὰ ἀναπνῇς, νὰ σὲ λακτοκοπίζω, 750
διότι βάνεις καὶ ἐσὺ τὴν ψῆφον σου, γαδούριν,
μὲ ἄλογον τὸ θαυμαστόν, τὸ φοβερὸν καὶ μέγαν.

Ἐμὲ σταβλίζουν πάντοτε ἀεὶ τὸν χρόνον ὅλον,
ταγίζουν καὶ ποτίζουν με καὶ κανακίζουσί με
καὶ ἀγαποῦσι με πολλὰ ὑπὲρ τὰ ζῷα πάντα.
Κοινῷ τῷ λόγῳ ἅπαντες καβαλικεύουσί με
οἱ βασιλεῖς, οἱ ἄρχοντες, ῥηγάδες καὶ σουλτάνοι
καὶ ἅπας ἄνθρωπος καλὸς καὶ ἅπας στρατιώτης,
μὲ σέλας χρυσοκόλλητας καὶ ἀργυροδεμένας,
‹μὲ› χαλιναροκαπίστελα ἀργυροχρυσωμένα, 760
‹μὲ› ἐντεληνομπροστέληνα, μὲ τὸ χρυσοπετάλιν,
ῥαμμένα μὲ τὸ χριμιζίν, ὅλα μὲ τὸ μετάξιν,
μὲ βροντοκούδουνα πολλὰ καὶ ἄλλας εὐμορφίας·
καὶ εἶμαι εἰς τὸν πόλεμον ὅλον κουβερτιασμένον
καὶ εἰς τὰ πανηγύρια καὶ εἰς τὰ κυνηγέσια.
Κτενίζουσιν, παστρεύουσιν καὶ ὁμαλίζουσίν με
καὶ ὥσπερ τὰς γυναῖκας των οὕτως μὲ ἀγαποῦσιν.

Ἄγωμε μὲ τὴν κάμηλον τὴν μακροσφονδυλάτην,
ὁποὺ φορτώνουν καὶ αὐτήν, ὥσπερ ἐσὲν τὸν ὄνον,
γομάρια ἀβάστακτα, φορτώματα μεγάλα· 770

ὁποὺ ἐπαρακάλεσεν αὐτὴ θεὸν τὸν Δία
νὰ τὴν ποιήσῃ κέρατα, ὡς ζῷον, εὐμεγέθη
κἀκεῖνος ὥρισεν εὐθὺς νὰ ἔναι κουτζοπτία
καὶ ᾽κόψαν τὰ ἀφτία της, ἐποῖκαν την καὶ κύμπον
καὶ ἓν πομπὴ καὶ γέλοιον καὶ κάθαρμα τῶν ζῴων.» *ἡ καμήλα*

Ὡς ἤκουσεν ἡ κάμηλος φθεγγόμενον τὸν ἵππον
καὶ κατ᾽ αὐτῆς ἀπέτεινεν ὕβρεις καὶ λοιδορίας,
εἰσῆλθεν καὶ ἐστάθηκεν καὶ αὕτη εἰς τὸ μέσον·
ὁ ὄνος δὲ καταισχυνθεὶς ἐστάθηκεν μακρόθεν.
Τότε φησὶν ἡ κάμηλος τοιαῦτα πρὸς τὸν ἵππον: 780

On hearing this, the horse was greatly angered
and spoke these words to castigate the donkey:

"Out of my sight at once, you shitty donkey!
Quickly, or else I'll stick my leg right out
and give you such a kick, it'll split your head
and crack your ribs; and I'll keep kicking you 750
as long as you still live and breathe, you jackass, 750
who dares compare your standing with my own,
that of the wondrous, great and fearsome horse!

I'm always housed in stables, all year round,
and people water, feed, and pamper me,
loving me far more than the other beasts.
It's common knowledge everybody rides me:
emperors, noblemen, and kings and sultans,
and every decent man and any soldier,
on silver-wrought and gold-embellished saddles,
with gold-and-silver–coated bridle and halter, 760
with straps both front and rear, with golden horseshoes,
all stitched in crimson and arrayed in silk,
with thunderous bells and other ornaments.
And in the battlefield I'm all decked out,
as well as during fairs and in the hunt.
They comb me and they clean me and caress me,
adoring me as much as their own wives.

Go keep that long-necked camel company,
who's loaded up, no differently from you,
with huge loads and unbearably large burdens— 770
the camel who once begged of Zeus the god
to give her horns appropriate in size, 772
which she deserved like any other beast; 772
whereby, without delay, he gave the order 773
that she be dock-eared. So they cut her ears, 773
as well as granting her a hunch to bear,
making her now an outcast and a joke 775 *The Camel*
and no more than a freak among the beasts." 775

The camel, hearing what the horse was saying,
the ridicule and insults aimed toward her,
entered the center stage and stood there, too.
The donkey, meanwhile, stood away in shame.
The camel then addressed the horse as follows: 780

«Τί ὠφελεῖ ἡ ἔπαρσις καὶ ἡ ἀλαζονεία (14)
καὶ τὰ πολλὰ καυχήματα τὰ ἔχεις, ἀλογάκιν;
Ἄκουσον καὶ νὰ σὲ εἰπῶ πολλὰ κακὰ τὰ ἔχεις.

Ὅταν γηράσῃς καὶ ἐσύ, βάνουν σε εἰς τὸν μύλον,
τυφλώνουν σε, κακότυχον, δέρνουν σε μὲ τὴν βίτζαν,
γυρίζεις καὶ σκοτίζεσαι ἡμέραν τε καὶ νύκταν,
ἐκδέρνονται οἱ κουτάλες σου, ὅλος ὁ σφόνδυλός σου
καὶ ἀπὸ τὸν κόπον τὸν πολὺν καὶ ἀπὸ τὴν σκοτίαν
οὔτε νὰ φάγῃς ἠμπορεῖς οὔτε νερὸν νὰ πίῃς·

καὶ ὅταν ἐξαπορηθῇς καὶ ἀποδυνατίσῃς, 790
ἐκβάνουν καὶ ὑπάγουν σε ἔξω εἰς τὸ λιβάδιν·
ἐκεῖ ψοφᾷς, κακότυχον, τρώγουν σε οἱ κοράκοι,
ἐκδέρουν τὸ δερμάτιν σου καὶ πολεμοῦν το τζάγγας
καὶ τὴν οὐράν σου κόπτουσιν καὶ κάμνουσιν τριχίας.»

Τότε πάλιν τὸ ἄλογον εὐθὺς ἀπιλογεῖται:
«Μωρὴ καμήλα, μυσερὴ καὶ καταβρωμισμένη,
κυμπόρραχη, πλατύποδε καὶ κοντοουραδάτη,
νὰ γύρευες, κακότυχη, τὸ πῶς σὲ θέτουν κάτω
καὶ βάνουν καὶ φορτώνουν σε γομάρια μεγάλα,
ἀπάνω δὲ καθέζεται αὐτὸς ὁ καμηλάρης 800
καὶ εἶσαι ἀργοκίνητος, ἀργὴ ὥσπερ χελώνη.

Φύγε ἀπὸ τὴν μέσην μας, παράσημον τῶν ζῴων,
καθὼς καὶ ὁ γαΐδαρος, ὁ λυκοφαγωμένος·
ὅπου γὰρ εὕρῃ καὶ αὐτὸν τὸν γάδαρον ὁ λύκος,
ἀσμένως ἀποδέχεται καὶ χαίρεται μεγάλως·
"Ἰδού, εὑρήκαμεν," φησίν, "τὸ ἐψημένον κρέας".»

Ἐντράπηκεν ἡ κάμηλος, φεύγει ἀπὸ τὴν μέσην,
τὸ δ᾽ ἄλογον ἀπόμεινεν μόνον καὶ μοναχόν του:
ὁ λύκος δέ, ὡς ἤκουσεν ἐκεῖ τὸ ὄνομάν του, *ὁ λύκος, τὸ ἄλογον*
ἐξέβη καὶ ἐστάθηκεν καὶ αὐτὸς εἰς τὸ μέσον 810
καὶ λέγει πρὸς τὸ ἄλογον ῥήματα τὰ τοιαῦτα:

«Πολλὰ ἐβαττολόγησας, λόγους πολυλογίας, (15)
καὶ ὕβρισας τὴν κάμηλον καὶ ὕβρισας τὸν ὄνον,
ὠνείδισας δὲ καὶ ἐμὲν πὼς ἐσθίω τοὺς ὄνους.
Λοιπὸν ἀρκεῖ σε τὰ πολλά, φεῦγε ἀπὸ τὴν μέσην.
Ἐγὼ εἶμαι ὠμόβορον, ἐσθίω γὰρ τὰ ζῷα,
οὐ μόνον γὰρ τὸν γάδαρον, καθὼς ἐσὺ ληρίζεις,
ἀλλὰ καὶ ἐσένα, ἄλογον, καὶ ὅλον σου τὸ γένος

"Now what's the point of all this arrogance, **(14)**
all this conceit and boasting, puny horse?
Listen, I tell you, you bear many ills.
For when your own turn comes to reach old age, 784
you're promptly put to work down at the mill. 784
And there they blind you, you unfortunate, 785
and beat you with a switch. So, night and day, 785
you get all dizzy, going round and round,
while both your flanks and your whole neck are flayed.
And you become so dizzy and fatigued,
you cannot eat or drink a sip of water.
And when you're finally all weak and helpless, 790
they take you off and put you out to pasture;
that's where you kick the bucket, poor, poor beast,
and ravens eat you. People skin you, then,
for boots, and cut your tail off to make ropes."

At once, the horse retorted to the camel:
"You stupid, loathsome, hunch-backed, short-tailed camel,
you flat-footed and outright filthy beast,
you would do well to ponder, my poor lady, 798
how people nail you down and load you up, 798
piling up massive burdens on your back,
the camel driver topping it all off, 800
and how you move then, slow as any tortoise.
Out of our way, you most ill-shaped of beasts,
you and the donkey, who's the feast of wolves;
for any time the wolf meets with this donkey,
he's thrilled to bits and joyfully receives him:
'Hullo', he says, 'we've found some roasted meat!'"

The camel was ashamed and stepped aside,
the horse now left behind and all alone.
But then the wolf, who'd heard his name invoked, *The Wolf, The Horse*
stepped up and stood on center stage himself 810
and uttered to the horse such words as follows:

"You've chewed the same tired nonsense over and over, **(15)**
cursing the camel, cursing the donkey, too,
and blaming me as one who preys on donkeys.
Well, I think you've said quite enough; get out!
I am a carnivore: thus, I eat beasts—
not only donkeys, as you've prattled here,
but you too, horse, and all your breed besides,

καὶ τὰ μικρὰ πουλάρια τὰ κάμνουν οἱ φοράδες·
ἐσθίω καὶ τὰ πρόβατα, ἐσθίω καὶ τὰς αἶγας 820
καὶ τὰ μικρὰ ἐρίφια καὶ τὰ ἁπαλὰ ἀρνία
καὶ τὰ μικρὰ δαμάλια, πολλάκις καὶ τοὺς χοίρους
καὶ ἄλλα ζῷα πάμπολλα, μικρά τε καὶ μεγάλα.
Ὅμως νὰ δικολογηθῶ μὲ ὅμοιόν μου ζῷον·
ἐσὺ δὲ φύγε ἀπ᾽ ἐδῶ, ἄλογον ψωριασμένον,
μὴ μᾶς κολλήσῃ ἡ ψώρα σου, ὁ βρῶμος τῶν πληγῶν σου.
Καιρὸς γὰρ ἦλθεν ἀπ᾽ ἐδῶ νὰ φύγῃς ἐκ τοῦ μέσου.»

Ἐξέβηκεν τὸ ἄλογον, παράμερα ἐστάθη.
Ὁ λύκος δὲ ἀπέμεινεν μέσον τοῦ συνεδρίου·
ἡ ἄρκος δέ, ὡς ἔβλεψεν ἱστέκοντα τὸν λύκον, 830
μεμονωμένον, μοναχόν, ἐστάθην εἰς τὸ μέσον
[ἐξῆλθεν καὶ ἐστάθηκεν καὶ αὐτὴ εἰς τὸ μέσον] 831a
καὶ λόγους ἐναπέτεινεν τοιούτους πρὸς τὸν λύκον:

«Πνιγάρη λύκε, θρασιοφᾶ ἀλλὰ καὶ νυκτοκλέπτη, **(16)**
ἐντρυπολόγε, μυσαρὲ καὶ νυκτοπερπατάρη, *ὁ ἄρκος*
εἰπὲ καὶ σύ, καυχίσθητι ὥσπερ τὰ ἄλλα ζῷα,
ἂν ἔχῃς μέλος τίποτες νὰ ὠφελῇ εἰς χρείαν,
εἰ μὴ τὸ ὅλον σου κορμὶν ἔναι ἄχρηστον παντάπαν.

Ὀνειδίζεις τὸ ἄλογον τὸ πῶς ποτὲ ψωριάζει
καὶ μᾶλλον ἐσύ, κάκιστε, ψωριάζεις πᾶσα χρόνον
καὶ κατακαλοκαίριον ἥλιον οὐδὲν βλέπεις, 840
ἀλλ᾽ εἰς τὰ δάση καὶ λογγοὺς εἶσαι κατακρυμμένος
καὶ τρώγουν σε οἱ κώνωπες, καὶ σφῆκες σὲ δακώνουν.»

Τότε ὁ λύκος ἔφησεν τοιαῦτα πρὸς τὴν ἄρκον:
«Μελισσοφάγα, μυσαρὴ καὶ κοντοποδαρέα
καὶ ἀλληθώρα καὶ στραβὴ καὶ χαμηλοβλεποῦσα,
βρωμοφηκάρα, παίγνιον τῶν μωροατζιγγάνων,
ἀχλαδοβαλανότροφε, μυρτοκουμαροφάγα,
οὐδὲ ἐσὺ ἔχεις καλὸν ἀπάνω σου τι μέλος,
καθὼς σὺ λέγεις καὶ ἐμέν, καθὼς μὲ ὀνειδίζεις.»

Πάλιν ἀπιλογήθηκεν ἡ ἄρκος πρὸς τὸν λύκον: 850
«Ἐγὼ ἔχω ὠφέλιμον εἰς ἰατροὺς μεγάλους·
ἀξούγγιν τὸ ἡμέτερον διὰ παντὸς τὸ χρῶνται
εἰς ῥεύματα, εἰς ἀλοιφάς, μὲ εἴδη μεμιγμένον,

including little foals that mares give birth to.
Likewise I prey on sheep, I prey on goats, 820
baby kids, tender lambs, and baby calves,
boars often, and many others, great and small.
I'd rather pick on someone my own size, though;
as for yourself, get lost, you scabby horse,
before we get infected by your mange
and by the stench that oozes from your wounds.
It's high time that you got away from us."

The horse walked out and stood off in the distance;
the wolf was left alone on center stage.
But when the bear saw how the wolf was standing 830
in splendid isolation, she stepped up
[she, too, stepped up and stood right next to him] 831a
and hurled such words as these toward the wolf:

"You! Strangler wolf, night thief and feral-eating, **(16)** *The Bear*
hole-dwelling, loathsome fiend who stalks by night,
why don't you boast like all the other beasts,
whether you've any useful parts to speak of?
Or could it be that no part of your body 837
is fit for use to anyone at all? 837
You mock the horse because at times it's mangy;
yet, worst of beasts, each year you get the itch!
And in midsummer you don't see the sun 840
but hide away in forests and ravines—
pumped bloodless by mosquitoes, stung by wasps."

The wolf talked back then to the bear like this:
"You honey-munching, loathsome, squinting dirtbag,
who never dares look up! You cross-eyed, stump-legged
mere toy for foolish gypsies to make sport with,
you who subsist on acorns and on pears 847
and feeds on myrtle and arbutus berries! 847
It's not as if there is a single part 848
of your whole body that's of any use, 848
as you've claimed of myself, in mocking me."

The bear replied back to the wolf and said: 850
"I am of use to doctors of renown,
who have employed my body fat of old
in ointments meant for discharge, all mixed in, 853
making a preparation highly useful 853

ποιοῦν σκευὴν πανεύχρηστον εἰς τὰς πληγὰς καὶ πάθη.
Ὅμως ἂς φύγωμεν μικρὸν ἔξω ἀπὸ τὸ μέσον,
νὰ ἔλθουν τὰ ὠμόβορα καὶ τὰ ἀνδρειωμένα
καὶ δυνατὰ καὶ ἄγρια θηρία τὰ μεγάλα,
πάρδος καὶ λεοντόπαρδος, νὰ δικολογηθοῦσι.»

Λοιπὸν ἀπέφυγον μικρὸν ὁ λύκος καὶ ὁ ἄρκος.

Πάρδος καὶ λεοντόπαρδος ἦλθασιν εἰς τὸ μέσον 860
καὶ εἷς τὸν ἄλλον ἔλεγεν: «Ἐγὼ εἶμαι ὁ καλλίων.» *ὁ πάρδος,*
Τὰ δόντια ἐφάγγριζαν καὶ ἐνεγκρυμματοῦσαν. *ὁ λεοντόπαρδος*
Ὅμως ὁ πάρδος προπετῶς ἐφθέγξατο τοιαῦτα
καὶ πρὸς τὸν λεοντόπαρδον τοιούτους λόγους λέγει:

«Ἐσὺ οὐκ εἶσαι φυσικόν, ἀλλὰ ἐξ ἡμισείας **(17)**
ἔχεις ἀπὸ τὸν λέοντα, ἔχεις καὶ ἀπὸ μένα.
Καὶ εἶσαι ζῷον πορνικόν, κοπελοαναθρεμμένον,
καθὼς δηλοῖ τὸ ὄνομα τὸ τοῦ λεοντοπάρδου.

Ἐγὼ δὲ πρὸς τὸ ὄνομα ἔχω καὶ τὴν ἀνδρείαν·
πάρδος γὰρ εἶμαι δυνατός, ὅλως ἀνδρειωμένος 870
καὶ πάντα τὰ τετράποδα ὅλα καταπονῶ τα.
Εἰς δύο μου πηδήματα ἢ καὶ πολλάκις τρία,
τὸ ζῷον, ὅποιον ἐστίν, φθάνω το καὶ κρατῶ το,
σφίγγω το μὲ τοὺς ὄνυχας, οὐ δύναται νὰ φύγῃ,
τρώγω το καὶ εὐφραίνομαι ἕως τὴν ὄρεξίν μου·
τὸ δ᾽ ἄλλον τὸ περίλοιπον ἀφήνω το καὶ φεύγω
καὶ οἷον ἄλλον εὑρεθῇ θηρίον, τρώγει τοῦτο.

Ἀκμὴν καὶ τὸ δερμάτιν μου ἔχουν το οἱ σουλτάνοι,
οἱ ἄρχοντες, οἱ εὐγενεῖς, μεγάλοι ἀμιράδες·
ἔχουν αὐτὸ καθίσματα ἀλλὰ καὶ ἀκουμπίζουν 880
καὶ εἰς τὰ προσκεφάλαια καὶ εἰς τὰς στρωμνὰς τῆς κλίνης·
ἐκεῖ γὰρ ὅπου εὑρεθῇ, ψύλλος οὐδὲν καθίζει.»

Τότε ὁ λεοντόπαρδος ἐφθέγξατο τοιαῦτα:
«Μηδὲν καυχᾶσαι, παρδαλὲ καὶ κοντοουραδᾶτε,
εἰς δύναμιν, εἰς πήδημαν καὶ εἰς τοὺς ὄνυχάς σου·
ὅσα γὰρ ἔχεις καὶ ἐσὺ χαρίσματα καὶ πράξεις,
οὕτως τὰ ἔχω καὶ ἐγὼ ὥσπερ καὶ σὲν τὸν πάρδον,
ἀκμὴν καὶ ὁ κατόπαρδος καὶ βασιλεὺς ὁ λέων.»

for curing any kind of wound or ailment.
Anyway, we should now step back a bit,
to let the brave, strong carnivores come forth,
those great, wild beasts, the cheetah and the leopard;
let them come forth now and debate their case."

So both the wolf and bear stood some way off.

Cheetah and leopard then arrived on stage, 860 *The Cheetah, The Leopard*
telling each other "I'm the better one!",
baring their teeth and lying both in ambush.
But then impetuously the cheetah spoke
and uttered to the leopard what here follows:

"You are no purebred; no, you are a crossbreed, **(17)**
having both something of the lion in you
and something else of me. And you're a beast 867
that's born in sin and brought up out of wedlock, 867
just like the very name of 'leo-pard' shows.

Now me—my gallantry goes with the name,
for I'm the mighty cheetah, brave past measure, 870
able to overpower any beast.
In just two bounds, or three at times, I reach
and pin down any animal I chase.
I clench it with my claws to stop it fleeing,
and then I eat it to my heart's content.
And what is left, I leave there and depart,
and any other passing beast consumes it.

Also my skin is valued by the sultans,
grandees and noblemen and great emirs,
who have it on their seats, and place it, too, 880
both on their pillows and their mattresses—
for anywhere it lies, no flea will land."

The leopard answered back to him as follows:
"No point in bragging, motley, short-tailed beast,
about your strength, about your bounds and claws,
for any deeds and merits you exhibit,
most certainly I share them with you, cheetah,
as do the cat-pard and our king the lion."

Ἀκούσας δὲ ὁ βασιλεὺς μεγάλως ἐθυμώθη *τὸ λεοντάρι*
καὶ πρὸς τὸν λεοντόπαρδον ἐφθέγξατο τοιαῦτα: 890

«Κρατεῖ με τὸ βασίλειον καὶ ἡ μεγαλειότης, **(18)**
ἡ ὄχλησις, ἡ ταραχή, ἡ μέλλουσα γενέσθαι·
ἀμὴ νὰ ἤπλωσα δαμὶν τὸ παλαμόχειρόν μου
καὶ νὰ σὲ ἔγγισα δαμὶν εἰς τὴν κατασαγοῦναν
καὶ νὰ σὲ ἐξεστόμωσα ἕως τὸν μήλιγγά σου·
τότε νὰ σ᾽ ἔμαθα καλὰ τὸ πῶς μοῦ συντυχαίνεις·
τὸν βασιλέα οὐδέποτε νὰ μὴν τὸν ἀναφέρῃς.

Ἀλλ᾽ ὅμως νῦν πρὸς τὸ παρὸν ἐβγᾶτε ἀπὸ τὴν μέσην,
νὰ ἔλθῃ ὁ ἐλέφαντας ὁ καὶ συγκάθεδρός μου,
νὰ εἴπῃ ὅσα καὶ αὐτὸς χαρίσματα τὰ ἔχει. 900

Καὶ ὅταν ἐκπληρώσουσιν καὶ ἀποποῦν οἱ πάντες,
τότε νὰ εἴπω καὶ ἐγώ, νὰ ὁρίσω εἴ τι θέλω
καὶ ὅ,τι πρᾶγμα βούλομαι ὡς βασιλεὺς καὶ λέων.»

Τότε ἐλθὼν ὁ ἔλεφας ἐστάθη εἰς τὸ μέσον *ὁ λέφας*
καὶ ταῦτα προσεφθέγξατο πρὸς τὴν κοινότην ὅλην:

«Ὥσπερ τις πύργος ἀσφαλὴς καὶ κατωχυρωμένος, **(19)**
φρούριον ἀπολέμητον καὶ δυνατὸν εἰς ἄκρον,
οὕτως ὑπάρχω καὶ ἐγώ, σφόδρα στερεωμένος·
ποιοῦσιν γὰρ ἀπάνω μου κάστρη μὲ τὰς σανίδας **(20)**
καὶ ξυλοπύργους δυνατούς, πολλὰ ὠχυρωμένους, 910
καὶ στέκουσιν οἱ ἄνθρωποι μέσα στερεωμένοι
καὶ πολεμοῦσιν ἰσχυρῶς πάντας τοὺς ἐναντίους
καὶ πάντας καταβάνουσιν, πάντας καταπονοῦσιν.

Ἀκόμη τὰ ὀστέα μου ποιοῦν μεγάλας χρείας,
βασιλικὰ κλινάρια, πατριαρχῶν σελία,
καθίσματα βασιλικά, θρονία δεσποινᾶτα
καὶ δοκανίκια γλυπτά, τορνοεμφωλευμένα.
Κρατοῦν τα οἱ ἐπίσκοποι καὶ οἱ μητροπολῖται
καὶ οἱ μεγαλοηγούμενοι μὲ τὰς μακρὰς γενειάδας·
ἀκόμη καὶ οἱ ἄρχοντες καὶ οἱ πραγματευτάδες 920
ἔχουσιν τα παιγνίδια, τετορευμένους σκάκους,
ταβλία καὶ ζατρίκια καὶ ὅσα τὰ τοιαῦτα.
Ποιοῦν μαχαιρομάνικα μεγάλων μαχαιρίων,
ὁμοίως καὶ εἰς τὰ μικρὰ ὡραιωμένα σφόδρα,
κτένια εὔμορφα πολλά, τὰ δένουν μὲ χρυσάφιν,

On hearing this, the king became enraged, *The Lion*
and spoke these words to reprimand the leopard: 890

"I am constrained by majesty and office, **(18)**
as well as by the uproar and the turmoil 892
which seem to be impending; otherwise, 892
if I would stretch my palm out just a smidgeon
and tap your lower jaw a tiny bit
and have your mouth tear off toward your temple,
I'd teach you to address me properly,
never to take the king's own name in vain.

For now, however, both of you get out
and let the elephant, who sits beside me,
come forth and list the merits he has, too. 900
And after that, when everyone is done, 901
and all have said what words they've had to say, 901
then will I speak as well and here dictate
whatever I decide as king and lion."

The elephant then came to center stage, *The Elephant*
and he addressed the whole assembly thus:

"Just like a tower, safe and fortified, **(19)**
a fort impregnable, firm to the end,
thus, too, stand I, robust beyond compare.
Thus bastions are built on me, made of boards, **(20)**
and solid towers made of wood, as well, 910
soundly fortified. Soldiers in these towers
stand resolute, fiercely combat their foes,
and overpower and defeat them all.

Also my bones are put to splendid uses:
in royal beds and seats of patriarchs,
emperors' chairs, armchairs of empresses;
and in carved staffs, with jewel settings lathed,
for metropolitans to hold and bishops
and for head abbots with their beards so long.
The noblemen and merchants have them, too, 920
in games they own: lathed chesspieces and chessboards,
backgammon boards, and all things of the sort.
And they make knife handles for fine, long knives
as well as for exquisite smaller ones,
and very pretty combs, all bound in gold,

ἀκόμη μὲ ἀσήμιον, σμαραγδοπλουμισμένα,
καὶ ἔχουν τα οἱ ἄρχοντες, οἱ γέροντες καὶ νέοι.
[Κτενίζουν τὰ μαλλία τους οἱ νέοι νεανίσκοι, 927a
κτενίζουν γρούντας τὰς ξαθὰς τὰς ἔχουσιν πολλάκις, 927b
ἀκμὴν καὶ οἱ ἀρχόντισσες καὶ οἱ ξαθὲς κουρτέσες, 927c
κτενίζουν τὰ μαλλία τους καὶ τὰς ξαθὰς πλεξούδας, 927d
ἀκόμη καὶ χωρίστριες τὰς ἔχουν οἱ κουρτέσες, 927e
χωρίζουν τὰ μαλλία τους αἱ νέες παιδοποῦλες, 927f
καὶ οἱ ξαθὲς οἱ δέσποινες διὰ τὴν πρεποσύνην.] 927g
Ἀλλ᾽ ἔχουσιν καὶ κάτοπτρα τὰ λέγουσιν καθρίπτες
καὶ βλέπουσιν τὸ σκίος τους αἱ νέες κορασίδες.
[Ταῦτα εἰσὶ τὰ ἀγαθὰ καὶ τὰ καλὰ τὰ ἔχω.]» 929a

Ὡς ἤκουσεν ἡ μαϊμοὺ ἐλέφαντος τοὺς λόγους— 930
—ὅλοι γὰρ ἐσυντύχασιν καὶ ἅπαντες ἀπεῖπον,
οὐδένας δὲν ἀπόμεινεν εἰ μὴ αὐτὴ καὶ μόνη·
ἐκρύπτετο δὲ ὡς πονηρὴ μέσον τοῦ συνεδρίου— *ἡ μαϊμοῦ*
[πολλὰ γὰρ ἔνι πονηρὴ πλέον τῆς ἀλωπούτζας] 933a
ἐπήδησεν δὲ καὶ αὐτὴ καὶ ἔστη εἰς τὸ μέσον
καὶ ταῦτα ἀπεφθέγξατο καὶ τῷ ἐλέφᾳ λέγει:

«Ἦλθες καὶ σύ, μακρόμυτε, μετὰ τῆς προμυτίδος, **(21)**
νὰ καυχισθῇς, νὰ ἐπαρθῇς, παράσημον τῶν ζῴων;
Ἔξω ἀπὸ τῆς φύσεως τῆς ἡμετέρας εἶσαι·
καβούρου τάξιν κέκτησαι μεγαλοχαχαλάτου·
ἔχεις ἀλλοῦ τὸ στόμα σου καὶ ἀλλοῦ τὴν προμυτίδα, 940
ἀλλοῦ συνάγεις βρώματα καὶ ἀλλαχοῦ τὰ τρώγεις.

Ξυλόποδε, παράσημε καὶ κάθαρμα τῶν ζῴων,
δίχα γονάτων γέγονας καὶ δίχα ἁρμονίας
καὶ στέκεις μονοστέλεχος νύκταν τε καὶ ἡμέραν
καὶ οὐ πίπτεις νὰ ἀναπαυθῇς ὥσπερ τὰ ἄλλα ζῷα,
οὔτε ἀνάπαυσιν μικρὰν ἔχεις ὡσὰν οἱ πάντες·

ἀλλ᾽ ὅταν θέλῃς νὰ ὑπνοῖς, ἱστέκεσαι ὀλόρθος
καὶ ἀκουμπίζεις εἰς δενδρὸν ἢ εἰς μεγάλην πέτραν
καὶ μετὰ φόβου στέκεσαι καὶ τρόμου καὶ κοιμᾶσαι·

καὶ ἂν νυστάξῃς πάμπολλα καὶ κοιμηθῇς βαρέα, 950
ἀλὶ σὲ σέν, κακότυχε, πῶς θέλεις ἐξηστρέψει,
νὰ γείρῃς ἐξανάσκελα, νὰ πέσῃς ἄνω κάτω,
οἱ πόδες σου νὰ στέκουνται ἀπάνω ὥσπερ ξύλα,
ποσῶς δὲ νὰ μὴ δύνασαι νὰ ἐγερθῇς ὀλόρθος.

and silver, too, and wrought with emeralds,
which noblemen possess, both young and old.
[The young lads use these combs to comb their hair; 927a
they comb that long blond hair they often have. 927b
Blond ladies of the court and noble dames 927c
will also comb their hair and their blond tresses; 927d
and ladies of the court adjust their partings. 927e
Young girls, it must be said, will part their hair, 927f
as do blond damsels, to look fair and decent.] 927g
They're even used in glasses, known as mirrors,
in which young lasses gaze upon their image.
[Such are my merits and advantages.]" 929a

Now when the monkey heard the elephant— 930
for everyone had spoken and was done,
and none was yet to speak but her alone,
as she'd concealed herself most cunningly, 933 *The Monkey*
craftily hiding in the conference 933
[being more cunning than the fox by far]— 933a
she jumped up front, in turn, and stood on stage
and spoke as follows to the elephant:

"So here you've come now, big-nose, with your trunk, **(21)**
to brag and boast, you ill-shaped animal!
You're nothing like the rest of us at all!
You've got the habits of a big-clawed crab:
your mouth is one place and your trunk is elsewhere; 940
you pick your food up here and move it there
to eat it. You deformed and wooden-legged 942
disaster in the realm of animals! 942
You're born with neither knees nor any joints,
and so you stand up rigid, night and day,
and you can neither ever have a lie-down, 945
like any other beast, nor can you rest— 945
not even just a bit, like everybody.
Instead, when you would sleep, you stand right up,
leaning against a tree or some large boulder,
and always stand in fear and sleep in dread.
And when you're drowsy and you fall asleep, 950
then woe betide you, O ill-fated beast: 951
you're twisted round and fall right on your back, 951
turned upside down, your legs up in the air,
just like so many wood boards! When that happens,
you are in no position to get up.

Καὶ ἔρχονται οἱ ἄνθρωποι ὁποὺ σὲ κυνηγοῦσιν·
εὑρίσκουν σε, σκοτώνουν σε καὶ καταλύουσίν σε
ὡς ἄνανδρον, ὡς ἀσθενῆν, μὴ ἔχοντα τί δρᾶσαι.
Καὶ σὺ ληρεῖς μὲ τὰ πολλὰ τὰ ψέματα τὰ λέγεις,
πὼς εἶσαι ζῷον μέγιστον, πάνυ ἀνδρειωμένον.

[Ὅμως ἀκμὴν νὰ σὲ εἰπῶ καὶ ἄλλον ἕνα λόγον] 959a
Πολλάκις δὲ οἱ ἄνθρωποι ποιοῦν καὶ ἄλλας πράξεις 960
καὶ τέχνας ἄλλας, ἄτυχε, πῶς νὰ σὲ καταλύσουν,
καὶ οὔτε ὕπνον θεωρεῖς νύκταν τε καὶ ἡμέραν·
ἀξινογλύφουν τὰ δενδρὰ ἢ πριονοκοποῦν τα
καὶ ἀποκόπτουν τα λοιπὸν εἰς ἄκρον νὰ κοποῦσιν
καὶ πᾷς ἐκεῖ νὰ κοιμηθῇς, ἐκεῖ νὰ ἀκουμπίσῃς·
τὸ δένδρον πίπτει, κρούει σου καὶ εἰς τὴν γῆν σὲ βάνει·
σκοτώνουν σε, ὡς εἴπαμεν, καὶ παίρνουν τὰ ὀστᾶ σου.
Αὐτὰ γὰρ εἶναι τὰ καλὰ καὶ τ' ἀγαθὰ τὰ ἔχεις.»

Τότε ὁ μέγας ἔλεφας εἰς ἄκρον ἐθυμώθη,
μετὰ σφοδρᾶς τῆς ἀπειλῆς τὴν μαϊμοὺν ἐλάλει: 970
«Φεῦγε, φαγγρίν, παράπτωμα, ἀκάθαρτον παράπαν,
μυσεροκακομούτζουνον, ψειροκονιδοφάγον·
ἐσθίεις τὰ ζωύφια, τὰς μυίγιας καὶ τοὺς ψύλλους
καὶ ἄλλα τὰ μικρότατα τῶν ἀκαθάρτων ζῴων.
Φεῦγε λοιπὸν ἀπ' ἔμπροσθεν, μὴ μαγαρίσῃς πάντας.»

Δρομαία δὲ ἡ μαϊμοὺ φεύγει ἀπὸ τὴν μέσην
ἀπὸ τὸν φόβον τὸν πολὺν τὸν εἶχεν τοῦ ἐλέφα,
καὶ μέσον ἀπεκρύβηκεν πάντων τῶν τετραπόδων.

Ὁ βασιλεὺς δ' ἀπόμεινεν λέων μεμονωμένος
καὶ πρὸς τὸ πλῆθος ἔφησε, τοιούτους λόγους εἶπεν: 980

«Ἀρκοῦσιν τὰ λεγόμενα τὰ εἴπασιν οἱ πάντες **(22)**
καὶ ὕβρεις καὶ ὀνειδισμοί, ἐπαῖνοι τε καὶ ψόγοι,
αἱ καυχησίαι αἱ πολλαὶ καὶ αἱ ἀντιλογίαι.

Ὁρίζω δὲ ἀπὸ τοῦ νῦν, λέγω καὶ ἀποφαίνω,
ἡ καθαρὰ καὶ ἄδολος ἀγάπη καὶ φιλία,
ὁποὺ ἐσυνεστήσαμεν μεθ' ὅρκου καὶ ἀγάπης,
ὁρίζω δὲ ἀπὸ τοῦ νῦν νὰ ἔν καταλυμένη,
νὰ στέκῃ μάχη δυνατή, καθάπερ καὶ τὸ πρῶτον, **(23)**
καὶ πάντα τὰ τετράποδα, τὰ αἱμοβόρα ζῷα,
νὰ τρώγουσιν τὰ καθαρά, ὥσπερ ἦτον καὶ πάντα, 990
ὁποῖον καὶ καταπονεῖ καὶ ἔναι εἰθισμένον.»

And then the men who hunt you down arrive;
they find you and they kill you and destroy you,
since, weak and helpless, you can't do a thing.
Yet with so many lies you've said, you babble
that you're a beast so very strong and great.

[But I have yet another thing to tell you:] 959a
people will often carry out more actions 960
and think up other methods to destroy you,
poor dear; so, day or night, you dare not sleep.
They axe the trees, or else they saw at them;
they cut them through and split them all the way.
And when you go to lean on them, to sleep there,
the tree falls, strikes you, pins you to the ground;
they kill you, like we said, and take your bones out.
Such are your merits and advantages."

At that, the mighty elephant, enraged,
threatened the monkey fearsomely as follows: 970
"Get out, you utter filth, you skeleton,
you offscouring! You louse-munching, nit-nibbling,
disgusting dirt-face who eats bugs, flies, fleas,
and all the other tiny filthy beasts!
Get off the stage, before you foul us all up!"

The monkey promptly ran away from there
out of her great fear of the elephant
and hid herself amidst the other beasts.

King Lion was left all alone on stage,
and he addressed the crowd along these lines: 980

"What everyone has said is quite enough; **(22)**
enough of all your mockery and curses, 982
enough of all your praises and reproaches, 982
your controversies and your drawn-out bragging.
Now, then, I state, declare, and order thus:
the pure and guileless peace and amity
that we have brought about through oath and concord,
I have determined, is henceforth dissolved.
We'll have fierce battle, rather, as before, **(23)**
and all bloodthirsty animals shall prey
upon the clean beasts, as has always happened, 990
as is the prevalent, long-standing custom."

Τότε νὰ εἶδες ὀδυρμοὺς καὶ δάκρυα μεγάλα *ἀρχὴ τοῦ πολέμου*
καὶ ὄχλησιν καὶ ταραχήν, τὴν ἔποικαν τὰ ζῷα,
νὰ εἶδες καὶ πηδήματα καὶ δρόμια ἐκεῖσε.

Ὁπού ἐκατεπόνεσεν, ἐδίωκεν τὸ ἄλλον,
ἔφθαναν, ἐδακῶναν τα καὶ ἐτινάσσασίν τα,
οἱ μὲν ἀπὸ τὸν σφόνδυλον, οἱ δὲ ἀπὸ τὴν ῥάχιν,
ἄλλοι δὲ ἀπὸ τὰ 'μίκωλα ἀλλὰ καὶ ἐκ τὴν κοιλίαν·
ἕτεροι ὡς ἐφθάνασιν καὶ ὅποθεν ὠρθῶσαν·
καὶ ἤκουσες καὶ τοὺς κλαυθμοὺς καὶ τὴν μεγάλην θλῖψιν 1000
καὶ τοῦ πολέμου ταραχὴν καὶ τὴν πολλὴν τὴν βίαν,
τὴν εἶχαν τὰ τετράποδα νὰ τρώγῃ ἓν τὸ ἄλλον.

Ἀμὴ νὰ διηγήσωμαι τὸν πόλεμον ἐκεῖνον
καὶ κατὰ μέρος νὰ εἰπῶ ὁποῖον ἔσχε τέλος
ἡ βία καὶ ἡ ταραχὴ ἡ τότε γεγονυῖα.

Πρῶτον εὐθὺς ὁ βασιλεὺς ἐπήδησεν ὁ λέων
καὶ τὴν βουβάλαν ἔδωκεν, καὶ πῆρε την καὶ κάτζεν.

Ἰδὼν ὁ βοῦς ἐκάκισεν ἀπάνω εἰς τὸν λέων **(24)**
καὶ σφόδρα ἐμουγκήθηκεν, ἐβόησεν μεγάλως:
«Βλέπετε τὸν πανάπιστον, τὸν ὁρκοκαταλύτην, 1010
ἀλλὰ καὶ τὸν ἐπίορκον καὶ ἀρχηγὸν τῆς μάχης.
Οὗτος οὐκ ἔνι βασιλεύς, οὐδὲ αὐθέντης ἔνι,
ἐπεὶ τὴν μάχην συνιστᾷ καὶ καταλεῖ ἀγάπην.
Καὶ ἂν ἦτον οὗτος βασιλεὺς καθὼς καὶ τζαμπουνίζει,
νὰ ὥρισεν νὰ ἐστέκετον πάντοτε ἡ ἀγάπη.
Ἐπεὶ οὖν ἔνι μαχοποιὸς καὶ ὁρκοκαταλύτης,
οἱ πάντες ἂς τὸν δώσωμεν μικροί τε καὶ μεγάλοι
καὶ ἂς τὸν ἀποκτείνωμεν ὡς ὁρκοπαραβάτην.»

Καὶ ἀπεφύσησεν ὁ βοῦς πρῶτον καὶ ἐκατέβη
καὶ σείει τὸ κεφάλιν του, κρούει τον κερατέα 1020
καὶ ὅλον του τὸ κέρατον εὐθὺς ἐκάτζεν μέσα
εἰς τὴν κοιλίαν λέοντος καὶ ἐξεντέρισέν τον.

Ἰδὼν ὁ πάρδος λέοντος τὸν θάνατον αὐτίκα, **(25)**
μεγάλως ἐλυπήθηκεν καὶ πρὸς τὸν βοῦν ἀντεῖπεν:

«Πόθεν νὰ ζῇ ὁ βασιλεύς, πόθεν οἱ ἄρχοντές του,
ἐὰν οὐ φάγῃ ἀπὸ σὲν καὶ ἀπὸ τοὺς ἑτέρους;»

Beginning of the War

You should have seen the lamentations then,
the mighty tears, the uproar and the turmoil 993
the animals all made! You should have seen 993
the running round and leaping that took place!
Whichever beast subdued and chased another,
would reach it, bite at it, and shake it round,
some from the neck and others from the back,
and from the buttocks and the belly, too,
with yet more animals arriving there, 999
grabbing their foes wherever they could manage. 999
You should have heard the crying and great sorrow, 1000
the battle's havoc and much violence
that swept the beasts up as they mauled each other.
But let me now relate in full that battle,
detailing what the outcome was of all
the violence and havoc that took place then.

First off, King Lion took a sudden leap,
striking and throwing down the buffalo.

On seeing this, the ox denounced the lion **(24)**
with mighty groans, and loudly crying out:
"See him! Untrustworthy oath-breaking fiend! 1010
Abolisher of oaths and first to strike!
This is no king, this is no decent leader,
for he dissolves our peace and brings on war.
Were he a king indeed, as he keeps babbling,
he should have bid that peace prevail forever.
Since he is an oath-breaking warmonger,
let all of us attack him, great and small,
and kill this king who violates his oath."

The ox then snorted and charged down against him.
He tossed his head, and struck him with his horn. 1020
And the entire horn instantly sunk through
the lion's gut and disemboweled him.

The cheetah, seeing how the lion died, **(25)**
was most distraught, retorting to the ox:

"How can the king and nobles make ends meet,
if not by eating you and all the others?"

Καὶ ἥπλωσεν τὸν πόδαν του ἀπάνω εἰς τὸ βόδι·
καὶ τὸ ἰδεῖν ὁ βούβαλος ἐσέβη εἰς τὴν μέσην,
κλότζον τὸν κλότζον ἔκρουεν τὸν πάρδον μὲ τοὺς πόδας,
ἀλλὰ καὶ μὲ τὰ κέρατα καὶ σόσπαστον τὸν κάμνει· 1030
καὶ μὲ τὴν βίαν τὴν πολλὴν καὶ τὴν ἀνάγκη ἐκείνην **(26)**
μικρὰν φωνὴν ἐλάλησεν ὁ πάρδος ἀπὸ χάμω:

«Ποῦ εἶστε, συντρόφοι ἀδελφοί, ὠμόβορα θηρία,
καὶ στέκετε καὶ βλέπετε καὶ οὐδὲν μὲ βοηθεῖτε;»
Εὐθὺς δὲ λεοντόπαρδος, εὐθὺς δὲ καὶ ἡ ἄρκος,
ὁ λύκος, ἡ ἀλώπηξ τε, ὁ σκύλος καὶ ὁ κάτης,
ὅλοι ἐκεῖ ἐδράμασι εἰς βοήθειαν τοῦ πάρδου·
τὰ ἕτερα ὠμόβορα καὶ τετράποδα ζῷα
εἰς μίαν ὥραν καὶ φωνὴν ἐσυνάχθησαν ἅμα
εἰς μάχην καὶ εἰς πόλεμον τῶν καθαρῶν τῶν ζῴων. 1040

Ὡς ταῦτα πάντα εἴδασιν τὰ καθαρὰ τὰ ζῷα, **(27, 28)**
ὡρίσασιν τὸν γάδαρον νὰ δώσῃ τὸ σαλπίγγιν,
ἡ κάμηλος δὲ νὰ βαστᾷ ζυγὴν ἀνακαράδας
καὶ νὰ τοὺς παίζῃ ὁ ποντικὸς νὰ μαδευθοῦσιν ὅλοι,
ὁ χοῖρος καὶ ἡ ἔλαφος, ἡ αἶγα, τὸ ἀγρίμιν,
τὸ πρόβατον, ὁ λαγωὸς καὶ τὰ ὅμοια τούτων,
τὸ ἄλογον δὲ ὡς γοργὸν ν᾿ ἀνεβοκατεβαίνῃ
καὶ νὰ ἀνδρειώνῃ δυνατὰ ὅλην του τὴν μερέαν.

Ἐδράμασιν δὲ καὶ αὐτοὶ ἀπάνω εἰς ἐκείνους **(29, 30)**
καὶ συγκροτοῦσιν πόλεμον καὶ θαυμαστὸν καὶ μέγαν. 1050
Ἐσέβη λεοντόπαρδος τὸν ἔλαφον νὰ δώσῃ
καὶ παλαμέα κρούει τον, διχοτομεῖ τον μέσα.

Καὶ χύνει χοῖρος ἀπεκεῖ ἀψὺς καὶ κατεβαίνει, **(31)**
κρούει τὸν λεοντόπαρδον καὶ ἐξεκοιλίασέν τον.
Εὐθὺς δὲ ἐχαμόδραμεν ἡ ἄρκος πρὸς τὸν χοῖρον·
οὗτος γυρίζεται γοργὸν καὶ κρούει καὶ τὴν ἄρκον·
ἐσκότωσε δὲ καὶ αὐτὴν μετὰ λεοντοπάρδου.

Ὁ σκύλος δέ, ὡς ἔστεκεν βλέπων τὰ γεγονότα, **(32)**
ἐβάβισεν ἀπὸ μακρά, ἐξύπασεν τὸν χοῖρον,
ἀνεβοεκατέβαινεν «βλέπετε καὶ σκοπεῖτε 1060
τὴν κακομήχανον αὐτὴν τὴν μεγαλομαστόραν,
τὴν ἀλωποὺ τὴν ἄπιστον τὸ πῶς καταμιτώνει
καὶ δείχνει ἀγάπην δολερὰν καὶ εἰς τὰ δύο μέρη.

And then he reached his leg out to the ox.
On seeing this, the buffalo rushed in,
and struck and struck the cheetah, kick for kick,
thrusting his horns as well, and thrashed him soundly— 1030
until the cheetah, forced and in dire straits, **(26)**
cried out from underneath, in straining voice:

"Where are you, brothers, comrades, carnivores?
Why do you stand there watching without helping?"
At once the leopard and the bear as well,
the wolf, the fox, the dog and cat all ran
to aid the cheetah down there. And the rest
of the carnivorous, four-legged beasts
in one voice, in one moment, all assembled
to battle and wage war against the clean beasts. 1040

The clean beasts, then, on seeing all of this, **(27, 28)**
bade that the donkey sound the call to arms;
the camel bear a pair of kettledrums,
and the rat beat on them, to gather all—
the boar and deer, the wild goat and the nanny,
the sheep, the hare, and all beasts of their kind;
and that the horse, fast as he is, should run
both up and down, boosting his camp's morale.

And so they, too, did rush against the others, **(29, 30)**
starting a great, formidable affray. 1050
The leopard ran right in to charge the deer,
struck with his palm, and split her down the middle.

The boar rushed down there briskly, like a torrent, **(31)**
striking and disemboweling the leopard.
At once the bear crawled over to the boar,
who swiftly turned around and struck her, too,
slaughtering thus the bear just like the leopard.

The dog, who stood by, following the action, **(32)**
barked from a distance, startling thus the boar,
while running up and down: "Watch her! Observe her! 1060
That mal-intriguer, that grand-master trickster,
the untrustworthy fox! See how she plots
and shows deceitful love toward both sides.

Τί στέκετε; Τί βλέπετε; Ἀμὴ ἀγωνισθῆτε.
Μὴ δειλιάσετε ποσῶς, ἀλλὰ ἀνδρειωθῆτε.»

Εὐθὺς ὁ χοῖρος ἔδραμεν, ἐπήδησεν ἡ αἶγα, **(33)**
τὸ πρόβατον, ὁ λαγωός, κριός τε καὶ ὁ τράγος,
ἐσάλπισεν ὁ γάδαρος, ἡ κάμηλος ὀρχᾶται,
κρούει τὰ ταβλαμπάσια ὁ ποντικὸς ἀπάνω,
τὸ ἄλογον δὲ ὡς γοργὸν ἀνεβοκατεβαίνει. 1070
Ποιοῦσιν ταραχὴν πολλὴν καὶ ὄχλησιν μεγάλην.

Κόπτει ὁ λύκος τὸ βουνίν, ἡ ἀλωποὺ τὸ δάσος, **(34)**
ὁ κάτης δὲ ἀνέβηκεν εἰς τὸ δενδρὸν ἀπάνω,
ἡ μαϊμοὺ ἀπέμεινεν, ἐσέβη εἰς τὴν τρύπαν.
Ἡλίου βασιλεύοντος ὁ πόλεμος ἐπαύθη
καὶ ἡ σκοτία τῆς νυκτὸς ἔσωσεν τούτους ἔξω.

Καὶ ἐπληρώθη τὸ ῥηθὲν διὰ τοῦ ὑμνογράφου:

«Ὁ βασιλεὺς οὐ σῴζεται ἐν πολλῇ τῇ δυνάμει
καὶ γίγας οὐ σωθήσεται ἐν πλήθει τῆς ἰσχύος.»

Ἔκτοτε οὖν καὶ μέχρι νῦν ἡ γεναμένη μάχη 1080
εἰς πάντα τὰ τετράποδα μικρά τε καὶ μεγάλα **(35)**
ἔμεινεν καὶ διέμεινεν εἰς πάντας τοὺς αἰῶνας.

[Δοξάζω σου τὸ ἔλεος Χριστέ μου παντοκράτορ, 1082a
ἀλλὰ καὶ σὲν πανύμνητε ἐλπὶς ἀπελπισμένων. 1082b
ἀμήν] **(36)**

What are you waiting for and staring at?
It's time to fight! Don't falter now; be bold!"

At once the boar ran in; at once the nanny, **(33)**
the sheep, the hare, the ram, the billy goat
leapt in; the donkey sounded the call to arms,
the camel danced, the rat struck at the drums;
the horse, fast as he was, ran up and down, 1070
all of them making turmoil and much uproar.

The wolf cut through the hills; the fox, the forest. **(34)**
The cat climbed to a treetop. And the monkey
was left behind and sneaked inside a hole.
Finally, as the sun crowned the horizon, 1075
the war came to an end. And then the night 1075
preserved them all away within its darkness.

Thereby the Psalmist's words became fulfilled:
"There is no king saved by the multitude 1078
of any host; nor is a mighty man 1078
delivered by much strength."

From that day forth, 1080 **(35)**
and to this day, the battle that took place 1080
endures amongst all beasts, both great and small—
and will abide with them forevermore.

[I glorify Thy Mercy, Christ Almighty, 1082a
Thou Ever-Praisèd Hope of the Despairing. 1082b
AMEN.] **(36)**

MANUSCRIPT C ILLUSTRATIONS

All illustrations are from manuscript C Graecus Seraglio 35 (ff. 31–75), reproduced here with the kind permission of Topkapı Saray Museum, Istanbul.

(A) King Lion; Leopard; Cheetah (f. 31r)
Λέων ὁ Βασιλεὺς· Λεοντόπαρδος· Πάρδος

The cheetah is depicted complete with spots and collar and with a long tail hanging down. The leopard looks like a standard lion rampant, though without much of a mane and with no dots at all. The lion, whose mane is luxuriant, scowls down at his attendants from his throne.

(B) King Lion; Dog; The Elephant; Rat; The Cat; Fox (f. 31v)
Λέων ὁ Βασιλεὺς· Σκύλος· Ὁ Λέφαντας· Πονδικός· Ὁ Κάτης· Ἀλώπηξ

This is the only time the elephant is depicted with tusks. On the bottom left, behind the rat, one can discern, Cheshire Cat–like, the outline of a cat—rather more convincingly drawn than the labeled hunchbacked cat facing the rat.

(C) The first page of text of the *Entertaining Tale of Quadrupeds* (f. 32r)

The title features an ornamental abstract symmetrical design right above it.

(1) They gave their papers in and held discussions (f. 34r)
Ἀπέδωκαν καὶ τὰς γραφάς, ἐσύντυχαν καὶ λόγους

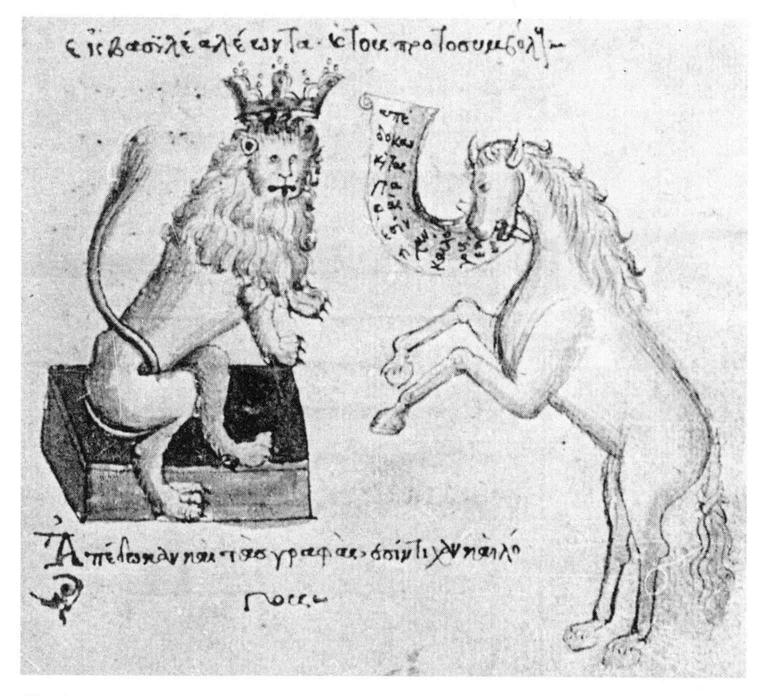

The horse faces the lion, speaking the next verse, "They gave their papers in and held discussions," as a ribbon—a commonplace of narrative art before the modern comic strip and its bubble. Tsiouni (1972:16) labels this illustration Λέοντος καὶ Γαϊδάρου, "Of a Lion and a Donkey," but we could not sight such a label anywhere.

(2) The Rat (f. 35v)
Ὁ πονδικός

(3) The Rat, The Humble Cat (f. 35v)
Ὁ πονδικός, Ὁ ταπεινὸς ὁ κάτης

(4) The Fox, The Hound (f. 38r)
Ἡ ἀλώπηξ, Ὁ κύων

(5) Fox, The Hare (f. 40v)
Ἀλώπηξ, Ὁ λαγωός

(6) [The Boar, The Deer] (f. 42r)

No caption is given.

(7) The Boar, The Sheep (f. 45v)
Ὁ χοῖρος, Τὸ πρόβατο

(8) The Sheep; The Sheep, The Nanny (f. 46v)
Τὸ πρόβατο· Τὸ πρόβατο, Ἡ αἶγα

The poem requires the right-hand "sheep" to be a billy goat; despite the (corrected) caption, that is what in fact has been drawn.

(9) The Buffalo (f. 49v)
Ὁ βούβαλος

(10) The Ox[, The Lion] (f. 50r)
Τὸ βούδι

(11) Cow; The Ox (f. 51r)
Ἀγελάδα, Τὸ βώδι

Presumably, *cow* is a later correction to *ox* (it is the topmost label), because the single bovine depicted has teats as well as horns. No cow figures in the poem, other than the buffalo's imprecise reference to the ox's milk in verse 597, so the presence of a cow is an interpolation on the part of the illustrator.

(12) The Ass, The Ox (f. 53v)
Ὁ ὄνος, Ὁ βοῦς

This is likely the notorious "fifth leg" picture.

(13) The Ass, The Ox (f. 54v)
Ὁ ὄνος, Τὸ βούδι

The illustrator repeats the preceding drawing (instead of presenting the correct pairing of horse and donkey)—this time with less emphasis on the donkey.

(14) The Camel, The Steed (f. 58r)
Ἡ κάμηλος, Ὁ ἵππος

(15) [The Horse, The Wolf] (f. 59v)

No caption is given.

(16) The Horse, The Wolf (f. 60v)
Τὸ ἄλογον, Ὁ λύκος

This is presumably an erroneous repetition of illustration 15 (as with illustrations 12—13), because the text has at this point introduced the bear.

(17) Leopard, Cheetah (f. 61v)
Λεοντόπαρδος, Πάρδος

(18) The King, The Leopard (f. 62v)
Ὁ βασιλεύς, Ὁ λεοντόπαρδος

(19) [The Elephant] (f. 63v)

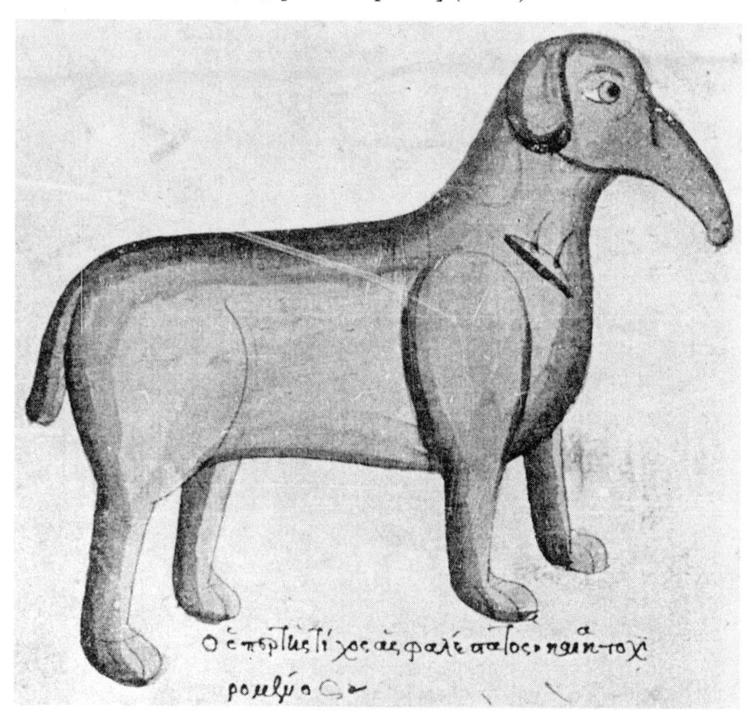

No caption is given. We do not know what the strange neck markings are; they appear on all three depictions of the elephant. It is not impossible that they are misplaced tusks.

(20) The King (f. 64r)
Ὁ βασιλεύς

The king appears in the middle of the elephant's speech, angrily facing his coregent's picture on the preceding page.

(21) Elephant, The Monkey (f. 65v)
Ἐλέφας, Ἡ μαϊμοῦ

The monkey is shown sitting on its haunches and gesticulating toward the elephant, much like an excitable human.

(22) King Lion (f. 67v)
Λέων ὁ βασιλεύς

(23) Camel, Cheetah, Cat, The Leopard, The Wolf, Fox, The Dog (f. 68r)
Κάμηλος, Πάρδος, Κάτος, Ὁ λεοντόπαρδος, Ὁ λύκος, Ἀλεπού, Ὁ σκύλος

Although Tsiouni (1972:17) does not indicate it, the animals are labeled. The animals are looking on at the lion on the preceding page declaring war; they are not yet fighting, contrary to Tsiouni's label ("An illustration of many animals fighting"). This also explains what the camel is doing in the middle of all the carnivores.

(24) The Ox, The King (f. 69r)
Ὁ βοῦς, Ὁ βασιλεύς

Goring the lion, the ox has cast him down from his throne (which looks uncannily like a shoeshine box), and his crown has been tossed to the side.

(25) Death of the King (f. 69v)
Θάνατος βασιλέως

(26) The Leopard [= Cheetah], The Ox (f. 70r)
Ὁ λεοντόπαρδος, Ὁ βοῦς

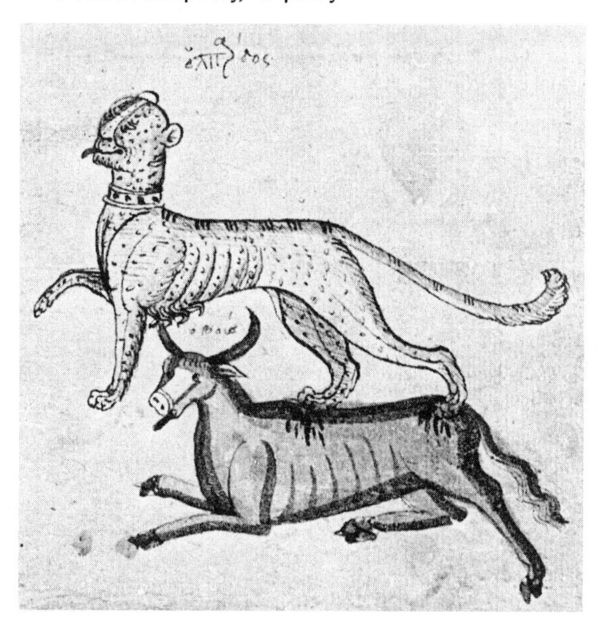

The cheetah is clearly drawn and is required by the poem at this point but has been mislabeled. The label is in fact Ὁ ΛΠάρδος ("*The L'Pard*"), an abbreviation not otherwise used by the illustrator for the leopard, so the illustrator may have intended to label the drawing as the pard (cheetah) after all.

(27) The Buffalo, The Cheetah (f. 70v)
Ὁ βούβαλος, Ὁ πάρδος

The cheetah is clearly "forced and in dire straits," being trampled by the buffalo and bleeding from the gashes made by the buffalo's hooves. The buffalo's horns, mentioned along with the hooves in verse 1030, are not displayed.

(28) The Wolf, Leopard, The Bear, The Dog, The Fox, The Cat (f. 71r)
῾Ο λύκος, Λεοντόπαρδος, ῾Η ἄρκος, ῾Ο σκύλος, ῾Η ἀλεπού, ῾Ο κάτης

This is the first time the bear appears in the illustrations. The illustration takes up the entire page. The animals have turned their backs to the buffalo and the cheetah on the facing page, even though the poem has the cheetah pleading for their help (verses 1032–33).

(29) The Horse (f. 71v)
Τὸ ἄλογον

(30) The Boar, The Deer, Buffalo [and other animals] (f. 72r)
Ὁ χοῖρος, Τὸ 'λάφι, Βούβαλος

The unlabeled animals in the rally of the herbivores are, from top to bottom, the ox, the (momentarily translucent) goat, and the sheep. The illustration takes up the entire page.

(31) Deer, Boar[, Leopard] (f. 72v)
Ἔλαφος, Χοῖρος

The gored leopard appears without a caption. C is the only manuscript in which the deer is not killed (verse 1052 omitted); consistently with this, the deer is shown fleeing rather than dying.

(32) Boar, Bear (f. 73r)
Χοῖρος, Ἄρκος

The boar and bear are depicted in a before-and-after illustration (labeled in both instances).

(33) Dog, Boar, Fox (f. 73v)
Σκύλος, Χοῖρος, Ἀλώπεξ

The boar is shown visibly startled by the dog (1059) and is turning his head back toward him.

(34) The Hare, The Boar, The Sheep, [The Ox,] The Ram, The Ass (f. 74r)
Ὁ λαγός, Ὁ χοῖρος, Τὸ πρόβατο, Ὁ τράγος, Ὁ ὄνος

Again, although Tsiouni (1972:17) gives no labels and describes the drawing as "an illustration of many animals fighting," the herbivores making their final attack are labeled (except for the ox).

(35) The Rat, The Camel (f. 74v)
Ὁ ποντικός, Ἡ κάμηλος

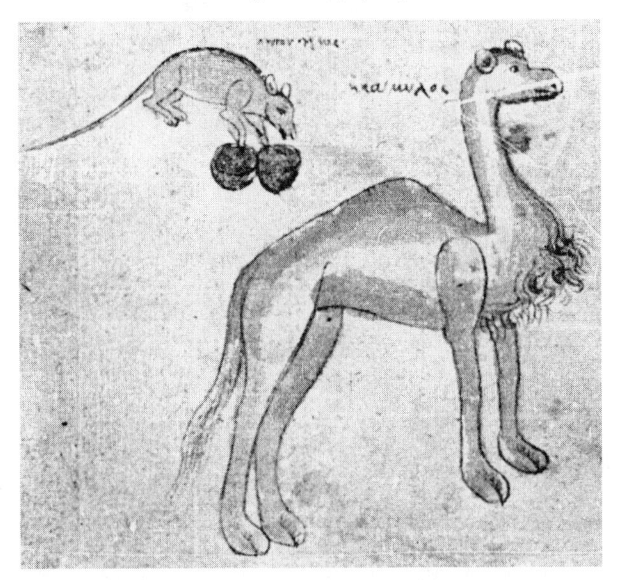

The rat is shown beating the kettledrums, though the illustrator has shrunk from showing him actually riding the camel.

(36) The Fox, The Wolf, The Cat, The Monkey (f. 75r)
Ἡ ἀλωποῦ, Ὁ λύκος, Ὁ κάτης, Ἡ μαϊμοῦ

The animals that have fled the battle are shown in their respective hiding places: the fox, barely visible in the top left, in what may be a depiction of undergrowth; the wolf on a craggy mountain top; the cat on top of a tree he is managing to dwarf; and the monkey, whose hindquarters alone are visible—and whose caption is likewise difficult to make out—seems to be hiding under a pile of rocks (presumably the *hole* of the poem). The illustration appears underneath the ornamental AMEN that concludes the text of C.

COMMENTARY

> Whether the Byzantines neglected to write about their daily lives, or someone did write something that has not survived—or has survived only to languish somewhere unknown—what is certain is that there are no available detailed accounts of those lives. Therefore only information scattered here and there, meticulously collected, may supply some indications clarifying the issue in question.
>
> —Konstantinos Sathas, *Ἱστορικὸν δοκίμιον περὶ τοῦ θεάτρου καὶ τῆς μουσικῆς τῶν Βυζαντινῶν*

The manuscripts cited are

- C Constantinopolitan (*Graecus Seraglio* 35)
- P Parisian (*Graecus Suppl.* 2911)
- V Viennese (*Vindobonensis Theol. Gr.* 244)
- L Lesbian (formerly *Lesbiacus* 92, now *Petropolitanus* 721)
- A St. Petersburgian (*Petropolitanus* 202).

Issues relating primarily to the standing of the original text are discussed in Textual Notes—though, of course, the distinction between topics discussed here and in that section is necessarily arbitrary.

1. **entertaining**. There is an extensive literature on the meaning of παιδιόφραστος (Dölger 1962a; Dölger 1962b; Michailidis 1970; Panagiotakis 1975; Trapp 1976; Tsiouni 1972:45–47; Tsolakis 1962; Vasiliou 1996:60–62). Part of this literature centers on the issue of which of the two readings to adopt: παιδιόφραστος is attested only in P, whereas the other manuscripts (but for A, whose beginning is missing) have the more straightforward πεζόφραστος, "expressed in prose." The lost Sirlet manuscript combined both in its title: Παιδιοφράστου διήγησις τῶν τετραπόδων ζῴων, πεζῇ φράσει, *The tale of quadrupeds by Paediophrastus (?), in prose expression* (Tsiouni 1972:45). Because the *Tale* is not in prose and παιδιόφραστος is clearly the *lectio difficilior* (i.e., the more difficult reading and therefore more likely to be original), this reading is preferred in scholarship.

An alternative hypothesis is that πεζός in πεζόφραστος meant "vernacular" as well as "prose"; both Dölger and Tsolakis have found instances of such usage in Byzantine literature. Tsiouni (1972:46) finds that "both words fit in our poem," and Ševčenko (1974:77) likewise calls the work *Story of the Quadrupeds Told in Jocular (or Simple) Style*; Tsiouni, however, finds that P's reading παιδιόφραστος accords better with the overall ethos of the poem. Because the language of the poem was probably not as peculiar a property as its humor, we have agreed. We have also been motivated by the fact that παιδιόφραστος has the weight of tradition behind it, being the title under which the *Tale* was published by Wagner—who primarily used P—as well as both its more recent editors, Tsiouni and Papathomopoulos.

The word παιδιόφραστος is not the *lectio difficilior* for nothing: its precise meaning is difficult to capture. The suffix -φραστος means "phrased, expressed," but the stem παιδιο- seems at first glance to refer to παιδίον, "child." The gloss is used by Krumbacher (1897:2.877), who refers to the *Tale* as *Die Kindergeschichte von den Vierfüsslern,* "The Children's Tale of Quadrupeds." But as Krumbacher himself finds, however liberal the Byzantines may have been about sexual morality (see abundant instances in the vernacular romances), this is clearly not a poem "expressed in a way fit for children" in either language or subject matter. (Krumbacher [1897:2.879] finds the *Book of Birds* a likelier candidate for didacticism: "While coarseness appears there too, at least the more gross obscenities are absent, and with its massive enumeration of bird names the work is like an ornithological compendium.") The opinion that has prevailed (Tsolakis, Vasiliou) is that παιδιο- refers instead to παιδιά, "fun," so that the word means "expressed for fun" (χάριν παιδιᾶς). We have felt "entertaining" a reasonable enough approximation to this. Trapp (1976:444) suggests the homonymous παιδειόφραστος, "expressed for education" (χάριν παιδείας); this is consistent with the prologue in which the word occurs, though, of course, not with the remainder of the poem. (See also discussion in "The Purpose of the *Tale.*")

A side effect of all this is the abbreviated form of the title. In translation, the word that stands out from the title is *Quadrupeds*, and the work is accordingly abbreviated as *Quadr.* in reference works (e.g., Psichari's [1886–89] and Jannaris's [1897] linguistic work). The title of Šandrovskaja's translation (1956a) leaves out the word for "entertaining" altogether (*Рассказ о Четвероногих,* "Tale of Quadrupeds"), though in the work itself she renders it as шуточный, "comical, facetious." In Greek, however, the most salient word is παιδιόφραστος, which is a hapax legomenon (a word attested only once in the language). The work is accordingly abbreviated by Greek authors as Παιδ. or Διήγ. Παιδ., "Entertaining Tale," not Τετρ., "Quadrupeds," and Παιδιόφραστος is the single-word designation of the poem current in modern Greek.

1. **quadrupeds**. The word τετράποδον, "quadruped," or τετράποδον ζῷον, "quadruped animal," is frequently used in the poem. We have avoided *quad-*

ruped in our rendering, retaining it only in the title and initial verses, for consistency with previous usage in the literature.

7. **false peace**. An experience late Byzantium certainly knew not a little about! Trapp (1976) points out that ψευδαγάπη, literally "false love," properly means "false peace," and the use of ἀγάπη, "love," to mean "peace" or "truce" is common in Byzantine writing:

> *Chronicle of Morea* H 6882–83: Τρέβαν ἐποίησε μετ' αὐτόν, ***ἀγάπην*** διὰ ἕναν χρόνον / διὰ νὰ ἐνεμείνῃ ὁ τόπος του 'ς ἀνάπαψιν κ' εἰρήνην
>
> [He made a truce with him, an ***armistice*** for one year, that his land might remain in tranquility and peace.] (Lurier 1964:266)
>
> *Chronicle of the Sultans* 29: Καὶ ἐγύρισε 'ς τὸν θρόνο του 'ς τὴν 'Ανδριανούπολι, καὶ ἐστερέωσε τὴν ***ἀγάπην*** μὲ τοὺς Ρωμαίους, μὲ τὸν βασιλέα Παλαιολόγο
>
> [And ⟨Bayezid I⟩ then returned to his court in Adrianople; here he confirmed his ***treaty of friendship*** with the Romans and their emperor Palaeologus.] (Philippides 1990:22)
>
> Della Porta 1.1305–8: Ἤξευρε, Λουνάρδο, ἐποίκαμέν σε / ἀποκρισάρην σήμερον, νὰ ὑπᾷς εἰς τὰ Παλάτια, / νὰ ἐσμίξῃς μὲ τὸν ἀμιρᾶν καί, ὡς δύνεσαι, νὰ ποίσῃς / ***ἀγάπην*** τέλειαν μετὰ μᾶς, τὰ σκάνδαλα νὰ λείψουν
>
> [Linardo, know we've made you / today an envoy; you'll go to Palatia ⟨Mendeşe⟩, / to meet the emir; as much as you can manage, / make perfect ***peace*** between us; end the troubles.]

(The gloss ἀγάπη, εἰρήνη: *pace,* "peace," is as late as Somavera 1977 [1709].)

Tsiouni glosses ψευδαγάπη as "false love" but ἀγάπη itself as both "peace" and "love." Though the primary meaning, "love," is also applicable here, we have preferred throughout our translation the secondary, diplomatic meaning of ἀγάπη, to emphasize the political tenor of the narration. (In 279 we have *friendship*, as more appropriate between two individuals normally at odds; in 986 we have *concord*, to avoid the absurdity of the lion bringing about peace through peace; whereas in 1063 we have *love*, as the sentiment affected by the fox.) Šandrovskaja (1956a) correctly renders the word as лживый мир, "deceitful peace."

11/12. **thirteen hundred sixty-four**. In the original, "On the six thousandth and eight hundredth, and toward seventy and another three years" (dating from the creation of the world, 5508 B.C. by Byzantine reckoning, which had stabilized by the tenth century—Grumel 1958:127). The year is usually cited as 1365 (6873–5508) rather than 1364 in the secondary literature (starting with Gidel 1866:331 and running at least up to Kazhdan 1991, s.v. DIEGESIS TON TETRAPODON ZOON). But in late Byzantium the year began on the first of September

(Grumel 1958:176), so the Western Anno Domini would not yet have changed over on the fifteenth of September, when the poem is set (verse 13). There is a long history of confusing the changeover of Byzantine dates:

> In practice, the rule is thus that for a date from January 1 to August 31, 5508 must be subtracted, whereas from September 1 to December 31, 5509 must be subtracted [6873 – 5509 = 1364; the rule is identically stated in Grumel 1958:220]. This rule is so obvious that it is beyond understanding why it has been paid so little attention until now, that almost all datings in the older Greek [paleographical] catalogues . . . need to be reexamined in this regard. (Gardthausen 1913:2.450)

17. **king**. Byzantine Greek distinguished between βασιλεύς, "emperor," and ῥῆξ, "king." The former is the absolute ruler and typically designates the Byzantine emperor, whereas the latter term (borrowed from Latin *rex*) refers to the lesser Western kings—including the emperors of the Holy Roman Empire, from Charlemagne on. (See also discussion under "Place of Composition.") As absolute ruler of the animal kingdom, the lion is a *basileus,* not a *rex*. This is consistent with the (pre-Byzantine) Aesopic conventions in Greek, as *basileus* is the older word. Moreover, the metaphorical use of *basileus* was possible in vernacular Byzantine Greek (e.g., *Callimachus and Chrysorrhoe* 763: Ἔρως παρὼν ὁ ***βασιλεὺς*** εἰς τοὺς ἐκείνων λόγους, "Love, the ***king***, was present at their words"). (The promotion of Cupid to king has been argued by Cupane [1974] to constitute a borrowing from French literature, so it originates from a domain where the *basileus/rex* distinction was foreign.)

At any rate, to call the lion an *emperor* in English would clash with the conventions of English language storytelling. We thus render βασιλεύς as "king" consistently when referring to the lion.

18. **fierce-eyed**. On the possible Physiologan provenance of "fierce-eyed," see "Fact and Fiction in the *Tale*'s Zoology." The adjective itself, ἀγριόφθαλμος, is first attested in the *Life of St. Nilus* (*xi* A.D.), referring to Ethiopians, and in the *Apocalypse of Leo of Constantinople* (*ix* A.D.?) (Trapp 1994–99, s.v.). Kriaras (1968–97) provides two glosses of ἀγριόφθαλμος: the *Tale*'s instance, glossed as "having fierce eyes," and instances in the *Belisariad* and *Imperios and Margarona*, glossed as "by synecdoche, having a fierce aspect; (of the sea) wild, stormy":

> Καὶ ὁ βασιλεύς, ὡς τὸ ἤκουσεν, ἐτρόμαξεν, ἐφύρτη
> καὶ ὥσπερ θηρίον ἄγριον καὶ ὡς δράκων φουσκωμένος
> καὶ ὡς θάλασσα ***ἀγριόφθαλμος*** λέγει τοὺς ἄρχοντάς του
>
> [On hearing this, the King was shocked and startled,
> and like a wild beast, like a puffing dragon,
> a sea ***fierce to the eye,*** he tells his nobles] (*Belisariad* χ 47–49).

The parallel with *Physiologus* manuscript M is compelling (see "The *Physiologus*"); there is no reason not to render ἀγριόφθαλμος as "fierce-eyed." Šandrovskaja (1956a) translates the word as *страшноглазый*, "terrible-eyed."

18. **twisting**. γαγκλαδοραδάτος is a compound of γαγκλάδα and ο(ὐ)ραδάτος, "tailed." The word γαγκλάδα is otherwise unattested in medieval Greek, but the stem γάγγλ- is widespread in modern Greek dialect (Academy of Athens 1933–84, s.v. γάγγλα, II), with meanings related to "twist" ("curve in road"; "twist"; "deceit"; "spiral-shaped embroidery"; "curve"; "ulcer"; "corner"; "wrinkle"). The variant γαγγλάδ- is more restricted (Academy of Athens 1933–84, s.v. γαγγλάδα), being attested in Crete (γαγλάδα), Apiranthos in Naxos (an old Cretan colony: gagλάδα), and Cephallonia (βagλάδα); for example, ὅλο ***γαγλάδες*** εἶν' ἡ βέργα, "that stick is full of ***twists***"; τσίτωσε τὸ σεδόνι, γιατὶ κάνει πολλὲς ***γαγλάδες***, "stretch out the bedsheet, because it's got a lot of ***folds***."

The stem appears to derive from postclassical γαγγλίον and the *Historical Dictionary of Modern Greek* spells it accordingly (as does Kriaras 1968–97 in the addendum to volume 10). In late antiquity, γάγγλιον (Liddell–Scott–Jones 1940, s.v.) was used to mean "encysted tumor on a tendon" or "aponeurosis"; for example, *Aëtius: Iatricorum* 15.9 (*vi* A.D., citing Philagrius, *iii/iv* A.D.): Τὸ ***γάγγλιον*** συναγωγή ἐστι νεύρου, τὰ πολλὰ μὲν ἐκ πληγῆς ἢ κρούσματος προηγησαμένου γιγνόμενον, σπανίως δ' ἐξ αὐτομάτου, "A ***ganglion*** is an accumulation of sinews, usually caused by a preceding wound or being struck, and only rarely arising on its own." The term *ganglion* is also used in modern medicine to denote a mass or knot of nerve cells, and this usage began with Galen as a comparison with the tumor (*De Usu Partium* 16.5). This sense is preserved in Pontic Greek (Academy of Athens 1933–84, s.v. γαγγλάζω), which uses the stem to refer to a cramp (particularly in the tendons), sprain, or itch. Outside the Pontus, this physiological sense is unknown and presumably was also unknown in medieval Greek, once the generalization was made from "tendon knobby or twisted through a tumor" to "knobby, twisted."

Tsiouni (1972) renders γαγκλαδοραδάτος as "knob-tailed," presumably inspired by the late antique medical term, but the main thrust of the modern meanings of γαγγλ- is "twisted," not "knobby." As discussed in "The *Physiologus*," "twisting" makes for a satisfying tie-in to the Physiologan account of the lion's tail. It also accords with the heraldic depiction of the lion's tail, as featured in manuscript C. Šandrovskaja 1956a has *с извилистым хвостом*, "with a winding tail."

19. **seat mate**. The word συγκάθεδρος, "seat mate," was in learned use in Byzantium to refer to prominent noble supporters of the incumbent emperor. The elephant is thus being singled out as particularly important to the king.

The elephant is not necessarily being called a coregent to the lion. The term does mean "coregent" in Cantacuzene's autobiography (*Historiae*):

ἀλλὰ καὶ πολλάκις βασιλεὺς Ἀνδρόνικος ὁ νέος Καντακουζηνὸν τὸν μέγαν δομέστικον ὅλῃ γνώμῃ καὶ πάσῃ σπουδῇ τοῖς βασιλικοῖς ἠθέλησε κοσμῆσαι παρασήμοις καὶ ***συγκάθεδρον*** αὐτῷ καὶ συμβασιλεύοντα ἀποδεῖξαι

[But often the younger emperor Andronicus, with full certainty and all haste, wished to decorate the Grand Domesticus Cantacuzene with imperial insignia and declare him his ***seat mate*** and coregent.] (1.239)

But in *Theophanes the Confessor* (124, 247), the person who is already the coregent is *honored* as a seat mate:

Τούτῳ τῷ ἔτει Ἰουστῖνος ὁ βασιλεὺς Τιβέριον, τὸν κόμητα τῶν ἐκσκουβιτόρων, υἱοποιησάμενος καίσαρα ἀνηγόρευσε καὶ ***συγκάθεδρον*** αὐτοῦ ἐποίησεν ἔν τε ταῖς ἱπποδρομίαις καὶ αἰσίαις ἡμέραις

[In this year the emperor Justin, having adopted Tiberius the comes excubitorum as his son, proclaimed him Caesar, and made him sit as his ***partner*** at the chariot races and on holidays.] (247)

And συγκάθεδρος could also simply mean "peer":

σύνθρονον δ' ὄντα τῶν θεῶν καὶ συγγενέα τούτων,
ὃν τετιμήκασιν αὐτοὶ ***συγκάθεδρον*** δεικνύντες

[⟨Darius⟩ being a throne mate of the gods, their kinsman,
whom they have honored, declaring him their ***peer***] (*Alexander Romance: Learned Poetic Version* 1814–15)

(See also *Ducas* 43.5; Socrates Scholasticus, *Historia Ecclesiastica* 7.20—referring to the "seat mate" of a Persian general; and Palladius, *Historia Lausiaca* G 62.1—where Constantius is the seat mate of the eparchs of Italy.) We have rendered συγκάθεδρος as "peer" in verse 109 of the *Tale*—where, as a plural, it cannot single out any individual as a coregent; the lion's συγκάθεδροι are more plausibly councilors or nobles.

20. **a beast** . . . See "The *Physiologus*."

22. **the cheetah and the leopard**. On the identification of the cats we have labeled "leopard" and "cheetah," see "A Conundrum of Cats."

22. **maligners**. Tsiouni (1972) glosses ἀποφουμιστής as "one who vaunts himself"; Šandrovskaja (1956a), as славословцы, "glorifiers", and Kriaras's dictionary (1968–97), as "boaster." As Karanastassis (in preparation) argues, however, the noun should here be understood as κακολόγοι, "maligners, detractors" (so in Kazazis and Karanastassis 2001, s.v. "he who maligns, who detracts, detractor"). Neither interpretation seems to have much to do with great cats; "maligner," however, fits well with the image of the corrupt courtier.

The verb ἀποφουμίζω is also attested in the *Historical Dictionary of Modern Greek* as a variant of ἀποθυμίζω, glossed (Academy of Athens 1933–84, s.v.) as "to grow angry and depart, be displeased, particularly with reference to children refusing to sit at the dinner table or to accept something offered to them; in general, to become enraged without a good reason." The felines in the poem are certainly irascible, but this seems to us a riskier interpretation.

30. **made decision**. βουλή can mean either "will" or "council, parliament" (as in 78, 109, 554). Here, ἐπῆραν CVL δίδουν P βουλήν, "they took/give will," like ἐβάλετε βουλήν, "you placed will," in 691, is a fixed phrase meaning "make a decision" (Kriaras 1968–97, s.v. βουλή, 2d):

> Ἐνταῦτα ***ἀπήρασιν βουλὴν*** τὸ πῶς ἠθέλαν πράξει·
> τὰ λόγια ἤσασιν πολλά, τὰ εἶπαν κ' ἐλαλῆσαν·
> τὸ γὰρ τὸ τέλος εἴπασιν νὰ ὀρθώσουν τὰ φουσσᾶτα
>
> [Then they ***took counsel*** as to how they should act; the words were many which they said and spoke; but in the end, they declared that they would get the armies ready.] (*Chronicle of Morea* H 8974–76; Lurier [1964:319])
>
> Ἐχθὲς ***ἐβάλαμε βουλὴ*** μὲ τὴν συντέκνισσά μου,
> τότες ὅντα τὴν ἔκραξα κι ἦλθεν ἐδῶ κοντά μου,
> τὰ κρίματα νὰ λύσωμε, ὁπό 'χεις καμωμένα,
> καὶ νὰ τὰ συγχωρήσωμε, νά 'ναι συμπαθημένα
>
> [Yesterday my in-law and I ⟨the Wolf and the Fox⟩ ***worked out***,
> when I invited her to come on over,
> that we'll absolve you of your sins committed,
> and shall forgive them, so they may be pardoned.] (*Fair Tale of the Donkey the Wolf and the Fox* 294e–h)

Tsiouni (1972) accordingly glosses βουλή in 30 as "decision, resolution." Šandrovskaja (1956a) seems to be in error here: они открыли совет, "they opened the council"—though she has the correct приняли решение, "took a decision," in 691.

36. **attending both of them**. Though in modern Greek νὰ τοὺς δουλεύει means "to tease them, to trick them" and this is what we would expect of the monkey, there is no attested Byzantine usage with this meaning (Kriaras 1968–97, s.v. δουλεύω), and the more probable meaning is the literal "to service them."

52. **who sucks down snakes**. See "Fact and Fiction in the *Tale*'s Zoology."

53. **the wild goat**. Although ἀγρίμι originally meant "wild beast" (Kriaras 1968–97, s.v. ἀγρίμι, 1; it is so used in the Judeo-Greek Pentateuch Genesis 7:14), there is no reason to doubt that it means here "wild goat," as it does in modern and renaissance Cretan Greek (Kriaras 1968–97, s.v. ἀγρίμι, 2: *Erotokritos* 2.645). The wild goat (ἀγρίμι) is named here distinctly from the (she-)goat (αἶγα), but it does not recur as a character in the debate, turning up again only in the final battle (1045).

54. **the glutton boar**. The original χοῖρος is ambiguous in later Greek between "boar" and "pig," as Vasiliou (1996:76) points out. In classical Greek, the word meant only "young pig" or "pig." The earliest instance we have identified of ἀγριόχοιρος, "wild χοῖρος = boar," is from the thirteenth century (*Pseudo-Zonaras* 1854). But χοῖρος is already used as both "pig" and "boar" in the tenth- to twelfth-century legislation *Ecloga ad Prochiron Mutata*:

"pig," 26.8: Ἐάν τις εὕρῃ ***χοῖρον*** ἢ πρόβατον ἢ κύνα ἐν πραίδᾳ, παραδώσει αὐτὸν ἐν πρώτοις τῷ κυρίῳ αὐτοῦ, εἶτα δευτερώσας καὶ παραγγείλας τὸ τρίτον οὐροκοπήσει ἢ τοξεύσει αὐτόν, ἀνέγκλητος ἔστω.

[If one should find a ***pig*** or sheep or dog eating from one's farmland and at the first instance hands it over to its master but after giving warning on the second instance cuts off its tail or shoots it with an arrow on the third, he shall be deemed void of offence.]

"boar," 26.15: Ἐάν τις κύνα τῆς αὐλῆς καταῤῥάξῃ ἢ σφάξῃ, δώδεκα νομίσματα ἀπολογείτω τῷ κυρίῳ αὐτοῦ. ἐὰν δὲ καὶ λαγγαῖος ἐστίν, δωσάτω τῷ κυρίῳ αὐτοῦ νομίσματα γ΄. εἰ δὲ διώκτης ἐλάφων ἢ ***χοίρων***, νομίσματα λ΄.

[If one should dash to pieces or slaughter a household dog, he shall pay restitution of twelve coins to its master; if it be also a hare-chasing ⟨?⟩ hound, he should pay its master ⟨another⟩ three coins; if a hunter of deer or ***boar***, thirty coins.]

In addition, the Byzantine scholiast on Aristophanes felt the need to point out that χοῖρος in *The Acharnians* did not mean the same as it did in contemporary Greek:

χοίρους γὰρ ὑμὲς σκευάσας: τοὺς παρ' ἡμῖν νῦν λεγομένους δέλφακας, λέγω δὴ τοὺς μικροὺς σῦς· οὓς οἱ ἀρχαῖοι χοίρους ἐκάλουν.

[χοίρους γὰρ ὑμὲς σκευάσας, "I'll pass you off as piglets": what we now call δέλφακας, "piglets"; that is to say, small pigs, which the ancients called χοίρους.] (*Scholia in Acharnenses* 739a)

The ambiguity between boar and pig also exists for the synonymous term used in the *Tale*, μοχθηρόν ("wicked" < μόχθος, "toil; distress") (419, 443):

"pig," *Ptochoprodromos* 3.197-8–197-9: καὶ ***μουχτερὸν*** ὁ κηπουρὸς ἔχει καὶ τρέφει τοῦτο / καὶ θρέφει καὶ τὸν κηπουρὸν καὶ μουχτερὸν ὁ κῆπος, "The gardener has a ***pig*** and feeds him, / and both the pig and the gardener are fed by the garden"; Somavera (1977 [1709]):

> μουκτερὸν, λαχτένδον, γουρουνάκι, γουρουνόπουλον (ζῶον): *Porcello, porchetto (animale),* "piglet (animal)."

> "boar," in a receipt from 1442–43 (Schreiner 1991:316): Ἔτι ὅταν ἀγόρασεν ἀπὸ τὸν Μοῦζο Γκελμι ***ἄγριο μουκτερὸ*** ἐδανήσατο σολδ(ια) ιζ΄, "Also, when he ⟨the abbot⟩ bought a ***wild boar*** from Muzio Ghelmi, he borrowed seventeenth soldi"; given as the gloss of the modern Pontic Greek reflex μουχτερός by Papadopoulos (1961), together with the proverbial citation Ἄν γίνεται τῆ μουχτεροῦ τὸ μαλλὶν μετάξ', γίνεται κι ὁ χωρέτς μὲ τὴν τάξ', "If a boar's hair can turn into silk, then a peasant can become tidy." (The fifteenth-century receipt was written by Cardinal Bessarion, who was himself from the Pontus.)

Tsiouni (1972:50) refers to the animal as both "pig" and "boar" on the same page. Šandrovskaja (1956a) renders the word as **свинья,** "pig," throughout, and Gidel (1866:316) likewise as *porc,* "pig." The mention of the animal's fang in 402 has decided us in favor of "boar," and we think it unlikely that a household pig would be capable of dispatching both the leopard and the bear (1053–57). The illustrator of manuscript C has likewise depicted the animal as a boar, complete with fangs.

The narrative itself brings up χοῖρος, on occasion, not as a participant in the story but mentioned in passing: the wolf boasts that he preys on χοίρους at the end of a list of farm animals in 822 (though followed by a generalization to all animals), and χοῖροι eat the dead dog on the farmyard's dungheap in 174. In these instances, the animal referred to may well be the pig rather than the boar. (In 255, on the other hand, the dog clearly hunts in the wild for boars rather than pigs.) Nevertheless, we have kept our rendering of χοῖρος as "boar" in those verses, as well, for consistency.

65. **witty**. The word ἀστεῖος derives from ἄστυ, "city," and literally means "urban, urbane, courteous." As a further development, the meaning "witty" is attested as early as Aristophanes (*Frogs* 901) and Plato (*Phaedrus* 227d). In modern Greek, the word has come to mean "funny," although this presumably involves a neoclassical revival of the later meaning of the word rather than a survival. (The neo-Atticist Kontos used it to mean "witty" and "artful" [Nikos Sarantakos, personal communication], but that is the exception that proves the rule: only Kontos would have attempted so thorough a revival.) And the word is routinely used in the Scholia to Lucian and Aristophanes to point out jokes. A comment like the following (in Tzetzes' *xii* A.D. scholia on Aristophanes' *Plutus*) is typical: ἱστέον δὲ ὅτι μειδιασμοῦ ἕνεκα παραπλέκει τὰ γελοῖα καὶ ***ἀστεῖα*** ταῦτα, "Note that he weaves in these laughable and ***amusing*** matters for the sake of laughter" (*Scholia in Plutum, recensio 1* 165). Kriaras (1968–97) glosses ἀστεῖος in this passage in the *Tale* as "amusing"; Vasiliou (1996:61) also understands ἀστεῖος here to mean "funny." Šandrovskaja (1956a), on the other

hand, renders it as **приветливые**, "courteous," and Tsiouni (1972) glosses it as "refined."

Within the poem, verse 65 corresponds structurally to verses 99 and 115, where the narrator and the lion respectively recapitulate the rat's invitation. In verse 99, ἀστεῖος discourse is conjoined with μετεωρισμάτων, "jests," in the next verse, and in verse 115 it is substituted by "jests." Although verse 99 may still be contrasting urbane discourse and jests, verse 115 makes it likelier that ἀστεῖος is to be understood as a synonym of "jests." In addition, C and V clearly use the word to mean "amusing" in the title of the poem (see Textual Notes). We have thus glossed the word as "witty" rather than "urbane" or "civil."

81. **throne**. The original meaning of θρόνος was "seat," but in modern Greek it can only mean "throne." In the *Tale* itself, the term is associated with King Lion in verse 108, where it clearly means "throne," but in verses 618 (θρόνους) and 916 (θρονία) it retains its original, mundane meaning. Verse 81 presents a problem, as the usage may be metaphorical: is the horse merely presented, matter-of-factly, as a seat for the person riding it, or does the horse make its rider feel like a king? Given the ambiguity of the passage, we have chosen to render θρόνος as both "seat" and "throne."

84. **neck so long**. σφόνδυλος, originally "vertebrum," could mean either "spine" or "neck" in medieval Greek; the latter meaning has died out in modern Greek but has survived in Cappadocia and Crete as "nape of the neck" and in the Peloponnese as "a blow to the nape of the neck" (Andriotis 1974 §5892). Here and in 768, Tsiouni (1972) glosses μακροσφονδυλάτος as "one with a long spine" and Šandrovskaja (1956a) as с длинными позвонками / длинно-позвоночным, "long-vertebra'd." But the *Book of Birds*, describing creatures with necks much more prominent than the rest of their spines, uses the term to mean "neck": Χαρὰ εἰς τὸν καλογερανὸν ὁπού ἦλθεν εἰς τὸν γάμον / μὲ τὸν μακρὺν τὸν ***σφόνδυλον***, καμάριν ὅλος ἔχει, "Well done to that fine crane who's come to the wedding, / with his long ***neck***, he's proud from head to toe" (59–60); ἄτυχε, ***ἀπιδοσφόνδυλε*** καὶ γριζοφορεμένε, "you wretch, ***pear-necked*** and dressed in gray" (236: of the *karkandzas*). Tsavare (1987) in fact glosses the same adjective μακροσφονδυλάτος in her edition of the *Book* as meaning "long-necked" (πού ἔχει μακρύ λαιμό): Εἰπέ με, κύκνε ἀσύσσουμε καὶ ***μακροσφονδυλάτε***, "Now tell me, you misshapen, ***long-necked*** swan" (7). (See also the use of ἐκσφονδυλίζω discussed in the commentary to verse 895.)

The extension of σφόνδυλος to "neck" is already ancient. Liddell–Scott–Jones 1940, s.v., claims Euripides *Electra* 841 as a potential instance: ὄνυχας ἔπ' ἄκρους στὰς κασίγνητος σέθεν / ἐς ***σφονδύλους*** ἔπαισε, νωταῖα δὲ / ἔρρηξεν ἄρθρα, "your brother rose on tiptoe and struck him on the ***spine***; his backbone broke apart," but the changeover had certainly taken place by the Septuagint: καὶ ἀποκνίσει ὁ ἱερεὺς τὴν κεφαλὴν αὐτοῦ ἀπὸ τοῦ ***σφονδύλου*** καὶ οὐ διελεῖ, "and ⟨the priest shall⟩ wring off his ⟨the sin offering's⟩ head from his ***neck***, but shall not divide it asunder." (Leviticus 5:8)

Although the camel's spine may be notorious for its apparent curvature, it is its neck, rather than its spine, that one would tend to call long—so much so that the giraffe was thought by the Greeks to be a hybrid of the camel and the pard (καμηλοπάρδαλις). We have translated the word in all instances as "neck." See discussion for verses 232, 619, 787, and 997.

86. **awkward**. We see no reason to follow Tsiouni (1972) in rendering as "obsessed" the word used here, κακογυρισμένη, "badly turned." Xanthoudidis (1927–28:355) has suggested this means "like a sack turned inside out," and Šandrovskaja (1956a) has потешая и развлекая их неуклюжими прыжками, "entertaining and amusing them with clumsy jumping." Compare the similar word κακοεντύλικτος, "badly wrapped" in the *Book of Birds* (37–38): Ἂν οὐ 'γερθῆς εἰς τὸ γοργὸν νὰ ἐπάρης τὰς ποδέας σου, / αὐτὰς τὰς ***κακοεντύλικτας***, καὶ ἐπάρης καὶ ὑπαγαίνης, "If you do not rise swiftly and move your legs, / those ***badly wrapped*** things, and be on your way."

The closest word to κακογυρισμένη attested in modern Greek in the *Historical Dictionary of Modern Greek* archives is κακοὔριστα, "difficult to turn" (Apiranthos, Naxos; HDMS 497:311), and the following excerpt from the Epirot Christos Christovasilis (1988:125): κι ἄρχισαν νὰ ***κακογυρίζουν*** τὸ σφαχτὸ ψηλὰ στὰ κάρβουνα, καὶ στοὺς καπνούς, σὰν ἄμαθοι ἀνθρῶποι ποὺ ἦταν, "They started ***badly turning*** the animal ⟨on a spit⟩ high above the coals and in the smoke, inexperienced as they were."

If we accept for this verse the reading "to dance her rump out" (νωτιδά: see Textual Notes), then "badly turned" here clearly means "moving awkwardly," particularly as "turn" was routinely used in medieval Greek to refer to movements of the entire body (commentary to verse 144.) An interpretation whereby "badly turned" refers to a bodily deformity is suggested by the camel's hump but does not seem to be very germane to the camel either hopping or shaking her rump. So it is less likely to hold here.

90. **pledges**. στοιχήματα, here and in 142, obviously does not have its modern Greek meaning of "bet," as Tsiouni (1972) glosses it. Rather, it has the meaning Lampe (1961) reports in *Theophanes the Confessor* (338), "pact":

> ἀκούσας δὲ Ἡράκλειος τὰ πραχθέντα ἀποστέλλει Κῦρον πρὸς τὸ πεῖσαι αὐτοὺς ἀναχωρῆσαι τῆς Αἰγύπτου τῷ πρώτῳ ***στοιχήματι*** καὶ ἀπελθὼν ὁ Κῦρος εἰς τὴν παρεμβολὴν τῶν Σαρακηνῶν ὑπεραπελογεῖτο ὡς ἀναίτιος ὢν τῆς παραβάσεως, καὶ εἰ βούλοιντο τὴν προτέραν ***συμφωνίαν*** ὅρκοις βεβαιῶσαι
>
> [When Herakleios had heard of these events, he dispatched Kyros to persuade the Saracens to depart from Egypt according to the former ***treaty***. So Kyros went to the camp of the Saracens and offered many excuses, saying he was innocent of the transgression and urging them, if they so wished, to confirm the former ***accord*** by oath.]

This meaning survives in Imbros and Thrace (Andriotis 1974 §5576) as στ'χῶ, "to arrange a lease," and in Chalcidica in Macedonia as στ'χῶ, "to hire oneself out to someone." The general modern Greek meaning, "bet," originates from its other attested medieval meaning, "what has been agreed upon or approved." This meaning is already used to gloss into the vernacular the Homeric περιδώμεθον, "wager," in Eustathius of Thessalonica's *Commentary on the Iliad* 4.769 (ὡς οἱ πολλοί φασι, "as the many say") and the Aristophanean περιδοῦ, "wager," in the *Scholia in Nubes (scholia anonyma recentiora)* 644a (κοινῶς, "commonly"); so the usage was current at the time of the *Tale* (see also Koukoules 1947–55 3.66)—but that makes it no more pertinent here as a sense of στοιχήματα. The word is postclassical; Liddell–Scott–Jones (1940) report only the meaning "deposit" in Eustathius, presumably as a misunderstanding of his vernacularism.

Koukoules (1947–55 2.1.274) reports the use of the word in the *Eparchicon* legal code (§22.1) to refer to a ring given to confirm a commercial transaction; this gives a third, related meaning, "pledge." The senses of "pledge," "pact," and "agreement" are too close, in any case, to insist on a differentiation in our translation. Šandrovskaja (1956a) translates the word as договор, "agreement," here, and обет, "promise," in 142.

92. **total**. Kriaras 1968–97 gives several definitions for καθολικός in medieval Greek: (1) universal (its original meaning); (2) entire; (3) perfect, complete; (4) major; (5) genuine, real, true; (6) Catholic. (The sense "genuine" has survived in Cyprus: Andriotis 1974 §2433.) The candidate meanings here are

- (1) universal; for example, Ducas 39.5: Ὁ δὲ τύραννος ἤρξατο ἡμέρᾳ Κυριακῇ συνάπτειν πόλεμον ***καθολικόν,*** "And the despot started on Sunday to wage ***universal*** war."
- (3) perfect, complete; for example, *Cypriot Love Songs* 133.12: θαρῶ ***καθολικῆς*** χαρᾶς ποτήριον νὰ πιοῦμεν, "I trust we shall drink a glass of ***pure*** joy" (the editor translates it into modern Greek as ολοκάθαρης, "totally pure").
- (5) genuine, real, true; for example, *Chronicle of the Sultans* 53: Ὁ Μουσταφᾶς δὲν ἔναι υἱὸς τοῦ πατρός μου μηδὲ ἀδελφός μου καὶ δὲν μᾶς ἐμοιάζει, διατὶ ὁ ***καθολικός*** μου ἀδελφὸς ὁ Μουσταφᾶς ἀπόθανε, "Mustafa is neither the son of my father nor my brother and does not even look like us. My ***true*** brother Mustafa is dead" (Philippides 1990:42–43).

Kriaras considers καθολικός here to have meaning (3); so does Tsiouni (1972) ("entire, whole, integral"). Šandrovskaja (1956a), on the other hand, uses the original meaning, (1) (всеобщую, "common, general"); the strong parallel to Ducas's example makes us suspect this is at work here, too. If anything, even meaning (5), "genuine," would be likelier in this diplomatic context than (3), "perfect." And in the context of the poem, where the animals tend to act fairly autonomously, it would be much more relevant to insist that absolutely everyone abide by the truce than that the truce be particularly heartfelt. So we believe

(1) applies here, though our rendering is deliberately ambiguous between (1) and (3).

Given the word used, καθολική (*katholiki*), one might at first glance wonder whether an allusion is being made to Catholicism—even if as a veiled pun, given the dominant senses of the word outlined above. The evidence suggests that the use of this word to refer to the Church of Rome was largely unknown in medieval Greek, however. For example, Makhairas, in his *Chronicle,* p. 576, has no problem in describing the "Latin" church as "apostolic" and the "Roman" (Byzantine) church as "catholic" (= "genuine, independent": sense 5.) Despite two hundred years of French rule in Cyprus and even while writing in a language heavily influenced by Old French, Makhairas never uses the adjective καθολικός to refer to the Church of Rome. For that matter, even as late (and as Catholic) an authority as Somavera (1977 [1709]) makes a distinction between "catholic" and "Roman Catholic": καθολικός is glossed as κοινὸς, *universale, commune,* "universal, common"; ἀληθινὸς, φυσικὸς, γνήσιος, ἴδιος, ἀυτὸς κ ἴδιος, "true, natural, genuine, proper, self-same"; and *proprio, genuino,* "proper, genuine." For Roman Catholicism, Somavera needs to resort to the Italian loanword κατόλικος; in fact (like *Florios and Platziaflora,* see discussion following), he ends up glossing *Catolico* as κατόλικος, ὀρθόδοξος, "[small-o] orthodox" (i.e., the opposite of heretical and/or Protestant—or of Greek Orthodox, for that matter, as far as the missionary Somavera was concerned).

There are only four instances in which καθολικός has been claimed to mean "Catholic" in medieval Greek. Philippides, in his translation of the *Chronicle of the Sultans,* provides one:

> ἐπειδὴ ἐπῆρε ὁ Σανταλὸς δοῦκας τὴν Φιορεντῖνα καὶ ἄφησε τὴν ***καθολική*** του γυναῖκα, ἔφυγε μὲ τὸν υἱόν της καὶ ἐδιάβη εἰς τὸ Ραγούζι μὲ τὸ βίον της, "Duke Sandalos had taken this Florentine woman and had deserted his ***Catholic*** wife, who had fled to Ragusa with her son and her fortune." (1990:87)

The *Chronicle of the Sultans* is late (early *xvii* A.D.), written in Italy, and based on Italian sources, so if any Greek work were to start using καθολικός to mean "Catholic," this would be it. Yet we have already seen that the *Chronicle* still uses καθολικός in its medieval sense, and because Sandalos's paramour was quite likely just as Catholic as his legitimate wife, we believe it means "proper, true" here as well.

Kriaras (1968–97) lists two instances of the sense "Catholic": one in the *Chronicle of Morea* and one in *Florios and Platziaflora.* The instance in *Chronicle of Morea* H 813 was written by a Catholic, so it does not necessarily indicate a larger tendency among the largely Orthodox Greek-speaking population; even so, it is still ambiguous:

> ὅλα τὰ ἐλαττώσασιν ἀφότου ἐχωρίσαν / ἀπὸ τῆς Ῥώμης Ἐκκλησίας, ποῦ ἔνι ***καθολική*** μας, "all these they ⟨the Orthodox⟩ distorted

when they separated from the Church of Rome, which is our ***Catholic*** Church." (Lurier 1964:89)

This is an odd thing to say if, as in modern usage, Catholicism is regarded as just another version of Christianity. But the author of the *Chronicle* hardly meant it like that, and a literal translation, "which is our *True* (or *Universal*) Church," would probably be closer to what he meant.

The use of καθολικός to mean "Catholic" in the romance *Florios and Platziaflora* (verse 1865) is notorious and has been much discussed; see Beaton (1996:137) and Ortolá Salas (1998:51–54) for summaries of the discussion. *Florios and Platziaflora* is an adaptation of the Italian *Cantare de Fiorio e Biancifiore*, and the verse concerns the mass conversion of the Saracens and their king in Rome, so it would hardly be a surprise if the translator simply copied across the original's reference to Catholicism as a translationism. The problem is that the verse appears to be self-contradictory:

> βαπτίζονται, χριστιανοὶ γίνονται παραυτίκα
> καὶ πᾶς λαὸς τῆς χώρας των, μικροί τε καὶ μεγάλοι,
> εἰς πίστην τὴν ***καθολικὴν*** Ρωμαίων ***ὀρθοδόξων***·
> καὶ ἡ Ρώμη διαλέγει τον Ρωμαίων βασιλέα·
> καὶ ἐβασίλευσε εὐσεβῶς τὴν πρεσβυτέραν Ρώμην.
>
> [They're baptized, and turn Christian at once—
> their country's people, too, both great and small—
> in the ***orthodox*** Romans' ***catholic*** faith;
> and Rome picked him to be the Romans' king;
> and piously he ruled the Elder Rome.]

Though the translator does feel the need to explain that this is "the Elder Rome" and not "New Rome" (Constantinople), this reference is lifted straight out of a Western romance. Yet the Greek text calls the Romans both "orthodox" and "catholic," and it cannot intend both to mean Christian denominations. After all, *Florios and Platziaflora* already uses καθολικός in its usual medieval sense (διὰ νὰ τὸν ἔχῃ εἰς θέλημα ***καθολικὸν*** δικόν του, "to have him bend ***completely*** to his will" [1330]). Ortolá Salas (1998:53), the most recent editor of the text, translates the contentious verse literally as *se convierten a la fe* ***católica*** *de los romanos* ***ortodoxos***; he concludes that although the poem is certainly speaking about Catholics, the translator meant nothing more by πίστην τὴν καθολικὴν but "true faith," as would be normal for medieval Greek anyway—just as ὀρθοδόξων means nothing more here than "holding correct belief, nonheretical." (As we have just seen, even four centuries later Somavera had no problem treating κατόλικος—this time "Roman Catholic"—and ὀρθόδοξος as synonyms.) So the "orthodox" here are "small-o orthodox" and the "catholics" are "small-c catholic": "in the right-believing Romans' true faith"—a more or less literal translation of the Italian original *la fede catolica e cristiana,* "the Catholic and Christian faith," with "orthodox" intended by the Greek translator as a contrast to Islam, not Eastern (or Western) Christianity.

Finally, the instance in the Vienna manuscript of the *Flower of Virtue* (287) displays all three of the traits already discussed: the usage is a literal translation from Italian; the translator also uses the term with its more common meaning of "proper" (in the same sentence, in fact—allowing for some liberty on the part of the translator; see Kakoulidi 1971:302); and in context, the adjective does not distinguish Catholicism from Orthodoxy, because it refers to the scriptures they have in common:

> Original: e per tanto in nome de la sanctissima Trinita cum la divina gratia intrando nelo odorifero e florido zardino sacratissimo del spirito sancto per la porta ***spetiosa*** delle sacre sancte scriture ***catholice . . .***
>
> Vienna manuscript translation: Καὶ διὰ τοῦτον εἰς τὸ ὄνομαν τῆς ἁγίας Τριάδος μὲ τὴν χάριν τοῦ Θεοῦ ἐμπαίνοντα εἰς τὸ μυρισμένον καὶ ἀθημένον περβόλιν τὸ ἁγιασμένον τοῦ ἁγίου Πνεύματος ἀπὸ τὴν πόρταν τὴν ***καθολικὴν*** τῶν ἁγιασμένων καὶ ἁγίων Γραφῶν τῶν ***καθολικῶν*** . . .
>
> [And for that reason, in the name of the Holy Trinity and through God's grace, entering the perfumed and flowering sanctified garden of the Holy Spirit through the ***virtual*** ⟨*spetiosa*⟩/***proper*** ⟨καθολικήν⟩ door of the sanctified and holy ***universal/catholic*** scriptures . . .]

In sum, it is unlikely that speakers of medieval Greek understood καθολικός as anything but "true" or "universal"; as Makhairas shows, the "Universal Church" would in fact be understood by them as the Church of New Rome rather than Elder Rome. So it is unlikely the *Tale* is making a pun here (for the motivation of which, see "The Attempted Church Union [1360s]," appendix 2) and unlikelier still that anyone would have picked it up, if it had.

100. **jests**. μετεωρισμάτων here, and the verb μετεωρισθοῦσιν in 115, had a range of meanings in medieval Greek encompassing pleasantries. Thus, Kriaras 1968–97, s.v. μετεώρισμα, gives it two meanings:

> "(a) talk about insubstantial or silly matters; joke, teasing": αγαπά τον πλούτον και την δόξαν, / την παρρησίαν την πολλήν, γέλια και παιγνίδια, / άχρηστα ***μετεωρίσματα***, δεινές αισχρολογίες, "he loves riches and glory, / much boldness of speech, laughter and games, / pointless ***jesting***, and terrible obscenities" (Nathaniel Bertos, *Stichoplokia* 1.98, cited from Kriaras 1968–97; that interpretation is also given to this instance in the *Tale*).
>
> "(b) discussion of something not real (in order to pass the time pleasantly . . .), empty talk, fantasy": οὐδὲν μὲ ἐφαίνετον ποτὲ ἀλήθεια τὸ

> λέγουν, / εἶχα το εἰς ***μετεωρισμὸν*** ν' ἀκούγω νὰ τὸ λέγουν, / τώρα θωρῶ τὰ ἔλεγαν ὡσὰν νά 'σαν προφῆτες, "it never seemed to me they spoke the truth; / I held it ***empty talk*** to hear them speak. / Now what they said, I see, as if they were prophets." (*On Exile* 125–127).

The similar noun μετεωρισμός is given three definitions by Kriaras 1968–97; besides "(b) discussion of something not real," there is "(a) joking, teasing; witticism" (the example given involves courting) and "(c) pleasantly whiling away the hours." The implication is that the lion wants light-hearted entertainment—not the heavy-handed insults and defiance he actually gets.

A fourth meaning of the stem is attested in Lampe 1961 (s.v. μετεωρισμός, D): "pride," usually with reference to Psalm 131 [130]:1: Κύριε, οὐχ ὑψώθη μου ἡ καρδία, οὐδὲ ***ἐμετεωρίσθησαν*** οἱ ὀφθαλμοί μου, "Lord, my heart is not haughty, nor mine eyes ***lofty***" (where the Septuagint used μετεωρίζω in its literal meaning of "hover, raise"). This usage would be more appropriate to the animals' tenor, if not the present context, and would probably have been a commonplace of theological education. However, it is the "jesting" meaning that has survived into modern Greek (Andriotis 1974 §4012: Corfu, Leucas, Peloponnese). Compare the Corfiot Konstantinos Theotokis's translation of *Hamlet*: γιὰ μιὰ χτυπιὰ γιὰ ***μέτωρο*** στὸ σβέρκο, "for a strike on the nape of the neck as a ***joke,***" original "or paddling in your neck with his damned fingers" (Shakespeare 1977:175).

109. **peers**. συγκάθεδροι, "seat mates"; see discussion at verse 19. P has a singular but female ἡ συγκάθεδρος, "seat mate," at this point, which cannot be the elephant (ὁ ἐλέφας, masculine); so it is not counterevidence to our claim that the otherwise plural "seat mates" here means just "peers."

109. **council**. See note on "senate" below (verse 111).

111. **senate**. The Greek text has γερουσία. The term is recorded in Lampe's (1961) and Trapp's (1994–99) Byzantine dictionaries as referring to the council of elders (monks) in monasteries and to an ecclesiastical council in general; for instance, Basil of Seleucia's *Life of St. Thecla*, 2.7 (*v* A.D.), speaks of the "senate of priests" (γερουσίας τῶν ἱερέων). In vernacular Byzantine Greek literature, γερουσία was used to refer to the Jewish Sanhedrin (*Sosanna* 9; *Della Porta* 1.1792, 2130); its use to refer to the Venetian senate is much later (1635: *Abbatios* 336). Though it was not referred to with the term γερουσία, there was a well-established institution at the time of village elders (γέροντες) acting as intermediaries between the state (Byzantine or Western) and the rest of the village (Jacoby 1989:23). Accordingly, Šandrovskaja (1956a) translates the word as совет старейшин, "council of elders."

One cannot rule out that the term is used here purely conventionally, with no concrete referent. Yet Gidel's rendering (1866:313) of the term in his summary as *sénat* is probably the most accurate, given the picture drawn here of an imperial court. The term γερουσία was used to refer to the senate through classical precedent (where it referred to any council of elders, including the

Roman senate). The institution survived in Byzantium, though, of course, in only a ceremonial role; Byzantine instances of γερουσία to refer to this body include historians such as Michael Attaleiates (*xii* A.D.) and Nicephorus Gregoras (*xiv* A.D.). (Kazhdan [1984:45] glosses it in Attaleiates as "the senior senators.")

In Christofilopoulou's dissertation (1949:11–33), the Byzantine terms for the senate are examined. Although the official name for the institution was σύγκλητος, "convocation" (Christofilopoulou 1949:13–14), there is plenty of precedent for the use of γερουσία in Byzantine historians. Given the kind of literature with which the *Tale*'s author seems familiar, it is more profitable to identify instances of γερουσία in the humbler chroniclers; such instances are to be had in John of Antioch, the continuators of Theophanes (though not Theophanes himself), Cedrenus, and Michael Glycas—though only Zonaras uses it as his main term, and many chroniclers do not use it at all (Christofilopoulou 1949:25–29). There is enough precedent in the chronicles, in any case, to assume the author was familiar with the archaic term for "senate" without recourse to special reading.

The same seems to hold for βουλή, "council," used in this verse; the term turns up by itself relatively infrequently in both the historians (Cantacuzene uses it on occasion) and the chroniclers (John Malalas, Pseudo-Symeon Magister, Cedrenus, Zonaras, and Constantine Manasses), but in combination with σύγκλητος (σύγκλητος βουλή) it is omnipresent in both historians and chroniclers (though still less frequent than σύγκλητος itself.)

A third term is used in this passage: συνέδριον, "assembly" (111), used in the remainder of the poem to refer to the assembled animals. The term was not used in Byzantium to refer to the senate outside the historian Theophylactus Simocatta (Christofilopoulou 1949:19), and given how broadly representative the animal assembly is, the imperial senate would probably not remind the author of the animal assembly. (By way of corroboration, an assembly including the army and clergy as well as the senate is called συνέδριον in *Anna Comnena* 1.189: Christofilopoulou 1949:21.)

By piling up terms of parliamentary representation, the author is giving a weighty picture of the court but does so redundantly. Three terms for the same institution are unnecessary, and the author probably does not mean each to allude to the Byzantine senate literally. These are rather conventional means of reference to the same imaginary entity—though Christofilopoulou (1949:31) does list the *Tale*'s instances of γερουσία and βουλή as vernacular names of the senate. Characteristic of its propensity to concrete reference, the *Book of Birds* refers to the senate with its proper name, σύγκλητος (259).

125. **brisk**. The adjective used here and in 183, ἀψός, and its now more common variant ἀψύς (1053), have four groups of meanings. (In the following, HD refers to the *Historical Dictionary of Modern Greek,* Academy of Athens 1933–84):

QUICK: "immediately" (Kriaras 1968–97, s.v. ἀψά, 2a–b; HD, s.v., 4): κ' ἔλα νὰ πᾶμε στὸν ἰατρὸν ***ἀψὰ*** νὰ σὲ ἰατρεύσει, "Let's go to the doctor so he can cure you ***immediately***" (*Eugena* 821); "soon" (Kriaras 1968–97, s.v. ἀψά, 2c; HD, s.v., 4): γιατὶ θωρῶ τὸ πῶς ***ἀψὰ*** πάγω νὰ σᾶς ἀφήσω, "for I can see that I will leave you ***soon***" (*King Rodolino* 4.510).

ANGRY: *Eustathius of Thessalonica: Commentary on the Iliad* 2.565: Τὸ δὲ «ἁπτοεπές» . . . δασύνεται καὶ δηλοῖ τὴν καθαπτομένην ἐν ἔπεσι καὶ ὑβριστικήν—ὅθεν ἡ συρφετώδης ἴσως ὑπολείξασα γλῶσσά φησιν ***ἁψοὺς*** τοὺς ἐν λόγῳ θρασεῖς, "The word '*ἁπτοεπές*' . . . with a rough breathing means attacking someone verbally and insulting—which the jumbled-up language ⟨vernacular⟩ has soaked up, equivalently, calling ***ἁψούς*** those who are impudent in word"; "quick to anger" (Kriaras 1968–97, s.v. ἀψύς, 1): κι' ***ἀψὺς*** ἂν εἶναι γὴ ἀγαθός, θὲ νὰ τόνε φοβᾶται, "Be he ***quick to anger*** or kindly, he will fear him" (*King Rodolino* 2.419)—"quick to anger" is the main modern dialectal meaning of the word (HD, s.v., 1a) and is also current in the standard modern language.

STRONG: "acrid" (Kriaras 1968–97, s.v. ἀψότης, 1): αὕτη δὲ ἡ ἀσπίς, ὅπου ἂν κεῖται εἰς τόπον ἅλωνος, καίει τὸν χόρτον τῆς γῆς, καὶ διὰ τὴν ***ἀψότηταν*** τῆς πνοῆς αὐτῆς ἀπὸ βημάτων τριῶν καίει τὸν χοῦν τῆς γῆς, καὶ ἀπὸ βημάτων ἑπτὰ οὐδὲν τολμᾷ τις πλησιάσαι διὰ τὴν τοῦ φαρμακίου ***ἀψότητα,*** "And that asp, wherever it lies in a threshing field, burns the grass of the earth, and through the ***acridity*** of her breath, from three paces she burns the soil of the earth, and from seven paces no one dares approach her, because of the ***acridity*** of the poison" (*Physiologus* 2.17); "fiery" (Kriaras 1968–97, s.v. ἀψός, 2; HD, s.v., 3): Διὰ νὰ δροσίσω καμπόσον τὸ πτωχὸν πλάσμα τὸ ἀνθρώπινον κατὰ τὸν ἀχαμνόν μου σκοπὸν καὶ ***ἀψὴν*** ἀγάπην μὲ γλυκειάν ἀποσκότισην, "to cool off somewhat the poor human creature according to my humble purpose and ***fiery*** love with sweet relief" (*Flower of Virtue* [Vienna ms.] 287—translating Italian *benche de carita* ***ardente***); "loud": μὴ μιλῇς ***ἀψά,*** μὴ διαβάζῃς ***ἀψά,*** "Don't speak ***loudly***, don't read out ***loud***" (dialects of Chios, Ainos) (Hatzidakis 1989–90 [1905–07]:1.169); "strong" (HD, s.v., 5b). So also in Somavera (1977 [1709], s.v. ἀψά): δυνατὰ, ψηλὰ, τρανὰ, *Alto, ad alta voce, forte, fortemente,* "loud."

RAW: "raw" (of metal) (Kriaras 1968–97, s.v. ἀψύς, 2; HD, s.v., 12): τ' ***ἀψὺ*** καὶ τ' ἄφτιαστο σίδερον δὲν μαλάσσει, "***Raw*** and unprocessed iron cannot be molded" (Soummakis, *Pastor Fide* 1.261, cited from Kriaras 1968–97).

According to Hatzidakis (1989–90 [1905–07]:1.169–70), ἀψύς is a back formation from ancient words such as ἀψίθυμος, "touch-humored" = "touchy, irascible," and ἀψίχολος, "touch-biled, irascible"; this is confirmed by the survival in medieval Greek of ἀψόθυμος (Kriaras 1968–97, s.v.). The back formation would have allowed both "quick" and "angry" to arise: "quick" as the meaning the prefix ἀψί- bears in the compound, "angry" as the meaning of the entire compound. One would expect the stem ἀψ-, "to light a fire," to have also played a part in this development—compare the English *inflammatory* and *fiery* and the medieval use of ἐξάπτω, "light up," to mean "get angry" (Kriaras 1968–97, s.v., B 3). The meaning "angry" for ἀψός is early enough to have been recorded by Eustathius of Thessalonica in the twelfth century. The other early instance is Glycas (1158–59) in verse 190 of the *Prison Verses*: Οἱ πόνοι ***ἀψὰ*** σὲ εἰσέβησαν κ' ἐκατεσκούρωσάν σε, "The pains have entered you ***ἀψά*** and darkened you entirely." This is clearly not "angrily"; Hatzidakis thought it meant "quickly," but Kriaras (1968–97, s.v., 1) believes it means "intensely" instead.

Of the meanings here, "raw" (or "coarse") is clearly a secondary meaning, derived from either "angry" ("rough") or "strong" and restricted to metal. The meaning "strong" also seems to be secondary, deriving from "angry." In this particular instance, ἀψός is likeliest to constitute a synonym of γοργός, "swift," but would still have carried a connotation of forcefulness; we have thus rendered it as "brisk." Tsiouni (1972) does not gloss the word, although it is clearly postclassical. Šandrovskaja (1956a) renders it as **порывисто,** "impetuously."

125. **humble**. ταπεινός has several possible meanings. Its original meaning is "low-lying, low in physical stature," as in ***ταπεινὰ*** νέμεσθαι, "to live in ***low*** regions" (Pindar *Nemean* 3.82); μὴν ἄγαν ***ταπεινὰ*** τὰ ὀστᾶ δεῖ εἶναι, "the bones should not be too ***short***" (Xenophon *De Re Equestri* 1.4). Its other meanings are metaphorical extensions of this:

- "lowly, of low rank, humble in status": for example, Isocrates *Panegyricus* 95, Ἡγοῦντο γὰρ ταῖς μὲν ***ταπειναῖς*** τῶν πόλεων προσήκειν ἐκ παντὸς τρόπου ζητεῖν τὴν σωτηρίαν, "for they considered that while it was natural for the ***weaker*** states to seek their security by every means."
- "mean, base": for example, Plato *Laws* 791d, ***ταπεινοὺς*** καὶ ἀνελευθέρους καὶ μισανθρώπους ποιοῦσα, "makes them ***lowly*** and mean spirited and misanthropic."
- "wretch": for example, *Leontius of Neapolis: Life of St. Symeon the Fool* 83, μηκέτι μοίχευε, ***ταπεινέ***, καὶ οὐκ ἐγγίζει σοι ὁ δαίμων, "Commit adultery no more, ***wretch***, and the Devil won't draw near you."
- "humble": Plato *Laws* 716a, ᾗς ὁ μὲν εὐδαιμονήσειν μέλλων ἐχόμενος συνέπεται ***ταπεινὸς*** καὶ κεκοσμημένος, "and she, again, is followed by every man who would fain be happy, cleaving to her with ***lowly*** and orderly behavior"; Matthew 11:29, ἄρατε τὸν ζυγόν μου ἐφ' ὑμᾶς καὶ μάθετε ἀπ' ἐμοῦ, ὅτι πραΰς εἰμι καὶ ***ταπεινὸς*** τῇ καρδίᾳ, "Take my yoke upon you and learn of me; for I am meek and ***lowly*** in heart"; James 4:6, διὸ λέγει, Ὁ θεὸς ὑπερηφάνοις ἀντιτάσσεται, ***ταπεινοῖς*** δὲ δίδωσιν χάριν, "Wherefore he saith, God resisteth the proud but giveth grace unto the ***humble***."

The last meaning was popularized through Christianity and is the main meaning to have survived into vernacular modern Greek.

If the term is meant literally, the author cannot mean that the cat is displaying Christian meekness: the cat displays nothing of the sort. Moreover, in 564 the lion describes the rat, conjoined with the cat, as εὐτελές, "lowly." So the author would instead be implying that the cat was low on the pecking order in the household. Compare *Ptochoprodromos* 3.273 P, using the same word: καὶ ἡμεῖς ἀδικούσαμεν τὸ ***ταπεινὸν*** κατούδιν, "and we have been unfair to the ***lowly*** cat." The other manuscripts of *Ptochoprodromos* have καὶ ἡμεῖς ἐκατεμπλέκαμεν τὸ ***πονηρὸν*** κατούδιν, "and we have implicated the ***cunning*** cat," so manuscript P might have meant "base" rather than "lowly." But *Ptochoprodromos's* cat is anything but cunning, serving as a scapegoat for the hungry cleric (see "Humor"), and in several instances in *Ptochoprodromos* 4 ταπεινός is clearly meant as "lowly." Such a moralizing interpretation of ταπεινός would in any case be too learned for the *Tale*.

On the other hand, it is quite possible that the author is being ironic with his use of ταπεινός and simply intends the meaning "meek, humble," to be immediately negated by what the cat actually says. This is what he does with the unambiguous use of ταπεινῷ to mean "humble" in 197, introducing the fox, and in the sheep's entrance in 421—compounded there with the unexpected "gently" (ἥμερα). It is difficult to decide between the two senses; our rendering is deliberately ambiguous between the literal "lowly" and the ironic "meek" in using "humble," a word just as ambiguous in English. Šandrovskaja (1956a) omits the adjective in her translation.

130. **bread-squanderer**. ψωμοκαταλύτη, literally "bread-destroyer." The verb καταλύω appears at verse 961, also in the sense "destroy." Both Šandrovskaja (1956a) (**пожиратель . . . хлеба,** "devourer of bread") and Tsiouni (1972) ("bread consumer") understand καταλύτης here to mean "consume" as in "eat," thereby making it synonymous with the adjacent τυροφᾶ, "cheese-eater." But in Kriaras 1968–97 the sense "consume, spend" is marginal (s.v. καταλύω, A.1.8a), with a single example pointing to "eat": Makhairas §563, καὶ οἱ Γενουβίσοι ἐπαρακαλοῦσαν νὰ ἐβγοῦν ἀπὲ τὴν Ἀμόχουστον οἱ ἀτύχοι ὅπου ***ἐκαταλυοῦσαν*** τὴν τροφήν, "And the Genoese were begging them to leave Famagusta—the poor creatures—because they were ***consuming*** their provisions." (In Liddell–Scott–Jones 1940, the "consume" sense is entirely absent.) Likewise in modern Greek dialect, the survivals of καταλύω almost always mean "destroy," and only in one locality (Halicarnassus) is the sense "consume" reported (Andriotis 1974 §3143). Because καταλύω is used to mean "destroy" both in the majority of medieval texts and in the *Tale* itself (961), we have preferred it also for this passage over the parallel with τυροφᾶ, "cheese-eater."

132. **buttermilk**. ὀξύγαλα, literally "sour milk," could be yogurt, curds/curdled milk, or buttermilk; it is glossed as all three in Eideneier (1991:255), as it occurs in *Ptochoprodromos* 3.179 (ἐπάρετε ***δρουβανιστὸν ὀξύγαλον***, γυναῖκαι!, "Come, ladies, get your ***churned-up sour milk*** here!"). The referent

of ὀξύγαλα is further discussed in Koukoules 1915:311–14 and 1947–55 2.1:240, 5.122. Although Koukoules discusses it as a drink, he also says that the churning (δρουβανιστόν) alluded to in *Ptochoprodromos* produced butter, and he considered "churned sour milk" to be the leftover buttermilk. He reports that the adjective δρουβανιστόν survived in Anatolia (Pontic and Cappadocian Greek), where buttermilk is both drunk and eaten dried. Kriaras (1968–97) likewise glosses the word as ξινόγαλα, "sour milk."

On the other hand, the Pontic Greek reflex ξύγαλα is glossed as γιαούρτι, "yogurt" (Papadopoulos 1961, s.v.), and Koukoules (1915:314) admits that although the adjective *Ptochoprodromos* uses, δρουβανιστόν, refers to buttermilk, the noun used in Anatolian Greek to refer to buttermilk is the Armenian τάν or τάνιν—normal yogurt is called ξυγαλὶ ὑλιστόν, "strained sour milk," instead. So although *Ptochoprodromos*'s "churned" may indeed refer to buttermilk as used in the Pontus, Pontic Greek uses the word ὀξύγαλα to refer to yogurt instead of buttermilk. Alexiou (1986:19) likewise believes that "*oxygalon* is probably yogurt, here beaten up to make a refreshing and frothy drink, much like the modern Turkish *ayran* (drink made with yogurt and water, mixed with snow or ice, rather than buttermilk), still sold on the streets of Istanbul."

At issue is whether the Byzantines knew of yogurt independently or learned of it through the Turks. If the latter is the case (as we suspect, particularly because yogurt—a Turkish word, after all—is much more prominent in Turkish than Greek cooking), "buttermilk" or "curds" is likelier in a text as early as the *Tale*.

133. **mollusks**. Šandrovskaja (1956a) translates ἁγνά literally as "pure things" (чистые вещи); the correct reading, "mollusks," adopted by Tsiouni (1972), was first pointed out by Xanthoudidis (1927–28:355), correcting Hesseling (1924:369). Koukoules (1947–55:5.86) gives a parallel in Agapios Landos's seventeenth-century *Geoponicon* §137 [139]: Ὅλα τά ***ἁγνά*** καί ὀστρακοδέρματα εἶναι πολλά κακοχώνευτα, ἤγουν σουπίες, καλαμάρια, ὄστριες, ἀχιβάδες, ἀτζομπάτοι καί τά ἐπίλοιπα, ἀμή χειρότερον ἀπό ὅλα εἶναι τό ὀκταπόδιον, "All ***mollusks*** and shellfish are difficult to digest, namely cuttlefish, calamari, oysters, scallops, ἀτζομπάτοι (?), and the rest, but the worst is the octopus."

139. **dip**. Tsiouni (1972) glosses χαλῶ as "thrust"; Eideneier (1976:459) points out that χαλῶ normally means "let go" ("loosen" in classical Greek) and here must mean "dip." Šandrovskaja (1956a) likewise translates it as опуская, "dropping; letting down, lowering; drooping." Compare the *Book of Birds* 44–45: ἐσὺ ὁποὺ τρῶς ἐκ τὸ πουρνὸν ὁλῶμα τὰ ὀψάρια / καὶ ὡς τὸ δισάκκιν τὰ ***χαλᾶς*** καὶ ὡς τὸ ταρπὶν τὰ ρίπτεις, "You who eat fish from morning on, all raw, / ***dropped*** to your bill and cast down to your belly?" The modern meaning of χαλῶ, "destroy," already present in the *Book of Birds* (634), is irrelevant here. See also discussion in "Of Mice and Timothy."

144. **how cats can move**. Although the sense is clear enough, the noun used

here, γυρίσματα τοῦ κάτη, "the turns of the cat," is not the most obvious. For an analogous interpretation, compare the following from *Ptochoprodromos:*

> Πανάχραντέ μου, κράτει την, ἐμπόδιζε, Χριστέ μου,
> μὴ παίξῃ ***κοντογύρισμα*** καὶ ἐπάρῃ τὸ ραβδίν μου
>
> [Thou Undefiled, restrain her; Christ, impede her;
> lest she ***swerve swiftly round*** and grab my staff] (1.175–76)
>
> καὶ τότε νὰ εἶδες, δέσποτα, πηδήματα νεωτέρου,
> καὶ καλογέρου ταπεινοῦ ***γυρίσματα*** καὶ κρότους/ψόφους
>
> [Then you should see, my lord, a young man's leaps,
> a humble monk's ***tossing-turning*** and noise.] (4.225)

Thus, "turns" could be used in medieval Greek to refer to the motion of the entire body.

Koukoules (1947–55:5, appendix, 24) interprets γύρισμα in the *Tale* in terms of someone threateningly circling an opponent, as in wrestling; compare *Achilleid* N 1559–60:

> Κανεὶς τοῦτον οὐκ ἔτρεψεν ἢ ἐνίκησεν πολλάκις,
> ἀλλ' ὅσοι τὸν ***ἐγύρευσαν*** {ἐγύρισαν: Hesseling 1919}, τὸ ἀλίμονον ἐπῆραν
>
> [Nobody turned him back or beat him often;
> whoever ***circled*** him found woe instead.]

But the cat is looking forward to making γυρίσματα *after* jumping at the rat, so the "turns" are not threatening moves, but outright combat against him.

146. **humble teeth**. We reject the literal meaning "small, low" of ταπεινά as being too learned for the *Tale*. Instead, we have preferred the figurative meaning "humble," meant here ironically. The cat is likelier to mean that his teeth are humble in status ("lowly") than meek, which is consistent with our interpretation of verse 125. This kind of self-abasement is typical of the poem; compare Commentary, verse 187.

158. **cajoled**. The word in the original, ἀκολάκευτον, occurs only in this passage in vernacular medieval Greek, according to Kriaras 1968–97. The primary meaning of the verb κολακεύω since antiquity has been "flatter" (Liddell–Scott–Jones 1940, s.v. 1, 2), so ostensibly the word means "unflattered." But it would be uncharacteristically metaphorical of the author to speak of the rat not being flattered by humans.

In learned Byzantine Greek, the word also meant "rough" or "ruthless," via "implacable"; thus, Michael Psellus has πάντα δὲ τῇ ***ἀκολακεύτῳ*** γαστρὶ χαριζόμενοι, "and granting everything to the ***implacable*** belly" (*Oratoria minora* 4.114), and the *Suda* uses it to gloss ἀμείλιχος, "implacable, relentless"; ἀθώπευτος, "unflattered, not open to flattery"; and δεινός, "fearsome; clever."

Yet it makes even less sense to speak of the rat as implacable, particularly as an animal that humans cannot placate.

However, the "cajole" sense is prevalent in the vernacular for κολακεύω: for example, Τοῦτον ὅλον ἐγίνετον διὰ νὰ μαλακτιάνουν τὸν θυμὸν τοὺς Γενουβίσους καὶ νὰ τοὺς ***κολακέψουν·*** καὶ ὀλλίγον ἐφελέθησαν, "All this was done to soften the wrath of the Genoese and to ***cajole*** them: and they got but little advantage from it" (*Chronicle of Makhairas* §338). In fact, Kriaras's (1968–97) first gloss of κολακεύω is κολακεύω, "flatter," καλοπιάνω "cajole." And Somavera (1977 [1709], s.v.) glosses ἀκολάκευτος as ἀχάϊδευτος, ἀκανάκευτος, "uncarressed, unpampered," *non accarezzato, et inadulabile,* "not caressed, and unflatterable." This accords with the treatment the rat notes humans deal out to the cat: independent minded as he is, humans have to make an effort to keep the cat on side.

170. **clubs**. On the ματζούκιον, "club" (mentioned also in 650 and 674), see Kolias 1988:177.

171. **walnuts rattling**. There might be precedent for the association of walnuts with noise in Leontius of Neapolis's fifth-century *Life of St. Symeon the Fool.* In one of Symeon's escapades (Festugière 1974:79–80), he enters a church at the beginning of Mass "walnuting" (καρυδίζων) and extinguishing candles (σβεννύων τὰς κανδήλας); he then goes on to pelt women with walnuts (ἐλίθαζεν τὰς γυναῖκας τοῖς καρυδίοις) from the pulpit. Krueger (1996:151) translates this as "he ***threw the nuts*** and put out the candles. When they hurried to run after him, he went up to the pulpit, and from there he pelted the women with nuts." Festugière (1974:133) translates it in the same way: "il ***jetait des noix*** et éteignait les cierges. Commes donc ils se précipitaient pour le chasser, il monte à l'ambon et de là bombardait les femmes avec ses noix." Festugière (1974:187) justifies his interpretation by analogy with the similar verb ἐλούριζεν "whipping" < λουρίον "strap," in the same text (Festugière 1974:90) and ἀκοντίζειν, "throw javelin at" < ἀκόντιον, "javelin."

Aerts (1986) believes that what is meant by καρυδίζων, rather, is cracking and eating the nuts:

> Festugière agrees with Rydén, but the interpretation is incorrect, in my opinion, for two reasons: (a) Just "throwing nuts" has been expressed by λιθάζειν τοῖς καρυδίοις; it is not very likely that καρυδίζειν should mean the same thing. (b) Festugière compares the act of καρυδίζειν with ἀκοντίζειν (throw a spear), but what is the "natural thing" to do with an ἀκόντιον (spear), namely "throw him" ⟨*sic*⟩, does not fit to a καρύδιον. The natural thing to do with a nut is to crack and eat it. This is obviously also Leontios' intention: Symeon the Fool behaves himself in an offensive manner, by making improper noise, cracking the nuts, and by eating them during the holy service. But this is not enough: he also extinguishes the candles! And for this act he uses of course the empty shells of the nuts!

Rydén (1970:90), who is responsible for the text of Symeon reproduced in Festugière (1974), reports that though he believes καρυδίζω means *Nüsse werfen,* "throw nuts," Darrouzès, in a book review of his earlier edition of Symeon, pointed out this was already covered by ἐλίθαζεν . . . τοῖς καρυδίοις, "pelt with walnuts," and was instead inclined to read καρυδίζω as *jouer aux noix,* "play with nuts," by reference to Koukoules (1947–55:1.171). But Koukoules in that passage is describing the Byzantine counterpart to games with marbles; it would be hard for Symeon to make an effective entrance into the church by stooping to the floor, knocking nuts out of a circle, and then getting up and snuffing candles. So Symeon is clearly making noise with the walnuts, disrupting the church service. It would be confusing to have Symeon throwing walnuts at people twice in the narrative, and walnut shells would not be particularly effective at snuffing out candles (as Aerts suggests), so that cannot be what is meant, either. Though it is not otherwise documented, we think it much likelier that Symeon was simply rattling walnuts in a bag.

The connection between walnuts and noise is clear, at any rate, and this association persisted from Leontius through to the *Tale.*

177. **haughty eyebrow**. The original (though only in P, as the other manuscripts omit this part of the verse) has just ὀφρύν, "eyebrow." But in postclassical Greek, "eyebrow" was used to refer to arrogance (our thanks to Nikos Sarantakos for pointing this out to us); we have added "haughty" to indicate this. Šandrovskaja (1956a) likewise translates the word here as **гордость,** "pride." The image invoked is one of raised eyebrows indicating pride; this image is absent in English proper but is present in the etymology of *supercilious.* It is also absent in modern Greek, which instead refers to "high noses" (ψηλομύτης)—looking down one's nose at the world.

But the image is not to be found in classical Greek either; none of the references in Liddell–Scott–Jones 1940 to this meaning of the stem (s.v. ὀφρυάζω II, "to be haughty, supercilious"; ὀφρυόομαι, "to be supercilious"; ὀφρῦς I.2, "scorn, pride") may be dated with any certainty before the third century B.C. (The noun ὀφρῦς, literally "eyebrow," is used in this sense in several epigrams in the *Palatine Anthology,* but most of its epigrams are postclassical.) The stem in this use was particularly popular with early church fathers (Lampe 1961, s.v. ὀφρυόω, "make conceited"; ὀφρυώδης, "proud"; ὀφρύωσις, "pride, superciliousness"); they often used it to allude to Psalm 131 [130]:1: Κύριε, οὐχ ὑψώθη μου ἡ καρδία, ***οὐδὲ ἐμετεωρίσθησαν οἱ ὀφθαλμοί μου***, οὐδὲ ἐπορεύθην ἐν μεγάλοις οὐδὲ ἐν θαυμασίοις ὑπὲρ ἐμέ, "Lord, my heart is not haughty, ***nor mine eyes lofty:*** neither do I exercise myself in great matters or in things too high for me." It would have been this patristic usage that made the usage known to later Byzantines.

The question is, was the *Tale*'s reference to arrogance as an eyebrow—quite unlikely to be coincidental—current in the vernacular of the time, or was it literary? The evidence suggests the latter. Kriaras (1968–97) lists this meaning only for the *Tale* and *Spaneas:*

Βλέμμα θρασὺ καὶ ἀναίσχυντον καὶ τράχηλος ὑψαῦχος
ὀφρύδιν σαλευόμενον καὶ ἀναπετασμένον

[A bold, insolent glance; a stiffened neck;
an ***eyebrow*** wavering and raised up high] (Vatican ms. 516–17)

Υιέ, αν έχεις χρήματα, υιέ, αν είσαι πλούσιος,
μη διασπάσεις τας ***οφρύς***, μηδέ κενοδοξήσεις

[If you have money, son, if you are rich,
don't be vainglorious, don't arch your ***eyebrows***.] (Mavrofrydis version P 415–16; cited from Kriaras 1968–97)

But the vernacular credentials of *Spaneas* are shaky, compared even with our fourteenth-century corpus: the poem appears in so many registers and variants, it may well have been originally written in a learned idiom. As seen, the expression is absent in modern Greek. And related words for arrogance derived from "eyebrow" needed to be glossed in Byzantine dictionaries (*Photius, Suda, Lexica Segueriana, Pseudo-Zonaras*). It is probably also no coincidence that the *Tale* uses the classical word ὀφρῦς rather than the vernacular ὀφρύδιον, much more common in medieval vernacular texts (see Kriaras 1968–97, s.v.; admittedly there is not much difference between the two, but the scarcity of the learned word in vernacular texts is telling).

But if the reference is literary, to what is it a reference? Nothing about the text would lead us to suspect a classical allusion, and this use of "eyebrow" is not to be found in the classical canon to which most Byzantines had access anyway. The usage turns up in Epictetus, which implies it was genuinely colloquial in Koine:

ὡς ἐρούντων ὅτι 'ἄφνω φιλόσοφος ἡμῖν ἐπανελήλυθε' καὶ 'πόθεν ἡμῖν αὕτη ἡ ***ὀφρύς***;' σὺ δὲ ***ὀφρὺν*** μὲν μὴ σχῇς· τῶν δὲ βελτίστων σοι φαινομένων οὕτως ἔχου

[and ⟨they⟩ say, "Here he is again, turned philosopher all of a sudden," and "Where do you suppose he got that ***high brow***?" But do you not put on a ***high brow***, and do you so hold fast to the things which to you seem best.] (*Enchiridion* 22.1)

However, the usage is absent in the three Koine texts in which we have been able to find most of the *Tale*'s learned words: the Septuagint, the New Testament, and Aesop (including the *Life of Aesop*). The closest we have found is Psalm 131:1, cited earlier; it is as unlikely that the author consulted Gregory of Nazianzen, St. Nilus, or the other church fathers who commented on it, as it is that he was familiar with Epictetus. However, Byzantine pupils would have still gotten some theology along with their reading lessons, so the association could have been made, at second hand, in the classroom.

The word may have also made its way into the *Tale* through the pages of a dictionary. Some corroboration for this lies in the fact that the word continued to be used in this sense, not only in learned late Byzantine writing (e.g., *Gregoras* 3.41: ἀλλὰ σκληρὰν καὶ οἷον εἰπεῖν ἡγεμονικὴν τὴν ***ὀφρὺν*** κατὰ πάντων ὅσοι θαλάττιον βόσκουσι βίον, "but a harsh and, so to speak, imperial ***haughtiness*** against those who lead a seafarer's life") but also in glosses in Byzantine dictionaries themselves; for example, *Pseudo-Zonaras* (1329): τέθεικε δὲ τὴν λέξιν ὁ Ἀπόστολος καταστέλλων τὴν ***ὀφρὺν*** τῶν Κορινθίων καὶ διδάσκων, ὡς οὐ παιδεύσεως, ἀλλὰ πίστεως αὐτοῖς χρεία, "The Apostle ⟨Paul⟩ used the word ⟨*maranatha*⟩ in condemning the ***pride*** of the Corinthians and teaching that they had need not of education but of faith."

So though the reference does not seem to have been colloquial, it may have still had enough currency among the educated to have been sighted or heard by the author. Though modern Greek does not use "eyebrow" to refer to arrogance, it *does* use the verb found here, κόβω, "cut, slash," to refer to humiliation or frustration: θα σου κόψω το βήχα, "I'll cut off your cough" (Sarantakos 1997:46); θα σου κόψω τον τσαμπουκά, "I'll cut off your swagger." We know that medieval Greek uses κόπτω in a very similar way—in fact, Pseudo-Georgillas uses κόπτω with ἔπαρσιν, "arrogance," just as the *Tale* does in verses 178 and 274:

> νὰ ὁμονοιάσουν ἐμπιστά, νὰ πᾶν κατὰ τὰ ἔθνη·
> τὴν πόλιν τῶν Χριστιανῶν, Λατίνων καὶ Ῥωμαίων,
> νὰ πάρουν ἀφ' τὰ χέρια των, νὰ ***κόψουν ἔπαρσίν*** των.
>
> [Let them ⟨Western Christians⟩ make concord and attack the Gentiles;
> take off their hands the Latins' and the Romans',
> the Christians' city; ***cut*** their ***arrogance***. (*Fall of Constantinople* 356–58)

So the author (or the scribe of P) may have adapted the learned allusion to this vernacular template, making a rather adroit play on words.

180. **place**. An insidious *faux ami,* the term used here, στασίδιον, only means "church stall" in modern Greek (so in Somavera 1977 [1709], s.v. στασίδι: *seditoio, sedile,* "seat"); Tsiouni (1972) glossed it accordingly as "a seat, a pew." But only the lion is depicted with a seat, and to postulate pews for each of the conference participants would introduce an anthropomorphism uncharacteristic of the *Tale*.

As it turns out, although the meaning "stall, pew" was already extant (e.g., *Acts of Docheiariou* 37.2, 37.18, dated 1361), στασίδιον still retained its original meaning as a diminutive of στάσις, "station, place to stand; (military) watch":

> νὰ ζιῶ ἀποκάτω εἰς μιὰ φτωχειά, τσ' ἀνάπαψης ***στασίδι***,
> ποὺ ἀλάφρωση τοῦ λογισμοῦ καὶ τοῦ κορμιοῦ ὕπνο δίδει
>
> [that I should live in a poor yet restful ***abode***,
> which gives relief to the mind and sleep to the body] (*King Rodolino* [*xvi* A.D.] 4.37–38)

(Compare *King Rodolino* 1.703; *Acts of Lavra* 158.2–7, where it refers to fishing spots [στασίδιον ἁλιευτικόν]; *Phocas: De Velitatione* 1.10; see also discussion in Steiner 1989:256–57.) Rather than the *Tale* making some obscure allusion to rats gnawing at church pews, it is likelier that the original meaning of στασίδιον is intended here. Šandrovskaja (1956a) correctly renders στασίδιον in her translation as **место**, "place."

187. **jolt you oh-so-gently**. Although ἀκροτινάζω literally means "edge-fling, edge-jolt," Byzantine usage was overwhelmingly for ἀκρο- to diminish the intensity of the predicate—as a perusal of Kriaras 1968–97 clearly shows. Compare, for example, ἀκροτρευλίζω, "to stutter," in *Father Wine* AO 114, V 112, L 79, S 165, where ἀκρο- cannot mean "edge," or ἀκροστέκομαι, "stand for a while," in *Pastor Fide (Cretan)* 4.3:104–6:

καὶ ἂν ἒν καὶ ***ἀκροσταθῇς ἐδῶ λιγάκι***
θέλεις τὴν δεῖ δεμένη,
σερμένην στὸν ναὸν νὰ τήνε πηαίνουν

[and if you ***stay here for a little***,
you'll see her bound,
and being dragged into the temple.]

This tendency has continued in modern Greek dialect (Andriotis 1974 §258); for example, ἀκροβοηθῶ, "help a little" (Crete), ἀκροκαθίσκω, "sit for a little" (Cyprus).

Counterexamples, where ἀκρο- intensifies rather than diminishes the force of the verb to which it is prefixed, are rare:

Ὅταν βαλθῇ ἡ εὔταρμη κ' ἐγρήγορή σου χάρη
τὸ ὁρίσης πράγμα νὰ γενῇ, δὲν ἔναι ν' ***ἀκροπάρη***

[When your bold, swift grace sets itself
to carry out its bidding, it should not be ***long delayed***.] (*Sklentzas* 3.14)

(Kriaras [1968–97] gives only two stems with intensifying ἀκρο-, against twenty-six with diminishing; the modern intensifying instance he gives, Cypriot Greek ἀκροφοοῦμαι, "fear greatly," is contradicted even by the usage of the same verb in medieval Greek: ἀκροφοβοῦμαι, "fear slightly.") Of course, several instances are difficult to resolve; for example, ἀκρογομάτος, "slightly fleshy (of lips)" in *Digenes* P 315:

τὰ δὲ χείλη της ἦσαν κόκκινα καὶ ***ὑπόπαχα*** καὶ ὡσὰν βαμμένα. Καὶ ἦτον ***ἀκρογομᾶτα*** καὶ ἔσταζεν ἀπ' ἐκεῖνα ἡ χαριτόβρυτος βρύσις

[and her lips were red and ***fullish*** and looked as if they were painted. And they were ***slightly/(quite) fleshy*** and the fountain of graces dripped from them.]

The use of a diminutive in this verse of the *Tale* echoes that in verse 143 ("a teensy jump") and 893–94 ("stretch my palm out just a smidgeon and tap your lower jaw a tiny bit"), although the events described there are anything but slight: the author is consistent in his use of understatement. So though the literal meaning of ἀκροτινάζω was probably just "jolt slightly" to the author, in its ironic use it does indeed mean "jolt greatly." (See also "Comedy".)

Šandrovskaja (1956a) has сильно встряхнула, "violently shake off," which assumes intensification rather than the ironic diminishing of force we have posited. Šandrovskaja was possibly misled by the similar phrase εἰς ἄκρον, "overly," used in 907 and 969. Tsiouni's (1972) gloss, "to shake something from its end, its tip," makes for a vivid image—the dog shaking the fox around by the tip of its tail—but it seems a little unrealistic, especially within the overall naturalistic world of the *Tale*. Physical plausibility has also made us prefer to read τινάζω as "jolt" rather than "fling."

197. **low-profile entrance**. In the original, ἐν ταπεινῷ τῷ σχήματι, "in humble form." A commonplace description of monks, it is repeated in the vernacular *Vita of the Esteemed Donkey* 176, as the fox describes how she impersonated a cat: Καὶ μὲ ταπείνωσιν πολλήν, ***μὲ ταπεινὸν τὸ σχῆμα***, / θεωρεῖ ἡ γραῖα πῶς ἔρχομαι, ἔχει το κάτος ἔναι, "And the old woman sees me coming with great humility, ***in humble form***, and thinks that it's the cat."

198. **tropically**. The word in the original (τροπικῶς) is the word that gave us *Hamlet*'s verse (3.2) "The Mousetrap. Marry, how? Tropically" (i.e., metaphorically).

200. **dog by nature**. It is possible that this is meant literally: "dog" was well established as a derogatory term (e.g., *Digenes* E 129, Ὦ ἀμιρά, πρωταμιρὰ καὶ ***σκύλε*** τῆς Συρίας, "Emir, first of emirs and ***cur*** of Syria"), and the fox could merely be stating that the dog deserves its poor reputation.

But it is likely that something subtler is going on. The modern Greek term for "dog" (σκύλος) used in the text has its roots in ancient Greek σκύλαξ, "puppy," with no obvious relation to classical σκῦλον, "arms stripped off a slain enemy" / σκυλεύω, "to loot, to plunder"; σκύλος, "pelt"; or σκύλλω, "mangle" (Frisk 1970, s.v. σκύλλω, σκῦλα). The fox, however, with her characteristic pedantry apparently sees a connection between these two meanings ("because your name and conduct go together"), and the dog confirms as much ten verses later: to mangle the fox's pelt stripped off her is exactly what he threatens to do. A similar wordplay turns up in the *Belisariad*:

> ἐκείνους ὁποὺ ***ἐσκύλευσεν*** ὁ μέγας Βελισάρις
> καὶ ἐφάνηκεν ἀπάνω τους ὡσὰν ***σκύλος*** λυσσάρης
>
> [Those whom the great Belisarius ***looted***
> and acted toward like a rabid ***dog***.] (ρ 483–84)

That the author was familiar with classical dictionaries we know from verse 335; we may be grateful, at least, that the fox's pedantry did not extend so far as to add the Homeric monster Scylla to her list. The pun between σκύλος and σκυλεύω has already been pointed out by Dölger (1964:205):

> Master Fox ⟨allowing for the change in gender in German⟩ shows off with etymological erudition, as we can see, but his audience has no understanding of grammar jokes. So the dog's response (verse 204ff.) cannot be ignored. . . .

We suspect that the dog understood the fox all too well.

211. **tanner**. The text refers to a γναφέα < classical γναφεύς, "fuller," and Tsiouni (1972) and Šandrovskaja (1956a) (сукновальню) translate it literally. But the fuller's business had to do with whitening cloth, not processing hides. Kriaras (1968–97) interprets the term here as "tanner," following the definition in Pseudo-Zonaras's dictionary, written at roughly the same time as the *Tale* (442):

> Γναφεύς. ὁ λευκαίνων τὰ ἱμάτια. κναφεὺς δὲ ὁ τὰ δέρματα ξύων. {ὅ ἐστι βάπτων}
>
> [*Γναφεύς*: he who whitens clothes. And *κναφεύς* is he who scratches hides {i.e., dyes them}.]

Because classical γναφεύς and κναφεύς are the same word, this presumably reflects a shift in the meaning of the word in Byzantium. This also applies to the verb forms of γνάπτω in 640 and 641, which Tsiouni (1972) also interprets literally ("fulled by a fuller," "having been fulled by a fuller")—although Šandrovskaja (1956a) hedges her bets with обработанной, обработанные, "processed."

Whereas γναφεύς occurs uniquely in the *Tale* in vernacular medieval literature according to Kriaras (1968–97), the related verb γνάπτω does occur in Renaissance Cretan Greek, meaning "to tan" rather than "to full" (Kriaras, s.v.):

> μηδὲ σοῦ δώσω τσὶ ξυλιὲς κεῖνες ποὺ σοῦ τοκάρου, / καὶ τὸ πετσί σου ***γνάψω*** το σὰ νά 'τονε γαϊδάρου, "or I'll give you the beating you deserve / and ***tan*** your hide as if it was a donkey's" (*Fortounatos* 1.113–14, also 3.94; the work's editor Vincent [1980] glosses the word as γδέρνω, "to skin," but the English metaphor "tan = beat" clearly applies here as well, and donkey skin is much better known for its abuse rather than its use).

And Somavera (1977 [1709], s.v.) glosses γνάφω as *conciar corame, ò cuoio,* "to tan stamped leather, or leather." This semantic transition is not remarked on in Koukoules (1947–52:2.1 197–98), who discusses γναφεῖς only as fullers and makes no allusion to this passage in the *Tale*. The word is rare in modern Greek: it appears in neither Babiniotis's nor the Triandafyllidis Institute's recent dictionaries, but Stamatakos's dictionary (1971) has the entries γναφαρ(ε)ιό, "place where wool is washed; place where hides are washed and processed," and γναφτός, "of hide or fleece, processed, has had its wool worked on"—which suggests the ambiguity has persisted into the modern language between "fulling" and "tanning." And unsurprisingly, the verb γνάφω survives in places like Crete:

> Ἐγάπησα κι ἐγὼ ὁ φτωχὸς μιὰν ξαναπαντρεμένη,
> πάω ν' ἀγγίξω στὰ βυζά, βρίσκω προβιὰ *γναμένη*.
>
> [Poor man, I've fallen for a remarried woman;
> I try to touch her breasts—and find ***tanned*** sheepskin.] (Lioudaki 1971 [1936]:291)

This belies Andriotis's (1974 §1703) report that γνάφω survives in the broader region of the Aegean only with its original meaning, "to full."

212. **alum** . . . **quicklime** . . . Alum and lime were both used as tanning agents, as was ash (verse 293).

212. **torment**. The text has δαμάζω, which in classical Greek has the primary meanings of "overpower" and "tame." The dog could have the quicklime metaphorically tame the insubordinate pelt. However, the meanings δαμάζω took on in the medieval vernacular are more promising:

> "torment": *Alphabetic Poems* 21.35 (*xv* A.D.): Συντρίψας, τύψας ὁ Ἀδὰμ τὰς παρειὰς ***δαμάζει,*** "Adam ***torments*** his cheeks, crushing them and striking them"; *Glycas: Prison Verses* 130–32: Τῆς φυλακῆς ἡ κάκωσις, ἡ τσίκνα, τὸ καρβούνιν, / ἐγὼ τὸ ἐξεύρω μοναχός, ἐμέναν καίει μόνον· / μόνος ἐγὼ ***δαμάζομαι*** κ' ἐγὼ τὴν πεῖραν ἔχω, "The smokiness, the coal ⟨grief⟩, the pains of prison— / only I know, and only me it burns; / it ***torments*** only me; I know it well."
>
> "subdue" (through metaphorical extension): *Physiologus (Vernacular)* 603–4: ἀδάμας τοίνυν λέγεται αὐτό τε τὸ πουλάκι, / διότι οὐ δαμάζεται, ἀλλὰ τὸ πῦρ ***δαμάζει,*** "this bird ⟨the salamander (!)⟩ is therefore called *adamas*; / it is not subdued, but rather it ***subdues*** fire."
>
> "subdue" (according to Eideneier [1991]) or "calm down" (according to Kriaras [1968–97]) in *Ptochoprodromos* 4.378: τοῦτο ⟨τὸ ἁγιοζούμιν⟩ ***δαμάζει*** πάντοτε, ἄναξ, τοὺς καλογήρους, "this ⟨broth⟩, my king, always ***subdues*** the monks" (though given how revolting Ptochoprodromos finds the broth and that the "subdue" sense is not attested anywhere else, δαμάζω could well mean "torment" here, too).

Somavera (1977 [1709], s.v.) reports two further senses: *macerare, mortificare la carne con austerità,* "to emaciate, to mortify the flesh through austerity," and *maturare, et maturarsi le nespole, le sorbe e simili, mezzare, mizzare, diventar mezzo,* "to mature, and to ripen, of medlars, sorb-apples, and the like; to overripen." The first sense is comparable to the Ptochoprodromic instance:

by ill-nourishing their flesh, monks tame and subdue it. The second sense draws an analogy between wildness and sourness, against tameness and ripeness; it is continued in Samos, where Andriotis (1977 §1745) reports for δαμάζου the sense "to lose its bitter taste (of olives)." The sense Andriotis reports for δαμάζου in Imbros on the other hand, "beat soundly," stands between "torment" and "subdue."

Tsiouni (1972) glosses δαμάζω in this passage as "to make supple," and Šandrovskaja (1956a) as обработают, "to process." Kriaras (1968–97) glosses δαμάζω in this instance as "destroy." It makes the most sense to have the dog refer to tanning, not as a normal industrial process of smoothing but explicitly as punishment for the fox; this coheres with the unambiguous use of κάψῃ, "burn," in the same verse. (The same verb accompanies δαμάζω in the verse from Glycas cited earlier.) So δαμάζω is unlikely to have been the normal tanners' term for their use of quicklime as a softening agent, and the intended meaning seems closest to Glycas's "torment" in figurative use. The sense "subdue" would be as plausible but, given the dog's hostile intentions, would probably not satisfy him. The same holds for the meanings suggested by Tsiouni (1972), Šandrovskaja (1956a), and Kriaras (1968–97), none of which are supported by any attested usage; the parallel with medlars and olives is not compelling enough to derive a meaning like "process, make fit for human use" ("tame").

213. **high philosophizing**. *Philosophy* (φιλοσοφία) was the usual Byzantine designation of intellectual pursuits in general (Koukoules 1947–55:1.1.124–25).

217. **You boast** . . . This is a structural inconsistency in the poem: the fox refers to claims the dog has not yet made! There are a few instances of such inconsistencies, as the author seems to have been rather relaxed about keeping the plot straight. For a recent proposal on resolving this particular disruption, see appendix 3.

232. **neck**. This is another instance in which σφόνδυλος means "neck" rather than "spine" (see verse 84): the dog is far easier to drag to its death by the neck than by the spine. Šandrovskaja (1956a) accordingly has горло, "throat."

246. **fart early and fart often**. The original has συχνοπυκνοκλάνῃς, "you fart frequently and densely."

252. **raw**. χλωρά, literally "green" (< χλόη, "first green shoot of plants"; compare χλωρὴν τὴν βέργαν, "green switch" [679]). We have not found a reference to "green meat" outside the *Tale*, but the analogy with green (fresh) vegetables is clear and classical as shown in Liddell–Scott–Jones 1940: Homer (*Odyssey* 9.379) applies it to green olivewood; Aristophanes (*Frogs* 559), to cheese; and Athenaeus (7.309b), to fish. The sermon *In Herodem et infantes*, attributed to John Chrysostom, uses χλωροκοπεῖσθαι, "freshly cut," to refer to the infants slaughtered while "fresh" by Herod (Migne 1857–87:61.701). Much later in Greek, the fox in the *Vita of the Esteemed Donkey* (145) boasts that she always eats χλωροφαγιάν, "fresh food"—which can hardly be vege-

table. Likewise in modern Greek, the adjective is used to describe curds (HDMS 802:85; Schinoussa, Cyclades), and fresh fish (ἔχομεν παστὰ καὶ ***χλώρια*** ὡς πεντὲξ ὀκάδες χώρια, "we've got salted and ***fresh*** ⟨fish⟩, up to five or six *okas* ⟨weight⟩ each" [HDMS 118:167, Kastria, Cynuria, Peloponnese]), whereas Somavera (1977 [1709], s.v.) glosses it as *fresco, parlando di latte, e frutti,* "fresh, of milk or fruit." And in verse 374 of the *Tale*, χλωρόν, "green," is again used for fresh meat as distinct from παστόν, "salted." Šandrovskaja (1956a) likewise has свежим, "fresh."

252. **cooked**. In ancient Greek, ἑψημένος as the participle of the verb ἕψω means "boiled"; for example, Herodotus 1.48: χελώνην καὶ ἄρνα κατακόψας ὁμοῦ ***ἧψε*** αὐτὸς ἐν λέβητι χαλκέῳ, "he had cut up a tortoise and a lamb and then ***boiled*** them in a cauldron of bronze"; *Aristotle: Problemata* 884b: καὶ ἐπὶ τὰς χύτρας τὰς ***ἑψημένας*** φυσώντων, "blowing on the ***boiling*** pots." In modern Greek, [ὁ]ψημένος as the participle of ψήνω has shifted in meaning to "roasted"; that is also how Tsiouni and Šandrovskaja (жареным) translate it.

In Cretan Greek, however, the verb ψήνω has shifted further to "cook" in general—so it can be applied to both soup and roast meat. In fact, Somavera (1977 [1709], s.v.) glosses ψήνω as both *cocere, cuocere,* "cook," and *rostire, arrostire,* "roast." Because "cooked" is more plausible as a term contrasted with "raw" than "roasted" is, one might reasonably suspect something similar to have happened here. Based on the use of the verb in 381 (see Commentary), which also seems to refer to cooking in general rather than roasting, we have followed this Cretan gloss. We do not currently have enough information as to how widespread this meaning was in medieval Greek (although ψήνω is glossed as *kochen,* "cook," in Oikonomu-Agorastu's popular remedy book [1982], and Somavera's gloss points to a widespread meaning).

252. **strangled**. The "strangled meats" (πνικτά) are meats obtained from smothered animals; their consumption by humans was prohibited by the church. For discussion of the frequently violated Byzantine taboos on meat, see Koukoules 1947–55:5.58–62 and Kolbaba 2000:35–36, 146–48. The animals might be smothered in two ways. One was by hunting animals, as described in Theodore Balsamon's eleventh-century commentary on the canon law:

> Τὰ δὲ ὑπὸ ὀρνέων θηρευτικῶν, ἢ κυνῶν, ἢ παρδάλεων θηρευόμενα καὶ ***πνιγόμενα***, πῶς παρά τινων ἐσθίονται, ἀγνοῶ. Σημείωσαι οὖν τὸν κανόνα, διὰ τοὺς Λατίνους τοὺς τὰ ***πνικτὰ*** ἀδιαφόρως ἐσθίοντας
>
> [How meats hunted and ***suffocated*** by hunting birds, hounds, or pards can be eaten by some, I know not. This law should be noted by the Latins, who eat ***strangled meats*** indiscriminately.] (Rallis and Potlis 1852–59:2.81)

The other was in traps: Koukoules (1947–55:5.60) cites a sixteenth-century canon law referring to animals "suffocated in snares": πνικτὰ εἰς τὰ βρόγχια.

The taboo is ultimately Jewish (Genesis 9:4) and was formulated early in Christianity:

> ἔδοξεν γὰρ τῷ πνεύματι τῷ ἁγίῳ καὶ ἡμῖν μηδὲν πλέον ἐπιτίθεσθαι ὑμῖν βάρος πλὴν τούτων τῶν ἐπάναγκες, ἀπέχεσθαι εἰδωλοθύτων καὶ αἵματος καὶ ***πνικτῶν*** καὶ πορνείας· ἐξ ὧν διατηροῦντες ἑαυτοὺς εὖ πράξετε
>
> [For it seemed good to the Holy Ghost, and to us, to lay upon you no greater burden than these necessary things; that ye abstain from meats offered to idols, and from blood, and from things ***strangled***, and from fornication: from which if ye keep yourselves, ye shall do well.] (Acts 15:28–29)

Origen, in the third century (*Against Celsus* 8.30), explains the taboo on strangled meats thus:

> τὰ δὲ ***πνικτὰ*** τοῦ αἵματος μὴ ἐκκριθέντος, ὅπερ φασὶν εἶναι τροφὴν δαιμόνων, τρεφομένων ταῖς ἀπ' αὐτοῦ ἀναθυμιάσεσιν, ἀπαγορεύει ὁ λόγος, ἵνα μὴ τραφῶμεν τροφῇ δαιμόνων, τάχα τινῶν τοιούτων πνευμάτων συντραφησομένων ἡμῖν, ἐὰν μεταλαμβάνωμεν τῶν πνικτῶν.
>
> [As to ***things strangled***, we are forbidden by Scripture to partake of them, because the blood is still in them; and blood, especially the odor arising from blood, is said to be the food of demons. Perhaps, then, if we were to eat of strangled animals, we might have such spirits feeding along with us.]

The most influential statement of the taboo in Byzantium is in John the Faster's *Penitential* (1895A), conventionally dated to the late sixth century: διερευνᾷν... ἢ αἷμα, ἢ ***πνικτὸν***, ἢ θηριάλωτον, ἢ θνησιμαῖον, ἢ ὀρνεοπάτακτον ἔφαγεν, "⟨The priest⟩ should also inquire. . . . Has he eaten blood, or something ***strangled***, something killed by an animal ⟨Lev. 5:2⟩, a carcass ⟨Lev. 11:8⟩, or something slain by birds?" The penitential was reproduced, in embellished form, in later variants (see Rallis and Potlis 1852–59:2.81, where it forms Canon LXIII of the Apostolic Canon law; Theodore Balsamon's commentary on this was cited earlier). For example, there is a Cypriot vernacular Greek penitential (Christodoulou 1983:453), dated to the period of Western rule (*xiii–xvi* A.D.), which states that Ὅστις τρώγ(ει) ζῷα ***πνικτά***, ἀκοινώνητος χρόνους β′ καὶ καθ' ἑκάστην μ(ε)τ(ανοί)ας σ′, "whoever eats ***strangled*** animals shall spend two years without Communion and shall perform two hundred prostrations a day."

The term πνικτά could also mean "steamed, stewed," as in classical Greek (Liddell–Scott–Jones 1940, s.v. πνικτός, II; πνίγω, II: "cook in a close-covered vessel, bake, stew"). This is the interpretation Xanthoudidis (1927–28:356), Šandrovskaja (1956a) (тушеным), and Tsiouni (1972) ("cooked in a close-covered vessel") gave the word here. We know from Koukoules (1947–55:5.67) that Byzantines ate πνικτὰ ᾦα, "steamed eggs." However, there is no instance known to us of πνικτά referring to stewed meats in *Byzantine* Greek, and Koukoules (1947–55:5.60) himself finds in this verse of the *Tale* proof that the taboo strangled meats were disposed of in this way. Dimitrakos (1936–50, s.v. πνικτοφαγία) sees a reference to eating stewed meat in the stem as used in Theophylact of Ochrid, *On the Errors of the Latins* 279, but as the title of the work should make obvious, Theophylact is not talking about stews but is referring to the same taboo as his contemporary Theodore Balsamon—and notes that Western clerics at least (Λατίνοις σώφροσιν, "the more prudent Latins") condemned the practice. In any case, the *Tale* already uses ἐκζεστόν to refer to boiled meat (372), and there is a logical contrast between χλωρά, "raw and fit for human consumption," and πνικτά, "raw and unfit for human consumption," both in opposition to ἐψημένα, "cooked, roasted." So we have adopted the meaning "strangled."

The reading given (ταγίζουν με χλωρά, πνικτά) is from P. The other manuscripts have some variant of ταγίζουν καὶ ποτίζουν με χλωρόπηκτα καὶ ὀψημένα κρέη, "they feed and water me with green-congealed (V: χλωρόπτηκα, "green-roasted[?]") and cooked meats." (L, as usual, gives up and has instead καλὰ ψημένα κρέη, "well-cooked meats.") The addition of "and water me" is clearly extraneous and extrametrical, so it can be dismissed. However, the use of a single, compound word where P has two words is noteworthy. The parallel with P suggests that the prototype of CVLA may have had χλωρόπνικτα, "green-suffocated"; the form might mean "freshly steamed" or "freshly strangled." The former is unlikely for the same reason the reading of πνικτά itself as "steamed" is unlikely. The latter would be an oddly metaphorical use of "green" to mean "newly," but it has some precedent in John Chrysostom's use of χλωροκοπεῖσθαι and the *Vita of the Esteemed Donkey*'s χλωροφαγιά (see note on "raw" immediately preceding). And a compound as odd as χλωρόπνικτα would clearly constitute the *lectio difficilior*, which the scribe of P would want to unpack into its less odd component parts. Still, "raw" meat makes perfect sense as something to feed a dog, and the distinction between "raw" (but slaughtered by humans) and "strangled" (i.e., slaughtered by animals) was culturally salient to Byzantine dog owners. So the reading in P would make perfect sense to a contemporary. We thus retain P's as the original reading.

254. **beads and bells**. Compare Nicephorus Basilaces, *In Praise of the Dog* (*Progymnasmata* 29.41–45):

> ἕτερον τοῖς περὶ τὸν τράχηλον ἀναδέσμοις ἐπαγαλλόμενον καὶ ταῖς ψηφῖσι γαυρούμενον καὶ τοῖς χρυσοειδέσι ῥυτῆρσι ἐναβρυνόμενον, ἡδεῖαν ὄψιν τοῖς θεωμένοις εἰ μή πού τις ἐξ ἀδάμαντος τὴν καρδίαν κεχάλκευται, γλαυκή τε τοῦτον ἔτεκε θάλασσα.

> [and ⟨you may see⟩ another ⟨dog⟩ rejoicing in the bands around his neck and strutting with its beads and proud of its golden leash, a sweet sight to behold—unless one's heart is perchance as hard as diamond, and he is "born of the blue sea"] ⟨to quote *Homer: Iliad* 16.34⟩.

The other examples Koukoules (1947–55:5.395) adduces of dog paraphernalia refer simply to dog leashes.

257. **to catch or beat**. Koukoules (1932:33) believes this refers to hunted bears and lions. Bears are a reasonable animal to read in here, but in fourteenth-century Byzantium lion hunting had surely become a mere literary topos (see Nicholas 1999:266–67).

270. **toff**. Tsiouni (1972) glosses the noun κορδῶναν as "strutting, used of a person who has put on airs." Šandrovskaja (1956a) omits the second half of this verse in her translation, so her gloss is unavailable. Hesseling (1924:310) objects that κορδῶναν—meaning "stupid, simpleton" (*dumme, einfältige Person*) in Triandafyllidis's dictionary (1963 [1909]:405) of medieval loanwords—ill befits the fox, and prefers A's κορδωμένη, "having airs." In any case, Tsiouni's gloss, rather than Triandafyllidis's, is adopted by Kriaras (1968–97), with the *Tale*'s the only instance attested from his corpus.

Triandafyllidis (1963 [1909]) gives his gloss in the context of discussing loanwords whose polysemy was inherited from the original language—which would imply that the meaning "stupid" of κορδῶνα originates in Italian. But the verb κορδώνομαι, "put on airs," is still extant in modern Greek (as used in A's participle), and nothing in the text suggests the meaning "stupid" for the corresponding noun of the other manuscripts: this would directly contradict the following verse. Moreover, the meaning "stupid" is nowhere attested to our knowledge for κορδών- in either medieval or modern Greek.

Kriaras (1968–97) derives κορδῶνα from κορδώνω, "to fasten a cord, to stretch"; how this relates to strutting (expressed in modern Greek by the passive of the verb) is not obvious. The passive of "stretch" may be the origin of the noun, with someone strutting termed "as taut as a cord," describing the way they bear their body (cf. the modern Greek expression σαν να κατάπιε μπαστούνι, "[proud as if] they swallowed a cane," or Epictetus *Discourses* 1.21.2, τί οὖν ἡμῖν ὀβελίσκον καταπιὼν περιπατεῖς, "Why, then, do you walk around in our presence as though you had swallowed a spit?"). In such a case, the noun κορδῶνα would be a back-formation from the verb: "she is taut like a cord" > "she is a 'corder.'" A similar development turns up in Somavera (1977 [1709]), where the medial verb κορδίζομαι, also derived from κόρδα, is glossed as *tendersi, rizzarsi,* "to stretch, to rise to one's feet." All the same, the Venetian-derived diminutive of κόρδα, κορδέλα, "ribbon," might point to a less problematic derivation: "proud as someone wearing a ribbon."

The Cretan Renaissance word κορδόγερος, "old man one wishes dead" (*Fortounatos* 4.71; Vincent 1980:223) exploits the same image but to a different end. The image underlying this formation, as Hatzidakis (1977:2.325, 445) argues, is of a corpse stiff as a taut cord, and Hatzidakis supplies comparable modern Cretan phrases (στσὶ χαρές σου τσὶ κορδιστές, "here's to your corded celebration" = "here's to your funeral"); Psychoundakis (1979:19), in his modern Cretan Greek translation of the *Odyssey*, uses ὁ κορμοτεντωτής ὁ χάροντας, "Death the Body-Stretcher," to the same end (*Odyssey* 2.100, for the Homeric τανηλεγέος θανάτοιο, "Death bringing long woe"). But this obviously has nothing to do with the fox's arrogance. See also Textual Notes, verse 612–12a.

271. **dear master and philosopher**. Literally, "my master-craftswoman and sophist" (τὴν μαστόρισσαν καὶ τὴν σοφίστριάν μου). Although σοφιστής, "sophist," was originally a paid teacher of grammar, the pejorative meaning "quibbler" familiar in English was already established in Aristophanes, Plato, and Demosthenes (Liddell–Scott–Jones 1940, s.v. σοφιστής, II.2). This meaning is also present in modern Greek, presumably through revival—although Somavera (1977 [1709]) does gloss σοφιστής as *sofista, cavigliatore, un cavilloso,* "quibbler."

However, the word itself is immediately derived from σοφία, "wisdom," and to someone unfamiliar with the intellectual politics of classical Athens, the term would have meant quite transparently "practitioner of wisdom." This is, in fact, how the stem was used in the medieval vernacular:

> *Mirror of Women* 157: λάλησε, ἅγιε Σολωμὼν, καὶ ***σοφιστὴ*** Σωκράτη, "speak, holy Solomon, and ***philosopher*** Socrates"
>
> *Della Porta* 1.1530: ⟨addressing Virtue⟩ μὲ τὴν πολλήν σου φρόνεσιν, μὲ τὰ ***σοφίσματά*** σου, "with your great prudence, with your ***wise advice***"
>
> *Life of Aesop: Vernacular* 1 §108: καὶ εἶπε του λόγους διδασκαλικοὺς καὶ ἑρμηνεῖες πολλὰ ***σοφιστικές,*** "and he spoke to him instructive words and most ***wise*** counsels"
>
> *Falieros: Story and Dream* 636: καὶ ἀπάνω ὅντε ***σοφίζομαι*** μ' ἔχεις παρατρεμένο, "just when I ***come to my senses***, you drive me mad" (interpretation defended in van Gemert 1980:164).

So there is no need to posit that the hare is making a pejorative classical allusion: he is literally calling the fox a philosopher. The other terms he uses (μαστόρισσαν, λογιωτάτην, φιλοσοφωτάτην, "master-craftswoman," "most scholarly," "most intellectual") likewise praise the fox's wisdom; the preceding κορδῶναν, "toff" (see the previous discussion), criticizes her pride but not her learning. The hare is obviously being sarcastic but is probably not giving himself away just yet.

Šandrovskaja (1956a) translates the word as софистке, which is a borrowing from classical Greek and thus carries the associations we've rejected; Tsiouni (1972) also invokes those associations in glossing it as "quibbler."

285. **sorceress**. The first controversy here is which reading to accept for the word. If we accept L's reading, ἀτζιγγάνα, as Tsiouni (1972) does, then ostensibly the fox is being called a Gypsy. There is a slight possibility that the word here means "miser" instead. The modern Turkish *çingene* (< Old Ottoman *çigâne*) has both meanings, and the modern Greek τσιγκούνης, "miser," is derived from *çingene*; there is precedent in this use of a Turkish ethnic term as a derogatory epithet in both modern Greek and Turkish τσιφούτης, "miser" < Turkish *çıfıt,* "Jew; miser." The Turkish word for "Gypsy," in turn, is presumably a loan from Greek ἀθίγγανος, "Gypsy"—although its meaning "miser" might be derived not from ἀθίγγανος but from Old Turkic *çıgañ,* Old Ottoman *çıgan,* "poor." This means that somewhere in Byzantine territory the word for "Gypsy" picked up the secondary meaning "miser." The question is whether it did so in Turkish alone or whether the doublet "Gypsy"/"miser" appeared in medieval Greek as well—with medieval Greek either borrowing the secondary meaning from Turkish or itself making the association between Gypsies and miserliness and passing it on to Turkish. (Our thanks to Nikos Sarantakos and Yusuf Gürsey for this information.)

Although modern Greek keeps the concepts "miser" and "Gypsy" distinct by using slightly different stems (τσιγγάνος, τσιγκούνης) and likewise rarely uses τσιφούτης to mean "Jew," this needs not have been the case in earlier stages of the language. In the context of the *Tale*, furthermore, the word τζιγγάνα is associated with notions of poverty (κλέπτρια καὶ τζιγγάνα, "thief and gypsy"); this would be fertile ground for the meaning "miser" to come to the forefront. However, this is an uncorroborated development, and the default assumption remains that "Gypsy" would be here meant as an ethnic slur, without any further specific associations.

On the other hand, the reading [ἀ]τζιγγάνα is attested only in L, which immediately makes it suspect. The other manuscripts have at 286 a word that differs from this by one letter: ματζιγγάνα (PCA), μαντζακάνα (V). V is obviously a distortion of PCA's form, and the emendation of ματζιγγάνα to [ἀ]τζιγγάνα would appear straightforward; it is the reading Wagner (1874) adopts in his edition without ever sighting L, and Šandrovskaja (1956a) likewise translates the word as цыганка, "Gypsy," without comment.

The initial μ, however, is puzzling, and there is nothing in the phonetic context to justify it. One might think of the Turkish practice of adding an initial *m-* to words to mean "of that ilk" (e.g., *kitaplar mitaplar,* "books and such"; cf. the Yiddishism *books, schmooks*). This practice is occasionally also used in contemporary Greek, and the *Mass of the Beardless Man* (A 225) does have the nonsense sequence ἄντζαλα μάντζαλα σάνταλα κλάνταλα. But the *Tale* is probably too early for such a Turkism to occur with non-Turkish nouns—particularly as it occurs on its own and not as ἀτζιγγάνα ματζιγγάνα.

The only remaining way to explain ματζιγγάνα that makes sense is by postulating *ματζικάνα, "sorceress," as a combination of the Italian *magica* and the Greek suffix -ᾶνος < Latin *-anus*. This would fit the context neatly: it is close in meaning to the following word, μαγγαναρέα, "magic-working; swindling" (see note following). But *ματζικάνα is problematic on several fronts. A word like *magicanus* is not attested; the closest Du Cange (1954 [1678]) has for medieval Latin is *magicarius*, and the closest modern Italian offers is the participial *magicante*. (English *magician* and French *magicien* apply the suffix *-ianus* instead.) We have no instances of *μάτζικα attested in Greek. Du Cange (1958 [1688], s.v.) finds μάτζια in Sachlikis, but this is in a passage in which Sachlikis is quoting Italian verbatim, and the word is presumably *mangia,* "eat!" rather than *magia,* "magic" (μάτζια, ἐμπέβρε, ἰνπρεγάδα, *mangia, embevre, impregada,* "eat, drink, I pray you (?)"; this is presumably a variant of *Strange Narrative* 584, which is a verse in Italian.

Our choice ends up being between a distorted ethnic term, which L has cleaned up latterly, and an otherwise unattested loan from Italian, which is linguistically odd (possibly because it has been nativized) but fits the context well. Papathomopoulos (2002) has chosen the latter (obviously the *lectio difficilior*) by insisting on the majority reading, so we tentatively translate this as "sorceress" rather than "Gypsy." We should also note that Gypsies were associated with the dark arts in Byzantium (Soulis 1961:146–47), so "Gypsy" could have been construed as "sorceress" anyway, and vice versa.

286. **innards-devouring**. Literally, "belly-and-cord–eating" (κοιλιοχορδοφᾶσα); as discussed in Koukoules (1947–55:5.56–57), χορδές, "cords," was the name given to the small intestine of goats and sheep, whereas κοιλιόχορδα, "belly-and-cord," is a name given to this day (allowing for dialectal variation) to cooked intestines and belly. Because, as Koukoules confirms, the Byzantines had no real problem eating offal (πατσάς, κοκορέτσι, and the Easter dish μαγειρίτσα remain popular among Greeks, notwithstanding European Union directives), the hare's pejorative reference is puzzling. This may be a rhetorical strategy of the hare's, emphasizing that the fox is carnivorous by having her eat even the offal of her prey.

286. **swindling**. The term used here, μαγγαναρέα, is derived from the word μάγγανον. The meaning of μάγγανον itself, however, is an involved matter and is not adequately dealt with in existing lexica. For that reason, we take some time in working out what its meaning encompasses.

(1a) The original meaning of μάγγανον is "means for charming or bewitching others; philter" (Liddell–Scott–Jones 1940, s.v., I; Lampe 1961, s.v. μαγγανεία, 1). In its meaning of "philter" it was associated in particular with φάρμακον, "drug; potion"; both stems, for example, are associated with the sorceress Circe in Aristophanes *Plutus* 310 (Οὐκοῦν σέ, τὴν Κίρκην γε, τὴν τὰ ***φάρμακ'*** ἀνακυκῶσαν / καὶ ***μαγγανεύουσαν*** μολύνουσάν τε τοὺς ἑταίρους, "You then, Circe, who mix up ***potions*** and ***use philtres*** and besmear your companions").

(1b) The μαγγαν- stem acquired a secondary meaning of "trickery, deceit." However, this meaning seems not to have been completely divorced from notions of sorcery. In particular, the two examples that Liddell–Scott–Jones 1940 use to illustrate the metaphorical meaning of μαγγανεύω as "play tricks" evoke notions of sorcery: Demosthenes 25.80 levels the charge at Aristogeiton that he "plays ***juggling tricks*** and professes to cure fits" (***μαγγανεύει*** καὶ φενακίζει καὶ τοὺς ἐπιλήπτους φησὶν ἰᾶσθαι) in consort with Theoris of Lemnos, a sorceress, and Julian *Against the Galilaeans* 340A terms "witchcraft" (not just "trickery") the practice of sleeping among graves in order to receive dream visions. The frequent patristic references to μαγγανεία as the wiles or tricks of the devil (Lampe 1961, s.v. μαγγανεία, 2) also involve the supernatural domain.

Two further elaborations of μαγγαν- involve sexuality (**2**) and fake sorcery (**3**). The analogy between sorcery and sexuality ("meretricious arts": Liddell–Scott–Jones 1940, s.v. μαγγάνευμα; Lampe 1961, s.v. μαγγανεία, 3, μαγγανεύω, 2) was commonplace—compare the English *bewitching*. For example, *Achilles Tatius* 2.38 claims of a boy that τὰ δὲ φιλήματα σοφίαν μὲν οὐκ ἔχει γυναικείαν, οὐδὲ ***μαγγανεύει*** τοῖς χείλεσι σινάμωρον ἀπάτην, "his kisses, to be sure, are not sophisticated like a woman's; they are no ***devastating spell*** of lips' deceit." The association with charlatans is made in Photius's dictionary entry for μαγγανευτής, repeated in the *Suda*: ὁ μιγνὺς παντοδαπὰ πρὸς φενακισμόν, "he who mixes all sorts of materials for the purpose of quackery" (also Liddell–Scott–Jones 1940, s.v. μαγγάνευμα, μαγγανευτήριον).

(**4**) Examples of μαγγαν- referring to trickery without a supernatural component are hard to come by. The two clearest examples we have found are patristic:

> καὶ οὐ παύεται στρέφων ὧδε, στρέφων ἐκεῖ, πάντα ***μαγγανεύων*** τί εἰπεῖν ἕως ἀνύσει τὸν σκοπὸν αὐτοῦ, ὁ τοιοῦτος οὐδέποτε πιστεύεται, "and he never ceases, turning to and fro, ***twisting*** everything he says until he accomplishes his aim; such a person can never be trusted." (Dorotheus the Abbot, *vi* A.D.; *Doctrina* 1721A) (Lampe 1961, s.v. μαγγανεύω, interprets the word as used here as "play tricks; of verbal subtlety.")

> μεῖζον τοῦ φιλεῖν τὸ ἀγαπᾶν. οὐδὲν ἐν αὐτοῖς σκολιόν, οὐδὲ στραγγαλιῶδες ἢ στρεβλὸν καὶ καμπύλον, πάντα εὐθέα, φανερά, οὐδὲν σοφιστικὸν οὐδὲ ***μεμαγγανευμένον*** ἔχοντα, "Love is greater than friendship; there is nothing twisted or knotted or crooked or curved about them—everything is straight and in the open, and there is no sophistry or ***trickery*** to them." (Hippolytus [attributed], *iii* A.D.; *Fragmenta in Proverbia* 39)

(**5**) Finally, μάγγανον had a second distinct meaning, which Frisk (1970, s.v.) considers original: "engine of war, catapult" (Liddell–Scott–Jones 1940, s.v., II; Lampe 1961, s.v., I; Kriaras 1968–97, s.v., 2), and by extension "windlass, crane; block of a pulley" (Liddell–Scott–Jones 1940, s.v., III; Lampe 1961, s.v., II; Kriaras 1968–97, s.v., 1). Thus a μαγγανάρι(ο)ς is a conjurer in early astrological texts (Liddell–Scott–Jones 1940, s.v., I) but a mechanical engineer in Pappus and Theophanes (Liddell–Scott–Jones 1940, s.v., II; Lampe 1961, s.v.). The sense was further elaborated in the vernacular: it came to mean a "press" (Kriaras 1968–97, s.v., 4), in which sense it remains extant in Cretan Greek (Xanthoudidis 1927–28:356). (This development has been paralleled in Germanic: Frisk considers German *Mange(l)*, English *mangle,* to be a related word.) And the *Tale* itself (289: Kriaras 1968–97, s.v. μάγγανον, 3; see Commentary) uses the noun to refer to a trap or snare (**6**) as a hapax legomenon. (Somavera (1977 [1709]) gives a seventh meaning, *telaio, telaro,* "loom," for μάγκανον, and *ricamare,* "embroider," for μαγκανίζω; we will ignore this here.)

So there is a wide array of notions to which μαγγαναρέα could be appealing. If we array the possibilities, however, they fall into three families:

(1) "magician" < "magical charm" (= 1a, 1b)
(2) "seductress" < "meretricious arts"
(3) "quack" < "quackery"
(4) "trickster" < "play tricks"
(5) "engineer" < "siege engine";
metaphorically, "artificer"
(6) "entrapper" < "snare"

For the animal kingdom and the kind of story the *Tale* tells, (2) and (3) are irrelevant. The two families of senses of μαγγαν- left, then, are that invoking the supernatural (1) and that invoking ingenuity (4, 5, 6). So if the hare is claiming supernatural activity for the fox, (1) applies. If not, one of the remaining meanings (4), (5), and (6) applies, though they are all quite close to each other: they all claim that the fox engages in deceit through her own intelligence.

Of these possibilities, Xanthoudidis (1927–28:356) considers (1) likelier for the *Tale* and (5) less likely. Šandrovskaja (1956a) adopts (1) (мерзкая фокусница, "villainous conjurer"). Tsiouni (1972) seems to adopt (4) ("mischief-making"), whereas Eideneier (1976:459) counterclaims that it should be understood as (1) ("magic-working"). Kriaras 1968–97 glosses it as (1) ("witch, enchanter, evil-doing"). Scholarly consensus thus seems to be that "magician" (1) is the correct gloss; however, we believe it is in fact one of (4)–(6): "trickster," "artificer," or "entrapper." To establish this, we appeal to both contemporary usage and the internal evidence of the poem.

The adjective itself, μαγγαναρέα, is a hapax legomenon. However, the stem μαγγαν- recurs several times in vernacular medieval Greek. As seen, Kriaras (1968–97) defines the noun μάγγανον as referring to various kinds of machinery but never as an allusion to either magic or deceit. With the noun so used, meanings (5) and (6) were readily available for any noun derived from it. And it would not have been much of a metaphorical extension to generalize *Theophanes the Confessor*'s noun (258) μαγγανάρις, "maker of siege machines," to its feminine version μαγγαναρέα, "an artificer."

Of the other words derived from μαγγαν- that Kriaras (1968–97) lists, μαγγανότζαγρα, "catapult–crossbow"; μαγγανέλλα, "siege machine" (from Italian); and μαγγανικόν ξύλον, "catapulting wood = catapult" are straightforward military references; they shed no further light on the issue. The word μαγγανοσανίδα, "board to press grapes with" (in Kriaras 1968–97, addendum, volume 14) derives from "press" and is similarly irrelevant. The remaining two nouns that look promising are μαγγάνη, glossed as "witch, enchantress," and μαγγανεία, glossed as "art of augury, artifice."

On closer inspection, these words prove to be disappointing. The first, μαγγάνη, occurs in the *Vernacular Oracles* (9.7, 10.9), in a passage so garbled and stripped of context that the work's editor Trapp (1964) admits to defeat with his gloss "Zauberin (?)":

Ἔλθη θέλει ***ἐξαλάττης***
τῆς μεγάλης τῆς ***μαγγάνης***,
καὶ νὰ τὸν ἐνδύσουν κάππαν (9)

Ἔλθη θέλει ***ἐξοβλάτην***
τὴς μεγάλης τῆς ***μαγγάνης***,
διὰ νὰ ἐνδύσουσι τὴν κάππαν (10)

[He shall come ἐξαλάττης/ἐξοβλάτην (?)
from the great ***witch***,
to be dressed in a cape.]

Kriaras's emendation of the unknown word to ἐκ θαλάττης, "from the sea," does not help much: a seafarer (or the sea itself) could just as easily be a trickster as a sorcerer. The same holds for the use of Μαγγάνης as a nickname (Koukoules 1947–55:6.486) and for Μάγγανον/Μάγγανα as a place name in Constantinople and elsewhere.

The other noun, μαγγανεία, is attested in Hermoniacus's *Iliad* (15.176) and the learned poetic version of the *Alexander Romance*. Despite Kriaras's gloss, the instance in Hermoniacus clearly refers to siege machines, even if μαγγανείαις is treated as synonymous with μεθοδίαις, "machination, trickery" (a confusion not uncharacteristic of Hermoniacus):

ἔποικαν καὶ ξυλοπύργους
πρὸς ἀφάνισιν τελείαν
τῆς χαράκωσης Ἑλλήνων
καὶ τῶν κατασκευασθέντων
πυργωμάτων τὲ καὶ τείχους

κροσσωτῶν γὰρ μεθοδίαις
σὺν ἑτέραις ***μαγγανείαις·***
τὰς λεγόμενας γοῦν σκρόφας
καὶ τοὺς λεγομένους κρίους
τοὺς ἐκείνων προμαχῶνας
ἐκατέρριξαν τοῦ τείχους.

[They made wood towers
to do away
with the Greeks' trench,
the walls and towers
with battlements
that they had built;
through trickery
and other ***engines***:
the so-called sows
and so-called rams
brought down the ramparts
of their walls.]

In the learned *Alexander Romance*, on the other hand, μαγγανεία refers to the trickery of the villain Nectenabo, sorcerer and king of Egypt. These tricks are clearly brought about through magic; for example, the form of voodoo with which Nectenabo repels his enemies is described as carried out κακομηχάνῳ τέχνῃ τε μεγίστῃ ***μαγγανείᾳ,*** "through evil-doing art and greatest ***witchcraft***" (52). This is the only firm example of a supernatural definition of the μαγγαν- stem in Kriaras; unfortunately, it is not from a vernacular work! (However, Caracausi 1990, s.v., does report κακομαγγανεία, *malvagio sortilegio* ["evil witchcraft"] from medieval Italy, in a legal document dated 1098.)

Our conclusion from contemporary usage is that the meaning "trickster" could have readily been derived at the time from μάγγανον, "siege machine," or the *Tale*'s hapax legomenon "trap" and is as plausible a gloss of μαγγαναρέα as "magician" is. The metaphorical use of μάγγανον to mean "trick" does not seem to have been vernacular and is not always distinct from sorcery in older usage, yet it, too, could have given rise to a nonsupernatural meaning of μαγγαναρέα. So any decision between the two types of meaning must be determined from internal evidence in the poem itself.

The allusion to magic-working that most scholars posit for the word in the *Tale* comes out of the blue in this passage. The fox is known as a figure of an intellectual, so one might imagine she dabbles in the dark arts. Furthermore, she is called in the poem either a Gypsy or, more likely, a sorceress—see Commentary 285. But the reading of (μ)ατζιγγάνα in 285 is very uncertain. And nothing else in what is said about the fox corroborates an appeal to the supernatural. Neither does the supernatural play any role with other animals: although the deer is said to behave at night like a demon (330), to flee as the devil does from incense (332), and to expel snakes through having its horn burnt (347), it is rather far from this to suggest that the deer actually exploits demonic powers. The description of the *Tale*'s animals is much too naturalistic for that.

On the other hand, plenty of what the fox does corroborates her description as a trickster: the hare has just described how he is deceived into friendship with her, and the fox is described elsewhere as "excelling in cunning" (28) and as a "grand-master trickster" (1061). In fact, the adjective used for "trickster" there, κακομήχανον, is the same word translated as "evil-doing" in the previous quotation from the learned *Alexander Romance*. The word literally means "evil-machining," but μηχανή in Greek, just like μάγγανον, came to mean "device, exercise of cunning" as well as "war engine" or "machine (in general)." So the term used in the *Tale* displays a parallel development to the sense postulated in (5).

We admit that the use of μαγγανεία in modern Greek, which displays the full range of meanings from "witchcraft" to "artifice," is rather tempting, especially in light of verse 285, which *may* be calling the fox a witch. But all the vernacular medieval examples of μαγγαν- we have seen are mechanical rather than supernatural; the *Vernacular Oracles* are too corrupt to provide an exception, and the instance from the *Alexander Romance* is not vernacular. So we conclude that no allusion to supernatural influence should be understood here; the usage in the *Tale* is likelier closer to that in Hermoniacus. Our gloss encompasses meanings (4)–(6). It would be hard to pick one meaning given the paucity of external evidence, but (5) and (6) are the only senses directly supported by vernacular medieval Greek.

287. **branch tips**. The ἀκρίδας mentioned here also mean "locusts," and this mistranslation is frequent for the New Testament: Matthew 3:4, Mark 1:6. (It makes much more sense for John the Baptist in the desert to be feeding on branch tips than insects.) The usage attested in Kriaras 1968–97 (s.v. ἀκρίδα, II) suggests that the word had survived in the vernacular:

> ***ἀκρίδας*** οὐ σιτεύομαι οὐδ' ἀγαπῶ βοτάνας, / ἀλλὰ μονόκυθρον παχὺν καὶ παστομαγειρείαν, "I eat no ***branch tips***, and I like no greens; / I'll take thick casseroles, and salted cooking." (*Ptochoprodromos* 2.103)

> Ὅτι πολλάκις εἰς πόλεμον ἐφάγετε κ' ***ἀκρίδα***, "for often in wartime you have even eaten ***branch tips***." (*Koroneos: Bua,* 70; Koroneos's account of an Albanian warlord's feats is fairly pedestrian and less likely than *Ptochoprodromos* to be making a biblical allusion.)

288. **raisins hanging there**. The original has just σταπίδας, "raisins" (cf. σταφίδια, "raisins," in 132); the *Etymologicum Gudianum* (s.v. σταφυλή) records σταπίς, ἀσταπίς, and ἀσταφίς as variants of "raisin" (the normal classical term was ἀσταφίς, and the normal modern term is σταφίς > σταφίδα),

and Somavera (1977 [1709], s.v. σταπίδα) gives σταπίδα and σταφίδα as synonyms. The word σταπίδα survives only in Thrace (Andriotis 1974 §5518), with the expected meaning. So clearly σταπίς and σταφίδα both mean just "raisin." But it seems to us unlikely that the fox is purposefully seeking out raisins where they have been laid out to dry in the sun (dried-on-the-vine raisins date only from the 1960s and are still experimental: May and Kerridge 1967). It is far likelier that the fox is pilfering grapes that had dried, uncollected, on the vine.

In times of famine, people were also known to subsist on grapes dried on the vine. For instance, in the famine of the Morea in 1455–56, people were reported as subsisting on γίγαρτα along with greens, shoots, roots, and hard-shelled fruit (Diana Wright, personal communication). (In classical Greek [Liddell–Scott–Jones 1940, s.v. γίγαρτον] this word meant a grape stone or olive stone, but Hesychius in his *vi* A.D. dialect dictionary already glosses γιγαρτίς as σταφίς, "raisin," and though the word is absent from Kriaras 1968–97, Giambattista della Porta, in his 1589 book *Magiae Naturalis* [4.24], refers to "Oil out of Grapes or Raisins—The Greeks called these *Gigarta*." Andriotis [1974 §1676] confirms this meaning in modern Greek dialect: Livisi, Karpathos, Pontus, Epirus.)

The fox's preoccupation with stealing grapes was of course immortalized in Aesop's fable of the sour grapes (fable 15).

289. **trap**. As discussed in the Commentary to verse 286, the *Tale*'s use of μάγγανον to mean "trap" rather than "catapult" or "press" is to our knowledge unique in vernacular medieval Greek and for that matter Greek in general. This seems to be related to the sense "press": a press is a machine that squeezes fruit, and a snare works by "squeezing" an animal. This sense probably also underlies modern Greek μαγγώνω, "squeeze, crush; get stuck; nab" (Andriotis 1983, s.v.—although he does not speculate on the particular sense of μαγγ(αν)ώνω < μάγγανον involved), so the sense must have formerly been more widespread.

303. **major merchant**. Tsiouni (1972) sees in the Italian word μαρκατάντος (Italian *mercatante*, Venetian *marcante*) a reference to an explicitly Western merchant. As the West had pretty much taken over Byzantine commerce by that time, we do not feel this assumption warranted: the word would easily have become generic. Šandrovskaja (1956a) translates the phrase as богатый торговец, "wealthy merchant." Kriaras (1968–97) adds that a μαρκατάντος was "typically active in distant lands," citing *War of Troy* 13586:

> εἰς Κρήτην ἐκατέβηκεν ὁ φρόνιμος Δυσσέας
> ἔνδον εἰς δύο κάτεργα, ἤσασι ***μαρκατάντων***·
> εἰς βυζάντια ἑκατὸν τὰ εἶχε καιρογεύσει
>
> [Prudent Odysseus then went down to Crete
> taking two galleys, which belonged to ***merchants***;
> he'd hired these paying a hundred bezants.]

This confirms the μαρκατάντος was a merchant rather than a mere trader.

The term survives in Crete as μαρκαταντιές, "lies, mischief" (an obvious semantic extension) and in Corfu as μαρκάντης, "peddler" (HDMS data). The latter contradicts the tendency of the Byzantine term to mean a merchant traveling the world, but with the Venetians ruling Corfu for six centuries (and Corfu using the Venetian form of the word), it may have taken on a more homespun connotation there.

306. **they put on undergarments**. If we assume a break between 305 and 306, as Tsiouni (1972) and Papathomopoulos (2002) both do through their punctuation, it is not clear that the undergarments or lining discussed (both termed ἐνδύματα, "garments/covers") have anything to do with hareskin. This passage (306–9) looks more like a digression on alternate ways of warding off the cold, following on from the hareskin hat of 302, and reminiscent of C's digression in 927a–g. Unlike that digression, 306–9 appears in all manuscripts, with only P preserving 309 (see Textual Notes). But if the text is changing the topic at 306, the change is pointless and connects awkwardly with the foregoing. Even if there is no break in 306 ("but also all the large-cloaked noble ladies . . . put on ⟨hareskin as⟩ undergarments for decorum"), there is no singular pronoun to refer back to the δερμάτιν, "skin," of 301, so verses 306–9 are still unconnected with the preceding discussion on hareskin and must be considered a digression. That said, we do have evidence that Byzantines used hareskin (as well as foxskin) to keep warm:

> Μόνον ἡ ὑπερβολὴ τοῦ ψύχους θανατοῖ με καθ' ἑκάστην, ἣν οὔτε ἀλωπῶν οὔτε λαγωῶν δέρματα, οὔτε ὅσα ἄλλα ἐπιτηδεύουσιν οἱ ἄνθρωποι εἰς θάλψιν παραμυθοῦνται, εἰ μὴ μόνον ἡ θηριακή, "The excess of cold alone is killing me every day—which neither fox- nor hareskins nor anything else people devise to keep warm can assuage, other than that medicine." (*Michael Choniates: Epistulae* 179)

Choniates is probably not referring just to a hat to see him through his illness, but the text of the *Tale* gives no clear indication that the undergarments in 306 are indeed made of hareskin.

The failure of the *Tale* to mention foxskin as well as hareskin may be part of the author's general bias against the carnivores; see "Subversion and Politics."

312. **to pick the gold**. See Koukoules (1947–55:2.1.229), who does not adduce examples from any other texts. Confirmation is given by the English encyclopedist Alexander of Neckham, who studied in Paris (late *xii* A.D.):

> The goldsmith . . . must also have a rabbit's foot for smoothing, polishing and wiping the surface of gold and silver. The small particles of metal should be collected in a leather apron. (Cited in Cherry 1992:24)

326. **foot-long whiskers**. The word used here, σπιθαμογένης, literally means "with a beard a span long" (< σπιθαμή, "span" + γένιν, "beard"); we have followed Eideneier (1976:459) in this interpretation. Šandrovskaja (1956a), along similar lines, has с челюстью в пядь величиной, "with chaps a span long." Tsiouni (1972) interpreted σπιθαμογένης as "short, belonging to a dwarfish family" (< σπιθαμή, "span" + γένος, "breed, kin," i.e., "from a breed a span tall"), which would have given "You two-toothed, crook-toothed loon of dwarfish stock." Although this line might have been more vivid, however, the accentuation of σπιθαμογένης cannot justify this conclusion: derivatives of γένος in Greek are uniformly stressed on the final syllable, as in εὐγενής, "noble = of good stock"; μονογενής, "only begotten = of single stock"; Διγενής, "Digenes, Twyborn, half-caste = of two stocks"; and νεογενής, "newly created" versus κακογένης, "ill-bearded" (*Mass of the Beardless Man* D 45); μακροασπρογένης, "long-and-white–bearded" (*Book of Fruit* 1.63–64: καὶ συμπέθερόν μου Πράσον τὸν ***μακροασπρογένην***, "and my in-law the ***long-and-white–bearded leek***"); and μαυρογένης, "black-bearded" (*Synadinos* 154: Καὶ ἦτον αὐτὸς ὁ κὺρ Γαλακτίων ὡς ν΄ χρονῶν ἄνθρωπος, ***μαυρογένης***, κοντός, "And Sir Galaktion was around fifty years old, ***black-bearded***, short").

Misaccentuation does occur in Byzantine vernacular texts, usually to force meter. The *Chronicle of Morea* is an egregious offender in this regard, and the *Tale* itself contains such instances as ἔλεφας for ἐλέφας, "elephant," in 904 (CVL); and οὔρην/οὔραν, "tail" (139 CVLA), a misaccentuation unique in Byzantine literature (the correct οὐράν is in P and elsewhere in the poem, e.g., 467). We are disinclined to posit such misaccentuation here, however, in the absence of any parallels for -γενης compounds in the volumes of Kriaras 1968–97 published so far.

Hares are not noted for their beards, unlike goats (470, where γένιν is also used), and the poem uses μουστάκιν instead for whiskers (34, 128). It is tempting to see in this odd reference to a beard an allusion to some contemporary human personage. Were this so, however, it would be the only such apparent allusion in the poem, which in all other respects keeps to a fairly literal description of animal physiognomy. We have therefore judged it likelier that "beard" is here a metrically convenient way of referring to the hare's "whiskers" (μουστάκιν).

Neither sense of (σ)πιθαμογένης has survived in modern Greek; the closest we have found is πιθαμόστομος, "having a big (span-long) mouth," in the village of "Kokkin. Hatz (?)" in the Peloponnese (HDMS 687:125). This points clearly to the "span-long whiskers" sense, as it emphasizes a large body part, rather than denigrating one's overall body size.

330. **the equal** . . . As in the West, Byzantine demons were most active during the night (Greenfield 1988:27, 257).

333. **just like the devil** . . . An early attestation of a common modern Greek proverbial expression (όπως ο διάβολος το λιβάνι: Papadopoulos 1950:35; Sarantakos 1997:72). The proverb is also present in Romanian (*Fuge ca dracul de*

ţamaîe) and Russian (Бежать как черт от ладана), which suggests that it is a notion of some antiquity in Orthodox Christianity. (Our thanks to Cristian Gaspar and Eugene Lomize for this information.)

Papadopoulos (1950:35) comments that "the phrase is based on the ancient belief of Eastern peoples and Greeks that demons cannot tolerate odors and the slightest hint of them turns them to flight." (See also Papadopoulos 1926:226; the earliest attestation he cites there is Justin Martyr, *Dialogue with Trypho* 85.3 [ca. A.D. 160]: ἤδη μέντοι οἱ ἐξ ὑμῶν ἐπορκισταὶ τῇ τέχνῃ, ὥσπερ καὶ τὰ ἔθνη, χρώμενοι ἐξορκίζουσι καὶ θυμιάμασι καὶ καταδέσμοις χρῶνται, εἶπον, "Now assuredly your ⟨Jewish⟩ exorcists, I have said, make use of craft when they exorcise, even as the Gentiles do, and employ fumigations and incantations.")

There is some precedent for the notion of incense expelling demons in late Byzantium (Greenfield 1988:265), although it appears that incense was used more frequently to conjure demons (Greenfield 1988:253–54). The modern Greek expression refers explicitly to the incense used in church; this was not a component of the official Byzantine procedure of exorcism (see Greenfield 1988:139–48). Although the precedents cited by Greenfield in popular demonology seem associated with explicit ritual, the notion reported in the *Tale* may reflect not an exorcism as such but a folk explanation of the liturgical use of incense—informed by such notions as the burning of deer horn to repel snakes (see "Fact and Fiction in the *Tale*'s Zoology").

335. **literary**. The word πτώξ occurs once in Homer (*Iliad* 17.676), and almost all subsequent usage seems to be either in imitation (Oppian, Manuel Philes, Attaleiates) or in commentary (Herodian, Eustathius of Thessalonica, Choeroboscus) of Homer. (In one instance, Theodosius the Deacon, *De Creta capta* 566, 589, the borrowing from Homer is secondhand, via George Pisides, *De Expeditione Persica* 3.24; Theodosius's own poem is in the homely Koine of *x* A.D., with little Homeric about it.)

Ševčenko (1974:78) is reminded by this verse of Michael Psellus's grammatical poem (*Poems* §6): 490 verses of grammar in iambic heptameter, with no less than 169 of them (271–439) rattling off obscure word definitions:

> Μάθε καὶ χρῆσιν, δέσποτα, σπανίων ὀνομάτων.
> Ἄγγαρος μὲν ὁ ἄγγελος, ἀγῆλαι τὸ σεμνῦναι.
> ἀγχέμαχος ὁ πολεμῶν ἐγγύθεν, στεφηφόρε . . .
>
> [Learn too, my lord, the use of words obscure:
> ἄγγαρος, "messenger"; ἀγῆλαι, "exalt";
> ἀγχέμαχος, "he who fights close", my liege . . .] (270–72)

But of course, the *Tale*'s author is not writing his own metrical dictionary but a narrative work in verse. At any rate, the author appears to intend nothing more than a throwaway remark. In fact, he packs in more detail here than Psellus, who gives only definitions and no etymologies.

335. **"fear."** Properly, πτήσσω meant "cower for fear," primarily of animals, though also "crouch in ambush" and "frighten" (Liddell–Scott–Jones 1940, s.v.).

338. **difficult to cook**. Here, too, we have translated the stem ψητ- as "cook" rather than "roast" against Tsiouni's (1972) "badly roasted" and Šandrovskaja's (1956a) rather liberal неудобоваримо, "indigestible." Kriaras (1968–97) glosses κακόψητα as "difficult to roast (ψήνεται) or boil (βράζεται)," confirming our broader interpretation of the stem. Compare 252, 381.

339. **painful to the stomach**. The difficulty in digesting hare meat was widely bemoaned in Byzantium (Koukoules 1947–55:5.51); for example, Psellus (*Poems* 9.207) classes hare meat, along with venison and beef, as μελάγχολον—"generating black bile" (and hence literally "melancholic"). Compare Commentary verses 381–82.

340. **unequalled**. Opinions on venison were in fact divided in Byzantium (Koukoules 1947–55:5.52). It was popular with hunters, but doctors frowned on it; for example, Oribasius (*iv* A.D.): κακόχυμος δὲ τούτων οὐδὲν ἧττόν ἐστι καὶ ἡ τῶν ἐλάφων καὶ σκληρὰ καὶ δύσπεπτος, "but nothing is worse out of these, when it comes to dryness, toughness, or difficulty in digestion, than deer meat" (2.28.11).

345. **tinder**. The ἴσκα is the fungus *Fomes fomentarius* (tinder fungus or touchwood, in Latin *esca*), used to light fires before the invention of matches; compare *Katzourbos* 2.179–80:

> Τὸ χιόνι ν' ἅψη δύνεται σὰν ***ἴσκα*** ἡ ὀμορφιά σου,
> καὶ νὰ μερώσῃς τὰ θεριὰ μπορεῖς μὲ τὴ θωριά σου
>
> [Your beauty can set snow on fire like ***tinder***,
> and you can tame wild beasts just with your gaze.]

350. **no longer** . . . See "Manuel Philes" in the introduction.

366. **semolina**. Koukoules (1947–55:6.84) names semolina bread (σεμιδαλᾶτον) as being reserved for abbots, while the monks made do with rusks (κιβαρόν: 367). Of course, this social distinction applied outside the cloister as well (Koukoules 1947–55:5.14).

367. **rusks**. On κιβαρόν, see Koukoules (1947–55:5.20–21):

> After "clean" ⟨including semolina⟩ and medium-quality bread came the so-called dirty (ῥυπαροί) or vulgar (χυδαῖοι) or (using the Latin word) κιβαροί or κιβαρῖται ⟨*panus cibarius,* "rations bread"⟩. They were so called, being made from dirty barley groats, namely mixed and unsifted, and were destined for paupers.

371. **with cabbage and with squash**. Such cooking is also attested in Symeon Seth and *Timarion* (Koukoules 1947–55:5.53):

> παρέκειτο δὲ αὐτῷ καὶ χύτρα χαλκῆ εὐμεγέθης κρεῶν ὑείων ταρίχων πλήρης καὶ κράμβης Φρυγίας, πιμελῆς τὰ πάντα μεστά, "Alongside him reposed a large bronze pot full of salt pork and Phrygian cabbage, all drenched with fat." (*Timarion* 17)

374. **fresh**. Another instance of χλωρός extended from "green" to "fresh" (see verse 252). Šandrovskaja (1956a) likewise has **свежее**, "fresh." Tsiouni's gloss "cooked" (1972) is unjustified.

376. **jars**. Jars were commonplace enough in Byzantine cooking that Koukoules (1947–55:5.62) reports two independent sources (*Manasses: Compendium Chronicum* 3457, 4835; canon law, Rallis and Potlis 1852–59:5.80) using the proverb ἀπὸ τοῦ γεύματος τὸν πίθον, "from the dinner, the jar" (i.e., I can tell what jar you used from what you have served).

378. **cheek-and-tongue meats**. καταμαγοῦλαν σύγλωσσην, "by-cheek with-tongue." Tsiouni (1972) regards these as two nouns and accordingly separates them with a comma. We agree with Xanthoudidis (1927–28:357–58) in regarding "with-tongue" as an adjective: "cheek meats that come with the tongue." Koukoules (1947–55:5.54) relates this verse with the preceding (see Textual Notes) and believes it refers to brawn being made out of cheek and tongue meats.

379. **cured tenderloins**. On the ἀπάκιν, see Koukoules 1947–55:5.49, 65; the cut of meat involved is glossed in Politis's edition of *Katzourbos* (1964:137) as ψαρονέφρι, "tenderloin fillet" (< ψοιάριον, "loin muscle" + νεφρόν, "kidney"). The word ἀπάκιν remains in widespread use in modern Greek dialect (Andriotis 1974 §821). The term was also extended in Byzantium to refer to human loins:

> Οὐ μὴν ἀλλὰ καὶ ἑκατέρωθεν τοῦ συνδέσμου τοῦδε κατέστρωσε τοὺς ῥαχίτας μύας τῆς αὐτῆς ἕνεκα χρείας, ἅμα καὶ ἀναπλήρωσιν τῶν κενῶν τόπων ἑκάστου σπονδύλου, ἀπὸ τοῦ πρώτου ἕως τοῦ εἰκοστοῦ καὶ τετάρτου. τούτους τοὺς ῥαχίτας μύας ὀνομάζει ἡ κοινὴ συνήθεια ***ἀπάκια***
>
> [But also on either side of the spinal cord He arranged the spinal muscles to this same end, as well as to fill the empty places of each vertebrum, from the first to the twenty-fourth. Common usage calls these spinal muscles ***loins***.] (*Theophilus Protospatharius: On the Construction of the Human Body* 5.5)

The Judeo-Greek Pentateuch accordingly uses the word to render Deuteronomy 33:11, "smite through the ***loins*** of them that rise against him": σύντριψε τ' ***ἀπάκια*** τῶν ἀντιστεκουμένων του.

As a dish, ἀπάκια were smoked and salted, and Koukoules (1947–55:5.65) states it was still prepared by Greeks in the twentieth century (Crete, Cephallonia, Cappadocia, Peloponnese) under that name. The most extensive reference to them is in *Ptochoprodromos* 3.240 (it is what the cat is blamed for eating by the guilty hero—see "Humor"); there it is referred to as ἀκρόπαστον, "slightly salted"; σύμπλευρον, "with ribs"; and σύλλαρδον, "with fat." Alexiou (1986:11) interprets ἀκρόπαστον as "smoked" and σύμπλευρον as "having sides" ("i.e., with a kind of skin?") and concludes that it is "some kind of smoked sausage." She is encouraged in this by the Cretan Renaissance comedies *Fortounatos* (5.55, 70) and *Panoria* (1.389, 2.18), where it is used in sexual allusion. The ἀπάκιν is in fact conjoined with the sausage (λουκάνικον) in the *Tale* and in *Fortounatos*. Eideneier (1991:237), in his edition of *Ptochoprodromos,* limits himself to saying that it is improbable that it means "meat from hindquarters" (*Hüftstück*) and gives Alexiou's interpretation. Šandrovskaja (1956a), on the contrary, renders it as **спинные части,** "back portions", while Tsiouni's (1972) gloss concurs with ours.

380. **and fatty meats**. The interpretation of πασπαλάδας has proven difficult. Etymologically, it is obviously related to πασπάλη, "fine flour"—but it is not obvious how. There is an added complication in the adjective with which they are described: Wagner (1874) and Tsiouni (1972) follow PV in adopting παραγεμισμένους, "stuffed," whereas Papathomopoulos (2002) goes with CLA in adopting παραμεμιγμένους, "mixed in," as a *lectio difficilior* (only the former survives in modern Greek—though CLA's participle recurs in verse 853 of all five manuscripts without its prefix).

Xanthoudidis (1927–28:358) identified πασπαλάδας with ὀμματιές, Cretan rice sausages (etymologically "blood sausages": αἱματίαι), because they are stuffed with barley groats. But Xanthoudidis's Cretan enthusiasm has had a poor track record, and the ὀμματιές that Nicholas has eaten, though stuffed, were not remarkably fatty. Besides, contrary to Xanthoudidis's gloss (χονδροκομμένα ἄλφιτα, "coarsely ground barley groats"), πασπάλη has been identified with *fine* flour since antiquity (Liddell–Scott–Jones 1940, s.v.).

Further information is provided by Koukoules (1947–55:5.62):

> Nowadays in Chalcidica, Karystos, Andros, Kyme, and Thera, πασπαλᾶς is the name of portions of pork boiled in fat and preserved in casks, elsewhere called σύγληνα. In Samos πασπαλιά or πασπάλη is simply the pork preserved and kept in a cask, probably named from πασπάλη or πασπαλιᾶ, flour fallen off the millstone, from which pigs are fed.
>
> That the medieval πασπαλᾶς would have been something like this, I have no doubt. So Xanthoudidis is incorrect in identifying stuffed πασπαλᾶς with blood sausage.
>
> What exactly is meant by stuffed πασπαλᾶς ⟨in Wagner's 1874 edition of the *Tale*⟩, I cannot say. Perhaps it means the delicacy made of flour and pork fat, now called πασπαρᾶς in Tinos, or that made of flour, stuffed with portions of pork or of bird entrails, as happens in Mani. Note in addition that in Karpathos πασπαρᾶς is the name of lamb and fowl stuffing.

We can add to this that in Aetolia and Acarnania, πασπαλᾶς is glossed as "small pieces of pork boiled with finely chopped leek and salt and pepper and preserved in fat" (HDMS 1041:530); similar mention is made in Geraki, in the Peloponnese, of "πασπαλᾶς with pig-dripping" (HDMS 889:273). This falls in line with the kinds of πασπαλᾶς described in Koukoules' first paragraph. The dish mentioned elsewhere in the Peloponnese, "a concoction from flour, oil, and water" (HDMS 785:247), sounds more like Koukoules' sweet from Tinos. In present-day Kasos (the island adjoining Karpathos), finally, πασπαράς refers to lamb stuffing (Sofos 1987:3.215): minced entrails, rice, onion, salt and pepper, raisins, and almonds.

If the "stuffed" reading holds (PV)—and this was the only reading available to him—then Koukoules' speculation in his third paragraph cited earlier seems appropriate: the transition from stuffed meat to stuffing, and the change in grammatical gender, is believable and would make the Maniot dish, involving pork stuffing in flour (batter?), the most plausible interpretation for the *Tale*. If we adopt "mixed in" (CLA) on the other hand, as Papathomopoulos (2002) does, the Aetolian dish is probably meant instead, and the meat is mixed with vegetables before being preserved (closer to Koukoules' first paragraph given). The πασπαλάδας obviously involve pieces of pork, and it is likelier for individual pieces of pork to be mixed into a kind of stew than for anything short of a suckling pig to be stuffed. Given how hard meat would have been to come by in general, we thus think the "mixed" reading, and the Aetolian dish, the likeliest interpretation here.

Šandrovskaja (1956a) uses the noncommittal **изделия**, "wares," whereas Tsiouni (1972) gives "pork meat boiled with fat, or simply cured, kept in an earthen cask."

381–82. **cook . . . add some of mine**. Koukoules (1947–55:5.53) claims this practice is also attested in *Timarion* §17, but this is not apparent in that text—although *Timarion* §31 does speak of a ζωμὸς . . . χοιρείᾳ πιμελῇ λιπαινόμενος, "broth . . . enriched with pig's fat," confirming that pig lard was used as flavoring.

The practice is attested explicitly in Agapios Landos's *Geoponicon* (*xvii* A.D.), though again involving pig fat rather than meat:

> Τό κρέας τοῦ λαγοῦ εἶναι ἀργοχώνευτον, γεννᾶ χοντρόν αἷμα, στύφει τήν κοιλίαν, φέρνει ἀυπνίαν, βλάπτει τούς μελαγχολικούς καί δείχνει κακά ὀνείρατα. Λοιπόν οἱ σπουδαῖοι μή τόν τρώγουσιν ἤ ἄς βάνουν καί λαρδί πολύ εἰς τό τσουκάλι νά ***συμψήνονται*** ἤ ἄλλο παχύ μέ σπλέτζες καί ἄλλα ἀρώματα, πλήν μόνον τόν χειμῶνα ἄς τόν τρώγουσιν οἱ αἱματώδεις καί νεώτεροι.
>
> [Hare meat is slow to digest, generates thick blood, causes stomach acidity, brings insomnia, harms the melancholic, and makes for bad dreams. So scholars should not eat it, or let them also put a lot of lard in the pot to ***cook with*** it or some other fat, with peppers and other spices; but let the young and the sanguine eat it only in winter.] (*Geoponicon* §79 [81])

Being Cretan, Landos uses ψήνω with the meaning "cook" rather than its mainstream Greek meaning, "roast" (see Commentary verse 252). However, as a flavor enhancer, pig lard—and pig meat even more so, as the boar says—would be far more effective in the pot than in the pan. In conjunction with the contrast between fresh (χλωρά) and ἐψημένα meats in 252, we conclude the poem uses the verb ψήνω consistently to mean "cook" rather than "roast."

386. ***Asperges***. In the Orthodox Church, the sprinkling of the congregation with holy water is a ritual reserved for special occasions (consecrations, major feast days) and is carried out using a sprig of basil. Its Catholic counterpart, *Asperges*, is part of the High Mass and (much to the Orthodox poet's disgust) is performed with a sprinkler made from pig bristles (Herbermann 2000 [1914], s.v. ASPERGES).

388. **wallow in the mires**. The expression βορβοροκύλισιν, "wallowing in the mires," would likely have already acquired by then the metaphorical meaning it has in contemporary Greek ("wallow in sin" via "mire of sin"); Lampe (1961) attests the latter as a metaphorical meaning of βόρβορος in such early church fathers as Clement of Alexandria:

> Οἱ δὲ σκωλήκων δίκην περὶ τέλματα καὶ ***βορβόρους***, τὰ ἡδονῆς ῥεύματα, καλινδούμενοι ἀνονήτους καὶ ἀνοήτους ἐκβόσκονται τρυφάς, ὑώδεις τινὲς ἄνθρωποι. Ὕες γάρ, φησίν, «ἥδονται βορβόρῳ» μᾶλλον ἢ καθαρῷ ὕδατι καὶ «ἐπὶ φορυτῷ μαργαίνουσιν» κατὰ Δημόκριτον.
>
> [And wallowing after the fashion of worms in swamps and ***mires***, the currents of pleasure, they graze on useless and foolish wantonness, being swinish men. For as they say, swine "enjoy the mire" rather than clean water and "lust for garbage" according to Democritus.] (*Protrepticus* 10.92.4)

For the metaphorical meaning in English, compare The Doors' "Light My Fire."

The stem βόρβορ-, "mire," which is also used with reference to the sheep in 414, the boar in 436, and the buffalo in 612, would have thus acquired a strong moral coloring, but it seems it remained in use in the vernacular in its literal meaning. Thus Kriaras (1968–97) cites Bishop Matthew of Myrae in his *History of Wallachia* (197–98) describing the corpse of Moyses Szekely (ruler of Transylvania, 1602–1604): νεκρός, γυμνὸς καὶ ἄθλιος, αἱματοκυλισμένος, / καὶ μέσα εἰς τὸν ***βόρβορον*** σὰν χοῖρος λασπωμένος, "dead, nude, and miserable; quite steeped in blood, / and in the ***mire*** all muddy like a pig." Furthermore, the *Vernacular Physiologus* (295) speaks of the *enhydros* as κυλίεται ςτὸν βόρβορον, "rolling in the mire." The *Chronicle of Makhairas*, a text not greatly indebted to classical Greek, gives even better evidence of survival: it uses the term in an unclassical neuter plural (βόρβορα, against the classical masculine singular βόρβορος), with no reference to swine or morality: καὶ 'διάβην ἀπουμέσα καὶ 'ποντίστην μὲ τὰ ***βόρβορα***, "And he wedged himself into the hole, and passed through the ***deep mud***" (§508). And in modern Greek dialect, βόρβορος is reported as surviving in various forms in Cyprus, the Pontus, Chalcidica in Macedonia, and Ainos in Thrace, all meaning "mud" (Andriotis 1974 §1513), whereas the related verb βορβορῶ, "to cast into the mud, to destroy" is reported from Crete (Andriotis 1974 §1515).

Of the four instances of the βόρβορ- stem in the *Tale*, this is the likeliest to have been used in the metaphorical, moralizing sense; see discussion in "Faith and Country." The survivals of the stem, however, indicate that it could have been used in the *Tale* quite neutrally, as a vernacularism.

391. **the thread**. The text has "placing a hair from me in the fathom" (ὀργυίαν). Hesseling (1924:310) thought the passage corrupt and preferred V's οὐρίαν, "urine" (?)/"tail" (?)—mentioning that pig hair, used to guide thread, is dipped in urine by saddle-makers to make it more flexible. (Recall the stiffness of boar hair in the Pontic Greek proverb cited in the Commentary to verse 54; the practice is also mentioned in the *Book of Birds* 289—see appendix 1.) Xanthoudidis (1927–28:360) counterargues that the P reading is correct, as the word ὀργυίαν was still in use in Greece, referring to linen thread used in such crafts—characteristically a "fathom" long (i.e., six feet). Koukoules (1947–55:2.1.215) adds that the "fathom" was waxed and used to pass through holes made by an awl. At any rate, the *Tale*'s is the only instance of ὀργ[υ]ία given in Kriaras 1968–97 referring to "thread" rather than "fathom."

394. **some thick** . . . The *Tale* uses the adjective *(i)psila* in three instances—394, 493, and 504—where it is ambiguous. The form as spelled in Tsiouni's 1972 and Papathomopoulos's 2002 editions, [ὑ]ψηλά, properly means "high, tall." Clearly, this makes little sense referring to paintbrushes or paintings, and a secondary sense of ὑψηλά needs to be brought up.

Tsiouni (1972:140, s.v. δεύτερον) was of the opinion that ὑψηλά, δεύτερα, and τρίτα here refer to grades of painting ("painting some fine, some second-grade, some third-grade"); she glosses ὑψηλά as "high-class." The division of wares into three grades was common in Byzantium; Koukoules (1947–55:4.399) quotes it in reference to shoes. However, we have judged it likelier that the poet refers to grades of paintbrush (rather than admitting that painters may paint third-grade paintings). Šandrovskaja (1956a) agrees in this and inserts after this verse the explanatory [кисточки], "small brushes."

An emendation that offers itself is the word for "fine" (applying to brushes), ψιλά; this reading was first suggested by Xanthoudidis (1927–28:360) and adopted by Šandrovskaja: **тонкие, средние и толстые,** "thin, medium, and thick." As it stands, the emendation cannot work: ψιλά is disyllabic, and the meter clearly requires a trisyllabic word, as is in fact displayed in all the manuscripts. However, at the time the poem was written, vernacular Greek was dropping initial unstressed vowels so that ὑψηλά was increasingly pronounced as ψηλά. It was possible for ψιλά (which has never had an initial vowel in Greek) to be hypercorrected to ὑψιλά as a counter to this tendency. The hypercorrection occurs uncontroversially in Oikonomu-Agorastu's fourteenth-century remedies (1982): κριθάλευρον ***ἰψιλόν,*** "***fine*** barley flour" (§213);

μαργαρίτας *ἰψιλούς*, ἀτρυπήτους κουκκία γ', "three unperforated ***small*** pearls" (§281); ἀγριομολόχην τρίψας τὰ φύλλα *ἰψιλά*, "grinding the leaves of the wild mallow ***finely***" (§301). Oikonomu-Agorastu glosses the word (which she spells phonetically) as *dünn*, "thin."

But the word ὑψηλά, "tall," itself could be metaphorically extended to mean "thick." Our best evidence for this comes from the *Tale* itself, where we argue for such an interpretation in 493 and 504 (see Commentary).

So the word *(i)psila* could mean either "thick" or "fine," and phonetics does not resolve the issue. The co-occurrence in the text of δεύτερα and τρίτα, "second, third," also does not resolve it. Koukoules (1947–55:2.1.225) refers to icon painters beginning their painting with an outline:

> As for painters and icon painters, we know that they used their paintbrush, ending in pig bristles ⟨*Entertaining Tale of Quadrupeds* 392⟩ to sketch the image they would paint at first with ochre, drawing white outlines, which they corrected on a second or third pass, placing the colors finally.

This suggests a "first" brush being coarser than the "second" and "third," corrective brushes. In contemporary icon-painting practice likewise, the "first" brush is the broadest, for large surfaces, the "second" is broad on one side and fine on the other, for painting flesh, and the "third" is very fine, for facial details (Lambrini Thoma, personal communication). A broad first brush would contradict *(i)psila* = "fine." Although readily applicable to a thick carpet (493), whose thickness is its height, "tall" seems forced for a thick brush. But its use to describe thick cassocks (504) is rather closer to the meaning we propose here. In all, it seems likeliest that the second brush is finer than the first and that in icon painting the order of using the brushes was what mattered. Thus, *(i)psila* in this instance can mean neither high quality (Tsiouni 1972) nor "fine" (Xanthoudidis 1927–28, Šandrovskaja 1956a) but rather "thick," consistent with verse 504.

401. **magnates.** μεγιστᾶν, "magnate," is a postclassical word; it is first attested in Menander (fragment 1035) and the Septuagint (forty-four times). In the New Testament, it shows up in Revelations (6:15, 18:23), where it is translated in the King James version as "great men."

The term could be used in Byzantium to refer to a senator; Christofilopoulou (1949:25–30) gives instances from the chroniclers George Monachus (*Chronicon* 2.645, 778) and the Continuator of George Monachus (766). However, the word was not intrinsically associated with aristocracy (Revelations 18:23: ὅτι οἱ ἔμποροί σου ἦσαν οἱ ***μεγιστᾶνες*** τῆς γῆς, "for thy merchants were the ***great men*** of the earth")—even though it is predominantly so used in the Septuagint, and μεγιστᾶν could easily denote the nobility of foreign nations (e.g., *Digenes* P 400: Διότις οἱ ***μεγιστάνοι*** καὶ ὅλοι οἱ σατράπαι ἔστελλάν τον χαρίσματα, "for the ***magnates*** and all the satraps ⟨Arab overlords⟩ sent him gifts"). The word is unglossed in Tsiouni 1972; Šandrovskaja (1956a) renders it as вельмож, вельможи, "grandees," in 401 and 500, and as магнаты, магнатов, "magnates," in 550, 567.

403. **bookbinders**. Although the Italian loan word σκούφια normally means "cap" in Greek, the σκουφάδες here are not hat makers, as Tsiouni (1972), Šandrovskaja (1956a) (шляпочники) and Koukoules (1947–55:2.1.215) have presumed, but bookbinders, and σκούφια in the next verse refers to book covers (the "caps" of books). There is only one other known instance of σκούφια used in this manner in Greek writing (Karanastassis, in preparation), but the sense is clear from context.

404. **to polish** . . . This practice was also extant in the West: Clanchy (1979:90) cites a twelfth-century English work including among the tools of the scribe "the boar or goat's tooth for polishing the surface to stop the ink running."

419. **boar**. Here and in 443, the text uses the synonym μοχθηρόν instead of χοῖρος. As established by other medieval texts and modern dialect (see note to verse 54), this clearly denotes a boar, rather than having the literal meaning "malicious, wicked" given by Tsiouni (1972). (See also the discussion in Legrand 1875:107–8.) Šandrovskaja (1956a) correctly translates the word as свиньи. Occasionally in medieval Greek the term was used to refer to donkeys instead (Schreiner 1991:466, so glossed also in Du Cange 1958 [1688]), but this has no bearing on our text.

424. **The Jew stinks** . . . This proverb survived into the twentieth century (Politis 1902:4.635) and also turns up in the *Book of Birds,* with reference to the pelican's pouch (καὶ ἀποθηκάριν τοῦ Μωσὲ γεμάτον σκυλινέαν, "⟨You⟩ satchel of Moshe's full of dog turds" [55]). Tsiouni (1972:28) does not comment further other than to say that Jews "were known as shopkeepers in Byzantium, as the above line indicates." But the proverb cannot be explained by mere Jewish shopkeeping, and in the context of the *Tale* a clear connection is made with feces. Likewise, neither editor of the *Book of Birds* seems aware of where the association comes from: Tsavare (1987:324) speaks of "a sarcastic allusion to the greed of the Jews, who hoarded in their storehouses whatever they found (even 'dog turds'), or to their storehouses, which smelled badly," whereas Krawczynski (1960:42–43) says "here the poet refers to Jewish storehouses, in which Jews piled up anything they could get hold of which might bring them profit."

However, the association clearly (and much more straightforwardly) originated in the practice of the exclusively Jewish tanners of late Byzantine Constantinople (Bowman 1985:21–24) collecting dog feces as material required in their profession. Until the early 1900s bating (the process of lowering the alkalinity of skins and making them pliable) was done using pigeon, hen, or dog dung. As was also the case in the West, Jews took on professions regarded as taboo to Christians—though their association with tanning did not commence until the Comnenan dynasty (Sharf 1995b:69). Benjamin of Tudela, who visited Constantinople in the 1160s, confirms how the stigmatized profession brought the Jewish community into disrepute:

> They live under heavy oppression, and there is much hatred against them which is engendered by the tanners, the workers in leather, who pour out their dirty water in the streets before the doors of their houses and defile the Jewish quarter. So the Greeks hate the Jews, good and bad alike, and subject them to severe restrictions and beat them in the streets and force them to hard labor. Yet the Jews are rich and good, kindly and charitable, and cheerfully bear the burden of their oppression. (Bowman 1985:335)

The Ottoman Constantinopolitan tanners, now Muslim (their Jewish colleagues having been expelled from Constantinople proper to Hasköy: von Hammer 1968 [1834]:1.2.41), are discussed in similar terms by the seventeenth-century traveler Evliyâ Çelebi:

> The offensive smell prevents great people from taking up their abode here; but the inhabitants are so accustomed to it, that if any person perfumed with musk approaches them they feel annoyed. They are wealthy people, a blessing they owe to the saint of tanners, Saint Ahurán, who one day having excrements in his apron, was asked what he had got; when, actuated by false shame, he replied "Money,"—and money it was. To the recollection of this miracle the tanners owe their wealth. (von Hammer 1968 [1834]:1.2.29–30)

> These tanners are a set of wild fellows, and men-dragons; who, if a criminal, or bloodstained villain takes refuge amongst them, refuse to deliver him up to justice, but they do not let him escape, but put him to the business of turning up dog's dirt, an occupation which causes him to repent of former crimes and to amend his life afterwards. (von Hammer 1968 [1834]:1.2.206)

As a reference to a tanner gathering dog dung, θήκη is likelier to refer to "satchel" than "storehouse"—notwithstanding ἀποθηκάριν in the corresponding instance in the *Book of Birds* being glossed by both Krawczynski (1960) and Tsavare (1987) as "storehouse" and Tsiouni (1972) glossing θήκη as "shop." There is Byzantine precedent for using θήκη to mean "storehouse" (*Digenes* Z 1225–28: Καὶ ὁ λαὸς τοῦ ἀμηρᾶ ἔφθασαν εἰς τὸ κάστρον, / . . . καὶ ἔβαλον τὰ πράγματα ἔνδοθεν εἰς τὰς ***θήκας*** / καὶ τὰ φαρία ἔθεντο εἰς τοὺς μεγάλους στάβλους, "And the emir's people arrived at the fort; and they put their things inside in the ***stores***, and they placed the steeds in the great stables"—corresponding to *Digenes* E's [600/601] καὶ ἔβαλαν τὸ πράγμα εἰς τὸ σπίτιν του, "they put the things in his house"). Likewise, the evidence at the *Historical Dictionary of Modern Greek* archives suggests the word in modern dialect means "storehouse" rather than "satchel." However, the primary use of θήκη given by Kriaras (1968–97, s.v., 1) was to denote a container rather than a building; thus, in *Panoria* 2.554, it denotes a scabbard (Βάλε στὴ ***θήκη*** τὸ σπαθί, "Put the sword in its ***case***"), consistent with standard modern Greek usage.

Note that in the example from *Digenes*, θήκη could mean "shelf" or "storeroom" rather than "storehouse." Accordingly, Šandrovskaja (1956a) rendered the word as ящик, "box."

We wish to thank Tassos Karanastassis for his insights on this note.

430. **her mouth** . . . The use of the verb "to shit" to indicate contempt is commonplace in modern Greek:

> [On an exhibition about the atomic bomb planned by the Smithsonian Museum, which was to point out that the Hiroshima and Nagasaki bombs were not a military necessity:]
>
> ShkwOhkane oi beteranoi, oi repoumplikanoi, oi stratiwtikoi, ki ena swro alloi na ta koukoulwsoune. ***Xesane*** tous istorikous, ***xesane*** kai to Smithsonian pou tolmouse na amfisbhthsei dhmosia thn anagkaiothta twn mpompwn.
>
> [Σηκωθήκανε οι βετεράνοι, οι ρεπουμπλικάνοι, οι στρατιωτικοί, κι ένα σωρό άλλοι να τα κουκουλώσουνε. ***Χέσανε*** τους ιστορικούς, ***χέσανε*** και το Smithsonian που τολμούσε να αμφισβητήσει δημόσια την αναγκαιότητα των μπομπών.]
>
> [The veterans, the Republicans, the military, and a host of others rose in an uproar, seeking to cover it up. They ***shat*** on the historians, and they ***shat*** on the Smithsonian, which dared dispute in public the necessity of the bombs.] (Yiannis Koutalos, re Re: Purauloi kai mpompes; Hellas mailing list, bit.listserv.hellas, December 5, 1996.)

However, the use of a direct object, indicating the object of contempt, is obligatory in modern Greek, and the same holds with the other medieval Greek scatological text, the *Mass of the Beardless Man*: the verb χέζω is frequent in the given meaning but always occurs with an object; for example, Ἐὰν μὴ ἅπαντες / ***χέσωμεν τοὺς σπανέας***, / δὲν θέλουν βγάλει γένια / καὶ ἀιλὶ ὤχ τὰ μάγουλά τους, "Unless all of us ***shit on the beardless men***, they shall not get beards, and woe to their cheeks!" (D 268–71). So the instance in the *Tale,* which lacks an object, is grammatically problematic.

The medial past form of the verb "to shit," χέστηκα, "I shat myself," is used in modern Greek as an expression of indifference (cf. English *I don't give a shit*). This has the advantage of not requiring a direct object, but the usage is not attested in medieval Greek to our knowledge. It is likelier that the *Tale*'s usage, employing the verb in the active voice, is the same as in the *Mass* and the Hellas mailing list, though with the sheep as only an implicit object of contempt.

Another possibility is that what comes out of the sheep's mouth is so foul (either literally its breath or figuratively its words) that the other animals defecate in order to emulate it. A third possibility (suggested to us by Nikos Sarantakos) is that the other animals defecated into the "philosopher's" open mouth as an expression of contempt.

433. **blood-brother**. The Byzantine institution of fraternization (ἀδελφοποιτός) was well established (Kazhdan 1991, s.v. ADELPHOPOIIA) and has generated debate recently on whether it was a form of legitimizing homosexual relationships (Boswell 1994; Rapp 1997). The custom—which had an associated church ritual—persisted into modern times in Greece and Albania (βλάμης; *vllam*) before falling afoul of the spirit of modernization. In fact, as Evliyâ Çelebi reports, in border regions like Ottoman Bosnia it was common for captives to become blood-brothers with their captors, "exchanging religions," and to pledge to protect each other's lives or else suffer damnation as apostates (Dankoff 1991:249–51).

Tsiouni (1972) glosses the word with the approximate "close friend"; Šandrovskaja's (1956a) собрат, "colleague" is likewise somewhat off.

446. **finest flour**. Compare *Aelian* 10.16:

> Ἡ ὗς καὶ τῶν ἰδίων τέκνων ὑπὸ τῆς λαιμαργίας ἀφειδῶς ἔχει, καὶ μέντοι καὶ ἀνθρώπου σώματι ἐντυχοῦσα οὐκ ἀπέχεται, ἀλλ' ἐσθίει, "The pig in sheer gluttony spares not even its own young, and if it comes across a man's body it does not refrain from eating it."

There is no reason to doubt the author of the *Tale* is speaking from observation rather than alluding to written sources. Rowland (1973:37–38) refers to several instances as late as the nineteenth century of pigs eating human flesh—with a predilection to ears.

458. **to offend us thus**. See appendix 3 on the ostensible inconsistency here.

486. **violet**. It is clear from contemporary texts that "purple" is to be preferred for ὀξέα (literally "sharp") over Tsiouni's "bright" (1972), the ancient meaning of ὀξύς as a color term:

> ἔπεψέν τους δύο κομμάτια παννὶν κοττένον σκαρλάτον, τὸ ἕναν τῆς τάμου Τζουάνας Λ' Ἀλεμὰν καὶ τὸ ἄλλον τῆς τάμου Τζίβας τε Σκαντελίου, ***ὀξὺν*** φίνον, "He sent them two pieces of scarlet cotton stuff, one to the Lady Joanna L'Aleman and the other to the Lady Echive de Scandelion, fine ***purple*** cloth." (*Chronicle of Makhairas* §245)

(See also Kriaras 1968–97, s.v.; Trapp 1976.) The Byzantine meaning is recorded in Du Cange (1958 [1688], s.v.) as *violaceus;* Koukoules (1947–55:2.1.186, 2.2.37) speaks of it as "deep red." The sense had also survived in early modern Greek, with Somavera (1977 [1709], s.v.) defining it as *paonazzo, pavonazzo, di color violato,* "purple, violet"; Andriotis (1974 §4425) reports this as surviving in modern times only in Karpathos as ἀξύς, "red." Šandrovskaja (1956a) likewise has фиолетовый, "violet."

489. **sundry pretty forms**. εἴδη καὶ θεωρίας, "items and decorations." Although the latter noun is the same word as English *theory*, its primary meaning in medieval Greek, inherited from classical Greek, is "view" or "appearance" (thus also in modern Greek θωριά.) The meaning "theory" originated from

“view”; the meaning “decoration” came about through the transition “view” (Kriaras 1968–97, s.v., 1a) > “appearance” (2a) > “good appearance, beauty” (2b) > “decoration” and is paralleled in the *Efforts and Studies* (*Κόποι καὶ Διατριβή*) of Archbishop Arsenius, 870–71 (cited from Kriaras): Ετέραν ***θεωρίαν*** τε ουκ είχεν ουδεμία, / χρυσίον ούτε κόκκινον ουδέ στιγμή τε μίαν, “⟨The queen⟩ had not a single ***decoration***; / not gold, not scarlet—not a single speck.”

The dialectal instances of the word attested at the *Historical Dictionary of Modern Greek* archives and Andriotis (1974 §2774) mean only “appearance”; this extension of the meaning of the word has thus not survived into the modern language. Šandrovskaja (1956a) renders the phrase as **виды и фигуры,** “views and figures,” and Tsiouni (1972) glosses the words as “thing” and “a thing beautiful to look at,” respectively.

492. **others of their rank**. The owners of the curtains described here are explicitly Westerners. See discussion in “Place of Composition.”

493. **thick**. As with 394, the interpretation of [ὑ]ψηλά is difficult. The ambiguity is not with ψιλά, “fine,” as this would be incongruous for πεύχια and σάκτια, the two types of carpet named in the manuscripts (see the following discussion). We thus reject the reading “fine,” although it was adopted by Šandrovskaja (1956a) (**тонкие**), presumably by analogy with 394. The clash is rather between the two secondary meanings of ψηλά: “tall” > “thick” and “high” > “high-class.” Unlike in 394, Tsiouni (1972) explicitly glosses ψηλά here as “high” rather than “high-class,” thus adopting the “thick” interpretation.

The use of “high” to refer to “noble” was commonplace in late Byzantium:

Belisariad Λ 292: ἐκ τὴν γενιὰν τὴν ***ὑψηλὴν*** θαρρῶν ἀπιλογήθην, “boldened by his ***high*** lineage, he responded”

Belisariad Λ 540: ὡς ἔχων αἷμαν ***ὑψηλὸν*** καὶ ἀπὸ γενιᾶς μεγάλης, “as one who has ***high*** blood and noble lineage”

Account of Famed Venice 15: πολλά ’τον μέγας καὶ ***’ψηλὸς*** καὶ ’πεικασμένος ἄρχων, “He was a great, ***high*** noble, marveled at”

Furthermore, the adjective that ψηλά is conjoined with in the *Tale*, μεγαλοπλουμάτα, “richly decorated,” also refers to quality rather than thickness. Nevertheless, it is hard to believe that the author did not intend—and his readers did not understand—“tall” here to refer to the primary meaning of [ὑ]ψηλά, namely, the more concrete quality of height associated with expensive carpets. This is also supported by our interpretation of verse 504.

493. **carpets**. P and Papathomopoulos (2002) have here σάκτια, which Ševčenko (1974:78) interprets as “prayer rugs.” The fact that sultan and emirs are seated (κάθεται) on these rugs—a posture which by no means could constitute a misunderstanding of Muslims kneeling to pray—makes it doubtful that prayer rugs specifically are meant by the word, whatever the word’s provenance.

Nicholas Prevezianos, for instance, lists in his account book in mid-fourteenth-century Chalcidica:

> ἔχω ὀκτῶ ***σακτιν*** (καὶ) ἀπανωσκέπ(ασμα) (καὶ) πτερνηστήρ(ια) αργυρα, καπούτζιν, (καὶ) ταμπάρ(ιον) στρογγυλ(ὸν), καμουχᾶν, "I have eight ***σάκτια*** and covers and silver spurs, a hood and a round cloak, and woven silk" (Schreiner 1991:87)

—all plausibly the possessions of a rich Byzantine nobleman. The association of the rugs with Muslim nobility probably has more to do with the renown of Muslim carpet making in both Persia and Anatolia.

The word (which is far from a hapax legomenon; see Schreiner 1991:104 for other instances) has caused previous scholars much trouble. Schreiner himself admits he had mistranslated it as "mantle" in an edition of Theodore Meletiniotes. Hesseling (1924:311) and Šandrovskaja (1956a:245) reject this "unknown" word in favor of CVLA's πεύχια. The word σάκτιν is not included in Tsiouni's glossary (1972) and is also conspicuous by its absence in the commentaries by Koukoules (1911–12) and Xanthoudidis (1911–12, 1927–28). We have been unable to identify a foreign source word for σάκτιον. Eideneier (1977) does not include it among the loanwords in the *Mass of the Beardless Man* and instead concludes that its usage there (B 109; see Eideneier 1977:320) exploits the ancient stem σαγ- so that the term is presumably cognate to σάγμα, "covering, cloak, saddle"; σάττω, "to pack, to load"; and σάκτας, "sack." Koukoules (1947–55:2.2.71) reports σάκτα meant "stuffing," from classical σακτός, "crammed, stuffed," and the kind of carpet alluded to must have something to do with this.

The CVLA tradition and Tsiouni (1972) have the word πεύχια, "carpets" (Koukoules 1947–55:2.2.73, 74, 85), which, although etymologically related to "prayer" (πεύχιν < ἐπεύχιον < ἐπί, "on" + εὐχή, "prayer, blessing"—the Continuators of Theophanes 319 explicitly assert this etymology), is likewise not inherently Muslim or otherwise religious in reference. Constantine VII Porphyrogennetus (*De cerimoniis* 465ff.) mentions their use at the imperial table; the *Belisariad* (χ 285, Λ 414) has the emperor order them spread in the streets for the general's triumphal march. Koukoules (1947–55:2.2.85) considers this simply the vernacular word for "carpet," in which sense it survives in Cyprus and Castellorizo, and Somavera (1977 [1709]) likewise glosses πέφκι as χαλί: *tapetto,* "carpet." Echoing the *Tale*'s usage, the instance in *Acts of Docheiariou* 49.9 (dated 1384) is defined by Oikonomidès (1984:261) as "a kind of carpet on which one lay down" and occurs in a listing of items belonging to the petitioner's bedroom effects. Likewise, *Acts of Lavra* 22 (dated 1017) contains a reference to κρεβατοστρώσιν ἤτοὶ επέυχιν, "a bed-covering, namely, an ἐπεύχιν." The *Tale* likewise goes on to imply that it is the σάκτια/πεύχια specifically, rather than wool in general, that people use for bedding (496).

495. **Greeks and Westerners**. See "Wording."

503. **gray clothes**. The word γρίζα properly means "gray clothes" (Tsiouni 1972: "grey garments") rather than "ecclesiastical clothes." Compare the following receipt written in the Greek community of Venice in 1470, where the word does not even refer to gray clothing but to gray cloth:

> ἠγόρασα τὸν Μαστρομαστθαῖον τετραβαγγελον διὰ λίτρ(ας) ι΄. χρεωστεῖ με τα: ὀφείλει ἐξ αὐτῶν τὰ ἔδωκ(εν) διὰ τ(ὴν) κυρ(ὰν) εἰς τὸ ***γρίζο***. τὸ κόπτει διὰ τὸν Πέτρ(ον) σκαπύτζ(ι)ν(ον) εἰς μπράτζα ε΄ (καὶ) τρεῖς κάρτας, τὸ μπράτζον λίτρ(αν) α΄, λίτρ(ας) ε΄ κ(αὶ) σόλδ(ια) ιε΄
>
> [I bought a Gospel book for Master Matthew for ten lire; he owes me it. He owes from it what he paid the lady for the ***gray material*** [*den grauen Stoff*]. He cut for Peter a piece of cloth (?) five and three-quarters ells long, at one lira an ell, which makes five lire and fifteen soldi.] (Schreiner 1991:109)

However, the context makes it clear that γρίζα are thought of as church clothes—as is confirmed by P substituting it with ῥάσι, "cassocks." What is not as clear is whether γρίζα is being used as a synonym for ῥάση, "cassocks," in the next verse—though P clearly thought it was.

Šandrovskaja's (1956a) **части одежды**, "thick clothes," seems to us unwarranted—even if she is translating P's ῥάσι, "cassocks, cloaks" (see the discussion following).

504. **thick**. A hypercorrect ὑψιλά, "fine, thin," as proposed for verse 394, could be considered here—particularly as the passage is reminiscent of *Ptochoprodromos* 1.59, where Eideneier (1991) emends τὸ ὑψηλὸν διβίκιν, "the tall [thick, high-class] blouse," to τὸ ψιλὸν διβίκιν, "the thin blouse." However, such a reading should be ruled out: ῥάσον, "cassock; coarse woolen clothing," has never referred to a thin garment, particularly if woven with serge, and verse 503 specifically refers to thicker wool. Tsiouni (1972) considers ὑψηλά here to mean "high-class," and though the ῥάσον was originally coarse, this is not impossible, given the use of serge and the author's concentration on an affluent urban clergy rather than peasant parishes. However, the other clerical garments listed are not praised any more effusively, and the sense "thick" is hard to avoid in light of the preceding verse ("out of coarser wool are gray clothes made"). Šandrovskaja's (1956a) **высокие**, "tall; superior" presumably uses the literal meaning "tall/long," which appears to us misplaced.

504. **cassocks**. Tsiouni (1972) glosses ῥάσον as "garment." The term originally refers to coarse wool. Its primary meaning in modern Greek is "cassock" (already attested in a church accounts book around 1328: Schreiner 1991:463). There are dialectal instances where it refers to a shepherd's cloak (Γι̯ὰ φέρε μου τὸ ***ράσομ*** μου, γι̯ατὶ κρυ̯αίνω, "bring me my ***cloak***, I'm getting cold": Vrakades, Icaria, HDMS 1224:119; Ὅποιους ἀγαπάει τοὺν ἄσσου πάει στοὺ σπίτι δίχους ***ράσου,*** "whoever loves the Ace ⟨playing cards⟩ goes home without

a ***cloak***": Pelion, HDMS 1089:9)—and this is the interpretation Xanthoudidis (1927–28:361) gave to the instance in the *Tale*. Given the following verses, however, the ecclesiastical gloss "cassock" is a reasonable choice—particularly as talk of laypeople's wool is delayed until verse 509. (On the history of ῥάσον, see Kahane and Kahane 1966:314–15.)

506. **metropolitans**. Tsiouni (1972) glosses μητροπολεπισκόπων as "metropolitan bishop," but Trapp (1976) sees here a dvandva compound, "metropolitan and bishop," and the term is broken up into two nouns in P (μητροπολιτῶν καὶ ἐπισκόπων, "of metropolitans and bishops") and V (ἐπισκόπων μητροπολίτων, "of metropolitan bishops").

508. **nuns**. For a description of Byzantine monastic clothing, see Koukoules 1947–55:6.102–3.

511. **covers**. Tsiouni (1972) glosses κέντουκλον as "a woolen saddle cloth partly colored," and the word derives from the Latin *centunculum,* "saddle cloth." Eideneier (1976:459) glosses κέντουκλον as "cover," after an edict by Diocletian, and Byzantine usage of κέντουκλον and its variant κεντούκλα applies it to any clothing or covering made from coarse wool or felt:

> κεράδες χειρομάχισσες, καλοοικοδέσποινές μου,
> προκύψετε, βηλαρικὰς ἐπάρετε ***κεντούκλας***
>
> [My handy housewives, my fair homemakers,
> peer out, and buy these woven ***covers***.] (*Ptochoprodromos* 4.190–91)

Koukoules (1947–55:2.2.23–24) defines it as "coarse fabric from the coarsest, shortest wool and the leftovers from carding, pressed and woven together. . . . With such fabric the poor made clothes for everyday use"—consistent with verse 509.

Though the κέντουκλον was part of the Byzantine soldier's armor (Kolias 1988:54–55), its use in the *Tale* in conjunction with δρομάχια, literally "sweat fighters," makes it refer to the horse—as was in fact more usual for κέντουκλον in Byzantine military writing, according to Kolias. The δρομάχιν thus would be closest to the horse's flesh, then the κέντουκλον as a cover, then the saddle, then the φέλεθρον, "saddle felt" (see Du Cange 1958 [1688], s.v. ἀφέλεθρον; < Latin *filtrum* < Germanic—cf. Old High German *filz*)—placed over the saddle.

512. **the wide-brimmed hats of state, the fur caps, the gold-embroidered caps**. The καπάσιν was a wide-brimmed hat worn by Byzantine dignitaries both civilian and ecclesiastical, including patriarchs and emperors. (It is what the rebel sky-lark is crowned with in the *Book of Birds*: see appendix 1.)

The other two pieces of headgear mentioned are Islamic in origin. The ζαρκούλιν (τζαρκούλια V; elsewhere in medieval Greek ζαρκουλᾶς: *Ducas* 21.12) (*zerqulā*) was a felt cap with a conical top embroidered in gold and associated in particular with the Janissary troops (*Ducas* 23.9; Du Cange 1958 [1688], s.v. ζαρκουλᾶς; Moravcsik 1956:2.120). The *Mirror of Women* (557–58) says that a hat makes a woman "look like a great big Turk / wearing a ***zarkoula***" (καὶ φαίνεται ὡσὰν Τούρκαρος, / ὁποῦ φορεῖ τὸν *ζαρκουλᾶ*). Ducas (23.9) describes the cap as follows:

> Τὸ γνωριστικὸν δὲ σημείωμα τούτων τὸ τῆς κεφαλῆς κάλυμμα, ὃ κατὰ τὴν κοινὴν γλῶτταν Ῥωμαῖοι ζαρκολᾶν λέγουσι· καὶ γὰρ κοινῇ πάντες Τοῦρκοι τὸ αὐτὸ χρῶντες ὡς κεφαλῆς περιβόλαιον, οἱ μὲν πάντες, ὅσοι ἐξ ἰδιωτῶν καὶ ἐξ εὐγενῶν τυγχάνουσι, κοκκινοβαφὲς τοῦτο χρῶνται, ὅσοι δὲ τῶν ἀλλογενῶν τῷ τῆς δουλείας ὑπέπεσον ζυγῷ γραφέντες δοῦλοι τοῦ ἀρχηγοῦ, οὗτοι λευκόχροα φοροῦσι τὰ τῆς κεφαλῆς περιβόλαια ἐκ πίλου λευκοτάτου, ἡμισφαιρές, ὅσον χωρεῖν κεφαλή, ἔχον περιττεῦον ἄνωθεν τῆς κορυφῆς, ὅσον καὶ σπιθαμῆς εἰς ὀξὺ καταλῆγον.
>
> [The identifying feature of these ⟨the Janissaries⟩ is their headgear, which the Greeks in the vernacular call *zarkola*. For all Turks use the same cap on their head. Any private citizen or nobleman has it dyed red, but those of outside origin who have fallen into the yoke of slavery and have been enrolled as slaves to the sultan ⟨i.e., Janissaries⟩ wear their caps white from whitest felt, hemispherical for as much as fits on the head, with a leftover part above the top up to a span long and a pointed ending.]

Grecu (1958:151), in his edition of *Ducas,* renders the *zerqulā* as "fez," but contemporary pictures of Janissaries show a much taller hat, with a pronounced cone. Du Cange (1958 [1688], s.v.) renders ζαρκουλᾶς as "a *circle,* or a band attached to the head, wrapped as a circle; commonly, *turban.*" But the contemporary witnesses he cites (Bullialdus—the astronomer Ismaël Bouillau, who wrote a translation and commentary on Ducas in 1649—and Leunclavius—Johannes Löwenklau, who wrote *History of the Turks* with a glossary in 1591) are clearly discussing the same headgear as Ducas. Du Cange's conflation with "turban" presumably results from the Ottoman habit of wrapping caps inside turbans (Jirousek 1995:24; Pallis 1951:75).

The *börk,* which was the distinctive headgear of the Janissaries by the sixteenth century (Jirousek 1995:29; Wratislaw 1862:4) seems unrelated: it had a flattened rather than conical top, with the back and front drawn together and a long plume hanging down. But Evliyâ Çelebi presumably has something like the *zerqulā* in mind when he reports in the 1630s that recruits to the Janissary corps are invested "with caps of red felt, which resemble the night-caps of Karagoz (the merry fellow in the Chinese shades)" (von Hammer 1968 [1834]:1.2.210; the hero of Turkish shadow puppetry *Karagöz*, Greek *Karagiozis*). And Çelebi speaks of *börk*-makers ("Burk-makers") as a guild distinct from the guild making felt caps for the Janissaries (von Hammer 1968 [1834]:1.2.207).

The σαρπούζιν (σαρπούζια [PC]; τζαρπούτζια [V]; τζαρπούζια [L]; σάρπουτζία [A]) is even more difficult to pin down and is not mentioned in

Moravcsik's compendium (1956) of Turkish loanwords into Byzantine Greek. The first candidate is the *sharbūsh* (Mayer 1952:27–28), the normal headgear of the military aristocracy in Egypt under the Bahri Mameluk dynasty (1250–1382); it was abolished by the Circassian Mameluk dynasty. This appears to have been a stiff cap with a triangular front, trimmed with fur. The *sharbūsh* was so characteristic of a Muslim knight that even a crusader is reported as being prepared to wear it as a friendly gesture to Saladin. Clerics, by contrast, wore turbans (*'imâma*), and a contemporary source reports of a cleric receiving military rank that "he was forced to leave the *'imâma* and wear a *sharbûsh*" (Mayer 1952:54).

The second candidate is the Turkish *serpuş*. This is derived from Persian *serpuš,* "head cover," and its dominant use in Turkish is to mean just "headgear." The word is so used in Kumbaracılar (1979) and Sevin (1973), both historical surveys of Turkish headgear, where it includes such heterogeneous items as *Yabancı Sefir Serpuşu,* "foreign ambassador headgear" (Kumbaracılar 1979:28—a rather typical eighteenth-century West European hat), and *Soytarı Serpuşu,* "clown hat" (29—a black cap with forked sides). (Neither source makes any mention of the *zerqulā*, speaking exclusively of the *börk*; they may have imposed unified terminology in their accounts.)

Although *serpuş* is glossed vaguely as "headgear" in most Turkish dictionaries, Kieffer and Bianchi (1835–37, s.v. SERPOCH) offer "calotte worn by Turkish women," and Thomson (1944, s.v. SERPUŞ), "calotte, skullcap (of priests), headgear." (The calotte is a close, round, brimless cap; the skullcap was worn by high-ranking clergy in Ottoman times as well [Pallis 1951:75], though enclosed in the obligatory turban.) If the word ever referred to a distinct piece of headgear, it would certainly not have been restricted to the military. For instance, the *serpuş* of the thirteenth-century Sufi mystic Shams al-Dîn Tabrîzî is reported displayed at the mausoleum of his disciple Mevlânâ Jalal-e-Din Rumi in Konya (el-Fers [1993:72]—although Seal [1995:187] mentions the *sikke*, a tall dervish cap, used in this function instead).

The military *sharbūsh* matches better the *Tale*'s overall tendency to speak of Muslims only in terms of their nobility and military, and the date would allow for the *sharbūsh*, still in use at the time the *Tale* was presumably authored. Although one might at first expect the *Tale* to refer more readily to Turkish than Egyptian artifacts, the modest *serpuş* does not seem like a promising candidate. Admittedly, the *zerqulā,* with which the σαρπούζιν is mentioned, is an unambiguously Turkish cap; there is no mention of anything like the *zerqulā* in Mayer's survey (1952) of Mameluk costume. But whereas the *zerqulā* recurs in Greek writing, the σαρπούζιν is never heard of again after the *Tale.* This would be odd if it referred to a contemporary generic Turkish cap, but it makes sense if it refers to an Egyptian cap that passed out of use quite early (1382). So, on the available evidence we are inclined to identify the σαρπούζιν with the Egyptian *sharbūsh*. This may allow a concrete *terminus ante quo* for the poem; see "Date of Composition."

The only instance known to us where the word may have survived in use in Greek is in Kozani in Macedonia, where σαρπόσ' refers to "a woolen cloth stuck to the rear part of the saddle to protect from cold" (HDMS 615:24). Although the material is right, the author is clearly not speaking of saddle cloths here. Perhaps this was a metaphorical extension of the original "skullcap" (a loan from Turkish is likeliest) to "something that fits like a skullcap."

It is unlikely that σαρπούζιν represents the *tarboosh*, presumed the Arabic version of the Persian *serpuš*, and the Middle Eastern counterpart to the fez (or in the seventeenth century [*tarpuş*] a tall pointed woman's cap out of silver brocade: Scarce 1987:53, 55–57). It is worth noting, finally, that the *Tale* does not mention the turban (Byzantine Greek φακιόλιν), the ubiquitous Turkish headgear worn by the majority of the population and by common soldiers and peasants in particular (Jirousek 1995:26). The peasant turban was—and remains, as Seal (1995:113) reports of clandestine continuing use in Turkey—little more than a wrapped scarf. The hats the *Tale* is describing in this verse are more artfully put together, and the sheep would be entitled to take greater pride in them.

515. **loafers**. The word used is παπούτζια < Turkish *pabuç*, "shoe" < Persian *babuč,* which Tsiouni (1972) and Šandrovskaja gloss as "shoe" (башмаков). The word is in modern Greek the generic word for "shoe," and this was certainly the case already in the sixteenth century, when *Bertoldo* (a Venetian chapbook and a translation from Italian) contained the line Ὅποιος σπέρνει τά ἀκάνθια, ἄς μήν περιπατεῖ χωρίς ***παπούτσια***, "Whoever sows thistles should not walk without ***shoes***" (22).

It is not as obvious that this was already the meaning of the word παπούτζια in the fourteenth century. The first instance in which the stem is mentioned, according to Koukoules (1947–55:4.398–99), is the twelfth century, when John Tzetzes (*Chiliads* 11.369.221) speaks of a newly appointed court orator as πετρομαχασκοπάπουτσον τζαγγάριον, ξυλοσούβλων, "wearing ⟨shoes⟩ with a gaping (χάσκων) front sole ⟨πετρομάχιον, "stone fighter"⟩, a cobbler, a wooden awl ⟨user?⟩." (The interpretation is Koukoules'; the work's editor, Kiessling (1963 [1826]), was unable to decipher the word.) We cannot judge from this whether the target of Tzetzes' ridicule was wearing generic shoes or specifically Muslim shoes, although this does seem to be an accusation of poverty, which makes an exotic allusion less likely. The next group of attestations, however, all from the thirteenth to fifteenth centuries, are quite ambiguous:

> Τὸ δικαίωμαν τῶν ***παπουτζίων*** τῶν ἀγοράζουν οἱ Σαρακηνοὶ, ἐντέχεται νὰ δώσουν τέλος τὸ δέκατον, "For the right to import [***shoes***] that the Saracens buy, they are taxed one-tenth." (*Assizes of Cyprus* 241, ca. 1250)

> φοροῦσι . . . ἔτι τε καὶ κάλτζας τοιαύτας, μετὰ ***παπουτζίων*** μαύρων, "They also wear such socks, with black [***shoes***]." (Description of the *cortinarii*, the emperor's tent servants) (*Pseudo-Codinus* 181, ca. 1340)

Προετοιμάζουσι πτωχοὺς δώδεκα, καὶ ἐνδύουσι τούτους ὑποκάμισα, κουρτζουβάκια καὶ ***παπούτζια***, "They prepare twelve paupers, and they dress them in shirts, breeches, and [***shoes***]." (Preparations for the ceremony of the emperor washing feet in commemoration of Maundy Thursday) (*Pseudo-Codinus* 228)

Φοροῦν στιβάνια τραγικὰ ὡσὰν εἶν' μαθημένοι,
παπούτζια καὶ γουνέλλες των, φοροῦν καμαρωμένοι
[They wear their goatskin boots, as is their wont;
they wear their [***shoes***] and coats, as proud as punch.] (Referring to Cretan villagers' parties)
(*Sachlikis: Strange Narrative* 188–89, ca. 1370)

διατ' ἦτον ἀξυπόλυτη κ' οὐδὲν εἶχε ***παπούτζια***
[For she was barefoot and she had no [***shoes***].] (referring to a Candia prostitute)
(*Sachlikis: Counsels* 2:507)

Καὶ θωρῶντα τον ὁ καραβοκύρης μὲ τὰ ***παπούγκια*** κατζούφτερνα, εἶπεν του· "Ἄμε 'ς τὸ καλόν· καὶ εἶνε ἀντροπὴ νὰ συντύχω μετά σου," "And when the captain of the ship saw him with his [***shoes***] trodden down at the heels, he said to him: 'Go about your business; it is a shame for me to be speaking to you'" (referring to a Nestorian Christian in Famagusta; the Nestorians had fled the Muslims from Syria) (*Chronide of Makhairas* §95, ca. 1432; in his glossary, however, Dawkins translates the word as "slippers").

In the *Assizes of Cyprus,* παπούτζια are still associated with Muslims. Already by the time of Sachlikis, they are associated with Orthodox commoners, although one passage identifies them with women, which is consistent with slippers. In *Pseudo-Codinus,* the shoes appear to be luxury items—there would be no point having paupers put them on otherwise (contrary to Tzetzes' allusion.) And in the rarefied atmosphere of the court, Pseudo-Codinus's παπούτζια could easily be slippers (although the work's editor, Verpeaux, translates them as *souliers,* "shoes"). Dawkins also vacillates in his rendering in Makhairas; as the Nestorians were Syrians, however, they might be expected to wear "Oriental" footwear.

The behavior of other Balkan languages is also illuminating. In both Turkish and Greek, the word is completely generic and includes shoes worn outside the house. In fact, Greek and Turkish share the expression "to hand someone his shoes" meaning "to dismiss someone" (του 'δωσα τα παπούτσια στο χέρι; *pabuçu eline vermek*: Papadopoulos 1953:51; Sarantakos 1997:204; Alderson and İz 1984, s.v. PABUÇ)—because guests would take their shoes off on entering a house, and put them on again on leaving. In fact, the Turkish word *pabuççu* (Alderson and İz 1984, s.v.) does not mean only "shoemaker," like its Greek equivalent παπουτσής, but also "attendant looking after peoples' shoes at a mosque, etc."

In the other Balkan languages, however, the Turkish loanword has not come to denote shoes in general but a particular kind of shoe: a slipper, associated specifically with women or with indoor use—that is, the particular kind of footwear imported from Turkey. (The sense "slipper" is maintained in Turkish itself, because Alderson and İz gloss *pabuç* as "shoe, slipper," but "slipper" in Greek is only παντόφλα—see note on **corkwood slippers** following.) Thus:

- In Bulgarian, dictionaries vacillate between the generic and specific senses: Stefanov (1914, s.v. папуци) has "woman's slippers"; Atanasova et al. (1980, s.v. папук) have "shoe"; and Chakalov, Ljakov, and Stankov (1961, s.v. папук) have "shoe; slipper."
- Similar vacillation appears in Romanian: Leviţchi (1960, s.v. PAPUC) has "slipper, mule; (generally) shoe," and Bantaş (1995 [1993], s.v. PAPUC) likewise has "slipper; shoe." (In Romanian, it is *pantof* < παντόφλα that is the truly generic word for "shoe.")
- In Macedonian Slavonic, Koneski's (1961–66, s.v. папук) dictionary has "(archaic) kind of shoe"—though given Koneski's role as a language planner, the "archaic" comment is presumably prescriptive.
- In Serbian and Croatian, the word is routinely glossed as "slipper" (Drvodelić 1953, s.v. PAPUČA [Croatian]; Grujić 1977, s.v. PAPUČA [Serbo-Croat]). In fact, the dictionary of the Serbian Academy (Stevanović 1967–71, s.v. папуча) explicitly glosses it as "a sort of light shoe that is worn only in the house."
- In Albanian (Newmark 1998, s.v. PAPUÇE), the word is glossed as "light woolen slipper worn in the house."
- In Hungarian (Országh 1953, s.v. PAPUCS), the word is glossed as "slipper; scuff, baboosh; mule."
- Finally, the association of the word with women's slippers is underlined by the presence of the expression "under the slipper," meaning "henpecked," in Hungarian (*papucs alatt van*), Romanian (*sub papuc; a fi sub papucul nevestei*), and Serbian and Croatian (*on je pod papučom*). Because that association is absent in Greek and Turkish, the equivalent expressions κάτω από το παπούτσι and *pabuç altında* would not make any sense.

Although in Turkish and Greek the term is now generic, referring to any footwear, it seems that the further one moves from Turkey, the more the term is associated with a particular type of shoe originally specific to the Turks. This would have also been the case when the word was first introduced into Greek.

As Sachlikis shows, παπούτζιν was not necessarily a *Turkish* shoe by the time the *Tale* was written, but it was likely still a specific kind of shoe, as is the case with the modern cognates north of Greece. This would also make sense in the context of a listing such as the *Tale*'s, where it is differentiated from the other types of footwear mentioned, and is unlikely to subsume them as the generic term "shoe." We have used *loafers*, accordingly, as a term for the kind of shoe probably involved.

515. **sandals**. No one has been able to this day to work out what a κλῶστρα is; the word does not appear anywhere else in Byzantine literature. Tsiouni (1972) has the guess "a kind of shoe (?)," and Šandrovskaja (1956a) admits defeat and does not translate the word. Xanthoudidis (1927–28:362) wonders whether the word has even been transmitted correctly in the manuscripts. The word seems to be etymologically related to κλώθω, "weave." In modern Greek dialects, κλῶστρα means things such as "spindle" and "woven cloth" though never "shoe": Cyprus κλῶστρος, "woven"; Imbros κλουστρός, "twisted"; Rhodes κλωστρός, "twisted, wrapped"; Calabria (Bova) *klóstra,* "thread; ball of wool; binding rope; bundle of wheat or barley"; Bithynia, Crete κλῶστρα, "weaver"; Zante κλώστρης, "a kind of spindle"; Epirus (Kokkinia, Grevena), Macedonia (Drymos, Thessalonica) κλώστρης, "spindle" (also Somavera 1977 [1709]: κλώστρια, κλώστρα: *filatrice, filatoia,* "spinning wheel"); Pontus κλῶστρα, "whetting stone (which twists around)." (Words from the archives of the *Historical Dictionary of Modern Greek.*)

We have guessed that it refers here to a type of sandal whose straps are made of woven ("twisted") wool. Trapp (1976:446) interprets it as *Schafwoll-schuhe (Filzschuhe)*—a shoe from wool, that is, felt, but the notion of weaving does not indicate felt to us. Koukoules (1947–55:4.401–2) likewise interprets the κλῶστρα as involving straps:

> Shoes, in accordance with their use, also had straps, with which they were fastened to the lower part of the foot or the shin, which were called ἱμαντάρια or with the Latin word κορρίγια (*corrigia*), to which may be added ζινίχια; such are the σπαρτία mentioned in a hagiographic text and the κλῶστρα mentioned in the *Entertaining Tale of Quadrupeds,* because the Greeks of Bova in Calabria call κλώστραν the strap with which something is bound, namely, originally something woven, twisted.

515. **boots**. The ὑπόδημα was the original generic term for footwear (Koukoules 1947–55:4.398), displaced in Greek by παπούτζιν. As its etymology shows ("under-tied"), it was itself originally a sandal, and Šandrovskaja (1956a) accordingly translates it as сандалий, "sandals." However, Koukoules (1947–55:4.410) argues that in Byzantium ὑπόδημα was used synonymously with τζάγγα, "boot" (see Commentary verse 794), based on both modern Greek dialect (also Somavera 1977 [1709], s.v. τζαγκί) and references in military manuals:

> ἐχέτωσαν δέ, εἰ μὲν δυνατόν, καὶ ***ὑποδήματα*** κοντά, διπλᾶ μέχρι τῶν γονάτων, εἴτε καὶ μονοπλὰ μέχρι τῶν μηρῶν, "If possible, let

them ⟨the foot-soldiers⟩ also have short ***footwear*** folded up to the knees or unfolded up to the thighs" (*Phocas: Praecepta Militaria* 1.20–22; as McGeer [1995:62, 205] and Kolias [1988:72–73] both explain, these denote boots combined with protective leggings, and elsewhere McGeer refers to ὑποδήματα as "boots").

Moreover, it would be odd for boots to be absent from this listing of footwear. That is the interpretation we have given the word here.

515. **corkwood slippers**. The word used here, φελλάρια < φελλός, "cork," survived in modern times in Macedonia, Thrace, Crete, and Bithynia (Koukoules 1947–55:4.416; Andriotis 1974 §6305, §6306) as a generic term for "slippers," and φελλός itself is glossed by Somavera (1977 [1709]) as γόβα, κοντούρα, μοῦλα: *pianella, pantoflo,* "mule, slipper." (The generic word in standard Greek, παντόφλα, is itself derived from earlier παντόφελλος, "all-cork," or possibly πατόφελλος, "cork-bottom": Andriotis 1983, s.v.) Šandrovskaja (1956a) accordingly translates φελλάρια as туфель, "slippers," whereas Tsiouni (1972) gives "cork-soled shoe," citing Sachlikis's use of φελλός;

> κι ὅποιος νὰ τὴν κρατῇ κρυφὴν βιάζεται νὰ τὴν παίρνῃ,
> ροῦχα καὶ μπόταις καὶ ***φελλοὺς*** καὶ ψούνια νὰ τὴν φέρνῃ
>
> [who keeps her ⟨a whore⟩ secretly hastens to buy her
> and bring her clothes and boots and ***mules*** and goods.] (*Counsels* 1.342–43)

524. **humble**. On the ambiguity of ταπεινός, see note to verse 125. The context here ("never dares look up" and the proverbial meekness of the sheep) weighs in favor of "humble," the dominant vernacular meaning of the word. Šandrovskaja's (1956a) малодушная, "faint-hearted," seems out of place; though ταπεινός was associated in antiquity with "submissive" (e.g., *Xenophon: Hiero* 5.4: ἐνδεεστέροις γὰρ οὖσι ***ταπεινοτέροις*** αὐτοῖς οἴονται χρῆσθαι, "for the needier the people, the ***humbler*** he thinks to find them"), Šandrovskaja's gloss is without precedent. The original meaning of ταπεινός, "low in physical stature," is even unlikelier here, as it would display higher learning than we have come to expect of the *Tale*. Although the meaning "wretch" so prominent in the *Life of St. Symeon the Fool* is more promising merely by virtue of being invective, the sheep looking down seems to us to indicate "humble" instead.

536. **fluff**. In classical Greek, the στοιβ- stem meant either "pile, heap" or "stuffing, padding" (Liddell–Scott–Jones 1940, s.v. στοιβάζω). In modern Greek, στοιβάζω means either "pile, heap up" or "cram, pack in"; the latter is an obvious generalization from "stuffing" and is unambiguously present in *Alexander Romance* ρ (published in 1529): ἐκεῖνοι ***ἐστοιβάκτησαν*** κ' ἐκλείσασι τὸν δρόμον, "They ***crammed together*** and closed off the road" (339). The "packing" sense was also present in medieval Greek: Du Cange 1958 [1688], s.v., glosses στοιβάζω as *accomodare,* ἁρμόζεσθαι, "to fit."

A similar use of στοιβάζω turns up in *Ptochoprodromos* 1.97: κάμνω ὑποκαμισόβρακα, ***στιβάζω*** τὸ βαμβάκιν, which Eideneier (1991) translates as *die Unterwäsche web ich selbst und **häufe auf** die Wolle,* "I weave the underwear myself and ***pile*** the wool [cotton] up." Housewives in Byzantium had to make their own clothes, and that is what Ptochoprodromos's aristocratic wife is bemoaning. What business a housewife had piling up (packing?) cotton, though, is not clear. And the problem with both interpretations for the *Tale* is that although one can both pile and pack wool or cotton, neither action has an obvious relation with cords.

There is in fact a third sense of στοιβάζω that has entered modern Greek but is not typically listed in Greek dictionaries: "fluffing." Fluffing wool and cotton to rid them of impurities is necessary for further processing them into textiles, and fluffing woolen and cotton processed textiles—clothing, blankets, and so forth—is necessary to maintain their quality. The latter, in particular, would be a commonplace household chore, so it is plausible for *Ptochoprodromos* to refer to it in this context. Until recently, this task was undertaken in Greece by a professional, a στοιβαχτής (in Cyprus a δοξαρᾶς), who would fluff cloth by twanging a bow against it (Tassos Karanastassis and Andrew Nicholas, personal communication). The same practice is clearly being alluded to here.

The semantic progression is "pile up cloth" > "make cloth fluffy (like it is piled up)" > "strike cloth to fluff it (by twanging)" > "strike." This "striking" sense is arguably present in the *Mass of the Beardless Man* A 313, which menaces the Beardless Man by saying that Παῖδες μὲ ραβδία καὶ ματσούκας γυρεύουσί σε, οὔριε, διὰ νὰ σὲ ***στοιβάσουν***, "Lads with sticks and clubs seek you, outcast, to [***strike***] you." This may be a sexual allusion ("'cram' you with their clubs"); two lines above, the text speaks of "the donkey's dick, on which he always sits," so that allusion wouldn't require much of a mental leap. But it seems likelier that all that is meant is "strike repeatedly." (The comparable example from *Mirror of Women* 813–14, καὶ ἀπὸ πίσω τὴν ***στιβάζει*** / καὶ καλά της τὴν ἐμπάζει, "and he [***crams***] her from behind / and sticks it well in her," is unambiguously sexual, but that sense could still be satisfied by an analogy to striking rather than filling.)

The term was also applied to the related process of carding, whereby wool fibers are straightened with a comb to prepare them for spinning. Thus, the Cretan accountant Manolis Varoukhas, listing various cotton household effects in a 1613 appraisal, ends with μπαμπάκι λητραις στ′ ***αστίβακτο***, υπερπυρα ιδ′, "six liters of ***uncarded*** wool, worth fourteen *hyperpyra*" (Varoukhas §852; the editors gloss the word as ποὺ δὲν ἔχει ***ξανθεῖ***, "which has not been ***carded***"). But the reference to the cords makes it unlikely that carding is meant here.

A further alternative, implicit in the spelling Hesseling and Pernot (1910) used in their earlier edition of *Ptochoprodromos*, is "bleach." In classical Greek, στιβεύς referred to someone who processes or whitens cloth; in modern Pontic Greek (Papadopoulos 1961, s.v. στιβίζω), the reflexes of that word, στιβίω and στιφίζω, refer to spreading cloth at the seaside and washing it in seawater to whiten it (see also Andriotis 1974 §5563, §5564). But again this does not explain the cords of the preceding verse ("into the cords / with which they fluff their wool and cotton, too") as satisfactorily as fluffing does, so we need not pursue it any further.

The word is unglossed by Tsiouni (1972); Šandrovskaja (1956a) has **связывают**, "bind," which is, of course, the most plausible thing to use cords for with wool and cotton, but nothing suggests στοιβάζω (or στιβάζω) ever had that sense.

558. **obscure**. Although the meaning of ἄτιμος in modern Greek is "dishonorable; scoundrel" and this meaning is old (Kriaras 1968–97, s.v. ἄτιμος, has examples from *The Rod of the Archpriests* and Defaranas *Instructive Words,* both *xvi* A.D.), the main meaning of the word was its original sense "unhonored," "of little account." Compare Theodore Prodromus, *To the Sebastocratorissa* 117 (cited from Kriaras): καθάπερ σκεῦος ***ἄτιμον ἀτίμως*** ἀπερρίφθην, "Just like a ***worthless*** vessel, I'm discarded, ***unworthily***"; Soummakis, *Pastor Fide* 4.1246 (cited from Kriaras): ζῆσε πάντα σ' ***ἄτιμος*** καὶ δόξης στερεμένε, "Live forever ***unhonored*** and deprived of glory." This interpretation harmonizes better with the preceding verse, amounting to its restatement. The ambiguity seems to have persisted: Somavera (1977 [1709], s.v.) glosses the word as *dishonorato, inhonorato, dishonorevole,* "dishonored, unhonored, dishonorable."

Tsiouni (1972) does not gloss the word because it is also classical (e.g., Sophocles *Oedipus at Colonus* 51: σήμαινε, κοὐκ' ***ἄτιμος*** ἔκ γ' ἐμοῦ φανεῖ, "Tell me, and you will not be ***without honor*** from me"); Šandrovskaja (1956a) has **презираемый,** "scorned," which reads too much into the term.

559. **brave and cowardly**. The words used, ἀνδρειωμένος and ἄνανδρος, are based on the stem ἄνδρ-, "man": the former literally means "manned" and the latter, "unmanly." The stem recurs often in the poem: 576a, 856, 869, 870, 957, 959, 1048, and 1065.

The dominant meaning of the words in medieval Greek are "brave" and "cowardly," the notion of "virile" being associated with "bravery." This is the only meaning that survives in modern Greek. However, there are indications of a secondary medieval meaning for the ἄνδρ- stem, "physically strong." (In classical Greek, this meaning seems to have applied only to inanimates, as a metaphorical usage, e.g., *Eupolis* 148: λαφύσσεται λαφυγμὸν ***ἀνδρεῖον*** πάνυ, "he eats gluttonously, with a most ***brave*** appetite": Liddell–Scott–Jones 1940, s.v. ἀνδρεῖος, II.3.) Although Kriaras (1968–97) attests only the meaning "cowardly" for ἄνανδρος in the vernacular, the word in *Ducas* 39.12 clearly means "weak":

> Ἀναβλέψαντες δὲ ὁρῶσι Τούρκους. Ἰδόντες δὲ εἰς φυγὴν ἔνδον ἐτράπησαν. Καὶ μὴ δυνάμενοι εἰσελθεῖν διὰ τῆς πύλης τῆς ἐπονομαζομένης Χαρσοῦ, στενοχωρούμενοι διὰ τὸ πλῆθος, οἱ μὲν ἀλκὴν περισσοτέραν ἔχοντες τοὺς ***ἀνάνδρους*** καταπατοῦντες εἰσήρχοντο.

[Looking up, they saw Turks. And on seeing them, they fled inside. Unable to enter through the gate called Charsos, and pressed by the throng, those with greater strength trod on the ***weaker*** and got in.]

Similarly, the verb ἀνδρειώνω/ἀνδρειοῦμαι/ἀνδρειεύω, of which ἀνδρειωμένος is a past participle, has the secondary meanings "increase; strengthen" (Kriaras 1968–97, s.v. ἀνδρειεύω; ἀνδρειοῦμαι; ἀνδρειώνω); for example, *Belisariad* Λ 55: ὅσον νὰ δράμῃ ἄλογον καλόν, ***ἀνδρειωμένον,*** "so that a good, ***strong*** horse may run"; *Erotokritos* 1.317: Κ' ἡ ἀγάπη, ποὺ στὰ βάσανα ***ἀντρεύγει*** καὶ πληθαίνει, "love that ***strengthens*** and grows plentiful through woe." So the words can mean either "strong/weak" or "brave/cowardly" and need to be resolved case by case.

In two cases, "brave/cowardly" is unambiguously meant: in 1048 and 1065, the horse and dog are obviously urging courage, not strength, on the herbivores. In another two, "weak/strong" are just as clear. In 957, the elephant is clearly weak in his predicament of being felled; his bravery is irrelevant to his inability to escape. In 959, likewise, the monkey is responding to the elephant's claims of might; the elephant has made no claims of bravery, but he has called himself "robust" (907), so "strong" must be meant there.

The remaining cases (576a, 856, 869–70) are discussed in their respective commentaries. In this instance, we have no clear arguments to resolve it one way or the other, because both "brave/cowardly" and "strong/weak" fit equally well in context ("great/small" [557], "honored/obscure" [558]), so we have stuck with "brave and cowardly," as the more frequent meaning of the words in medieval Greek. (See also Textual Notes verse 576.)

Tsiouni (1972) does not gloss the adjectives. Šandrovskaja (1956a) consistently translates the words in the poem in terms of bravery and cowardice (even with the elephant: **как немощного труса,** "as an impotent coward" [957], **очень мужественное,** "very courageous" [959]); she was presumably unaware of the secondary meaning of the stem.

571. **offscourings**. The word used here (in all manuscripts) and in 971 (P only) is παραπτώματα, literally "fallings beside." This word first appeared in Koine, in Polybius, Diodorus Siculus, and the Septuagint: it meant "blunder," "defeat," and "transgression" (Liddell–Scott–Jones 1940, s.v., 1, 2, 3—compare *falling off the wagon*). The latter is the meaning featured in both the Septuagint and the New Testament (e.g., Matthew 6:14: ἐὰν γὰρ ἀφῆτε τοῖς ἀνθρώποις τὰ ***παραπτώματα*** αὐτῶν, ἀφήσει καὶ ὑμῖν ὁ Πατὴρ ὑμῶν ὁ οὐράνιος, "for if ye forgive men their ***trespasses***, your heavenly Father will also forgive you"). Inevitably, this is the meaning that prevailed in medieval Greek (Lampe 1961, s.v.), and with the exception of the orator Sopater using it in the fourth century to refer to defeats of the Thebans (Διαίρεσις Ζητημάτων 207), almost all Christian-era usage of the term we have sighted in the *Thesaurus Linguae Graecae* (2002) corpus has been moralistic in tenor, influenced by its biblical usage. (Sopater himself is traditionally identified with the pagan orator that Constan-

tine the Great is said to have executed in order to prove his Christian bona fides.) Accordingly, Šandrovskaja (1956a) translated the noun as грешники, "sinners," in 571. (In 971, she follows CVL's reading instead: с нашей средины, "out of our way.")

But παράπτωμα means "a falling aside," not "a faller aside," so the shift from action to agent that Šandrovskaja proposes is peculiar. The only other instance of which we know in medieval Greek (learned or vernacular) where παράπτωμα might mean anything different from "transgression" is regrettably too obscure to be of much help; it is from Meletius's *De natura hominis* (§26; *ix* A.D.), in a discussion of the derivation of names for the penis:

> ψωλὴ δὲ, παρὰ τὸ ἐμφυσάσθαι κατὰ τὴν ὄρεξιν τῶν ἀφροδισίων· καὶ ὅτι φυσῶδες φύσει ***παράπτωμα*** ἐστίν, "and it is called *ψωλή* because it inflates during venereal excitement and because it is an inflatable ***παράπτωμα*** by nature ⟨?⟩."

Although Meletius was a monk as well as a medical author, his discussion is quite dispassionate, and there is no reason to think παράπτωμα here means "something involved in transgression." We cannot rule out textual corruption in the passage: the second phrase appears in only one out of the two manuscripts of the work.

It seems unlikely that the *Tale*'s author is thinking of the small animals and the monkey (971) as "transgressions." And given that both the ox, here, and the elephant (971) rail on their adversaries' insignificance and poor hygiene, it seems peculiar for them to be speaking of transgressors. What we suspect has happened here is that the author is not using παράπτωμα in its accepted sense.

Originally παράπτωμα was the classical nominalization of the verb παραπίπτω, "fall beside." This verb had a range of meanings in antiquity, including "befall," "flatter," and "go astray" (Liddell–Scott–Jones 1940, s.v.); παραπέφτω survives in modern Greek in the sense "to be mislaid, to get lost," and Glycas (1158–59) used it in the sense "to go astray, to err," as in *Prison Verses* 270: Ἡ παπαδιὰ ***παρέπεσεν***, ἐξύβρισε τὴν κοίτην, "The priest's wife ***has gone astray***; she has dishonored their bed." (We thank Tassos Karanastassis for the reference.) The author had enough education to have heard the word παράπτωμα and to have realized that it corresponds to the verb παραπίπτω/παραπέφτω (the vernacular nominalization would have been παραπέσιμον). Whether through ignorance or design, we believe, he connected παράπτωμα to the verb instead of following its established use. In this context, it is likeliest he used the literal meaning of παραπίπτω rather than the moralizing sense to which Glycas appeals: a παράπτωμα would have been something that falls aside or something that gets mislaid—in other words, rubbish. So Tsiouni (1972) was correct to reject the conventional sense of παράπτωμα and gloss it as "something unworthy that should be thrown away."

Interestingly, the author seems to have serendipitously returned to the earlier nonmoralizing usage of the word, comparable perhaps to the precept attributed to Secundus (*Sentententiae* 13; *ii* A.D.), who defined a gladiator as Τύχης παράπτωμα, "Fate's refuse."

571. **The hell with you**. ἀποσκορακίζω < ἀπό, "from, away" + classical σκορακίζω < ἐς κόρακας, "to the crows," the classical equivalent of "to hell" (in Liddell–Scott–Jones 1940, s.v. κόραξ, "go and be hanged") and an expletive much beloved of Aristophanes. Thus, ἀποσκορακιστῆτε corresponds, as Eideneier (1976:459) points out, not to Tsiouni's gloss "get lost" but to "go to hell"—though it would be pedantic to argue the strength of the English rendering of classical Greek invective embedded in a vernacular medieval Greek text. Šandrovskaja (1956a) has **проваливайте**, "get lost"—a rather strong expression in literary Russian.

This is the only instance of the word attested in vernacular medieval literature; the other instance Kriaras (1968–97) cites is in a letter by the scholar Nicephorus Blemmydes, which cannot properly be counted as vernacular. However, the word is to be found in the Septuagint, though perhaps not used as forcefully as in Aristophanes:

> βοηθός μου γενοῦ, μὴ ***ἀποσκορακίσῃς*** με καὶ μὴ ἐγκαταλείπῃς με, ὁ θεὸς ὁ σωτήρ μου, "thou hast been my help; ***leave*** me not, neither forsake me, O God of my salvation" (Psalms 26:9)

> ὡς ὕδωρ πολὺ ἔθνη πολλά, ὡς ὕδατος πολλοῦ βίᾳ καταφερομένου· καὶ ***ἀποσκορακιεῖ*** αὐτὸν καὶ πόρρω αὐτὸν διώξεται, "The nations shall rush like the rushing of many waters: but God shall ***rebuke*** them, and they shall flee far off" (Isaiah 17:13)

The word was glossed in Byzantine dictionaries (*George Choeroboscus: Epimerismi in Psalmos* 137; *Etymologicum Gudianum*; *Etymologicum Magnum*; *Hesychius*; *Lexica Segueriana: Collectio verborum utilium*; *Photius*; *Suda*; *Pseudo-Zonaras*), so it does not seem to have been vernacular. It has survived in Mani in the Peloponnese (Andriotis 1974 §1048), but a single archaic modern dialect is not enough to establish widespread earlier usage. Still, turning up as it does in Psalms, ἀποσκορακίζω would have been a word any Byzantine at school would have learned early.

576a. **weak-limbed and powerless**. Of the two adjectives, κακόχειρα literally means "ill-handed"; the word is not attested elsewhere in Greek. The classical antonym εὔχειρ, "good-handed = dexterous," would suggest the meaning "clumsy"; but it makes more sense in the context of the ox's belittlements to characterize the smaller animals as weak limbed rather than clumsy. In fact, the behavior of κακο- in Kriaras (1968–97) actually suggests "ugly-limbed" (κακόδοντος, "bad-toothed = ugly-toothed" [*Tale* 425]; κακομούσουδος, "ill-faced"; κακομούσουρος, "ill-faced"; κακομούστακος, "ill-moustached"; κακομύτης "ill-nosed"; κακότριχος, "ill-haired"; κακογένης, "ill-bearded = having a weak [or ugly?] beard"). But as invective, "ugly-limbed" makes little sense here.

Both words used in this verse are ambiguous (κακόχειρα: "weak-handed," "ugly-handed," "clumsy-handed"; ἄνανδρα: "cowardly," "weak"). The use of ἄνανδρα here, however, suggests weakness rather than ugliness or cowardice (on which see Commentary verse 559): the ox, as mentioned, describes the smaller animals as "ill-fated," "despised," and "puny" (576), to which 576a has already added κακόχειρα as well as ἄνανδρα. And because κακόχειρα and ἄνανδρα are likeliest to be meant as synonyms, we should pick for both the sense they have in common, which is weakness. We thus render ἄνανδρα as "powerless."

Somavera (1977 [1709], s.v.) includes in his dictionary κακοχερικόν: *cattivo principio,* "inauspicious beginning." Now, κακοχερικόν (literally "ill-handedness") is derived from κακόχειρος, "ill-handed," just as ποδαρικό, "luck," is derived from πόδι, "foot" (alluding to entering a house with the right foot as an auspicious omen). So there is a possibility that κακόχειρος meant "ill-fated" rather than "ill-footed." (Compare, for example, the Cretan custom of καλή χέρα, "good hand," whereby children are given money by their adult relatives on New Year's Day.) This would make κακόχειρος a synonym of κακορρίζικα, "doomed," in the verse before, and κακότυχα, "ill-fated," in the verse after. (The closest parallel to κακόχειρος in Kriaras 1968–97, κακοπόδαρος, literally "ill-footed," means not "ugly-footed" or "weak-footed" at all but "ill-fated"; compare καλοπόδαρος, "good-footed = lucky," also in Kriaras.) But we have no independent evidence of κακόχειρος ever having been used this way, and it is safe to assume that whenever the author could make a synonym pair, he did. Neither of the two possible meanings of ἄνανδρα could be a synonym of "ill-fated," so we retain the literal reading "weak-limbed."

588. **get past your lips**. ἐξεχειλίσῃς, literally "[push] out from the lips." The normal meaning in modern Greek is "spill over" (past the lips = brim of a vessel), so already in Somavera (1977 [1709], s.v. ξεχειλίζω): *sgorgare, straboccare, traboccare, riboccare, sboccare, spandersi l'acqua, ò simili,* "overflow, spill, of water and such." But there is precedent for the meaning "utter" in the *Byzantine Iliad* 688–89 (καὶ ποιὸς τὸ πρῶτον νὰ τὸ πῇ καὶ νὰ τὸ ***ξεχειλίσῃ*** / νὰ φανερώσῃ τὴν ἀρχὴν τοῦ ἔρωτος τὴν τρῶσιν, "who'll be the first to speak and ***utter*** it / and to reveal the onset of Love's gnawing"), and there are occasional parallels in modern Greek dialect (Patmos, HDMS 690:248: τίς ἔχει στόμα νὰ σοῦ πῇ νὰ σοῦ τὸ ***ξεχειλίσῃ***, "who has a mouth to tell and ***utter*** it to you"; Kozani, HDMS 613:39: ξεχλιάζω: συνδιαλέγομαι, "converse").

594. **in all assignments**. The buffalo is not mentioned as a farm animal in Byzantine reference works (e.g., Kazhdan 1991). However, there is good evidence for its use. Schreiner (1991:145, 198) records two mentions in financial transactions of buffalo, the former from the first half of the fourteenth century—though the purpose to which they were put (whether agricultural or dietary) is not clear. The use of the buffalo in farmwork, especially in demanding tasks, is attested in contemporary censuses from the monasteries of Iviron and Hagia Lavra in Mount Athos (Angeliki Laiou, personal communication). For instance,

Acts of Lavra 109 (dated 1321) contains several mentions of agricultural buffalo; these are discussed in the same terms as cattle, either ploughing (ζευγάρια, "[yoked] pairs") or grazing (ἀργά, "idle"). Thus, Eudocia, the widow of Xenos Lemnaios in the village of Loroton, has "two pairs, of which one are buffalo" (109.108). Most buffalo mentioned in that census are from Loroton and almost always as the second pair of cattle owned by a household; of the ninety-six cattle (ζευγάρια, βοΐδια) from the village, twenty-four are buffalo.

Compare also Manuel Philes' testimony (*Poems* 1.191.55–60):

> Πλὴν οὐδ' ἐφικτὸν ἐκ νομῆς βουβαλλίδα
> Μόνην προελθεῖν εἰς νομὴν ἀλλοτρίαν,
> Εἰ μή τις αὐτὴν ἢ παραζεύξας λάβοι
> (Τὸ σύννομον γὰρ εὐμενὲς τῷ συννόμῳ),
> Ἢ δίφρον εὑρὼν ἐκ τροχῶν εἰργασμένον,
> Καὶ τινὰ βαλὼν τοῖς σφυροῖς ποδοστράβην

> [A buffalo will not go from one pasture
> alone into another one, however—
> unless one either yokes it to another
> (for fellow-grazer favors fellow-grazer)
> or finds a chariot-board that's wrought with wheels
> and places there a snare to trap its ankles.]

Buffaloes continued to be used for agriculture and milk around Ottoman Constantinople, as attested by Evliyâ Çelebi's description of a procession of guilds in 1638:

> The peasants pass with rude sandals on their feet, coarse cloaks (*abbá*), and headdresses framed of wire in different forms. They lead bulls, oxen, and buffaloes with gilt horns, and silken saddle cloths and covers, yoked together, and carry in their hands the implements of agriculture. They drive the buffaloes as if they were ploughing and sowing, and say: "The seed comes from me, the blessing from Thee! give it, O God, give it." (von Hammer 1968 [1834]:1.2.119)

> The Milkmen of buffaloes (*Sújián Shúreh*) are a thousand men, with two hundred shops. . . . They milk the buffalo-cows, and pass, crying: "Who buys buffalo-milk." They have fine fat cattle. (von Hammer 1968 [1834]:1.2.142)

To this day, Hatzis's patisserie in Thessalonica advertises its use of buffalo milk, taken from one of the last buffalo herds in Greece.

601. **cabbage**. In classical Greek λάχανα referred generically to "greens," and it is so glossed by Tsiouni (1972) ("vegetables, greens"). In standard modern Greek, however, it is the normal word for "cabbage" (greens are now the adjectival λαχανικά), and Šandrovskaja (1956a) translates it accordingly as ка-

пустой. Kriaras (1968–97) also glosses medieval λάχανον simply as modern λάχανο, "cabbage."

But the older meaning of λάχανο was slow in dying. Apart from the compounds that have survived in the modern language (λαχανικά, "greens"; λαχαναγορά, "vegetable market"; λαχανόκηπος, "vegetable garden"), Koukoules (1947–55) mentions the Byzantine ἀγριολάχανον/λεπτολάχανον, "wild λάχανον," of which mallow is an instance (5.89), and χρυσολάχανον, "gold λάχανον" (5.91), which he considers "of the same nature" as spinach and beets (*Ptochoprodromos* 2.41; Eideneier [1991] glosses χρυσολάχανον as *Gartenmelde,* "orache"). Ambiguity is also apparent in Pseudo-Zonaras's thirteenth-century dictionary. On the one hand he glosses the classical κράμβη, "cabbage," as λάχανον (used by Koukoules [1947–55:5.93] as evidence to identify λάχανον as cabbage; compare the *Book of Fruit*'s Lord Κραμπολάχανος [2.39], combining κράμβη and λάχανον). But Pseudo-Zonaras also glosses several instances of greens as kinds of λάχανον: ἀδράφαξις; ἄνθρησκα; ἄσσαρ; βλίτον, "blite"; βουπρῆστις, "similar to mustard"; βράκανα, "wild herbs" (according to Liddell–Scott–Jones 1940); γηθυλλὴς, "similar to the leek"; σκάνδιξ, "chervil" (*Pseudo-Zonaras,* s.v. διασκανδικίσας); θύμβρον, "savory"; ἰφίη, "spike-lavender." And even among the examples Kriaras adduces from the vernacular for λάχανον, one refers clearly to the gathering of greens endemic to this day in Greek rural cuisine:

> Μία γυναίκα λόγιασε . . . νὰ πάγει νὰ μαζώνει / ***λάχανα*** κεῖ στὰ τρίγυρα, καὶ στὰ χωράφια σώνει, "A woman thought . . . she'd go gather ***greens*** in the surroundings, and she arrived at the fields." (Tzane Bounialis *The Cretan War* 239 [258])

So in the medieval vernacular, λάχανον was ambiguous between "greens" and "cabbage," and this ambiguity has persisted in vernacular dialects. For example, Papadopoulos's (1961, s.v.) dictionary of Pontic Greek gives only the gloss "cabbage," but Halo (2000:51) records her Pontic mother's reminiscence "there were fava beans and cabbage and a green we called *lahana* that Mother dried for winter soups." The ambiguity also persisted in early modern Greek: Somavera (1977 [1709]) glosses the plural λάχανα as *ogni sorte di herbaggi di giardino buoni di mangiare,* "all kinds of garden greens that are good to eat," and the singular λάχανον as κραμπὶ, κραμβὶ (χορτάρι), *cavolo (herba),* "cabbage (vegetable)."

Given the *Tale*'s propensity to synonymy (see note following), however, there is little reason to doubt that "cabbage" is meant here.

601. **"Phrygian."** φρυγία; in P ὀφρύγια, presumably hypercorrectly preposing an initial unstressed vowel (as vernacular medieval Greek regularly dropped them—see verse 394). As Xanthoudidis (1927–28:364) points out, φρύο < φρυγίον is the Cretan Greek word for "cabbage" (also attested in Karpathos, Rhodes, Ainos in Thrace, and indirectly in Chios: Andriotis 1974 §6391). So

"Phrygian" should be understood here as an alternative medieval vernacular name for "cabbage." The term turns up in the ninth-century *Geoponica* 12.1.2–3 (a gardening manual) as φρυγιατικόν and occurs in *Ptochoprodromos* 2.42 (see note following) in combination with the classical κράμβη (φρύγιον κράμβην, "Phrygian cabbage"); it is also so mentioned in the contemporary *Timarion* §17 (see Commentary verse 371). See also Eideneier (1964:333); the transition from "Phrygian" to "cabbage" was first remarked on by Hatzidakis (1989–90 [1905–07]:2.222) in 1893.

602. **kohlrabi**. γοῦλα and its diminutive γουλί, like their Latin equivalent *colis*, can mean either a kind of turnip or "stalk/heart of a vegetable"—particularly in association with cabbage. This applies both in early modern Greek (Byzantius 1874, s.v.) and present-day Greek. The passage in question sounds like an enumeration of distinct kinds of vegetable (cabbage, turnips, beets)—particularly given the reading in P, discussed in Textual Notes. There are two issues to resolve: first, whether γοῦλα here refers to a distinct vegetable rather than a vegetable stalk, and second, if so, to which particular vegetable it refers.

The kind of turnip denoted by γοῦλα seems to be variable. Modern Greek dictionaries gloss the word as "beet, beetroot" (Giannakopoulos and Siarenos 1978, s.v. γουλί). However, Byzantius (1874, s.v.) glosses the word more multifariously as "Γαστορίς. *chou-navet* (rutabaga), *chou-rave* (kohlrabi), *chou de Siam* (rutabaga), *turneps* (turnip)."

Kriaras (1968–97) lists the "turnip" meaning of γοῦλα/γουλίν as occurring only in the *Tale* and *Ptochoprodromos*. Eideneier (1991) glosses the instances of γουλίν and γοῦλα in *Ptochoprodromos* (2.42, 3.197–7, respectively) as *Rübe,* "turnip," and interprets the instances of the compounds λαχανόγουλα, "cabbage-γοῦλα," and σευκλόγουλα, "beet-γοῦλα," (3.197–6) as pleonastically referring to vegetables ("cabbage and turnip," "beet and turnip") rather than stalks ("cabbage stalk," "beet stalk"). He thus glosses the words as *Kohlrübe,* "rutabaga"—the same compound in German; compare French *chou-navet,* "rutabaga"—and *Runkelrübe,* "beet," respectively. If γοῦλα meant "stalk" in σευκλόγουλα, the noun σευκλογουλᾶς, "beetroot-gardener" in 3.197–11 would make little sense—especially as 3.197–6 refers to λαχανόγουλα and σευκλόγουλα being planted. In the very next verse, γούλας might just refer to cabbage hearts still (P: καὶ κὰν ψωμὶν ὁ κηπουρὸς νὰ χόρταινα καὶ ***γούλας***, "and as a gardener I'd have my fill of bread and ***cabbage-stalks***"); the alternative reading (K—C of the *Tale*) χλεμπόνας, "honeydew melon," does not help disambiguate. In 2.42, however, a distinct vegetable is probable as the sense of γοῦλα, coming as it does at the end of a long list of vegetables—even if it yet again cooccurs with "cabbage": σπανάκιν, χρυσολάχανον, ***γογγύλιν***, ματζιτζάνιν, / φρύγιον κράμβην καὶ ***γουλὶν*** καί ἀπὸ τὸ κουνουπίδιν, "spinach, orache, ***γογγύλιν***, eggplant, / Phrygian cabbage and ***γοῦλα*** and some cauliflower."

In all, though the evidence from *Ptochoprodromos* is not incontrovertible, it appears plausible in medieval Greek for γοῦλα/γουλίν to refer to a distinct vegetable, and such a reading is preferable in this context. The reading of verse 602 in P (see Textual Notes) confirms that γοῦλα is to be understood as a separate vegetable. So we do not interpret the word here as referring to "fat cabbage hearts."

The second issue is identifying the γοῦλα as used in Byzantium. *Ptochoprodromos* 2.41–42, as cited previously, clearly intends γογγύλιν and γοῦλα to be understood as distinct; Eideneier (1991:241) believes γογγύλιν here means "kohlrabi, turnip cabbage" (*Kohlrabi*) and γοῦλα, "turnip" (*Rübe*). Winterwerb (1992:210), working under Eideneier's supervision, likewise identifies the γογγύλιν in the *Book of Fruit* with *Brassica oleracea* var. *gongyloides—Kohlrabi, Kohlrübe,* "kohlrabi, rutabaga." However, the γογγυλ- stem is consistently associated in Greek with the turnip (Liddell–Scott–Jones 1940, s.v. γογγυλίς, "turnip, *Brassica rapa*": γογγύλη is given as a colloquial variant of γογγυλίς [classical Greek]; Sophocles 1900, s.v. γογγύλιν = "γογγύλη, turnip" [medieval Greek]; Trapp 1994–99, s.v. γογγυλίδι, γογγύλι(ο)ν, γόγγυλον, "*Rübe* [turnip]" [learned medieval Greek]; Du Cange 1958 [1688], s.v. γολγόσιον, "*Rapa* [turnip], Γογγόλη" [medieval Greek]; Byzantius 1874, s.v. γογγύλιον, "*navet* [turnip]" [early modern Greek]; Giannakopoulos and Siarenos 1978, s.v. γογγύλι, "turnip" [modern Greek]).

Because we identify the γογγύλιν with a turnip and the γοῦλα is distinguished from the γογγύλιν in *Ptochoprodromos*, the γοῦλα cannot be a turnip. It must therefore be by elimination a kohlrabi, rutabaga, or beet. But a beet must likewise be rejected as an interpretation of γοῦλα, given how verse 602 of the *Tale* continues in CVLA—distinguishing γούλας from beets (σεῦτλα). In P, as discussed in Textual Notes, γοῦλα seems to be identified with a kind of cabbage. The remaining two candidate vegetables are both named as turnip–cabbage hybrids (***kohlrabi***: Italian *cavolo rapa,* "cabbage turnip"; German *Kohlrabi* < *cavolo rapa* with the added influence of *Kohl,* "cabbage"; French *chou-rave,* "cabbage-*rapa*"; English *turnip cabbage*. **rutabaga**: German *Kohlrübe,* "cabbage-turnip"; French *chou-navet,* "cabbage-turnip"). The kohlrabi looks somewhat more like a cabbage—the bulb is not in fact a root, as is usual with members of the turnip family, but a green or purple swollen stem routinely regarded as a turnip–cabbage hybrid. The rutabaga, on the other hand (also known in English as *yellow turnip*), looks nothing like a cabbage. For that reason we render γούλας as "kohlrabi."

Koukoules (1947–55:5.94) identifies the instances in both *Ptochoprodromos* and the *Tale* with cabbage hearts, pointing out that cabbage hearts are still cooked with pork in Aetolia (Koukoules 1947–55:5.93). He gives only the classical γογγύλις as the Byzantine name of a distinct vegetable of the turnip family (Koukoules 1947–55:2.1.209, 5.95)—even though Byzantius (1874, s.v. γουλί) mentions φραγκολάχανον, "Westerners' cabbage," as the name the turnip (γουλί) "was first given in Constantinople." What we have found is thus at odds with Koukoules' conclusion.

Of the existing renderings, Tsiouni (1972) has "root, beet-root," whereas Šandrovskaja (1956a) has стеблями, "stalks, stems."

610a. **verbosity betokens foolishness.** ζαβία, and its corresponding adjective ζαβός, literally mean "crooked" and can mean either "devious" or "foolish" in both medieval and modern Greek dialects:

> Medieval: ***devious*** (Kriaras [1968–97]): *Assizes of Cyprus* 203 (ζαβά, ζαβός, ζαβόν).
>
> Medieval: ***foolish*** (Kriaras [1968–97]): *Erotokritos* 4.10 (ζαβά); *Fortounatos* 3.146, *Erotokritos* 3.774 (ζαβάγρα); *Fortounatos* 3.151, *Erotokritos* 4.376 (ζαβός); Morezinos *Bed of Solomon* 438 (ζαβωμένος).
>
> Modern: ***devious***: HDMS: Macedonia (Siatista, Kozani; Aidonohori, Kozani; Eratyra, Kozani), Samos, Thessaly (Stagiades), Euboea (Avlonari), Leucas, Peloponnese (Ligour. [?]), Thrace (Soufli; Sisanion).
>
> Modern: ***foolish***: HDMS: Tinos (Isternia), Naxos (Apiranthos), Thera. Dictionaries of Somavera (1977 [1709], s.v. λωλός, *Pazzo, mezzomatto, grossolano*), Weigel (1804).

The dialect division seems to be between the mainland ("devious") and the Aegean ("foolish"). Likewise, in medieval and early modern Greek, the locus of the "foolish" meaning seems to be Crete. However, the evidence is too narrow to derive conclusions; the Cretan instances of "foolish" are from the seventeenth century, whereas the Cypriot instances of "devious" are from the thirteenth century. As Moutsos (1970) argues, "devious" is the initial meaning (Moutsos, in fact, derives the word from ζάβολος < διάβολος, "devil"), but ζαβός could easily have acquired its secondary meaning, "foolish," by the time of the *Tale*.

Tsiouni (1972) gives "crookedness, trickery," but the context weighs toward "foolishness," as Kriaras (1968–97, s.v.) and Eideneier (1976:459) have proposed: cunning is not typically realized through verbosity. Šandrovskaja (1956a) also has глупости, "foolishness." Although the dialectal distribution weakly suggests the meaning "devious" is prevalent in the region whose language is closer to the *Tale*'s (i.e., the more archaic Aegean), it is not strong enough evidence to contradict this.

612. **bred in lakes.** The *Tale*'s buffalo is not the Midwestern buffalo familiar to North American readers (genus *Bison*) but the water buffalo (*Bubalus bubalis*) indigenous to the Middle East and the Balkans.

616. **inkhorns.** The term used here, καλαμάρια, is not of course a reference to squid (*calamari*). Neither (as a modern Greek speaker might expect) does it refer to the pens stored in the pen cases mentioned in the same verse. Rather, it is an earlier station on the circuitous path that καλαμάριον has taken in Greek.

The word is derived from κάλαμος, "reed," which the ancients used as a writing implement, sharpening the portion of reed between two adjacent nodes.

The Greek for reed node is κόνδυλος, and its derivative κονδύλιον is the term that persisted as meaning "pen" into modern times. However, κάλαμος (Latin *calamus*) continued to be used into Byzantine times for "pen," and pens were stored in what was called, in Latin, a *theca calamaria,* "reed case." This implies that καλαμάριον meant, in the first instance, a pen case. By metonymy, however, καλαμάριον came to denote not just "pen case" but also the ink case it was put next to; this is reported as early as Origen (*ii–iii* A.D.) in his commentary on Ezekiel 9:2 ("and one man among them was clothed with linen, with a writer's ***inkhorn*** [***qeceth***] by his side"):

> οὐδὲ γὰρ ἡγοῦμαι παρ᾽ Ἕλλησι σημαίνεσθαι διὰ τῆς ***κάστω*** φωνῆς *πινακίδιον γραφέως ἔχειν ἐπὶ τῆς ὀσφύος αὐτοῦ.* Τῶν δὲ Ἑβραίων τις ἔλεγε, τὸ καλούμενον ***καλαμάριον***, τουτέστι ***κάστω***

> [Nor do I believe that ***qeceth*** means in Greek "he had a scribe's tablet by his side." Rather a certain Jew has said "the so-called ***calamarium***, namely ***qeceth***."] (*Selecta in Ezechielem* 800)

> Likewise Jerome (A.D. 413), in his own commentary on Ezekiel:

> cesath cum ab Hebraeo quaererem quid significaret, respondit mihi Graeco sermone appelari *καλαμάριον* ab eo quod in illo calami recondatur. Nos atramentarium ex eo quod atramentum habeat dicimus. Multi significantius thecas vocant, ab eo quod thecae sint scribentium calamorum.

> [When I asked a Jew what *cesath* meant, he told me that it was called καλαμάριον in Greek because the *calamus* is stored in it. We call it *atramentarium,* "inkwell," because it contains ink. Many call it more clearly *theca,* "case," as it is a case for writing reeds.] (Wattenbach 1958 [1896]:224–25)

Eventually, the "ink case" meaning prevailed in Greek (Koukoules 1947–1955:1.2.79). Because squids produce ink, the word καλαμάριον was applied to squid as well, gradually displacing τευθίς—certainly by the time of *Ptochoprodromos* (4.320).

Since antiquity, horns were used to make ink containers. (That the same conclusion was arrived at in the West is shown by the use in English of *inkhorn.*) These were typically a simple horn tip, either set in a hole on the scribe's desk (Wattenbach 1958 [1896]:242–43) or carried with him in his belt. Thus, Gregory Antiochus's eulogy on Nicholas Cataphlorus (*xii* A.D.; *Epitaphia* 1, 71) describes Death finding the scribe at work:

> πῶς τε ἡ δέλτος ἀνεπτυγμένη τῷ σκιμποδίσκῳ ἐπέκειτο καὶ πῶς ἐπὶ τῆς ἀγκάλης τῷ μάκαρι ἡ ***μελανδόχος*** καὶ τῇ λαιᾷ μὲν ὁ τόμος ἐπὶ καρπῷ, τῇ δεξιᾷ δὲ ὁ δόναξ ἐπιδακτύλιος

[how the writing tablet ⟨manuscript⟩ lay unfolded on the small couch and how the ***inkwell*** lay on the dear departed's bent arm, with the volume ⟨being copied⟩ to the left, on the wrist, and the reed ⟨pen⟩ to the right, on the finger.]

References to inkhorns persist in English into the nineteenth century (Henry Wadsworth Longfellow 1934:149, "Evangeline: A Tale of Acadie" 1.3: "While from his pocket the notary drew his papers and ***inkhorn***").

In modern Greek the word now occurs in its original sense almost exclusively in the formulaic expression χαρτί και καλαμάρι, "paper and ink stand," meaning "to the utmost detail" (as if it has been written down: Sarantakos 1997:258). The expression formerly included κοντύλι, "pen," as well as ink stand and paper (*Sachlikis: Strange Narrative* 23: ἐπιάσα τὸ κονδύλι μου χαρτὶν καὶ καλαμάριν, "I've picked my pen up, ink and paper, too"; *Apokopos* 474; *Erotokritos* 4.460), yet it is already reduced to just paper and inkhorn in the sixth century (*Leontius of Neapolis: Life of John the Almsgiver* 347: ᾐτησάμην οὖν εὐθέως χάρτην καὶ ***καλαμάριν,*** καὶ τὰ λεγόμενα κατ' ἔπος παρεσημειούμην, "So I immediately asked for paper and ***inkhorn,*** and I noted down what was said word for word"). Compounded with the fact that inkhorns are no longer to be seen, this may lead modern Greek speakers to read καλαμάρι as meaning "pen." There are hints that this confusion is old (see Textual Notes, verse 616), but because it was inkwells that were made of horn and pens themselves remained reeds, the *Tale* is clearly talking about an inkwell, not a pen.

618. **seats**. Though σελία (translated as "seats" here and in 915) literally meant "folding chair," Byzantine terms for chairs were frequently confused (Koukoules 1947–55:2.2.77–78).

619. **necks so finely shaped**. The term used in the original, σφονδυλοτορνεμένας, "*sfondylos*-lathed," is difficult. Šandrovskaja (1956a) avoids the conundrum by translating only the second component: **выточенных,** "ground down." Tsiouni (1972) applied the "obvious" interpretation of σφόνδυλος as "whorl" to interpret this as "whorl-lathed." Her definition of the term is thus "shaped on the lathe into a circular whorl that balances and twirls a spindle." But the whorl is a weight attached to the spindle, not the distaff, so it does not seem to us to make sense to have a distaff be whorl-lathed. We have therefore made use of the second meaning of σφόνδυλος extant in medieval Greek, "neck" (see verse 84).

Given that distaffs often had elaborate heads carved at their ends, we thus took σφονδυλοτορνεμένας to mean "neck-lathed." Koukoules (1947–55:2.2.114) reports that ox horns were set on the surface of distaffs in Byzantium—although the only evidence he presents for this comes from the *Tale*.

624. **fix them to their bows**. On Byzantine bowstrings, see Kolias (1988:216–17). The use of ox sinews in bowstrings is confirmed by Eustathius of Thessalonica (*Commentary on the Iliad* 1.662, 714), who uses the Homeric term νευρά, "sinews > bowstrings," as do the vernacular versions of the *Iliad* (*Hermoniacus*

8.190; *Loukanis* 17.289—itself an adaptation of *Hermoniacus*). Otherwise in vernacular medieval Greek, the Italian term κόρδα is normal instead (*Digenes* E 820; *Eustathius of Thessalonica: Commentary on the Odyssey* 2.267) (Kolias 1988:216); they are the "strings" to which the deer refers in 344 and the goats in 535. Sinews used for bowstrings continued into Ottoman times; thus Evliyâ Çelebi in 1638:

> They ⟨the Bow-ring–makers⟩ adorn their shops with these rings stuck on the thumb to bend the arrows, and hold the sinew with, made of all kinds of horns and fish bones. (von Hammer 1968 [1834]:1.2.197)
>
> After them comes the chief of the bowmen, and the chief of the bowmen of the Okmaidán surrounded by their troops, with bows bending and sinews thrilling. (von Hammer 1968 [1834]:1.2.200)

624. **crossbows**. On the Byzantine crossbow (τζάγκρας L, τζάγρας CVA, τζάκρας P, with only the modernizing L giving its conventional form), see Kolias 1988:239–53.

624–25. **arrowheads**. These two verses use the verb νευρώνω three times—taking as objects "bows," "crossbows," and "arrows," and here translated as "fix," "[fix]," and "fasten." With reference to bows and crossbows, it is obvious how sinews are to be used. It might not be as immediately obvious how sinews applied to arrows. We understand the latter case to mean "fasten together the component parts of the arrow (shaft, head)." Corroboration comes from various sources from late antiquity (Kolias 1988:218), including Ammianus Marcellinus's account (31.15.11) of Emperor Valens's warfare against the Goths in A.D. 378:

> animadversum est a nostris isdem telis barbaros uti, quibus petebantur. ideoque mandatum est ut ***nervis*** ferrum lignumque conectentibus ante iactum incisis emitterentur arcu sagittae, quae volitantes vires integras servabant, infixae vero corporibus nihil vigoris perdebant, aut certe, si cecidissent in vanum, ilico frangebantur.
>
> [Our men noticed that the barbarians were using the same missiles that had been hurled at them. And so it was ordered that the ***cords*** by which the barbs were fastened to the shaft should be partly severed before the arrows were shot from the bows; these during the flight kept their whole strength, and when they were fixed in the bodies of the enemy lost none of their effectiveness, or at any rate, if they found no mark, were at once broken.]

As Kolias (1988:219) points out, "The binding between the arrowhead and the shaft could be firm or loose, depending on whether the shaft should become detached from the arrowhead after shooting—something the aforementioned incised sinews could influence." (Our thanks to Taxiarches Kolias for bringing this to our attention; the other sources mentioned in Kolias are *Anonymus De Obsidione Toleranda* 50; Procopius *Bella* 6.5; Paul of Aegina 6.8.)

We cannot be sure that the Homeric use of νεῦρον as "string attaching an arrowhead to its shaft" (*Iliad* 4.151) would have survived (as Eustathius's bowstring did) and engendered the appropriate definition of νευρώνω for arrows, but this is the interpretation of the passage that makes the most sense. In any case, because sinews were the strings par excellence of Byzantium just as they were in Homeric times, the Byzantine term could be readily devised independently of Homer. The term survives, moreover, in modern dialects, denoting binding in northern Greece (cf. the mention of "bindings" in verse 627)—νεύρουμα, "fast binding of a farm animal at the knees to make its legs numb and force it to limp so that it will not be able to escape during transport": κεχουνά, bρέ, νὰ τοὺ ***νιβρώσῃς!***, "Hey, ***bind*** that one!" (HDMS 837:123–24: Lemnos); νευρώματα, "nooses holding the filling to the wood base of a saddle" (HDMS 1144:15: Vria, Pieria, Macedonia); Ἀφοῦ βάλουν τὴ σικαλχά, ράβουν τοὺ πετσὶ (= δέρμα) καὶ τοὺ ***νιφρώνουν*** (συνδέουν) τὸ ξυλίκι μὲ τὴ στρώση, "When they place the σικαλιά (?), they sew the leather and ***bind*** the stick with the flooring" (HDMS 1081:88: Vlasti, Kozani, Macedonia). We have also been told by an elderly native of Polykastano in Kozani (met by Baloglou on a plane flight, May 1996) that νεύρωμα refers to the binding of a growing tree to a supporting stick.

Šandrovskaja (1956a) translates the verb neutrally as снабжать [жилами], "to supply [sinews]."

630. **white bait**. Fanciful as it sounds, this is confirmed in *Sachlikis: Counsels* 1.219: Byzantine fishermen used to tie their fishhooks using hair from boars, horses, or oxen. Sachlikis speaks of τ' ἀγκίστριν μὲ τὴν τρίχα, "the hook with the hair" (cited in Koukoules 1947–55:5.333 erroneously as from *Sachlikis: Strange Narrative*; Koukoules also refers to *Aelian* 12.43). On white bait, see Koukoules 1947–55:5.80–81.

635. **a mighty dick**. The νεῦρον to which both the ox and the donkey refer was already ambiguous in antiquity between the two meanings it carries in the *Tale*: "nerve, sinew, tendon" (622) and "penis" (635). The latter meaning is attested in Plato the Comic, in the fourth century B.C., and is also used by Galen and Callimachus (Liddell–Scott–Jones 1940, s.v. νεῦρον, V); Koukoules (1947–55:6.536) mentions its survival in central Greece, Crete, and the Cyclades and that Eustathius of Thessalonica (*Commentary on the Iliad* 4.667, comment on *Iliad* 22.499) confirms its colloquial use in the twelfth century:

> ὡς δῆλον ἐκ τοῦ «οὐκ ἐθέλει νεύρων ἐπιήρανος εἶναι», ἤγουν ἐράστρια τοῦ κατ' ἄνθρωπον σπερματικοῦ νεύρου. διὸ ἐπάγει «καὶ στύματα μισεῖ», ἤγουν αἰδοίου τάσεις. τὸ δὲ τοιοῦτον νεῦρον Ἀριστοφάνης ἐν Ὄρνισι κοινῶς εἶπεν, ***ὡς οἱ πολλοὶ λέγουσιν***, οἱ δὲ σεμνότεροι δέμας καλοῦσι.

> [As is obvious from ⟨Plato the Comic's⟩ "she does not wish to be pleasant to νεῦρα"—namely, a lover of the human sperm-producing νεῦρον, to which he adds "and she hates hard-ons," that is, the erection of the

pudendum. And Aristophanes called this a νεῦρον frequently in the *Birds*, ***as the many ⟨now⟩ say***, whereas the more solemn call it δέμας ⟨"body"⟩

The whip βούνευρον, "ox *neuron*" is defined in Lampe's dictionary (1961) of patristic Greek as a whip made out of ox *tendons* rather than an ox penis; it is mentioned frequently in Byzantine sources. Koukoules (1947–55:1.1.102) also refers to the βούνευρον, used to whip schoolchildren, as made of "raw ox tendons"—although of the two instances he mentions, Herodas (*iii* B.C.) has a teacher threaten a child with an ox *tail* (βοὸς κέρκος: *Mimiambi* 3.68), whereas Nicholas Mesarites (*xiii* A.D.) speaks of arithmetic teachers βοείοις ***νεύροις*** ὠμοῖς κατακόπτοντας ἀνηλεῶς τὰ παιδάρια, "mercilessly cutting down children with raw ox ***nerves***" (*Description of the Church of the Apostles* §10).

But the ox makes it clear that he is speaking of a penis rather than tendons. In fact, the ox penis (βοϊδόπουτσα) was still in use as a whip in rural Greece in the early twentieth century (Tassos Karanastassis, personal communication), and its memory persists:

> Tis gunaikes, ws gnwston, prepei na tis xtupas mono me birtsoual triantafulla :-)
> [—Τις γυναίκες, ώς γνωστόν, πρέπει να τις χτυπάς μόνο με *βίρτσουαλ* τριαντάφυλλα:-)]
>
> Oute me birtsoual ***boidopoutsa*** den 8a thn xtupaga! Ki auto akoma a3ia ths dinei!
> [—Ούτε με *βίρτσουαλ* ***βοϊδόπουτσα*** δεν θα την χτύπαγα! Κι αυτό ακόμα αξία της δίνει!]
>
> [—As is well known, women should only be struck with virtual roses :-)
>
> —I wouldn't even strike her with a virtual ***ox dick***! Even that'd be paying her too much attention!] ("Asteras Amaliadas," Re: Peirasmos tou Xristou kai Or8odo3h 8eologia . . .; Hellas mailing list, bit.listerv.hellas, December 8, 1997)

As Nikos Sarantakos informs us, demonstrators had certainly transferred the term to riot police clubs by 1980. In fact, the ox penis (*pinto de boi*) is still in use as a torture implement in Brazil (Rodley 2001).

Moreover, the ox has already talked about sinews a few verses previously, without mentioning a whip made of them. So the *Tale*'s whip is the modern implement, made of an ox penis, rather than the whip from ox tendons referred to by Lampe (1961). Šandrovskaja (1956a) decorously renders this instance of νεῦρον as член, "member." Gidel (1866:318) misses the point and speaks of *nerfs,* "nerves."

636. **thrash soundly**. μαγκλαβοκοποῦσιν is derived from the weapon μαγκλάβιον, whose denotation varied between "whip" (*Pseudo-Codinus*) and

"staff, club" (all other Byzantine literature; etymology: Latin *manus,* "hand" + *clavus,* "nail; rudder") (Kolias 1988:179). Although this passage suggests the former (and the compilation of Pseudo-Codinus was roughly contemporary to the *Tale*), it does not decide the issue, as the verb could have just as easily have been used figuratively ("beat as if with a club") as literally ("to whip"). The translation of the word, in any case, is not affected. Tsiouni (1972) glosses the word as "to beat up," and Šandrovskaja (1956a) as бьют ремнями, "beat with straps" (i.e., Pseudo-Codinus's interpretation.)

637. **all sorts of felons**. Koukoules (1947–55:6.54–55) finds that the whip was used in Byzantium not only for punishment but also in trial by ordeal—and indeed to extract confessions not only out of the accused but also out of witnesses (*Basil of Caesarea: Homily on Psalm VII*; Migne 1857–87:29.244):

> Ἐτασμὸς κυρίως ἐστὶν ἡ μετὰ πασῶν βασάνων προσαγομένη ἔρευνα παρὰ τῶν κριτῶν τοῖς ἐξεταζομένοις, ἵνα οἱ κρύπτοντες παρ' ἑαυτοῖς τὰ ἐπιζητούμενα τῇ ἀνάγκῃ τῶν πόνων εἰς τὸ ἐμφανὲς καταστήσωσι τὸ λανθάνον.
>
> [Properly, examination is an investigation conducted through all means of torture by judges on the subjects of interrogation—so that those who keep to themselves the facts sought after are compelled through pain to bring to light what was concealed.]

Witnesses are not mentioned in the *Tale*, but the fact that judges rather than guards whip felons implies that trial by ordeal is meant here, too.

640. **tanned**. Here and in 641, the modern rather than ancient meaning of the γναφ- stem is used; see Commentary verse 211.

644. **donkey**. The donkey has already been singled out for his genitals (verse 82). Unlike the prevalent attitude in the West (as Irmscher 1956:54 points out), the donkey in Greek is proverbially associated not with stupidity but with pig-headedness and deficient social graces.

646. **let fly a little fart**. ἐτζιληπούρδισεν literally means "farted and squirted," but the word picked up two secondary meanings early on. The first is reported in Somavera (1977 [1709]), who glosses τζιλιπουρδῶ as *calcitrare, ricalcitrare,* "kick back," and glosses separately τζιλιπουρδιανὸν ἄλογον as *calcitroso cavallo,* "recalcitrant horse." (Somavera is certainly not censoring anything with his gloss because the word is immediately preceded by τζιλίζω, τζιρλίζω: *squaccarare, squaccherare, squacquarare,* "get the squirts.") This is probably the sense in *Vita of the Esteemed Donkey* 310: Ὁ γάδαρος βολήσει τον, ***τσιλιπουρδᾶ*** καὶ κροῦ τον, "The donkey throws him off, ***kicks back,*** and strikes him."

The second meaning involves tricky behavior, and when the *Donkey Tale* uses the verb to refer to the fox rather than the donkey, this is presumably the sense meant (rather than the fox somehow kicking back):

Εἰς τὰ κρυφὰ κλεψίματα καὶ τὰς ’πιδεξιοσύνας
ὁμοιάζω τὴν μητέρα μου ἐκείνην τὴν ἁγίαν,
εἰς τὰ ***τσιλιπουρδίσματα*** ὁμοιάζω τὸν πατήρ μου.

[In secret thieving and dexterity
I am most like unto my saintly mother,
whereas in ***farting round*** I'm like my father.] (*Vita of the Esteemed Donkey* 146–48)

Εἰς τὰ κρυφοκλεψίματα κ’ εἰς τὴν τεχνολογίαν,
ὁμοιάζω τὴν μητέρα μου ἐκείνην τὴν ἁγίαν.
Κ’ εἰς τὰ ***τσιλιπουρδίσματα*** κ’ εἰς τὴν ’πιδεξοσύνη,
ὁμοιάζω τοῦ πατέρα μου κ’ εἰς τὴν γληγοροσύνη.

[In secret thieving and in artfulness,
I am most like unto my saintly mother.
In ***farting round*** and in dexterity
I'm like my father, and in swiftness, too.] (*Fair Tale of the Donkey the Wolf and the Fox* 146–48b)

This second sense is the one to have survived: the verb's denotation in modern Greek is "to fool around; to womanize" (cf. Australian English *piss-fart around*) and even extends to "play" (in Pyli, Kos, τσουλούπουρδο means "hide-and-seek": HDMS 890:300).

There is one modern dialect instance where the verb is used to mean "fart at someone as an insult" (HDMS 958:42, Neohori, Central Greece). This may be also intended by the fox in the *Fair Tale of the Donkey the Wolf and the Fox* (141i–j):

Οἱ σκύλοι σὰν γροικήσουσι, ***τσιλιπουρδῶ*** καὶ φεύγω,
καὶ δὲν τοὺς χρήζω τίποτες, μὰ τρέχοντας χορεύγω

[When hounds are on to me, I ***fart*** and depart;
I owe them nothing, so I run and dance.]

But it does not seem to match the donkey's demeanor in the *Tale* that he should be willfully insulting the audience. So we do not believe this semantic extension need be postulated for the *Tale*. Tsiouni (1972) glosses the word as "fart for joy"; this appears somewhat exaggerated.

Šandrovskaja's (1956a) брыкнулся, "bucked," uses Somavera's gloss, but it is nonsense for the donkey to be running while kicking back (711: there Šandrovskaja [1956a] censors out the reference, with двигаясь то в одну, то в другую сторону, "moving now to one and now to the other side").

654. **lust**. The Greek stem used, οἶστρο- literally means "gadfly," but in medieval Greek it was used exclusively to refer to lustful passion or excitement (Kriaras 1968–97, s.v.):

Τοῦτο ἔναι τοῦ διαβόλου
γέννημα καί σπέρμα,
νά πληθύνη καί τόν ***οἶστρον***
εἰς τόν κόσμον τοῦτον ὅλον

[This ⟨woman⟩ is the devil's
spawn and child
multiplying ***lust***
in this whole world.] (*Ptocholeon* P 250–53)

The transition is as old as Herodotus: ἐπεάν σφεας ἐσίῃ ***οἶστρος*** κυΐσκεσθαι, ἀγεληδὸν ἐκπλέουσι ἐς θάλασσαν, "when the ***desire*** of spawning comes on them ⟨fish⟩, they swim out to sea in schools" (2.93). The expression has also been recapitulated in modern Greek, where the proverbial expression μύγα τον τσίμπησε, "a fly has bitten him" (Sarantakos 1997:177) refers to erratic behavior.

The *Tale* speaks specifically of being "moved by lust": οἰστροκινηθῶ, "⟨when⟩ I am lust-moved" (P); εἰς οἶστρον κινηθῇ, "it is moved in lust" (C); εἰς οἶστρον κινηθῇς, "you are moved in lust" (A); εἰς ἄστρον κινηθῇ, "it is moved in [star]" (VL). The word οἰστροκινηθῶ is a hapax legomenon, and the correlation of movement and lust is likewise unusual. Although οἶστρος does survive in modern Greek dialect, meaning both "horsefly," "be bitten by a horsefly," and "excitement, anger, bad mood" (Andriotis 1974 §4344, §4345), it is fairly unrecognizable compared with the original (ἔστρος, ἔστρο, ὀστρεός, 'στριός, οἰστρίγκα, ἀστριάζου, 'στριάζομαι). And the word is unfamiliar to VL, which substitute οἶστρον with ἄστρον, "star." (There is a slight chance this is a regional variant of οἶστρος, given the Leucadian ἀστριάζου, "be bitten by a horsefly," but a simple misunderstanding is rather likelier.) All this might make one suspect that the use of οἶστρο- is bookish and that the author is aware of the original sense of οἶστρον, "gadfly," particularly in its mythological associations with Io (the paramour of Zeus concealed as a cow, which a gadfly sent by Hera pursued through Egypt). This is an allusion otherwise unattested in the medieval vernacular, even though the same image of a mad cow bitten by a fly underlies the modern Greek expression given above.

The stem itself does turn up in other vernacular works: *Ptocholeon, Apollonius of Tyre*, and the *Vernacular Physiologus*—though not, to our knowledge, in the romances, possibly because it devalues love. This means that οἰστρο- must have been reasonably accessible to literate Byzantines, even if not necessarily colloquial. And the stem does turn up in the Septuagint:

Hosea 4:16: ὅτι ὡς δάμαλις ***παροιστρῶσα παροίστρησεν*** Ισραηλ, "For Israel ***slideth back*** as a ***backsliding*** heifer" (in the Greek, clearly "frenzied").

4 Maccabees 2:3: νέος γὰρ ὢν καὶ ἀκμάζων πρὸς συνουσιασμὸν ἠκύρωσε τῷ λογισμῷ τὸν τῶν παθῶν ***οἶστρον***, "For when he was

young and in his prime for intercourse, by his reason he nullified the ***frenzy*** of the passions" (though Maccabbees, unlike the rest of the Septuagint, was originally written in Greek and was if anything hypercorrectly Atticist).

At any rate, the collocation of οἶστρος and κινῶ, "move (to emotion or action)" appears to be postclassical. The author may have gotten it either from Photius's *Lexicon*, which repeats *Timaeus the Sophist*'s definition of the Platonic οἰστρᾷ as συντόνως καὶ μανικῶς κινεῖται, "move violently and manically"—or likelier from the work *On the races of India and the Brahmans*, spuriously attributed to Palladius and quoted frequently by the chroniclers: οἳ καὶ εὐκρατότεροι λέγονται εἶναι οἱ μῆνες ἐκεῖνοι καὶ ***οἶστρον κινεῖν,*** "and those months ⟨July and August⟩ are said to be more temperate and to ***stir lust***" (Palladius *De Gentibus Indiae et Bragmanibus* 1.13; Cedrenus 1.268; George Monachus *Chronicon* 36; George Monachus *Chronicon breve* 77; Michael Glycas *Annales* 269; Suda, s.v. Βραχμάν). The expression was also popular with the scholiasts (*Scholia et glossae in Oppiani halieutica* 1.252, 1.473, 3.622, 4.142; *Scholia vetera in Prometheum vinctum* 559a) and seems to have been first used by St. Nilus of Ancyra (*iv* A.D.) in his *Commentary on the Song of Songs*, proem 3, 29 (καὶ οὐ βακχείᾳ ἐρωτικῇ πρὸς ***οἶστρον*** ἐμμανῆ ***κινηθέντος*** ὑπὸ τοῦ πάθους, "and not ***moved*** by passion through erotic intoxication toward manic ***lust***"; see also Photius *Amphilochia* 14.10; Psellus *Opuscula Logica* 16.150).

So the author could easily have come across the word in his education, however limited it may have been. But although there are comparable classical compounds (οἰστρήλατος, "driven by a gadfly," and οἰστροδίνητος, "driven round and round by a gadfly," in Aeschylus), there is no reason to assume the author had ever heard of *Prometheus Bound* or is making an allusion in any way classical.

655. **Western saucer**. This verse involves a hapax legomenon, which defeated Šandrovskaja (1956a) (possibly for reasons of obscenity rather than lexicography): she does not translate the verse. Tsiouni's guess (1972) at the meaning of σαλτζαρόλιν CA (σαρσαρόλιν PV, σαλταρόλιν L) was "a kind of hat" (repeated by Vasiliou 1996:65), but we have been unable to find explicit justification for this. Tsiouni (1972) may have had in mind the comparable passage from *Vita of the Esteemed Donkey* 324–28, where the fox, just struck overboard by the donkey, fearfully relates to the wolf her narrow escape from a fate worse than death:

Ὁ θεὸς μᾶς ἐλευθέρωσεν, νὰ μὴ μᾶς θανατώσει.
Ἐκ τὴν κοιλιάν του ἐξέβαλεν ὡσὰν ἀπελατίκι
μακρύν, χοντρὸν καὶ ἔμπροσθεν εἶχεν ὡσὰν καπούσι.
Ἀλλ' εἰ τὴν δώση μιὰ φορὰν ζωὴν ποσῶς οὐκ ἔχει,
ἐγύρεψεν κ' ἐμὲν πολλά, μήνα μὲ κουκουδώση.

[God has preserved us, so he has not killed us.
Out from his belly he produced a club,

long, thick, and sort of hooded up the front.
Once struck by it, one is deprived of life;
and sure he sought me out, to stick it in me.]

(The "hood" to which the Fox refers, καπού[τ]σιν, was a Capuchin hood.) However, Tassos Karanastassis (in preparation) has identified the *Tale*'s σαλτζαρόλιν as a sauce warmer, or "saucer," with the proper form of the word attested in CA (*saltsarolin*); compare modern Greek σαλτσιέρα (***saltsiera***) < Italian *salsièra,* "saucer."

665. **Dick-O-Matic**. ψωλογομάριν, literally "dick-donkey." The word γομάριν is a diminutive of γόμος, which in Koine had come to mean "a beast's burden" (first recorded in Babrius 7.11, *ii* A.D.; in classical Greek, it meant a ship's cargo). This is the meaning γομάριν has in verse 770. Loads were so inextricably linked with donkeys that already by 1432, γομάριν had come to mean "donkey" or at least "beast of burden" (*Chronicle of Makhairas* §650: ἐδιαλαλήσαν εἰς τὴν Λευκωσίαν καὶ εἰς ὅλην τὴν Κύπρον, ὅτι . . . οὐδὲ ***γομάριν*** νὰ ἔλθῃ ἀππέξω τῆς χώρας, "a proclamation was made at Lefkosia and in all Cyprus that [. . .] nor should any ***beast with a load*** come into the town"), a meaning it continues to have in modern Greek. Indeed, "donkey" (or at least "beast of burden") must already underlie the *Tale*'s ψωλογομάριν.

CVL have "bread-donkey" or, using the classical meaning of the stem, "morsel-donkey" (ψωμογομάρι CV, ψομῶν γομάριν L), against ψωλογομάριν P, ψωλογόμαρε A, "dick-donkey." The CVL reading obviously is the *lectio difficilior*, but though the donkey is indeed referred to as carrying flour in 667, it seems odd to single out bread in particular as the donkey's burden. Moreover, it is the donkey's claims of being well endowed to which the horse is responding, so the stemmatically independent P and A must preserve the original reading, and both Tsiouni (1972) and Papathomopoulos (2002) have adopted it accordingly. Given usage elsewhere in the poem, there is no reason to suspect any deliberate bowdlerization on the part of CVL.

Instead of refusing to translate the obscenity, Šandrovskaja (1956a) has an apparent emendation, which she does not otherwise comment on: чесоточное животное, "scabby beast," which suggests ψωρογομάρι, "lousy donkey." Hesseling (1924:313) reports that Sathas had attempted the same emendation. Like CVL's reading, this differs from P only in the third letter. The similarity of ρ and μ would explain the odd ψωμογομάρι, and λ and ρ sound similar, but we prefer to give the horse a chance to respond to the donkey's endowment.

676. **looting**. On the Byzantine attitude to animal trespass, known in Byzantine law by the Latin term πραῖδα < *praeda,* "plunder" (whence *prey* and *predator*), see Commentary 54 and 678. The term (spelled πρέδα by Tsiouni [1972], who glosses it as "spoil") was obscure enough to confuse the scribes: only P transmits it accurately. CLA drop a letter, making it παῖδα[ν], "torment." Instead of L, it is V here that recasts the word, to πταῖσμα, "fault"; this is the reading Šandrovskaja (1956a) adopts (провинность).

678. **cut your ears and slash your tail**. Both were common retaliations against animals found roaming in a stranger's farm. The practice was commonplace enough that the *Farmer's Law* (*vii–viii* A.D.) pays a lot of attention to what should happen to animals found trespassing:

> Ἐάν τις εὕρῃ βοῦν ***πραιδεύοντα*** καὶ οὐ δώσει αὐτὸν τῷ κυρίῳ ἀπολαμβάνων τὸ βλάβος, ἀλλ' ὠτοκοπήσῃ αὐτὸν ἢ τυφλώσῃ ἢ οὐροκοπήσῃ, οὐ λαμβάνει αὐτὸν ὁ κύριος αὐτοῦ ἀλλὰ λαμβάνει ἄλλον ἀντ' αὐτοῦ.
>
> [If a man finds an ox ***doing harm*** and does not give it to its master on being paid for the damage done, but cuts its ear or blinds it or cuts its tail, its master does not take it but takes another in its place.] (*Farmer's Law* 48)
>
> Ἐάν τις εὕρῃ χοῖρον ἐν ***πραίδᾳ*** ἢ πρόβατον ἢ κύνα, παραδώσει αὐτὸ ἐν πρώτοις τῷ κυρίῳ αὐτοῦ· εἶτα καὶ παραδώσας δεύτερον, παραγγελεῖ τῷ κυρίῳ αὐτοῦ· τὸ δὲ τρίτον οὐροκοπεῖ ἢ ὠτοκοπεῖ ἢ τοξεύει αὐτὸ ἀνεγκλήτως.
>
> [If a man finds a pig ***doing harm*** or a sheep or a dog, he shall deliver it in the first place to its master; when he has delivered it a second time, he shall give notice to its master; the third time he may cut its tail or its ear or shoot arrows at it without incurring liability.] (*Farmer's Law* 49)

An echo of this practice is found in the modern Greek saying σαν το σκυλί στ' αμπέλι, "like a dog in a vineyard," referring to an unlamented death (Papadopoulos 1953:39; Sarantakos 1997:227).

The chapter of the *Ecloga ad Prochiron mutata* (*x–xii* A.D.) dealing with animal trespass quotes the *Farmer's Law* and includes donkeys in its listing:

> Ἐάν τις εὕρῃ βοῦν ἢ ὄνον ἢ ἵππον ἐν ἀμπέλῳ ἢ ἐν ἀγρῷ ἢ ἐν ἑτέρῳ τόπῳ ***πραῖδαν*** ποιοῦντα, καὶ οὐ παραδώσῃ αὐτὸν τῷ κυρίῳ αὐτοῦ ὡς μέλλων αὐτὸν ἀπαιτεῖν ἅπασαν τὴν ***πραῖδαν***, ἀλλὰ φονεύσῃ ἢ κλάσῃ ἢ τυφλώσῃ ἢ ὠτοκοπήσῃ ἢ οὐροκοπήσῃ, οὐκ ἄρει αὐτὸν ὁ κύριος αὐτοῦ, ἀλλὰ λαμβάνει ἄλλον ἀντ' αὐτοῦ.
>
> Should one find an ox, donkey, or horse in a vineyard or farm or other place committing ***trespass***, and does not surrender it to its master to demand restitution for the entire ***plunder*** but instead kills it, wounds it, blinds it, cuts off its ears, or cuts off its tail, its master shall not receive it back but shall have another in its place. (*Ecloga ad Prochiron mutata* 26.7)

679. **rein you in by force**. βάνουν καὶ χαβώνουν, literally "put and bridle"; Šandrovskaja (1956a) renders it as **валят и бьют**, "throw down and thrash." Of the two verbs, χαβώνω means "bridle, put the bit in the mouth of a beast" (e.g.,

χάβουσ' τοὺ γουμάρ,' "bridle the donkey": HDMS 552:338, Zagoria, Epirus; HDMS 449:63, Samothrace), derived from χαβιά, "bridle" (Andriotis 1983, s.v.). It is used metaphorically to mean "immobilize":

> Ἄμα σὶ δῆ οὐ λύκους πρῶτα, σὶ ***χαβῶν'*** καὶ δέ gρένεις dίπ, "If the wolf sees you first, it ***immobilizes*** you and you cannot speak a word." (HDMS 888:105, Sparta, central Greece)

> Μ' ἔφαγε τὸ βράδυ ἕνας σκορπιὸς καὶ μὲ ***χάβωσε*** ἀπ' τὸν πόνο, "A scorpion-fish bit me last night and ***immobilized*** me with pain." (HDMS 817:135, Othoni)

Farmer's Law §48 (see note, verse 678) provides that a donkey caught trespassing should not be returned to its owner if it has been mutilated. So there would be little point in a farmer, on catching a wandering donkey, proceeding to both mutilate the donkey (678) and bridle it (679) if χαβώνουν indeed means "bridle." The farmer would have no reason to bridle the donkey if he intended to return it, whether mutilated after repeated warnings to its owner (*Farmer's Law* §49) or not. And even if the farmer was allowed to confiscate the offender under the older principle of *noxae deditio* (*Basilica* 60.2.1, 60.3.39; *Attaleiates: Legal Compilation* 35.10; *Synopsis Basilicorum* Z 1.1.3; *Synopsis Minor* Z.10), it seems pointless to mutilate an animal of which one intended to take ownership. So it is likelier that χαβώνω here has its metaphorical meaning of "immobilize." If the farmer abused the donkey, it would be to drive it away ultimately—though he would have to immobilize it first, both to stop it causing further damage and to be able to maltreat it. We have exploited the similar ambiguity in English of *rein you in*.

Although βάνω is a multifarious verb of medieval Greek (Kriaras's 1968–97 dictionary lists sixty-nine meanings), the only promising definitions are (1a) "throw down, subdue" (as used by Šandrovskaja [1956a]; compare *Rime of Imperios* 898: καὶ κονταριὰν τοῦ κτύπησα καὶ κάτω τόνε ***βάνω,*** "I struck him with the lance and ***threw*** him down") and (39) "rush against" (*Hermoniacus* 20.219: Ἀχιλλεὺς εὐθὺς γὰρ ***βάνει*** / πρὸς τὸν Ἕκτοραν μὲ λόγχην, "Then Achilles ***rushed*** at once / against Hector with a lance"). The first definition is said to "usually" require the adverb κάτω, χάμω, "down," which is absent here, and the second is inappropriately dramatic, even though μὲ τὴν χλωρὴν τὴν βέργαν, "with a green switch" corresponds nicely to *Hermoniacus*'s μὲ λόγχην, "with a lance."

The use of βάνουν here is thus odd. Kriaras's 1968–97 dictionary itself (s.v. βάνω, II) adopts Xanthoudidis's emendation (1927–28:366) to χαώνουν καὶ λαβώνουν, "destroy and injure." However, Xanthoudidis shows that he does not understand the χαβόνουν of P; likewise Wagner (1874), whose edition Xanthoudidis used, misrepresents βάνουν as λαβώνουν. The manuscripts are consistent in these two words (L having the alternative form βάλουν for the former), and there is no real reason to suspect textual corruption. The emendation that Xanthoudidis proposes, and that Šandrovskaja appears to have followed, is in any event quite fanciful.

We see two possible interpretations of βάνω here. If βάνω is understood to be a synonym of χαβώνω, as we suspect, it would mean "put in a spot, immobilize," akin to Kriaras's and modern Greek's βάνω κάτω, "subdue; pin down." If not, the verb could be understood as a modal, "set forth"; compare modern Greek βάνω μπρος. Neither of these meanings is attested in Kriaras 1968–97.

Tsiouni (1972) leaves βάνουν unglossed and offers the literal gloss "bridle" for χαβώνω.

681. **freak**. The word κάθαρμα occurs four times in the *Tale*. Here and in 775, it is used in conjunction with πομπή, "procession; someone guilty of an offence (adultery, theft, gambling, etc.) and paraded to ridicule on a donkey" (*outcast*; see Koukoules 1947–55:3.184–208), and γέλοιον, "[figure of] laughter." In 942, it occurs with the obscure ὀξύποδε (see Commentary) and with παράσημον, "misshapen." In 971, finally, it occurs in VL with μιασμένον, "defiled," and C substitutes for it πομπή, "outcast." This would make κάθαρμα mean something like "figure of ridicule."

Of course, matters could not be that simple. The word, derived from καθαρός, "clean," originally meant "that which is thrown away in cleansing" (i.e., garbage) and in particular "offscourings, refuse of a sacrifice." According to the scholiasts (e.g., *Scholia in Plutum* 454), it also denoted the φαρμακός, "scapegoat," a person ritually expelled (and possibly in some instances killed) during a festival or a natural disaster to appease the gods. Because the scapegoat was typically a criminal, the word is actually used in classical Greek primarily as invective, attributing baseness and criminal intent to someone; Demosthenes was particularly enamored of it. In the translated Greek texts available as of this writing on the Perseus website (Crane 2002), it is rendered accordingly as "worthless scoundrel," "infamous beings," "runagate," "blackguard," "scum of the earth," "outcasts," and "rascality."

This usage continued in Byzantium in the learned language. Tzetzes (*Epistulae* 6.10), for example, writes:

> καὶ παραινῶ ἱκετεύων σε ἐπ' ὄνου ἢ χοίρου τιτανοχρίστου δημεῦσαι αὐτὸν καὶ τῆς σῆς ἐξελάσαι χειρός, πτῶμά τι καὶ μορμολύκειον ὄντα καὶ ***κάθαρμα*** καὶ τῆς σῆς εὐγενείας ἀλλότριον. εἰ δ' οὔ, ὑπέρ γε τὸ μῆλον ἐκεῖνο τῆς Ἔριδος τὸν ὀσμίλον τοῦτον εὑρήσειας.
>
> [And I urge and beg you to parade him on a donkey or pig smeared with chalk and discard him from beside your hand, for he is a wreck and a bugbear and a ***rascal*** and alien to your lordship. If you do not, you will find that stinker (?) to be even worse than the legendary Apple of Discord.]

And in the winter or spring of 1382–1383, Demetrius Cydones (*Epistulae* 259) writes:

> καὶ ὡς ἔοικεν εἵμαρτο καὶ τοῦτον νῦν Τούρκοις δουλεῦσαι, ἵνα μηδεὶς Ἑλλήνων κἂν πάλαι τεθνηκὼς ἢ τὴν τῶν ***καθαρμάτων*** τούτων ὕβριν ἐκφύγῃ
>
> [And it seems even this is our lot, to become slaves to the Turks, so that there may be none even of the long dead ancient Greeks to escape insult from these ***scum***.]

The word is also present in modern Greek—though most likely reintroduced through *katharevousa,* the neoclassical attempt to revive the ancient language. As used nowadays, the word is little different to how Demosthenes and Cydones used it: it constitutes "fighting words" and denotes someone ruthless and immoral.

This is a strong word for the animals to be throwing around, and one has reason to suspect its effect is milder in the *Tale*. Both Kriaras (1968–97) and Šandrovskaja (1956a) translate the word as "insignificant" (ничтожество, though in 942 Šandrovskaja has урод, "monster"). That meaning fits the *Tale* somewhat better, but the origin of the gloss is puzzling to us: it is absent from the obvious sources (Du Cange 1958 [1688], Liddell–Scott–Jones 1940, Sophocles 1900), and it seems unlikely to us that Kriaras consulted Šandrovskaja. Neither source justifies its gloss.

In addition, the *Tale* is the only work for which Kriaras attests the invective definition in the entirety of vernacular medieval Greek. This, along with its reference to a long-forgotten pagan ritual, leads one to suspect that κάθαρμα was a bookish term. Kriaras also finds it once, in a spelling dictionary, with its literal meaning "rubbish": Λύματα, τὰ ***καθάρματα***, ταῦτα ψιλά μοι γράφε, "λύματα means ***rubbish***; write this with an ⟨u⟩psilon" (*Metrical Dictionaries* 2.141). But this is hardly a dictionary glossing into the vernacular and merely shows that the word was known to those Byzantines with enough learning to care about spelling.

The only other vernacular medieval Greek works we know of containing κάθαρμα are the recently published vernacular translations of the *Life of Aesop*, which in its original form was lowbrow Koine reading matter like Aesop himself. In the vernacular versions (first excerpt following), the use of κάθαρμα is clearly an artifact of translation, because the original (second excerpt following) also has Aesop routinely called a κάθαρμα by his master and his fellows:

> Ἐγύρισε ὁ πραματευτὴς καὶ ἰδὼν τὸν Αἴσωπον ἐγέλασεν καὶ λέγει· "Πόθεν τὸ ἀπόκτησες αὐτὸ τὸ τζηκκάλι; Καλαμίου ῥίζα ἔναι τάχα ἢ ἄνθρωπος; Αὐτὸς ἂν τὸν ἔλειπεν ἡ συντυχία, ἐπαρωμοίαζεν ὥσπερ ἀσκὸς φουσκωμένος. Τί μὲ ἐμπόδισες ἀπὸ τὴν στράταν μου, ὦ Ζηνᾶ, διὰ τὸ ***κάθαρμα*** αὐτό; Καὶ ἔλεγα ὅτι ἔχεις κανένα πρᾶγμα καλόν." Ὅμως ὡσὰν εἶπεν αὐτὰ ὁ πραγματευτής, ὑπῆγεν τὸν δρόμον του.
>
> [The merchant turned, and seeing Aesop, he laughed and said: "Where did you get this saucepan from? Is this perchance the root of a cane

or a human? This one, had he no speech, would resemble a puffed-up sack. What did you stop me on my way for, Zenas, for this ***κάθαρμα***? And here I was thinking you had something good for me." And when the merchant said this, he went his way.] (*Life of Aesop: Vernacular* 1 §14; Zenas is proposing to sell Aesop to a slavetrader.)

Θεασάμενος οὖν ὁ ἔμπορος τὸν Αἴσωπον καὶ μέγα γελάσας ἔφη "πόθεν σοι ἡ χύτρα αὕτη; ῥοιζοκάλαμόν ἐστι ἢ ἄνθρωπος; Οὗτος τῆς τερατομαχίας σαλπιστής ἐστιν. Εἰ μὴ φωνὴν εἶχεν, ἀσκοκήλη ἦν. Ἵνα τί, ὦ Ζηνᾶ, τῆς ὁδοῦ πεπλάνηκάς με ἕνεκεν τοῦ ***καθάρματος*** τούτου;" Καὶ ταῦτα εἰπὼν ἐπορεύετο.

[When the merchant saw Aesop, he said, laughing heartily: "Where did you get this pot from? Is this a cane root or a human? This is the very bugler at the battle of monsters. If he had no voice, he would be a leather bladder. Zenas, why did you take me out of my way on account of this ***κάθαρμα***?" And saying this, he went off.] (*Life of Aesop* [W: mss. SBPTh] §14: Koine original)

Yet the passage quoted, in fact, solves the quandary. Unlike the instances we have seen, the slavetrader has no reason to attribute criminal intent to Aesop. He might readily drive Aesop off a cliff—which as Papathomopoulos (1999a:144) points out, is exactly the fate Aesop meets at Delphi. But as far as the slavetrader is concerned, that would be on account of his proverbially ugly looks, not his behavior (even though Aesop gives his eventual master Xanthus good reason to call him a rascal, with the tricks he plays on him). The usage of κάθαρμα in the *Life of Aesop* matches the *Tale* better, particularly in its combination with παράσημον, "misshapen," and γέλοιον, "object of ridicule." In fact, though Papathomopoulos translates into modern Greek the word in the equivalent passage of the Koine version W (mss. MORNLo) as κάθαρμα, "scum" (1999a:46), in the vernacular translations he glosses it as "miserable slave, filthy" (Papathomopoulos 1999b:158). The other vernacular translations of the *Life* give even clearer evidence: 3 §14, a translation of the Planudean version of the *Life* that uses the same word κάθαρμα, renders it as ἀκάθαρτον πρᾶγμα, "filthy thing"—probably not far from how the author of the *Tale* understood the word.

The near match to κάθαρμα as used in the New Testament might likewise have led to such an association. Paul (1 Corinthians 4:13) speaks despairingly of his mission, saying ὡς ***περικαθάρματα τοῦ κόσμου*** ἐγενήθημεν, πάντων περίψημα, ἕως ἄρτι, "we are made as ***the filth of the world***, and are the offscouring of all things unto this day" (King James Version; most modern translations have "scum of the earth"). The word Paul uses is merely the plural of κάθαρμα, with the prefix περι-, "around," added; some manuscripts of the epistle in fact segment the phrase as the soundalike ὡσπερεὶ καθάρματα, "as if we were scum." (Demonstrating the equivalence of the two terms, *Life of Aesop* G §14 uses the longer word in its version of the slavetrader's speech;

Papathomopoulos [1990a:51] translates it there as "utter filth.") Whether Paul intended the literal meaning "something cleaned right up," "utter filth," or the pagan allusion "scapegoat, outcast," a less learned reader of the Epistles might have concluded that the reference to rubbish meant something along the lines of worthlessness (as Kriaras [1968–97] and Šandrovskaja [1956a] have postulated) or an outcast in general. The genitive in "filth of the world" may also explain the *Tale*'s consistent use of the word in the phrase "κάθαρμα of the beasts" (τῶν ζῴων).

Given this, κάθαρμα appears to be used here in the sense of "ugly, freak" and is thus synonymous with παράσημον. We have rendered it as "freak" here and in 775 and (allowing ourselves some rhetorical license) as "disaster" in 942 (where Šandrovskaja's [1956a] урод, "monster," moves along the same lines).

690. **this tale**. What follows is a detailed variation on an Aesopic fable, which has survived to this day in Cyprus (see "Aesop and Folk Tale"). The donkey is portrayed as an exploited worker, and the notion of social protest is evident. This is the only time that the poet takes a break from the animals' endless disputation.

691. **made a resolution**. See Commentary verse 30.

693. **king**. Of course, the poem names here the *basileus*, the emperor, but the conventions of English storytelling would make that word sound out of place. See also Commentary verse 17.

695. **extra loads piled on your back**. The original has "the top loads (ἀπανωγόμια < ἀπάνω, "above" + γόμος, "load") they place on your middle." Tsiouni (1972) glosses the word—yet another hapax legomenon—as "a beast's load placed on it's [*sic*] back," whereas Šandrovskaja (1956a) has сверхпоклажу, "cargo on top." The sense they give is of an extra load on a donkey, placed on top of it rather than hanging from its sides, as was usual. The interpretation is Xanthoudidis's (1927–28:366), using P's reading ἀπανωμιγόμια < ἀπάνω, "above, in addition to" + μιγόμιν < ἡμιγόμιον, "half-load," in Cretan Greek the half of the load slung over one side of the donkey, whether in a sack or a basket.

Kriaras (1968–97, s.v. ἐπανωγόμιον) interprets the majority manuscript word as "extra load," which uses a legitimate meaning of the prefix (ἀ)πανω-; comparable instances in modern Greek are πανωτόκι, "above interest = excessive interest, usury," and πανωπροίκι, "extra dowry, requested after the dowry has already been agreed upon." The word απανωγόμι is reported to survive in the sense "extra load" in Cretan and Cypriot Greek (see "Aesop and Folk Tale": πουπανωγόμαρον). But even if P extrapolated ἀπανωμιγόμια from ἀπανωγόμια, the two senses are in effect the same (as Šandrovskaja [1956a:221] has already argued), and it is doubtful that the two words ever meant anything different. One cannot load as much on top of the donkey as on both sides, so the only way to do so is to get the donkey to carry both side loads and top loads; the top load is by necessity an extra load. Moreover, P uses ἀπανωγόμι(ν) in 715 and 725, like the other manuscripts, so it is unlikely the scribe of P actually intended anything different.

701. **donkeys**. As Eideneier (1976:459) points out, the adjectival form ὀνικά means "donkeys" and not "species of donkeys" as glossed by Tsiouni (1972) (so Šandrovskaja 1956a: ослами, "donkeys"); compare the originally adjectival Tsakonian δεντρ̌ικό, "tree" < δέντρον (Costakis 1986). The term enjoyed wide use in Byzantium (Kriaras 1968–97, s.v.) and survives in Cyprus and Karpathos in various forms (Andriotis 1974 §4409), among which is the Cypriot γονικόν (the form used in CLA).

708. **mile**. The Byzantine mile (Kazhdan 1991, s.v. MILION) was either 4,200 or 4,500 Byzantine "feet" in length; that makes it 1.3 or 1.4 kilometers, that is, 0.8 or 0.9 imperial miles.

729. **this good news**. The noun used here, συχαρίκιν, originally referred to congratulatory presents (Lampe 1961, s.v. συγχαρίκιον):

> ἐν αὐτῷ δὲ τῷ καιρῷ ὁ βασιλεὺς τῶν Ἰνδῶν πέμπει ***συγχαρίκια*** τῷ Ἡρακλείῳ ἐπὶ τῇ τῶν Περσῶν νίκῃ, μαργαρίτας καὶ λίθους τιμίους ἱκανούς, "At the same time the king of India sent ***gratulatory*** gifts to Herakleios on the occasion of his victory over Persia, namely pearls and a considerable number of precious stones." (*Theophanes the Confessor* 335)

This is the meaning reported by Somavera (1977 [1709], s.v. τὰ συγχαρίκια, τὰ συχαρίκια): *La mancia, ò il presente che si fà per la congratulatione,* "the gratuity or present given as congratulations."

In modern Greek, the word is always used in the plural and has three meanings as defined in Babiniotis (1998, s.v. συγχαρίκια): (1) "money or gift to one who announces pleasant news" (so also in Byzantius 1874, s.v. συγχαρήκια/σχαρήκια); (2) "(synecdoche) pleasant news"; (3) "congratulations." The first meaning is obviously the original, although it already represents a change away from Theophanes' gift to the recipient of good news toward a gift to the messenger. The following is a modern instance ambiguous between (1) and (2):

> Ἔτρεξε κι' ἕνας, Ἄσπρο Πουλάρι τόν λέγανε καί βρῆκε τόν Λουδοβῖκο στή φυλακή.
> —Μπάρμπα, τοῦ λέει, τί μοῦ τάζεις;
> —Πουρκουά;
> —Γιά τά ***σχαρίκια***, ρέ χλέα! Τόν ἐχθρό σου τόν Τουράν Σάχ τόν καθαρίσαμε. Νά δές τά χέρια μου, δικά του εἶναι τά αἵματα!
>
> [One guy ran, called White Foal, and found Louis ⟨IX⟩ in prison.
> —Nuncle, he tells him, what'll you pledge me?
> —*Pourquoi*?
> —For the ***congratulatory presents***, you shmuck! We knocked off your enemy, Turan Shah. Look at my hands, it's his blood!] (Tsiforos 1987:313)

However, with the death of the custom of rewarding messengers in modern Greece, that meaning seems to be moribund, too. Of the twenty-eight instances of the word found online (January 2002: search for *sygxarikia, sugxarikia, syxarikia, suxarikia,* συγχαρίκια, and συχαρίκια on www.google.com, groups.google.com, and www.alltheweb.com; repetitions not counted), twenty-one involve the dominant modern meaning of the word, which is "congratulations"—probably by association with the also plural neoclassical synonym, συγχαρητήρια:

> Yiannis Koutalos, in an immanent manifestation of deity, wrote:
Euxaristw, euxaristw, alla ta ***sugxarikia*** sthn 0eothta pou katadexthke na plhktrologhsei me ta anaksia daxtula mou.
[Ευχαριστώ, ευχαριστώ, αλλά τα ***συγχαρίκια*** στην θεότητα που καταδέχτηκε να πληκτρολογήσει με τα ανάξια δάχτυλά μου.]

[Thank you, thank you, but your ***congratulations*** should go to the deity that deigned to type through my unworthy fingers.] (Yiannis Koutalos, To statous tou xaou; Hellas mailing list, bit.listserv.hellas, February 3, 1997)

The exceptions are almost all quotations of earlier texts, although the "gift to newsbearer" sense is occasionally remembered by a contemporary speaker:

ema0a prox0es eva veo kai favtastnka oti av dev to exete ma0ei ap'allou 0a sas kakokardize va mou dwsete ta ***suxarikia***.

[έμαθα προχθές ένα νέο και φαντάστηκα ότι αν δεν το έχετε μάθει απ' αλλού ⟨δεν⟩ θα σας κακοκάρδιζε να μου δώσετε τα ***συχαρίκια***.]

[I heard some news the other day, and I imagined that, if you haven't already heard it from someone else, you will ⟨not⟩ mind giving me the ***gifts for the newsbearer***. ("Kosmas," Avupotaktoi kalws va mas er0ete; Hellas mailing list, bit.listserv.hellas, August 23, 2001; the "news" is a proposed reduction in military service for citizens over forty returning to Greece.)]

The meaning "good news" that Babiniotis (1998) reports arises by synecdoche: συγχαρίκια are given on receipt of good news, so they come to stand for the good news itself. This definition of the word was unfamiliar to us. However, we have identified two premodern instances of the word used in this sense (at least the first of which is ironic):

καὶ γράψαν μίαν διαταγὴ εἰς τὸν Καραϊσκάκη οἱ καλοὶ πατριῶτες καὶ τὄλεγαν, ὅταν κιντύνευε ἡ πατρίς, ὅταν νἄστιβε ὁ Καραϊσκάκης καὶ οἱ συντρόφοι του τὰ πουκάμισά τους, ἐκίναγε τὸ αἷμα ἀπὸ τὴν Ἀράχωβα, ἀπὸ τὸν Ἔπαχτο, ἀπὸ τὸ Δίστομον κι' ἀπὸ τὸν καθημερινὸ πόλεμο, τότε ἔγραψαν τοῦ Καραϊσκάκη καὶ τὄπαιρναν τὰ ***συχαρίκια*** ὅτι διόρισαν τὸν Τζούρτζη—κι' αὐτὸς νά εἶναι εἰς τὴν ὁδηγίαν του. (Makriyannis 1907:229; written around 1829)

[And they wrote out an order to Karaiskakis, did these good patriots, when the country was in danger, when Karaiskakis and his comrades had but to wring out their shirts and there'd have dripped from them the blood from Arachova, from Naupactos, from Distomon, from the battle day by day; they wrote then to Karaiskakis and bore him the ***glad tidings*** that they had appointed Church, and Karaiskakis was to be under his command.] (Makriyannis 1966:131)

Στον Νικολό Ράπτη (Τουρλαρονικολό) πήγαν τα ***συχαρίκια*** πως η νύφη του Αικατερίνη γέννησε ένα κοριτσάκι «άσπρο σαν το γάλα». Τότε ο Δημ. Πατίλης (Πατλομήτρος) είπε: «Ας ήταν παιδί (δηλ. αγόρι) κι ας ήταν μαύρο σαν το τηγάνι.»

[They brought Nicholas "Tourlaronikolos" Raptis the ***good news*** that his daughter-in-law Catherine had given birth to a little girl "white as milk." Then Dimitris "Patlomitros" Patilis said: "If only it was a boy, he could have been black as a frying pan."] (Papathanasopoulos 1998:152, reporting an early twentieth-century exchange from the village Perista in Aetolia and Acarnania)

Of the four meanings for the word we have found ("congratulatory gift," "gift to newsbearer," "good news," "congratulations"), it makes no sense in the *Tale*'s passage for a gift to be involved; the donkey is a messenger, but he says he will give the συγχαρίκιν, not receive it. The assembled donkeys are not messengers, so "gift to newsbearer" can be ruled out. Moreover, the only thing the donkey has to give is the good news itself; this also rules out Theophanes the Confessor's "congratulatory gift."

So only one of the later meanings can be involved: "good news" or "congratulations." Tsiouni (1972) glosses συχαρίκιν as "good news, cheerful news," picking the former, whereas Šandrovskaja (1956a) chooses the latter, поздравить, "to offer congratulations." The donkey could be congratulating his fellows on the good news, but "giving" the good news itself (in the form of the physical document) is a much more obvious thing for him to intend to do. We accordingly use Tsiouni's rather than Šandrovskaja's rendering.

Corroboration comes in contemporary works such as the Grottaferrata *Digenes* and *Callimachus and Chrysorrhoe*, in which συγχαρίκιν is clearly used in this sense:

Ἔλευσιν δὲ τὴν ἑαυτοῦ πάντες ἀναμαθόντες
εἰς τοὺς οἴκους ἀπέτρεχον εἰπεῖν τὰ ***συγχαρίκια***

[Everyone learnt of his arrival
and ran to the houses to bring ⟨tell⟩ the ***good news***] (*Digenes* G 3.310–11)

τὸ ***συγχαρίκιν*** γράφουσιν ὡς πρὸς τὸν βασιλέα,
πέμπουσι ταύτην τὴν γραφὴν μετὰ σπουδῆς μεγάλης

[they write the ***good news*** to the emperor,
they send the following letter with much haste] (*Callimachus and Chrysorrhoe* 2124–25)

Callimachus and Chrysorrhoe's editor Prichard (1956) likewise translates the word as *la bonne nouvelle,* "the good news."

732. **till I piss**. See "Aesop and Folk Tale."

763. **thunderous bells**. The word used here (βροντοκούδουνα in all the manuscripts) has survived in modern Greek dialect (Academy of Athens 1933–84, s.v. βροντοκούδουνο), referring to "a kind of edible fungus similar in shape to a little bell," and Kriaras (1968–97, s.v.), glosses it as almost the same ("a small aromatic plant that looks like a bell"). But it is absurd to decorate a horse with mushrooms, and the compound would have also been understood, then and now, literally as a kind of bell. In fact, the *Historical Dictionary of Modern Greek* itself presumes that βροντοκούδουνα in the *Tale* refers to "a kind of little bell," and Kazazis and Karanastassis (2001, s.v.) correct Kriaras's definition to "thundering bell."

Though the *Historical Dictionary of Modern Greek* does not attest any modern dialectal instances of βροντοκούδουνο as a kind of bell, various terms derived from βροντή, "thunder," are used to refer to cowbells or other bells worn by animals (Academy of Athens 1933–84, s.v. βρονταλίδι, βροντάρι, βροντήσιος). Moreover, in Crete the traditional three-stringed musical instrument, the λύρα, is distinguished from the larger, four-stringed βροντόλυρα, "thunder lyra," whereas in Almyros in Thessaly the word βρονταράδι is recorded in a folk song as referring to musical instruments in general (Academy of Athens 1933–84, s.v.). So to call the bells worn by a horse "thunder bells" matches a pattern well established in modern Greek. And the practice of adorning horses with bells itself was old enough to have been attested in the Hebrew Scriptures (Zechariah 14:20: "In that day shall there be upon the bells of the horses, holiness unto the Lord"). The word was understood to refer to a bell by both Šandrovskaja (1956a) (звонкими колокольчиками, "sonorous handbells") and Tsiouni (1972) ("loud-ringing bell").

764. **all decked out**. The original has κουβερτιασμένον (P), κουβερτωμένον (CVL), μουβερτωμένην (A), "covered," from Venetian *coverta.* The term literally means only "covered," and in modern Greek κουβέρτα means "blanket." However, the medieval term is almost always applied to horses (κουβέρτα: *Florios and Platziaflora* 538; *Achilleid* N 379; *Imperios and Margarona* 106, 385; κουβερτιάζω: *Theseid* 11.35: *Alexander Romance* V 60). The only exceptions (*Chronicle of Makhairas* 554, "ship deck"; *Chronicle of Morea* H 7698, 7724, "bedspread") seem to be derived from the French *couverture* instead. As it turns out, then, the *Tale* is echoing here the language used in the Byzantine romances of chivalry.

Byzantine horse armor was made of "hide, felt, lamellar, or mail" (Kazhdan 1991, s.v. ARMOR); we have already seen a reference to felt used in this function in verse 511.

771–75. **the camel who once begged** . . . This is an Aesopic fable from the horse about the camel (see "Literary Parallels"), whose overall depiction in the poem is not particularly flattering. In fact, the camel is the only "useful" animal that has not been permitted to brag of her merits and has been omitted from the Herbivores' Call (40–54).

775. **freak**. See Commentary verse 681.

787. **flanks**. The word used, κουτάλες, literally "spoons," means "shoulderblade" when applied to humans. Applied to horses, Kriaras (1968–97) believes it means "rump" (καπούλια); so Ricks's (1990:147) translation of *Digenes* E 1546–47: Καὶ ἐγὼ ραβδέαν ἔδωσα τὴν φάραν 'ς τὰς ***κουτάλας*** / καὶ ἀνάσκελα ἐξήπλωσεν ἡ θαυμαστὴ ἡ φάρα, "And I gave the mare a club-blow on its ***haunches*** / and the wonderful mare was stretched out on its back." But if Digenes is attempting to upend his Amazon rival's horse, it makes more sense to shove it over from the side, rather than making it somersault by striking it on the rear. Moreover, the legs and flanks of a horse are more reminiscent of spoons than are its haunches. So Jeffreys's (1997:153) rendering seems to us more plausible: "I gave the charger a blow on the ***flanks*** with my stick / and the marvellous charger collapsed with its legs in the air." As for the horse in the mill, its flanks are what will be rubbing against the wall, so they would be flayed long before its rump. Hence, we believe κουτάλες refers to "flanks." Tsiouni (1972) does not gloss the word; Šandrovskaja (1956a) has ушей, "ears" (!).

787. **neck**. The horse's σφόνδυλος is flayed through rubbing against either the wall of the mill or its harness. In either case, this is unlikely to involve the horse's back, so once again (see Commentary verse 84) σφόνδυλος is to be interpreted as "neck"—despite Šandrovskaja's (1956a) позвоночника, "spine." On the Byzantine use of horses in the mill, see Koukoules 1947–55:2.1.204.

788. **dizzy**. σκοτία literally means "darkness" (explicitly translated into the modern Greek σκοτεινάδα in L) and hence would here indicate blindness. But the secondary meaning of σκοτία, "dizziness," is already attested for the more frequent cognate noun σκότος in classical Greek (Hippocrates *Epidemiae* 5.23; Aristotle *Historia Animalium* 584a), to the extent that it has displaced "darkened" as the meaning of the verb σκοτίζομαι in verse 786; this verb has undergone its own semantic shift in modern Greek to "be concerned." That the ambiguity was in force in Byzantium is confirmed by the fact that *Ptochoprodromos* 3.233–36 puns on the two meanings "dizzy" and "blind":

> ***σκότος*** δὲ πάλιν ἀφεγγὲς τὸν ***σκοτασμόν*** μου κρίνω,
> ὃν ἔχω τότε, βασιλεῦ, ὅταν ψωμὶν οὐκ ἔχω,
> καὶ γὰρ μὴ ἔχων τί φαγεῖν ***σκοτίζομαι*** τῇ πείνῃ
>
> [I call my ***dizziness*** unlighted ***darkness***,
> which I endure when I lack bread, Your Highness;
> with naught to eat, I'm ***dizzy*** through my hunger.]

At any rate, the horse has already been blinded (785), so there is no point in having the world grow even darker for it. Šandrovskaja (1956a) has **огорчения,** "distress," which seems to refer to the modern Greek development of the word (cf. σκοτούρα, "distress"); we think it unnecessary to take this further step. Tsiouni (1972) leaves the word unglossed, implying that she preferred the older, classical meaning, "darkness."

In modern Greek dialects, the meaning "darkness" for σκοτία is attested in the Pontus (Ordu, Trebizond, Antreanti), Cappadocia (Misti), and Ithaca. The meaning "dizziness" is attested in the Cyclades (as σκοθι̯ά: islands of Melos, Paros, Naxos [Apiranthos], Thera, Tinos, Sifnos), in Cythera, in the Dodecanese (islands of Patmos and Astypalaea), and in the Peloponnese (Mani [Xehori], Lefktra, Kardamas, Saidona, Platsa) (data from *Historical Dictionary of Modern Greek* archives; see also Andriotis 1974 §5434). And "dizziness" is the only sense attested in Somavera (1977 [1709], s.v. σκοτίζω, σκοτίζομαι: *stordire, infoscare altrui la testa con molte parole, & abbucinare,* "to dizzy, to darken another's head with many words, and to bugle [?]"). Other than Ithaca, the original "darkness" meaning is restricted to the archaic dialects of Anatolia, which were already cut off from the mainstream development of Greek by late Byzantium. The "dizziness" meaning, on the other hand, occurs throughout southern Greece and is presumably of some antiquity. This bears out the validity of our choice.

794. **boots**. τζάγγας, according to Triandafyllidis (1963 [1909]:449) a Perso-Syrian loanword, *ein Art Stiefel,* "a kind of boot." In fact, the word is Parthian: the term is first attested in Latin by the historian Trebellius Pollio, citing a letter (possibly fictitious) by Emperor Gallienus (A.D. 260–268): *Misi autem ad eum . . . **zanchas** de nostris **Parthicas** paria tria,* "I am sending to him, moreover . . . three pairs of ***Parthian shoes*** from our own supply" (*Trebellius Pollio: Vita Divi Claudii* §17). Likewise the *Codex Theodosianus* (14.10.2, 14.10.3) reports that these shoes were banned from use in Rome, along with the just as foreign *bracae,* "trousers," in A.D. 397 and 399 (*usum **tzangarum** adque bracarum intra urbem venerabilem nemini liceat usurpare,* "no one is allowed to use trousers or ***tzangas*** within the venerable city"; *intra urbem Romam nemo vel bracis vel **tzangis {tzancis}** utatur,* "within the city of Rome no one shall use trousers or ***tzangas***"). Lewis and Short (1879, s.v.) accordingly gloss the word as "**zancha**, **zanca** or **zanga**. A kind of soft Parthian shoe."

In Greek, the term shows up as early as the *Paschal Chronicle* (*vii* A.D.; 614: τὰ γὰρ ***τζαγγία*** αὐτοῦ ἦν ἀπὸ τῆς χώρας αὐτοῦ ῥουσαῖα, Περσικῷ σχήματι, ἔχοντα μαργαρίτας, "His ***boots*** ⟨Tzathios's, crowned king of the Lazes by Justin I⟩ were from his own country, red, in Persian form, with pearls") and in the Greek translation of the fourth-century Syriac sermons of Ephraem the Syrian (*Sermo asceticus,* 1.126: Μὴ σήμερον ἀνυπόδετος, αὔριον δὲ ***τζάγγην*** ἢ καλίγην ἐπιζητεῖς, "Don't go barefoot today, only to ask for ***boots*** or shoes ⟨Latin *caliga*⟩ tomorrow"). As Koukoules (1947–55:4.409) argues, the term had spread to mean the boots worn "by farmers, poor workers and soldiers," that is, a generic term for "boot." This is clear even in the earliest examples: although the *Paschal Chronicle* is referring to exotic footwear worn by royalty within the Persian cultural sphere, the translations of Ephraem speak of it as footwear for commoners. (See also Kazhdan 1991, s.v. TZANGION.)

That τζάγγα referred to a common kind of footwear is further confirmed by the survival of the professional term τσαγγάρης to mean "cobbler" in modern Greek, though the word for the boot has disappeared from most dialects of the language. The word did survive in Cappadocia and the Pontus (Dawkins 1916:617 [ǰavǰí], Papadopoulos 1961, s.v. τζαγκί[ν]), denoting in both dialects a knee-high boot; in Chios, meaning "boot"; and in West Crete, in the adjective τσαgᾶτος, "wearing shoes, wearing boots" (Andriotis 1974 §6116). And Somavera (1977 [1709], s.v. τζαγκί) still knows of it as πόδημα, *stivale grande per l'acqua,* "large boot for use in water."

In Byzantium τζαγγάρης was used for "cobbler" in general and not specifically "boot maker"; the distinct term τζαγγᾶς was used for the maker of imperial boots (Koukoules 1947–55:4.398). Accordingly, τζαγγάρης is also used in this generic fashion in the *Tale* (389, 514), without being restricted to a maker of boots. The τζάγγα itself, however, was uncontroversially a boot.

The reading τζάγγας is Xanthoudidis's emendation; see Textual Notes.

802. **ill-shaped**. The adjective παράσημος (also used in 937 and 942; παρασημία in CVL 802 and 937) properly refers to counterfeit currency ("missigned," "misstamped"), although Aristophanes early on applied it metaphorically to people (*Acharnians* 517–18: ἀλλ' ἀνδράρια μοχθηρά, παρακεκομμένα, / ἄτιμα καὶ ***παράσημα*** καὶ παράξενα, "but some badly minded troublemaking creeps, some worthless ***counterfeit*** foreign currency"); by extension, it was also used to refer to "false" or "incorrect" (i.e., non-Attic) expressions (Liddell–Scott–Jones 1940, s.v., I.2).

The term survived in use in the vernacular, with the "counterfeit" sense yielding to "ill-shaped, misshapen." The *Mass of the Beardless Man* uses the adjective quite frequently to refer to its target, almost always as an epithet, but at least once tying it to the Beardless Man's body: Ὄρη καὶ βουνοὶ γελῶσιν αὐτόν, ὅταν ἴδωσι τὴν ***παράσημον*** αὐτοῦ μορφήν, "Mountains and hills shall laugh at him, when they see his ***ill-shapen*** form" (D 116). (The vernacular translation of the *Life of Aesop,* on the other hand, uses the word to mean "witty": the Koine *Life of Aesop* W [variant MORNLo] §32: στωμύλος μοι ὁ σαπρὸς φαίνεται καὶ ***εὐτράπελος,*** "this rotten man seems to me talkative and ***witty***" is rendered in 1 §32 as καὶ πολύλαλος φαίνεται ὁ σαπρὸς καὶ ***παράσημος,*** "this rotten man seems talkative and [***witty***].") Somavera (1977 [1709]) glosses the adjective παράσημος as ὁποῦ εἶναι ὄξω ἀπὸ τὴν φύσιν, "that which is outside of nature," *mostruoso, stormato,* "monstrous," and he glosses the phrase παράσημον πρᾶγμα, "παράσημος thing," as παρασούσουμον, παράπλασμα, μόστρο, *mostro, monstro,* "monster." And in modern Greek dialect, Andriotis (1974 §4681) records the stem surviving in Vytina in the Peloponnese (παράσημος), Tsakonia (παράσημο), and Crete (παράσουμος)—all meaning *verkrüppelt, verstümmelt,* "crippled, maimed"—and in northern Thrace (παρασήμι) as the noun *Mißgeburt,* "freak." All these senses converge on παράσημος referring to someone whose appearance is extraordinary and unpleasant—not an unreasonable comment to make of the camel.

In each instance in the *Tale*, the word appears in the context παράσημον τῶν ζῴων, "ill-shaped one of the beasts"; in the final instance, it is combined with another word associated with τῶν ζῴων: κάθαρμα, "freak." In the first two instances, παράσημον is in the neuter, agreeing with ζῷον, "animal" and appears to be used as a noun ("ill-shaped one of the beasts" patterned after κάθαρμα τῶν ζῴων, "freak of the beasts"—on which formula see Commentary verse 681). As far as we can tell, this shift of the adjective to the corresponding noun is unique in the *Tale*, because everywhere else in classical and medieval Greek the noun παράσημον refers to an emblem (cf. modern Greek, "medal"), a marginal note, or a password (Liddell–Scott–Jones 1940, s.v.; Sophocles 1900, s.v.)—not directly related to the adjective παράσημος, if one excepts the rare use "birthmark" (Liddell–Scott–Jones 1940, s.v., II.1.b). In fact, the noun and the adjective were associated with distinct genres: the noun ("emblem, note, password") almost always occurs in historical writings, whereas the adjective ("false, misshapen") is most popular in theological writing. The Thracian noun παρασήμι (freak), identified by Andriotis (1974), however, and Somavera's separate entry (1977 [1709]) for παράσημον πρᾶγμα show that the *Tale*'s author wasn't the only person to have come up with the adjective-to-noun transition of παράσημον in the history of Greek. The form used in CVL, παρασημία (802 and 937 only), is a nominalization unattested in classical Greek—and is if anything even closer to παρασήμι and παράσημον πρᾶγμα.

Tsiouni (1972) glosses the word as "badly made"; Šandrovskaja (1956a), as нескладный, "unharmonious," in 802 and 937 and нелепый, "absurd," in 942.

803. **feast of wolves**. As Trapp (1976) correctly points out, although -φαγωμένος can mean "bitten," "worn down," or "eroded" as well as "eaten" in modern Greek, the only plausible gloss for λυκοφαγωμένος is "eaten by wolves" rather than Tsiouni's "bitten" (1972). The past tense of the participle is not a problem: the horse is not referring specifically to the donkey standing before him, and in any case modern Greek is deficient in present (= progressive) passive participles. Šandrovskaja (1956a) has добыча, "booty; prey," which moves along the same lines.

806. **found some roasted meat**. Similar to the modern Greek expressions πέσαμε στο ψητό, "we have fallen onto the roast" = "we have fallen upon a great opportunity," and έρχομαι στο ψητό, "to come to the roast" = "to get to the point" (Sarantakos 1997:267).

824. **pick on someone my own size**. "To the Chechens, the wolf ('Borz') is the most respected and famous animal in nature. The explanation for this is that: 'the lion and the eagle are the symbols of strength, but they attack only the weak animals. The wolf however, is the only beast that dares to attack a

stronger animal. Its lack of strength is compensated for by its extreme daring, courage and adroitness. If he loses the struggle, he dies silently, without expression of fear or pain. And he dies proudly, facing his enemy'" (Usmanov 1999; the she-wolf is a symbol of Chechnya).

833. **night thief**. The term νυκτοκλέπτης also turns up in *Ptochoprodromos* 4.555, where the destitute hero complains that, in his rags, he will be taken for a "night thief." The term there clearly means "burglar" or "robber" (Eideneier 1991:216 renders it as *Räuber* "robber," and for the *Tale* Šandrovskaja [1956a] has ночной вор, "night burglar"), so the form "night thief" may well have been a commonplace word for "burglar" rather than an innovative compound. Compare the law in the *Prochiron* 39.4 (early x A.D.): Ἐὰν τὸν ***ἐν νυκτὶ κλέπτοντα*** φονεύσῃ τίς, τότε ἀτιμώρητος μένει, ὅτε μὴ ἠδύνατο δίχα κινδύνου ἰδίου φείσασθαι αὐτοῦ, "If one should kill a person ***thieving at night***, then he shall go unpunished, for he could not have spared him without danger to his own person."

833. **feral-eating**. Tsiouni (1972) glosses θρασιοφᾶς (θρασιοφᾶ CV, θρασίοφα L, θαρσιοφᾶ A, θρασοφά P) as "rash, daring"; presumably she regards the word as a synonym of θρασύς, "rash," which is unwarranted, as the second part of the word clearly means "eating" (-φᾶς < -φάγος). The first part of the word is θράσιο-, which is reminiscent of modern Greek θρασίμι, "animal carcass, carrion." Šandrovskaja (1956a) accordingly has пожиратель гнилого, "devourer of the rotten." Thavoris (1969) points out that the word θράσιος or θράσος is still extant in modern dialects, meaning both "carcass" and "animal let loose." Rejecting Hatzidakis's (1977:1.587–88) earlier derivation, proposed in 1910 (θρασός < classical σαθρός, "decayed"), Thavoris derives θράσιος from θρασίμι, which in turn he derives from the classical θηράσιμος (Byzantine θηρασιμόν, attested in Du Cange 1958 [1688]) "hunted animal"; the semantic chain is "hunted animal" > "wild animal" > "killed wild animal" > "carrion" OR "wild animal" > "domesticated animal let loose like a wild animal." Thavoris (1969:452) counts the instance in the *Tale* as the earliest attestation of θράσιος, and Kriaras (1968–97) concurs.

The problem is, which of the two interpretations of θράσιος to give here: does the wolf eat carrion, as is the dominant modern meaning of the word, or game, as is its etymological meaning? Kriaras hedges his bets by introducing both glosses: "eating wild animals (αγρίμια), carrion (θρασίμια)." However, because there is no occurrence of θρασίμι or θράσιο in medieval Greek, we cannot appeal to direct usage of the word. All we can be sure of is that "wild game" is the etymologically prior meaning of θράσιος, and we prefer it for reasons of caution over the later meaning, "carrion"; our rendering, "feral-eating," reflects this. Although the eating of carcasses was taboo in Byzantium (Koukoules 1947–55:5.59–60) and is a more plausible feature to use as an insult, it does not match with wolf behavior: although wolves will eat dead prey if no live animals are available, they do not do so by preference (Fiennes 1976:119).

Reportedly wolves are not averse to human corpses (Fiennes 1976:119), but as θράσιος is used to refer to a human corpse only marginally (1b in the following list), this meaning may be ruled out. Moreover, the bear calls the wolf in the same phrase a "strangler" (πνιγάρη), which clearly means he kills his own prey.

The foregoing gives a simplified account of the meaning of θράσιος, which has in fact diversified prodigiously in Greek dialect. For completeness, the various meanings of θράσιο reported by Thavoris (1969) from *Historical Dictionary of Modern Greek* material should be listed.

1. **animal carcass**: πάγει θράσιο τὸ ἀρνί, "the lamb has gone *thrasio*" = "it has not been slaughtered on time, has died naturally."
1a. **useless, unproductive**: "lazy"; "cowardly"; "infertile land"; "dirty water"; "wasted effort."
1b. **sickly, dying**: "sickly (of sheep)"; "unhealthy place"; "thirsty"; "prematurely dead"; "suddenly dead."
1c. **tasteless, gamey**: "tasteless"; "unbuttered food"; "unboiled meat."
2. **running free, unbound**: τὰ πρόβατα τά 'χω θράσα, "I've left the sheep *thrasa*" (Andros, Tinos).
2a. **bountiful**: "producing much milk" (Leucas); "blooming (of plant)" (Messenia).

There seems to be little potential in the meanings grouped under (1), even though they constitute the majority of the modern meanings of θράσιος. The meaning "prematurely dead," for example, is normally associated with humans and would display an atypical sentimentality applied to the wolf's more usual prey. Speculation on how tasty the wolf's fare is would be similarly unprofitable, and we have already rejected the interpretation "carrion." As can be seen, on the other hand, the postulated original meaning "wild animal" is nowhere attested in modern Greek, and "unbound" (whereby the wolf would be eating a sheep or goat either escaped or allowed out of the pen) is a minor component of its current range of meanings. In fact, so inconsistent is "unbound" with the main trend of meanings of θράσιος that its secondary meaning "bountiful" (2a) directly contradicts the prevalent secondary meaning, "useless" (1a).

The archaic meaning actually preserved in (2) is "free-ranging," not "wild," and one might be tempted to interpret θρασιοφᾶς as "eating free-range sheep," "eating sheep that have not been penned in." Depredations of the wolf against domestic livestock would have been of greater concern to a human than wild game: it is what the wolf boasts of in 817–23, and θρασιοφᾶς is immediately followed by νυκτοκλέπτης, "night thief"—which, by postulating ownership, clearly refers to domestic rather than wild prey. If the two nouns are connected, then θρασιοφᾶς should also refer to depredations against free-range livestock. Now, in the original the two nouns are separated by ἀλλὰ καί, "but also." However, usage in the *Tale* of ἀλλὰ καί is such that one cannot tell whether the second term is used in contrast to the first or in corroboration—compare 63, literally "the unclean *but also* the bloody," versus 96, literally "the clean and domestic *but also* the bloody." If θρασιοφᾶς is a synonym of νυκτοκλέπτης, it refers to (free-range) livestock. If it is an antonym, it can refer to either wild game (as opposed to livestock) or free-range (as opposed to penned) livestock. Because all three interpretations are possible, νυκτοκλέπτης cannot decide the meaning of θρασιοφᾶς.

Attractive as the interpretation of θρασιοφᾶς as "eating free-range animals" is, in any case, it would still involve a regionally restricted modern usage (two adjacent islands in the Cyclades), unattested in medieval times. And if sheep had been left free ranging or allowed to escape in an area known to have wolves, the bear would be better advised to insult the shepherd than the night-thieving wolf for the inevitable result. We thus regard "feral-eating" as the most conservative interpretation.

842. **pumped bloodless**. See Commentary verse 1002.

844. **honey-munching**. The text has μελισσοφάγα, "bee-eating," which Tsiouni (1972) and Kriaras (1968–97) gloss literally as "one who eats bees." But to have the bear eating insects is absurd; the animal named μελισσοφάγος in modern Greek is a bird, the bee-eater or tomtit (genus *Merops*), as already defined in Somavera (1977 [1709]): μελισσοφάγον (πουλὶ): *aparicolo, lupo delle api (ucello),* "bee-eater (bird)." The *Tale*'s usage is obviously a straightforward synecdoche instead, with "bee" standing for "honey," as Gidel (1866:326) already understood it. Šandrovskaja (1956a) likewise has едок меда, "eater of honey." One might compare the words used in the fifteenth-century astrological work *A Boy Born in the Time of the Zodiac*: μελισσογένης, "bee-bearded"; μελισσίθριξ, "bee-haired"; μελισσοπούγουνος, "bee-chinned" (Kriaras 1968–97, s.v. μελισσογένης, μελισσόθριξ, μελισσοπώγωνος), clearly denoting "honey blond," though the editor Kakoulidi-Panou (1980:86) admits those word formations are not vernacular. A bee is highly unlikely to be something hair color is compared to—besides which, bees are hardly exemplars of yellowness. Kriaras's derivation of the words from the adjective μελισσός, "bee-colored" (Cretan Greek: Hatzidakis 1989–90 [1905–07]:1.148), is beside the point: μελισσός would have already meant "honey-colored" by synecdoche anyway.

845. **squinting**. Tsiouni (1972) has given στραβός its main modern Greek gloss when applied to vision, "blind." However, στραβός is glossed in Liddell–Scott–Jones 1940 (s.v.) as "squinting." Etymologically, στραβός is derived from στρέφω, "turn, twist," and so means "cross-eyed." This is what most older usage indicates. The word first appeared in Koine, and Phrynichus (*ii* A.D.), who as an Atticist prescribed against it, relates it to the Attic στρεβλός, also derived from στρέφω: στρεβλός: ὁ διάστροφος τοὺς ὀφθαλμούς, ἀλλ' οὐχὶ στραβός, "*στρεβλός*: one whose eyes are distorted, but not *στραβός*" (*Preparatio sophistica* 108). This sense persisted long in Byzantium; for example, Eustathius of Thessalonica and many other Byzantine lexicographers erroneously define the Homeric φολκός, "lame," as follows:

Ἔστι δὲ φολκὸς μὲν ὁ ***στραβός***, ὁ τὰ φάη, τουτέστι τοὺς ὀφθαλμούς, μὴ ὀρθὰ ἔχων ἀλλὰ ἐστραμμένα καὶ παρειλκυσμένα τῆς κατὰ φύσιν ὀρθότητος, "And φολκός ⟨φαολκός⟩ means ***cross-eyed***, he whose φάη, that is, eyes, are not straight but turned and drawn aside from their natural straightness." (*Commentary on the Iliad* 1.314)

Pseudo-Zonaras likewise (again erroneously) glosses ἑτερόφθαλμος, "one-eyed," as στραβός, ἀλλοθεώρης—where ἀλλοθεώρης is merely the older form of ἀλλήθωρος, "cross-eyed," the adjective used in this same verse. Conversely Somavera (1977 [1709]) glosses στραβός, στραβομάτης, "στραβός-eyed" as *guercio, cieco d'un occhio,* "cross-eyed, blind in one eye." This identification of στραβός with "cross-eyed" has passed into English: the medical term *strabism* refers to being cross-eyed.

But there is a long distance from "cross-eyed" to "blind," and there is evidence for στραβός having the intermediate meaning "myopic" or "night-blind." Liddell–Scott–Jones (1940, s.v.) reports that στραβός was glossed into contemporary Latin as *luscus,* "half-blind." Du Cange's dictionary (1958 [1688]) seems to attest all three meanings: his definition of στραβάρα is *luscitio,* "night-blindness"; *vitium oculorum,* "eye defect"; but he then cites Meursius's (1614) dictionary in which the Homeric ἀλαοσκοπή, "blind man's watch = inattentiveness," is glossed as τύφλωσις τῶν ὀφθαλμῶν, "blindness of the eyes" (classical), ***στραβάρα*** τῶν ἀμματιῶν, "***blindness*** of the eyes" (vernacular). And Du Cange's definition of στραβομάτης, "στραβός-eyed" (s.v. ὀμμάτη) is *strabo,* "squinting,"; *torvus,* "grim"; *aspectu obliquus,* "looking askance"; στράβων, "squinting"; βλοσυρωπός, "grim-looking"—all of these more likely alluding to "cross-eyed."

So we have three candidate senses: "cross-eyed"; "myopic"; "blind." Given the context, the sense "blind" can safely be rejected, as in fact Trapp (1976:446) has already done: it is odd for the bear to be both blind and looking downward (χαμηλοβλεποῦσα). Trapp interprets στραβός as *schielend,* "cross-eyed," instead, and this has the advantage of making ἀλληθώρα καὶ στραβή one of the synonym pairs so beloved of the author. Though a fumbling and maltreated bear may have seemed myopic to an observer, the synonym to ἀλληθώρα seems a safer bet, so we have opted for "squinting," to be understood as "cross-eyed."

The word στραβός generalized early on, from "cross-eyed" to "crooked": στραβοπόδης, "crooked-legged," is attested as early as Herodian (*ii* A.D.); compare στραβοκερέα, "crooked-horned," in verse 468 of the *Tale*. Šandrovskaja (1956a) uses this sense (кривой) but it is implausible here: στραβή occurs between two adjectives referring to vision (verse 845 literally has "and cross-eyed and στραβή and downwards-looking"), and it is not clear why the bear would be referred to as having a crooked body.

846. **dirtbag**. The word βρωμοφηκάρα, "case of filth" (φηκ- being a common dialectal variant of θηκ-, "case") is otherwise unattested in medieval

Greek, but compare βρωμοθήκη recorded in Imbros as an insult directed to a woman (Andriotis 1955:227). A chamberpot may be meant. The emendation of V (originally spelled βρομοφυκάρα, "filth-seaweed" [?], in the manuscript) dates from Hesseling (1924:314).

The readings of P, κορμοφηκάρα, "body case," and C, βορμοφηκάρα, are presumably corrupt.

846. **foolish gypsies**. Eideneier (1976:459) suggests μωροατζίγγανος means "swarthy (< Moorish) Gypsy" (μορο-), rather than "foolish Gypsy" (μωρο-), comparing it semantically with *Father Wine* V 13: μαυροκατζίβελλος, "swarthy (< black) Gypsy." Kriaras (1968–97) has adopted this reading of the *Tale*'s word in his dictionary, adding that the Gypsies might have been called black because of their getting dirty in their traditional occupation as blacksmiths. The prefix μορο-, "Moorish," is Italian (< *moro,* "dark") and in vernacular Byzantine literature appears otherwise only in a dvandva (μοροκαταλάνοι, "Moors and Catalans") in Pseudo-Georgillas's *Fall of Constantinople* 416; this suggests the word would have been understood as a noun ("Moors and Gypsies") rather than an adjective ("black Gypsies"). The word on its own occurs in the *Mass of the Beardless Man* and frequently in post-Byzantine literature (written under Venetian rule), but it consistently means "Moor" rather than "black" in general: compare Koroneos *Bua* 31: Ἡλίου ἀνατέλλοντος ἔσωσ' ὁ χαρτοφόρος / ποῦ ἥλιος τὸν μαύρισε, καὶ γίνετον ὡς ***Μόρος,*** "At sunrise did the messenger arrive; / tanned by the sun, he looked just like a ***Moor***."

As a further instance, Trivolis considered "Syrian" to be an instance of μόρος: ἕνας μπαζαρκάνος / ***μῶρος***, ποὖτονε Σουριάνος, "a ***Moorish*** merchant, who was Syrian" (*Tagiapièra* 77–78). Syrians may be swarthier than Greeks, but they are not, properly speaking, "black." This confirms that μόρος in Greek—much like *Moor* in Western Europe—referred more to the region and religion of the Middle East than to the color of Africans' complexion. This was a general trend for the time; for example, a Venetian chronicler in 1496 used *moresca* to mean "Arabic" (i no sa franco, ma i ha la lengua greca, ***moresca*** e turca, "they ⟨two Lebanese brothers⟩ did not know Frankish ⟨any Western European language⟩, but they did know Greek, ***Moorish***, and Turkish": Cortelazzo 1970:92). Somavera 1977 [1709] does define μῶρος as μαύρος, *un moro, un negro,* "a Moor, a black man," but this definition is late and still treats μόρος as a racial rather than color term.

By contrast, there is ample precedent for the use of μωρο-, "foolish," as a prefix in the *Tale* (e.g., 525: μωρόλαλος, "foolish-talking"; "swarthy-talking" would make no sense) and elsewhere in medieval Greek (Kriaras, 1968–97 s.v. μωροθαύμαστος, μωροκόπελο, μωρολόγι/μωρολογία/μωρόλογος/μωρολογῶ). (The use of μωρο- to mean "slightly," as in μωρογεμάτος, "fullish," however, seems irrelevant: there is no point in saying the bear trainers are "slightly Gypsy.") And it seems a stretch to posit the use as a color term of "Moorish" instead of the normal Greek μαυρο-, "black," to describe swarthiness (cf. 665: μαυροπείσματος) in a text where the influence of Italian is relatively slight—particularly as the word is not used in medieval Greek as a color term at all but as a racial term.

Even if μωρο- were understood as a racial term, however, its use in this passage would imply either that Muslims/Moors, in addition to Gypsies (see note following) were bear trainers (dvandva: "mere toy for Moors and Gypsies to make sport with")—something for which we have no evidence—or that Byzantines conflated Muslim Moors with Gypsies ("mere toy for the Moorish Gypsies to make sport with"). Greeks did conflate Gypsies with Middle Easterners enough to call them γύφτοι < αἰγύπτιοι, "Egyptians" (also the etymology of *Gypsy*), but we are not aware of Gypsies being called specifically Moorish anywhere else in medieval Greek, and the insistence on the precise racial affiliation of bear wards seems an odd comment to make. Moreover, such an interpretation of μορο- would certainly make this the earliest attestation of μόρος, "Moor," in Greek, by up to a century—which in itself is reason to be skeptical. We have thus not adopted μορο- in either of its senses—Eideneier's (1976) reading ("swarthy") or "Moorish"—and have preferred μωρο-, "foolish," as have Šandrovskaja (1956a), Tsiouni (1972), and Papathomopoulos (2002).

846. **to make sport with**. To this day, Gypsies tour villages in Greece and all over the Balkans with dancing bears. These are trained to dance by being forced to jump on burning coals to the sound of drums. (A Greek proverb states that νηστικό αρκούδι δεν χορεύει, "a hungry bear will not dance.") The Byzantines spoke of Gypsies in the same breath as bearkeepers (e.g., Theodore Balsamon, in Rallis and Potlis 1852:2.444–45) but do not seem to have generally identified them as the same people (Soulis 1961:146–47). The identification was certainly in place by 1638, by Evliyâ Çelebi:

> The Leaders of Bears (Ayijián) are Gipsies who have no patron ⟨saint⟩; they inhabit the quarter called Shah Mahalleh, in the suburb of Balát. They appear in public processions, being attached and belonging to the hunters, in their train. They number about seventy men, having strange names, such as Káryághdí, Awára, Dúraják, Binbereket, Bazi-oghlí, Sívrí-oghlí, and Haiwán-oghlí, leading bears by double chains, with cudgels in their hands, and playing on tambourines. If from time to time a bear gets up, they cry, "O Wassil! now show thy skill; they took thee from the mountain, and have bred thee like a man. Wheels turn in the garden in watering it, why shouldst thou not turn in dancing." Saying such idle words as these, they pass playing the tricks before the Aláï-koshk ⟨Imperial pavilion⟩. (von Hammer 1968 [1834]:1.2.146)

853. **discharge**. ῥεύματα is not glossed by Tsiouni (1972); Šandrovskaja (1956a) renders it as **ревматизме**, "rheumatism," and the same meaning is presumed by Koukoules (1947–55:5.418) in his discussion of the passage, using the modern Greek word ρευματισμοί. No other examples of bear fat used in Byzantium for medical purposes are named by him.

In classical and postclassical Greek, ῥεῦμα and (by extension) ῥευματισμός meant "rheum, sickly discharge." For example, Aëtius in the seventh century (*Iatricorum* 16.63) cites Archigenes' definition of menstruation as Ὁ καλούμενος γυναικεῖος ῥοῦς, ***ῥευματισμός*** ἐστι χρόνιος τῆς ὑστέρας, "the so-called womanly flow is a chronic ***discharge*** of the womb." The same holds for *rheumatismus* in classical Latin, though the term was used in general to refer to some flow in the body causing disease and had "become in course of time merely a loose, lay expression implying pain of obscure origin" (Copeman 1964:120). This development in Latin was paralleled in Greek; for example, the same Aëtius refers to gout (ποδάγρα) and arthritis (ἀρθρῖτις) as ἀσθένειά ... τῶν ἄρθρων χρονία ***ῥευματική*** "a chronic ***rheumatic*** disease of the joints" (*Iatricorum* 12.2)—but in his discussion in the ensuing chapters, he makes it obvious that by "rheumatic" he is referring to the humors of the body (melancholic *rheuma*, phlegmatic *rheuma*, etc.). He also speaks of ἡμικρανίαι γὰρ καὶ σφάκελοι καὶ ***ῥευματισμοὶ*** τῆς κεφαλῆς, "migraines and convulsions and ***ῥευματισμοί*** of the head" (*Iatricorum* 7.96), and ἐλευθεροῖ μὲν τὸν ὀφθαλμὸν τῶν ***ῥευματισμῶν,*** "ridding the eye of ***ῥευματισμοί***" (*Iatricorum* 7.60), referring to the surgical excision of pterygia (tissue growing over the cornea—*not* associated with discharge); pterygia themselves, Aëtius claims, are caused by "ῥευματισμοί of the head." So in medieval Greek medical usage, the term would have referred to both "discharge" and "pain originating from the presumed flows of the humors." The former usage continued into early modern Greek: Somavera (1977 [1709]) glosses ῥεματίζω as *esser pieno di catarri,* "be full of catarrhs."

The modern use of *rheumatism* to refer exclusively to a form of arthritis dates only from Guillaume de Baillou in 1591, in his *Liber de Rhumatismo* published in 1642 (Copeman 1964:121). Furthermore, this shift affected only *rheumatismus* and not *rheuma*. Thus, *rheum* in English retains its original meaning of "discharge" in Shakespeare and later writers. As we argue later, the transition had nothing to do with Byzantium, and the modern Greek use of ρευματισμός to mean "rheumatism" must be considered a returning loan (*Rückwanderer*) from Western European languages. We therefore reject Šandrovskaja's (1956a) interpretation as rheumatism—even though the use of carnivore fat as a cure for rheumatism is commonplace (Turnbull-Kemp 1967:157) and bear cub fat was prescribed as such a remedy as recently as 1838 (Copeman 1964:viii).

The normal Byzantine term for rheumatism in its modern sense seems to have been "arthritis" (ἀρθρῖτις) or "arthritic (joint) pains" (ἀρθριτικὰ πάθη) (Jeanselme 1920; Koukoules 1947–55:6.32–33; ἀρθρῖτιν νόσον, "arthritic illness," in *Prodromus: For a Live Fox*: see "Subversion and Politics," endnote 108)—although Koukoules includes the *Tale*'s ῥεύματα in his discussion. We have no evidence that Aëtius's usage of ῥευματισμός to refer to arthritis was continued, particularly in the vernacular. Thus, Staphidas (pp. 10, 11) speaks of ῥεμματισμός as distinct from ἁρμοπονία, "joint aches"; his treatment for "rhemmatism" is νὰ ἀλειφθῇ μέλιν καὶ νὰ θέσῃ ἀπάνω κύμινον κοπανισμένον καὶ κρησαρισμένον, καὶ νὰ τὸ φασκιώσῃ καλὰ καὶ νὰ ὑπνώσῃ, "smear honey and place on it ground and sifted cumin, bind it well, and have him sleep." And a contemporary popular remedy speaks of ῥέμμα, "current; discharge" (flow of humors in the body causing pain?) in an incantation against headaches (κεφαλαλγίαν):

> Ὁ Κύριος ἡμῶν Ἰησοῦς Χριστὸς ἐν τόπῳ κρανίου ἐσταυρώθη, καὶ ἐτάφη, καὶ ἀνέστη· καὶ σὺ, ***ῥέμμαν, ἀγριόρρεμμαν***, ἔξελθε καὶ ἀναχώρησε ἀπὸ τὸν δοῦλον τοῦ θεοῦ δεῖνα, καὶ ἄγωμε εἰς τὰ ἄγρια ὄρη, ἔνθα σημαντηρίου φωνὴ οὐκ ἀναβαίνει· φεῦγε, δαιμονικὸν συναπάντημα, ἀπὸ τὸν δοῦλον τοῦ θεοῦ δεῖνα.
>
> [Our Lord Jesus Christ was crucified in a place of a skull and was buried and is risen; and you, ***current***, ***wild current***, come out and leave from the servant of God so-and-so and go to the wild mountains, where the voice of the bell does not rise to; leave, thou demonic encounter, from the servant of God so-and-so] (*Remedies* 19)

The vernacular remedies published by Oikonomu-Agorastu (1982) point squarely to ῥεῦμα meaning "discharge." Of the remedies, §210 and §287 are for the "rheum" (ρέμαν) of eyes; §97, for "rheumatizing = discharging" (ρευματιζομένων) eyes; and §106, for "rheumatizing" gums. The comparable terms for the head could be understood likewise in terms of discharge or in association with pain caused by an internal flow of "humors" (§70: Περὶ τοῦ στῆσαι ρεῦμα κεφαλῆς, "to stop the rheum of the head"; §141: Περὶ ρεουσῶν τριχῶν κεφαλῆς, "for discharging hairs on the head"; §182: Περὶ κεφαλῆς ρεούσης, "for a flowing = discharging head"; §275: Περὶ ρέμαν κεφαλῆς, "for the rheum of the head"). Indeed, the use of bear fat attested in the *Tale* is probably that also invoked in Oikonomu-Agorastu's remedy §54:

> Περὶ πληγὴν κεφαλῆς. . . . Ἄλλον: ἄρκου λίπος ἄλειφε καὶ ἀλῴπεκος καὶ ὑγιάνει καὶ τρίχας φύει παραδόξως, "For a wound to the head. . . . Alternatively: Smear bear fat and fox fat, and it will recover, and grow hairs wondrously."

The word πληγή, "wound," can also mean a sore, and the discharge of hairs in remedy §141 suggests some kind of sore associated with hair loss.

The use of bear fat in a cure for baldness, which appears to be invoked in remedy §54, is explicitly mentioned in remedy §71 (Περὶ τρίχωμα κεφαλῆς ὁποὺ ἔχει λειψάδιν . . . τὴν δὲ ἄλλην κατακόψας τηγάνισον μετὰ στέατος ἄρκου, "On hair on the head which is lacking . . . and chop up the other ⟨lizard⟩ and fry it in bear fat") and is repeated from Aëtius (*Iatricorum* 2.155), whereas the vernacular *Hippiatrica* (*Excerpta Ludgunensia* 68) advises that bear fat should be used to repair horsetail hair. This is the tradition the *Tale* seems to follow. The use of bear fat as a cure for aching falcon feet (*Vulgar Bird Lore* 552–53: ***Ἀξούγγιν ἀρκῷον*** θερμανεῖς ** κακκάβιν καὶ τοὺς πόδας αὐτοῦ συχνῶς ἀλείψεις, "Heat ***bear fat*** ⟨in a⟩ cauldron and rub its feet continuously") is likely related to its use against rheumatism instead.

The use of the same preposition (εἰς) twice in the verse, meaning "***in*** ointments ***for*** rheum," is awkward but not impossible. The alternative that ῥεῦμα here derives from its main meaning "current," referring to some kind of lotion (***in*** ointments, ***in*** lotions), is attractive but unsubstantiated.

856. **brave**. The ambiguous ἀνδρειωμένα is used here (see Commentary verse 559). The adjective co-occurs with "strong," but this could mean either that it is intended as a synonym or that it adduces bravery as another trait of the felines. However, because the cheetah goes on to emphasize what we consider to be his bravery (using the same ambiguous adjective!—see Commentary verse 870), we have chosen "brave" for consistency.

862. **baring their teeth**. See Commentary verse 971.

862. **lying both in ambush**. The word as it appears in the manuscripts, ἐνεγκριματοῦσαν, has tripped up many a scholar. Tsiouni (1972) provides no gloss for it, though it is clearly a postclassical term. Xanthoudidis (1927–28:367) was led by the reading ἐγκρεομανοῦσαν of P to emend the passage to ἀγγριομανοῦσαν (< ἀγγρίζω, "rage" + μανίζω, "be angry"). The other four manuscripts, however, point to ἐνεγκριματοῦσαν quite clearly (ἐνεγκριματοῦσαν in CVL, ἐνεκριματοῦσαν in A). Wagner (1874) read V as ἐνεγκριμασοῦσαν, and this is reminiscent (as Šandrovskaja 1956a:247 suggests) of μασοῦσαν, "chewed," but Wagner's reading is inaccurate. Šandrovskaja's [залязгали и заскрежетали] зубами, "made noise with and gnashed their teeth," for τὰ δόντια ἐφάγγριζαν καὶ ἐνεγκριματοῦσαν seems to have been influenced by Wagner's reading.

Karanastassis (in preparation) derives the verb from ἐν, "in" + ἔγκρυμμα, "ambush; hideout," that is, "to wait in ambush," leading to a present tense ἐνεγκρυμματῶ. (The spelling of the word changes accordingly to ἐνεγκρυμματοῦσαν, and that spelling has been adopted by Papathomopoulos [2002].) A similar verb, ἐγκρυμματώνομαι < ἐγκρυμματώνω, "to hide" (lacking the initial ἐν), is attested in *Troika* (534), referring to the Greeks hiding (in ambush) inside the Trojan horse:

> τότε οἱ ἄνδρες ὅπου ἦσαν ἔσω εἰς τὸ ξυλάλογον ***ἐγκρυμματωμένοι*** ἐξέβησαν μετὰ σιωπῆς ἐπιδέξια, "Then the men that were ***hidden*** inside the wooden horse deftly came out in silence."

The word ἐνεγκρυμματῶ involves a repetition of ἐν as a prefix within the word (ἔγκρυμμα itself is derived from ἐν, "in," and the perfective stem κρυμμ-, of κρύπτω "hide"); this is infrequent but not unheard of in Byzantine Greek (see Trapp 1994–99 under ἐνεγ-).

A variant of the verb is also attested in a manuscript Latin–classical Greek–modern Greek dictionary from around 1500; there ἐγκριματεύω (again without the initial ἐν) glosses into modern Greek the pair ἐνεδρεύω–*insidior,* "lie in ambush" (Decharme 1873:105). Proving that the confusion the *Tale*'s verb has provoked is not unique, the dictionary's editor thought the verb was a misspelling of ἐγκληματεύω, "commit a crime"!

867. **brought up out of wedlock**. κοπελοαναθρεμμένον, literally "brought up (ἀναθρεμμένον) by an unmarried girl (κοπέλα)" or "brought up as a bastard" (κοπέλιν—see Kriaras 1968–97, s.v., 5). The two interpretations of this hapax legomenon are identical, though Tsiouni (1972), Hesseling (1924:314), and Šandrovskaja 1956a (взращенное девкой), all adopt the first.

868. **leo-pard**. In Greek, λεοντόπαρδος < λέων, "lion" + πάρδος, "pard (= leopard, panther); animal we have identified as cheetah in this poem." (See "A Conundrum of Cats.")

869. **goes with the name**. Given the etymological joke made at verse 200, one might suspect the cheetah is attempting something similar here. But as it turns out, though a profusion of Byzantine texts suggest an etymology of πάρδαλις/πόρδαλις (the classical version of πάρδος, "pard"), nothing is promising. The majority of sources (*Etymologicum Gudianum* 452; Eustathius of Thessalonica, *Commentary on the Iliad* 4.5; *Etymologicum Magnum* 652; *Scholia on the Iliad (D scholia)* 17.20; Theodore Meletiniotes *Scholia on the Iliad* 17.20) derived the word from προ[σ]άλλεσθαι, "to leap toward," which has no immediate relation to gallantry or strength, and nothing is made of the potential correlation with the cheetah's leaping in 872. Pseudo-Zonaras's πόρον ἅλλεσθαι, "crossing by leaping" (1509; attributed to Orus the Milesian) is no more promising. As for the *Scholia on Oppian's Halieutica*'s (1.386) πέρδω + ἅλλομαι, "to fart while leaping," the *Tale*'s cheetah is brazen but probably not *that* brazen—and it is a shame the author does not seem to be familiar with the source: he could have put it to very good use.

870. **brave past measure**. For the proverbial bravery of the "pard," compare Trivolis: *Tagiapièra* 8–9, written to commemorate a minor naval victory by the Venetian Giovanni Antonio Tagliapietra (Tagiapièra) in 1520: σοπρακόμου ἀξιωμένον, / πὄχει τὴν ψυχὴν ὡς ***πάρδος,*** "the man invested with the rank of captain, who has a soul like a ***pard***." (Irmscher [1956:37] translates it in his edition as *Leopardenseele,* "soul of a leopard.") Other late medieval Greek instances are gathered in Nicholas (1999:268–69).

The cheetah uses the ἄνδρ-, "man," stem here (ἀνδρειωμένος) and in 869 (ἀνδρείαν), on which see Commentary verse 559. It is not impossible that the cheetah is boasting of his physical strength rather than his bravery—particularly as he boasts in the next verse of a physical feat. If the "pard" had come to be associated with maleness in particular (as the modern Pontic Greek πάρδος, "tomcat," suggests), the use of ἀνδρειωμένος may even have been a deliberate wordplay. Nonetheless, the extensive tradition of associating "pards" and bravery has swayed us in favor of "brave."

878. **valued by the sultans**. See "Untraced Beliefs."

884. **motley**. In manuscripts CVL, the leopard calls the cheetah πάρδαλε; in P, he says παρδαλέ (A is missing). The word πάρδαλος is a variant (*Aelian* 1.31) of πάρδαλις, the original Greek word for "leopard"; the term was sup-

planted in the vernacular by πάρδος. Derived from this word is the modern adjective παρδαλ(ωτ)ός, "motley" (already in Somavera 1977 [1709], s.v. παρδαλωτός: *versicolore come il leopardo,* "variegated like the leopard"). So CVL have the leopard calling the cheetah with its normal appellation, the noun "pard," whereas P has the adjective "motley." The difference between the two cannot be explained by forcing a word to match the meter (unlike the cases discussed in Commentary verse 326), because both words match the meter. There is precedent for a similar misstressing unmotivated by meter, however, with φλυαρέ, "chattering" (normally φλύαρε) in 216 V, 263 CV, and 649 CV.

The use of "and" followed by the adjective κοντοουραδάτε, "short-tailed," in the original is more consistent with an adjective than a noun ("Boast not, motley and short-tailed [one]" rather than "Boast not, pard and short-tailed [one]"), though admittedly the boundary between adjective and noun is always fluid in Greek. The introduction of a synonymous appellation for the cheetah would be strange, though not without precedent: the boar, the horse, the fox, the donkey, and the dog are all doubly named. In all, it is far likelier for the leopard to comment on the cheetah's appearance as "motley" as well as "short-tailed." We have thus chosen this reading here.

Rather than interpret the misstressed CVL πάρδαλε as an early variant of παρδαλέ, "motley," we believe P preserves the original reading, with the CVL forming a quite plausible scribal misreading: because a pard is being referred to, a scribe would readily correct "motley" to "pard."

888. **cat-pard**. On what evidence there is for identifying the κατόπαρδος, see "A Conundrum of Cats."

889. **enraged**. The leopard, which is absent in the *Physiologus*, was first introduced into Western bestiaries only in the thirteenth century. Ironically, it has been claimed that the leopard was introduced to take the heat off the bestiary lion, who as a symbol of royalty had been newly imbued with nobility and mercy. Traditionally, the lion was depicted as bloodthirsty and cruel; these traits were now politically inconvenient and were instead passed off to the leopard (Haist 1999:8–12). The *Tale*'s lion, ever the Oriental despot, has obviously not been kept up to date with the latest Western developments.

892. **seem to be impending**. See "The Hero" for discussion of this turning point in the poem's plot.

894. **lower jaw**. Kriaras (1968–97) translates this noun, κατασαγοῦνα, as κάτω σαγόνι, "lower jaw" (s.v. κατωσαγούνα; so also Tsiouni [1972] and Šandrovskaja [1956a]: нижней челюсти), but he translates κατασάγονον in the Judeo-Greek Pentateuch and κατωσάγουνον in the *Mass of the Beardless Man* as πηγούνι, "chin" (s.v. κατωσάγονο). Obviously these are the same word, and there is no distinction to be made between a feline's chin and lower jaw.

895. **tear off**. The text has ἐξεστόμωσα, "to [put] the mouth out," or, with the modern meaning of the prefix (ξε-), "to unmouth"—in either case, namely, to dislocate the mouth. Tsiouni (1972) glosses it as "to tear the mouth," and Šandrovskaja (1956a) as **выбил бы тебе зубы,** "your teeth will come out," which

is an extrapolation. Kriaras (1968–97) glosses it as "make the mouth crooked" (s.v. ἐκστομώνω), which is close enough. There are similar verbs in Kriaras: ἐξεντερίζω, "disembowel" (*Tale*, verse 1022) < ἔντερον, "intestine"; ἐκσφονδυλίζω, "break the neck" (or, as glossed in Kriaras, "break the spine": *Digenes* G 4.137–38, στρέψας τὸν τράχηλον αὐτοῦ ***ἐξεσφονδύλισέ*** το / καὶ παρευθὺς ἀπέψυξεν εἰς τὰς χεῖρας τοῦ νέου, "He twisted its neck and ***snapped its spine*** / and immediately it expired in the young man's hands").

914. **bones**. The author will not necessarily have known that ivory is derived specifically from tusks rather than other elephant bones; in fact, he may not have known that elephants have tusks at all. (Compare the illustrator's confusions on the elephant's tusks, pointed out in "Manuscript C Illustrations.") Homer knew the word for "elephant" to refer only to ivory (*Iliad* 5.583: ἐκ δ' ἄρα χειρῶν / ἡνία λεύκ' ***ἐλέφαντι*** χαμαὶ πέσον ἐν κονίῃσιν, "and the reins, white with ***ivory***, fell from his hands to the ground in the dust"), and the elephant is first named as an animal with tusks by Herodotus (Liddell–Scott–Jones 1940, s.v. ἐλέφας). Yet long after Herodotus, Greek writers continued to call ivory "elephant bones"; for example Eustathius of Thessalonica (*Commentary on the Iliad* 2.151) comments on *Iliad* 5.583 as follows:

> Ὅτι τὰ τοῦ εἰρημένου Πυλαιμένους ἡνία λευκὰ λέγει ἐλέφαντι, διότι κατὰ συνήθειαν παλαιὰν ἀστραγάλους ἐλεφαντίνους ἑκατέρωθεν εἶχον, δι' ὧν εἷλκον αὐτὰς οἱ ἡνίοχοι. Ὅρα δὲ ὅτι καὶ ἐνταῦθα ***ἐλέφαντα*** τὸ ἐλεφάντινον ἔφη ὀστοῦν, ὡς καὶ ἐν τῷ «***ἐλέφαντα*** γυνὴ φοίνικι μιήνῃ».
>
> [He calls the aforementioned Pylaemenes' reins white with ivory, because according to an old custom they had elephant knucklebones on either side, with which charioteers would pull on them. Observe that here, too, he calls ***"elephant"*** the elephant bone, just as in "As when a woman staineth ***ivory*** ⟨***"elephant"***⟩, with scarlet."] [*Iliad* 4.141]

So there was a long tradition of Greeks being familiar with ivory but with only a vague notion of where it came from.

916. **armchairs of empresses**. Tsiouni (1972) renders δεσποινάτα as "of a lady"; the term δέσποινα could be used for any noble woman, and Kriaras (1968–97) agrees with Tsiouni on this passage. We follow Trapp (1976) and Eideneier (1976:459), however, in translating it more like "of a queen," which fits the context better. P has δεσποτάτα, "of a lord" or "of a bishop"; Šandrovskaja (1956a) has властителей, "of a ruler."

The word θρόνος originally meant just "seat" rather than "throne" (Liddell–Scott–Jones 1940, s.v.), and the diminutive θρονίν had come to mean just "seat" by the time of Falieros, in the early 1400s:

> Βάνω *θρονὶν* καὶ λέγω της: «Ἔλα, κερά, νὰ ζήσης,
> θωρῶ σε 'τι ἦλθες μὲ σπουδή, κάτσε νὰ ξατονήσης.»

[I placed a ***seat*** and told her ⟨Fate, visiting the poet in his dream⟩,
"Come, lady, I pray you,
I see you have come in haste, sit down and rest."] (*Enypnion* 115–16)

(See also Andriotis 1974 §2880: θρονί has retained the sense "armchair" or "choir stall" in modern Greek dialect, and we have already translated θρόνος as "armchair" in verse 618.) So we can only prefer "empress" over "lady" or "queen" by virtue of its juxtaposition in the text with the emperor.

921. **games they own**. In the absence of any meaningful punctuation in the original manuscripts, the text could also be read with a full period at the end of 920, with the nobles and merchants, as well as the senior clergy, holding the staffs. But the differentiation drawn between secular and clerical authorities, through a period at the end of 919, makes more sense to us. Šandrovskaja (1956a) and Papathomopoulos (2002) likewise put a semicolon at the end of 919; Tsiouni (1972) leaves the passage unpunctuated. Kriaras (1968–97) glosses δεκανίκιν/δοκανίκιν (the "staff" of 917, derived from δεκανός, "deacon") as meaning either "churchman's staff" or "crutch"—but not as a secular emblem of office, so nobles would be unlikely to hold them.

921. **lathed chesspieces and chessboards**. The original refers to σκάκους (from the Italian word for chess, *scacchi*) and ζατρίκια (derived from the Persian word for chess, *šaxrats*). (On chess in Byzantium, see Koukoules 1947–55:1.1.219–21.) Tsiouni (1972) glosses σκάκους as "a kind of chess," but there is no reason the two words should refer to different variants of the game; *Ducas* 16.9 says explicitly that Bayezid and his son were playing ζατρίκιον, ὃ οἱ Πέρσαι σαντρὰτζ καλοῦσιν, οἱ δὲ Λατῖνοι σκάκον, "*zatrikion*, which the Persians call *santradz* and the Latins *skako*."

Because the σκάκους are described as "lathed," we believe the Italian word here refers to chesspieces. (In Italian, a single *scacco* is a chesspiece, whereas the plural *scacchi* refers to the game.) Likewise, because ζατρίκια are conjoined with backgammon boards (ταβλία: the sequence is "lathed σκάκους, ταβλία, and ζατρίκια"), we believe the Persian word refers here to chessboards, although properly both terms presumably refer to chess sets (as in verse 618). Of course, given the propensity of medieval Greek literature to synonymy, there is nothing preventing either σκάκους or ζατρίκια from referring to chesspieces, although the intervening word for backgammon is inconsistent with how such synonyms appear in the *Tale*.

Šandrovskaja (1956a) omits σκάκους, translating the passage as для игры: выточенные [из слоновой кости] / тавли, шахматы, "for games: lathed [from ivory] / backgammon, chess."

922. **backgammon boards**. On the Byzantine game of backgammon (ταβλίον), ultimately of Roman origin (*tabula aleatoria*), see Koukoules 1947–55:1.1.200–204. The game involved dice and the moving of pieces on a board, like modern backgammon; the word survives with that meaning in modern Greek (τάβλι).

929. **image**. The text has σκίος (C), σκίον (P), σχίος (L), ἤσχιον (V): "shade, shadow." Tsiouni (1972) glosses it as "shadow"; Šandrovskaja (1956a), translating by the meaning, as отражение, "reflection." For the extension of "shadow" to "image" or "simulacrum," compare *Theseid* 12.39 (cited from Kriaras 1968–97, s.v. ήσκιος): γι' αγάπη-του κεινού που τόσα τον ηγάπας, / οπού ακόμη φαίνεται ο ***ήσκιος***-του ομπρός-σου, "for the love of him that you loved so / that still his ***image*** appears before you." There was plenty of precedent for this transition in meaning from "shadow" to "phantom" (already in Homer, e.g., *Odyssey* 10.495: τοὶ δὲ ***σκιαὶ*** ἀΐσσουσιν, "but the other ***ghosts*** flit about aimlessly"); from late Byzantium, compare *Achilleid* N 1919: οὐδὲ τοῦ κόσμου τὸ λοιπόν, ἀλλὰ ***σκιὰ*** τὰ πάντα, "so nothing of the world, then; all's a ***shadow***," and the inscription in the Dormition Church at Nicaea cited by Ševčenko (1974:77): ὄναρ τὰ πάντα καὶ ***σκιᾶς*** οὐδὲν πλέον, "Everything is a dream and nothing more than a ***shadow***."

Kriaras (1968–97) does not attest the meaning "reflection" for ήσκιος outside the *Tale*. However, the only instance for which Liddell–Scott–Jones 1940 (s.v.) attests the meaning "reflection" for the classical σκιά, "shadow," is in fact postclassical:

> ἐλαίου πλήρη κρατῆρα τιθέασιν, οἱ δὲ κολοιοὶ ἐπιβάντες τῷ χείλει ἀφορῶντες εἰς τὴν ***σκιὰν*** ἑαυτῶν ἄλλους κολοιοὺς ὁρᾶν νομίζουσιν· εἶτα ἐπιπεσόντες τῷ ἐλαίῳ, ὡς πρὸς τοὺς ἑταίρους δῆθεν κατιόντες, ἁλίσκονται συγκολληθέντες τὰ πτερὰ τῷ ἐλαίῳ
>
> [They place a bowl full of oil, and the jackdaws, landing on the rim and looking at their ***reflection***, think that they are seeing other jackdaws; then they fall into the oil, trying to go over to their apparent companions, and are captured as their wings are stuck together from the oil.] (*Scholia vetera in Iliadem* 17.755b1)

942. **disaster**. See Commentary 681.

943. **nor any joints**. See "Fact and Fiction in the *Tale's* Zoology."

957. **can't do a thing**. The confusion this time arises from classical Greek: the verb used here, δρᾶσαι, looks like classical δρῶ (future δράσω), "act," and Šandrovskaja (1956a) accordingly renders it as не знающего, что делать, "not knowing what to do." But δράσσω also exists as an independent verb in medieval Greek, derived from the classical verb δράσσομαι, "grasp" (surviving in that sense in Thera, northern Thrace, and the Pontus: Andriotis 1974 §1959). Kriaras (1968–97) glosses δράσσω as meaning only "grab," and the verb is clearly used in that sense in 281 (where Šandrovskaja [1956a] has схватываешь, "grasp").

For all that the verb is ambiguous between "grab" and "act" in medieval Greek—even within a single work:

> ***Δράσσει***, περιλαμπάνει τον κ' ἐκεῖνος τὸ κοράσιον

[She ***grabs*** and embraces him; and he, too, the maiden.] (*Florios and Platziaflora* 1677 L)

Οὕτως λοιπὸν ***ἐδράξασιν*** οἱ πάντες ὑπηρέται·
δένουσιν χεῖρας ὄπισθεν βιαίως καὶ τῶν δύο

[So all the servants ***acted*** thus;
they bound both their hands behind them forcefully.] (*Florios and Platziaflora* 1743–44 L)

But although in Byzantine Greek the verb is used to mean "grab, seize, capture," it is not used to mean specifically "hold on to." So although we cannot rule out that it means "hold on to (a tree)" here, we have preferred the other sense instead and interpret it as "do."

959a. **another thing to tell you**. See "The *Physiologus*" and "The Misfit."

964. **split right through**. One would expect that the hunters almost cut the tree down so that the tree is felled only when the elephant leans on it. But the author's choice of words is clear: when referring to cutting, ἀποκόπτουν always means "cut thoroughly" (Kriaras 1968–97, s.v. ἀποκόπτω, 1; e.g., *Ecthesis Chronica* 48: ***ἀπέκοψε*** δὲ τὴν κεφαλὴν τοῦ Καραγκιὸζ μπασία καὶ τῶν μετ' αὐτοῦ, "and he ***cut off*** the head of Karagöz Pasha and his followers"; *Digenes* P 411: Ὁ θάνατος ***ἀπέκοψεν*** τὸ ἄνθος τῆς νεότητός μου, "Death has ***severed*** the flower of my youth") and never "almost cut [down]." The phrase εἰς ἄκρον is a common intensifier in this part of the *Tale* (907, 969) and means "to the extreme"; it cannot mean "at the extremity" = "on the edge of the trunk," as it is missing the definite article that would allow such an interpretation (εἰς ***τὸ*** ἄκρον νὰ κοποῦσιν).

In the *Tale*'s world, a tree can be sawed through and not fall but stand precariously, waiting for just the right amount of pachydermal pressure. This is a premise no more absurd than trapping elephants this way in the first place. Šandrovskaja (1956a) has the same general sense: затем подсекают до конца, чтобы подломить, "then they cut it from underneath until the end so that it may be broken underneath."

971. **skeleton**. Various interpretations are possible for φαγκρίν. The meaning that we propose, and that has survived in modern Greek dialects, is "something translucently thin"; φαγκρίν is considered cognate to φέγγω, "shine," via φεγγάριν, "moon" (Andriotis 1983, s.v.). For the meaning "shine," compare the use of the corresponding verb φαγγρίζω in Τ' νύχτα τὰ μάτια τ'ς γάτας ***φαγγρίζ'***, "At night, the cat's eyes ***shine***" (HDMS 1059:195, Plateousa, Peloponnese). For the meaning "thin," compare φαγκρί «λεπτόσαρκος», "thin" (***ἐφάνgρισες*** κακόμοιρο, "You've ***gotten thin***, poor thing": HDMS 346:151, Vourvoura, Cynuria, Peloponnese). In Kardamena, Kos, both meanings are preserved in φαγγρίζω: Τώρα πού̃ναιν νέα ***φανgρίζ-ζει*** κόμη, αὔριον νὰ δοῦμεν, "Now that she's young, she's still ***shiny*** (= beautiful, shining like the sun); let's see tomorrow . . ."; Ἤδειξεν dου καλὰ ἡ ἀρώστεια, ***ἐφάνgρισεν***!, "The illness has taken hold of him well; he's ***emaciated***!" (HDMS 926:600).

The verb φαγγρίζω, “show,” has in fact already turned up in the *Tale* in verse 862, referring to the cheetah and leopard baring their teeth; this is the only instance we know of it being used transitively. The semantic pathway would be φέγγω, “shine” > φέγγος, “light, gleam” > φεγγάριον (diminutive), “light” > “moon” > φεγγαρίζω, “shine (like the moon)” > φεγγρίζω, “shine faintly” > φαγγρίζω, “let shine” > “be translucent” (attested in Byzantius 1874, s.v.: διαφαίνω, *paraitre à travers; être transparent*; Somavera 1977 [1709] gives this definition for φεγγίζω) > φαγκρίν, “something translucent.” In baring their teeth, the cheetah and leopard could be considered either to let them gleam (shine) or to make them visible (a less likely further extension of φαγγρίζω). The “gleam” interpretation has already been proposed by Xanthoudidis (1927–28:367).

Possible alternatives include “sea bream” (φάγρος, the word that looks like φαγκρίν the most in ancient Greek; cf. HDMS 612:117, from Skyros, where φαγκρί refers to a sparse-toothed fish) and Tsiouni’s (1972) “ugly as a phantom” (tantamount to our proposal). Šandrovskaja (1956a:248) suspects a connection with the Arabic *faqîr,* “need, requirement,” so that φαγκρίν would mean “poor, unfortunate person.” The Arabic word has entered modern Greek both directly (φακίρης, “Indian magician”) and via Turkish (φουκαράς, “pauper” < *fukara*) (Andriotis 1983, s.v.). Of the two, the latter conveys a strong sense of pity, whereas the former is semantically distant, so we do not regard them as promising interpretations. Somavera’s (1977 [1709]) φεγγαριάζομαι, *esser lunatico,* “be a lunatic,” presumably a calque from the Italian, is also unlikely to be relevant to the monkey.

997. **neck**. As elsewhere in the *Tale* (see verse 84), we have translated σφόνδυλος as “neck,” the neck being a likelier place for an aggressor to grab on to than the spine. In this we differ from Šandrovskaja (1956a), who has позвонок, “vertebrum.”

1002. **mauled each other**. The original has νὰ τρώγῃ ἓν τὸ ἄλλον, “to eat one another.” Vasiliou (1996:75) has claimed on the basis of this verse that the carnivores win the battle and that the ensuing narration with a herbivore victory is a subsequent accretion. We discuss this more broadly in appendix 3; in the following we consider the linguistic aspects of the expression.

The verb τρώγω originally meant “gnaw, munch,” applied to herbivores according to Liddell–Scott–Jones 1940. In modern Greek, its principal meaning is “eat,” a meaning acquired in Koine (Liddell–Scott–Jones 1940, s.v., III); however, it has a wide range of figurative use. Two instances have already been seen in the *Tale*: the wolf in 842 is “pumped bloodless [literally “eaten”] by mosquitoes, stung by wasps,” and the goat is described in 468 as πετροφαγωμένη, “rock-eaten” = “worn down by rocks” (“boulder-tumbled”). So τρώγω has the secondary meanings of “wear down” and “eat away.” One could interpret τρώγω here as a further extension of “eat away,” now meaning “bite away” or otherwise “injure.” This is something herbivores could do as well as carnivores, and such usage might have been informed by the classical use of τρώγω.

Also worth mentioning is another figurative use of τρώγω: the medial τρώγομαι, "I am eaten" (properly interpreted as a reciprocal), meaning "I am arguing"; for example, τρώγομαι με το γείτονα, "I am eaten (reciprocally) with the neighbor" = "The neighbor and I eat at one another" = "I am at odds with my neighbor." Such reciprocals can also be expressed with the two parties as a joint subject: τρωγόμαστε, "We are eaten" = "We are eating at each other" = "We are at odds," and the modern proverbial expression τρώγονται σαν τα σκυλιά, "they are eaten [i.e., they eat each other—they are fighting] like dogs." This construction is also present in languages neighboring Greek (Joseph 1994:512: Albanian *hahet me,* Bulgarian *jade se sa,* Rumanian *manânca cu*), which testifies to its antiquity. The medial construction could readily have been reformulated—if not originally expressed—by an explicit reciprocal such as ἓν τὸ ἄλλον, which is precisely what the text presents.

Šandrovskaja (1956a) has когда один стал поедать другого, which constitutes a literal gloss. The context admits either of the two interpretations, "bite/injure" or "eat/fight"; we have used "mauled" as a compromise (weighing in favor of "bite").

1007. **throwing down**. The text has the lion literally "sitting" after latching on to the buffalo: τὴν βουβάλαν ἔδωκεν, καὶ πῆρε την καὶ κάτζεν, "he struck the buffalo, and he took her and he sat." The intended meaning is clear ("throw to the ground") and it is not necessary to assume that the buffalo was killed. (The notion that the buffalo is killed—see appendix 3—seems to originate in Gidel's paraphrase [1866:322]: *D'abord le lion s'élance sur la génisse et la tue,* "First the lion hurls himself onto the heifer and kills her.")

There is no precedent in Byzantine vernacular Greek for the use of "seat" to mean "kill." The closest parallel from the period appears to be the use of καθίζω, "seat," to mean "besiege" in the *Chronicle of Morea*:

> δι' οὗ ἔνι ἀπολέμητον θέλει νὰ τὸ ***καθίσῃ***
> τῆς γῆς καὶ τῆς θαλάσσης γὰρ θέλει νὰ τὸ φυλάξῃ
> φύλαξιν τε καὶ ***κάθισμα***, ἕως νὰ τὸ ἐπάρῃ
>
> [since it was unassailable, he wished to ***besiege*** it by land and by sea and to set up a blockade and ***siege***, until he would take it.] (P 2898–2900; Lurier [1964:156])

But by distinguishing the siege from the conquest, the *Chronicle of Morea* uses καθίζω to mean "sit in waiting" rather than "subdue by seating." So this is not truly a parallel usage. Likewise, the use in the *Belisariad* of καθίζω to mean "kill" (χ 191, 202) is associated with impalement ("seat someone on the stake"); there are no comparable large sharp objects available to the lion.

At any rate, the subject of the verb is likeliest the lion, coordinated as it is with two preceding verbs with the same subject. The verb used, κάτζεν, is both transitive ("seated") and intransitive ("sat down"), but in the absent of an object (unlike the preceding verbs), the transitive meaning is implausible. So Šandrovskaja's (1956a) одолел его и сел, "he overcame her and he sat down," which is a fairly literal translation, is likely correct.

Although "sitting down" seems quite strange in this context, there are intransitive instances of the verb suggesting something more abstract, like "go down": σὰν ***κάτσει*** ὁ ἥλιος, νὰ ἔρτει πρὸς μεσωθιὸ τὸ φουσσᾶτο, "when the sun ***is down***, he shall come into the camp again" (Judeo-Greek Pentateuch, Deuteronomy 23:12); καὶ ἤτονε μὲς στὴ λάσπη ***καθισμένο***, "and it ⟨the galley⟩ had ***settled*** into the mud" (*Raid on Paros* 660). This seems to be the sense appealed to here: the lion strikes the buffalo, drags her along with him, and sinks to the ground.

1007. **buffalo**. Among the enmities of animals, Aelian (5.48) includes πρὸς βουβαλίδας καὶ ταύρους λέοντες, "lions towards buffaloes and bulls." He is cited in this regard by Manuel Philes (*On the Features of Animals* 693–94). But it is unnecessary to postulate that the author was familiar with Aelian or Philes here, just as it is in the remainder of the poem: there are only three herbivores in the *Tale* that could plausibly attack the lion, namely, the boar and the buffalo/ox pair. And there is nothing implausible about a buffalo and a lion being at odds—buffalo being characteristic (and feisty) prey for the lion. They are certainly more plausible as rivals than the other pairs listed by Aelian—including carrion-crow and owl, swan and serpent, titmouse and donkey, fox and hawk, bull and crow, and yellow wagtail and horse.

1013. **brings on**. The original meaning of συνιστῶ is "contrive, organize, put together" (Liddell–Scott–Jones 1940, s.v. συνίστημι, III); Demosthenes (15.3) uses the same terminology as the *Tale*: ***συνέστησαν*** ἐφ' ἡμᾶς τὸν τελευταῖον τουτονὶ πόλεμον, "They ***concerted*** the last war against us." The "recommend" meaning, current in modern Greek, is late and initially involved only people as its object ("bring together as friends"; "recommend one to another"): Liddell–Scott–Jones 1940 (s.v., IV) report the extension from "recommending people" to "recommending actions" in only one inscription, dating from 143 B.C. (Dittenberger 1915–24 §679.90, from Magnesia in Asia Minor: καὶ ἡ παραναγιγνωσκομένη ἐ[πι]στολὴ οὐθαμῶς ἡμῖν ***συνίσ[τη*** ἃ ἐπ]οίησαν οἱ Πρ[ι]ηνεῖς, "And the letter read out publicly did not by any means ***recommend*** to us what the Prienians did")—though thereafter it is commonplace in Koine and the church fathers (Lampe 1961, s.v., 1.C.2).

At first sight this would make one suspect that the verb as used in the *Tale* is a vernacular usage ("recommend")—the more so as the form used in the *Tale*, συνιστᾷ < συνιστάω rather than συνίσταται < συνίστημι, is postclassical, first occurring in Aristotle (*De Generatione Animalium* 777a6: ἐξ ἧς ***συνιστᾷ*** τὴν γένεσιν ἡ φύσις, "from which Nature ***forms*** the animal in generation"). However, although the form used in the *Tale* is postclassical, just as in Aristotle's passage, Aristotle's meaning is classical, and so is the *Tale*'s: the classical meaning "bring on war" makes more sense here than the postclassical meaning "call for war," because the lion has started the battle himself. And the author would have found very similar expressions in the Septuagint: the expression συνίστημι πόλεμον/μάχην, "to start a war/battle against," occurs in 1 Maccabees 1:2, 1:18, 2:32, 3:3; Daniel 7:21; and 1 Ezra 1:27, 2:17. Various redactions of the *Alexander Romance* also have a similar expression (α 2.12.3; β 2.19; γ 2.19; Learned Poetic version 2652, 3816). So the author could easily have learned this usage through his Koine reading. Corroboration of the learned usage of συνιστῶ in the *Tale* comes from verse 986, where the verb is again used in its Koine form (ἐσυνεστήσαμεν < συνιστῶ instead of συνιστάμεθα < συνίστημι) but with its classical meaning ("brought about")—in that instance referring to peace instead of war.

Šandrovskaja (1956a) has возбуждает сражение, "arouses combat," which concurs with our rendering.

1034. **Why do you stand there** . . . The plaint of the fallen cheetah is comical enough without claiming, as Dimaras (1972:46) does, that it alludes to heroic folk song.

1043. **kettledrums**. The ἀνακαράδας are the Arabic *naqqārat* (singular *naqqāra*); the term refers to hemispherical drums in general and covers both the larger kettledrums borne on horseback or camelback into battle and the smaller versions played in the lap by musicians on social occasions. The kettledrums were introduced into the West (English *nakers*, French *nacaires*, Italian *nacchere*), where they were worn on the belt of minstrels; however, it seems from the entries in Kriaras 1968–97 that the drum was associated in Byzantium with military use, whether in battle or ceremonially:

> Καὶ τὴν αὐγὴν ἐχέρισαν ὄργανα τοῦ πολέμου,
> τρουμπέτες, βιόλες, μπίφαρα, τύμπανα, ***ἀνακαράδες***
> καὶ μουσικὰ πανέμνοστα, ἀπλήρωτα τὰ εἶχαν.
>
> [At dawn, they took up warlike instruments:
> trumpets, viols, shawms, drums and ***kettledrums***,
> and wondrous fiddles that they had past counting.] (*Belisariad* χ 271–73; on Belisarius's triumphant return to Constantinople)
>
> Καὶ τὰ σπαθία ἔσυραν, λάμπουν τὰ ἅρματά τους,
> τρουμπέττα εὐθὺς ἐλάλησαν, ὄργανα, ***ἀνακαράδες***,
> μὲ τὰ ἅρματα, μὲ τὰ σπαθιὰ καὶ ἔκαμαν μέγαν φόβον.
>
> [They drew their swords, their weapons gleamed. At once,
> trumpets blared, instruments and ***kettledrums***;
> with swords and weapons, they caused quite a fright.] (*Chronicle of Tocco* 622–24)
>
> Ἑτοιμασθέντος οὖν καὶ καβαλλικεύσαντος τοῦ βασιλέως, οἱ ἀνακαρισταὶ κρούουσι τὰ ***ἀνάκαρα***, σαλπίζουσι δὲ καὶ οἱ σαλπιγκταὶ ὁμοίως καὶ οἱ βυκινάτορες δι᾽ ὀργάνων ἀργυρῶν. . . . Γίνεται μέντοι τὸ τοιοῦτον, εἰ κατὰ τὴν πρωΐαν τύχοι καβαλλικεύων ὁ βασιλεύς· μετὰ δὲ τὸ γεῦμα καβαλλικεύσειν μέλλοντος οὐδαμῶς γίνεται τοῦτο. Ἡ δὲ αἰτία ἀγνοεῖται.

> [When the emperor is ready and rides the horse, the kettledrum players strike the ***kettledrums***, and the buglers bugle as do the horn players, with silver instruments. . . . And this occurs if the emperor happens to go riding in the morning; but if he is to ride after lunch, this never occurs. The reason for this is unknown.] (*Pseudo-Codinus* 172–73)

Of the three forms the word took in medieval Greek, Kriaras (1968–97) defines νάκαρο as "metal drums covered with skin, played usually in pairs, by military musicians (usually a small band of percussion and wind instruments accompanying military campaigns)"; ἀνακαράς, as "a kind of drum"; and νιάκαρο (Venetian *gnacara*), as "drums or rattles (cf. νάκαρο)"—used, again with bugles and horns, to announce the entry of Nikostratis, lord of Macedonia, in *Erotokritos* 2.230.

1052. **struck with his palm**. The noun παλαμέα, "a strike of the palm" is a nonce-formation in the *Tale* but is clear enough and morphologically consistent (κονταρέα, "blow of the lance," is especially common in medieval Greek literature; the modern reflex suffix -ιά is productive, e.g., κονταριά, "blow of the lance," σουβλιά, "skewering"; μαχαιριά, "knife stab"). Hesseling's emendation (1924:314) to παλαμναῖᾳ, "with a murderous (blow)," is thus unnecessary.

1053. **briskly**. See verse 125. As pointed out in 125, the adjective ἀψός means both "brisk" and "irate." The boar here has much more to be upset about than the provocations taken umbrage to in 125 and 183. However, P has γοργός, "swift," here, indicating that its scribe, at least, understood ἀψός to mean "brisk," just as it does elsewhere in the poem, referring to the cat (125) and the dog (183). And the poem's tendency to synonymy is consistent with the author expressing quickness twice in the sentence, both in this adjective and in the verb χύνει, "pours [himself]; rushes." For consistency with the rest of the poem, we have used the sense "brisk" here, too.

Šandrovskaja (1956a) has стремительно, "vehemently."

1069. **drums**. In the original, ταβλαμπάσια. As was the case with drums in general in the European Middle Ages, these are Arabic in origin; compare Arabic *ṭabl,* "drum" (which is the etymon of the Turkish *davul* and the Greek *daouli*, essentially the same instrument: Sadie 2001, s.v. *Ṭabl*). The specific drum referred to here is the Turkish *tablbaz,* "small hawking drum" (Karanastassis, in preparation). These drums were presumably small cylindrical hand drums and distinct from the hemispherical kettledrums named in 1043—though it is not certain the poem intends these to be understood as different instruments. (The illustration in C clearly shows the rat beating kettledrums.) The word is unknown to Šandrovskaja (1956a:249) ("a word of unknown origin . . . possibly it is a kettledrum") and Tsiouni (1972) ("a musical instrument").

On the *ṭabl*, the *New Grove Dictionary of Music and Musicians* (Sadie 2001, s.v. *Ṭabl*) has the following:

> Arabic generic term for drums. It is particularly applied to double-headed cylindrical drums in the Arab Middle East. . . . The cylindrical drum is central to Islamic musical cultures; it is used in military bands

> and is also played at village ceremonies such as weddings, circumcisions and funerals and on religious occasions. . . . In Islamic countries the cylindrical drum is often played with the shawm in rural music and in military bands; trumpets, kettledrums and cymbals may be added to create larger ensembles.

1075. **sun crowned the horizon**. This line may appear more poetic than it actually is: modern Greek routinely refers to the "reigning sun" instead of the "setting sun." Our translation offers one explanation for the origin of this expression—another being that the sun is most magnificent when it is about to disappear behind the horizon. By extension, "reign" in modern Greek (βασιλεύω) can mean "die" or "vanish"; for example, George Seferis writes of μιὰ σαΐτα τιναγμένη ξαφνικὰ ἀπὸ τὰ πέρατα μιᾶς νιότης ***βασιλεμένης***, "an arrow shot suddenly from the confines of a ***vanished*** youth," in his poem "In the Manner of G.S." (Seferis 1995:106–7).

Quite possibly, this particular meaning of βασιλεύω is first attested in the *Tale*; the examples that Kriaras gives are from the sixteenth century (*Pastor Fide* [Soummakis] 5.475; *Digenes* Z 194). P describes the sunset far more traditionally, as the sun's "eveningfall" (ἑσπέρας), in an additional line (1075a: ἐπέτυχε τότε δυνατὸς ἑσπέρας τοῦ ἡλίου, "Then chanced a splendid ***setting*** of the sun"). The history of this use of "reigning" is examined by Kriaras (1937) and Lindenburg (1978 [1961]).

1078–79. ***There is no king*** . . . Septuagint, Psalms 33 [32]:16, οὐ σῴζεται βασιλεὺς διὰ πολλὴν δύναμιν, καὶ γίγας οὐ σωθήσεται ἐν πλήθει ἰσχύος αὐτοῦ, "There is no king saved by the multitude of an host: a mighty man is not delivered by much strength." Allowing for the need to recast the verse in heptameter, the *Tale*'s version is quite close to the Septuagint. (Not that the next verse in Psalms offers the herbivores much comfort: ψευδὴς ἵππος εἰς σωτηρίαν, ἐν δὲ πλήθει δυνάμεως αὐτοῦ οὐ σωθήσεται, "An horse is a vain thing for safety: neither shall he deliver any by his great strength.")

1082. **will abide with them forevermore**. The original has "the battle that took place stayed and persisted among/for the beasts." The linguistically obvious interpretation is that the battle continued. But the choice of διέμεινεν, "persisted," an emphatically static verb, along with the vagueness of the preposition εἰς, allows a construal in accordance with what has preceded; whether or not the war continues on in the animal kingdom, the battle is certainly over. Šandrovskaja (1956a) has **не прекращается и продолжает,** "did not cease and continues." Gidel (1866:322) likewise has *sont restés en querelle,* "have remained in combat," and Krumbacher (1897:2.878) has *leben die vierfüssigen Tiere in ewiger Feindschaft,* "the quadrupeds live in eternal enmity."

Vasiliou (1996:76) interprets διέμεινεν here as referring to the results of the battle:

> If, on the other hand, we conclude that there is no discrepancy between verses 1003–79 and the concluding verses 1080–82, which would lead to the excision of the latter, then we end up with the illogical conclusion

that the result of the battle now constitutes the prevailing state of the animal kingdom.

But this seems to us the least plausible alternative linguistically: the memory of a battle can persist (διέμεινεν), particularly given the vagueness of the preposition εἰς ("for, to, among"; in this context plausibly "in the minds of, as far as they were concerned"), and a state of battle can remain (ἔμεινεν). But if the intended meaning is for the aftermath of a battle to continue ("the battle that took place endures and will abide" > "the victory that took place remains the case"), it would be strange for the narrator to speak of the battle itself persisting rather than the victory. It is far simpler to suppose that if a battle is spoken of as enduring, what is meant is the process of battle (the ongoing hostility) rather than its effects (the herbivores' victory).

TEXTUAL NOTES

. . . nor a wedding without laughter, nor a scribe without error . . .

—Cephas Diogenous, A.D. 1404 (quoted in I. Hutter, ed., *Corpus der Byzantinischen Miniaturenhandschriften*)

We have noted here the major discrepancies between the manuscripts of the *Tale*. The full *apparatus criticus* may be found in Tsiouni (1972) and Papathomopoulos (2002).

Title 1–2. **Amusing verses** . . . These two verses appear in CV before the start of the poem, with only the second verse appearing in L. P repeats the first verse of the poem as its title instead. (Manuscript A is missing the first few pages of the poem.) Vasiliou (1996:60) argues that CV's is likely to be the original title of the poem, with P's title a later interpolation, following the Byzantine practice of using the first line of a poem as its title.

1. **entertaining**. See Commentary.

4–5. **as written** . . . On the textual discrepancies here, see appendix 3.

6. **So understand** . . . Eideneier (1976:456) regards this verse, present only in P, as a superfluous repetition of verse 5. The acrostic discovered by Sofianos (1996) (see appendix 3) may disprove this.

8. **hoping audaciously** . . . CVL have βούλονται μὲν ὡς ἄθεοι ἡμᾶς κακῶσαι τέως, "willing, as godless ones, to abuse us meanwhile."

10. **power**. P changes this to "prayer, blessing" (ἰσχύν to εὐχήν).

10a. **So here, my friend** . . . Omitted in P; see discussion, appendix 3.

18. **twisting tail**. L is defeated by γαγκλαδοραδάτος and instead has καὶ μάλιστα δραστικός τε, "and active indeed."

34. **as the cat's companion**. Somewhat overrealistically, L has διὰ φαγὶν τοῦ κάτου, "for the cat's food," presumably by misanalysis of συντροφίαν (C), συνδροφίαν (P), "company," which literally means "eating together."

36. **attending both of them**. Tsiouni (1972) and CL have νὰ τοὺς τὰ λέγῃ, "to tell them things," which in modern Greek could be interpreted as either "to chat to them, to tell them tales" or "to tell them off." PV, Šandrovskaja (1956a), and Papathomopoulos (2002) have νὰ τοὺς δουλεύῃ, "to work for them"; Eideneier (1976:456) also prefers this reading, which turns up in verse 83 as well (PCVA; there it is only L that has τὰ λέγῃ).

40. **this horrid, sudden embassy**. On the herbivores' call, see appendix 3.

44. **long-eared**. Rather than the form μεγαλάπτην (for μεγαλαύτην) (defended as a hypercorrection already by Koukoules [1911–12:371], who adduces contemporary parallels), Eideneier (1976:456) follows Politis's re-edition (1966–67) in preferring both here and in verse 327 P's μ[ε]γαλόπτην—which would on face value mean "big-eyed." Besides 327, where only V has μεγαλάπτη and PCLA have μεγαλόπτη, Eideneier adduces verse 678, where CA have ὀπτία for V's ἀπτία, P's αὐτία, and L's ὠτίας, "ears."

In 678, however, the poem clearly talks about docking the donkey's ears, rather than its eyes (!). So even if there is evidence to reconstruct μεγαλόπτην, there is no reason to think the author meant anything by ὀπτ- but a further hypercorrection for αὐτ-, "ear," rather than "eye." The same holds for verse 774, where the camel's ears are given as ἀπτία in CV and πτία in LA; ἀπτία in all manuscripts in 328; and "dock-eared" in 773 appearing as κουτζοπτία in VLA. In fact, similar hypercorrections occur elsewhere in Byzantium, in addition to the early twentieth-century instances reported by Koukoules (1911–12): Kriaras (1968–97, s.v. ἀφτίον) gives ἀπτίν in Sachlikis and the *Consolatory Speech on Misery and Happiness (Λόγος Παρηγορητικὸς περὶ Δυστυχίας καὶ Εὐτυχίας)*, ὀφτίν and ὀπτίν in the *Codex of Popular Remedies,* and πτίν in Georgillas and the *Flower of Virtue.*

Our rendering as "big-eared," which exploits a much more salient characteristic of the hare than its eyes, thus stands.

49. **They came and gathered there all through the day**. Before verse 49, P has a blank space, presumably for a rubric to be filled in.

61. **that all the animals assemble**. Verse omitted in CL. The text still makes sense without it ("the lion orders . . . the clean, domestic beasts and the unclean and bloody to one place"), but verse 61 is likelier to be original, as it supplies a verb otherwise missing in the lion's order. Whether or not the verse is original, its presence can be counted as evidence of contamination between P and V.

63. **bloody**. P here uniquely uses σαρκοφάγα, "flesh-eating," rather than the poem's usual ὠμόβορον, "raw-eating"/αἱμόβορον, "blood-eating."

71. **in all their feasts**. PV (again potentially an instance of contamination) use εὐωχίαν, "good cheer, feast," a somewhat obscure Koine word (see "Language"). The other manuscripts of the *Tale*, defeated by this difficult word, preserve versions of the straightforward ἡσυχίαν, "in peace and quiet."

76–8. **And only then . . . and his council**. Verses 76–78, which recapitulate verses 59, 61, and 64, are attested only in P. The narrative can stand without these verses, though it becomes a little abrupt, and in context the verses are redundant, because the purpose of the herbivores securing "a lasting peace and friendship" is obviously to allow the conference to take place. So these verses may constitute an interpolation; see appendix 3.

82. **of giant dick and balls**. L has καμηλορχιδάτον, "and camel-like balls," but clearly this is contamination from context (verse 84), as the donkey has nothing to be jealous of the camel for in this regard.

86. **her rump out**. PVL here have νὰ πηδᾷ, "to hop," which is the reading Tsiouni (1972) adopts. CA have a different reading, νωτιδά C νωτηδά A, which Hesseling (1924:309) interprets as dancing "with her rear" (νῶτα)—"that is, it does a 'hindquarters dance' comparable to humans' 'belly dance.' . . . One could allow that the author of the poem has coined an amusing neologism, which was ill-understood by its copyists: νωτιδά goes very well with ὡς κακογυρισμένη, 'ungainly'" (see Commentary). The word νωτιδά is clearly the *lectio difficilior* and looks very similar to the other manuscripts' νὰ πηδᾷ, "to hop." That it is absent from both P and VL is not necessarily a problem, if we accept Papathomopoulos's (2002) postulated contamination between the two branches. We have thus adopted this reading here. The term could conceivably also be interpreted as "backward," but the peculiarity of the camel's gait makes that unlikely. Šandrovskaja (1956a) sidesteps the issue and has потешая и развлекая, "amusing and entertaining."

124. **If any of you . . . and decent**. The verse is omitted in P; even if we take on face value its spelling in 123 P so that it has καὶ οὗτος ἀποφθέγξατο, "and this one declared," instead of καὶ οὕτως ἀπεφθέγξατο, "and he declared thus," the gap in P is still noticeable. L is the only manuscript to have "thus," which both Tsiouni (1972) and Papathomopoulos (2002) adopt, rather than "this one"; the two sound identical, and this hardly makes any real difference in the meaning. Šandrovskaja (1956a) also goes with L rather than PCVA, using так, "thus."

134–35. **and grain . . . consumed by people**. Verses 134–35 are omitted in V.

138. **unsealed**. Papathomopoulos (2002) emends the extrametrical ἀβούλον of P to ἀβούλλωτον, "unsealed"; CVLA and Tsiouni (1972) have ἀσκέπαστον, "uncovered." It does make more sense to speak of a pitcher of oil as unsealed than as uncovered, but the difference is not great. On the other hand, the form ἀβούλλωτος is attested in Trapp (1994–99, s.v.) and is extant in modern Greek. Other than this instance, the stem ἀβούλλ- is unattested in Kriaras 1968–97; this may make this the *lectio difficilior* but may well simply be an accident, because the stem is attested in Trapp's learned texts, even though it is not a classical word (βοῦλα is from Latin *bulla,* "bubble, knob," and is cognate to *papal bull,* because such documents were sealed with the pope's seal).

151. **trying to argue . . . as follows**. The redundant verse 151 is absent in the oldest witnesses, P and C.

161. **and pet you**. L has καὶ κολακεύουνέ σε, "and cajole you," by imitation of verse 158.

178. **conceit and arrogance**. CVL (A is missing) reduce verses 177–78 to the single verse εὐθὺς τινάσσει (τινάς C, τινάξει L) τὴν (omitted: L) γοῦναν (γοῦνα L) σου καὶ ὅλην (ὅλη V) τὴν ἔπαρσίν σου, "he'll jolt your fur—and arrogance—at once."

186. **seized**. Papathomopoulos (2002) follows Eideneier (1976:456) in adopting the *lectio difficilior,* ἀλίσκωσα, against Šandrovskaja (1956a) and Tsiouni (1972), who used the modernizing L's πήδησα, "leapt." The form involved is garbled in the older sources:

- ναχήσβοσα in P
- ν' ἀλίσκωσα (emended to ἀλίσκω σε) in V according to Wagner (1874)
- ν' ἀλήσβωσα in CV according to Tsiouni (1972)
- ναλίσκωσα = ν' ἀλύσκωσα in CV according to Eideneier (1993:275)
- ναλήσκοσα = ν' ἀλίσκωσα V ν' ἀλήσβωσα C according to Papathomopoulos (2002)
  (A is missing at this point.)

The interpretation of this grammatically odd form is controversial. Xanthoudidis (1927–28:355) saw in it ν' ἀλύκτησα, "barked," a modern form derived by metathesis from the ancient ὑλακτῶ. Eideneier (1993) saw in it a reflex of ὑλάσκω, "bark," a variant of ὑλακτῶ, through an analogical metathesis. More conservatively, Kriaras (1968–97), after Hatzidakis (1989–90 [1905–07]:1.128), prefers it as an analogical active voice of the classical passive ἀλίσκομαι, "seize" (in accordance with Wagner [1874]). That is the reading we have adopted here, requiring as it does the least violence to the word form. We agree with Eideneier, however, that the verb should be in the aorist indicative (ἀλίσκωσα), for consistency with the rest of the sentence, and thus reject Wagner's present tense emendation ἀλίσκω σε, "seize you." Papathomopoulos (2002) concurs with our reading.

191. **and some she eats . . . from drinking**. Verse missing in VL.

193. **infinite**. CV and Papathomopoulos (2002) have ἄπληστος, "insatiable," whereas PL and Tsiouni (1972) have ἄπειρος. In connection with "injustice," ἄπειρος can mean only "infinite" (so Tsiouni 1972, "immense"; Šandrovskaja 1956a, бесконечную) < πέρας, "limit," as confirmed by the synonymous ἄπληστος. The homonymous stem ἄπειρ- < πεῖρα, "experience," means in both ancient and Byzantine Greek "inexperienced" (of people) rather than "unexperienced, untold" (of events). PL's reading is more emphatic, but CV's reading conforms to the usage in all manuscripts in verse 710.

204. **Has Madam Fox** . . . P is in the third person; the other manuscripts, and Tsiouni's and Papathomopoulos's texts, are in the second. We have used the third person as stylistically appropriate to English, rather than to support P here—although that reading was adopted by Dölger (1964:205).

210. **and skin your tail**. The manuscripts here are confused: P repeats σύρω, "pull off," from the first half of the verse; VL have χάψω, "swallow, bite down"; C has δάρω, the ancient verb for "skin"; and A has κιδάρω, which is ostensibly

nonsense. P can be rejected: the scribe would readily have repeated the first available verb if faced with a difficult reading. Tsiouni (1972) adopts VL's "bite down," which is hyperbolic—and given that the dog is in business with the furrier (211), doesn't make much sense. Šandrovskaja (1956a) has **вытянуть,** "stretch; extract"; as far as we can tell, she is adopting P's reading.

In fact, the modern verb for "skin" is γδάρω < κδάρω < ἐκδάρω < ἐκ, "from" + δάρω, "skin." The medieval form of the verb already turns up elsewhere in the poem: 293 κδάρουν CA (γδάρουν PVL); 683 ἐκδέρει CA, ἐγδέρνει PV, γδέρνει L; 793 ἐκδέρνουν AV, ἐκδέρουν CL, ἐδέρνουν P. (The present tense stem varies between δερ- and δερν-; the former is the older form.) So CA prefer the more archaic form of the verb; they are not being deliberately antiquarian about this, as the elision of the initial unstressed vowel in (ἐ)κδάρω is a characteristically medieval phenomenon. We suspect CA preserved an original κδάρω here, too, though with some tampering: C removed the postclassical prefix (ἐ)κ-, whereas A interpolated the vowel ι, either for euphony or because its scribe didn't quite understand the verb. The other manuscripts, just as clearly uncomfortable with the older form of the verb, got rid of it here. The older κδάρω certainly explains A κιδάρω better than would the newer γδάρω.

213. **high philosophizing**. CA may be punning by referring to "high" (ψηλήν), "fine [or trivial] wisdom" (ψιλοσοφίαν).

221. **whether you've stolen . . . at something**. Verse omitted in V.

226. **No, everywhere you go . . . stand**. Verse omitted in V. In both 221 and 226, the passage makes sense without the omitted verse, and V tends to edit out redundancies, though these verses are clearly authorial.

234. **wipe you out**. Papathomopoulos (2002) prefers, as a *lectio difficilior,* P's ἀφανίζου, "vanquish, destroy," over CVLA's ἀφήνουν, "leave behind," which both Šandrovskaja (1956a) and Tsiouni (1972) had adopted. The parallel usage of ἀφήνω in 876 is not enough of a counterexample to rebut this.

241a. **you just spend . . . inside a hole**. Verse omitted in P; verse 241a is not necessary for the passage to make sense, because verse 242 can be taken as qualifying 243 rather than 241a.

254. **They even put a collar . . . beads and bells**. Verse 254 is absent in VL.

255a. **goats both wild and tame**. Hesseling (1924:309), like Wagner (1874), regards verse 255a, literally "wild goats, [tame] goats, and all such" (absent in P), as redundant.

269. **such merry-making words as these to her**. Here CA insert 269a: καὶ μὲ μανίαν καὶ θυμὸν λέγει πρὸς τὴν τοιαύτην, "and spoke to her with vehemence and anger." This seems inconsistent with χαροποιούς, "merry-making," and the hare's subtle argumentation. C reuses the formula καὶ μὲ μανίαν καὶ θυμὸν in 664a (see note).

271. **dear master and philosopher**. P has "my master-craftswoman and partner" (τὴν μαστόρισσαν καὶ τὴν συνδρόφισσάν μου), which seems overly ironic.

274. **and brought him down . . . broken**. Verse omitted in V.

276. **before the conference**. PV use here the formula μέσον τοῦ συνεδρίου, "in the middle of the conference," which Papathomopoulos (2002) adopts, rather than CLA's μέσον τοῦ πλήθους ὅλου, "in the middle of the entire crowd," which was adopted by Tsiouni (1972). The argument for PV's reading is that it is more consistent with the overall usage of the text (the *usus*); because the formula is so characteristic of the text, it is more likely as a reading. The counterargument (supported by 281; see note) is that scribes increasingly tended to quote formulas they had already seen in the text when copying it, so a repeated formula cannot constitute a *lectio difficilior.*

281. **by the neck**. CVLA implausibly intrude here the formula μέσον τοῦ συνεδρίου, "in the middle of the conference," rather than P's μέσον ἐκ τοῦ τραχήλου, "by the middle of the neck." This illustrates the scribes' tendency to repeat existing formulas in the text, whether or not they actually make sense where they ended up.

285. **sorceress**. See Commentary.

300. **golden**. CVLA, Šandrovskaja (1956a), and Papathomopoulos (2002) have χρυσᾶς, "golden," whereas P and Tsiouni (1972) have ἔμορφας, "shapely." CVLA's reading repeats "gold" (χρυσᾶ) from the preceding verse, and it is likelier for a copyist to have increased the repetitiveness of the work than decreased it, given what we know of medieval scribes (cf. verse 281). On the other hand, Papathomopoulos (personal communication) believes that the repetition is appropriate to the hare's bragging and that "shapely" by contrast would be much too bland in context.

309. **against the brutal cold**. Verses 307 and 309 end identically (διὰ πολλὴν ψυχρότην); verse 309 occurs only in P, and Eideneier (1976:456) regards it as a redundant interpolation. Verse 309 sits somewhat awkwardly grammatically, and we are inclined to agree. Removing it would not make the grammar of 308 any worse: verse 308 has no verb, because the clitic placement in verse 309 indicates that it is a relative clause (τὰ ἔχουσιν instead of ἔχουσίν τα: Mackridge 1993), and its verb is implied by parallelism with 306, whether or not 309 follows.

315. **back in the assembly**. This reading adopted by Papathomopoulos (2002) is P's μέσον, "in the middle," whereas CVLA and Tsiouni (1972) have ἔξω, "outside." In fact, μέσον, "middle," is used ambiguously in the text, referring to either the audience or the podium, and so can here easily report the fox returning to her spot (as well as recapitulating an established formula); see "Imagery."

344. **everything like that**. Instead of καὶ ἄλλα τούτων ὅσα, "everything like that," L has ἁλατομπουγκία, "salt pouches." A adds 344a: δεσμεύουσι τὰ ζῷα ποιοῦσι καὶ ζωνάρια, "They tie up animals and make belts, too"—the first half of which extrametrically repeats verse 533.

Instead of verse 344, P has ἀκόμη καὶ τὸ κέρας μου πληρώνει ἄλλην χρείαν, "Also my horn is put to further use." This seems merely to anticipate verse 348.

370. **cookery**. P and Papathomopoulos (2002) have "in any cookery" (μαγειρείαν), whereas CVA and Tsiouni (1972) have καρυκεία (on which see "Language"); L, confused as usual by archaic words, has "in any household" (κατοικίαν). Tsiouni interprets καρυκεία as "seasoning," whereas Kriaras (1968–97, s.v.) has "cooking of food with καρύκη (sauce)," and the word is glossed by Liddell–Scott–Jones (1940, s.v.) as "cooking with καρύκη; hence, rich cookery." It does seem that καρυκεία also had the meaning "spices" in Byzantium: Theophylact of Simocatta (7.13.6; *vii* A.D.) reports that when the Khagan of the Avars requested "Indian καρυκείας" from Emperor Maurice, πέπερί τε ἐξέπεμψε καὶ φύλλον Ἰνδικὸν κασίαν τε καὶ τὸν λεγόμενον κόστον, "he sent pepper, Indian leaf, cassia ⟨a spice like cinnamon⟩, and the so-called *kostos.*" The word is similarly used by Eustathius of Thessalonica (*Commentary on the Odyssey* 2.245), among others.

Šandrovskaja (1956a) has **стряпин,** "cooking," which could easily be a translation of P rather than the other manuscripts.

372. **it's fine when boiled . . . else**. Verse omitted in P.

377. **brawn**. Here Papathomopoulos (2002) adopts Koukoules' (1911–12:372) emendation πολεμοῦσιν με πηκτήν (P: πτικήν) over Tsiouni's preference (1972) for πολεμοῦσιν μὲ τὴν γῆν (CVLA), "they work with the earth." The emendation has also been accepted by Šandrovskaja (1956a:244–45): **студень,** "brawn, jelly." Tsiouni surmises πτικήν is a corruption of ὄπτησιν, "cooking, roast," but the elision of the stressed initial vowel necessary for ὄπτησιν > πτικήν is problematic, and the specific term "congealed = brawn" matches better with "and all the like," literally "and other such" (μὲ ἄλλα τὰ τοιαῦτα) (i.e., foodstuffs). P has already avoided the adjective πηκτός in 252, although as noted there (see Commentary), the use of "congealed" by other manuscripts at that point is presumably not original.

383. **no scent at all**. Or, as C puts it: χωρὶς ἐμοῦ τὴν μυρωδίαν ποσῶς χάριν οὐκ ἔχουν, "without my scent there is no grace about them."

414. **dips her belly in mires and shit**. In PCV σκατοβορβορόκοιλη; this compound defeats the usual suspects A, which renders it as κατοβροβορόσκυλε, "cat–mire–dog" (anything but a sheep), and L, which conflates the sheep with its environs, giving σκατοβόρβορος αὐλή, "shit-mired courtyard."

422. **You've bragged and bragged . . . boar**. V has πολλὰ καυχᾶσαι φλυαρὲ καὶ κοπρολόγε χοῖρε, "You brag a lot, babbling, shit-talking boar."

423. **local**. P (and V, misspelled), with relentless logic, think ἐπιχώριος should be ἐπιχοίριος, "pigological."

434. **of butting brow**. Papathomopoulos (2002) prefers κοῦτλαν, "goat's brow; headbutt" (PCLA), following Hesseling (1924:311), rather than Tsiouni's use (1972) of κοῦτζαν "doll; tuft of thread" (V; glossed as "beard" by Tsiouni). Šandrovskaja (1956a) has **бодливый,** "butting," also following Hesseling. Xanthoudidis (1927–28:360) defends the V reading, and the extension of "tuft of thread" to "goat beard" is not implausible, but Hesseling's reading seems to us far likelier.

The word κοῦτλα is attested in Kriaras 1968–97, with the meaning "headbutt," in the Cretan Greek translation of *Pastor Fide:*

σὰν λιόντας μανισμένος
ὀπ' ὦρες φεύγει καὶ ὦρες
πετᾶται καὶ ἀπαντήχνει
τοῦ ἄμερου τοῦ ταυριοῦ τὶς θυμωμένες
κοῦτλες

[like an angry lion
who sometimes flees and sometimes
springs up and responds to
the wild bull's angry
headbutts] (4.2.176–80—though the work's editor Joannou [1962] interprets it as *Hörner,* "horns")

Modern Greek has as words for "forehead" the similar κούτρα < Latin *scutra,* "flat dish," and κούτελο < κότυλον, "cup"; κοῦτλα seems to be a blend of the two. The normal modern word for "headbutt" is κουτουλιά, for which Andriotis (1983, s.v.) accepts an etymology from κονδυλίζω, "trip over," though the similarity to κούτελο is obvious and has been appealed to in an alternative etymology (by Filindas) cited in Andriotis.

What this means is that there is a steady (and unsurprising) traffic in Greek between terms for "forehead" and "headbutt" (for κούτρα, cf. the verb κουτρῶ in the Judeo-Greek Pentateuch, Exodus 21:31). So κοῦτλα could refer to both, and in the case of a goat, probably does. In the modern dialects, κοῦτλα turns up in the meaning "accidental headbutting" (Symi); "hornless goat" (Samothrace [κ'τούλα], Symi—presumably the goat is "all forehead"); "horns" (κούτουλα: Siphnos); "forehead" (Kasos). In Aravani in Cappadocia, κουτούλα had come to mean "head" rather than just "forehead" (hence βιλλιοῦ μ' τὸ κουτούλα, "the head of my penis"), but there is no reason to posit such a transition here.

The word κοῦτζα in modern Greek dialects, by contrast, means "tuft of thread" (Karpathos, Nisyros, Symi, Ionia, Smyrna, Halicarnassus, Schinoussa, Rhodes, Icaria, Peloponnese [Kampos, Laconia; Lefktra?]); "tuft of wool" (Lefktra); "noose of thread" (Oitylon, Pelponnese; Lesbos); "stick placed in each turn of the warp" (Karpathos, Kythnos, Fourni, Siphnos); "roots, shoots of vegetable" (Crete); "wart" (Pontus); "beard of corn" (Vourles, Ionia); "ear of wheat" (Rhodes); "nest" (Mani). Though κοῦτζα has never been applied to a goat beard to our knowledge, the extension of "tuft" has already gone as far as corn. Nonetheless, none of these readings suggests that this reading is superior for this passage to κοῦτλα, which is also clearly the superior reading stemmatically. (Words from archives of *Historical Dictionary of Modern Greek.*)

A possibility that has not been raised until now is that V's κοῦτζαν may also mean "headbutt"; this is the meaning of Venetian *cozzada* (Boerio 1960

[1867], s.v.), Italian *cozzo*. We have no evidence of that word ever entering Greek, however.

439. **flesh**. CLA and Šandrovskaja (1956a) have εἴδη, "goods," instead of P's κρέη, "meats," a reading that Hesseling (1924:311) prefers—though neither Tsiouni (1972) nor Papathomopoulos (2002) adopt it, and we agree that it is much too generic.

439–43. **and snakes and reptiles . . . not only dead.** V deletes verses 439–43, censoring any mention of the boar's cannibalism. That V has done so deliberately becomes plausible from its verse 444. In the other manuscripts, "putrid" (σαπημένον) is singular, agreeing with the dead boar (μοχθηρόν) mentioned in 443. V, however, makes it the plural σαπημένα, to agree with the plural nouns "dead meat" (κρέατα ψοφισμένα) and "both worms and dung" in 438, the verse it places before 444. Similarly, it uses a plural rather than singular copula (ἔναι rather than ἔνι [CA], ἔν' [P]; L's modern εἶναι is ambiguous in number). So V has changed 444 to conceal its omission of 439–443.

460. **like we do**. The Greek is somewhat awkward here; all manuscripts give outright nonsensical readings, although they also all point clearly to Tsiouni's emendation (1972) ("but rather like us, the yours [τὰ σοῦ] you should have company"), which Papathomopoulos (2002) adopts. Hesseling's emendation (1924:311) to "like us, you too" (καὶ σύ) does not necessarily help. We do not feel, at any rate, that our rendering is too far off the mark.

The expression τὰ σοῦ, "the yours," may be an analogical formation from colloquial Greek σε τα μάς, "to the us," coined by analogy with the metanalysis με τα μάς, "with the us/ours" < μετὰ μᾶς, "with us" (e.g., *Della Porta* 1.1308, ἀγάπην τέλειαν μετὰ μᾶς, "perfect peace between us"). See also note to verse 961.

463. **talked right back**. CVLA and Tsiouni (1972) have ἔφησεν, "spoke," whereas P, Šandrovskaja (1956a), and Papathomopoulos (2002) have ἔρισεν, "quarreled with, competed." The poem consistently introduces animals with fairly colorless verbs of speaking; ἔφησεν itself is used in 262, 352, 428, 664, 746, 843, and 980. Furthermore, the usage of ἔρισεν in medieval Greek as outlined by Kriaras (1968–97) is almost all "compete" rather than "quarrel with" (although the "quarrel" sense has survived in at least Karpathos and the Pontus: Andriotis 1974 §2521). Even for the sense "quarrel with" there is no medieval evidence of which we know that it was used as a verb of speaking. And obviously, given phonetic writing and Byzantine script, the two verbs ἔφησεν and ἔρισεν are exceedingly easy to mistake for each other. Papathomopoulos (2002) prefers ἔρισεν as a *lectio difficilior* and appeals to classical rather than medieval use of ἔρισεν as a verb of speaking (e.g., Demosthenes 9.11: καὶ παρ' ἡμῖν ***ἤριζον*** οἱ πολλοὶ Θηβαίοις οὐ λυσιτελήσειν τὴν ἐκείνου πάροδον, "most people here at Athens ***contended*** that his passage through Thermopylae would be anything but a gain to the Thebans"). We are not convinced, but the difference is minor, and our rendering is intended to cover both senses.

477. **succulent**. Tsiouni (1972) has εὔνοστα, by emendation of P's ἔνοστα, and Papathomopoulos (2002) adopts this. Šandrovskaja (1956a) also follows P with вкусны, "delicious," and though the other manuscripts do not have this reading, one cannot blame her: their readings make little sense. VLA have σύνοχα, "joined together; in agreement," which is absurd referring to meat. This seems to be a desperate attempt to emend C's εὔνοχα, which is meaningless and clearly a corruption of εὔνοστα.

480. **by many craftsmen**. C appends (redundantly) 480a: πρῶτον τὸ κέρας τοῦ κριοῦ χρῶνται αὐτὸ τεχνῖται, "First off, the ram's horn is employed by craftsmen."

486. **red . . . blue**. The full list of colors is present only in P; CVLA reduce 486–87 to a single verse: κόκκινα, μαῦρα, κίτρινα, χρειώδη πρὸς τὴν τέχνην, "red, black or yellow, needed in their trade."

491. **queens**. P replaces ῥήγαινες, "queens," with εὐγενεῖς, "nobles," which is more suspect as a reading: it is redundant given the following verse, which mentions two kinds of Western nobles.

493. **carpets**. See Commentary.

494. **sultan and emirs are seated**. On L's ὁ βασιλεὺς δὲ κάθεται καὶ ὅλοι μεγιστᾶνοι, "where the emperor [*basileus*] and all grandees repose," see "Relation among the Manuscripts."

496. **mattresses**. L has εἰς σκαμνὶ ἀπάνω, "on their sofa(s)" (cf. Koukoules 1947–55:4.22; Byzantius 1874, s.v. σκαμνί).

499. **unto every realm**. P and Papathomopoulos (2002) have εἰς ἅπαντα τὰ πέρατα, "to all the bounds/frontiers"; CVLA and Tsiouni (1972) complete this elliptical expression extrametrically as εἰς πάντα τὰ πέρατα τῆς γῆς, "to all the bounds of the earth."

503. **gray clothes**. See Commentary.

506. **metropolitans**. See Commentary.

509. **I mean leftovers**. The reading is P's and is adopted by Papathomopoulos (2002). CVLA, Šandrovskaja (1956a) and Tsiouni (1972) have κάμνουσιν κοινοὶ ἀνθρῶποι, "And common folk make [the other coarse stuff]." It is difficult to choose between the two. The use of λέγω, "I mean," in P sounds like an interpolation, but a similar expression recurs in 544. P's reading is extrametrical (Papathomopoulos [2002] emends ἀπομοναρέα to ἀπομονάρια)—but CVA are just as extrametrical with their κάμνουσιν, and L's modern Greek form κάμνουν, while fitting the meter, is hardly likely to be authorial.

What weighs against CVLA is that common people *make* the clergy's clothes, just as they make felt products, so CVLA doesn't add any new information to 503 (unless we interpret κάμνουσιν as "use," which seems unwarranted). Moreover, it would be odd if the subject of making clothes is unstated in 503 and made explicit only in 509 as the "common folk." On the other hand with P's reading, the subject in 509 is probably not even human but the wool itself (cf. 497), so no incompatibility with 503 arises: the subjects in the two verses are distinct. So we concur with this reading, and it makes sense for mattresses and caps to be made of wool leftovers, as distinct from the finer-quality cloth used to make the clothes of the nobility and the coarser cloth used to make cassocks.

537. **I don't know what to say**. We follow PL, Šandrovskaja (1956a), and Papathomopoulos (2002); CVA and Tsiouni (1972) have ἔχω τινὰ νὰ λέγω, "I could say a few things." Because the goat refuses to speak any further (539), the former reading makes more sense—unless we construe the goat as checking herself before embarking on yet another tirade, just as the buffalo does in 609–10.

540. **no dumb ewe**. CLA and Papathomopoulos (2002) have "I will not brag a lot—like you, dumb ewe" (ὡς σὺ λωλοπροβάτιν) instead of PV and Tsiouni's (1972) homophonous "I will not brag a lot—like the dumb ewe" (ὡς ἡ λωλοπροβάτα). CLA's reading is supported by Vasiliou (1996:79). Although there is something appealing about the nanny dropping hints to the ewe in the third person, the use of the second person in the very next line makes the PV reading implausible, and we agree with CLA. Our rendering, however, encompasses both versions.

541. **inanities**. The word used by P, ληρήματα, appears to be unknown to CVLA; both here and in 586, they substitute a form of ῥήματα, "words." The corresponding verb, ληρίζω, seems to have offered them no such difficulty in 817 and 958.

542. **How you've puffed yourself**. L here appends 542a–b: καὶ τέλος ἀνεχώρησαν οἱ τρεῖς τους ἐκ τὴν μέσην, / καὶ εὐθὺς ἤλθασιν αὐτοὶ μέσον τοῦ συνεδρίου, "And finally the three departed then. / And they came onto center stage at once" (or "amidst the assembly": see note 315). L has done this to compensate for the fact that its source text (the antecedent of VL) is missing verses 545–82, including the sheep's departure; L is attempting to repair the connection between the end of the goats' speech and the ox and buffalo in middiscourse. That this makes a hash of 543–44, which are still preserved in L, is testimony of L's maladroitness, and the ambiguity of the connecting formula makes it impossible to tell whether the bovines are coming or the goats are going.

544. **formidable large animal**. L has ζῷον ἄξιον ποὺ πρέπει νὰ τὰ λέγῃ, "some worthy animal that has to speak."

557. **is such that both . . . alike**. Verse 557 is present only in P; its omission in CA results in problematic syntax (no copula).

570. **the ox impertinently setting forth**. Verse 570 is present only in P, but though the juxtaposition of 569 and 570 is awkward, 575 makes it clear it is the ox who is doing the talking and not the pair of ox and buffalo. So verse 570 is not inaccurate and may easily have been omitted as seemingly redundant by the scribe of the archetype of CA (VL are missing here), rather than interpolated by P.

576a. **weak-limbed . . . beasts**. This verse is present only in C. At this point in the manuscript, C and P are the only witnesses (VL are missing a page, and

A is on one of its many lacunae), so it is hard to tell which manuscript is more faithful to the original.

580. **orderly**. P (the only other witness to the text at this point) has εἰς τοὺς ἰδίους τόπους, "in their own places."

602. **and with beetroot, too**. P, echoing the preceding line, has καὶ εἰς τὰς γούλας τὰς χοντράς, τὰ λέγουνε κουροῦκλες καὶ εἰς τὰς σεύκλας, "and fat kohlrabi, too, known as κουροῦκλες, and with beetroot, too." As a result, the verse is extrametrical, so the κουροῦκλες of 602 are clearly P's interpolation.

Xanthoudidis (1927–28:364) is unfamiliar with the word κουροῦκλες, although he reports that in Paxi (south of Corfu), according to the archives of the *Historical Dictionary of Modern Greek,* it denotes a kind of dark cabbage (λαχάνου, which in context presumably means "cabbage" rather than "vegetable"). Sampson (1972:113) also reports the word, in Skopelos (off Thessaly), although he glosses it there simply as λάχανον, "cabbage." Triandafyllidis (1963 [1909]:424) glosses the instance in the *Tale* as *ein Art Kohl,* "a kind of cabbage," and derives it (with a question mark) from vulgar Latin **colucula,* an unattested diminutive of *colis,* "stalk; cabbage"; compare medieval Latin *colucula,* "distaff" (Du Cange 1954 [1678], s.v.) as a diminutive of classical *colus.*

603. **main courses**. P has "at noon" (γιῶμα), a term sounding very similar to "main (afternoon) meal" (γεῦμα), from which it is in fact etymologically derived (Andriotis 1983, s.v. γιόμα).

610a. **verbosity betokens foolishness**. Verse 610a is absent in P.

612–12a. **You mud-and-quagmire–weltering . . . shithead**. Verse 612a is absent in P and V. (This may constitute evidence of contamination between P and V.) It is also absent in Šandrovskaja 1956a. The individual manuscripts at this point read as follows:

Βορβοροκωλοκύλιστε, ***φλυαροσκοτολόγε***	612 P
Βορβοροπηλοκύλιστε, ***φλυαροκοπρολόγε***	612 V
Βορβοροπηλοκύλιε, λιμνοαναθρεμμένη,	612 L
πολλὰ μοῦ ἐτζαμπούνισες, ***φλυαροκορδολόγε***	612a L
Βορβοροπηλοκύλιστε, λιμνοαναθρεμμένη,	612 C
πολλὰ μοῦ ἐσταμπούνισες, ***φλυαροκορδολόγε***	612a C
Φορβοροπηλοκύλιστε, λιμνοαναθρεμμένε,	612 A
πολλὰ μοῦ ἐτζαμπούνισες, ***φλυαροκορδολόγε***	612a A

Obviously the words in boldface derive from the same word in the prototype. So a solution that repeats the same word twice, as Tsiouni (1972) does, is unacceptable and does not correspond to any extant manuscript:

Βορβοροκωλοκύλιστε, ***φλυαροσκατολόγε*** (P) 612
πολλὰ μοῦ ἐτζαμπούνισες, ***φλυαροκορδολόγε*** (CLA) 612a

[You arse-in-quagmire-rolling, babbling bullshitter!
You've chattered quite enough, you babbling braggart!]

In 612 P has φλυαροσκοτολόγε, "babbling darkness-talker" (an obvious misspelling of φλυαροσκατολόγε, "babbling shit-talker"), and V has φλυαροκοπρολόγε, "babbling dung-talker." CLA, however, insert two hemistichs, starting here with λιμνοαναθρεμμένη, "bred in lakes." In 612a P and V are absent, and CLA have φλυαροκορδολόγε, "babbling pride-talker" (?—cf. κορδῶνα, 270). It seems likely that PV have coalesced 612 and 612a, whereas CLA supplanted an original φλυαροκοπρολόγε with the orthographically similar φλυαροκορδολόγε. P went further, supplanting φλυαροκοπρολόγε with the semantically similar φλυαροσκατολόγε but misspelling it as φλυαροσκοτολόγε. So if we accept verse 612a as valid, then we must also accept the "added" material in 612: 612 must have ended in λιμνοαναθρεμμένη, "bred in lakes."

Furthermore, if the reading of P is abandoned for the second half of 612, it should probably be abandoned for the first half as well, for reasons of consistency. The epithet βορβοροκωλοκύλιστε, "quagmire-arse-rolling," is present in P only, whereas all the other manuscripts have βορβοροπηλοκύλιστε, "quagmire-mud-rolling." The compounds in the *Tale* involving three parts—excluding those where the second is a prepositional prefix to the verb in the third: ἀλευροκαταχέστη (159), τορνοεμφωλευμένα (917)—uniformly group the first and second together as synonyms: συχνοπυκνοκλάνῃς (246), κοιλιοχορδοφᾶσα (286), σκατοβορβορόκοιλη (414), τζιλοπορδοκοπῶντα (711), ἀχλαδοβαλανότροφε (847), μυρτοκουμαροφάγα (847), μυσεροκακομούτζουνον (972), ψειροκονιδοφάγον (972). The one exception is κονδοποδαρομύτα (844, CVLA only), though there the first term qualifies both the second and third (as both are body parts), whereas in βορβοροκωλοκύλιστε all three parts are semantically distinct. (See appendix 5 for glosses.) It is unlikely that the adjective here constitutes such an exception: within the grammatical system of the *Tale*, "quagmire-and-mud–rolling" is far likelier than "arse-in-quagmire–rolling." We thus propose the following text:

Βορβοροπηλοκύλιστε, λιμνοαναθρεμμένη, 612
πολλὰ μοῦ ἐτζαμπούνισες, ***φλυαροκοπρολόγε.*** 612a

Papathomopoulos (2002) had originally disagreed with our choice for the bolded word and had chosen the emendation φλυαροπορδολόγε, "babbling fart-talker." In doing so, he appealed to the fact that both babbling and farting involve sound, so the compound is semantically more coherent than the alternatives. Papathomopoulos also appealed to Alexiou's emendation (1954:271) of *Fortounatos* 4.71: κορδόγερος, "cord–old man," to πορδόγερος, "farting old man." But as we have noted in our commentary to verse 270, it is not at all obvious that *Fortounatos* needs emending here, and neither Kriaras (1968–97) nor *Fortounatos*'s latest editor, Vincent (1980), have adopted Alexiou's reading.

If we are to accept one of the three extant readings as original, φλυαροκορδολόγε is clearly the *lectio difficilior,* but this does not adequately explain how the other readings (particularly P's) came into being, and V's reading is *difficilior* enough to be near nonsense. In restituting the original word, then, we need something that could have plausibly engendered all three of φλυαροσκατολόγε, φλυαροκοπρολόγε, and φλυαροκορδολόγε. Papathomopoulos's solution requires the steps φλυαροπορδολόγε > φλυαροκορδολόγε CLA (one letter changed); φλυαροπορδολόγε > φλυαροσκατολόγε (metonymizing farts to shit) (> φλυαροσκοτολόγε P [miscopied])> φλυαροκοπρολόγε V (by synonym). By retaining a form that has actually appeared in a manuscript, we believe our account is more economical, requiring only two real changes instead of three: φλυαροκοπρολόγε (archetype, V) > φλυαροκορδολόγε CLA (two letters changed, still an easy conflation to make); φλυαροκοπρολόγε > φλυαροσκατολόγε > φλυαροσκοτολόγε P. This would seem to violate the rule on three-part compounds we have formulated, because babbling and dung cannot be understood as synonyms. But the -λόγος suffix, "person occupied with," seems to have been almost empty semantically, as witnessed by its derivational use in the *Tale* (240, 327, 834). The three-part compound κλαδοτρυπολόγε in 327 likewise does not make synonyms of its first and second terms.

The meaning "mud" of πηλός in βορβοροπηλοκύλιστε, "mud-and-quagmire–weltering" was secondary even in antiquity to the meaning "clay." The meaning "mud" has not survived into the standard modern language but is still discernible in certain contexts (πηλοφόρι, "mud-carrier = mortar board"). The old meaning died out quite late (Somavera 1977 [1709] glosses πηλός as both πηλόν: *fango, creta, poltiglia, argilla,* "mud, clay, mush," and λάσπη: *fango, malta,* "mud, mortar"); in fact it remains in widespread use in modern dialect (Andriotis 1974 §4885), particularly in the plural πηλά (used also in verse 447). So the term πηλός, meaning "mud," could well have been extant in the vernacular of the time without the author needing to appeal to classical Greek.

616. **pen cases**. The inferiority of P's (and Wagner's [1874]) reading (ποιοῦν τὰ καλαμάρια, ποιοῦν κονδυλογράφοι, "they make their inkhorns, penmen/pens make them"), which disrupts the balance of the verse relative to the other manuscripts (literally "they make inkhorns, they make pen cases"), was pointed out by Hesseling (1924:313). Wagner himself found V's reading "apparently preferable" (*praestantius videtur*), and Hesseling adds "one might say it is the only reasonable reading." It has been accordingly adopted by Šandrovskaja (1956a), Tsiouni (1972), and Papathomopoulos (2002).

The nominative case of P's κονδυλογράφοι makes nonsense of the verse, but it is not obvious whether the term (a hapax legomenon, according to Kriaras 1968–97) means "pen," as Kriaras suggests, or "penman." However, the corresponding verb κοντυλογράφω "to pen, to write with a κονδύλιν" in *Della Porta* (1.53) suggests "penman," consistent with the behavior of the suffix -γράφος in Greek in general, and this is how Hesseling had interpreted it.

Though the term κονδυλοθήκη, "pen case," is a hapax legomenon, something like it is mentioned in *Erotokritos* 1.1423–24, describing the hero's study:

> σκριτόριο εἶχε ὁλάργυρο, καδέγλα χρουσωμένη,
> ***καλαμαρθήκη*** πλουμιστὴ καὶ μαργαριταρένη
>
> [he had a desk of silver, a golden chair,
> a ***pen case*** decorated, set with pearls.]

Kriaras (1968–97) glosses the word as a case for καλαμάρια (i.e., inkwells: see Commentary verse 616), but the work's editor Alexiou (1980) more plausibly describes the piece of office furniture named as "καλαμάρι (inkwell) and pen case." And Somavera (1977 [1709]), who glosses καλαμάρι as *calamaro,* "inkwell," glosses καλαμαροθήκη as στούκιον, "[pen] case," *pennaruolo, pennaiuolo, pennaruola,* "pen case." This incidentally shows how interchangeable the senses "pen" and "inkwell" remained for καλαμάριν.

618. **chess sets**. The Italian word σκάκους < *scacchi* gave the scribes much grief. PCA have εἰς κάκους, swallowing up the initial sigma. V tries to make sense of this by shifting the stress down, giving εἰς κακούς, "in the bad ones." L seems thoroughly unfamiliar with the game and has εἰς σκάμους, which looks like "in sofas" (εἰς σκάμνους); in 921 L is the only manuscript to distort the word on its second appearance, giving εἰς σάκους, "in sacks."

620. **spearheads**. P has σκουτελίων, "plates," instead of κονταρίων, "spears."

621. **and many other necessary products**. P has (extrametrically) λέγω δὲ καὶ ἑτέρας πλειόνας δουλείας τορνεμένας, "and, I say, many other lathed products."

635. **mighty**. CVL have παχύν, "thick," instead of P's δυνατόν, "mighty," whereas A extrametrically combines the two as παχὺν δυνατόν, "thick, mighty." VL also have παχύν, "thick," in 645 instead of PCA μακρόν, "long."

635. **long and fiery**. VL have δυνατὸν καὶ μέγα, "mighty and large," instead of PCA's μακρὺν (μακρὸν P) καὶ πυρωδάτον.

646. **brayed**. There are two medieval Greek words for braying, as Eideneier (1995) discusses: (ὀ)γκανίζω, *[o]ganizo,* and (ὀ)γκαρίζω, *[o]garizo.* Both have survived into modern Greek, although γκαρίζω is the form used in the standard language. The -ρ- infix is also normal for modern animal-call verbs, as Eideneier (1995:176) points out (μουγκρίζω, "growl"; νιαουρίζω, "meow"; γρύζω, "oink"). Tsiouni (1972) uses the *gar-* form in her edition, and Papathomopoulos (2002) the *gan-* form.

Eideneier (1995:178) notes that C "retains" the *gan-* stem, whereas the more recent manuscripts prefer the modern *gar-* stem. He speculates that the *gan-* stem is what the author must have used and that Tsiouni (1972) was influenced in her edition by her standard Greek primary education. In actuality only V uses one form consistently, although Tsiouni does indeed impose the *gar-* form uniformly on her text. In order of the antiquity of the manuscripts, the proportion of *gan-* to *gar-* is C 3:2, P 4:2, V 0:6, A 3:3, L 2:4. (The instances of the stems in the *Tale*, of which the last is missing in C, are 646, 710, 716, 718, 728, 730.)

This weakly suggests *gan-* is the original form, and although the two oldest members of their families, P and C, swap usage erratically, they never both support *gar-*. But the evidence is too confused to allow a definitive conclusion as to which form the author used—if indeed he did not use both.

650. **thick as a cudgel**. Carried away by the similarity of μεγαλοματζουκᾶτον to another prominent epithet in the *Tale,* P has the donkey's penis be μεγαλομουστακᾶτον, "big-moustached."

654. **stirred by lust**. See Commentary.

657a. **The ox and buffalo departed then**. This verse is present only in VL, but though it is absent in the two best witnesses of the text, verse 658 sounds abrupt without it, so it is either original or a good emendation by the scribe of the prototype of VL. Šandrovskaja (1956a) includes it in her text, explicitly appealing to V, as do both Tsiouni (1972) and Papathomopoulos (2002).

661. **He ran . . . posed**. Verse 661 is present only in P. Its choppy syntax of four unconnected verbs—literally "he ran up, he ran down, he shook, he bended"—is uncharacteristic of the poem (though two unconnected verbs are frequent enough—e.g., verse 264), so it may be an interpolation. Admittedly, ἐσείσθην, ἐλυγίσθην, "(s)he shook, (s)he bended," is a commonplace formula describing graceful movement of both horses and women (Kriaras 1968–97, s.v. λυγίζω), which has survived into modern Greek (cf. the Cretan song couplet το ***σείσμα*** και το ***λύγισμα*** που κάνεις του κορμιού σου / σκλαβώνουνε τον άθρωπο μα δεν το βάνει ο νους σου, "The ***bending*** and the ***shaking*** of your body / enslaves a man—but you do not suspect it"); so the asyndeton is not necessarily that much of a problem. Likewise, the first two verbs recur as a compound in verses 1047 and 1070, referring again to the horse. But in fact this makes the interpolation even more suspect; scribes were particularly prone to inserting formulas from other works they had been copying (although, because P consists only of the *Tale,* we know nothing of what else its scribe was familiar with).

Tsiouni (1972), Šandrovskaja (1956a) (встала), and Wagner (1874) all read ἐσείσθην, "shook," as ἐστάθην, "stood"; Papathomopoulos's reading (2002) is more plausible, because it invokes the chivalric formula.

663. **neigh**. Tsiouni (1972) and PL give essentially the modern word for neighing (ἐχλιμίντρισεν L, ἐχιλιμήντρισεν P). Papathomopoulos (2002) and CVA have ἐχρημάτισεν, which literally means "to do business with" or "to serve as." But, of course, the verb should be identified with the classical ἐχρεμέτισεν, "neighed," and may be a portmanteau of the classical and the modern word. Bakker and van Gemert (1988) reconstruct the classical verb ἐχρεμέτιζαν

for *Belisariad* ρ 810, based on χρεμέτιζον in manuscript P; the printed editions of that version of the work (including M, the surviving apograph of the earliest edition) have ἐχλιμίτιζαν (cf. *Alexander Romance* ρ 2919, χλιμίτηξε), which may show that the classical form had already become unfamiliar by the sixteenth century (although Somavera [1977 (1709)], who is normally scrupulously vernacular, has χρεμετίζω and χειλιμοντρῶ—similar to P's ἐχιλιμήντρισεν—as synonyms).

664. **along these lines**. C allows the horse his day in court (664a–c):

καὶ μὲ μανίαν καὶ θυμὸν λέγει πρὸς τὸν τοιοῦτον,
καὶ λόγους ἐπεμφθέγξατο ὅλους μετ' ἀληθείας,
ὀνειδισμοὺς καὶ ὕβριτας πρὸς αὔτον ταῦτα ἔφη.

[and said to him with vehemence and anger
and uttered forth these words, all truthfully,
speaking these mockeries and insults to him.]

665. **Dick-O-Matic**. See Commentary.

666. **burden you, poor fool**. The reading is PA's (φορτώνουν ἄτυχε); the other manuscripts have a variant of φορτώνουσι ταχύ, "burden you so swiftly" or "burden you in the morning."

671. **trunks**. P has "onions" (κρόμμυα), which has crept in among the building material as a soundalike to "trunks" (κορμούς).

673a. **and any kind . . . pile it up**. P omits this verse, and the passage reads well without it. Šandrovskaja (1956a) does not include it in her translation, though it is ostensibly based on VLA.

676. **looting**. See Commentary.

685–88. **And if you come . . . bite your lips**. The delightful episode of the donkey by the brook (685–88) is attested only in P.

688. **bite your lips**. P has the somewhat garbled καὶ νὲ καὶ ἀποδαγκάνει, "and yes (?) and it thoroughly bites." We almost know what is meant here, but all interpretations offered have their problems. Wagner (1874) has emended the passage as καὶ σέν' ἀποδαγκάνει, "and you it thoroughly bites"—a reading Xanthoudidis (1927–28:366) doesn't think helps. Tsiouni (1972) has emended it to καῖνε καὶ ἀποδαγκάνεις, "they burn and you thoroughly bite."

Tsiouni's emendation (1972) is the most plausible and is what we and Papathomopoulos (2002) have adopted. But (ἀπο)δαγκώνω in medieval Greek (Kriaras 1968–97, s.v.) is used in the active voice to indicate someone biting something else; if the donkey is biting his own lip out of pain, this should have been the medial ἀποδαγκάνεσαι. If the verb is indeed meant to be active and what bites (stings) are the beatings (ῥαβδακές), then the verb should have been plural: ἀποδαγκάνουσι.

If the verb is meant to be both active and singular, then this might be construed as the donkey's master "stinging" the donkey. But although Kriaras

(1968–97) claims the sense "torment" for δαγκώνω (s.v. δαγκάνω, 4—ἀποδαγκώνω itself is a hapax legomenon), this seems far likelier to involve abstract subjects, as a metaphorical usage, than refer to human agents. (Kriaras's example given is Bounialis, *Κατάνυξις ὠφέλιμος διὰ κάθε χριστιανόν* [cited from Kriaras] 378: ὁ ἔρωτας φλόγα πολλὴν ἀπάνω τους θὰ βάνη / καὶ γιὰ παρηγοριά τωνε θέλει νὰ τοὺς ***δακάνη***, "Love shall cast a mighty flame on them; and for their solace, it shall ***sting*** them.") And Kriaras himself, adopting the Wagner (1874) reading for his lemma on ἀποδαγκάνω, admits the word is used in this passage "with some exaggeration, because the subject is a human." In this context, we might even say it would be perverse. So the least problematic interpretation is that the donkey is biting his own lip in pain, with the active instead of the medial used either for metrical convenience or elliptically.

691. **you donkeys**. V has "you Bugdans" (βουγδάνοι). Bogdan is a Slavonic proper name and was frequent in the fifteenth and sixteenth centuries as a name of Moldavian voevods; from the sixteenth century onward, the Ottomans began referring to the whole of Moldavia as *Bogdan*. Whether this reference to Moldavia is a double (or single!) entendre is difficult to say at this remove. (Our thanks to Liliana Simeonova for bringing this to our attention.)

693. **and sent him all the way**. L swaps verse 693 with 694, leading to an avoidable syntactic gap.

697. **should be abolished**. We have agreed with Papathomopoulos (2002) in following P's subjunctive νὰ ῥίσῃ, "that he should order [that it be abolished]," rather than ὥρισε (CV), ὅρισεν (A), and ὅρησε (L), "he ordered." CVLA's readings, in using the indicative aorist, make no sense: they have the narrator presupposing the king has already banned the practice. (Šandrovskaja [1956a] likewise has the subjunctive **чтобы он постановил**, "so that he may decide," whereas Tsiouni [1972] followed the indicative ὥρισε.) In reality, of course, this makes very little difference to the translation. It is more straightforward to read P as "order" ([ὁ]ρίσῃ) rather than "say" (ῥήσῃ), given that CVLA also uses the verb "order," so we accept Papathomopoulos's emendation to ὁρίσῃ.

717–18. **letting fly farts . . . amidst his braying**. Verses 729a–730 are a repetition of 717–18, and Eideneier (1976:456) suggests these need not both be present in the text (also in Eideneier 1995:179); he is inclined to omit 717–18, trusting C, which lacks them. In context, 730 is a necessary clarification of 731, whereas the sense does not suffer if either 717–18 or 729a is omitted; therefore 730 must be original. However, 729a is present only in C and A (which usually patterns with C); this makes one suspect it is verse 718 moved down by C. VL agree with P in preserving 717–18; though this may have resulted from contamination, it still makes it likelier that 717–18 is an old reading. Even more worrying, A, though a quite corrupt manuscript, retains all four verses, although nothing in C—which must have looked a lot like the prototype of A—would encourage A to retain or reconstruct 717–18.

It seems likelier to us that both verses 717–18 and 730 are original, all being attested in both families. The prototype of CA would have copied 718 to the newly interpolated 729a, passing all four verses down to A, whereas C noted the resulting repetition between the two pairs of verses and reacted by deleting the original instance, 717–18. (C overwhelmingly tends to add rather than delete, as shown in "Relation among the Manuscripts," but it has also deleted verse 1052.)

722. **donkeys**. Reflecting the prejudices of the time, the scribe of L had originally written here ἐβραίων (*sic*), "Jews," before substituting γαϊδάρων, "donkeys," back in.

727. **you assembled**. All manuscripts have ἡμετέραν, "our [assembly]," but Wagner (1874), Šandrovskaja (1956a) (**ваше сборище**), Tsiouni (1972), and Papathomopoulos (2002) have all chosen to read this as ὑμετέραν, "your [assembly]." The two words sound identical in modern Greek (which is why it no longer uses them), but clearly only the latter makes sense, unless the donkey is somehow appealing to corporate identity.

728. **I brayed . . . farts aplenty**. CVL and Tsiouni (1972) have ἐγκάνιξα ἐκ τὴν χαράν, ἐφώναξα μεγάλως (ὀλίγον VL), "I brayed with joy, I cried out mightily" ("slightly" VL); PA, Šandrovskaja (1956a), and Papathomopoulos (2002) have ἐγκάρισα (ἐγάνισα A), ἐφώναξα τζιλοπορδοκοπῶντα, "I brayed, I cried, I let fly farts aplenty." Both versions copy expressions used elsewhere in the text: PA are close to 711 φωνάζοντα καὶ τρέχοντα τζιλοπορδοκοπῶντα, "called them out, running and farting merrily on the way," but CVL are only two verses down from 726: ἐγώ δὲ ἀπὸ τὴν χαρὰν τὴν εἶχα τὴν μεγάλην, "and out of the delight that overwhelmed me"; literally "and out of the mighty joy I had." In fact, the mention of joy in 726 makes its repetition in 728 suspicious, particularly as it also ends up echoing 710 rather closely: the tendency in the *Tale* is for repetitiveness to increase rather than decrease as scribes copied each other (see Textual Notes 281). We thus agree with Papathomopoulos that PA is the original reading; this is also supported stemmatically, because P and A are independent witnesses.

729. **this good news**. Continuing the tenor of PA, C has the donkey say πορδοκοπῶν εἰσέδραμα, "I sped up, farting."

Hesseling (1924:313) thinks the verse should read νὰ δώσουν συγχαρίκιν, "that *they* [rather than *I*] should give congratulations." No manuscripts support this reading, which would be grammatically awkward, as the messenger has already started addressing the donkeys referred to in the second person; and the messenger congratulating the others on their mutual good fortune does not seem any more out of place than the others congratulating him. In fact, the confusion arises because of the obscurity of the word used: see Commentary.

729a. **Letting fly farts . . .** See verses 717–18.

738. **they keep placing**. P has πάντοτε ποτὲ οὐδὲν σᾶς λείπει, "it is always never absent from you"—which in actuality makes more sense than one might think. . . .

740. **donkey**. Possibly influenced by the *Donkey Tale*, L has "Mister Donkey" (κυρ' γάδαρος).

747. **Out of my sight at once, you shitty donkey**. Reiterated in C as 747a: φύγε ἀπὸ τὴν μέσην μου, φύγε ἀπ' ἔμπροσθέν μου, "Out of my way, out from in front of me."

752. **the wondrous, great and fearsome horse**. C, recalling 81, has μὲ ἄλογον τὸ θαυμαστὸν καὶ θρόνον τῶν ἀνθρώπων, "the wondrous horse, the seat and throne of men."

762. **stitched**. Tsiouni (1972) has βαμμένα, "dyed," in her edition, following Wagner (1874). Šandrovskaja (1956a) has also followed suit, with окрашенными в темнокрасный цвет, "painted in dark red color." This is a word absent in the manuscripts: CVA have καμμένα, "burnt," and PL ῥαμμένα, "stitched." The use of crimson stitching in equestrian gear is not unreasonable, and we do not think the emendation warranted, so Papathomopoulos (2002) and we have both used PL's reading.

771. **begged of Zeus the god**. P judges this too pagan and substitutes ἐπαρακάλεσεν καὶ αὔτη τὸν θεόν μας, "who once herself did beg our God." Hesseling (1924:313) thinks it unlikely that P's is the original reading or that the other family of manuscripts (of which he knew only VL) inserted a classicizing reading. In this we concur, and the god's capricious response is at odds with the remote Christian deity (although perhaps not with the modern Greek folkloric treatment of Christ: see, for example, Loukopoulos 1940). Aesop was accessible enough to scribes for them to correct "God" to the "Zeus" of the fable the horse is repeating, but it is far likelier that Zeus was censored out than added back in. Šandrovskaja (1956a), on the other hand, rejects the reading of her own manuscript family in favor of P.

776. **hearing what the horse was saying**. P here follows the precedent of other transition passages in the *Tale* in having ὡς ἤκουσεν ἡ κάμηλος ἐκεῖ τὸ ὄνομάν της, "the camel, hearing that her name was mentioned." This does not mention the horse, so verse 777, which has the horse as its implicit subject, would make no sense.

777. **aimed**. Instead of ἀπέτεινεν, "directed," V has ἀπέκτεινεν, "slew."

793. **boots**. τζάγγας is Xanthoudidis's emendation (1927–28:367) for what the manuscripts actually give, which is τζάπας (τζάπα V, τζυπᾶς A). The confusion between γγ and π was easy given the script of the time, so the emendation is plausible. To accept it, though, we have to rule out that τζάπας made any sense.

The main meaning of τζάπα/τσάπα, in medieval and modern Greek alike, is "hoe, pickaxe," from the Italian *zappa*. This is the sense under which it is listed in Du Cange 1958 [1658]. It is not clear to us how horseskin could have anything to do with pickaxes. Somavera (1977 [1709], s.v. τζάπα) lists another meaning for the word, which is no more promising: *paletta da giuocare la palla,* "board with which to play ball"; πινακίδα, τόρα: *paletta da imparar l'a, b, c, à i putti,* "board to teach the ABCs to children."

A third sense of the stem τσαπ- has to do with coating or embroidering, typically in some precious metal. Thus, *Imperios and Margarona* 106, 385; *Belisariad* χ 338, N² 258, ρ 391; *Achilleid* N 1621 have χρυσ(ι)οτσάπωτος, "gold-embroidered" (of a horse cover or saddle, or in the *Achilleid,* of a nobleman's clothes); *Digenes* E 12, A 340, P 319, ἀργυροτσάπωτα, "trimmed with silver" (of a horse's hooves); *Belisariad* χ 280, N² 300, ρ 461, ὁλοτσάπωτος, "all-covered" (referring to the royal tents adorned with golden bells); Judeo-Greek Pentateuch Exodus 25:11, καὶ νὰ *ζαπώσῃς* αὐτὸ μάλαμμα καθάριο, "And thou shalt ***overlay*** it ⟨the Ark⟩ with pure gold." In this sense, the stem actually refers to the same thing as the silverwork and goldwork described for the horse's saddles, bridle, halter, and shoes in *Tale* 759–61.

The word is clearly not Greek; Alexiou (1985:246) proposes it is derived from Old French *chape,* "overcoat," or *chapé,* "wearing an overcoat"—hence, "coated." The etymology is eminently plausible; but because medieval Greek already had κάππα (which of course derives from the Latin ancestor of *chape, cappa*), the French word itself seems not to have entered Greek. And even if it had, horse leather is a poor choice for making an overcoat. We therefore think that Xanthoudidis's emendation is correct and that the scribal error, strangely unemended by subsequent scribes (A's confused τζυπᾶς doesn't count) dates from the prototype manuscript. Tsiouni (1972) and Papathomopoulos (2002) have adopted this reading. Šandrovskaja (1956a) speculates that the term refers to "some kind of special instruments with the help of which the hide of a dead animal is prepared," but we find no corroboration for such a sense.

795. **At once, the horse retorted to the camel**. The verse is omitted in CVA, and L has reconstructed it on its own, independently: καὶ παρευθὺς τὸ ἄλογον πρὸς τὴν καμήλαν λέγει, "Immediately the horse said to the camel." (The difference in wording means this shouldn't be considered an instance of contamination.) That L felt the need to reconstruct this verse confirms that its absence must be a fault in CVA, as all transitions between speeches are accorded at least a verse of narrative in the text. (The omission of 858–59 in CVLA truncates but does not eliminate the narrative transition there; see note.)

813. **cursing the donkey, too**. The wolf's speech, as noted in "Meter" (endnote 168), is characterized by a deliberate repetitiveness, which is obvious in Papathomopoulos's edition (2002). Tsiouni's edition (1972) follows P, which seems to have gone out of its way to avoid that repetition, substituting the repeated words with ὁμοίως, "similarly"—in this verse (ὕβρισας) and in 820 (ἐσθίω). However, P does not change the repetition in 821–22; in fact, it moves μικρά, "small," up to 821 so that the repetition there is contained in a single verse. (V follows P in 821 and CLA in 822; as a result, it manages to repeat μικρά three times.)

The repetitiveness occurs in the same speech as the deliberate accumulation of anapests in 810–14 (see "Meter"), which has also been suppressed in P, and the literal repetitions are more striking as a literary effect than the bland usage of "similarly" (which also replaces πολλάκις, "often," in 822). We thus agree with Papathomopoulos's text as respecting the intent of the author.

817–18. **not only donkeys . . . besides**. Verses 817–18 are omitted in A. We cannot explain this as the scribe toning down the savagery of the wolf's speech, because the scribe leaves in verse 819, the harshest verse of all.

831a. **she, too, stepped up . . . next to him**. This verse is attested only in C. PVL have 831 as μεμονωμένον, μοναχόν, ἐστάθη εἰς τὸ μέσον, literally "isolated, alone, she ⟨the bear⟩ stood in the middle." This reading stands on its own and is adopted by Papathomopoulos (2002). In the context of PVL's verse 831, C's 831a is incoherent. Verse 831 in CA, however, reads μεμονωμένον {ἐμόνον A}, μοναχόν, μέσον τοῦ συνεδρίου, "isolated, alone in center stage." In other words, C moves εἰς τὸ μέσον, "in the middle," from 831 to 831a and repeats the entire phrase μέσον τοῦ συνεδρίου, "center of the conference," from 829 to 831, supplanting ἐστάθη εἰς τὸ μέσον, "took center stage." C (or its antecedent) is thus manipulating verse 831 in order to accommodate its verse 831a, presumably inserted because its scribe realized that the transition from the wolf to the bear was too rushed.

PVL is abrupt enough to make one suspect that C preserves a reading closer to the original, with PVL (for which Papathomopoulos [2002] posits contamination) contracting C 831 and C 831a into a single verse. This is reminiscent of CLA 612–12a corresponding to PV 612 (see note). Observe that C 831 is the only instance in the *Tale* where the phrase "in center stage" occurs twice during a transition from one animal to the other, making it repetitive. Papathomopoulos (2002) prefers PVL, placing 831a in brackets as a dispreferred reading.

837. **Or could it be . . . to anyone at all**. As Eideneier (1976:456) points out, P has verse 837 but not 838–42, whereas the other four manuscripts have 838–42 but not 837. So it is unlikely both verse groupings originate in the prototype. Verse 837 ("Or could it be . . . to anyone at all") is more likely to be redundant than 838–42, because it is merely an elaboration of 836 ("whether you've any useful parts to speak of?"). However, Šandrovskaja (1956a), Tsiouni (1972), and Papathomopoulos (2002) retain all the verses in their editions following Wagner (1874).

840. **in midsummer**. CA have κατακαλοκαίριον, "and in the summer" (as two words: κατὰ καλοκαίριον—so read by Tsiouni [1972]), or "in the middle of the summer" (as one word—so read by Papathomopoulos [2002]), rather than V's κάθε καλοκαίριον, "and each summer." (P is missing this verse, and L omits the particle, substituting the unrelated πούπετε, "anywhere.") Hesseling (1924:314) thinks CA make more sense; this seems valid to us ("you don't even get to see the sun in midsummer ⟨when it is at its brightest⟩"). The prefix κατά- recurs two verses later, in κατακρυμμένος, "well-hidden"; this makes the prefixed reading likelier.

844. **stump-legged**. The reading (καὶ κοντοποδαρέα) is P's and is followed by Šandrovskaja (1956a), Tsiouni (1972), and Papathomopoulos (2002). CVLA have κονδοποδαρομύτα, "short–legged-and-nosed." As observed in the tex-

tual note to 612–12a, κονδοποδαρομύτα is an exception to the overall behavior of three-part compounds in the *Tale* (the first two parts are not synonymous), which makes it suspect.

858–59. **the cheetah and the leopard . . . some way off**. These two verses are attested only in P. We have already noted in "Plot" that the transition between the bear and the felines is rushed, so to omit these two verses would make it excessively curt: the narrator is not given an opportunity to announce the departure of the disputants, and for the bear to describe the "brave, strong carnivores" without naming them, only to have them burst in at 860, seems unnecessarily abrupt.

862. **lying both in ambush**. See Commentary.

867. **born in sin**. Rather than CVA πορνικόν, "whorish" (consistent with the low moral repute the leopard enjoyed in the Middle Ages as a product of miscegenation—see Commentary and "Fact and Fiction in the *Tale*'s Zoology"), P has πονηρόν, "evil; cunning." CVA's reading is more consistent than P's is with κοπελοαναθρεμμένον, "brought up out of wedlock," in the same verse (see Commentary).

880–81. **place it, too**. The verse as it stands in PCA (L is absent here) is asymmetrical; it is literally "they have it ⟨as⟩ seats, but they also lie/place/touch and ⟨both⟩ on the pillows and on the mattresses." So verse 880 in those manuscripts joins a noun with a verb whose arguments are in 881. In an attempt to emend this imbalance, V (whose reading was adopted by Wagner [1874], and consequently both Šandrovskaja [1956a] and Tsiouni [1972]) changes the verb in 880 (ἀκουμπίζουν, "lie/place/touch") into a noun as well: ἔχουν αὐτὸ καθίσματα ἀλλὰ καὶ ***ἀγκουμπιστήρια,*** "they have it as seats but also as [***couches***]." However, this leaves the nouns of 881 high and dry; making them arguments of a verb, as in PCA, leaves the verse much less repetitive.

The verb ἀκουμπίζω originally meant "to lie, to recline" (from the Latin *accumbo*); this meaning is still prevalent in medieval Greek (Kriaras 1968–97, s.v. ἀκουμπίζω, A.1a.) As a transitive verb, it can mean "to place" (Kriaras 1968–97 s.v., B.3a; from "to make something recline"). There is no overt object here (verse 880 does not read ***τὸ*** ἀκουμπίζουν, "they place ***it***"), so this interpretation is grammatically difficult. Nevertheless, such an interpretation makes explicit what the skin has to do with pillows and mattresses, rather than merely implying it. (That the skin is still the topic being discussed is clear from 882; interpreting the verb as "recline" would be changing the topic to refer to human posture.) Moreover, the author is probably elliptically understanding the object of ἀκουμπίζουν to be the same as the object of the first hemistich's verb (ἔχουν αὐτό, "they have it"). So "place" is the sense we have chosen for the verb here, rather than "recline."

However, the verb also came to mean "to lean on" (Kriaras 1968–97, s.v. ἀκουμπίζω, A.2; ἀκουμπῶ, A.1), which is the meaning the verb has in verses 948 and 965, so that the verb appears in the *Tale* in both senses. (This is not the only time this has happened in the *Tale*; cf. πολεμῶ: "make" in 377 versus "attack" in 407.) The verb ἀκουμπῶ accordingly survives in standard modern Greek, meaning "lean on," and by an extension already medieval (Kriaras 1968–97, s.v. ἀκουμπῶ, A.2), "touch."

As it turns out, V makes a misstep in its emendation. Kriaras (1968–97) lists V's use of ἀγκουμπιστήρια as meaning "seat, couch, place where one rests." Šandrovskaja (1956a) similarly renders the term (спинки кресел) as "back of an armchair." These renderings exploit the original sense of ἀκουμπίζω, "recline." But all the other attested instances of a noun derived from ἀκουμπίζω exploit not the "recline" meaning at all (which would still plausibly be associated with pillows and mattresses) but the "lean on" meaning:

> *Erotokritos* 4.327: ὁ γονὴς θυμᾶται,
> πὼς ηὗρεν εἰς τὰ γερατιὰ θάρρος κι ***ἀκουμπιστήρι***,
> "The parent then recalls
> he's found, in old age, solace and ***support.***"
>
> *Pastor Fide (Cretan)* 4.3.84: στὸν κόσμον ἦταν μόνο ἀπομονάρι,
> μόνο ραβδὶ καὶ ***ἀκούμπιστρο*** τοῦ γέρου,
> "She was the one thing in the world left for him,
> the old man's one ***support*** and staff was she."
>
> *Paraphrase of Nicetas Choniates* 171: τὸ γὰρ ***ἀκουμβιστήριον*** ξύλον ἐν ᾧ ἠκούμβιζεν ὡς καχεξίᾳ δῆθεν παλαίων, "the ***support***, a staff on which he leaned pretending to suffer the infirmity of the old."

Likewise Somavera (1977 [1709], s.v.) glosses ἀκουμπιστῆρι as *appoggiatoio,* "support." We doubt ἀγκουμπιστήρια meant anything other than "walking stick" to V's scribe, either, and conclude he made a cane, rather than an easy chair, of leopard skins simply because he got carried away with the symmetry of his emendation.

882. **will land**. Both Tsiouni (1972) and Papathomopoulos (2002) have adopted V's οὐδὲν καθίζει, "does not sit [land]"; C has ἐκεῖ οὐ στέκει, "does not stand [stay] there," and P has οὐκ ἔστιν ὅλως, "does not exist at all." (LA are absent.)

884. **motley**. See Commentary.

894. **and tap . . . a tiny bit**. Verse 894 (literally "and touched you slightly on the lower jaw") is attested only in P.

897. **never to take . . . in vain**. Verse 897 is omitted in V.

902–3. **and here dictate whatever I decide**. P here has καὶ τότε νὰ ὁρίσω / ὁς εἴ τις ἔχω θέλημαν, "then will I decide as [?] whatever desire I have"; CVL have νὰ ὁρίσω εἴ τι θέλω / καὶ ὅ,τι {εἴ τι L} πρᾶγμα βούλομαι, "I will dictate whatever I wish and whatever I decide." As the grammar of P is obviously distorted at 903 (ὁς is meaningless), CVL are likelier to preserve the original text. Tsiouni (1972) follows P for 902 and CV for 903; Papathomopoulos (2002) follows CV for both. Šandrovskaja (1956a) follows P, trying to make sense of ὁς as ὡς, "as": и вынесу решение, / как имеющий свою волю, "and I will support my decision, / as it is available to my will."

906. **tower**. CVL have τοῖχος, "wall"; the comparison of elephants to walls is commonplace in the *Alexander Romance* (see "Fact and Fiction in the *Tale*'s Zoology").

906. **safe**. Rather than PV's ἀσφαλής, CL use the superlative ἀσφαλέστατος, "safest," which throws the meter out.

916. **emperors' chairs**. P has this verse after verse 917 ("and in carved staffs . . ."); because the poem goes on to spend verses 918–19 talking about the staffs, P is obviously in error here.

919. **with their beards so long**. C adds 919a: καὶ οἱ πρωτοπαπάδες γοῦν καὶ οἱ ἀρχιμανδρῖται, "and protopopes, and archimandrites, too." An archimandrite is the superior of a monastery or a group of monasteries, a church official equivalent to a Catholic prelate (Herbermann 2000 [1914], s.v. ARCHIMANDRITE). Protopopes in the Byzantine Orthodox Church were church officials ranking just below bishops and corresponding to Catholic deans. In Constantinople the protopope was a senior church official, whereas in the countryside he could act as the bishop's delegate (Herbermann 2000 [1914], s.v. PROTOPOPE). In territories under Catholic control, the protopope could also be the leader of the local Orthodox community, reporting to the Catholic bishop (Richard 1989:45).

924. **as well as for exquisite smaller ones**. This verse appears only in P.

926. **and silver, too**. P, Papathomopoulos (2002), and Tsiouni (1972) have the text as ἀκόμη μὲ ἀσήμιον, "also/even with silver." CV have καὶ μὲ ἀσήμιν ἀκομή, placing the word for "even" at the end of the hemistich rather than its beginning. The CV reading goes against the sixteen other times an "even" word occurs at the start of a hemistich—even though the word used, the distinctly medieval form ἀκομή, is infrequent in the poem (158 L, 373 P, 628 P—all at the beginning of the verse) and thus would at first sight be the *lectio difficilior*. See discussion in "Structure" (endnote 125) on the distribution of words in meter.

927. **both young and old**. P has καὶ γραῖες καὶ μεσόγραις, "old and middle-aged (women)."

927a–g. **The young lads . . .** This passage appears only in C and is not included in either Tsiouni's (1972) or Papathomopoulos's (2002) text. We do not dispute its exclusion; its wording seems to us too repetitious even for the *Tale*. We have included it, if for no other purpose, to demonstrate that elephants prefer blondes.

929. **gaze**. Rather than βλέπουσιν, V has the lasses pilfering (κλέπτουσιν) their image.

929a. **Such are my merits and advantages.** This verse is present only in C; the monkey hearkens back to it in 968. The repetition seems too facile to be valid; in fact, the very verse meant to be repeating it, 968, is absent in CVL—so the repetition does not occur in any extant manuscript. By including both verses in their editions, Tsiouni (1972) and Papathomopoulos (2002) imply that the original contained both verses, with P dropping the former, C the latter, and VL both. It seems more economical to have one of PC transpose the verse from one speech to the other and have VL drop that single verse; the verse in question would have been all the more mobile as it is a formula in the text. (That the formula was added independently by P and C is not impossible, but the structural parallel between the two places it appears makes it unlikely.)

The other occurrence of the formula, 235, is found in all manuscripts in the second person, addressed by the fox to the dog. This makes it derisive in its first instance; so if the author is repeating himself, it is more obvious for him to be repeating 235 in 968 than in 929a: the comment appears there in the same derisive tenor, in the same person, and with an animal of similar reputation to the fox (see 933a). The instance in 929a, on the other hand, is quite different in tone. So if one of the two has to be chosen as consistent with the rest of the poem, it should be 968, leaving 929a as the interpolation. There is additional circumstantial evidence for C tampering with the text here, rather than preserving the original reading, in that C has already interpolated 927a–g just above and 933a just below.

All the same, what purpose the transposition to 929a would serve is unclear. Verse 929a could be setting the elephant up for a fall with the monkey's derisive repetition of it in 968, but because no such repetition actually occurs in any manuscript, it seems foolhardy to posit this. The scribe of C may have intended to ridicule the elephant simply by having him vainly utter self-praise that 235 has already undermined; that done, 968 would no longer have been necessary.

933a. **being more cunning . . . by far**. Verse 933a appears only in C. It does something uncharacteristic of the *Tale*: having the narrator pause to give an explanation. And C has already tampered with the text nearby, at 927a–g and arguably 929a. This is consistent with an interpolation.

939. **big-clawed**. The word μεγαλοχαχαλάτου appears in P and is based on a word for "claw" (χαχάλα < χηλή) that now survives in Crete (Kriaras 1968–97, s.v. μεγαλοχαχαλάτος). It is obscure enough to have defeated the other manuscripts: L omits it, whereas C and V render it as variants of "big-cabbaged" (μεγαλολαχανάτου C, μεγάλου λαχανάτου V).

942. **wooden-legged**. All the manuscripts here have ὀξύποδε, "sharp-footed = swift-footed." Even though Nonnus refers to the elephant as brisk footed (*Dionysiaca* 33.278–79: καί τις ***ἀερσιπόδης*** ἐλέφας παρὰ γείτονι λόχμῃ / ὄρθιον ὕπνον ἴαυεν, ὑπὸ δρυὶ νῶτον ἐρείσας, "and a certain ***brisk-footed*** elephant slept by a neighboring copse, leaning his back beneath an oak tree"), the reference does not make much sense in this context. Šandrovskaja (1956a) has кривоногий, "crooked-legged"; this is just a guess and if anything contradicts the *Tale*'s belief (verse 20) that elephants had no joints.

Tsiouni (1972) has suggested ξυλόποδε, "wooden-footed, wooden-legged," as an emendation, which Papathomopoulos (2002) has accepted. This has the advantage of linking seamlessly with verse 953. A similar construction occurs in the prenuptial agreement in the *Mass of the Beardless Man* (D 1686)—which also features the old canard about the elephant's unbending legs:

> ὑποδήματα ψεύτικα ζευγάρια β′ καὶ ἕτερα ***ξυλοποδήματα*** ζευγάρια τρία, διὰ νὰ χέζεται στεκόμενος ὥσπερ λέφας καὶ νὰ τσιρλᾶ τὲς ἀρίδες του·
>
> [Two (2) pairs of shoes, fake, and three (3) pairs of ***wood footings***, that he may shit himself standing like an elephant and splatter his limbs.]

How a wood footing as a shoe is meant to impede the bending of knees is not obvious. Eideneier (1977:312), in his edition of the *Mass,* concludes that this is a "comical portrayal of an impossibility," and disputes (against Koukoules 1947–55:4.417) that the Byzantines actually had wooden clogs (although Koukoules does provide independent evidence).

Likelier here is the meaning borne by ξυλοπόδαρον, which in Du Cange (1958 [1688], s.v.) and routinely in the modern dialects (HDMS data) means "stilt, wooden leg": the image is made much more plausible in that case. In *Apokopos* 220, ξυλόποδο, "wood leg," is used to mean "a thin leg that looks wooden" (κ' οἱ φράροι μὲ ***ξυλόποδα*** ἐξεζωνᾶτοι τρέχουν, "the friars, with their ***wooden legs,*** run without belts on"), paralleled by the adjective ξ(υ)λουπόδαρους, "having long and thin legs," recorded in Aetolia and Acarnania (HDMS 1041:486). This hardly seems promising as a parallel for an elephant leg, but the notion of inflexibility may have engendered this secondary meaning. Something very similar to what the *Tale* must have had in mind is given in the verb ξυλοποδαριάζω, ξυλοποδαριάζομαι, "get wooden legs = be tired from standing up for a long time" (HDMS 927:138; Psakhna, Euboea).

The *Mass of the Beardless Man* suggests two other possible restorations of the text. One fits the elephant better: ξυγγόποδε < ὀξυγγόποδε, "fat-legged," by analogy with ξυγγόκωλε, "fat-arsed" (*Mass* D 150–53: Ὦ σπανὲ καὶ παράσημε, / ὦ τριγένη καὶ τρίκωλε, / σκατογένη ἅμα δὲ / καὶ ***ξυγγόκωλε,*** "O thou beardless freak, thou three-whiskered and three-arsed, thou shit-bearded and also ***fat-arsed***!"). This has the advantage of explaining the initial o- in ὀξύποδε, which in the case of ξυλόποδε could be explained only by analogy or reanalysis. (It does entail a metrically inconvenient extra syllable, however.) On the other hand, "wooden-legged" matches better what the poem then goes on to say about the elephant's alleged lack of joints—in particular his legs standing "up in the air, just like so many wood boards" (953). The other similar word in the *Mass* is ὀξυντόκωλε, "pointy-arsed" (presumably "bony-arsed"; e.g., *Mass* A 167), but this seems even less applicable to the elephant. For that reason, we have retained Tsiouni's emendation (1972) in our rendering.

The only other apparent emendation is ὀξαποδῶ, "Out-of-Here," a euphemism in modern Greek for the devil, but it seems strained to call the elephant satanic. The word occasionally has the milder meaning in modern Greek dialect of "someone messy" (HDMS 632:14; Maistros, eastern Thrace), but this does not seem much help either. The word (unattested in Kriaras 1968–97) may at the time have meant just "outcast," but we have no independent evidence of this; neither does such a meaning show up to our knowledge in any modern dialect.

946. **like everybody**. VL have ὡς οἱ ἀνθρῶποι, "like people," and C has ὡς πάντας τοὺς ἀνθρώπους, "like all people." The introduction of humans as a standard of comparison is decidedly odd at this point, so this variant reading has not been taken up.

949. **stand in fear and sleep in dread**. Papathomopoulos (2002), like Eideneier (1976:456), rejects the reading from P that Tsiouni (1972) had adopted, καὶ μετὰ φόβου στέκεσαι καὶ τρώεις καὶ κοιμᾶσαι, "and stand and eat and sleep in fear." The reading in VL, adopted by Šandrovskaja (1956a), is καὶ στέκεσαι φοβούμενος μὲ τρόμον καὶ κοιμᾶσαι, "and you stand fearful with dread and you sleep," which is incoherent. C has καὶ στέκεσαι φοβούμενος καὶ τρόμου καὶ κοιμᾶσαι, "you stand fearful and of dread [*sic*] and you sleep", which points to Papathomopoulos's solution (2002): the genitive τρόμου, "dread," of C agrees with the genitive φόβου, "fear," of P, so Papathomopoulos combines the start of 949 P with the end of 949 C. This makes an obvious allusion to the formulaic expression φόβος καὶ τρόμος, "fear and dread," also used in verse 248; this expression is first attested in the Septuagint (Exodus 15:16: ἐπιπέσοι ἐπ' αὐτοὺς φόβος καὶ τρόμος, "Fear and dread shall fall upon them"; Judith 2:28; Psalms 54:6 [55:5]) and is still in use in modern Greek.

952. **turned upside down**. CVL have νὰ ἐγερθῇς, κακότυχε, "to get up, poor one." From this point on the elephant clearly remains down, and CVL seem merely to be anticipating 954, without much forethought.

956. **and destroy you.** C has καὶ παίρνουν τὰ ὀστᾶ σου, "and extract your bones [= tusks? see Commentary verse 967]," and its scribe may be anticipating the recapitulation in 967.

959a. **But I have . . . to tell you**. P omits this verse, which seems redundant; Šandrovskaja (1956a) once again abandons her manuscripts in doing likewise. Both Tsiouni (1972) and Papathomopoulos (2002) retain it—the latter as a dispreferred reading.

961. **to destroy you**. C elaborates (961a–b):

καὶ πράξεις καὶ καμώματα τὰ θέλεις ἐγροικήσει,
ἐσὺ καὶ ὅλοι ἅπαντες ποὺ στέκουσιν μεδέμας.

[and tricks and acts which you will hear from me,
both you and everyone who stands with ⟨stature/bindings⟩].

The final word, μεδέμας, does not exist in Greek. If analyzed as μὲ δέμας, it still makes little sense, either as the Homeric word for "stature" (incongruous with the modern μέ, "with"), the word Eustathius of Thessalonica mentions as a euphemism for "penis" (see Commentary verse 635), or as the modern word "binding"—which is already used in verse 627 but would be clearly out of place here, besides being grammatically odd. If δέμας, "stature," is somehow an allusion to the size of elephants, then "everyone who stands" would be referring to the collective of elephants (cf. 120, "all his breed"), but the monkey has little reason to refer to them here. A further alternative is that another noun, such as δέος, "awe" (cf. φόβου, "fear," in 949), is intended.

Papathomopoulos (2002) ingeniously emends μὲ δέμας as μεδ' ἔμας, "with us"; this would have the monkey make her threat only before the assembled animals, which fits the context very well. The emendation is not unproblematic: both μεδ(έ) and ἔμας are rare medieval forms of μετά, "with," and ἐμᾶς, "us" (Kriaras [1968–97, s.v. μετά] only attests the former in *Digenes* E and the *Battle of Varna*). Nonetheless, it is the only way to make sense of the passage.

966. **falls, strikes you**. Both Tsiouni (1972) and Papathomopoulos (2002) follow P (τὸ δένδρον ***πίπτει, κρούει*** σου). Šandrovskaja (1956a) likewise gives a translation consistent with P and not her base manuscripts VL[A]: **дерево падает, ударяет тебя,** "the tree falls, strikes you." A has no text here; CVL have, with minor differences, "the tree ***strikes***, ***throws*** you, pins you to the ground" (L: τὸ δένδρον ***κρούει*** καὶ ***ῥίπτει*** σε), a reading Vasiliou (1996:80) prefers as more realistic:

> For whomever has even an elementary knowledge of wood cutting, the verb "strikes" seems unnatural, because a tree, once cut down, falls not on the side from which it is being pressured but to the opposite side. Thus, the falling tree cannot hit the elephant but can only drag him along and throw him to the ground.

This is somewhat disingenuous, we must point out, because in fact all manuscripts use the verb κρούει, "strikes." And we have already seen (Commentary verse 964) that realism is not the author's primary concern in this passage. Neither is there any reason to think κρούει means anything but "strikes"; the closest meanings Kriaras (1968–97) lists to "drag" are "rush against" (s.v. κρούω, I.A.3) and "shake" (s.v. κρούω, I.A.8):

> Μὴ θηρίον σὲ ***ἔκρουσε*** καὶ ἐτάραξε φόβος / ἢ τίς κακὸς σ' ἐβάσκανε βλέπων σου τὴν ἀνδρείαν, "Has a beast ***rushed*** at you, so that fear has shaken you? / Or has a malicious man given you the evil eye, on beholding your manliness?" (*Digenes* Z 1776–77)
>
> ἄνεμος ἡμερούτσικος ***ἔκρουσεν*** τὰ δέντρα, "A peaceful wind ***shook*** the trees." (*Achilleid* L 746)
>
> καὶ νὰ τὸν ***ἔκρουε*** σεισμός, καὶ νά 'πεφταν οἱ πίροι, "Would that an earthquake ***shook*** it ⟨the wine barrel⟩ and the plugs fell off." (*Father Wine* AO 28).

968. **Such are your merits and advantages**. See 929a.

971. **skeleton**. The manuscripts vary in the precise form of their invective here. VL (V with rickety meter) have Φεῦγε ἀπὸ τὴν μέσην μας κάθαρμα μιασμένον (L), Φύγε ἀπὸ τὴν μέσην μας ἀκάθαρμα διόλου μιασμένον (V), "Get out of here, you {thoroughly} polluted freak." C prefers Φεῦγε ἀπὸ τὴν μέσην μας πομπὴ μαγαρισμένη, "Get out of here, you unclean outcast." (A

is missing the end of the text.) The words παράπτωμα, "offscouring," and φαγκρίν, "skeleton," adopted in Tsiouni's (1972) and Papathomopoulos's (2002) critical editions (see Commentary verses 571 and 971) are unique to P.

972–73. **louse-munching nit-nibbling**. VL describe the monkey as μυσεροκακομούστακον, "disgusting dirt-whiskers," and V goes on to claim that the monkey is ψαροκονιδοφάγον, "fish-munching nit-nibbling," in both cases through straightforward misreadings.

973–74. **who eats bugs, flies, fleas . . . filthy beasts**. CVL's reading, adopted by Tsiouni (1972), is ἐσθίεις ψύλλους, ψείρας τε καὶ πάντοτε δακώνεις / καὶ ἄλλα τὰ μικρότατα τῶν ἀκαθάρτων ζῴων, "you eat fleas, lice, too, and forever bite / and [= also] other tiny filthy beasts." CVL's "forever bite" is awkward in that it interpolates a new verb, which interrupts the listing of the monkey's diet. The effect is syntactically awkward: "and" (καί) needs to switch from a conjunction in 973 to a focal particle in 974 ("also") for the sentence to make sense. Even then, it seems out of place, because the connection between "fleas and lice" and "other tiny filthy beasts" is strong enough to make "forever bite" look out of place. We thus agree with Šandrovskaja (1956a) and Papathomopoulos (2002) that P preserves the original reading.

985. **guileless**. Instead of ἄδολος, P characterizes the peace and amity, inadvertently rather more accurately, as ἄδηλος, "unknown, uncertain, groundless."

999. **wherever they could manage**. The manuscripts are confused here. C has ἐφθάναν, "arrived; caught up," which merely repeats the first half of the verse ("others, as they arrived, and ***arrived*** from anywhere") and so cannot stand. VL have ἐπιάναν, "got, grabbed"; this is the reading Tsiouni (1972) adopted, and it makes eminent sense ("others, as they arrived/as they caught up, and ***grabbed*** from anywhere"). Papathomopoulos (2002) has preferred P's ὀρθῶσαν as the *lectio difficilior.* The *lectio difficilior* it clearly is, but it can only stand if it actually makes sense in context.

The literal meaning of ὀρθώνω is "to stand up" or "to stand something up." Although the image of a ship standing on the horizon (*Chronicle of Makhairas* 588) may be attractive, applied to quadrupeds it becomes nonsensical. The dominant medieval meaning of ὀρθώνω is "to prepare" (transitive and intransitive), but this would be anticlimactic here: the other animals are shown in action in the melee, whereas these would be merely getting ready. And if ἐφθάνασιν in the first half of the verse means not "arrive" but "catch up," then "prepare" makes no sense at all. The verb φθάνω in fact does mean "catch up" in the other two instances it occurs in the poem, 873 and 996—but because verses 992–94 structurally echo 102–5, which speak of the arrival of beasts, an "arrival" meaning is still possible here. Still, the notion of arrival is already conveyed in the poem by other verbs: ἀπεσώθησαν (38), ἦλθεν (720). So "catch up" is likelier than "arrive" as the sense of ἐφθάνασιν in this verse, too, making it unlikely that ὀρθῶσαν means "prepare."

Even if ἐφθάνασιν does mean "arrive" however, there are grounds to accept Kriaras's reading of the verb here (1968–97, s.v. ὀρθώνω, I.B.6) as "manage to, be able to." For starters, there is the parallel verb κατ-ορθώνω, whose primary meaning since antiquity has been "achieve." The transitive meanings Kriaras records for ὀρθώνω include "manage, achieve" (I.A.15) and "realize, execute" (I.A.16):

> . . . μὴ πιάσῃ καὶ πιέτε / τοσὸν κρασὶν μετ' ἐκεινοὺς τοῦ νὰ σᾶς σκανταλίσῃ / καὶ χάσωμεν τὰ ἐλπίζομεν νὰ ἔχωμεν ***ὀρθώσει,*** "But, you be careful that you do not chance to drink so much wine with them that it befuddles you, and we lose what we hope to ***prepare***." (*Chronicle of Morea* H 8302–4—so Lurier's translation, but the parallel passage in *Chronicle of Morea* P has τὸ ὀλπίζομεν ***κερδέσει,*** "what we hope to ***gain***," and, of course, that is the meaning that makes sense in this context [Lurier 1964:303].)

> καὶ ἐὰν σὲ φανῇ καλόν, οὕτως νὰ τὸ ***ὀρθώσω*** (διορθώσω H), "and if it seems agreeable to you, thus shall I ***arrange*** the matter." (*Chronicle of Morea* P 6961; Lurier 1964:268)

Both these meanings are quite close to that posited for the instance in the *Tale*. And "manage" is also a very close semantic match to the verb in the first hemistich: the beasts are said to attack as they "caught up" and wherever they "managed." Both phrases describe the opportunity for the carnivores' attack, giving parallelism between the two. Such parallelism would not obtain for VL's reading: "as they caught up" still describes opportunity, but "wherever they grabbed" indicates manner.

Because the extension from "prepare" to "bring about" to "manage" for ὀρθώνω is semantically plausible and the resulting verse is rhetorically better balanced, we accept Papathomopoulos's reading (2002). Šandrovskaja (1956a) avoids the issue by using нападали, "attacked."

1001. **the battle's havoc and much violence**. This verse (which basically expands on 1000) is missing in P.

1004. **detailing what the outcome was**. P has καὶ κατὰ μέρος λέξομαι λεπτομερῶς εἰς ἄκρον, "and in its particulars shall I relate, to the utmost detail"; see appendix 3.

1013. **for he dissolves our peace and brings on war**. V amusingly gets these the wrong way round: ἐπεὶ τὴν μάχην κατελεῖ καὶ συνιστᾷ ἀγάπην, "for he dissolves our war and brings on peace."

1016. **warmonger**. P has κακοποιός, "evildoer," instead of μαχοποιός.

1023. **cheetah**. In L ὁ λεοντόπαρδος, "the leopard"—which leads to inconsistencies with the ensuing verses. L's scribe has apparently seen the words "cheetah" and "lion" next to each other in the original (πάρδος λέοντος) and conflated them into λεοντόπαρδος. P has ἰδὼν δὲ πάρδος τὸ παρὼν θέαμα τὸ τοῦ λέου, "the cheetah, seeing the present spectacle of the lion."

1024. **retorting to the ox**. L adds the redundant 1024a: καὶ λόγους ἐναπέτεινε τοιαῦτα πρὸς τὸν βόδι, "And spoke unto the ox such words as these."

1031. **dire straits**. CVL have the absurd "love" (ἀγάπην) as a slip of the pen for "dire straits" (ἀνάγκην).

1040. **war against the clean beasts**. VL have πόλεμον {πόλεμον δὲ V} τῶν ἀκαθάρτων ζῴων, "war of the impure beasts," which, of course, means the same thing. In the Greek, the bare genitive used is ambiguous between "war of" and "war against."

1048. **boosting his camp's morale**. C adds in reiteration (1048a–b):

καὶ ἐσυνάχθησαν ὁμοῦ ὅλοι εἰς ἕνα τόπον,
εἰς μάχην καὶ εἰς πόλεμον τῶν αἱμοβόρων ζῴων.

[and they all assembled in a single place,
to battle and wage war against the bloody beasts.]

1052. **struck with his palm**. C omits this verse; it is tempting to think its scribe Agiomnitis was censoring out the one instance of a herbivore being killed.

1060. **while running up and down**. As observed by Vasiliou (1996:77; see appendix 3), there is an asyndeton here that our translation smoothes over; CVL have

ἐβάβισεν ἀπὸ μακρά, ἐξύπασεν τὸν χοῖρον,
ἀνεβοεκατέβαινεν «βλέπετε καὶ σκοπεῖτε
τὴν κακομήχανον αὐτὴν τὴν μεγαλομαστόραν. . .»

[⟨the dog⟩ barked from afar, he startled the boar,
he was going up and down—"Watch and observe
that mal-intriguer, that grand-master trickster."]

P is missing the first half of 1060 and of 1061:

ἐβάβισεν ἀπὸ μακρά, ἐξύσπασε τὸν χοῖρον,
«βλέπετε καὶ σκοπήσετε τὴν μεγα^{λ} μαστορίαν. . .»

[⟨the dog⟩ barked from afar, he startled the boar,
"Watch and observe that grand-master trick."]

In neither family is there the expected formula introducing a speech. It is tempting but speculative to suggest that the archetype had for verse 1060 something like ἀνεβοεκατέβαινεν, τοιούτους λόγους εἶπεν, "he ran both up and down and spoke these words"—the poem then continuing with 1061 P. This would make CVL displace the speech formula so it can fit in the description "that mal-intriguer," whereas P deleted the whole verse. But such an intervention raises more questions than it solves, so we cannot take it any further.

1062. **plots**. Instead of καταμιτώνει, L (with typical obtuseness) has καταγλυτώνει, "saves her skin."

1064. **It's time to fight**. P has μηδὲν γὰρ φοβηθῆτε, "for do not fear," which is too similar to the next verse to be satisfactory.

1066. **nanny**. Some confusion is shown in the roster among the manuscripts: CVL substitute τὸ βόδιν, "the ox," for P's ἡ αἶγα, "the nanny."

1067. **billy goat**. Continuing the confusion, L (and C, before it corrects itself) confuse τράγος, "billy goat," with a hitherto unheard of ταῦρος, "bull."

1070. **fast as he was**. P has χιλιμιντρᾶ, "neighed."

1070. **ran up and down**. VL elaborate (1070a), repeating 1048: καὶ νὰ ἀνδρειώνῃ δυνατὰ ὅλην του τὴν μερέαν, "boosting his camp's morale."

1073. **to a treetop**. VL have the cat, as well as the wolf, go εἰς τὸ βουνίν ἀπάνω (L), ἀπάνω εἰς τὸ βουνίν (V), "up the hill"—disrupting the symmetry of the narrative.

1075. **sun crowned the horizon**. See Commentary.

1082a–b. **I glorify . . . AMEN**. These verses are present only in C. The expression ἐλπίς ἀπελπισμένων, "hope of the despairing," was used (as ἀπελπισμένων ἐλπίς) in Byzantine theological writing, as an epithet of God:

> οὗτος θλιβομένων παράκλησις, καταπονουμένων ἀντίληψις, ***ἀπελπισμένων ἐλπίς***, ἀπεγνωσμένων βοηθός, ξένων παρηγορία, "He is the Consolation of the Sorrowful, the Succor of the Oppressed, ***the Hope of the Despairing***, the Aid of the Desolate, the Solace of Strangers." (Alexander of Cyprus [*vi* A.D.?] *Praise of Apostle Barnabas* 865)

> πέλεις γὰρ ***ἀπελπισμένων ἐλπίς***, "For Thou remainest ***the Hope of the Despairing***" (Patriarch Nicholas I [*ix–x* A.D.], *Miscellaneous Writings* §206)

> μακροθυμίας τε καὶ ἀνεξικακίας ἀκένωτε θησαυρέ, πλανωμένων ὁδηγέ, πεπτωκότων ἀνόρθωσις, ***ἀπελπισμένων ἐλπίς***, ἀπεγνωσμένων παραμυθία, "Thou Unemptying Treasure of Forbearance and Long-Suffering, Guide of the Wandering, Restoration of the Fallen, ***Hope of the Despairing***, Solace of the Desolate." (Michael Critobulus [*xv* A.D.], *Prayer* 12)

V, for its part, simply concludes with Τέλος τῶν τετραπόδων ζῴων, "The End of the Quadrupeds."

APPENDIX 1

THE *TALE* AND THE *BOOK OF BIRDS*

> We are led from this to two possibilities: either the *Tale* is older and consequently more "primitive," or it is a not particularly successful attempt at an imitation of the *Book of Birds*.
>
> —I. Tsavare, *῾Ο Πουλολόγος*

The *Book of Birds*

The *Book of Birds* is a poem of 668 verses, handed down to us in seven manuscripts. This number makes it one of the most popular medieval Greek works, equaling the count for the *War of Troy* though not quite reaching the two dozen of *Spaneas*—whose moralizing was more congenial to monastic copyists. The *Book of Birds* was also firmly associated with the *Entertaining Tale of Quadrupeds* through its textual history: four of the five manuscripts of the latter (all but the deviant Parisian, which contains no other texts) also contain the *Book of Birds*.

Its story goes something like this: the eagle, king of all the birds, invites the rest of the bird kingdom to be present at his son's wedding. Six verses in, the birds start to argue with each other: fourteen pairs of birds, one wild and one domesticated, chime in—the wild bird mocking the tame, and the tame countermocking the wild and retorting, in strict order. At the end of the poem, the eagle intervenes to ensure that order is maintained in his kingdom (652–68):

῾Απάντων τούτων τῶν ὀρνέων ἀλλήλων μαχομένων,
ὁ βασιλεὺς ἐλάλησεν, σταυραετὸς ὁ μέγας:

«῎Ορνεα καὶ πουλία μου, μικρά τε καὶ μεγάλα,
οὐδὲν σᾶς ἤφερα ἐδῶ διὰ νὰ γενολογᾶστε·

διὰ τιμὴν σᾶς ὅρισα, ἤλθετε εἰς τὴν χαράν μου,
νὰ φάγετε, νὰ πίετε καὶ νὰ χαρῆτε ἅμα,
οὐχὶ δὲ νὰ δικάζεσθε καὶ νὰ γενολογᾶστεν.
Ἀφῆτε γοῦν τὴν ὄχλησιν, κάθεσθε σιωπῶντα,
μὴ ὁρίσω τὸν ἱέρακα εἴτε καὶ τὸν πετρίτην, 660
ζάγανον τὸν ἐξάκουστον, πάλιν ἱεροφάλκον,
σεβοῦσιν εἰς τὴν μέσην σας, ἄρξωνται νὰ σᾶς τρῶσιν,
καὶ γένη ὁ γάμος μακελεῖον καὶ ἡ χαρμονὴ σφαγεῖον!»

Ἤκουσαν ταῦτα ὅλα τους, ἐσίγησαν αὐτίκα,
ἀφήκασιν τὴν ταραχήν, ἐπαύσασιν τὰς ὕβρεις,
εἰρηνικά, ἀνόχλητα ἐπλήρωσαν τὸν γάμον.
Περιπατοῦσιν ἄλαλα μὲ ἴδιαν τους σοφίαν,
ὑψιπετῆ γὰρ χαίρουνται, ἀμέριμνα διάγουν.

[And as the birds all fought against each other,
the king spoke up, the mighty golden eagle:

"Listen, my fowls and birds, both great and small,
I did not bring you here to cuss each other.
I bade you come to honor my rejoicing,
so you could eat, drink, and make cheer together
and not to argue and to cuss each other.
So cease this tumult now and sit in silence,
or I will have the hawk, the peregrine, 660
the famed pied falcon, or the bearded vulture
rush in among you and start eating you
and turn this wedding feast into a slaughter, 663
and turn this celebration into carnage!" 663

They all heard this and held their peace at once;
they ceased their turmoil and left off their insults,
and peacefully, refraining from disturbance, 666
they followed through the wedding to its end. 666
They walk unspeaking, with their own good sense;
they fly high merrily and live carefree.]

This is a very political end to what is in fact a very political poem. The work is full of allusions to contemporary enemies of the empire—be they French, Tatars, or Bulgarians. And it goes further: consider the following description (287–304) by the pheasant of the bird called *paragialitis* ("by-coast"), conventionally thought to be the flamingo (Tsavare 1987:148–49):

Ἐμὲν τὰ λέγεις, ἐλεεινέ, ταῦτα, παραγιαλίτα;
Οὐκ εἶσαι ἐσὺ τσαγγάρη υἱός, τοῦ πετσοκαταλύτη,
ὁποῦ ἐκαθέσθουν καὶ ἔραπτες μὲ τὴν χοιρνὴν τὴν τρίχαν

καὶ ὑπῆγες καὶ ἐδανείστηκες ὁκάποθεν λογάριν 290
{AZ: καὶ γέλασες ὁκάτιναν κἐδῶκε σε λογάρι}
καὶ ἠγόρασες τὴν θάλασσαν καὶ ἐγένου τοπικάρης,
{AZ: καὶ ἀγόρασες τὴν ἁλυκὴν καὶγίνης ἁλυκάρης}
καὶ ἠστόχησεν ἡ θάλασσα, καὶ ἐγένης τὸ καθόλου
μυριοχρειωμένος, ἄτυχος καὶ μυριονειδισμένος;
Οἱ χρεωφειλέται σύρνουν σε τὰ ὑπέρπυρα νὰ δώσης,
καὶ ἐσὺ κομπώνεις, λέγεις τους ὅτι κρυμμένα τὰ ἔχεις.
Καὶ ὅπου καθίσης εἰς ἀκτήν, πάλιν εἰς ἀκρωτήριν,
σηκώνεις τὸ κεφάλιν σου καὶ πάλιν δείχνεις κάτω,
καὶ λέγεις ὅτι, ἠστόχησα, οὐκ ἔναι ὁ τόπος οὗτος.
Ἐγὼ οὐ λέγω ψέματα, οἱ πάντες τὸ θωροῦσιν
ὅτι τσαγγάρη υἱός εἶσαι, τοῦ πετσοκαταλύτου· 300
καὶ γὰρ κρατεῖς καὶ τὸ σουβλὶν στὸ στόμα σου καὶ τρέχεις,
καὶ τὸ κεφάλιν σου νὰ σῆς, ὁπόθεν καὶ ἂν εἶσαι,
τοὺς χρεωφειλέτας νὰ γελᾶς, οὐκ ἔναι ὁ τόπος οὗτος,
καὶ πάντα τρέχεις, περπατεῖς, γελᾶς τους καὶ διαβαίνεις·

[You tell me this, you miserable flamingo?
Aren't you a cobbler's son, a leatherworker's,
who used to sit and work with a boar's bristle
and went and borrowed cash in hand from someplace, 290
{Manuscripts A and Z: and went and swindled cash in hand from
someone,}
and bought the sea and turned administrator?
{Manuscripts A and Z: and bought the salt flats and turned manager?}
The sea went under; you became a zero,
unlucky, in the red, and in the bad books.
Your creditors keep chasing after you 294
so you can give back their *hyperpyra*, 294
and you deceive them, telling them they're hidden.
And when you're seated by the coast or cape,
you raise your head and point back down again,
saying, "I can't recall! This isn't the place!"
I tell no lie, and everyone can see it,
that you're a cobbler's son, a leatherworker's; 300
you hold your awl in your mouth and run about
and shake your head, wherever you may be,
to cheat your creditors—"this isn't the place!"
and yet you run, walk, cheat them, and get past them.]

The Byzantines loved a good just-so story as much as anyone else; the *Physiologus* is testimony enough to that. But to adduce failed business ventures involving salt flats in order to explain a flamingo's gait is more than a little far-fetched. And when we find out from John Cantacuzene's *Historiae* (Makris 1993:403) that Alexius Apocaucus, the bête noire of the 1340s civil war, started off his career by swindling his way into the Byzantine salt flats monopoly, the conclusion seems inevitable:

> οὗτος γὰρ δὴ ὁ παρακοιμώμενος ἐκ Βιθυνίας ὡρμημένος καὶ ἄσημος ἐκ φαύλων φὺς, τὰ πρῶτα μὲν ὑπεγραμμάτευσε πολλοῖς τῶν τὰ δημόσια χρήματα εἰσπραττόντων ὀλίγου ἕνεκα μισθοῦ, ἔπειτα τῷ τοῦ βασιλέως ἐμισθοφόρησε θείῳ Ἀσάνῃ τῷ Ἀνδρονίκῳ. εἶτ' ἐκείνου ἀποστὰς, προσεχώρησε στρατηγῷ τῷ τῶν ἑσπερίων θεμάτων δομεστίκῳ, τοὺς δημοσίους ἅλας τότε ἐφορεύοντι. εὐφυὴς δὲ φανεὶς καὶ πρόθυμος πρὸς τὴν ὑπηρεσίαν, χρήματα ἐπιστεύθη παρ' ἐκείνου, ἵν' ἐλθὼν πρὸς βασιλέα, (Ἀνδρόνικος δὲ ὁ πρῶτος ἦν), πείσῃ στρατηγῷ καὶ εἰς τοὐπιὸν ἔτος τὴν διάθεσιν ἐγχειρίζειν τῶν ἁλῶν. ὁ δὲ τὰ μὲν χρήματα ὡς ἴδια βασιλεῖ παρεσχηκὼς, ἐπαγγειλάμενος δὲ καὶ διπλασίω τῶν ὑπὸ στρατηγοῦ παρεχομένων τῷ βασιλικῷ αὐτὸς εἰσφέρειν ταμιείῳ, πείθει βασιλέα ἐκείνου προελέσθαι καὶ τῶν ἁλῶν παρέχειν τὴν ἀρχήν.
>
> [For this chamberlain started out in Bithynia, born of commoners in obscurity. First he served under many collectors of public moneys, for slight salary. Next he was in the pay of the uncle of the emperor, Andronicus Asan. Then, moving on from him, he joined a general who was *domesticus* over the western regions and overseeing at the time the public salt flats. Appearing intelligent and eager in his service, he ⟨Apocaucus⟩ was entrusted by him with money to take to the emperor (Andronicus the elder) and to convince him to continue his mandate to manage the salt flats for the coming year. But he handed over the money to the emperor as his own, and promising to gather twice as much as the general did for the imperial coffers, he convinced the emperor to give him preferment and to entrust him with the management of the salt flats.] (Cantacuzene 2.89)

The conclusion becomes even more certain when we find out that Apocaucus built his forts on the coast, as befits a "by-coast" bird (Makris 1993:404):

> Βοᾷ δὲ καὶ αὐτὰ μονονουχὶ φωνὴν ἐκπέμποντα λαμπρὰν τὰ τῶν αὐτοῦ γε οἰκιῶν οἰκοδομήματα, μέχρι νῦν τὴν ἐκείνου κακίαν ἐκτραγῳδοῦντα· λέγω δὴ τὸ τῶν Ἐπιβατῶν φρούριον· ἔπειθ' ὅσα περὶ τὸ τεῖχος τῆς βασιλευούσης τῶν πόλεων ἤγειρεν, οἷον ἀμφίβιον καὶ γῇ καὶ θαλάσσῃ μεριζομένην ἔχοντα δίαιταν. πύλας γὰρ ἑκατέρωθέν σφισιν ἐτίθετο πρός τε γῆν καὶ πρὸς θάλασσαν· ἵνα διωκόμενον ἐκ θαλάττης ἤπειρος ὑποδέχοιτο, καὶ τοὐναντίον αὖθις φεύγοντα τὴν ἤπειρον ἡ συνοῦσα καὶ, οἷον εἰπεῖν, ναυλοχοῦσα τριήρης παρὰ τὴν οἰκίαν γίνοιτο παραπομπὸς ἐπ' ἀπίστου στοιχείου θαλάττης ἄχρι τῆς νήσου Πριγκίπου, ἢ ὅποι τῆς τύχης ἄγοι τὸ πέρας

αὐτόν. ἔστησε γὰρ κἀκεῖ, καὶ ὁπηδήποτε καταφυγεῖν ἐβούλετο, φρούρια καὶ πύργους οὐρανομήκεις.

[Even the very buildings he constructed cry out with a shrill voice, singing of his evils to this day. I am referring to the fortress of Epibatae and then to those he erected at the walls of the Queen of Cities—having an amphibious lifestyle, sharing both land and sea. For he placed gates on either side, facing both land and sea; if he were pursued by sea, the mainland would let him in. And conversely, if he should flee from the mainland, his accompanying boat, "lying in wait" so to speak, would convey him across the treacherous element of the sea to the island of Marmara or to whatever end Fortune would lead him. For there, too, and wherever else he might wish to seek refuge, did he set up fortresses and towers as tall as the sky.] (Gregoras 2.585)

And the *karkandzas* bird (for which Makris 1993:395–96 rejects its established identification with the guinea fowl, on historical and linguistic grounds) is vituperated by the hen as follows (241–47, 254–56):

Μωρέ, πάντες σε ξεύρουσιν, ἀπὸ τὴν Ρώμην ἤσουν,
καὶ εἰς τὸ Σπιτάλιν ἔποικες φρέρης κἂν ἕξι χρόνους,
καὶ εὑρῆκαν σε μὲ Φράγκισσαν, καβαλαρίου γυναίκαν,
καὶ ἐδείρασίν σε τὰ πολλά, καὶ ἐκ τοῦ δαρμοῦ τὴν βίαν,
ἐγέμισαν τὰ ὀμμάτια σου αἷμαν τῆς κεφαλῆς σου·
οἱ πάντες τὸ γινώσκουσιν, οὐδὲν τὸ λέγω ψέμα,
ἔκτοτε γὰρ καὶ μέχρι νῦν οὐκ ἔποικες μαλλία. . . .
Ἐκ τὴν κατάραν, ἄτυχε, ἐκείνου φρὰ Λιβέρη,
ὁποὺ σὲ ἐκούρευσεν ποτὲ εἰς ἐκεῖνον τὸ Σπιτάλιν,
ἐκέρδισες καὶ τοὺς δαρμοὺς καὶ τὴν κακοτυχίαν.

[Fool, everybody knows you've come from Rome
and were a friar over at the Hospice[1]
six years or so, and one day you were found 243
tarrying with a Western knight's young wife, 243
and then they beat you soundly; so much so,
your eyes filled up with blood flowed from your head.
Everyone knows it, and I tell no lie,
from then on to this day you've grown no hair. . . .
From Fra Liveri's curse, unlucky soul,
who shaved your hair once over at the Hospice,
you have gained naught but beatings and misfortune.]

Again, these are not the usual exploits of a guinea fowl or any other bird the *karkandzas* may be taken as representing. A definite allusion is being made to an event in the domain of human behavior, and specifically the Knights Hospitaller, although its referents are obscure to us today. What the hen goes on to say about herself (just before extolling her meat) seems no less allusive—and out of place with poultry as we know it (259–62):

> ἐγὼ πουλία τὰ γεννῶ ἢ πάλε τὰ ἀναθρέφω,
> ἐξέβησαν ἐπίσκοποι, ἔξαρχοι καὶ παπάδες,
> καὶ Βαρδαριῶτες κόπελοι, κουρτέσοι ἀπεσταλμένοι,
> καὶ περπατοῦν εὐγενικά, παλατοαναθρεμμένα.
>
> [The chicks I bear, or rather I bring up,
> have turned out bishops, exarchs, priests as well,
> lads of the Vardar,[2] emissaries of the court;
> and they walk nobly, bred in palaces.]

A further unusual feature of the *Book,* amenable to political interpretation, is the conspicuous absence of the two nations from which Byzantium had the most to fear at the time, the Serbs and the Turks—though virtually every other nation with which Byzantium had contact is mentioned by name, even the trading republic of Ragusa (modern-day Dubrovnik in Croatia). Tsavare (1987:110) believes this is because the Turks had failed to impinge on the popular imagination until 1331, the year the Ottomans conquered Nicaea, capital of the erstwhile Byzantine Empire in exile, and showed Byzantium they meant business. But Makris (1993:407) points out that Turks from various tribes were raiding Byzantium throughout the thirteenth century, and, after all, if we agree with Tsavare's own assumption (1987:352) that the "lads of the Vardar" were Turkic tribesmen, then Turks have also turned up in the poem in the excerpt just given. Makris also does not believe one can appeal to Nicaea as a watershed; he prefers to see the omission of the Turks and Serbs from the peoples besmirched in the *Book* as acknowledgment of their alliance with John VI Cantacuzene in the civil war.

If we are to follow Makris's interpretation, the *Book* was written by supporters of John Cantacuzene as an oblique polemic against his untrustworthy protégé Alexius Apocaucus. In view of the *Book*'s "happy" ending, such an interpretation would be fully consistent with Cantacuzene's persistent (and ultimately successful) efforts to make peace with the young emperor John V Palaeologus during the 1341–47 civil war. One is further tempted to associate the domesticated birds with Cantacuzene's noble friends and the wild birds with his rebellious adversaries, identifying King Eagle—if not an abstract symbolism for law and order—with John VI Cantacuzene rather than John V Palaeologus.[3] But even if we do not accept Makris's exegesis of the *Book,* the fact remains that there are unmistakable political allusions there. This immediately invites comparison with the *Tale.*

The *Book* Versus the *Tale*

The *Book of Birds* and the *Entertaining Tale of Quadrupeds* are works that naturally group together. The association was made by Byzantine scribes just as readily as by modern scholars: more manuscripts house both poems than either alone. They have the same premise of a convention of beasts; a similar propensity to colorful insult; didactic-seeming listings of uses and functions of beasts; a king figure running the proceedings; and an implied though unclear connection with current political realities. Furthermore, it is likely that the *Book* preceded the *Tale*: using different arguments, both Makris (1993) and Tsavare (1987) agree that the *Book* was written in the early fourteenth century. Tsavare's (1987:110) *terminus ante quem* is 1331, the Turkish conquest of Nicaea. Makris's (1993:408) *terminus* is Apocaucus's death in 1345, because the *paragialitis* he identifies with the grand duke is only mutilated by the king's troops, not killed (319–23). As argued in "Date of Composition," the *Tale* is generally thought to have been authored at least two decades later. Given also their very similar structure, it is reasonable to assume that the *Tale* started off as an imitation of the *Book* (Tsavare 1987:111; Makris 1993:411; Vasiliou 1996:81).

Yet the two works make a very different impression on the reader. The *Book of Birds* supports the "natural order of things," rejoicing in the torture to which the *paragialitis* ends up subjected by the eagle's forces (315–23), and denigrates birds as paupers, foreigners, or members of the underclass. It makes clear allusions to contemporary events, going so far as to name people and places.[4] It concocts elaborate narratives about the birds—which have little to do at times with the physical bird but are darkly allusive. Even when its allusions are obscured, they are not concealed; it is obvious that something deeper is being meant. Finally, it has a very strict structure; point then counterpoint, point then counterpoint, through fourteen pairs of tame and wild birds, with the speeches themselves strongly formulaic.

As we have seen, the *Tale* is much more chatty. The speeches themselves flow more easily and do not take part between contrasting pairs but between members of the same camp. The *Tale* starts and ends with an explicit programmatic statement—which the *Book* lacks.[5] But where the *Book* is explicit in its political satire, the animals in the *Tale* ascribe to themselves and each other nothing out of place in the barnyard. If social satire is being made in the *Tale*, it is subtle indeed. And finally, whereas the *Book* presents itself as an apologist for the established order, the *Tale*—when its social thrust is made explicit—calls for overthrow of the powerful and justice for the weak. The question thus arises: what was the connection between the two works, and what light can this shed on the Byzantines' view of the world?

As Makris (1993) has pointed out, one of the major differences between the *Tale* and the *Book* is that the *Tale* refers only to familiar animals whereas the *Book* refers not only to commonplace hens, geese, and seagulls but also to birds not mentioned elsewhere in Greek writing, such as the *karkandzas* and the *paragialitis*. To go further, the *Tale* refers at length to sundry particularities associated with its subjects, either through natural history or the lore of the time. In the *Book,* on the other hand, there is probably much less actual ornithology than previous researchers, including its most recent editor Tsavare (1987), have claimed. This discrepancy had not been previously noted, because scholars have assiduously attempted to identify the species of all the birds mentioned in the *Book* and have read into it the ornithology that Makris (1993) claims is absent. But if, as Makris argues, the identifications are wrong and at least some of the birds are fabrications used as a basis for Cantacuzenist propaganda (e.g., the "by-coast" is a dig at Apocaucus's military strategy and not a flamingo at all), then the entire conception of the two works is different.

This strengthens the case that the *Tale* is an imitation of the *Book,* limiting itself to the familiar occupants of the barnyard rather than engaging in the characteristically Byzantine pastime of inventing a fantastical menagerie. The absence of specific political and contemporary allusions in the *Tale* indicates that its author parted ways with the *Book.* He does not conceal his intent as the *Book* does—or, if he does, he is extremely circumspect about it—and he does not attempt to emulate the allusiveness or obfuscation of the *Book.* The *Tale* emulates the *Book*'s structure, simplistically as Tsavare (1987:125, 129) claims, substituting the fearful symmetries of the *Book* with an easygoing chattiness. But the outlook of the two has turned out very different. Appendix 2 considers the possibility that the *Tale* is a kind of response to the ideology that engendered the *Book,* if not the *Book* itself.

The Alternate Ending

Two late manuscripts of the *Book of Birds,* A (sixteenth century—distinct from the *Tale*'s St. Petersburgian A and also containing a partial history of the Ottoman conquests) and Z (seventeenth century) do not contain the *Tale.* They do, however, contain an alternative ending to the *Book*'s story, strongly reminiscent of the *Tale.* Rather than the birds "holding their peace" and "walking unspeaking," they stage a coup d'état. The alternative AZ ending departs from the other manuscripts at line 519 (response of the raven to the pigeon) and goes on for 133 lines.[6] Here are lines AZ 58–133, following the duck's argument with the *smyrilios*:[7]

᾿Ασκορδιαλὸς ὡς ἤκουσεν τῆς πάπιας τὰ λόγια,
ἐξέβηκεν, ἐκάθισε κοντὰ εἰς τὸ πλευρόν της:

«Χαρὰ στὴν πάπια, λέγει της, τὴν φιλοσοφωτάτην, 60
τὴν εὐγενούσαν, τὴν καλήν, μὲ τὸ μεγάλον γένος.»

Σπουργίτης καὶ ὁ κόσσυφας ἐκάθουνταν κοντά του,
ἀνάγκαζαν τὸν σκορδιαλὸν διὰ νὰ φιλονικήση
καὶ νὰ γκαρδιώση τὸν λαόν, τὸ πλῆθος τῶν ὀρνέων.
῎Ηρξατο δὲ ὁ σκορδιαλὸς τοιούτους λόγους λέγει:

«Ἀκούσατε ὅλα τὰ πουλία καὶ πλῆθος τῶν ὀρνέων,
ἐσεῖς καλὰ ἐγνωρίζετε, ὅλα κατέχετέ τα,
τὸ πῶς ὁ μέγας βασιλεὺς εἰς τὴν χαρὰν ἐτούτην
ἐκάλεσε στὴν τάβλαν του, στὸν γάμον τοῦ παιδίου του, 70
ὅλον τὸ πλῆθος τῶν πουλίων, μικρά τε καὶ μεγάλα.
Ἀτός του μᾶς ἐκάλεσεν καὶ ἤλθαμεν εἰς τὸν γάμον,
καὶ τώρα, ὡς μὲ φαίνεται, καὶ ἐσεῖς ἐβλέπετέ το,
ἀπὸ τὸ μέσον ἤρξαντο τινὲς νὰ φοβερίζουν
πῶς εἶναι ἀρχοντόπουλα, ἀπὸ μεγάλον γένος,
πῶς ἔχουν συμβουλάτορας πάππους καὶ ἐξαδέλφους.
Ἂς εἶναι ὡς ἐσυντύχασιν καὶ τ' ἄλλα τὰ πουλία,
διὰ τὴν φήμην καὶ χαρὰν μεγάλου βασιλέως,
δίχως νὰ φοβερίζουσιν, ὡς ἔκαμεν ἐτοῦτος,
ποὺ 'παίρνεται στὴν εὐγενείαν κι ἔχει τὸ προβελέντζιο.
Τί τοὺς φελᾶ ἡ εὐγενεία καὶ τί τὰ προβελέντζια, 80
ὅταν ἡμεῖς οὐ θέλομεν νὰ τοὺς ὑποκλιθῶμεν;
Ἂν ἦτον καὶ ὁ βασιλεὺς μόνος χωρὶς τὸ πλῆθος,
δὲν τὸν ἀξάζει ἡ βασιλεία, ἀλλ' οὐδὲ ἡ ἐξουσία.»

Ἀκούοντες τὰ λόγια του τὸ πλῆθος τῶν ὀρνέων
ὁποὺ ἦσαν ἀπὸ τὴν χαρὰν τοῦ οἴνου μεθυσμένοι,
ὅλα μὲ θάρσος ἤρξαντο νὰ βρίζουν τὸν σμυρίλιον
καὶ νὰ καταδικάζουσιν ὅλον τ' ἀρχοντολόγι.
Ἀκόμη καὶ τὸν ἀετόν, τὸν μέγαν βασιλέα,
λέγουσιν πῶς εἶναι ἄδικος, ποιεῖ στραβὰ τὴν κρίσιν,
διατὶ ἔχει συμβουλάτορας ὅλους τοὺς κυνηγάρους. 90
Πολλὰ ἐπαινοῦν τὸν σκορδιαλὸν διὰ τὴν πολλὴν σοφίαν,
τὴν λογικήν, ρητορικὴν καὶ τὴν μεγάλην τόλμην,
πῶς ἤρξατο κι ἐσύντυχεν κατὰ τοῦ βασιλέως.
Καὶ διὰ πλέον ἔπαινον ὁμοφωνοῦν τὰ ὄρνεα
καὶ στένουσιν τὸν σκορδιαλὸν εἰς θρόνον ὡς ἀφέντην,
καὶ στὸ κεφάλι βάνουν τον καπάσι τοῦ φορέσαν,
οἱ πάντες νὰ τὸν βλέπουσιν καὶ νὰ τὸν προσκυνοῦσιν.

Ὁ ἀετὸς ὡς ἤκουσεν τοὺς λόγους τῶν ὀρνέων,
καὶ τὴν μεγάλην σύγχυσιν ποὺ γίνεται εἰς αὖτα,
μεγάλως ἐθυμώθηκεν, τῆς ὥρας ἀγριώθην. 100
Τότε γυρίζει ὁ γέρακας, λέγει τοῦ βασιλέως:

«Ἐβλέπει ἡ βασιλεία σου τὴν τόλμην τῶν ὀρνέων!
Δὲν σώνει ἡ ὕβρις ἡ πολλὴ ποὺ μοῦ 'καμε ὁ λούπης,
ἀμὴ πάλιν ἡ πάπια ἤρξατο νὰ ὑβρίζη
τὸν ἀντρειωμένον, τὸν φρικτόν, σμυρίλιον τὸν μέγαν·
χωρὶς νὰ ἔχουν τήρησιν ἀπὸ τὴν ἀφεντίαν σου,
μᾶλλον τολμοῦν κατηγοροῦν, βρίζουν τὴν βασιλείαν σου,
τὸ πῶς ποιεῖς παράδικα, καὶ κάμνεις στραβὴν κρίσην·

καὶ ἔστεψαν τὸν ἀσκορδιαλὸν αὐθέντην νὰ τοὺς κρένη,
διὰ τὴν σοφίαν του τὴν πολλὴν καὶ τόλμην ὁποὺ ἔχει.» 110

Σηκώνεται ὁ μηλάδελφος ὁμοῦ μὲ τὸν πετρίτην
καὶ τὸ ξιφτέρι μετ' αὐτούς, λέγουν τοῦ βασιλέως:

«Αὐθέντη, μέγα βασιλεῦ, ἁπάντων τῶν ὀρνέων,
ἰδοὺ βλέπομεν σήμερον τὸ πλῆθος τῶν ὀρνέων,
κάμνουν μεγάλην σύγχυσιν κατὰ τῆς βασιλείας σου·
ἂν οὐ ποιήσῃς παίδευσιν εἰς αὖτα, ὡς τοὺς πρέπει,
βγάνουν σε ἐκ τὸ βασίλειον, παίρνουν τὴν αὐθεντία σου.»

Εὐθὺς γυρίζει ὁ βασιλεὺς καὶ στέλνει τὸ ξιφτέρι,
νὰ φέρῃ ὀμπρὸς τὴν πάπια, τὸν σκορδιαλὸν ἀντάμα.
Τὰ ὄρνεα ὁμοφώνησαν, διώχνουν τὸ ξιφτέρι· 120
ἐστράφη εἰς τὸν βασιλέα, χωρὶς αὐτοὺς νὰ φέρῃ.
Ὁ βασιλεὺς ἐκάκισεν καὶ σφόδρα ἐθυμώθη.
Σηκώνεται μετὰ θυμοῦ καὶ μὲ πολλὴν μανίαν,
ὁμοῦ καὶ οἱ συμβουλάτορες ὑπᾶν κατὰ τὰ ὄρνεα.
Κρούει ἀετὸς τὸν γερανόν, πετρίτης δὲ τὴν πάπιαν,
μηλάδελφος τὴν ὄρνιθα, ὁ γέρακας τὸν λούπην,
ξιφτέρι τὸ ὀρτύκιον, σκορδιαλὸν ὁ σμυρίλιος·
κρούει ἡ ὠτίδα στὸ νερόν, ὁ πελαργὸς στὸ δάσος,
ὁ καπικάνος, ὡς γλήγορος, ἐμπαίνει εἰς τὴν λίμνην,
ὁ κύκνος παίρνει τὸν γιαλόν, κυκνέας τ' ἀκρωτήρι, 130
ὁ γλάρος σὲ νησόπουλον, ἡ χήνα στὰ λιβάδια,
ἡ ὄφια ἐβούτησε, ἐχώθη εἰς τὸ βάθος,
ἡ πάωνος καὶ ἀφασιανὸς ἐμπῆκαν στὰ παλάτια.

[The skylark, hearing what the duck had said,
came out, sat down beside her, and exclaimed:

"Well done there, duck, most intellectual, 60
you good and noble bird of mighty lineage!"

The sparrow and the blackbird sat beside him,
and urged the skylark on to pick a fight
and give heart to the people, all the fowls.
The skylark then spoke out such words as follow:

"Listen, all birds! Listen now, all you fowls!
You know it well, and you are all aware
that for this celebration the great king
invited to his table all the birds,
both great and small, to be at his son's wedding. 70
Himself he bade us be here at this feast;

and now it seems to me—and you can see it—
that some here have begun to threaten us
that they are nobles, born of mighty lineage,
with grandfathers and cousins councilors.
The way the other birds already spoke
to honor and make proud our mighty king
is how it should be, with no threats like this bird's,
who boasts of his noblesse and *privilegia*.
What use are their noblesse and *privilegia* 80
if we refuse to do obeisance to them?
Were the king all alone, without his crowds,
then he would merit neither reign nor power."

The fowls all, drunk with the good cheer of wine,
on hearing what the skylark had exclaimed,
started to rashly curse at the *smyrilios*
and to condemn the whole nobility.
Even the eagle, the great king himself—
they said he was unjust and had poor judgment,
for hunting birds were all his councilors. 90
They praised the skylark for his awesome wisdom,
his rhetoric, his logic, and his daring
in speaking out against the mighty king.
And, to his further praise, unanimously
the birds enthroned the skylark as their ruler,
and on his head they placed the wide-brimmed cap[8]
so all could pay respects on seeing him.

The eagle, hearing what the birds were saying,
and the great tumult happening among them,
was greatly angered, instantly enraged. 100
The hawk then turned toward the king and spoke:

"Your majesty can see the fowls' defiance!
As if the kite had not bad-mouthed me enough,
the duck now seeks to denigrate the brave,
the terrible, the great *smyrilios*,
with no respect toward your majesty.
Indeed, they dare accuse and curse your reign,
claiming you are unjust and have poor judgment.
And they have crowned the skylark as their lord
to rule them, for his wisdom and his daring." 110

Then the *miladelfos*,[9] the peregrine,
the sparrow hawk rose up and told the king:

"Our lord and mighty king of all the fowls,
today we see the fowls make mighty tumult
against your rule. Now either teach them all
the lesson they deserve, or you will find
they'll drive you from your throne and seize your power."

The king then turned and sent the sparrow hawk
to bring the duck and skylark in before him.
Of one accord, the fowls all drove him off; 120
he went back to the king without his charge.
The king flew in a rage and was irate.
He rose in anger and with virulence,
and with his councilors rushed at the fowls.
The eagle struck the crane; the hawk, the kite;
the sparrow hawk, the quail; the peregrine,
the duck; the *miladelfos* struck down the hen, 127
and the *smyrilios* struck down the skylark. 127

The bustard hit the sea; the crane—the forest;
the pelican, quick as he was, the lake;
the swan fled to the beach; the heron—the cape; 130
the gull—an islet, and the goose—the meadow;
the diver plunged into the depths; the peacock
went to the palaces, as did the pheasant.]

It is clear that the *Book*'s AZ ending is heavily influenced by the *Tale*'s ending. This is demonstrated by their proximity not only in content but in style as well: there exist considerable linguistic and structural similarities between the AZ ending and the entirety of the *Tale* (Tsavare 1987:182–85),[10] whereas lines 1–518 and the traditional ending of the *Book* are not strongly reminiscent of the *Tale*. This view does not contradict the widely shared opinion that the *Book* preceded (and possibly influenced) the *Tale*. It is entirely possible that the *Tale*'s author got his inspiration from a manuscript containing the *Book*, while a couple of decades or centuries later a scribe copying a manuscript containing both the *Book* and the *Tale* modified the former's ending according to the latter, possibly compensating for the *Tale*'s omission from the new manuscript: recall that manuscripts AZ of the *Book* do not contain the *Tale*.

Yet a closer look shows that matters are not as simple as might be assumed. Because the alternative ending may constitute our first attested response to the *Tale*, it is worth spending some time on it.

There are some fundamental differences between the AZ ending and the *Tale*'s ending. One is that although both endings involve a rebellion and a battle, the ruling class, defeated in the *Tale*, emerges victorious in the AZ ending. Although King Lion is killed, King Eagle survives a rebellion and retains power. But one has to be careful in identifying what counts as the ruling class: the structure of power is different in the two poems' kingdoms. King Lion, although king of all animals (verse 17), is clearly associated with the carnivores (and, more broadly, the undomesticated animals). But King Eagle is neutral, siding if anything with the domesticated birds: he firmly punishes the *paragialitis,* a wild bird (318–23), and in the end he suppresses the rebellion of birds from both camps with the help of various hawks (AZ ending 122–33). Of these, the hawk proper (falcon) is defined as domesticated (owing to its hunting skills) in the poem's main body.

None of the other hawks or the leaders of the revolt are mentioned in any of the exchanges among the birds in the poem proper. In fact, the other hawks are just alluded to in the traditional ending, where the mere threat of their intervention quashes any possibility of a rebellion (659–68). However, AZ insists on depicting a picture of noble councilors surrounding the king. The leaders of the attack against the rebel birds (the hawk, the sparrow hawk, the peregrine, and the *miladelfos* [Bonelli's eagle]) are named, not only as the *smyrilios's* influential kin in his exchange with the duck (AZ ending 25–57) but also explicitly as the king's four councilors, in a verse AZ sneaks in after verse 3 (main poem). Thus, although the *Tale* has two roughly equal camps, one of which forms the king's party, the *Book* features King Eagle's central authority rather than a ruling class standing behind him or supported by him: his forces lie largely outside the body of birds attending the convention. AZ purposefully gives King Eagle a broader power base in the form of the hawk councilors, but even they are more of a pretorian guard than the considerable army that King Lion marshals.

Not only do AZ end differently from the *Tale,* but their battle also comes about differently. In the *Tale* the king seems fed up with the incidents of infighting and relaunches the time-old war between herbivores and carnivores. In AZ, on the other hand, there is a clear revolt against nobles who claim family ties with the powerful (as the *smyrilios* has done to the duck); the rebel skylark receives the Byzantine equivalent of the crown, the *kapasin*; and an explicit revolutionary program is articulated ("if we refuse to do obeisance to them").

The motives of a scribe dissatisfied with the *Book*'s traditional happy ending (which had fully respected King Eagle's authority) and adding a battle where King Eagle nevertheless still retains power call for scrutiny. A very simple explanation is that some anonymous scribe, who did not want to see King Eagle defeated under any circumstances, still liked the description of the *Tale*'s battle and decided to spice the *Book* with a similar final scene. This possibility gains ground given the *Tale*'s omission from AZ. Another explanation along similar lines would be that our scribe wanted to make a moral example of those who dare question authority; this argument was made by Zoras (1954:25–26) on first presenting the Z manuscript:

> We have thus [in the *Book of Birds*] two types of variant, of which one ends with the peaceful coexistence of the birds, while the other ends

> with their conflict. Both have didactic content, in that the first solution teaches the need for mutual love and general peace, while the second teaches the principle that no power can change the laws of nature and the established order, and any attempt to change them shall prove in vain and in the end shall meet with failure.[11]

The more important question, with regard to the interrelation of AZ and the *Tale,* is which came first. It is usually assumed that AZ is a late imitation, in line with the late date of the manuscripts, and the coherent tradition of the other five, earlier manuscripts. However, the very notion that the king could be overthrown and replaced by a popular ruler seems more appropriate to late Byzantium than the dominion of the *Sublime Porte* or the *Serenissima.* The *kapasin* is Byzantine; nothing in the Ottoman or Venetian realm would have suggested a parallel. And AZ's treatment of the *paragialitis* has more parallels to Apocaucus's career as discussed by Makris (1993:405–7) than do the other manuscripts: AZ refer explicitly to salt flats and swindling, whereas the other manuscripts speak generically of the sea and borrowing.

If the AZ variant was the original redaction of the *Book*, then the topical references readily fall into place. In that case, the *Tale*'s ending would necessarily have been an imitation of the *Book*'s rather than the other way round. It would have constituted a dilution of an AZ ending into something more generic: a battle of the weak and the strong rather than a concrete allusion to the civil war. The specifics that the AZ ending supplies of revolt and suppression would have been supplanted in that case with a more commonplace all-out battle—better suited to the camps of animals the *Tale* contains and their long-established hostility. And an ending featuring the king's death would be likelier to devise the closer the end of Byzantium drew.

Tempting as all this is, the evidence weighs against the priority of AZ's ending over the *Tale.*[12] Five manuscripts give a version of the *Book* without this ending; the first date from the mid-fifteenth century. This means the traditional version of the *Book* had been in existence for a long time. AZ are later, so the prospect that they preserve an earlier text in its entirety is problematic. As noted, the language and style of the AZ ending is out of place with the rest of the *Book* (Tsavare 1987:182–85), though not with the *Tale.* For example, the AZ ending features few of the characteristic formulas of the *Book* but several of the *Tale*'s, including its concluding verses. The reference to four hawkish councilors is less likely to be something suppressed from the *Book* in two different places by a scribe without exceeding cunning than something added in by a scribe with a point to make about councilors. And the reference to councilors itself is likely to be a borrowing from the *Tale,* which supplied a ready model. The leopard and cheetah are entirely believable as the lion's frontmen, whereas AZ's quadrumvirate seems to exist primarily to supply the *smyrilios* with a pedigree: they are not otherwise integrated into the birds' exchanges (unlike their feline counterparts in the *Tale*) and look very much like an extraneous interpolation. The interpolation is nonetheless very much deliberate, as the adaptor of AZ went out of his way to insert an allusion to the councilors in verse 3 (main poem), hundreds of verses before they actually come up.[13]

Accepting the established view of AZ, then, we have an instance where someone in the fifteenth or sixteenth century—in all likelihood, a denizen of either the Ottoman or the Venetian realm—modified the *Book* into its AZ version to express a specific moral message.[14] The message is ultimately one of conformity and seems likelier to have come from those dominions: in a thriving and stable regime, expressions of satisfaction with the standing order would be likelier than the overt dissent triggered in a time when central authority had been weakened and alternatives could be pursued. The Byzantine-seeming references—the *kapasin*, the parallels with Apocaucus—are odd in such a scheme. It is possible that the adaptation built on an earlier version of the text, with a more explicit treatment of Apocaucus, but this does not explain the use of the *kapasin* in the interpolated ending. Perhaps the ending was added while the memory of Byzantine ceremonial headgear was still fresh.[15] Even if the ending was authored outside Byzantium, the adaptor would still have had ample incentive to encourage obeisance to the sultan or the doge by drawing a parallel with the more congenial Byzantine emperor of yore. Which of the sultan or doge inspired this obeisance is hard to say, but the use of the explicitly Italian word προβελέτζια for "privileges" suggests the latter.[16]

The alternative we must reject might at first seem obvious; namely, that AZ adapted the *Tale* as a deliberate or even protonationalist expression of dissent against the foreign overlord. If the adaptor wished to make a revolutionary parable of the aristocratic *Book* by imitating the *Tale,* he would have followed the *Tale* all the way through to an overthrow of the Establishment, rather than allow King Eagle to suppress the revolution. In any event, even the seventeenth century was still too early for an articulate nationalism: though rebellions were recurrent in the Ottoman Empire, the prevalent ideology of the time remained that the sultan was the overlord of the Christians by the grace of God and as punishment for their sins.[17]

In any event, AZ's response to the *Tale* is a reading that rejects the poem's rebelliousness and supplants it with an explicit act of suppression; the adaptor took on the tenor of the *Tale* but not its story. In the end, the politics of AZ match the politics of the mainstream *Book of Birds* and is not so great a deviation from its central message as one might assume, judging by its tumultuous ending.

The manipulations in AZ form an obvious contrast with the coexistence in four manuscripts (all written during the Ottoman period) of both the *Tale* and the traditional version of the *Book:* the scribes of these manuscripts display no political inclination in their selection of poems and do not attempt to alter one or the other in order to articulate a political message. The discrepancy in the politics of the two epic bestiaries were overpowered by their narrative similarities and destined them to a curious coexistence.[18]

Notes

1. A hospice was a monastery of the Knights Hospitaller.
2. The Vardariots (Βαρδαριῶται) were palace guards to the emperor; they were named from the River Vardar, the main river of Macedonia. There is controversy about their ethnicity; Pseudo-Codinus speaks of them as "Persians" (i.e., likely of Turkic origin), and Tsavare (1987:352) concurs in this, but it is usually assumed they were in fact Hungarians (Kazhdan 1991, s.v. VARDARIOTAI).
3. We refer the reader to Nicol 1996 (a biography of John Cantacuzene largely based on his own memoirs) for further details on that period and potential insights on the *Book*.
4. An example is the Geoffrey who seems to be mentioned in verse 112 (Makris 1993:408–9).
5. The didacticism avowed in the *Tale* also goes unmentioned in the *Book*—save for the title inserted in manuscript C alone (also containing the *Tale*) and clearly in imitation of the *Tale*, though in rather more learned language:

   > Πουλιολόγος τῶν ὀρνέων πάντων· λόγος δὲ δικασίμου ἴσος διὰ μέσου τους ψέγοντα τὸν πέλας, τὸν ἑαυτὸν φημίζων εὖ, καὶ τινὸν ἐχέφρον νόημα πρὸς τέρψιν καὶ μάθησιν ἀνθρώπων τε καὶ νέων παράδειγμα πολλάκις
   >
   > [The Book of Birds of all the fowl; an equally divided telling of an argument between them, reproaching their neighbor, praising themselves well, and yielding up prudent meaning for the delight and learning of people and frequently as an example to the young.]

6. In addition to the alternate ending, AZ alter the hawk's speech (379–415) significantly and omit the exchange between the crow and the turtledove (416–66).
7. As the *smyrilios* is mentioned only in the alternative ending, it is not included in Tsavare's study (1987) of bird names. We have been unable to identify the bird. Whether this indicates that the bird never really existed and is some kind of topical allusion is not something we can decide at present. The tantalizing parallel with the Cretan rebel Constantine Smyrilios, active in 1341, can be rejected: the *Book*'s *smyrilios* is not counted among its rebels and does not strengthen the case for a Venetian provenance of the poem (see discussion following).
8. The *kapasin*; see Commentary verse 512.
9. The Bonelli's eagle, more commonly in Greek σπιζαετός (*Hieraaetus fasciatus*: Handrinos and Dimitropoulos 1999:114).
10. We can add to Tsavare's list (1987) the instance of the superlative φιλοσοφωτάτη, "most intellectual," in AZ 579—the only superlative in the poem and parallel with the three out of the six superlatives in the *Tale* referring to the fox: παμπονηροτάτη, "most cunning," 28; λογιωτάτην, "most scholarly," 272; and φιλοσοφωτάτην, "most intellectual," 272.
11. Though we do not have the space to investigate it here, the redactor of the AZ version may also have wished to avoid the traditional version's allusions

to prosperous or victorious foreigners from verse 518 on: the φράγκικον μαχαίριν, "Westerners' dagger," in 523; the newfangled Western invention of the compass in 541–42; the Tatars in 632–33 who looted τὴν Ρωμανίαν ὅλην, "the whole of 'Romania' (Byzantium)," in their search for the fleeing horned owl; and so on.

12. Nonetheless, we suspect the body of AZ preserves some old readings in its account of the *paragialitis* and may reflect in part an earlier redaction of the poem. The changes from the specific to the generic may reflect a cover-up after the loss of the Cantacuzenists in 1354 or, as Makris (1993:406–7, 410) argues, an updating of the poem for an audience unfamiliar with the details of mid–fourteenth-century politics.
13. Of course, one might suppose that all mention of the four councilors was consciously suppressed from an original AZ redaction as an unpalatable contemporary reference. But there is so much allusiveness left in the traditional redaction that one is at pains to see why the four councilors would have been singled out.
14. This is not to say that the traditional ending is necessarily original, either; Makris (1993:411) believes neither ending is likely to reflect the original conclusion of the *Book* during the civil war.
15. The patriarch in Constantinople, who had authority over the Greek Orthodox subjects of the Ottoman Empire, went on wearing the *kapasin* long after the fall of the city, as depicted in contemporary woodcuts; Kriaras (1968–97, s.v. καπάσιον) gives sixteenth- and seventeenth-century examples of the word used with contemporary reference (*Rod of the Archpriests*, *Stavrinos the Vestiary, Archbishop Arsenius*), and the word is contained in Somavera's (1977 [1709], s.v. καπάσι) dictionary, where it is glossed as σκιάδι, *cappello, capello,* "hat."
16. The form προβελέτζια is unlikely to reflect an older loan into Byzantine Greek from Latin *privilegium*. The form of the word borrowed earlier was πριβιλέγιον, without a coronal *g* (Pseudo-Maurice *Strategicon* 2.8.2; John Laurentius Lydus *De mensibus* 1.23; *vi–x* A.D. and *vi* A.D., respectively).
17. So already Ducas (*xv* A.D.) of his grandfather Michael Ducas, who had fled the Cantacuzenian civil war to the emirate of Aydin:

    Καὶ τὴν μετοικίαν ὡς πατρίδα ἐνηγκαλίσατο καὶ τὸν ἀλλογενῆ καὶ βάρβαρον ὡς θεόστεπτον ἔσεβε καὶ ἐτίμα, εἰς νοῦν λαμβάνων τὰς ἀτασθαλίας τῶν Ῥωμαίων καὶ προβλέπων, ὡς ὅτι ἐν ὀλίγῳ πάντα τὰ τῆς Θρᾴκης καὶ μέχρι Δανούβεως ὑπὸ χεῖρας τῶν Τούρκων πεσοῦνται καὶ αὐτοκράτορες φανήσονται ὡς ἐν ὀλίγῳ, καθὼς καὶ πρὸ ὀλίγου ἐν Φρυγίᾳ τε καὶ Ἀσίᾳ καὶ τῶν ἐπέκεινα ἐγένοντο, Θεοῦ παραχωροῦντος διὰ τὰς ἀνομίας τῶν τότε πολιτευομένων Ῥωμαίων καὶ ἡμετέρων ἀποπάππων.

    [And he embraced his new home as his motherland, and he revered and respected the foreigner and barbarian as one divinely crowned, because he bore in mind the presumption of the Romans and predicted that in a short while all of Thrace up to the Danube would fall to the hand of the Turks and that shortly they would become overlords, as they had just become in Phrygia and Asia Minor and beyond—God yielding this boon to them for the sins of the Romans then in power, our forefathers.] (*Ducas* 5.5)

For the seventeenth century, compare the following by Patriarch Cyril Loukaris, the most progressive Greek churchman of his age, written in 1627 (*Against the Jews*; Valetas 1947:1.147–48):

> Πὼς ἡ ἀνατολικὴ ἐκκλησία νὰ εἶναι κακὰ κατεστεμένη δὲν τὸ ἀρνούμεθα. Ἀλήθεια, βασιλεία δὲν ἔχομε, ὅτι ἔτζι ἠθέλησε νὰ μᾶς παιδεύσει ὁ θεός, διὰ τὲς ἁμαρτίες ὁποὺ κάμνομε, ὄχι διατὶ δὲν ὑποτασσόμεθα τὸν Πάπα. [...] Μάλιστα διὰ νὰ συμφωνήσουσι μὲ τὸν Πάπα εἰς τὴ ψεματινὴ σύνοδο τῆς Φλωρεντίας οἱ ἄγνωστοι ἐκεῖνοι ὁποὺ ἦσαν ἐκεῖ, διὰ τοῦτο ὁ θεὸς ἐπαρεχώρησε καὶ ἐχάθη ἡ βασιλεία, ὅτι δὲν ἤλπισαν εἰς τὸ θεό, ἀμὴ ἔκαμαν συμφωνία μὲ τὸν πάπα, διὰ νὰ τοὺς δώσει βοήθεια καὶ ὁ θεὸς ἄλλως ἐπαρεχώρησε καὶ ἦλθε μέγας ἀφανισμός.
>
> [That the Eastern Church is badly oppressed, this we do not deny. It is true that we have no empire, for thus did God wish to torment us for the sins we commit—and not because we will not subjugate ourselves to the pope. . . . Indeed, it is because those nobodies present there agreed with the pope in the bogus Council of Florence ⟨1438⟩ that God allowed the empire to be lost—for they did not place their trust in God but made an agreement with the pope so that he could give them aid. But God allowed a different outcome, and there came great desolation.]

18. There are further though less strong possibilities to account for the two texts' similarities, such as an initial version of the *Tale* faithfully imitating the *Book* and favoring the ruling class (with or without a battle) that has not survived—which would raise similar questions on the motives of the scribe who altered it, presumably long before it found its way into the four manuscripts. Such possibilities are obviously related to both the *Tale*'s political meaning, if any (appendix 2) and the authenticity of its ending (appendix 3).

APPENDIX 2

HISTORICAL INTERPRETATIONS

Yet note that it has meaning, too, and depth.

How seriously should we take this stern warning in verse 5 of the *Tale*? After all, many researchers who have dealt with the *Tale* have taken this at face value and considered the *Tale* an allegory. The answer depends, among other things, on the authenticity of the *Tale*'s prologue (which we discuss in appendix 3). But assuming for now that the prologue (1–10) is authentic, what can we make of the statement? Did the *Tale* have a deeper meaning for its author? Is it related to one or more historical events in or around fourteenth-century Byzantium? And is there any evidence for such an interpretation outside the disputed prologue, in the main body of the poem?

As argued in appendix 1 there is a strong possibility that the author of the *Tale* was familiar with the *Book of Birds,* which Makris (1993) has argued to be related to the civil war of the 1340s. Assuming this, it is tempting to conjecture that the author read through the *Book*'s political message and subsequently articulated a novel message in the *Tale,* be it as a response to the *Book* or an allusion to an unrelated incident. Yet as we have just argued, the *Tale*'s political meaning, if any, is much harder to detect than that of the *Book*. Unlike the *Book,* the *Tale* gives no names or places and makes no detectable specific allusions. It is not impossible that there had once been such references, only to be removed later on by scribes to whom they made no sense. But then why did the *Book* not meet a similar fate? One would have to assume that the *Tale*'s very structure made it easier to remove such named references, so their removal is imperceptible to us now, and such an assumption is far-fetched, as we have already explored in "'No purebred.'"

In view of the difficulties in attaching a political meaning to the *Tale*, our conjectures should be restricted to major historical events. We cannot rule out that the *Tale* might have alluded to a minor occurrence, but in that case its decoding based on the information now available would be virtually impossible. Still, there was no major historical event in fourteenth-century Byzantium in which a leading figure worthy of identification with King Lion was killed. And although one need not assume that every single animal corresponds to a historical figure, there can be no comprehensive historical interpretation leaving the lion unidentified. There are two ways of overcoming this difficulty. One approach is to conveniently assume that the *Tale*'s ending (992–1082) is inauthentic and that King Lion is not killed after all (a possibility discussed in appendix 3). The other solution is to propose that the anonymous author used King Lion's death as a metaphor (for someone's fall from grace or loss of power, for example) or a fictional happy ending, focused perhaps on the death of an otherwise undefeatable enemy. Both of these possibilities are examined in what follows—along with the possibility that no political allusions are made in the text at all.

Is There Allusion?

In the mid-fourteenth century, the Byzantine Empire was rapidly going downhill, and contemporary scholars knew it. In Alexius Makrembolites' *Dialogue Between the Rich and the Poor,* the rich are quite candid about the state of the empire when they defend themselves for being less generous than their forebears:

> Ἀλλ᾽ ἀγνοεῖτ᾽, ὠγαθοί, τὴν τῶν πραγμάτων ἀφθονίαν, ὁπόση τις ἦν τὸ κατ᾽ ἐκεῖνου καιροῦ, ἀκμαζούσης τῆς ἀρχῆς ἡμῶν καὶ τῆς πίστεως. τὰ πέρατα γὰρ κατείχομεν πάσης τῆς γῆς, νῦν δ᾽ οὐδεμιᾶς ἡμῖν σατραπείας ἔδαφος ὑπολέλειπται· καὶ ὅτι πάνθ᾽ ὅσα ἦσαν ἡμῖν ὑποχείρια ἔθνη τότε, εἰς πάντα νῦν ἡμεῖς ἐδουλώθημεν, οὕτω τῆς κοσμαγωγοῦ προνοίας ἄνω καὶ κάτω φερούσης τὰ πράγματα, καὶ κατὰ ἔθνη τὸ κράτος μεταθεμένης· καὶ ὅτι οὐδεὶς ἦν τότε πένης, οὐδὲ αἰχμάλωτος· νῦν δ᾽ εἵλωτες σχεδὸν πάντες καὶ τρισαιχμάλωτοι. καὶ τί ἂν ἔχοιμεν δρᾶσαι, εὐαρίθμητοι ὄντες ἡμεῖς πρὸς πλῆθος ἄπειρον; καὶ γὰρ καὶ εὕρεσιν θησαυροῦ πολυταλάντου τότ᾽ ὁ κρατῶν οὐ προσήκατο, ἀλλὰ καταχρῆσθαι τῷ εὑρηκότι προσέταξε· νῦν δὲ καὶ τὰς τῶν τεθνεώτων οὐσίας ὑπ᾽ ἐνδείας ἁρπάζουσιν, ἐπείπερ αἱ πρόσοδοι αὐτῶν ὀλιγώθησαν. (Ševčenko 1960:213)
>
> [But you are leaving out of consideration, O good friends, the flourishing state of affairs which prevailed at that time. Our Empire and her religion were at their height and we had in our possession the farthest reaches of the earth. Now no territory of a province is left to

us. You also forget that now it is we who are enslaved by all those peoples who were then under our sway. It is thus that the world-governing Providence guides affairs in ebb and flow and transfers sovereignty from one people to another. Furthermore, at that time there was no one who was poor or prisoner of war, whereas now almost all are helots and "thrice imprisoned." What can we do, few as we are compared with the vast multitudes of the poor? And if at that time a rich treasure was to be found, the emperor did not appropriate it but ordered the finder to utilize it; but now, forced by need, they even seize the property of the dead, for their sources of revenue have diminished.] (Ševčenko 1960:225)

Makrembolites may have been more forthright than most of his contemporaries, but he was by no means alone in his realization. The greatest Byzantine intellectuals of the fourteenth century—Gregoras, Cydones, Metochites—already referred to the empire as "remains," "dregs," and "refuse" (Ševčenko 1961:173). As early as 1364—the year when the *Tale* is set—Demetrius Cydones wrote to a Greek Catholic priest that the city would fall within the year (Ševčenko 1961:186):

ἴσθι δὲ ὡς εἰ μηδὲ νῦν εἰς ἔργον ἄξουσι τὰς κατὰ τῶν ἀσεβῶν ἀπειλάς, ἀλλ᾿ ἐν τῷ ψηφίζεσθαι καὶ παρασκευάζεσθαι καὶ τοῦτο παρέλθοι τὸ ἔτος, ἁλώσεται μὲν ἡ μεγάλη Πόλις—τοῦτο γὰρ μόνον οὐχὶ φωνὴν ἀφιέντα διδάσκει τὰ πράγματα—κρατηθείσης δὲ ταύτης περὶ τὴν Ἰταλίαν καὶ τὸν Ῥῆνον ἀναγκασθήσονται πολεμεῖν τοῖς βαρβάροις. οὐκ ἐκείνοις δὲ μόνον, ἀλλὰ καὶ πᾶσιν ὅσοι τὴν Μαιῶτιν καὶ τὴν Βόσπορον καὶ τὴν Ἀσίαν ὅλην οἰκοῦσιν. [...] Καὶ μηδεὶς ἀδυνάτων τούτους ἐπιθυμήσειν οἰέσθω. εἰ γὰρ μόνοι καὶ πένητες ὄντες οἱ βάρβαροι τοσαῦτ᾿ ἔθνη καὶ πόλεις δουλεύειν ἠνάγκασαν, πῶς οὐ ῥᾷστον τοσαῦτα προσλαβόντας καὶ τῶν ὑπολοίπων καταφρονῆσαι; βέλτιον οὖν μεθ᾿ ἡμῶν ὑπὲρ τῆς Πόλεως πολεμῆσαι τοῖς Τούρκοις ἢ πρὸς πάντας ἐφεξῆς ἀγωνίζεσθαι, μᾶλλον δὲ κινδυνεύειν. τούτοις τοῖς λόγοις κινῶν αὐτοὺς καὶ δίκαια ἐρεῖς καὶ ἀληθῆ καὶ συμφέροντα. καὶ βουλευέσθωσαν γενναῖόν τι δρᾶσαι, μᾶλλον δὲ δράτωσαν. ἤδη γὰρ οὐ χρεία βουλεύεσθαι, ἀλλὰ βεβουλεῦσθαι.

[You should know that, if even now they ⟨the West⟩ do not convert their threats against the infidels into action but rather let this year, too, pass with voting and preparations, then the Great City shall fall—for this is what the facts show, all but speaking for themselves. And when it is conquered, they will be forced to fight against the barbarians in Italy and on the Rhine—not just against them, but against all those who dwell in Scythia ⟨the Golden Horde⟩, the Bosphorus, and the whole of Asia. . . . And no one should think that they are wishing for

> the impossible. Though on their own and paupers, the barbarians have forced so many nations and cities into servitude. How is it anything but easy for them, who have already taken so much, to think but little of the rest? So it is better ⟨for the West⟩ to fight with us against just the Turks for the City now than for them to struggle against—indeed, to be imperiled by—everybody in the future. If you encourage them with these words, you will be speaking justly, truthfully, and in our interest. And they shall decide to do something brave—or rather, they shall go ahead and do it. For it is already time, not to keep deciding, but to take the decision.] (*Cydones* 93)

Cydones may have been crying wolf at the time, but he had good reason for his apprehension.

To argue in favor of a historical meaning of the *Tale,* conceived in this atmosphere of turmoil and doom, one should not rely exclusively on the prologue or the conclusion, as the authenticity of both has been questioned. But there is fruitful evidence to be uncovered elsewhere in the poem. Although conventions are a commonplace of epic poetry, the detailed description of the two diplomatic missions (29–102)—totally absent from *The Book of Birds*—seems to be there for an external purpose: they are nowhere near as comical as the subsequent dialogues, so the author would have little motivation to include them were it not for the political atmosphere they create. Moreover, the *Tale*'s subversive character and overall plot strongly suggest a specific peace conference that went the wrong way from beginning to end, or at least a mockery of the peace conferences of the author's time in general.

Of course the *Tale*'s allusion to historical events becomes far more plausible when the prologue and the conclusion are taken into account. The prologue refers to powerful enemies that might be overcome with God's help. The conclusion shows the strong party (carnivores) defeated by the weak (herbivores): a struggle that does not have the expected outcome and would require a radical imagination from an author not inspired by a particular historical event—or a rare author radically opposed to the established order. If we do assume the *Tale*'s historicity, then who are its combatants meant to represent—does it allude to a national or a class struggle? In other words, were the herbivores the Byzantines and the carnivores their powerful enemies, or were the herbivores the paupers of Byzantium and the carnivores its aristocrats?

The prologue and the conclusion of the poem appear to make opposite claims in this regard. The prologue speaks openly of the "nations" drawing "false peace" with "us." This makes no sense if the conflict alluded to is internecine, but it matches closely the diplomatic travails of Byzantium during the civil wars (Tsiouni 1972:36–38). The conclusion, just as openly, places the battle in the realm of class conflict: it incorporates the cheetah's credo of exploitation (1025–26: "How can the king and nobles make ends meet, / if not by eating you and all the others?"); the biblical quote at the poem's end (1078–79: "There is no king saved by the multitude / of any host; nor is a mighty man / delivered by much strength"); and the acknowledgment, even in the middle of his denouncement, by the ox of the lion as his monarch (1014–15: "Were he a king indeed, as he keeps babbling, / he should have bid that peace prevail forever").[1] An interpretation of these utterances along the lines of a conflict between states is still possible but rather less obvious. Because the authenticity of both the prologue and the conclusion has been called into question, however, we should reach a conclusion only based on the picture painted by the poem proper.

Once the prologue is over, the poem begins by presenting us with two rival camps, the herbivores and carnivores. The ruler of the carnivores is also ruler of all the animals and is acknowledged as such. His court is held in awe, though it is also denigrated—his courtiers, the great cats, are called "maligners." The herbivores have no corresponding leader, although they do hold councils and appoint emissaries. The elephant may be their representative at the palace as coregent—assuming, of course, that the poet even realized a beast of such magnitude is a herbivore (see "Fact and Fiction in the *Tale*'s Zoology"). The elephant is in general an enigmatic figure, whose allegiance is never made explicit, and he mysteriously disappears from the battle scene—possibly taking refuge elsewhere, more plausibly merely standing aloof from the whole melee (see "The Misfit"). The two camps are involved in detailed diplomacy and pacts. The constituents of the carnivores' embassy, the cat, rat, and monkey, form a curious group, whereas the herbivores' counterpart also contains a figure of fun in the camel (see "Plot"). And although the title given to the lion (*basileus,* "emperor": see Commentary verse 17) may simply come from the Greek fable tradition and not be an explicit association of the lion with the Byzantine *basileus,* the lion does appear on the scene with all the trappings of empire: advisors, an entourage, an assembly, and a healthy dose of pomp.[2] These elements at the start of the poem all concur with a political interpretation.

There are also arguments against the *Tale* having any political interpretation, which should be presented. King Lion's death, as already mentioned, is an argument against the *Tale*'s historicity. Just as puzzling for a historical interpretation is the elephant's disappearance from the battle: if the elephant represents someone important enough to be a kind of coregent, simply forgetting to bring him into the battle is curious. However, the author is not meticulous about plot consistency in the poem, at least in the form we have. And although we attempt interpretations of several peculiar inconsistencies, there is always the possibility that the author was simply inattentive. We have also already presented structural arguments (see "The Misfit") for why the omission of the elephant would be convenient to the author. In the same way, the peculiarities in the narrative that we investigate in appendix 3 may simply result from ignorance rather than deliberation.

Another argument for an ahistorical *Tale* could be the reference to September 15, 1364—not known to be the date of anything important in Byzantine history (though it could obviously have served to obfuscate the date of an actual event). And the flow of the *Tale* proper confounds any political interpretations of its prologue and conclusion: both enemy camps plausibly denoted by the carnivores, the nobles and the Westerners, are referred to in glowing terms in the animals' descriptions (see "Subversion and Politics" and "Faith and Country"). The animals within each camp spend more time arguing with each other than with their opponents; this is an inventive narrative strategy (see "Structure"), but it is difficult to identify any factions these internecine conflicts may have depicted. The contradiction between the prologue and the conclusion could be resolved by postulating subsequent accretions in the poem (see appendix 3), but it would be easier explained with the author ahistorically generalizing about the nature of conflict. The final piece of evidence against a political interpretation of the *Tale* is perhaps the most compelling: once the arguing is underway, the programmatic statements of "false peace" are lost in the ensuing barrage of insults, vignettes, and catalogs. It is difficult to see a satirist interpolating this much into a poem with "hidden meaning" unless he has done a better job of concealing his intent—and his target—than one might reasonably expect.

We nonetheless venture to offer two possible historical interpretations, one following the class model ("The Civil Wars"), and one following the national/religious model ("The Attempted Church Union"). Needless to say, in each case we offer no conclusive proof for the proposed interpretation. Given the nature of the poem, we doubt that such a proof would ever be possible; the allusions in the *Tale* are nowhere near as fertile as what Makris (1993) was able to exploit for *The Book of Birds*. What we can do is present indicative suggestions for and against both interpretations and a few plausible identifications of particular animals (though by no means claiming that the *Tale* is a roman à cléf). It is fair to say, in any event, that we employ these interpretations of the *Tale* to help the reader get a better notion of fourteenth-century Byzantium and its fortunes.

The Civil Wars (1341–1347, 1351–1354)

> Otherwise the ability to impose a universal peace—that is, to divert all aggression to their own wars—was a dream of kings rather than a reality.
>
> —P. Terry, *Renard the Fox*

Following Andronicus III's death on June 15, 1341, his longtime friend and advisor John Cantacuzene ended up acting as regent for the nine-year-old heir to the throne, John V Palaeologus. One day after his coronation on October 26, 1341, and following a general assembly, the people of Adrianople (present-day Edirne) revolted against him and what remained of Byzantium's aristocracy after the previous civil wars. Similar revolts followed in many other cities and a new civil war broke out, craftily incited by Cantacuzene's former protégé, Alexius Apocaucus. With the help of the emirs of Bithynia and Aydin, Cantacuzene gained ground against the old guard in Constantinople, amid substantial devastation of the countryside by the Turkish forces. Meanwhile, his former ally Stephen Dušan of Serbia captured the city of Serres in eastern Macedonia and crowned himself emperor of the Serbs and the Romans on April 16, 1346. With Alexius Apocaucus assassinated on June 11, 1345, Cantacuzene finally won the civil war and returned to Constantinople in early February 1347. Showing unusual clemency toward his enemies, he appointed himself and the fifteen-year-old John Palaeologus co-emperors of the Romans, with double coronations taking place in late May 1347.

About four years of internal peace followed, though the empire was granted little respite: it was buffeted by the arrival of the Black Death, further Serbian advances threatening Thessalonica, divisive theological debates centered around the doctrine of hesychasm, and war against the Genoese colony of Galata, right across the Bosphorus from Constantinople. In the summer of 1351, John Palaeologus, stationed in Thessalonica and egged on by Stephen Dušan, began to conspire against his co-emperor. Once again he had the support of the lower classes, those embittered by the incursions of Cantacuzene's Turkish allies, and the opponents of hesychasm (a religious movement that Cantacuzene vigorously supported). Civil war broke out anew, and John Palaeologus eventually prevailed, returning victorious to Constantinople on November 30, 1354. An earthquake that ruined Gallipoli in March 1354 and allowed the Turks to gain a foothold there for good had already marked the beginning of the end for Cantacuzene (if not the Byzantine Empire itself): he spent the rest of his long life as a monk, often acting as an advisor for John Palaeologus.

The existence of the two co-emperors is quite suggestive for anyone familiar with the *Tale,* as is the general assembly that Cantacuzene convened shortly after his 1347 coronation (Nicol 1993:220). One can formulate a scenario where King Lion is identified with John Cantacuzene (not killed but ousted from public life); his "seat mate" the elephant, with John Palaeologus (an emperor ultimately as weak as the *Tale*'s elephant); the carnivores, with the aristocrats (supporters of Cantacuzene); and the herbivores, with the largely unprivileged folk who stood behind John Palaeologus.

There are several features of the poem supporting such an identification. The ruler of the carnivores is the universal emperor of the beasts; this makes an identification with the Byzantine emperor of the time easy. The psalm cited at the end of the poem speaks of a "giant" as well as a "king"; Tsiouni (1972:39) sees in this an allusion to the considerable political power that Cantacuzene had accumulated even before becoming emperor. The carnivores fleeing at the end of the battle are reminiscent of the nobles fleeing for their lives from the cities in revolt during the civil war (Tsiouni 1972:41). Moreover, the herbivores' diplomatic activities and councils are hardly out of place and need not suggest embassies between nations; as Tsiouni (1972:44) points out, such activity characterized the confusion of the Cantacuzenian civil war.[3] The mixed-up embassy that the lion sends out is more plausibly seen as a mix-up of classes than a mix-up of nations or creeds. Tsiouni (1972:43–44) has interpreted it as comprising the three classes of the common folk (rat), the clergy (monkey), and the nobles (cat). Her suggestion is inspired by an assembly of these three classes in the city of Verroia, which as a result joined the camp of Cantacuzene:

> Ἄρμπενος δὲ εἰς Βέῤῥοιαν ἐλθών, τά τε Κράλη γράμματα παρείχετο ἀναγιγνώσκεσθαι ἐπ᾽ ἐκκλησίας καὶ τὰ βασιλέως τοῖς ἐπιτηδείοις κρύφα διεδίδου. Βεῤῥοιῶται δὲ καὶ πρότερον μὲν τὰ βασιλέως ᾑρημένοι οἵ τε ἄριστοι ὁμοίως καὶ ὁ δῆμος ἦσαν, καὶ τότε δὲ ὑπὸ τοῦ Τριβαλῶν πολέμου πιεζόμενοι, (πολλὰς γὰρ αὐτοῖς καὶ συνεχεῖς ἐποιοῦντο τὰς ἐφόδους, καὶ κακῶς ἐποίουν τὴν χώραν ληϊζόμενοι,) καὶ συνορῶντες ἤδη, ὡς ἐν χρῷ κινδύνου καθεστᾶσι δουλεύειν Τριβαλοῖς ἀναγκαζόμενοι, ἄλλως τε καὶ ὑπὸ τῶν ἀρίστων ἐναγόμενοι, (πλὴν γὰρ ὀλίγων τὰ βασιλέως ἦσαν πάντες ᾑρημένοι,) ἐψηφίσαντο τὴν βασιλέως κάθοδον· αὐτίκα τε ᾑροῦντο πρέσβεις, ἐκ μὲν τῶν ἀρίστων Ἀστραπήρην, τοῦ δήμου δὲ Ἀλληλούϊαν, ἐκ τῶν κατειλεγμένων δὲ τῷ κλήρῳ τῆς ἐκκλησίας Σύρον ὠνομασμένον, καὶ ἔπεμπον πρὸς βασιλέα, τάχιστα δεόμενοι ἥκειν πρὸς αὐτούς. οἱ πρέσβεις δὲ ἐπεὶ ἧκον, τήν τε ἀρχαίαν εὔνοιαν τῆς πόλεως ἐδήλουν βασιλεῖ καὶ ὡς, τοῦ πολέμου τοῦδε τοῦ συγγενικοῦ Ῥωμαίοις κεκινημένου, μετέωροι αὐτοὶ ἦσαν καὶ τὴν αὐτοῦ ἐπιδημίαν ἦγον δι᾽ εὐχῆς καὶ πρόθυμοι ἦσαν αὐτῷ προσνέμειν ἑαυτοὺς καὶ τὸν πόλεμον συγκατεργάζεσθαι.
>
> [When Armpenos came to Verroia, he brought the letters of the kral ⟨King Stephen Dušan of Serbia⟩ to be read in an assembly, and he secretly gave out what was happening with the emperor to those friendly to him. But the Verroians had already joined with the party of the emperor, both the nobles and the people, and they were pressed at the time by the war with the Serbs (who made many and frequent raids against them and harmed them in plundering their land). And realizing that they had been placed very near to the danger of being forced into servitude to the Serbs but also being urged on by the nobles (for all but a few had gone over to the party of the emperor), they voted for the emperor to come down to them. Forthwith they selected envoys, Astraperes from the nobles, "Hallelujah" from the people, and from those chosen to the clergy one named Syrus; and they were sent to the emperor to ask him to come over to them as quickly as possible. When the envoys arrived, they declared the city's ancient favor toward the emperor and that, since this internecine warfare among the Romans had begun, they had been in suspense, praying for him to come

to their side; and that they were eager to offer themselves to him and to fight beside him in the war.] (*Cantacuzene* 2.353)

We cannot be sure that the author of the *Tale* realized the elephant was a herbivore. If he did not and fell instead into the same trap as the vernacular *Physiologus* (see "Fact and Fiction in the *Tale*'s Zoology"), this would make the elephant inherently belong to Cantacuzene's side, and an identification with the emperor John V Palaeologus becomes problematic.[4] However, the identification of John V with the elephant becomes more plausible in view of Manuel Philes' early fourteenth-century poem *Exposition on the Elephant,* dedicated to Emperor Michael IX. The poem offers a fairly accurate and detailed description of the elephant's exotic features, as an example of how incomprehensible the emperor's nature itself is to his subjects. On top of that improbable comparison, the poet wishes in his conclusion that the emperor should live as long as an elephant—300 years, to be exact:

Ἀλλ᾽ εἴγε φασί, Βασιλεῦ, τὸ θηρίον,
ὃ μηδὲν εἰς ὄνησιν ἀνθρώποις φέρει,
κἄν τισιν ἴσως τὴν γλυφὴν τῶν ὀστέων
πρὸς θρύψιν ἁβρότητος ἀπλήστου τρόπου,
εἰς τρὶς ἑκατὸν συντεθέντας ζῆν χρόνους,
σὺ παντὸς ἐλέφαντος ὀφθείης πλέον
βιοὺς δι᾽ ἡμᾶς τῶν ἐτῶν σου τὸν δρόμον·
ἐχθρὸς δὲ πᾶς, ἢ δῆλος ἢ κεκρυμμένος,
πρὸ τῶν ποδῶν σου χοῦς βραχὺς γένοιτό σοι
θεοῦ τὸ σεπτὸν εὐγενίζοντος κράτος
καὶ τῆς ἀληθοῦς τοῦ θεοῦ λοχευτρίας,
ἐφ᾽ ἣν βεβαιοῖς τῆς ψυχῆς τὰς ἐλπίδας,
Αὐτόκρατορ μέγιστε, τοῦ γένους λέον.

[But if they say, O king, this animal
(which bears no profit to humanity—
except perhaps sculpting its bones, for some,
whittling at luxury insatiable)
lives up to thrice one hundred years in all,
yet may you live the course of your years through
longer than any elephant, for our sake.
And may all enemies, covert or open,
be crushed to finest dust before your feet,
you who make prosper the august dominion
of God, and Her who truly bore Him forth—
in Whom you have established your soul's hopes,
O greatest emperor, lion by breed.][5]

(Philes *Exposition on the Elephant* 369–81)

This is clearly an animal with imperial pretensions and unlikely to be merely one of Cantacuzene's sidekicks. In fact, Manuel Philes identifies the emperor with both the elephant and the lion, calling the emperor "lion" in the poem's first and last lines. So if the author was aware of either Philes' poem or similar descriptions, the imperial identification of the elephant makes sense. Such an identification might also explain the elephant's absence from the final battle: it would be impolitic to debase the author's emperor figure to the level of the bloodthirsty combatants.

Tsiouni (1972:40) proposes an alternative identification of the elephant, as a class traitor: "the elephant according to the poem, being completely insensitive and thick, could have easily deserted his own kind." The example she gives of Alexius Apocaucus, however, is not apt: Apocaucus was elevated from poverty by Cantacuzene but by the time of the civil war was overtly populist and siding with Palaeologus. Situating Apocaucus-as-elephant among the Cantacuzenist carnivores would make no sense, because Apocaucus had ostensibly gone back to the side of "the people."

Of the conspicuous personalities within the *Tale*, the fox could represent any number of intellectuals, if she is not a generic figure. If the fox is to be a turncoat, however, as the dog (himself a traitor) claims during the battle (1060–63), she is likelier to be a turncoat to her class than her people: the intellectual in Byzantium typically arose from the poor and identified himself with the rich. As seen, the Byzantine intelligentsia rarely had much time for the common folk, and even those intellectuals who expressed vague concern about the exploitation of the poor were shocked and repulsed by the Zealot rebellion in Thessalonica (Ševčenko 1974:85).

Going out on a limb somewhat, one might also identify the monkey, who was so critical of the elephant, with Patriarch Philotheus, a friend of Cantacuzene who succeeded Patriarch Callistus in September 1353 and was an outspoken critic of Palaeologus. On Palaeologus's victory on November 30, 1354, Philotheus went into hiding in a secret recess of St. Sophia (Nicol 1993:129), just as the *Tale*'s monkey, instead of following the cat to a treetop, found her hideout in a hole (verse 1074):

> πάντων δὲ μάλιστα φόβος κατέσχε τὸν πατριάρχην Φιλόθεον οὐ πάνυ μικρὸς διὰ τὸ πάνυ τοῦ συμπτώματος ἀπρόοπτον καὶ αἰφνίδιον· καὶ γὰρ ὁ χθὲς βρενθυόμενος καθιεροῦν τὸν ναὸν εἰς βεβαίωσιν τῆς παλαμικῆς αἱρέσεως ἀνίερος τήμερον ὤφθη καὶ μάλα τι σφόδρα θεοῦ καὶ ἱερωσύνης ἀνάξιος. ὅθεν ἐπεὶ μὴ λελογισμένα πράττειν μηδὲ συνέσει προσήκοντα παρέχουσιν οἱ τοιοῦτοι καιροί, καὶ μάλισθ᾽ ὅτε καὶ θεήλατός τις ἐλαύνοι πληγή, ἐξέστη καὶ οὗτος τοῦ καθεστῶτος εὐθὺς φρονήματος, καὶ ξυννενοηκὼς ἀνύποπτον μόνον εἶναι τὸν ἐπὶ θάτερα κρυπτῆρα μέρη τῆς τοῦ θεοῦ σοφίας λεγόμενον φοῦρνον, ἔνθα καὶ ᾧ τοὺς τῷ θείῳ προσιόντας βαπτίσματι χρίεσθαι μύρῳ νενόμισται, ἔψουσιν ἐν πενταετηρικαῖς

περιόδοις ἢ καὶ πλείοσιν ἴσως καὶ ἥττοσιν ἐνίοτε κατὰ τὴν τῶν ἄλλοτ' ἄλλων βούλησιν καὶ χρείαν πατριαρχῶν, ἐν τούτῳ φυγὼν ὑπότρομος καὶ περιδεὴς ὁ χθὲς διώκτης θρασὺς ἐπὶ πολλαῖς ἐκρύπτετο ταῖς ἡμέραις, ἠχρειωμένος καὶ μάλα ἀπαγορεύων τὸ ζῆν.

[The greatest fear of all took hold of the Patriarch Philotheus, all the greater because the mishap was unforeseeable and sudden. For he who just yesterday was haughtily dedicating the church to the assertion of Palamas's heresy ⟨hesychasm⟩ was today seen to be unholy and indeed quite unworthy of both God and divine office. Thus, because these times do not allow for rational action nor what befits prudence—the more so when a plague sent by God is about to strike—he, too, immediately distanced himself from the established sentiment. And realizing that the only place beyond suspicion was the so-called oven above the other crypts of the Church of God's Wisdom ⟨St. Sophia⟩, where the myrrh with which it is customary to christen those coming for holy baptism is boiled every fifty years (or more, and sometimes less, according to the will and need of different patriarchs from time to time)—fleeing there trembling and fearful, he who was just yesterday an impudent persecutor hid for many days, useless for anything and indeed giving up on life.] (*Gregoras* 3.247)

Tsiouni (1972:40) sees in the monkey, so ill fitting with her carnivore companions, a turncoat figure like the fox, being "more cunning than the fox by far" (933a).

If the *Tale* represents this scenario, incorporating the defeat of the lion, it would have been written some time after Cantacuzene's defeat—perhaps even as late as 1364, when the poem is set—by one of his enemies, possibly as a response to *The Book of Birds*. It is indeed plausible that an opponent of Cantacuzene, aware of the *Book*'s mockery of Apocaucus (as argued by Makris 1993), decided to take revenge by anonymously and obliquely attacking the still influential monk Joasaph, as Cantacuzene was known after 1355.

An interpretation along these lines seems to underlie most prior discussion of the *Tale*'s political intent, although it is seldom made explicit. This is the direction in which Sathas's (1972 [1872–94]:7.xxxvii–xxxix)[6] and Tsiouni's (1972:42) interpretations are oriented. Sathas believes the *Tale* refers explicitly to the assassination of Alexius Apocaucus and the Constantinopolitan mob's vengeance on the assassins ("there is a massacre of the innocent by their allied brethren on the orders and the encouragement of the emperor himself"). Sathas attempts to squeeze the *Tale* into the scenario by positing that 1365 should be read as 1345—and indeed dates the mob's attack, through the testimony of the *Tale*, to September 15, three months after Apocaucus's murder. Needless to say, Sathas's exegesis does not stand the test of time.

Tsiouni had come up with similar suggestions to those presented here in her preface, placing some emphasis on the Adrianople assembly and the very first revolt against Cantacuzene (Tsiouni 1972:42), which she finds similar to the herbivores' assembly and murmurs of discontent at the start of the poem. Šandrovskaja (1956b:181; 1960:11) likewise accepts that there is political intent to the *Tale*, although she does not say what it might be.

Dölger, Hunger, and E. Jeffreys, on the other hand, place the poem in the broader context of class conflict. Dölger (1964:204–6) concentrates on the depiction of the fox, finding in the poem satire against the intelligentsia and/or the court. Hunger (1958:287) finds in the epic bestiaries an "outlet for the embitterment accumulated in the people against a small, politically strong clique of courtiers and 'scholars,' who on the basis of their formal learning lived a drone's life in the court." (However, the only poem Hunger investigates in any detail is the *Donkey Tale*.) And Jeffreys (Kazhdan 1991, s.v. DIEGESIS TON TETRAPODON ZOON) states tentatively that "the conflict between the carnivores (the aristocracy?) and the herbivores (the people?) must reflect the civic turmoil of the late 14th C."[7]

Of course the most convincing suggestion, fully valid thirty years later, is Tsiouni's concluding statement: even if the poem does not refer to specific events, there is little doubt that whether on purpose or not, it reflects this turbulent period as a whole.

The Attempted Church Union (1360s)

> When the lion from the heavens ceases to lend its customary warmth to the earth, the lion will die!
>
> —"Pasquilli," cited in S. A. Bedini, *The Pope's Elephant*

John Cantacuzene was destined to play an important role in state affairs thirteen years after his abdication. When Pope Urban V sent to Constantinople Paul of Smyrna (the so-called Latin patriarch of Constantinople) and Prince Amedeo of Savoy in order to negotiate the details of an ecumenical church council to discuss the reunification of the church, it was Cantacuzene who discussed with Paul the prospects for such a synod. Remarkably, the whole record of the June 1367 debate between Paul and Cantacuzene survives to this day, featuring monk Joasaph's vigorous defense of his Orthodox faith and tactful criticism of the pope's authoritarianism and intransigence:

> Ἢν δ' οὐ γένηται κατὰ τὴν ἐμὴν τοιαύτην βουλήν, ἀλλὰ καθὼς σὺ ζητεῖς γενέσθαι κατὰ τὸ παρὸν ἀλογοπραγήτως, οὐ μόνον οὐχ ἕνωσις, ἀλλὰ καὶ ἀρχὴ διαστάσεως, τῆς προτέρας χείρων, μέλλει γενήσεσθαι. Καὶ γὰρ ἡ τοιαύτη τῆς ἐκκλησίας διάστασις εἰς τοσαύτην προέβη τὴν ἀτοπίαν ὡς καὶ βούλεσθαί τινας τῶν ὑμετέρων τοὺς τῆς ὄντας τῆς ἡμετέρας ἀναβαπτίζειν· καὶ γὰρ ὁ τῆς Οὐγγρίας ῥὴξ ἀδεῶς τοῦτο ποιεῖ, ἐξ οὗ ἀνεβάπτισε μὲν πολλούς, μετὰ τῶν

> ἄλλων δὲ καὶ τὸν τοῦ βασιλέως Βουλγάρων τοῦ Ἀλεξάνδρου υἱόν, ὡς δῆθεν ἀνωφελοῦς ὄντος τοῦ ἡμετέρου βαπτίσματος. Καὶ τίς χρεία τοῦ λέγειν με τόν τε δεῖνα καὶ τὸν δεῖνα; Αὐτὸν τὸν βασιλέα τὸν υἱόν μου ἐκεῖσε εὑρισκόμενον καὶ ζητοῦντα βοήθειαν παρὰ τοῦ ῥηγὸς κατὰ τῶν ἀσεβῶν πολλὰ κατηνάγκασεν αὐτός τε ὁ ῥὴξ καὶ ἡ μήτηρ αὐτοῦ καὶ οἱ τούτων ἄρχοντες ἀναβαπτίσαι αὐτόν τε καὶ τοὺς μετ' αὐτοῦ, εἰπόντες ὡς ἀλλοτρόπως οὐ δυνάμεθα δοῦναί σοι ἂν μὴ τοῦτο πρότερον γένηται.
>
> [If things do not happen as I advise you but according to your current irrational plans, then there will be, not church union, but the onset of a division even worse than before. And this division of the church has reached such a point of absurdity that some of your people want to rebaptize the members of our church! The king of Hungary has already done so unstintingly: he has rebaptized a great number of them, most notably the son of the king[8] of Bulgaria Alexander, as if our baptism is of no benefit. And why should I speak of such and such? Even the emperor my son ⟨John V Palaeologus, Cantacuzene's erstwhile ward⟩, who was there seeking from the king help against the infidels, was greatly pressured by the king, his mother, and the leaders there toward a second baptism, for both himself and the members of his entourage, and was told that otherwise he would obtain no aid unless that took place first.] (Meyendorff 1960:173)

What came out of those negotiations was not an ecumenical church council, much less a union of the Orthodox and Catholic churches, but a reverse mission: in an unprecedented move, John V Palaeologus went to Rome in October 1369, preceded by Demetrius Cydones, an old friend of Cantacuzene and a convert to Catholicism. While in Rome, John V announced his own conversion to Catholicism (Nicol 1993:270–71). As Nicol (1996:154) aptly states, Cydones' conversion was intellectual, based on his understanding of Latin theology. The emperor's conversion, however, was purely political, motivated by a last-ditch effort to gain Western support against the advancing Turks.

The unusual importance of the two diplomatic missions suggests the possibility of the *Tale* alluding to the attempted church union. In such a model the Latins would be the carnivores and the Byzantines would be the herbivores, with John V Palaeologus identified with the elephant (as previously discussed) and Pope Urban V identified with King Lion. The power the pope enjoyed over the world would have been obvious even to the Byzantine people. And though their own emperor remained the "one true ruler of the world," identifying the pope with the lion is not out of the question—particularly if the lion is shown to be dishonorable and cunning. The ambivalence and aloofness of the elephant has been pointed out earlier but strangely enough is less of a problem for this interpretation: by converting to Catholicism, the emperor's allegiance would itself have been called into question; this would make the elephant treasonous—something that would be difficult to say under the civil war model.

Though the case for such an interpretation is somewhat weaker than the previous and it has not been attempted until now in the literature, there are some indications favoring it. As mentioned in "Faith and Country," there is hostility expressed toward Catholicism in the boar's monologue. The poem's prologue has a clear program of enemy nations and false peace treaties (although as we discuss in appendix 3, its authenticity has been called into question), and the poet could have easily regarded the West, particularly Venice and Genoa, as rich predators living off the impoverished Byzantines. The adjective we have translated as "total" in verse 92 (μεθ' ὅρκου βεβαιώσαντες ***καθολικὴν*** ἀγάπην, "confirming ***total*** amity by oath") is καθολικήν: the author might be alluding to the fact that the Latins called their church *Catholic,* "universal"—although the Orthodox were no less inclined to call their own church catholic, and the word's primary meaning remained "universal, total" (see Commentary). The oath pledged at the start of the poem, and violated at the end, is consistent with a state treaty and reminiscent of the pope's repeated failure, since the days of Michael VIII Palaeologus, to follow through his promises to Byzantium with substantial military aid. And the date of 1364 is much closer to this scenario than the civil wars; the correspondence between the Catholics and the Orthodox would have been set in motion around that time.

If we accept this model, the embassy could include the cat as Paul of Smyrna (the cat's ingratitude to humans in defecating on their flour might reflect a view of Paul as a fifth column within the empire) and the rat as Prince Amedeo, his partner in the embassy. And once again, the monkey could be Patriarch Philotheus, criticizing the emperor as being deceptively strong, picking up food (with his trunk) in one spot and eating it elsewhere (his mouth) (941)—a possible reference to the emperor's begging for help abroad, as Cantacuzene relates, and at the much-hated Vatican in particular. In the inverse embassy, one of the ambassadors could in turn be Cydones, who had converted to Catholicism. None of the herbivores in the poem are turncoats (a privilege confined to carnivores—so that cases of Greeks such as Syrgiannes[9] could not form part of the poem); but the horse's expansive story might just be an indirect allusion to Cydones' "misplaced" learning.

Clearly this model, appealing as it might be, presents several problems. First of all, one would have to accept that the conference does not correspond in scope to actual events (the projected ecumenical church council, encompassing the entire Christian church, was reduced to an imperial visit to Rome in 1369) and was followed by a completely imaginary happy ending: Pope Urban V (King Lion) was not murdered or otherwise defeated, as the *Tale*'s author might have wished. But such an ending was not unheard of in literature during those desperate times. For example, the *Belisariad,* probably written somewhat later than the *Tale* and known to have originated in Constantinople (Bakker and van Gemert 1988:34–42), features several fictional Byzantine victories scored by the general's son, after the general himself was defamed and blinded. Likewise, there is a problem with John Palaeologus being a συγκάθεδρος, "seat mate," of Urban V right from the beginning (when the invitation to the herbivores was made).

Another difficulty is Patriarch Philotheus's improbable participation in Urban V's diplomatic mission, in the guise of the monkey. But a careful reading of the poem in conjunction with the events of June 1367 may yet show otherwise: the monkey does not go back, empty-handed, with the cat and rat (79) and is not mentioned along with them when the rat delivers their message (55). The only thing the author states about the monkey is that the cat and rat had her by their side, in order to amuse them (CL) or serve them (PV) (36). This does not contradict the poor opinion the author seems to hold of the monkey. On the other hand, the monkey escapes together with the other surviving carnivores at the end of the battle. If this is not merely a matter of the author's lapse of attention, it could be attributed to some ill feeling toward Patriarch Philotheus, whose embarrassing hiding out in St. Sophia's "oven" was probably still remembered.

Likewise, the rat's defection to the herbivores during the battle (1044, 1069) could reflect on the author's feelings toward Amedeo of Savoy: after all, he was a cousin of the emperor (brother of the emperor's mother, Anne of Savoy), so there was always a possibility that he would eventually side with the Byzantines.[10] Finally, the description of King Lion's court sounds more like Constantinople than the Vatican; but the references to seat mates, peers, and a senate might be entirely conventional, particularly given an audience unfamiliar with the intricacies of papal politics, and one could still draw equivalences between imperial and papal institutions.

What are the prospects for the *Tale* expressing such a program against the union of the Catholic and Orthodox churches? As we pointed out in "Faith and Country," the author does not attack the neighbors of Byzantium at all (except for the prologue, and that in passing), and the mockery of the Latins is slight if not questionable. But the author may have had reasons for hiding his real agenda: after all, the emperor himself had converted to Catholicism. And who might the author be in such a case? Most likely he would be a devout Orthodox Christian, possibly a monk, worrying about the future of his faith (rather than his empire) and trying to warn his people about the futility of trying to come to terms with the Catholics. Moreover he would be someone hopelessly dreaming of a miraculous destruction of the Western church, or at least Pope Urban V. And he would quite likely be someone of influence, well aware of the details of the attempted church union—a process that certainly started before the June 1367 debate, possibly as early as September 1364, the date the poem was set—and the Byzantine Empire's desperate situation.

If we accept such a program, the *Tale* could have been written by someone in Cantacuzene's inner circle. Indeed, unlikely as it might seem, one might entertain the romantic identification of the author with monk Joasaph himself.

He seems to have abruptly stopped writing his memoirs by late 1369, breaking off his narrative at Patriarch Philotheus's reinstatement in October 1364 without mentioning the June 1367 negotiations. One can imagine Joasaph stopping his memoirs in indignation over what was going on in Rome—the first manuscript appeared two months after John V and his entourage arrived there—and entering a mood of allegorically ridiculing everything and everyone, with no more attention to either historical detail or high language.

Notes

1. These facts about the conclusion have already been pointed out by Tsiouni (1972:39–40).
2. See Commentary verse 111 on γερουσία, "senate." The presence of three councils in the lion's court, all the same—βουλή, "council"; συνέδριον, "assembly" (the actual animal convention); γερουσία, "senate"—suggests the author is working at overkill rather than verisimilitude.
3. Tsiouni (1972) mentions, besides the assemblies in Adrianople and Verroia (see dicussion immediately following), the assembly of the loyalists in Constantinople convened by Patriarch Calecas (Cantacuzene 2.420); the embassy to Cantacuzene of the nobles, people, and clergy of Vizye offering surrender (Cantacuzene 2.490); and the assembly in Thessalonica convened by Alexius Apocaucus's son John, likewise to surrender the city to Cantacuzene (Cantacuzene 2.569).
4. The author might be making a distinction between the emperor's underprivileged supporters, as herbivores, and the emperor himself, as a mighty carnivore. But that would be tantamount to saying that there is no difference between the lion and the elephant: both Cantacuzene and Palaeologus are privileged carnivores, both preying on the people. The view is fairly accurate but necessitates more political maturity than one might reasonably expect of the period.
5. Or possibly "the people's lion."
6. Sathas (1972 [1872–94]:7.xxxvii) explicitly says that "the victims, assembling strategically for battle, repel the hostile members of their race." To consider carnivores and herbivores as members of the same "race" (ὁμοφύλους) only makes sense if one is reading the *Tale* in terms of internecine conflict.
7. Of the remaining commentators enumerated by Tsiouni (1972:34–35), Xanthoudidis (1927–28:353–54) brings up the inevitable reference to a Cretan rebellion taking place in 1364–65. (Šandrovskaja [1956b:194] argues explicitly against him.) Gidel (1866:323) holds the poem is didactic and doubts that any political allusion is to be found in it (330). Krawczysnki (1960:1) likewise holds that the *Tale* and *Book* satirize human follies rather than politics. Zoras (1956:32) accepts on face value both the claims of the *Tale*, that it is didactic and that it is "not lacking in a deeper allegorical character."

   Dimaras (1972:45) and Politis (1973:36) hold the poem is mainly didactic (though the latter finds the didacticism overwhelmed by the humor). And Krumbacher (1897:2.878) says that "just as little sense as the assertion that the poem is intended for children is made by the 'deeper meaning' that the author claims lies in his animal fable—the only point of comparison is the eternal enmity raging among humans as among animals." Knös (1962:151) is noncommittal: "There has been a tendency to see in these [epic bestiaries] allusions to social/political trends of the time—which is quite plausible, although it is difficult to identify precise indications." However in what he goes on to say Knös likewise concentrates on the didactic or moralizing intent of the poem.

Outside those mentioned by Tsiouni, Beck (1971:175) characterizes the *Tale* as having a "parodic rather than satirical character in its presentation." Vasiliou (1996) shares this view and in addition claims both the prologue and the conclusion to the poem, where its programmatic claims are made, to be inauthentic (see appendix 3).

8. Note that Cantacuzene uses here the Byzantine terms *basileus* for the Orthodox Bulgarian king and the Latin term *rex* for the Catholic Hungarian king. See discussion in "Place of Composition" and Commentary verse 17.
9. Syrgiannes, one of Andronicus III's coconspirators against Andronicus II, fled to Dušan in 1334 and made territorial gains on his behalf in Macedonia (Nicol 1993:176–77).
10. See Nicol (1993:263ff.); Ostrogorsky (1968:538).

APPENDIX 3

STRUCTURAL ISSUES

Decline has its own charm.

—Vasiliki Tsiouni-Fatsi, January 1996

Although there are lacunae and interpolations in the various manuscripts of the *Tale,* the sequence of verses itself is consistent across the manuscripts, with two minor exceptions (P swaps 916 with 917; L swaps 693 with 694). Therefore, the ordering of the verses has not been questioned by scholars until recently. Vasiliou (1996) represents an important step forward in the analysis of the text; he has raised serious questions about the authenticity of the poem's prologue and conclusion and about the arrangement of the dog's and fox's dialogue. These questions are important for our understanding of the text, and we discuss in some detail Vasiliou's conclusions. We also discuss our own observations on outstanding structural issues in the text.

Prologue

There are several problems with the prologue to the *Tale* (1–10), of which scholars have been aware since Krumbacher (1897:2.878).

One issue is that the prologue is recorded differently in the different manuscripts of the text. The discrepancies are minor but sufficient to affect our overall conclusions:

Διήγησις παιδιόφραστος περὶ τῶν τετραπόδων. P
Διήγησις παιδιόφραστος περὶ τῶν τετραπόδων
ἀνα ἀναγινώσκωνται καὶ χρῶνται ταῦτα παῖδες,
οἱ φοιτηταὶ καὶ νεαραὶ διὰ τὴν εὐνοστίαν·

γέγραπται γὰρ εἰς ἕνωσιν μαθήσεως καὶ πόθον.
Ἔχουσιν δ' ὅμως ἔννοιαν καὶ βάθος τὰ τοιαῦτα,
νοῆσαι μόνον ἀκριβῶς τὴν ἔννοιαν τὴν ἔχουν.

[*An entertaining tale of quadrupeds.*
An entertaining tale of quadrupeds,
for youngsters, students, and young girls to read,
and to employ for all of its good fun,
as written to conjoin learning and pleasure.
Yet note that it has meaning, too, and depth.
So understand exactly what it means.]

Στίχοι ἀστὴ πρὸς τὸ περίχαρον γενέσθαι τὸν ἄνθρωπον. C
Καὶ οἱ μῦθοι ἔνι περιχαρεῖς πάνυ.
Διήγησις πεζόφραστος περὶ τῶν τετραπόδων
ἵνα ἀναγινώσκοντες καὶ χρῶνται ταῦτα παῖδες,
οἱ φοιτηταὶ καὶ νεαροὶ διὰ τὴν εὐγνωστίαν·
γέγραπται γὰρ εἰς ἕλκυσιν μαθήσεως καὶ πό$^{\theta}$.
Πλὴν κεκρυμμένην ἔχουσιν ἔννοιαν οὐκ ὀλίγην.

[*Amusing verses for one's merriment.*
And all its stories are most comical.
A tale colloquial of quadrupeds,
for youngsters, students, and young men, who've read it,
to employ as well for all of its good knowledge,
as written to draw out and stir up learning.
Yet it conceals no little sense within.]

Στίχοι ἀστὴ {*ἀστεῖοι* L} *πρὸς τὸ περίχαρον γενέσθαι τὸν ἄνθρωπον.* VL
Καὶ οἱ μῦθοι ἔνι περιχαρεῖς πάνυ.⟨V⟩ / *Καὶ μῦθοι εἰσὶ περιχαρεῖς τε πάνυ.*⟨L⟩
Διήγησις πεζόφραστος περὶ τῶν τετραπόδων
ἵνα ἀναγινώσκωνται καὶ χρῶνται ταῦτα παῖδες,
οἱ φοιτηταὶ καὶ νεαροὶ διὰ τὴν εὐνοστίαν {ἐμνοστίαν L}.
Πλὴν κεκρυμμένην ἔχωσιν {ἔχουσιν L} ἔννοιαν οὐκ ὀλίγην.

[*Amusing verses for one's merriment.*
And all its stories are most comical.
A tale colloquial of quadrupeds,
for youngsters, students, and young men to read,
and to employ for all of its good fun.
Yet it conceals no little sense within.]

First of all, the poem proclaims itself as devised for "youngsters, students, and young men to read, / and to employ for all of its good fun, / as written to conjoin learning and pleasure" (2–4). This is the reading given by P and by VL for verse 3 (they are missing verse 4), and it has been adopted by Wagner (1874), Šandrovskaja (1956a), and Tsiouni (1972)—namely, by all scholars who have worked with it prior to Papathomopoulos (2002). This sets both a pedagogical and entertaining purpose for the poem. C, which Papathomopoulos follows for these verses, is more explicitly pedagogical, referring to "good knowledge" (εὐγνωστίαν) rather than "good fun" (εὐνοστίαν), and explicitly speaking of drawing out (ἕλκυσιν) and stirring up (πόθ[ον]) learning rather than merely conjoining (ἕνωσιν) learning and pleasure (πόθον; πόθου Tsiouni). Moreover, the word παιδιόφραστος, as discussed in the Commentary, is genuinely ambiguous between "entertaining" and "educational"; CLV avoid it outright and use πεζόφραστος, "prose-phrased; colloquial" instead. But as has been repeatedly pointed out, the poem does not make for likely pedagogical material, for all its utilitarian observations (see "Purpose of the *Tale*"). If we agree that the *Tale* is not pedagogy but entertainment, then this mildly contradicts what PVL say it is about (as they still speak primarily of how entertaining the poem is) and it contradicts what C says more strongly.

Second, the prologue makes an explicit programmatic claim about the duplicity of foreign nations, which, as Vasiliou (1996) observes, are absent from the poem proper. As we have already seen in appendix 2, the prologue is contradicted by the class interpretation apparent in the conclusion and supports only the interpretation of the poem along state/religious lines.

Finally, the poem proper starts at verse 10a (omitted in P): "So here, my friend, let me set forth this tale." The "friend" (φίλε μου CV, φίλη μου L) that CVL introduce appears out of the blue and is certainly not anticipated by the poem's dedication to "youngsters, students, and young men," who are unlikely to be counted as the poet's "friends."[1]

As a result, the prologue is inconsistent with the remainder of the poem, particularly as it stands in C. Vasiliou (1996:62–68) concludes from this that the prologue (1–10a) is not authentic but is rather an attempt to add historical value to an ahistorical poem, prompted by the explicit date given for the animals' convention. Now, the prologue, as well as the conclusion, is present in all of C, V, L, and P. The fifth manuscript, A, is missing the first sheet of its quire and the last 215 verses; there is no reason to suspect it would not also have contained the current prologue and conclusion in its missing pages. Therefore, this interpolation would need to have taken place very early on in the text's history. Still, we cannot dismiss the possibility that the prologue is inauthentic. As Beaton (1996:269) points out, the very convention of prologues in Byzantine vernacular narrative poems did not materialize before the fifteenth century. The *Tale*'s is the earliest instance attested, which makes it immediately suspect—particularly as Beaton associates such "exordia" with the popularization he postulates for the vernacular poems, away from the court and into a more general audience. Such popularization became possible only with the breakdown of Byzantine institutions (Beaton 1996:225–26); and in fact Beaton uses this to argue that the introduction to the romance *Belthandros and Chrysantza* is a sixteenth-century interpolation (269). It is possible to raise the same argument against the *Tale*'s prologue.

The moral lesson the *Tale*'s prologue presents would have been as topical in the fifteenth as the fourteenth century. For instance, one can easily imagine the prologue being added in a reprise of the poem for political purposes, say as an anti-Unionist manifesto before the Council of Florence (1438–1439)—or for that matter, as a moralizing reprise of a poem whose original political intent had been forgotten. In fact, if the poem was originally intended as a deliberate allusion to the civil wars (see appendix 2), then the prologue can be understood only as a subsequent reinterpretation: a poet with a specific message in mind concerning the civil wars would not hint at a different message at the poem's outset, which speaks of foreign nations (verses 7–10). If the poem was never intended to be political, on the other hand, the prologue might still have resided in the original as a sententious platitude or a clumsy attempt to elevate the poem. Whether or not the poem has a programmatic intent, the inconsistency in the manuscripts on how instructive the *Tale* is meant to be is perplexing.

Not all the evidence adduced supports the inauthenticity of the prologue, however. For example, the mention of "friend" could easily be a conventional rhetorical strategy of the time.[2] The solitary "friend," it should also be noted, appears in a line missing from one family of manuscripts. It is entirely possible that here, as elsewhere, the prototype of the CVLA family added a redundant verse—something that occurs not infrequently in the text and only rarely with the interpolators paying close attention to the preceding context. So by itself, it is not a compelling argument for inauthenticity.

Moreover, the prologue, by speaking of external enemies of "our" people that "draw with us false peace," was clearly written in a Byzantine-held region—something that narrows the window for its date of composition, although it still does not make its inauthenticity impossible. The fact that there is evidence for Byzantine authorship within the poem itself (see "Place of Composition") is partial evidence for the authenticity of the prologue: we know at least that the prologue and poem were not written under different regimes.

In all, some indications that the prologue is extraneous deserve to be taken seriously, although we are not as committed as Vasiliou (1996) to its inauthenticity and not all his arguments are equally compelling. This justifies our strategy in appendix 2 of evaluating the possible political interpretations of the poem separately from the prologue.

Conclusion

Having called into question the authenticity of the prologue, Vasiliou (1996:72–77) proceeds to question the conclusion also—namely, verses 1003 to 1079, starting from "But let me now relate in full that battle" and ending with the quotation from Psalms. Vasiliou sees this as another addition to the text, intended to fulfill the programmatic statement of the prologue. Indeed, the conclusion is the most overtly political segment of the poem, but unlike the case of the prologue, we are unconvinced by Vasiliou's argument and find no clear reason to reject the authenticity of that segment.

Internal Inconsistencies

A major problem with Vasiliou's argumentation is that it reproaches the conclusion, not only for inconsistencies with the poem proper but also for internal inconsistencies. The presence of internal inconsistencies would prove the inauthenticity of the conclusion only if they were not characteristic of the main poem and thereby hinted at a different author. Yet not only are there inconsistencies in the poem proper (e.g., the goats reproaching the ewe, as discussed later), but the internal inconsistencies of the conclusion itself are nowhere near as many as Vasiliou claims and in fact echo at times inconsistencies within the poem proper.

For instance, the βουβάλα (she-buffalo) is presumed by Vasiliou (1996:76) to be killed in verse 1007, whereas the βούβαλος (he-buffalo) turns up in verse 1028, attacking the cheetah. The gender of the buffalo oscillates in the poem proper (546, 611), so there is no reason to suppose, as Tsiouni (1972:53) did, that these are two distinct animals. If anything, the vacillation in gender of not only the buffalo but also the deer (340 versus 351, 1051 versus 1045) and bear (C: 1055 versus 1056) is a factor connecting the main poem and the conclusion: some animals change grammatical gender throughout the poem. Therefore, Vasiliou contends, the buffalo, one and the same animal in 1007 and 1028, would appear to have risen from the dead.

But there is no need to attribute any more carelessness to the author than necessary: the verb used in verse 1007 is not "killed" but κάτζεν, "seated down, threw down"; it could be used to mean "kill," but that is not a necessary part of its definition (see Commentary verse 1007). Because the ox kills the lion as soon as the lion throws the buffalo down, the lion has not necessarily had the time to do his worst to the buffalo. Such analysis might be more minute than the poet himself probably had in mind, but it shows the battle scene is not necessarily incoherent.

Vasiliou (1996:75–76) sees a similar resurrection claimed for the cheetah, between verses 1030 and 1031. But the cheetah is not disemboweled by the buffalo, as Vasiliou contends. Rather, the buffalo "struck and struck the cheetah, kick for kick, / thrusting his horns as well, and thrashed him soundly." The predicate used in verse 1030 is σόσπαστον, "all smashed up," with an emphatic prefix surviving in Cretan Greek; there is no reason to think it means "disemboweled," even if the buffalo has gone to work on the cheetah with his horns. It is all the more unlikely that the poet forgot that the cheetah had been killed, because the cheetah speaks up, not after a decent interval allowing the author to get distracted, but in the very next verse. And when the cheetah does speak, the author makes sure we know he is not in peak physical condition.

Vasiliou (1996:76) also finds fault with the dog accusing the fox to the herbivores in verse 1060 of duplicity, when this has not been displayed in the battle scene. The last we saw of the fox was in verse 1036, when she was loyally running along with the dog to the cheetah's aid; but it is entirely consistent with the fox's folk image that she should be a turncoat. And the dog's sudden accusation to that effect is not clumsy but astutely cinematographic in its delivery—the more so as the dog himself is being disloyal in informing the herbivores and egging them on (1064). The author's treatment of the dog also makes dramatic sense: the dog is from the outset a domestic animal, associating with herbivores more than carnivores in his daily life and (as a domestic animal) the only carnivore the author has allowed to praise himself at length. He can thus switch camps, going over to the "useful" animals, much more inconspicuously than the fox. As it turns out, the dog is not depicted actually attacking any animal (though he joins the other carnivores in their rally: 1036). And unlike the fox, the dog is not forced to flee with the other carnivores at the end of the poem. His treason, one might say, is passive and subtle enough to cover up by accusing the fox instead.

As for the improbability of herbivores slaughtering carnivores in the battle, it is indeed inconsistent with nature (Vasiliou 1996:76), but it *is* consistent with the ensuing quote from Psalms (1077–79). So the conclusion is not being internally inconsistent and on this point is dramatically consistent with the very end of the poem (1080–82)—the authenticity of which Vasiliou accepts. Because we are in the world of fable, moreover, the miraculous end of the battle is hardly reason to rule out the conclusion as inauthentic.

Inconsistencies with the Poem Proper

What remain, then, are the putative inconsistencies of the conclusion with the remainder of the poem. But the case here is no more convincing. There is an ambiguity in the final verse of the poem, which Vasiliou does accept as authentic: is it the memory of the great battle that persists among the beasts, is it its effects, or is it the battle itself that continues on? The first interpretation would make more sense if the battle was taken as a political statement; the third interpretation merely states that despite the herbivores winning the battle, the war continues. Vasiliou (1996:76) inclines toward the second interpretation, that it is the battle's effects that persist, and concludes that either the battle (with its victorious herbivores) contradicts the final verse or, if both are accepted, that we must also accept the absurdity of the herbivores now running the animal kingdom. But Vasiliou's interpretation of the final verse, where the herbivores have won the war as well as the battle, seems to us the least plausible alternative linguistically (see Commentary verse 1082).[3] In fact, if the author is referring to effects persisting from the battle, it could just as easily be the carnivores' enduring resentment as the herbivores' one-off victory that is meant. At any rate, if the battle was written as an allegory, the physical realities of the animal kingdom would hardly be uppermost on the poet's mind—the more so because the herbivores' victory represents wishful thinking: neither the poor of Byzantium, nor Byzantium itself, were to see such a victory in the remaining days of the empire.

There is a double telling of the battle in the *Tale*; first in verses 992–1002 (which Vasiliou accepts as authentic) and then in 1003–79. Vasiliou (1996:76) believes the first battle clearly shows the carnivores victorious, and because the second battle contradicts the first, the second must be inauthentic. But it is not self-evident that the first battle does show the carnivores victorious; it merely states that "Whichever beast subdued and chased another, / would reach it, bite at it, and shake it round" (995–96). Because this is an allegorical battle in the domain of fable, it is not inconceivable for carnivores, as well as herbivores, to be chased, subdued, bitten, and tossed. This does not rule out the buffaloes and the horses getting the better of the cheetahs and the wolves.

The one verse that would seem to establish a carnivore victory is 1002; but as discussed in the Commentary to that verse, τρώγω, the verb used there, has a range of metaphorical meanings in Greek beyond "eat." We have accordingly rendered the verb in 1002 as "mauled" rather than "ate." Similarly, expressions in the first telling of the battle such as "mighty tears" (992) and "uproar and turmoil" (993) are attributed to the beasts as a collective and not to one side. So the two versions of the battle do not contradict each other. The remainder of the first battle, especially in the context of a fable, is perfectly consistent with the second.

It is true that the first battle account is too short to stand on its own: it mentions no names and limits itself to generalities, whereas the transition to the second battle says that what follows provides more detail (κατὰ μέρος) about the battle. And such a brief, perfunctory ending to the poem would be singularly anticlimactic, given the author's elaborate leading up to the battle within the poem proper: the embassies, the lion's recurring threats, the monkey's impudence, the accelerated pace of narration, and so on. Furthermore, the "you should have seen's" of the first telling of the battle (992) echo the "you should have seen's" of the initial general assembly (103–7), which introduce the lion's first speech. The first telling thus itself sounds like an introductory passage rather than a conclusion. So the two tellings of the battle may still be counted as a unit.

This does not eliminate the fact that there are two battle narrations, a redundancy that is suspect (though less so if the first narration does not say who won). There is something clumsy about the connecting passage, verses 1003–5; Vasiliou (1996:77) is right in pointing out that as they stand in Tsiouni's edition (1972), the last two verses in "But let me now relate in full that battle, / detailing how it all turned out, / the violence and havoc that took place then" make more sense swapped. Then again, the transitions between speeches in the main poem are not always effected any more elegantly. And in fact, the awkwardness is an artifact of Tsiouni using CLV for 1004 but P for 1005. The manuscripts on their own are coherent, and by following one group of manuscripts for both verses (CLV) Papathomopoulos (2002) avoids this problem:

Ὅμως νὰ διηγήσωμαι τὸν πόλεμον ἐκεῖνον, P
καὶ κατὰ μέρος λέξομαι λεπτομερῶς εἰς ἄκρον
τὴν βίαν καὶ τὴν ταραχὴν τὴν τότε γενομένην

[However let me now relate that battle,
and in its particulars shall I relate, to the utmost detail,
the violence and havoc that took place then.]

Ἀμὴ νὰ διηγήσωμαι {διηγήσωμεν L} τὸν πόλεμον ἐκεῖνον CLV
καὶ κατὰ μέρος νὰ εἰπῶ ὁποῖον {ὅποιον L} ἔσχε τέλος
ἡ βία καὶ ἡ ταραχὴ ἡ τότε γεγονυῖα {γεγονυῖαν L}

[But let me now relate that battle,
and in its particulars shall I speak of what sort of an outcome
the violence and havoc that took place then had.]

The other inconsistencies that Vasiliou finds in the battle narration are no more compelling. For instance, the alliance of animals that were swearing at each other just a moment ago is not an inconsistency, as Vasiliou (1996:75) contends: we knew from the very start of the poem proper that there were distinct herbivore and carnivore camps, and for all their insults, we are hardly surprised that the two camps end up fighting each other, rather than among themselves. In fact, the internecine strife within the camps makes the poem more interesting: the two camps are not tediously harmonious state armies but disputatious, arrogant, engagingly individualistic animals, who have scores to settle between each other (cheetah and leopard, ox and buffalo, wolf and bear, deer and boar)—yet, when the chips are down, are loyal to their side. Recall that it is the boar, the deer's vociferous critic (353–56), who avenges the deer's death (1053–54).

Likewise, the inglorious defeat of the cheetah does not show the writer is unaware of the cheetah's bold claim in the main poem that "I'm the mighty cheetah, brave past measure, / able to overpower any beast" (870–71), as Vasiliou (1996:75–76) claims. Quite the opposite: the poet may well have delighted in pulling the cheetah down a notch or two. And the presence of the rat among the herbivore armies in battle shows an inconsistency, not in the battle scene (because rats *are* primarily herbivores) but in the introductory embassy, where the rat represents the carnivores. This inconsistency, in fact, which is organic to the poem, strongly suggests a political allusion (see appendix 2). The failure to disclose the fate of the elephant has also already been touched on: the poet would be inclined to leave him out of the battle for reasons of poor zoology and may have had additional political motivation in doing so (see "The Misfit" and appendix 2).

The redundancy of verse 1057 after 1056 that Vasiliou (1996:77) points out in Tsiouni's edition (1972) (αὐτὸς γυρίζεται γοργὸν καὶ σφάζει καὶ τὴν ἄρκον, / ἐσκότωσεν δὲ καὶ αὐτὴν μετὰ λεοντοπάρδου, "he turned swiftly around and slaughtered the bear, too; / so he killed her, too, together with the leopard") is irrelevant: redundancies are hardly unknown in the poem proper, and the inconsistency is again internal to the conclusion. Moreover, once again this turns out to be an artifact of Tsiouni following CLV in 1056 but P in 1057. On their own, CLV introduce some variety by switching to the passive; and P avoids the redundancy altogether by having the bear first struck and only then killed. By following P's reading at the end of 1056 as more coherent with 1057, Papathomopoulos (2002) also avoids this infelicity:

οὗτος {οὕτως L} γυρίζεται γοργὸν καὶ σφάζει καὶ τὸν {τὴν V} ἄρκον· CLV
ἐσκοτώθη {σκοτώθη L} δὲ καὶ αὐτὸς {αὐτὴ V} μετὰ λεοντοπάρδου

[he was turned swiftly round and slaughtered the bear, too,
so (s)he ⟨the bear⟩ was killed, too, together with the leopard.]

αὐτὸς γυρίζει δὲ γοργὸν καὶ κρούει καὶ τὴν ἄρκον· P
ἐσκότωσεν δὲ καὶ αὐτὴν μετὰ λεοντοπάρδου

[and he turned swiftly round and struck the bear, too;
so he killed her, too, together with the leopard.]

Nor are the grammatical points adduced by Vasiliou (1996:77) to argue for the inauthenticity of the conclusion any more convincing. The triple use of καί, "and," in verse 1050 has at least some similarity with 219; it is an exaggeration to describe it as a "unique phenomenon" in the *Tale,* as Vasiliou (1996:77) does, and syntactically it is not particularly distinctive. Neither is the unique instance of a temporal infinitive with a definite article in verse 1028 (καὶ τὸ ἰδεῖν ὁ βούβαλος, "on seeing this, the buffalo . . .") sufficient evidence of different authorship within a text of this size—this is a construction rather commonplace in Byzantine Greek and first attested in the tenth century (Xanthoudidis 1914:181–84; Mihevc-Gabrovec 1973).[4]

One linguistic point worthy of attention that Vasiliou brings up is the asyndeton in 1060. Verse 1060 has no verb of speech for the dog's speech. This is another stylistic infelicity, which may indicate textual corruption (see Textual Notes verse 1060). Again, however, the mere presence of textual corruption does not indicate that the conclusion is inauthentic.

We might mention at this point a further inconsistency with the main poem not remarked on by Vasiliou: verse 1067 introduces the ram (κριός), only here distinguished from the ewe (προβάτα) or sheep in general (πρόβατον). This distinction is not the same as that made between the billy goat (τράγος) and nanny goat (αἶγα), both of which have already been mentioned as distinct individuals in the main poem (453, 522, 578). The ram has merely been mentioned obliquely by the ewe (479, 480) as her "brother and [her] flesh and blood," and the ewe is still on her own in verse 579. But this is hardly a major foul-up; the bear also turns up late in the poem without having been introduced alongside the other carnivores at the beginning of the poem, and this does not mean there is anything inauthentic about the bear. In all, then, we see no compelling inconsistencies between the poem proper and the conclusion.

Inconsistencies with the Prologue

The prologue of the *Tale* presupposes its conclusion. A form of the poem with the prologue's program ("Yet are we saved by just, inviolate oaths"), unfulfilled by a final battle punishing the oath-breaking carnivores, is inconceivable. And the ox's recollection of the lion's oath in 1011 and 1013 is a major argument for the interconnection between the prologue and conclusion. Moreover, the mention of the lion breaking his oath in the conclusion contrasts with the three appeals to the oath in the poem proper (92, 141, 562), where the animals are described as restrained by it. The prologue's mention of the oath, on the other hand, is quite vague and does not tie in immediately with the poem's plot. We suggest that rather than the conclusion being written to fulfill the prologue, the prologue is, if anything, a response to the conclusion, whether contemporaneous or subsequent, and the question of the conclusion's authenticity is not dependent on that of the prologue. Disproving the prologue's authenticity, therefore, does not disprove the conclusion's authenticity, as Vasiliou (1996:76) has presumed.

The prologue of the *Tale* presupposes the battle in the conclusion, with its surprise ending: the conclusion has the weak defeating the strong, and the prologue speaks of Byzantine righteousness prevailing against the might of its enemies with God's help (8–9). It makes much more sense to view the emphasis on the inviolability of oaths (9) as a response to King Lion's violation of his own oath in the conclusion than vice versa. So if an adaptor wrote the prologue, he was working on a version of the poem containing the conclusion rather than a version where the carnivores prevailed (as Vasiliou [1996:76] suspects the original to have been). He thus either followed another adaptor who added the conclusion or himself added both prologue and conclusion.

Now if the same adaptor added both the conclusion and the prologue and had a political allusion in mind, then he was contradicting himself: as discussed in appendix 2, the prologue alludes to enemies of Byzantium, whereas the conclusion points to class conflict within Byzantium. If the same adaptor was at work on both, on the other hand, but did *not* have any political allusions in mind, then the political contradiction may be accidental—but in that case it is hard to see any point in adding the prologue, with its clearly political language. In addition, the language of the prologue is archaistic, whereas the language of the conclusion (up to the final few verses) is vernacular, as discussed in "Language."[5] A single author could modulate his style, and even his scope, like this; but it seems unlikely for an interpolator to decide to add both an archaic, patriotic prologue to the poem and a subversive, vernacular conclusion. So it is unlikely that a single person wrote both the prologue and the conclusion.

But if a single adaptor devising both prologue and conclusion is to be ruled out, two separate adaptors are no more promising a solution. With two adaptors at work, the first adaptor would need to have added the conclusion (as a protest against the mighty of the time, be they the aristocracy or the enemies of Byzantium), and the second adaptor would need to have added the prologue as some form of wishful thinking, which would make sense only in pre-1453 Byzantium. Moreover, these adaptations would need to have taken place early enough for two families of manuscripts to have emerged some time between, say, 1370 and 1461. This makes the second adaptor something of a second gunman theory: it introduces unnecessary complexity into the account, and we reject it, too. Because we have already dismissed the likelihood that a single adaptor wrote both the prologue and the conclusion, and we have established that the prologue presupposes the conclusion, it follows that whether or not the prologue is authentic, the conclusion groups together with the main poem.

There is one final indication in favor of the authenticity of the conclusion: the coexistence in most manuscripts of the *Tale* and the *Book of Birds* (see appendix 1). If the *Tale* was originally more like the *Book* in tenor and initially lacked its rebellious conclusion, then we would have to postulate that the adaptation of the *Tale* in a more populist direction, complete long before 1461, left the *Tale*'s seat mate, the *Book,* untouched (at least until the AZ ending was written—possibly for a couple of centuries). This would need to have happened even though the adaptor would likely have found the two works in the same codex and copied them into the same codex—with ample opportunity, therefore, to modify the *Book* as well. This adds one more implausibility: if the *Tale* was altered by a populist adaptor, it would make all the sense in the world to change the more strongly aristocratic *Book* also; but this has not taken place in any codex containing both works.

We note in passing that Vasiliou's (1996) primary motivation in disputing the authenticity of the prologue and conclusion of the *Tale* was to dispense with the notion, so prominent in both, that there is a political interpretation to the *Tale*. A *Tale* without them is less overtly political; but there is still enough going on in the poem proper—which incorporates the convention and the first telling of the battle—to allow political interpretations to be formulated. The removal of the conclusion and prologue would, if anything, reinforce the anti-Unionist interpretation of the *Tale* (see appendix 2): the absence of a herbivore victory would be a fitting moral example of what happens to those who place too much faith in the Latins . . .

If we accept the conclusion as genuine, our poet is shown to be much more inventive and slyly humorous than we might have first thought. Even if it is not genuine, the conclusion, almost certainly written by a Byzantine subject, is a unique document of dissent for its time, making the poem that has served as its vehicle also unique in Byzantine literature.

Dog and Fox

The final part of the poem where Vasiliou (1996:68–72) finds textual problems is the exchange between the dog and the fox. The interaction of the two beasts involves five speeches: fox's first speech (199–201: "Hey, dog, what are you crapping on about?"), dog's first speech (204–13: "Has Madam Fox come out to play the sophist?"), fox's second speech (215–36: "My, don't we brag a lot! You foulest hound"), dog's second speech (240–59: "You burrow-dwelling, highlands-native fox"), and fox's third speech (263–64: "Enough, you stinking, blathering, lying hound!").

Vasiliou believes there is a problem with the position of the dog's second speech: each of the animals' interactions involves no more than two speeches on the part of each member of the pair; only here does an animal get a third speech. Therefore, two of the dog's speeches presumably represent a single speech split up. This argument is not convincing: in contrast to the strict thesis–antithesis structure of the *Book of Birds,* the disputation in the *Tale* is much more fluid, with speeches varying in length from a couple of verses to near a hundred. And the fox's final speech is nothing more than a two-verse explosion of impatience. Structurally, it could just as easily be counted as part of the transition between the fox–dog and fox–hare episodes, as it could be counted as an independent speech. This structural argument is therefore not compelling.

More convincing is the other point raised by Vasiliou: in verses 217–19, the fox accuses the dog that

> You boast of hunting hares and other beasts,
> goslings and partridges and other birds;
> that people love you greatly and they pet you.

The dog has said nothing of the sort—at least, not before verse 217; for in verses 249–59, the dog does indeed claim that

> Now me, I'm raised within the midst of men:
> in royal courts, imperial palaces,
> . . . .
> And then I hunt
> for deer and boars, for goats both wild and tame,
> hares, and whatever else you'd care to mention.
> Why, even when it comes to large, strong beasts,

which I'm not strong enough to catch or beat,
I frighten them by barking, and they flee,
as do the partridges and other birds.

There are four ways to make sense of this temporal displacement. First, the fox displays, among her many talents, a psychic capacity previously unremarked upon. Though the hare does call the fox a sorceress in verse 285 (see Commentary), this possibility can probably be dismissed. Second, the omniscient narrator is preparing the ground for the latter statement with some poetic license: see Commentary verse 200. But one could see some sarcastic effect in such an anticipation, if true, at 200; nothing of the kind turns up in 249–59, so there would be no good reason for the author to do this. Third, the poet simply forgot when to mention what. Such wholesale incompetence is somewhat unlikely, though we have already had opportunity to remark on the author's inattention to detail.

The final option is that in the original text the dog had indeed spoken of partridges and hares before the fox rebukes him for it and that our extant text has undergone disruption. This suggestion makes a good deal of sense, although it leads to some juggling around of the text's verses, and we have preferred not to carry it out in our text. According to Vasiliou (1996:72), the proper order of verses here should be as follows:

196–98	Transition to fox–dog episode: "The fox, then, having heard the dog insult her . . ."
199–203	Fox's speech and turning: "Hey, dog, what are you crapping on about? . . ."
204–13	Dog's speech: "Has Madam Fox come out to play the sophist? . . . ," followed immediately by
240–59	Dog's second speech, which with the first makes up a single speech in sum: "You burrow-dwelling, highlands-native fox . . ."
214	Transition to fox's response: "The fox turned to the dog and answered thus."
215–36	Fox's second speech: "My, don't we brag a lot! You foulest hound . . . ," followed immediately by
263–64	Fox's third speech, which makes up a single second speech in sum: "Enough, you stinking, blathering, lying hound! . . ."
265–66	Conclusion: "And so the dog departed from the scene . . ."

Under this arrangement, verses 260–62 ("The fox, however, having heard the dog"), introducing the fox's third speech, are omitted as spurious, as are verses 237–39 ("Slightly embarrassed at the fox's insults, / the dog, now feeling bilious and embittered, / stood to one side and spoke such words as these"), introducing the dog's second speech. There is indeed a problem with verses

237–39: the first two sound like the dog is withdrawing, whereas the third (literally "and he spoke words and utterances like these") has him joining back in.

To resolve the inconsistency between 237–38 and 239, Vasiliou has chosen to delete all three verses. One may be tempted to make 237–38, which vividly show the dog in retreat, replace the pale verse 265 ("And so the dog departed from the scene") as a more satisfactory conclusion of the episode. One should resist the temptation, however. Vasiliou's emendation is at least economical in that it postulates only one displacement, that of the dog's second speech of some twenty verses, swapped with the fox's second speech of twenty-three verses—not an implausible number to be explained, we suggest, by a shuffled or misturned loose page in a prototype.[6] We have at least an indirect precedent for this in P swapping 916 and 917, and L swapping 693 with 694, clearly due to inattention. To introduce any more verse shuffling, however, becomes implausible. On the other hand, if the jumbling was deliberate on the part of the scribe, rather than an accidental jumbling of sheets, then of course all bets are off.

All the same, there is something rather abrupt (or at least anticlimactic) about the juncture that Vasiliou (1996) proposes, between the savage threat of 209–13 and the ridicule of 240–48. In fact, the interpolation of 240–59 between 208 and 209 would make just as much sense in literary terms as an alternative scenario: the dog questions the fox's impertinence, paints an unflattering vignette, praises his own good fortune, and ends on a high note with a threat to the fox. Even the page-swapping hypothesis could still stand, with some squeezing: the twenty-line speech would now be swapped with a twenty-seven-line passage. Under this version, of course, now it is the transition between 208 and 240 that becomes abrupt (though perhaps less so than 213–40).

One should point out that the kind of temporal displacement exemplified by the dog and the fox is not unique to them. Verse 458 provides a similar instance with the sheep and goats, as discussed in the following section. Moreover, each rearrangement we have discussed has the disadvantage of displacing verse 255 ("I hunt for . . . hares and whatever else you'd care to mention") much too far from verse 267 ("The hare, who'd heard his name brought up down there"): the narrator consistently introduces animals into the poem by having them respond to another animal's mention of them; but the interval involved is typically under ten verses—not around thirty, as would end up happening here if we went ahead with the rearrangement. So the text we have may well reflect the original text after all.

Sheep and Goat

The goat in 458 ("Now, sheep, you ought not to offend us thus") appears to respond to insults the sheep does not get to utter for another eight verses (466: "what need had I of services like yours, to embarrass me?"). This is a similar case to the dog-and-fox exchange noted by Vasiliou (1996—though he has not commented on it), and it calls for explanation—particularly as it is one of the few places the new beast's arrival on the scene is not obviously set up by what the previous beast has just said.

The first explanation one would attempt, after Vasiliou's approach to the dog and fox, would be to propose another textual perturbation. The prospects for anything of the sort, given the present arrangement of the text, are not promising. The text as we have it looks as follows:

428–35	Boar to sheep
436–49	Sheep to boar
450–52	Boar leaves
453–56	Goats enter
457–62	Goat to sheep I (A)
463–70	Sheep to goat (B)
471–520	Sheep monologue (C)
521–23	Goats prepare to address sheep (D)
524–28	Goat to sheep II (E)
529–44	Goat monologue (F)

To resolve the apparent anticipation of 466 in 458, B would have to move before A. Now, BC and EF must go together, as animals in the poem respond to their opponents before launching into their own monologues. Moreover, EF must follow BC, because F introduces the next pair of animals to speak and E itself starts with mockery of the sheep's self-praise in C. This places some restrictions on what the possible reorderings of the text can be.

These restrictions come into play when considering the main difficulty with reordering A and B: the start of B, 463–65, is an expression of impatience toward the goat. If the sheep is not responding to the goat's disparagement in A, then what has got her so worked up? The only other thing in the speeches that could give the sheep offense are the goat's insults in E. But this would lead to the ordering DEFBCA, which violates the rules we have already set up (EF follows BC) and gives a rather arbitrary rearrangement of the text, or BCDEFA, which makes the goat's speech abruptly resume addressing the sheep in A and disrupts the transition to the bovines already set up in 544.

The only other ways to reorder the text are with A between the two major speeches, BCDAEF (deleting the connecting verse 457 "But then the nanny spoke these saucy words," which would clash with D), or with A deleted completely (BCDEF). In either case, we still have to explain why B starts with such a negative reaction; the only apparent answer is that the sheep is offended at the very entrance of the goats. This means that the sheep and goats have had some prior dealings to which we have not been privy.

Even if, for a moment, we accept that there has been bad blood between them, BCDAEF is still problematic in other ways. Speech A mocks the boar; it is immediately connected to the boar's departure in its present location but would be some sixty verses removed from it in the rearrangement—one would have to wonder why exactly the nanny has chosen to bring the boar up again after so long an interval. (For BCDEFA it would be even further away: eighty-six verses.) Moreover, A and D have the goats speaking in the plural, whereas E has the nanny speaking in the singular throughout (with the exception of 535: "Also our guts are made into the cords"). So it is difficult for A and E to form part of the same speech, switching from plural to singular halfway.

Thus, we can explain the apparent anticipation of B by A either by positing that it originally used to follow it or by claiming it is a subsequent accretion. But if the original order used to be BCDAEF or BCDEFA, there is little obvious reason for someone to choose to transpose the five-verse passage A to the start. And if A was added in later, it is just as puzzling why an adaptor would choose to inflate the role of the nanny. In both cases, though we have settled an unresolved allusion in A (458: how the sheep offended the goats) by moving it after B, we now have a new unresolved allusion in B (463–65: why the sheep is offended by the goats)—which we can settle only by positing some unexplained bad blood between the sheep and goats.

But if such bad blood can explain 463–65, might we not explain the reference in 458 to something likewise outside what was said in the speeches? If we can do so, we will save ourselves the trouble of reordering or deleting passages. Tsiouni (1972:51), for instance, supposes that the goats "scold the sheep for allowing the filthy animal to speak badly of them." But one hardly sees how the sheep could have prevented the boar from saying anything. In fact, the sheep manages to silence the boar with devastating effect.

Too devastating an effect, in fact; and it is this, we claim, to which the goats take offense—something that, unlike the posited bad blood of the rearranged version, can be seen in the poem concretely. The boar associates the sheep with the fox, the wolf, the dog, the billy goat, and the nanny goat (429–34). In her response, the sheep ends by castigating the boar for comparing himself with clean beasts (448–49: "Yet you compare your name and reputation / with that of purest, spotless animals!"). The boar has explicitly compared himself with the deer and the hare (360–68, 381–83); but the sheep may instead have in mind what the boar has just said about her (429–34)—and because the fox, the wolf, and the dog are not "clean" in the *Tale*'s worldview, those clean beasts that the boar has just lumped together are the sheep herself and the goats. Whether or not that is what the sheep had in mind while castigating the boar, that is how the goats seem to construe it; and in defending the goats on their behalf (as they see it), the sheep has been presumptuous, just as the goats were about to do the job themselves: the goats are already on their way to respond to the boar; they had gotten up on hearing not the sheep but the boar speaking (453–54)—only to arrive on the stage with nothing to do in 455, with the boar already in retreat.[7] So the sheep has committed a double impropriety against them. The use of λοιδορήσῃς, "abuse, revile, rebuke," in the goats' speech (458) is a little odd, and we have taken the liberty of adjusting the rendering to "offend"—for the sheep has certainly given offense.[8]

There is one more linguistic feature that suggests that the goats find themselves forestalled. Modern Greek, like English, would normally express this anticipation with a pluperfect ("*had* come out and stepped in the middle of the audience before they heard the sheep forestall them"). However, the fourteenth-century Greek tense system was in flux (Browning 1983:80–81), and the *Tale* has no pluperfect or perfect verbs: as is frequently the case in modern Greek, the aorist acts as the default past tense. So the aorist of 455's ἐξῆλθον καὶ ἐστάθησαν could be ambiguous in the *Tale* between simple sequence ("they came out [to speak together] . . . but then the nanny spoke [against the sheep]") and anticipation ("they had come out [to speak against the boar] . . . but then the nanny spoke [against the sheep]").

The foregoing analysis may seem pedantic; but we feel it appropriate compensation for the neglect and misreadings the *Tale* has suffered. Subtleties like the timing of the goats arriving on stage can easily escape the casual reader, who assumes they are at center stage because of what was narrated immediately before. Yet the *Tale* deserves a more careful reading and has been more skillfully put together than has been generally acknowledged.

The Herbivores' Call

In "Orality" it was pointed out that the best instance in the *Tale* of the structural repetition characteristic of oral narratives is the correspondence between the carnivores' call to assembly (17–39) and the herbivores' (40–54). But as discussed there, the appearance of orality can be generated not only in an oral poem but also in a written poem emulating an oral poem. The provenance of the herbivores' call is made even more suspect because it is attested only in P. It was thus either inserted by the scribe of P or dropped by the scribe of the CVL archetype. By including it in their texts, Tsiouni (1972) and Papathomopoulos (2002) have decided that the passage is authorial. Still, the evidence for the episode's authenticity should be scrutinized.

There is a parallelism between the two calls, though it is not as strong as elsewhere in the *Tale*:

In one place all the clean, domestic beasts,	Seeing this horrid, sudden embassy,
the bloody and loathsome in another ***plain***.	they gave out word and law, to make it known
There sat the king of all the animals,	that all of them—the great and small alike—
the fierce-eyed lion, with his twisting tail.	should gather ***in one place***, a smooth, flat ***plain***.

His seat mate was the mighty elephant,
a beast with neither joints, nor knees, nor ankles;
and close to him he had two chief advisors—
the cheetah and the leopard, those maligners.
Other bloodthirsty beasts were also there:
the wolf, who stalks by night and drinks fresh blood;
the dog, obedient and dear to men,
consuming and devouring any foodstuff;
and furthermore the fox, of bushy tail,
who strangles hens and who excels in cunning.

They sent the long-eared hare to be their crier,
as swift of foot and quick, to gather all,
and bid them see the noble delegates,
to pay them compliments, to make them welcome,
and see their documents and hear their words.
They came and gathered there all through the day.
And so the ox sat by the buffalo,
the much-flogged donkey and the wondrous horse,
the deer, who sucks down snakes, the goat as well,
the wild goat and the sheep, the glutton boar—

The "one place" (ἕναν τόπον) and "plain" (πεδιάδαν) of 42–43 echo the corresponding terms in 15–16. King Lion sits down with the elephant when the carnivores meet in 17–19. Likewise the larger herbivores, the ox and buffalo, sit together in 50. Both passages include a catalog of animals with their properties; the description of each is more extensive in the carnivores' assembly, but that is balanced out by the greater number of herbivores. Although the parallelism is there, it is not so close as to suggest oral-like narrative thrift, and the herbivores' call could easily reflect a written echo of the carnivores', either by the author or by a scribe.

The absence of the herbivores' call in the manuscripts other than P does not make for any less coherent a text, which is evidence against an excision. Each of CVL preserves a coherent reading at this point—excusing L's confusion on who was doing the calling (A is absent for the beginning of the text):

Ἀπῆλθαν, ἀπεσώθησαν κατὰ τὸ ὡρισμένον	38 (P)
εἰς τἄλλα τὰ τετράποδα τὰ καθαρὰ τὰ ζῷα.	39
. . . .	
ἀπέστειλαν καὶ ἔκραξαν τοὺς ἀποκρισιάρους,	54
τὸν κάτην τε καὶ τὸν ποντικόν	55

[They left, and they arrived as was arranged	38
at all the other, clean beasts' meeting place.	39
. . . .	
They called and sent out for the delegates,	54
the cat and rat.]	55

Ἀπήγασιν καὶ ἔσωσαν εἰς τὰ ἕτερα ζῷα.	38 (CV)
Ἀπέστειλαν καὶ ἔκραξαν τὰ καθαρὰ τὰ ζῷα [*nominative*]	39
κάτην τε καὶ τὸν ποντικόν {πονδικόν V}	55

[They left and came to where the other beasts were.	38
The clean beasts then did call and send out for	39
the cat and rat.]	55

Ἐπῆγαν γοῦν καὶ ἔσωσαν εἰς τὰ ἕτερα ζῷα.	38 (L)
Ἀπέστειλαν καὶ ἔκραξαν τὰ καθαρὰ τὰ ζῷα [*accusative*]	39
κάτος τε καὶ ὁ ποντικός	55

[They left and came to where the other beasts were.	38
The clean beasts then were called and sent out for	39
by cat and rat.]	55

The text of the call is not noticeable by its absence from CVL. P has already stretched out CVL's verse 38 to its verses 38–39; it could just as easily have stretched out CVL's 39 into its 54 (a minor alteration, in any case) and interpolated a herbivore call. And there may be an analogue for such an interpolation a few verses further: P alone contains the herbivores' response in 76–78, which looks cobbled together from verses in the rat's speech to them (59, 61, 64); it is problematic to presume that the scribe of the prototype of CVL omitted both 40–54 and 76–78 from the prototype, by either accident or design.

The *Tale*'s manuscripts do not otherwise abbreviate the poem's long catalogs; the "elephants prefer blondes" episode in C is clearly an interpolation rather than a deletion from the other manuscripts. Although a deletion would satisfy the desire to avoid redundancy, the manuscripts do not excise anything more than a verse here and there (see "Manuscripts"). It would thus be uncharacteristic of CVL to have suppressed such an extensive episode, which gives the opportunity to introduce a panoply of epithets.

The text has plenty of parallelism around this point. The parallelism in 76–78 is admittedly "spurious" (postauthorial), yet the resemblance between the carnivores' embassy (31–37) and the herbivores' (80–86)—the strongest instance of parallelism in the *Tale*—cannot call the authenticity of the latter into question, as the herbivores' embassy is attested in all the manuscripts. Given this tendency to parallelism at the beginning of the poem and what would have seemed an inexplicable failure of the original to match the one call to assembly with another, the temptation would have been irresistible for the scribe of P to fill in the gap with a separate gathering.[9]

A missing leaf in the prototype of the *Tale,* we note, would account for the gap: sixteen verses are involved, and at this point of the *Tale* the manuscripts have around that many verses per page.[10] The smoothness of the transition in CVL, however, would make the loss of a page at precisely that point quite a coincidence and should be rejected. In our opinion, then, verses 40–54 do not originate with the author of the *Tale*—a conclusion we seem to be the first to have published—but rather serve as clear testimony of the scribes' liberty to right what they regarded as lapses of structure in their vernacular texts.

Diogenes

> Diogenes used to say, "Other dogs bite their enemies, but I bite my friends, to save them."
>
> —John Stobaeus, *Anthology* 3.13.44

We have already seen that the prologue of the *Tale* is in some respects unusual compared with the rest of the poem. Sofianos (1996) has pointed out another unusual feature of the prologue, hitherto unnoticed: the first nine verses of the poem, including verse 6 (whose authenticity has been disputed by Eideneier [1976:456]), spell out the acrostic ΔΙΟΓΕΝΟΥΣ, "of Diogenes."

The acrostic is a prominent characteristic of learned Byzantine poetry; it is featured in many a Byzantine hymn. For it to turn up in a vernacular Byzantine poem, removed as it appears to be from the norms of the Byzantine scriptorium, is surprising. It has several consequences for our understanding of the poem.

The first is to confirm, once again, the written provenance of the poem. The acrostic is not a characteristic of oral poetry, although Greek folk song did continue the medieval tradition of the alphabet poem (each stanza starting with the next letter of the alphabet). The acrostic is consistent with the other scattered allusions to the world of the literate in the poem—the Homeric word for "hare," the etymologizing of "dog," the raw materials for bookbinding, the fox's command of grammar. This is a piece of cleverness, however, that is alien to vernacular medieval writing. That an acrostic turns up in the conclusion of the *Mass of the Beardless Man* (ΓΕΛΩ ΣΕ, "I Laugh at You") is the exception that proves the rule: the *Mass* features this kind of parodic cleverness throughout and is conceived in entirely different terms than the *Tale*.

The second surprise is the very desire to make the work eponymous—even if the name turns out to be associated with a scribe adding the prologue rather than the original author of the work. The corpus of mainstream vernacular medieval poetry is consistently anonymous. Glycas's verses are early (1158–59), experimental, and outside the vernacular tradition. The attribution of the *Ptochoprodromos* cycle (and some short vernacular love poems: Legrand 1891) to Theodore Prodromus is still controversial. *Callimachus and Chrysorrhoe* has been attributed to a Byzantine nobleman—but on the basis of a third party's epigram (Manuel Philes') and not uncontroversially (Beaton 1996:104, 246); the romance itself says nothing about who wrote it. Cretan poetry is almost all eponymous; but it, too, comes from a very different tradition—pioneering the use of rhyme and typically looking to the West. Its poetry is often intensely personal, as was certainly the case with its three earliest exponents, Della Porta, Sachlikis, and Falieros. In Byzantine territory, where we believe the *Tale* to have originated, there is no precedent for eponymous vernacular poetry. This makes the acrostic all the more startling.

These two elements show that the *Tale's* prologue was conceived rather differently than the rest of vernacular medieval poetry. Of course, the acrostic says nothing about whether the prologue was written by the same poet as the remainder of the *Tale* (although Sofianos [1996:385–86] is confident that this proves its authenticity). Indeed, because it is so uncharacteristic of the poem's milieu, one could easily adduce it as evidence *against* the prologue having been written by the same author as the rest of the poem. At any rate, the fact that someone along the chain of transmission of the poem (whether the original poet or an unknown interpolator) introduced an acrostic and a possibly authorial name into a vernacular poem is momentous enough. That the person responsible may have been removed by a generation or so from the rest of the poem does not detract from his originality, either in this regard, or in the political content of the prologue.

The acrostic also fails to provide proof of the inherent superiority of the Parisian manuscript, as Sofianos (1996:386) contends, despite the fact that the Parisian is the only manuscript to preserve all verses comprising the acrostic. To the acrostic and verse 377 (μὲ πτικήν) that Sofianos employs as evidence of P's reliability, we need only adduce such counterexamples as P omitting verse 124 (so that the rat says nothing before the cat responds); the deer being characterized as ὁ φόβος, "fear," instead of ἄφοβος, "fearless" (319); or the boar accusing the deer and hare of boasting of κέρατά σας, "your horns," instead of κρέατά σας, "your meats" (361)—not to mention the considerable liberties with the text that we argue P has taken in "Manuscripts" and in this appendix.

One may wonder what the chances are that the acrostic is accidental, especially as none of the manuscripts actually give the acrostic as it appears in the modern edition: the trusted witness P itself slips and has ἀνα, "in proportion to," instead of ἵνα, "so that," for verse 2 so that its acrostic actually reads ΔΑΟΓΕΝΟΥΣ; C has ΔΙΟΓΠΟΒΣ (omitting verse 6); and VL, ΔΙΟΠΟΒΣ (omitting 4 and 6). However, ἀνα in P is a genuine slip-up (it repeats the start of the following word), and P is often proved as valuable a witness to the *Tale* as V and C. So we assume the default hypothesis that the acrostic is indeed intentional. The odds against this being accidental, even with the manuscript distortion taken into account, are still overwhelming. The distortions do indicate, however, that the acrostic cannot have been especially highlighted in the work's textual tradition; the scribes simply did not notice it.

There is a chance all the same that the scribe of P, who we have already seen took more than one liberty with the text, found ΔΙΟΓΠΟΒΣ in his source text and twisted it into ΔΙΟΓΕΝΟΥΣ. Eideneier (1976:456) has already argued that verse 6, which makes the acrostic in P, is redundant (see Commentary verse 6); he also argues for the superiority of CVL in verses 5 and 8, whose initials differ from those of P. It is hard to tell whether P or CVL preserve the original verse 5. CVL speaks explicitly of "hidden meaning," which ultimately seems a less substantiated claim to make than P's "meaning and depth." But because the prologue may well be a later addition, its programmatic claim need not match the *Tale*'s plot exactly.

Similarly, verse 8 (see Textual Notes) has clumsy archaisms in both versions (ἄρδην, "utterly," in P; τέως, "meanwhile," in CVL); this makes both versions as likely (or unlikely) as each other to be authentic. The verse's accusations of the enemies of Byzantium as "godless" in CVL may seem hyperbolic but match nicely the mention of God in verse 10. CVL also contains μέν, "on the one hand," in verse 8, which matches the contrastive δέ, "on the other hand, but" in verse 9; without the μέν, P is still grammatical, but δέ does not seem quite the right particle to follow its verse 8. Then again, the misuse of classical particles in semilearned Greek is notorious. In all, we cannot reject the possibility that the acrostic is the invention of the scribe of P.

Diogenes is unlikely as the given name of a Byzantine scholar. It is an extremely infrequent name (although there was a martyr Diogenes [died A.D. 345], whose feast day is December 5, and we know of early Christian clergy[11] by that name), whereas the neoclassical propensity of Greeks to take on the pagan names of their forebears was still several centuries in the future. This means that the name was in rare use, but it had not completely vanished; for example, the Emperor Romanus IV Diogenes, defeated at Matzikert (1071). There are two Palaeologan instances of which we know for the name. The first (Trapp 1976–95 §91792) was Diogenes from Kos, the owner of a mill that he had donated to the monastery of St. John the Theologian in Patmos by May 1259.

The second instance (Trapp 1976–95 §91793, formerly §5423) is more interesting. This was Cephas Diogenous, a priest and scribe from Aetolia, who wrote the manuscript *Oxoniensis Cromwell* 5 in 1404 (Hutter 1977–97:3.1 §173); as Hutter concludes, the scribe could not have learned his rather mannered handwriting in Aetolia and must have written the manuscript in either Constantinople itself or another major center for book production.

The scribe's name is odd for two reasons. The first name, Cephas, is the Aramaic form of "Peter" (John 1:42); it is likely to be an affectation for "Peter" rather than the scribe's original name. The other peculiarity is that the surname is in the genitive: "of Diogenes" (i.e., "son of Diogenes"). Such genitive surnames are to be found in modern Greece, particularly in Cyprus, where the surname Diogenous is now commonplace. They were not normal in Byzantium, however, where surnames tended to be either locational or nicknames. So Cephas Diogenous was likely someone of enough intellectual pretensions to toy with his own name. An additional pretension of Diogenous's is shown in the fact that his manuscript is the only one in its genre to feature a system of abbreviations of comparable complexity (Hutter 1977–97:3.1 §173).

Diogenous's manuscript, *Oxoniensis Cromwell* 5, contains Psalms with commentaries; it was donated to the Bodleian Library by Oliver Cromwell in 1654. At the end of the manuscript, Diogenous wrote a colophon and an epigram, the latter in iambic heptameter (more or less). The fact that the scribe had intellectual pretensions, was active in the right time frame, tried his hand at verse, and had an unusual surname matching the *Tale*'s acrostic are all strong circumstantial evidence for Cephas Diogenous being the author of the *Tale*'s prologue.

That said, we are not convinced this was in fact the case. The meter of the epigram is a little too rickety and the language a little too pretentious: δέλτος, "writing tablet," is Homeric, and θύτης, "sacrificer," is more pagan than Christian as a term for "priest" (though the prologue's νέμει, "share out," is admittedly also archaic: see "Language"). Because it is impossible to prove one way or the other whether Cephas Diogenous was involved with the *Tale*, all we can do is give the one piece of original writing we have from the scribe and let the readers draw their own conclusions.

[ὁ] θέλ(ων) τὴν δέλτον δέρκ(ων) ταύτ(ην) διαναπτύξαι,
κατὰ τρυφ(ῶν) καὶ θεωρ(ῶν) τοῦ γράψ(αν)το(ς) τὴν τέχνην,
[μὴ] προτιμήσας μέμψοιτο μάλλον δὲ κ(αὶ) εὐχέσθω.
[εἰ] γὰρ καὶ σφάλ(ων) ἥμαρτ(ον) τοῦτο ἐξ ἀγνωσί(ας)
ἄν(θρωπ)ος γὰρ εἰμὶ θνητὸ(ς) κ(αὶ) πρὸ(ς) παλαίω πάθει
[ε]ὔστοχον γὰρ κ(αὶ) ἀλαθ(ὲς) μόνω Θεῶ τυγχάν(ει)
ἡμεῖς δὲ σκοτεινωτ(α)τ(α) πάθει περιπλακέντ(ες)
[ἠ]χρίωτο ἐν σώματ[ι] κ(αὶ) τῆς ψυχῆς τὸ κάλλο(ς),
καὶ ἴσ(ως) γε μικρὰ τ(ῆ)ς τέχνης μικροτέρ(α). 10
[ἠ]λλοίωτο ἠχρίωτο φεῦ μοι τῶ ταλαιπώρ(α)
πεπλήρωτο γὰρ εἰς ἐμὲ ὁ τοῦ Χ(ριστο)ῦ μου λόγο(ς)
ὅτι τὸ ἔχοντι πολλ(ὰ) δοθήσετ(αι) καὶ ἔχει,
καὶ τὸ λοιπ(ὸν) ἃ δεῖ κλῆρ(ον) κατέχω [. . .] .
[ε]ὔχεσθαι ὑπερεύχεσθαι, ἀφ' (ὧν) γράψ(ας) κατέχω
καὶ Κηφ(ᾶς) Αἰτωλὸ(ς) γὰρ κέκληται ὁ ταῦτα [ξ]ύσ(ας)
[ἀ]νάξιος τε θύτ(ης) τ' οὐπίκλ(ην) ὁ Διογένους.
εὔξασθε οὖν συγχωρήσατε αἰῶν(ος) ἐς τελευτήν.

[ἐ]γράφη σὺν Θ(ε)ῶ τὸ παρὸν βιβλίον παρ' ἐμοῦ τοῦ
ἀναγεγραμμένου διὰ χειρὸς κόπου καὶ ἐξόδου τοῦ γράψαντος, καὶ
ἔχοντος ἐν μηνὶ δεκεβρίω εἰς τὰς ιε̄ ἰνδικτιῶνος ιγ′ ἔτους ͵ςϡι̅γ̅ καὶ
οἱ ταύτην τὴν β[ίβλον] βλέποντες καὶ θεωροῦντες εὔχεσθέ μοι διὰ
τὸν Θεὸν καὶ μὴ καταρᾶσθε ὅτι οὔτε [. . . three to four words . . .]
οὔτε γάμος ἀγέλαστος οὔτε γραμματικὸς ἄσφαλ[. . .], ἐπεὶ καὶ ἐγὼ
χωρικόγ [. . . three to four words . . .].

[Who would leaf through this writing, looking at it,
enjoying the writer's art and viewing it,
let them not choose to mock but wish me well.
If error was my fault, 'twas ignorance;
for I am mortal, with the old affliction—
sagacity and infallibility

are God's alone. But we have been entwined
by darkest passions, and our souls' own splendor 9
has been corrupted, also, in our bodies— 9
just like the minor details of ⟨my⟩ craft. 10
Changed and corrupted: woe to me, poor wretch,
for what my Christ said is fulfilled in me:
he who has plenty shall be given more;
and so I have the share that's due to me.

. . . .

Wish well, wish very well, for what I've written
and now do know. And he who scratched this down 16
is known as Cephas the Aetolian, 16
unworthy sacrificer, surnamed Diogenous.
So wish well, and pardon in the age to come.

The present book was written with God's help by myself the aforementioned, through the manual labor and expenses of the writer, it being the fifteenth of the month of December, in the thirteenth year of the indiction, in the year 6913 [A.D. 1404], and those of you seeing and viewing this book, wish me well for the sake of God, and curse not, for neither is there . . . nor a wedding without laughter, nor a scribe without error . . . , and moreover I am a villager. . . .] (Hutter 1977–97:3.1.263–64)

If Cephas Diogenous was not involved, then the name—as literary as the acrostic that conceals it—might enclose some sort of allusion that now escapes us. It certainly shows the composer of the prologue had some learning and was not so fanatic a Christian as to hold pagan wisdom in contempt.[12] Diogenes the Cynic, "The Dog" (*iv* B.C.), was renowned for holding human institutions up to ridicule; whether he would have been pleased with the association the *Tale* may have made with him is a question best left to the imagination.

Notes

1. L's "friend" is female, but L gets confused throughout the manuscript, so this should not be taken as indicating the poem was used in pioneering efforts to educate women.
2. Compare, for example, Ἀλλὰ, ***φίλε***, καὶ περὶ αὐτῶν τῶν χρειωδεστέρων προγυμνασμάτων μάνθανε, "But, ***friend***, you should also learn about the more necessary *progymnasmata*," in an anonymous rhetorical textbook (*Περὶ τῶν ὀκτὼ μερῶν τοῦ ῥητορικοῦ λόγου*: Walz 1968 [1833–35]:3.590) or Γίνωσκε, ὦ ***φίλε***, καὶ τὰ ὀνόματα τῶν ποιητῶν, "Know, O ***friend***, the names of the creators ⟨of gold⟩" in an alchemical text (*Ὀνόματα τῶν χρυσοποιητῶν*: Berthelot and Ruelle 1888:2.25).

3. If it is the battle itself that continues, on the other hand, then there is no inconsistency between the herbivores winning the battle in the *Tale* and the war between carnivores and herbivores continuing unabated.
4. L, as usual, is uncomfortable with premodern expressions and substitutes the temporal infinitive with the participial καὶ τότε ἰδὼν.
5. Note in particular that the language of the conclusion is basically the same as that of the poem proper (see "Language") and that it shares characteristic formulas and phrases with it (not counting the omnipresent μικρά τε καὶ μεγάλα, "great and small," there is also ὠμόβορα θηρία, "carnivorous beasts," 1033 and 23; τὰ καθαρὰ τὰ ζῷα, "clean beasts" 1041, 1040 [genitive] and 39, 69; μεγαλομαστόραν, "grandmaster," 1061, referring to the fox—compare μαστόρισσαν, "master [craftswoman]," 271, with the same referent; the recurring use of εὐθύς, "immediately" [112, 122, 150, 435, 611, 773, 795; 1006, 1021, 1035, 1055, 1066]; and so on).
6. At the dog's second speech, P10v has fifteen verses (239–53); C39v, sixteen verses (237–52); L194r, twenty-one verses (239–41, 241a, 242–53, 255, 255a, 256–57); and A7v, fifteen verses (241, 241a, 242–54). Because the prototype must have been fairly similar to the surviving manuscripts, a fifteen-to-twenty-verse page in the prototype is not out of the question. V is written as prose, so V92r has sixty-four verses (239–41, 241a, 242–53, 255, 255a, 256–73, 275–302).
7. This might explain the seemingly curious use of "but" (ὅμως) in 457: the nanny intended to speak against the boar *but* is forced to check the sheep for her presumption instead. However, it is likelier that "but" refers to the fact that whereas the two goats had set out to speak together (456: ὁμοθυμαδόν, "as one"), the nanny ends up speaking alone. Verse 456 and its ὁμοθυμαδόν are a closer target for 457's "but" than the goats reacting to the boar at 453–54.
8. Another possibility is that the goats object to the sheep failing to defend them explicitly in her rebuttal to the boar. But this would be extraordinarily petty of the goats and would make their use of λοιδορήσῃς even more odd.
9. In assembling animals for his roll call, the scribe of P looked not only to the plot of the poem proper but also to the listing in the final battle; that is the only other place in P where the wild goat (ἀγρίμιν) is mentioned (1045). (The other manuscripts also mention it as the hunting dog's prey in 255a, but P is missing that verse, so its scribe could not have used it.)
10. P2v has fourteen verses (34–47); C33r, seventeen verses (30–39, 55–60, 62); L189r, twenty verses (34–39, 55–60, 62–69); A1r, thirteen verses (64–75, 79). V is written as prose, so V90r has forty-two verses (1–3, 5, 7–10, 10a, 11–39, 55–68).
11. For instance Diogenes, archimandrite of the Monastery of St. Thalassius in A.D. 536 (*Acta Conciliorum Oecumenicorum* 3.68).
12. Recall also the reference to Zeus (771)—which scandalized the scribe of P into censoring it (see Textual Notes).

APPENDIX 4

CYPRIOT SONGS RESEMBLING THE *TALE*

The common elements of their linguistic and architectural structures, their meter, the limitless variety of equivalent meanings contained in their hemistich formulas, all seem to show us that these works were recited by "bards" of their time, before an audience subject to the same continuous transformation through tradition as the reciting bard himself.

—H. Eideneier, *Μεσαιωνική ποίηση καί οἱ ἀπολήξεις της σέ νεώτερα κυπριακά τραγούδια*

I

Δκιαλαλημὸν ἐκάμασιν, δκιαλαλημὸν ἐποῖσαν
Δκιαλαλημὸν ἐκάμασιν, τὰ ζώδκια νὰ κριθοῦσιν
Νὰ πᾶσιμ μέσα στοῦ καδῆ, νὰ ξημολοηθοῦσιν
Τζ'αὶ μέσ' τὴγ κρίσιν ἄφοα οὖλλα γιὰ νὰ τὰ ποῦσιν.
Τζ'αὶ ὁ λαὸς ἦταν γλήορος, τζ'ι' ἀνέβημ μέσ' τὴγ κρίσιν
Τζ'ι' ἄρτζ'εψεν τὰ κρηάτα του τζεῖνος νὰ τὰ χουμίση.
—Ἐμὲν ὅνταμ μὲ παίξουσιν τζ'αὶ βάλουμ με ξυδᾶτο
Καθένας βοῦκκος μου ἀξίζει ἕνα χρυσὸ δουκᾶτο.
Τζ'αὶ νάσου τζ'αὶ τὸ σ'οίρουλλα τζ'ι' ἀνέβημ μέσ' τὴγ κρίσιν
Τζ'ι' ἄρτζεψεν τὰ κρηάτα του τζεῖνος νὰ τὰ χουμίση. 10
—Ἐμὲν ὅνταμ μὲ σφάξουσιν τζ'αὶ βκάλουν τὰ λαρτιά μου
Γεμών' ἐφτὰ κοῦμνες σωστές, δίχως τὰ σαρτζ'ερά μου.
Τζι' ὁ ποντικός, σκαθθόνουρος τζ'αὶ 'λλιομουστακᾶτος,
Διπλὸν τραππήδιν ἔκαμεν τζ'αὶ ἔκατσε στὴν τσαέρα
Τζι' ἔκλωθεν τὸ μουστάτζ'ίν του μὲ τὴμ πολλὴμ μανιέρα.
—Τζ'αὶ φέρτε μου τὸγ κάττομ μου πῶχω μιτά του μάσιη.
Τζ'ι' ἐφέραν του τὸγ κάττον του, ποὖσ'εμ μιτά του μάσιη.
—Βρὲ κάττε, βρὲ βρωμόκαττε, βρὲ γαῖμα βρωμισμένο,
ποὺ κάθεσαι μέσ' τὲς γωνιὲς τζ'αὶ βρίσκεσ' ἁγιασμένος.
—Βρὲ ποντιτζέ, σκαθθόνουρε τζ'αὶ 'λλιομουστακᾶτε, 20

Ἄν εὕρῃς τζ'αὶ τσιμπὶγ κλαππὸ τζι'αὶ μπῇς μέσ' τὸ τζ'ελλάρι
Φορτώννουν τὴ ραχούλλασ σου ξυλιὲς ἕνα γομάρι.
Τζ'αὶ νάσου τζ'αὶ τὸγ κούελλον τζι' ἀνέβημ μέσ τὴγ κρίσι
Τζι' ἄρτζεψεν τὰ βυζάτζια της τζ'είνη νὰ τὰ χουμίσῃ
Τζι' ἄρτζεψεν τὰ μαλλάτζια της τζ'είνη νὰ τὰ χουμίσῃ.
—Ἐμὲν ὄνταμ μὲ κουρέψουσιν τζ'αὶ κάμουμ με καυκάρα
Πάω στὰ σ'ειλοπόταμα τζ'αὶ τρώω μιὰν τζ'ινάρα
Τζ'αὶ φέρνω στὰ μαλλάτζ'ια μου τοῦ κόσμου τὴν ἀσπράα
Τζ'αὶ φέρνω τὰ βυζάτζια μου μ' ἕναλ λαήνι γάλα.

[The beasts sent out a call, they sent out word;
the beasts sent out a call they should be judged;
they'd all go to the judge[1] and there speak out
and without fear tell all within the judgment.
The hare was swift, he stepped up in the judgment
and started praising how his meat was grand:
"When I am killed and cooked in vinegar,
each mouthful of me's worth a full gold ducat."
And look! The little pig stepped up to judgment
and started praising how his meat was grand: 10
"When I am slaughtered and my fat removed,
seven clay pots do I fill—my meat aside."
The blister-tailed,[2] sparse-whiskered rat was next:
he double-somersaulted to a chair
and twirled away his whiskers with great pride:
"Bring me the cat; I've got it in for him!"
They brought the cat; he had it in for him.
"You cat, you stinking cat, you filthy blood,
sitting in corners,[3] skinny as a saint."[4]
"You blister-tailed, sparse-whiskered bloody rat! 20
If you get any chance to board the cellar,
a ton of beatings rains down on your back."
And look! The ewe stepped up to judgment next
and started praising how her dugs were grand,
and started praising how her wool was grand:
"When I am shorn and bald, I go away
down to the creek and eat an artichoke.
My wool then gains all whiteness in the world,
a pitcherful of milk comes to my dugs."]
(Papaharalambous 1945–46:262–63; dictated to the teacher S. Kypragoras in Kythrea; singer not named)

II

Ἦρτε βουλὴ 'ποῦ τὸν Θεὸν τὰ ζῷα νὰ κριθοῦσιν
ἐπολοήθην κούδελλος κὴ ἐκεῖ χαμαὶ καὶ λέει,

κὴ ἐμέν' ἂν μὲ κουρέψουσι, μέ κάμουσι καυκάραν,
'πάω 'ς τὰ χειλοπόταμα καὶ τρώω ἀρκοκινάραν,
καὶ φέρνω τὰ βυζούδια μου ἕναν λαήνην γάλαν.
'Επολοήθην ὁ λαγὼς καὶ λέει καὶ λαλεῖ τους,
κὴ ἐμέναν ἂν μὲ παίξουσι καὶ κάμνουν με 'ξιδάτον,
κὴ ἔρτῃ καιρὸς καὶ φέρουν με καὶ βάλουν με 'ς τὸ πιάτον,
ἀξίζει τὸ κομμάτιν μου ἕνα χρουσὸν δουκάτον.
'Επολοήθην χοίρουλλος κὴ ἐκεῖ χαμαὶ καὶ λέει, 10
κὴ ἐμέναν ἂν μὲ σφάξουσι καὶ 'βκάλουν τὰ λαρτιά μου,
τρῶσι καὶ ξηφαντόννουσι 'ποῦ τὰ λουκάνικά μου,
καὶ λυοῦσι καὶ ταὶς μήλλαις μου καὶ τηανίζουν πίτταις,
τρῶσι καὶ οἱ ἄρκοντες ταὶς 'μέρες καὶ ταὶς νύχταις.

[It was the will of God, the beasts be judged.
The ewe responded, and she said down there:
"If I am shorn, if I am bald, I go
down to the creek and eat an artichoke:
a pitcherful of milk comes to my dugs."
The hare responded, and he said and told them:
"If I am killed and cooked in vinegar,
and time comes when they serve me in a plate,
a morsel of me is worth a full gold ducat."
The pig responded, and he said down there: 10
"If I am slaughtered and my fat removed,
they eat and feast upon my sausages;
they melt my fat off, too, and fry up pies,
and nobles eat them day and night."]
(Sakellariou 1890–91:2.203–4)

III

Παπάδες τζ'αὶ πνεμματιτζ'οί,
ἄλλοι ποὰ τζ' ἄλλοι ποτζ'εῖ,
νὰ μάθουσιν τὴ ψαρτιτζ'ήν,
ἔτσι χουμιστιτζ'ήν.
Τζ' ἕνας πὸν ἐγούλεψεν,
ππαράες τοῦ ἐγύρεψεν,
τζ' ἐγιώνι, ποὺ τοῦ δούλεψα,
ππαράες τοῦ ἐγύρεψα.
Τζ'αὶ κάμνει μου ἐτσὰς κουτσ'ιὰ
τζ'αὶ παίζει μου τὴν ταμπουτσ'ιὰν 10
τζ'αὶ ποῦ ν' νὰ πάω νὰ ρκωθῶ,
τὸ ξένον, τ' ἀρφανόν!
Τζ'αὶ πκιάννω τὸ γαδοῦριμ μου,
τὸ γέρημογ κουντοῦριμ μου

τζ'αὶ πάω κάτω 'ς τὴν 'Ορὰν
τζ'αὶ πκιάννουν τζ'αὶ τσιμπὶν νερὰ
τζ' ἐκάτσαν τζ' ἐστεγνώσαμεν
τζ' ἔπειτα στεφανώσαμεν.
Τζ' ἐπηλοήθην τζ' εἶπεν τους, τζ'αὶ λέει τζ'αὶ λαλεῖ τους,
νὰ σσάξουσιν τοὺς πετεινούς, 20
τζ'αὶ περσινοὺς τζ'αὶ φετεινούς,
νὰ μὲν ἀχήκου ζωντανούς.
Τζ' ἦρτεβ βουλὴ ποὺ τὸθ Θεὸν
τὰ ζῷα νὰ κριχοῦν.

Τζ'εῖ ποὺ τ' ἀκού' ὁ ποντικὸς ἔδωσεμ μέσ' 'ς τὴγ κρίσιν,
ἐδιπλώθην τζ' ἐτριπλώθην
τζ' ἔκλωσεν τὸ μουστάτζ'ιν του μὲ τὴμ πολλὴμ μανιέραν.
Τζ'αὶ φέρτε μου τὸγ κάττομ μου, πό 'χω μασ'ὴμ μιτά του.
«Βρὲ κάττε, βρὲ βρωμόκαττε, βρὲ γαῖμαβ βρωμισμένον,
ποὺ κάχεσαι μέσ' 'ς τοὺς σταχτούς, σὰν τὸν ἁγιασμένον. 30
—Βρὲ ποντιτζ'ὲ σπανόνουρε τζ'αὶ λλίομ μουστακᾶτε,
τωρὰ μ' ἐτίμηες, τωρὰ νὰ σὲ τιμήσω
τζ' ἐτσὰς τὰ λλιοβουττήματα μαζὶς σὂν νὰ δειπνήσω.»
Τζ'αὶ ποὺ τ' ἀκού' ὁ σ'οιραλλός, ἔδωσεμ μέσ' 'ς τὴγ κρίσιν,
ἀρτσ'εύκει τὰ κριάτα του τωρὰ νὰ τὰ χουμίσῃ.
«Τζ' ἐμὲν ἁντὰμ μὲ σφάξουσιν τζ'αὶ βκάλουν τὰ λαρκιά μου,
γεμώννουσιν ἑφτά κοῦμνες ἀποὺ τὰ σαρτσ'ερά μου.
Μονάχες ποὺ τὲς μίλλες μου, ποὺ κάμνουσιν τὲς πίττες,
τρῶσιν τζ'αὶ ξηφαντώννουσιν τὲς μέρες τζ'αὶ τὲς νύχτες.»
Τζ'εῖ ποὺ τ' ἀκού' ἡ κουελλιά, ἔωσεμ μέσ' 'ς τὴγ κρίσιν, 40
ἀρτσ'εύκει τὰ μαλλούδκια της τωρὰ νὰ τὰ χουμίσῃ.
—'Εμέναν [ἁντὰμ] μὲ κουρέψουσιν τζ'αὶ πκιὰσουν τὰ μαλλιά μου
τζ'αὶ πάρουν τα 'ς τὲς Περασ'ιὲς τζ'αὶ κάμουν τα τσ'ουχάες,
ποὺ τὰ φοροῦν οἱ ἄρκοντες, φοροῦν τα τζ' οἱ ἀγάες.
Τζ' ἐμέναν [ἁντὰμ] μὲ κουρέψουσιν τζ'αὶ κάμουμ με καυκάραν
τζ'αὶ πάω πά 'ς τὸ σ'ειλοπόταμον τζ'αὶ φάω μιὰν τζ'ινάραν
τζ'αὶ φέρνουν τὰ βυζούδκια μου ἕναλ λαῆνιγ γάλαν.»
Τζ'εῖ ποὺ τ' ἀκούει ὁ λαός, ἔωκεμ μέσ' 'ς τηγ κρίσιν,
ἀρτσ'εύκει τὰ κριάτα του τωρὰ νὰ τὰ χουμίσῃ.
«'Εμὲν ἁντὰμ μὲ παίξουσιν τζ'αὶ κάμουμ με ξυᾶτον 50
τζ'αὶ πάρουμ με 'ς τοὺς ἄρκοντες τζ'αὶ βάλουμ με 'ς τὸ πκιᾶτον,
κάμνει κάθε κομμάτιμ μου ἕνα χρυσὸφ φουκᾶτον.»
Τζ'εῖ ποὺ τ' ἀκού' ἡ ἀλουποῦ, ἔδωσεμ μέσ' 'ς τὴγ κρίσιν.
«Τζ' ἐμὲν ἓν τζ'αὶ κρινίσκουμ με ππασ'άες γιὰ μουλλάες,
γιατ' ἔφα' ὄρνιθες παλιές, ἔφαα τζ'αὶ πουλλάες.
Μέσα 'ς τὴμ μέσην τοῦ χωρκοῦ εἶσ'εμ μιὰγ καλορκίτσαν,
εἶσ'εμ μιὰν ὄρνιθα ψηλὴν τζ' ἔκραζέν τηγ καβάκαν,

πού τὸ φτερὸν τὴν ἔπκιασα τζ῾ ὁ νοῦρος ἐκοράκαν.»
Ἔβκαλέν τημ πὰ ᾿ς τὸ βουνόν, ἔφαέν την τζ῾ ἐπρίστην,
ηὗρεν τζ῾ ἄμμον τζ῾ ἐτζ῾υλίστην. 60
«Ἄδ᾿ ἀμμάδκια δκιὰφ φωστήρκα,
ἄδε πόδκια δκιὰλ λαμπάδκια,
ἄδε φκιὰ γιὰ σκουλαρίτζ῾ια!»
(Ἀχτυπᾷ τζ῾ ἔναγ γυρὸν νὰ χορέψῃ, ἐπκιάστημ πὰ ᾿ς τὸ παγίδιν)
«Ἄδ᾿ ἀμμάδκια δκιὰς στραβά,
ἄδε πόδκια δκιὰγ κουτσά,
ἄδε νοῦρον σὰγ κοντάριν,
πκοιὸς τὸς σώννει νὰ τὸμ πάρῃ;»

[Priests and confessors, too,
one here, another there,
should learn to chant in church,
a skill so well renowned.
A man who had not worked—
he asked him for some money.
And I, who'd worked for him—
I asked him for some money.
And he just gave me beans
and played a number on me. 10
Where will I seek a loan,
stranger and orphan I!
So I take up my donkey,
my poor old short-tailed beast,
and go down to Orá.
Then we got caught in rain;
we stayed till we got dry,
and then we had a wedding.
He answered and responded, spoke and told them:
Now let them kill the roosters, 20
this year's and last year's, too,
and leave not one alive.
And 'twas the will of God,
the beasts be judged.[5]

The rat, on hearing this, stepped up to judgment.
He double-triple somersaulted
and twirled away his whiskers with great pride:
"Bring me the cat; I've got it in for him!
You cat, you stinking cat, you filthy blood,
sitting in ashes, skinny as a saint."[6] 30
"You sparsely whiskered, bald-tailed bloody rat!
You've honored me, and now I'll honor you!

At sundown[7] I will dine along with you."
The pig, on hearing this, stepped up to judgment
and started praising how his meat was grand:
"When I am slaughtered and my fat removed,
my flesh will fill up seven full clay pots,[8]
just with my fat, with which they fry up pies;
they eat and feast on them, both day and night."
The ewe, on hearing this, stepped up to judgment 40
and started praising how her wool was grand:
"Now when I'm shorn and all my wool is gathered,
it's taken overseas and turned to serge;
it's worn by noble Greeks and noble Turks.
When I am shorn, when I am bald, I go
down to the creek and eat an artichoke.
A pitcherful of milk comes to my dugs."
The hare, on hearing this, stepped up to judgment
and started praising how his meat was grand:
"When I am killed and cooked in vinegar, 50
I'm taken to the nobles in a plate;
each piece of me's worth a gold Phocas coin."[9]
The fox, on hearing this, stepped up to judgment:
"Pashas and mullahs won't pass judgment on me
for eating up old hens or eating fowl.
An old nun dwelled there in the village center;
she had a tall hen, which she called Kavaka.[10]
I seized her by the wing; her tail got caught."

She took her to the mountain, ate and swelled.
Then she found sand and rolled. 60
"Look at these eyes like beacons,
look at these legs like candles,
these ears so fit for earrings!"

("She tries to dance a bout, and she is seized in the trap.")[11]
"Look at these eyes, so blind,
look at these legs, so lame,
look at this tail, a lance:[12]
who's got enough to buy it?"]
(Hatzioannou 1934–37:629–31; dictated by Christophis Michailis, from Agros, seventy years old, illiterate)

Notes

See also discussion in "Survivals of the *Tale.*" For glosses, we have consulted Giangoullis 1988–90. Thanks also to George Apepsitos, Stavroulla Herodotou, and Stavros Nicholas.

1. The term used is καδῆ < Turkish *kadı,* constituting as Papaharalambous (1945–46:262) admits a recent element of the song.
2. σκαθθόνουρε, literally "beetle-tailed." The term could mean "blister-tailed" (σκάθθαρος, "foot corn"; σκαθθαρωτός, "looking like it has 'beetles' on its surface"). The word also sounds quite similar to Hatzioannou's corresponding σπανόνουρε, "bald-tailed"—which uses the same adjective as was used to describe the victim of the *Mass of the Beardless Man.*
3. Or "fireplaces" (γωνιές).
4. In Cypriot Greek, "sanctified" (ἁγιασμένος) also means "skinny," the allusion being to the popular church icons of emaciated ascetics.
5. Hatzioannou (1934–37:631) believes the foregoing to have originally been a separate song.
6. See Papaharalambous's version (1945–46).
7. λλιοβουττήματα, usually in Cypriot Greek λιοβουττήματα. See discussion in "Survivals of the *Tale,*" endnote 79.
8. Note the contrast with Papaharalambous's version, in which the fat rather than the meat fills up the pots.
9. φουκᾶτον < φωκᾶτον, a coin minted by Nicephorus II Phocas; the interpretation is Hatzioannou's (1934–37:631). However the word sounds very similar to δουκᾶτον, "ducat," mentioned in the equivalent verse in Papaharalambous's version. The memory of the ducat would have persisted in Cyprus longer than that of a coin minted in the tenth century, of which a single example was to be found in the Cypriot Museum in 1937, so this may just be an accidental distortion.
10. At this point the song alludes to the *Donkey Tale*:

    Καὶ μία χήρα ἄπορος, καλὰ οὐκ ἐθεώρειεν,
    εἶχεν καὶ ὄρνιθαν χοντρὴ κ' ἐλάλειέ την Καβάκαν.

    [And one poor widow, who could not see well,
    she had a fat hen, which she called Kavaka.]
    (*Vita of the Esteemed Donkey* 161–62)

    Καὶ χήρα μία κακότυχη καλὰ οὐδὲν ἐθώρειε,
    νὰ 'γέρθη δὲν ἐδύνετο, νὰ κάτση δὲν ἠμπόρειε,
    Καὶ σπίτι δὲν ἐπότασε, ἀμ' εἶχε μία μπαράκα,
    εἶχε καὶ ὄρνιθα παχιὰ κ' ἐλάλειέν την Καβάκα.

    [A badly off widow, who could not see well,
    could not stand up and couldn't sit down either;
    she owned no home and only had a hut.
    She had a fat hen, which she called Kavaka.]
    (*Fair Tale of the Donkey the Wolf and the Fox* 161–62)

11. Prose in the original; as often happens in such transcriptions, the singer forgot the verses of the song here and gave the gist of them in prose.
12. Presumably, stretched like a lance (as the fox tries to escape the trap).

APPENDIX 5

COMPOUND EPITHETS

> Examining the artistic features of the work, one readily notices that through the character of his expressive devices, its author is oriented toward the classical Greek epic (mainly Homer). Among the traditional-epic artistic features that occur frequently in the *Tale* one should reckon the constantly repeated formulas, the complex epithets, the self-glorification of the heroes, and their defamation of their adversary. Hence the slowness of the action of the fable and the distinctive thoroughness of the exposition.
>
> —V. S. Šandrovskaja, "Византийская Басня «Рассказ о Четвероногих (XIV в.)»: Художвенные Особенности и Язык Памятника"

This listing incorporates all compound adjectives, verbs, and epithets in the *Tale* whose first component is a major part of speech (verb, noun, adjective). Asterisked words are well established in classical, medieval, or modern Greek and do not constitute nonce formations.

Verse	*Form*	*Gloss*
Title 1, 1	παιδιόφραστος (πεζόφραστος VCL)	entertainingly (?) phrased P; prose-phrased VCL 1
15, 32, 62, 96	εὔχρηστα*	good-used (= useful)
16, 63, 96, 816 PL, 1038 P, 1048b C	(αἱ)μοβόρα, αἱμοβόρων*	blood-eating
18	ἀγριόφθαλμος	savage-eyed
18	γαγκλαδοραδάτος	twisting-tailed
24	νυκτοβαδιστής (νυκτοβραδιαστής V)	night-stepper; night-eveninger V
25	αἱματοπότης	blood-drinker
27	φουντοουραδάτη	bush-tailed
28	ὀρνιθοπνίκτρια	hen-choker
33	νυκτοβλέπει	night-sees
34, 127	μεγαλομουστακᾶτον, μεγαλομουστακᾶτε	big-moustached

35, 127, 188	μακρύουρον, μακρύουρε, μακροουραδάτην (μικροουραδάτην L 188)	long-tailed; small-tailed L 188
35, 127, 936	μακρύμυτον, μακρόμυτε,	long-nosed
44, 327	μεγαλάπτην, μεγαλάπτη	big-eared
45	γοργοπόδαρον	swift-footed
47	φιλοφρονήσουσιν*	friend-think (= welcome)
51	πολυρράβδης	much-sticked (= much-flogged)
52	φιδορούφος	snake-sucking
53	πολυφάγος	much-eating
58	γερομουστακᾶτος	old-mustachio
82	μεγαλόψωλον (μεγαλόνευρον VL)	big-dicked
82	μεγαλορχιδᾶτον (καμηλορχιδάτον L)	big-balled; camel-balled L
84, 797	κυμπόρραχην, κυμπόρραχη	hunch-backed
84, 768	μακροσφονδυλάτην	long-necked
86	κακογυρισμένη	ill-turned
130	τζυκαλογλεῖφε	pot-licking
130	τυροφᾶ	cheese-eating
130	ψωμοκαταλύτη	bread-destroying
144	σκατοποντικέ	shit-rat
155	στακτοκυλισμένε	ash-rolled
159	ἀλευροκαταχέστη	flour–thorough-shitting
187	ἀκροτίναξα	edge-fling (= slightly fling)
216	σαλιαρομυξιάρη	drooling-snotty
233	λιθοβολοῦσι*	stone-cast
233, 666, 674, 739	ῥαβδοκοποῦν, ῥαβδοκοποῦσι(ν)*	staff-work (= beat)
238	πικροχολιασμένος (πικροχιλιασμένος P)	bitter-biled; bitter-thousanded P
240	τρυπολόγισσα	hole-working
240	βουνοαναθρεμμένη	mountain-bred
246	συχνοπυκνοκλάνης (συχνοπίνης κλάνης V)	often-densely–fart; often-drink fart V
247	κακοκοιμᾶσαι L	ill-sleep
252	χλωρόπηκτα CA; χλωρόπτηκα V; χλωρόπνικτα (*emendavimus*)	fresh-congealed (?) CA, freshly-cooked (?) V, freshly-strangled (*see* Commentary)
254	χανδρατοκουδουνᾶτον	beaded–belled

269	χαροποιούς*	joy-making
286	κοιλιοχορδοφᾶσα	belly-entrail–eating
292	μπαινοεβγαίνῃ*	enter–exit (= go in and out)
304	μεγαλομανδοῦσες	big-mantled
322, 422	φλυαροκόπε	chatter-working
326	δυόδοντε	two-toothed
326, 425	κακόδοντε (καμύδοντε 425 CA)	bad-toothed; suffering-toothed (?) 425 CA
326	σπιθαμογένη	span-bearded
327	κλαδοτρυπολόγε	branch-hole–working
338	κακόψητα*	ill-cooked
339	κακοστόμαχα*	ill-stomached
353	κοψόουρε	cut-tailed
358	κοντολογημένα*	short-worded
366	σεμιδαλαφράτον (σεμιδαλαυράτον V)	semolina-fluffy; semolina-floured (?) V
379	παχυλαρδάτας	fat-larded
385	ἀξιόλογον*	noteworthy
397	σεβοπροσκυνοῦσιν	revere-worship
399	ἱστορογραφίζουσιν (ἱστοριζογράφουσι P)	story-write; story-draw P
399	χρωματοπλουμίζουν (χριματοπλουμίζουν V)	color-decorate
413	βρωμομυξαρέα (βρωμομυξιαρίλα L)	filthy-snotty
414	σκατοβορβορόκοιλη (κατοβροβορόσκυλε A; σκατοβόρβορος αὐλή L)	shit-mire–bellied; cat-mire-dog A; shit-mired courtyard L
422	ἐμεγαλαύχησας*	big-boast
425	κοπροαναθρεμμένε	dung-bred
431	προβατομυξαρέα	sheep–snotty
436	σκατόχοιρε	shit–boar
436	βορβοροκυλισμένε	mire-rolled
459	λωλότραγον	dumb billy goat
461	κοπροφάγου*	dung-eating
462	πλατυνορρούθουνου	flat-nostriled
465, 577, 591, 785, 792, 951, 952 CVL	κακότυχη, κακότυχον, κακότυχα, κακότυχε*	ill-fortuned
468	στραβοκερέα	crooked-horned
468	πετροφαγωμένη	stone-worn
477	εὔνοστα* (εὔνοχα C; ἔνοστα P)	tasty

477	εὐστόμαχα* (εὔστοχα P)	good-stomached; well-aimed P
488	ὡραιοπλουμισμένας	beautiful-decorated
493	μεγαλοπλουμᾶτα	big-decorated
504	τζοχοϋφανδωμένα	serge-woven
525, 591	μωρόλαλον	stupid-uttering
525	κακόστομον*	bad-mouthed
529, 540, 579	λωλοπροβατίνα, λωλοπροβάτιν, λωλοπροβάτα	dumb-ewe
541, 812	ἐβαττολόγησας*	Battus-speak (= stammer)
552	ἐπολυλογήσασιν	much-speak
552	ἐμακρυλογῆσαν	long-speak
576	κακορρίζικα*	ill-fated
576a	κακόχειρα	ill-handed
584	παχυλοπετζάτας	fat-fleshed
585	πολυψαλιδάτη	much-scissored
612	βορβοροπηλοκύλιστε VC (βορβοροκωλοκύλιστε P; βορβοροπηλοκύλιε L; φορβοροπηλοκύλιστε A)	mire-arse–rolling; mire-mud–rolling VCLA
612	λιμνοαναθρεμμένη (λιμνοαναθρεμμένε A; φλυαροσκοτολόγε P φλυαροσκατολόγε *emendavimus*; φλυαροκοπρολόγε V)	lake-bred CLA; babbling-darkness–talking (= babbling-shit–talking) P; babbling-dung–talking V
612a	φλυαροκορδολόγε ACL	chattering-pride–talking
619	σφονδυλοτορνεμένας	neck-lathed
636	μαγκλαβοκοποῦσιν	club-work (= beat)
646	ἐτζιληπούρδισεν*	squirt-fart
647, 729 C	πορδοκοπῶν (τζιλοπορδοκοπῶν 647 P)	fart-working; squirt-fart–working P
650	μεγαλοματζουκᾶτον	big-clubbed
651	ῥουθωνοκεφαλᾶτον	nostril-headed
654	οἰστροκινηθῇ P	frenzy-move
657, 824, 858	δικολογηθοῦμεν, δικολογηθῶ, δικολογηθοῦσι*	trial-speak (= argue)
665	μαυροπείσματε	black-stubborn
665	ψωλογομάριν (ψωμογομάρι VC)	dick–(beast of) burden; bread–(beast of) burden VC

674	ματζουκοκοποῦν	club-work (= beat)
675	σουβλοκοποῦν	awl-work (= prod)
689	πομπογάδαρε	ridicule–donkey
696, 739	βαρεοφορτώνουν, βαρυφορτώνουσι*	heavy-load
711, 728	τζιλοπορδοκοπῶντα	squirt-fart–working
747	σκατογάδαρε	shit–donkey
750	λακτοκοπίζω*	kick-work
759	χρυσοκόλλητας	gold-stuck
759	ἀργυροδεμένας*	silver-bound
760	ἀργυροχρυσωμένα	silver-gilded
773	κουτζοπτία (κουτζουἀπτία P)	lame-eared
797	πλατύποδε*	flat-footed
797, 884	κοντοουραδάτη, κοντοουραδᾶτε	short-tailed
801	ἀργοκίνητος*	slow-moving
803	λυκοφαγωμένος	wolf-eaten
816, 856, 989 VCL, 1033	ὠμόβορον, ὠμόβορα, ὠμοβόρα*	raw-eating
833	θρασιοφᾶ	feral-eating
833	νυκτοκλέπτη*	night-thief
834	ἐντρυπολόγε (τρυπολόγε P)	in-holes–working
834	νυκτοπερπατάρη	night-walker
844	μελισσοφάγα	bee-eating
844	κοντοποδαρέα* (κοντοποδαρομύτα V, κονδοποδαρομύτα CL, κονδοποδαρομύτη A)	short-legged; short–leg-and-nosed VCLA
845	ἀλληθώρα*	other-looking (= cross-eyed)
845	χαμηλοβλεποῦσα*	low-looking
846	βρωμοφηκάρα (κορμοφηκάρα P)	filth-case; body-case P
846	μωροατζιγγάνων	foolish Gypsies
847	ἀχλαδοβαλανότροφε	pear-acorn–fed
847	μυρτοκουμαροφάγα	myrtle-arbutus–eating
867	κοπελοαναθρεμμένον	girl-bred
917	τορνοεμφωλευμένα	lathed-nested
926	σμαραγδοπλουμισμένα	emerald-decorated
939	μεγαλοχαχαλάτου (μεγαλολαχανάτου C)	big-clawed; big-cabbaged C
942	ξυλόποδε Tsiouni ὀξύποδε PCVL	wooden-legged; fast-legged PCVL

963	ἀξινογλύφουν* (τζηκουροκόπτουν L)	ax-chop
963	πριονοκοποῦν	saw-work
972	μυσεροκακομούτζουνον Tsiouni (μυρεκακομούτζουνον P, μυσεροκακομούστακον VL, μυσεροκακομούστανον C)	ugly-bad–muzzled; ugly-bad–whiskered VL
972	ψειροκονιδοφάγον	lice-nit–eating
1010, 1016, 1018 V	ὁρκοκαταλύτη(ν), ὁρκοκαταλύτης	oath-destroying
1016	μαχοποιός (κακοποιός* P)	battle-maker; evildoer P
1016 P, 1018	ὁρκοπαραβάτης, ὁρκοπαραβάτην*	oath-violator
1030	σόσπαστον	equal-broken (= very broken)
1047, 1060, 1070	ἀνεβοκατεβαίνῃ, ἀνεβοεκατέβαινεν, ἀνεβοκατεβαίνει*	ascend-descend (= go up and down)
1055	ἐχαμόδραμεν	low-run (= crawl)
1061	κακομήχανον*	ill-devising
1061	μεγαλομαστόραν	grand master

APPENDIX 6

FORMULA DENSITY IN A SAMPLE OF THE *TALE*

> And when the Bishop heard it, he procured a carriage and pair,
> while his heart was full of woe, and in a state of despair;
> he organised three search parties without delay,
> and headed one of the parties in person without dismay.
>
> —William McGonnagal, *Tragic Death of the Rev. A. H. Mackonochie*

In the following, formulas are indicated as follows (after Jeffreys 1973:183 and Papathomopoulos and Jeffreys 1996:lxxxii–lxxxv): hemistichs that are definite formulas set in boldface and underscored, whereas possible hemistich recurrences are only underscored. In the listing of comparable hemistichs, the following conventions hold:

- α and β refer to first and second hemistichs.
- = *200α* ~ means that the hemistich is fully identical to that hemistich.
- = *200α* followed by a quotation of the hemistich means that the hemistich, although not identical, differs so slightly that it should be considered a certain recurrence.
- = *200α* followed by a quotation in parentheses means the same, for an instance deemed a possible repetition.
- *cf. 200α* followed by a quotation indicates a similarity of wording that has not been counted as a formulaic repetition according to the criteria set in the introduction; the corresponding instances in the text are in italics.

Ἔχουν το εἰς τὰ λάχανα, τὰ λέγουσιν φρυγία
καὶ εἰς τὰς γούλας τὰς χοντράς, ἀλλὰ καὶ εἰς τὰ σεῦτλα,
τρώγουν το καὶ οἱ ἄρχοντες ὕστερον εἰς τὸ γεῦμα,
ὀλιγοστόν, δαμίτζικον ὡς διὰ νὰ χωνεύσουν.

Ἀκόμη καὶ τὸ κέρας μου *μεγάλην χρείαν κάμνει*·
ποιοῦν κερατοβούκινα, βαστάζουν τα στρατιῶτες

καὶ εἰς τὰ κυνηγέσια ἀλλὰ καὶ εἰς φουσσᾶτον.
Καὶ κροῦν τα καὶ φωνάζουσιν καὶ κράζει εἷς τὸν ἄλλον.
Ἔχω καὶ ἄλλα πλείονα χαρίσματα νὰ εἴπω,
ἀλλὰ ἀφήνω τα λοιπόν, **οὐκ ἔξεστί μοι λέγειν**· 610
πολυλογία γὰρ ἐστὶ τεκμήριον ζαβίας.» 610a

Τότε ὁ βοῦς ἐφθέγξατο εὐθὺς πρὸς τὴν βουβάλαν:
«Βορβοροπηλοκύλιστε, λιμνοαναθρεμμένη,
πολλά μοῦ ἐτζαμπούνισες, φλυαροκοπρόλογε. 612a
Ὅσα εἶπες διὰ λόγου σου **καὶ ὑπερεκαυχίσθης**,
ταῦτα γὰρ ἔχω καὶ ἐγὼ καὶ ἄλλα πλεῖον τούτων.

Πρῶτον ἐμὲν τὸ κέρας μου χρῶνται καλαμαράδες,
ποιοῦν τὰ καλαμάρια, ποιοῦν κονδυλοθήκας,
ἀλλὰ καὶ οἱ τορνάρηδες *εἰς ἅπασάν των χρείαν*,
εἰς θρόνους, εἰς σελία τε, εἰς σκάκους, εἰς ταβλία,
εἰς ἠλακάτας τορνευτάς, σφονδυλοτορνεμένας,
εἰς ἄκρας κονταρίων τε, εἰς ἄκρας λαντζονίων 620
καὶ εἰς ἑτέρας πλείονας δουλείας ἀναγκαίας.

Δεύτερον πάλιν νὰ εἰπῶ καὶ περὶ τῶν νευρῶν μου·
ἔχουν τα οἱ μαΐστορες, τζαγκράδες, δοξαράδες.
Νευρώνουν τὰ δοξάρια, νευρώνουν καὶ τὰς τζάγκρας.
Ἀκόμη καὶ ὁ σαγιτᾶς νευρώνει τὰς σαγίτας
καὶ ὁ σελᾶς καὶ σαμαρᾶς *χρῶνται καὶ οὗτοι ταῦτα*
καὶ ὅπου δ᾽ ἂν καὶ χρειαστοῦν, εὑρίσκουν με εἰς δέμαν.

Ἀκόμη καὶ τὸ εὐτελές τὸ ἄκρον τῆς οὐρᾶς μου,
χρῶνται αὐτὸ οἱ ἁλιεῖς εἰς ἄγραν τῶν ἰχθύων,
τὰς λέγουσιν ἀθερινάς, τὰς μικροτάτας πάνυ. 630

Ἀκόμη ἔχω νὰ εἰπῶ *καὶ νὰ λαλήσω ἄλλον*·
πολλάκις γὰρ ἂν εὑρεθοῦν καὶ γύναια ἐκεῖσε
καὶ νὰ ἀκούσουν τὸ παρὸν ἀπόφθεγμα καὶ ῥῆμα,
ἂν τύχῃ νὰ γελάσουσιν καὶ νὰ ἐμνοστευθοῦσιν.
Ἔχω καὶ νεῦρον δυνατόν, μακρὸν καὶ πυρωδάτον,
ὁποὺ τὸ ἔχουν οἱ κριταὶ καὶ μαγκλαβοκοποῦσιν
τοὺς κλέπτας καὶ τοὺς ὑβριστὰς καὶ πάντας κακεργάτας.

Περὶ δὲ τοῦ πετζίου μου **οὐκ ἔχω τί νὰ λέγω**·
ὥσπερ ὑπάρχει γὰρ τὸ σόν, οὕτως καὶ τὸ ἐδικόν μου
καὶ ὡς ὠμὸν καὶ ὡς γναπτόν *εἰς ἄλλας πάσας χρείας*. 640
Κάμνει λουρία εὔμορφα, γναμμένα μὲ τὴν στῦψιν,
χαλιναροκαπίστελα, ὀπισωμπροστελήνας
καὶ ἄλλα τούτων ὅμοια ἃ χρῶνται οἱ σελάδες.»

Ὡς ἤκουσεν ὁ γάδαρος βοὸς τὴν καυχησίαν,
πῶς ἒν τὸ νεῦρον του μακρὸν καὶ ἐξεπυρωμένον,

δαμὶν ἐτζιληπούρδισεν, ἐγκάνιξεν ὀλίγον,
πορδοκοπῶν εἰσέδραμεν, **ἐστάθη εἰς τὸ μέσον,**
ἐμπρὸς τ᾽ ἀπτία του ἔστησεν **καὶ πρὸς τὸν βοῦν ἐλάλει:**

«Ψέματα λέγεις, φλυαρέ, καὶ περισσὰ καυχᾶσαι·
ἐγὼ ἔχω νεῦρον τὸ παχύν, μεγαλοματζουκάτον, 650
μακρόν, παχὺν καὶ στιβαρόν, ῥουθωνοκεφαλάτον,
μὴ μόνον μεγαλώτερον παρὰ τὸ ἐδικόν σου,
παρὰ ᾽περβαῖνον ἅπαντα **τῶν τετραπόδων ζῴων.**

Καὶ ὅταν εἰς οἶστρον κινηθῇ καὶ πυρωθῇ ὀλίγον,
ὁμοιάζει τὸ κεφάλιν του φράγκικον σαρσαρόλιν·
Ὅμως ἐκβᾶτε τὸ λοιπόν, **ὁ βοῦς καὶ τὸ βουβάλιν·**
ἐγὼ δὲ καὶ τὸ ἄλογον **νὰ δικολογηθοῦμεν.**»

Τότε ὁ βοῦς καὶ ὁ βούβαλος ἐξέβησαν ἐκεῖθεν, 657a
ἀπῆγαν καὶ ἐστάθησαν **μετὰ τοῦ συνεδρίου.**
Τὸ φοβερὸν δὲ ἄλογον **ὡς ἤκουσεν τοὺς λόγους,**
πηδηματίτζιν ἔποικεν, ἐφόβισεν τοὺς πάντας. 660
Ἀνέβην, ἐκατέβηκεν, ἐσείσθην, ἐλυγίσθην,
τράχηλον ἐκαμάρωσεν, ἐτίναξε τὴν χήτην.
Μεγάλως ἐχρημάτισεν, **ἐστάθη εἰς τὸ μέσον**
καὶ πρὸς τὸν ὄνον ἔφησεν ῥήματα τὰ τοιαῦτα:

«Εἰπέ με, μαυροπείσματε, εἰπέ, ψωλογομάριν,
πῶς σὲ φορτώνουν, ἄτυχε, **πῶς σὲ ῥαβδοκοποῦσι.**
Φορτώνουν σε τ᾽ ἀλεύρια, σιτάριν καὶ κριθάριν,
τὰ ὄσπρια, τὰ φάβατα **καὶ ὅσα τούτων εἴδη,**
φορτώνουν σε καὶ τὸ κρασίν, ὀξίδι καὶ ἐλάδι
καὶ κουβαλεῖς καὶ τὸ νερόν, τ᾽ ἄχερα καὶ τὰ ξύλα, 670
τὰ χόρτα καὶ τὰ φρύγανα, κορμοὺς καὶ εἴ τι ἄλλον,
τὰς πέτρας, τὰ χαλίκια, τὰ βήσσαλα, τὸ χῶμα
καὶ ὅσα χρῶνται οἱ ἄνθρωποι **εἰς ἅπασαν δουλείαν,**
ταγισερὰ καὶ βρώματα ἀπάνω σου τὰ θέτουν. 673a
Ῥαβδοκοποῦν, σκοτώνουν σε *καὶ ματζουκοκοποῦν σε,*
σουβλοκοποῦν τὸν κῶλον σου μὲ σίδερα καὶ ξύλα.

Πολλάκις ἂν σὲ εὕρουσιν καὶ νὰ ποιήσῃς πραῖδαν,
ὁκάπου εἰς ἀμπέλια καὶ εἰς σπαρμένας χώρας,
κόπτουσιν τὰ αὐτία σου, χαράσσουν τὴν οὐράν σου
καὶ βάνουν καὶ χαβώνουν σε μὲ τὴν χλωρὴν τὴν βέργαν
καὶ οὔτε πίνεις οὔτε τρῴς οὔτε σεῖς τὴν οὐράν σου, 680
καὶ εἶσαι κάθαρμα, πομπὴ *καὶ γέλοιον τῶν ζῴων.*

Καὶ ἂν τύχῃ νὰ ᾽ναι καὶ κακὸν σαμάριν τὸ σὲ στρώνουν,
ἐγδέρνει καὶ τὴν ῥάχιν σου, πληγώνει τὰς πλευράς σου
καὶ τρώγουν σε συζώντανον κόρακες καὶ κουροῦνες.
Καὶ ἂν ἓν καὶ εὕρῃς καὶ νερὸν καὶ νά ᾽σαι φορτωμένος,

γυρίζεις καὶ τὸν κῶλον σου καὶ βρέχεσαι καὶ στέκεις
καὶ κάμνεις νοικοκύρην σου καὶ σκᾷ ἀπὸ τὸ κακόν του
καὶ δούδει σου καὶ ῥαβδακές, καῖνε καὶ ἀποδαγκάνεις.

Ἀκόμη, πομπογάδαρε, νὰ σὲ εἰπῶ καὶ ἄλλον,
τὸ ἤκουσα ἀπ' τοὺς γέροντας καὶ τοὺς προπάτοράς μου. 690
Ἐσεῖς ἐβάλετε βουλὴν τοιαύτην οἱ γαδάροι
καὶ ἕναν ἐξελέξατε τὸν εἴχατε φρονέα
νὰ ἀποστείλετε αὐτὸν ἕως τὸν βασιλέα,
νὰ δεηθῇ καὶ νὰ εἰπῇ καὶ νὰ παρακαλέσῃ
διὰ τὰ ἀπανωγόμια τὰ βάνουν εἰς τὴν μέσην
καὶ βαρεοφορτώνουν σας ὥστε νὰ ἀναπνῆτε,
μὲ ὁρισμὸν προστάγματος νὰ ὁρίσῃ νὰ τὸ κόψουν.
Ὁ βασιλεὺς δ' ἐπήκουσεν τὴν δέησιν τοῦ ὄνου·
κατὰ τὴν ὥραν ὥρισεν καὶ πρόσταγμαν ἐποῖκεν
καὶ ἔγραφε καὶ ὥριζε πάντας γαδουρολάτας 700

605β cf. 402β ποιεῖ καὶ τοῦτο χρεία, 513β κάμνει μεγάλας χρείας, 914β ποιοῦν μεγάλας χρείας
607α ~ 765β
610β = 539β ἂς οὐκ ἐξόν μοι λέγειν
611α cf. 428α τότε ὁ χοῖρος ἔφησεν, 843α τότε ὁ λύκος ἔφησεν
611β cf. 780β τοιαῦτα πρὸς τὸν ἵππον, 832β τοιούτους πρὸς τὸν λύκον, 843β τοιαῦτα πρὸς τὴν ἄρκον
(612α = 436β βορβοροκυλισμένε)
612αα cf. 208α πολλὰ μοῦ συντυχαίνεις, 812α πολλὰ ἐβαττολόγησας
613β = 542β ~, 553α καὶ ὑπερεκαυχίσθησαν
614α = 405α πολλάκις ἔχω το καὶ ἐγώ, 887α οὕτως τὰ ἔχω καὶ ἐγώ
(614β = 344β ἄλλα τούτων ὅσα, 487α ἄλλα τούτων πλείονα)
617β cf. 640β εἰς ἄλλας πάσας χρείας
620α cf. 620β εἰς ἄκρας λαντζονίων
620β cf. 620α εἰς ἄκρας κονταρίων τε
621α cf. 487α καὶ ἄλλα τούτων πλείονα
626β cf. 2β καὶ χρῶνται ταῦτα παῖδες
631α = 959α ὅμως ἀκμὴν νὰ σὲ εἰπῶ
631β cf. 593α καὶ νὰ λαλήσω ῥήματα
632α = 676α πολλάκις ἂν σὲ εὕρουσιν
638β = 537β ~
640β cf. 617α εἰς ἅπασάν των χρείαν
642α = 760α ~
643α cf. 487α ἄλλα τούτων πλείονα
644β cf. 181α ὁ κύων δὲ ὡς ἤκουσεν, 260α ὡς ἤκουσεν ἡ ἀλωποῦ, 267α ὁ λαγωὸς ὡς ἤκουσεν, 419α τὸ πρόβατον ὡς ἤκουσεν, 450α ὁ

χοῖρος δὲ ὡς ἤκουσεν, 453α ἡ αἶγα δὲ ὡς ἤκουσεν, 745α τὸ ἄλογον ὡς ἤκουσεν, 776α ὡς ἤκουσεν ἡ κάμηλος, 809α ὁ λύκος δέ, ὡς ἤκουσεν, 930α ὡς ἤκουσεν ἡ μαϊμοῦ
647β = 122β ~, 183β ~, 663β ~, 831β ἐστάθην εἰς τὸ μέσον, 904β ~, 934β καί ἔστη εἰς τὸ μέσον
648β = 582α καὶ πρὸς τὸν βοῦν ἐλάλησεν
(649β = 152α μεγάλως καὶ καυχᾶσαι)
653β = 14β τὰ τετράποδα ζῷα, 61α τὰ τετράποδα ζῷα, 341β ~, 1038β καὶ τετράποδα ζῷα
656β = 546α ὁ βοῦς δὲ και ὁ βούβαλος, 555β πρὸς βοῦν καὶ τὸ βουβάλιν, 657α τότε ὁ βοῦς καὶ ὁ βούβαλος, 581β ~
657β = 824α ὅμως νὰ δικολογηθῶ, 858β νὰ δικολογηθοῦσι
657aα = 569α ~; see also 656β
(658α = 180α ἀπῆλθεν καὶ ἐστάθηκεν, 195α ἐξῆλθεν καὶ ἐστάθηκεν, 315α ἐξέβη καὶ ἐστάθηκεν, 455α ἐξῆλθον καὶ ἐστάθησαν, 548α ἐξῆλθον καὶ ἐστάθησαν, 580α ἀπῆλθον καὶ ἐστάθησαν, 778α εἰσῆλθεν καὶ ἐστάθηκεν, 810α ἐξέβη καὶ ἐστάθηκεν, 831aα ἐξῆλθεν καὶ ἐστάθηκεν)
658β = 195β ~
(659α = 81α τὸ ἄλογον τὸ φοβερόν)
659β = 546β ὡς ἤκουσαν τοὺς λόγους
660α = 317α ~
661α = 1047β ν' ἀνεβοκατεβαίνῃ, 1060α ἀνεβοεκατέβαινεν, 1070β ἀνεβοκατεβαίνει
663β = 122β ~ etc.; see 647β ~
664α = 746α ~
664β = 239β καὶ ῥήματα τοιαῦτα, 811β ~
666β = 739β νὰ σᾶς ῥαβδοκοποῦσιν
668β = 134β ~
673β = 514β εἰς πᾶσαν του δουλείαν, 531β εἰς πᾶσας τὰς δουλείας, 590β ~, 594β εἰς ὅλας τὰς δουλείας
674β cf. 233β οἱ δὲ ῥαβδοκοποῦν σε
676α = 632α πολλάκις γὰρ ἂν εὑρεθοῦν
678α = 774α καὶ κόψαν τὰ αὐτία της
679α cf. 799α καὶ βάνουν καὶ φορτώνουν σε
681β cf. 775β καὶ κάθαρμα τῶν ζῴων, 802β παράσημον τῶν ζῴων, 937β παράσημον τῶν ζῴων, 942β καὶ κάθαρμα τῶν ζῴων
(685α = 245α νὰ εὕρῃς πούπετε νερόν)
(689β = 478α ἀμὴ νὰ εἴπω τὰ λοιπά, 959α ὅμως ἀκμὴν νὰ σὲ εἰπῶ)
693α cf. 73α στείλωμεν οὖν γε καὶ ἡμεῖς
695α = 715β καὶ τὸ ἀπανωγόμιν, 725β καὶ τὸ ἀπανωγόμιν, 738α καὶ τὸ ἀπανωγόμιον
696β = 739β νὰ σᾶς βαρυφορτώνουσι
700α = 724α καὶ ἔγραφεν καὶ ὥριζεν

BIBLIOGRAPHY

> Only then, after they come in direct contact with their small format, with their blue, gray or green covers, often smelling of cheese, olives, or sardines, and after they feel the crude and faded paper in their fingers, often spoiled by oil or butter stains, do they realize that they are holding a book for the masses.
>
> —G. Veloudis, *Ἡ Φυλλάδα τοῦ Μεγαλέξαντρου*

Texts

Translations are our own unless a source has been explicitly indicated in the following.

Abbatios. Legrand (1880–1913:1.331–38).
Account of Famed Venice. Bouboulidis (1967).
Achilleid L. Hesseling (1919).
Achilleid N. Smith (1999).
Achilles Tatius. Gaselee (1969 [1917]). *Translation:* Winkler (1989).
Acta Conciliorum Oecumenicorum. Schwartz (1914–40).
Acts of Docheiariou. Oikonomidès (1984).
Acts of Lavra. Lemerle, Guillou, and Svoronos (1970–82).
Additamenta in Etymologicum Gudianum. de Stefani (1965 [1909–1920]).
Aelian. Schofield (1921). *Translation:* ibid.
Aeschylus: Agamemnon. Murray (1955). *Translation*: Smyth (1926).
Aeschylus: Persians. Murray (1955). *Translation*: Smyth (1926).
Aesop: Fables. Hausrath and Hunger (1959).
Aesop: Proverbs. Perry (1952).
Aëtius: Iatricorum 1–4: Oliveri (1935). *Iatricrorum 5–8*: Oliveri (1950). *Iatricorum 12*: Kostomiris (1892). *Iatricorum 15*: Zervos (1909). *Iatricorum 16*: Zervos (1901).
Agatharchides. Müller (1855:1.111–94).
Alexander of Cyprus: Praise of Apostle Barnabas. van Deun (1993:83–122).

Alexander Romance α. Kroll (1926).
Alexander Romance β. Bergson (1965:1–192).
Alexander Romance ε. Trumpf (1974).
Alexander Romance E. Lolos and Konstantinopoulos (1983).
Alexander Romance ρ. Holton (1974).
Alexander Romance V. Mitsakis (1967).
Alexander Romance Φ. Veloudis (1977).
Alexander Romance: Learned Poetic version. Reichmann (1963).
Alphabetic Poems. Kakoulidi (1964).
Ammianus Marcellinus. Rolfe (1958). *Translation:* ibid.
Ammonius: *Fragmenta in Joannem.* Reuss (1966:196–358).
Anonymus Treu. Treu (1880). [unsighted]
Apokopos. Alexiou (1979).
Apollonius of Tyre. Wagner (1874:248–76).
Aristophanes: Acharnians. Coulon and van Daele (1923–30:1.12–66). *Translation*: Henderson (1992).
Aristophanes: Frogs. Coulon and van Daele (1923–30:4.85–157).
Aristophanes: Plutus. Coulon and van Daele (1923–30:5.89–147). *Translation*: O'Neill (1938).
Aristophanes of Byzantium. Lambros (1885).
Aristotle: De Generatione Animalium. Drossaart Lulofs (1965). *Translation*: Peck (1942).
Aristotle: Historia Animalium. Beck (1965). *Translation:* ibid.
Aristotle: *Problemata.* Bekker (1960 [1831]).
Arsenius: *Efforts and Studies.* Zampelios (1859–60). [unsighted]
Assizes of Cyprus. Sathas (1872–94:6.3–497).
Athenaeus. Kaibel (1965–66 [1887–90]).
Attaleiates: History. Bekker (1853).
Attaleiates: Legal Compilation. Zepos and Zepos (1962 [1931]:7.409–97).
Babrius. Perry (1965).
Basilica. Scheltema, Holwerda, and van der Wal (1953–88).
Basilaces. Pignani (1983:133–38).
Basil of Caesarea: Hexaemeron. Giet (1968).
Basil of Caesarea: Homilies on the Psalms. Migne (1857–87:29.209–494).
Basil of Seleucia: *Life of St. Thecla.* Dagron (1978).
Batrachomyomachia. Allen (1912:5.168–83). *Translation:* Parnell et al. (1872:29–54).
Battle of Varna. Moravcsik (1935).
Belisariad. Bakker and van Gemert (1988).
Belthandros and Chrysantza. Egea (1998). *Translation*: Betts (1995:1–32).
Bertoldo. Dalla Croce (1988).
Bertos: *Stichoplokia.* Aposkiti-Stammler (1974). [unsighted]
Book of Birds. Tsavare (1987).
Book of Fish. Winterwerb (1992:138–54).
Book of Fruit. Winterwerb (1992:252–53).
Bounialis: The Cretan War. Bounialis (1995 [1681]).
A Boy Born in the Time of the Zodiac. Kakoulidi-Panou (1980).
Byzantine Iliad. Nørgaard and Smith (1975).

Byzantine Reckoning Book. Hunger and Vogel (1963). [unsighted]
Callimachus and Chrysorrhoe. Pichard (1956).
Cantacuzene: Historiae. Schopen (1835).
Cat and Mice. Bănescu (1935).
Cedrenus. Bekker (1838–39).
Chalcocondyles: *Historiae*. Darkó (1922–27).
Choeroboscus: *Epimerismi in Psalmos*. Gaisford (1842).
Choniates, Michael: Epistulae. Lambros (1879–80:2.1–357).
Chronicle of Makhairas. Dawkins (1932). *Translation:* ibid.
Chronicle of Morea. Schmitt (1904). *Translation:* Lurier (1964).
Chronicle of the Sultans. Zoras (1958). *Translation:* Philippides (1990).
Chronicle of Tocco. Schirò (1975).
Clement of Alexandria: Protrepticus. Mondésert (1949).
Codex of Popular Remedies. Amantos (1951).
Codex Theodosianus. Momsen (1990 [1903]).
Comnena, Anna: Alexiad. Leib (1937–45).
Consolatory Speech on Misery and Happiness. Lambros (1906).
Constantine of Rhodes. Matranga (1971 [1850]:624–32).
Constantine VII Porphyrogennetus: De cerimoniis. Reiske (1829).
Critobulus: *Historiae*. Reinsch (1983:11–207).
Critobulus: Prayer. Reinsch (1983:12*–15*).
Cydones. Loernetz (1956–60).
Cypriot Love Songs. Siapkara-Pitsillidou (1976).
Cyranides. Kaimakis (1976).
Defaranas: *Instructive Words*. Karaiskakis (1934–37). [unsighted]
Della Porta. Manousakas (1995).
della Porta, Giambattista. della Porta (2001 [1658]).
Demosthenes. Butcher and Rennie (1903–31). *Translation*: Vince and Murray (1935–39).
Digenes A. Miliarakis (1881).
Digenes E. Jeffreys (1997:237–75). *Translation:* ibid.
Digenes G. Jeffreys (1997:1–235). *Translation:* ibid.
Digenes P. Paschalis (1926).
Digenes Z. Trapp (1971).
Diodorus Siculus. Vogel and Fischer (1888–1906).
Dorotheus the Abbot: Doctrina. Migne (1857–87:88.1611–1838).
Ducas. Grecu (1958).
Ecloga ad Prochiron Mutata. Zepos and Zepos (1962 [1931]:6.216–318).
Ecthesis Chronica. Lambros (1979 [1902]).
Ephraem the Syrian. Frantzolis (1995 [1988]).
Epictetus: Discourses. Schenkl (1965 [1916]:7–454). *Translation:* Oldfather (1995–96 [1925–28]:1, 2.1–437).
Epictetus: Enchiridion. Schenkl (1965 [1916]:5*–38*). *Translation*: Oldfather (1995–96 [1925–28]:2.482–537).
Erotokritos. Alexiou (1980).
Etymologicum Gudianum. de Stefani (1965 [1909–20]); Sturz (1973 [1818]:229–584).
Etymologicum Magnum. Gaisford (1967 [1848]).

Eugena. Montselese (1995 [1646]).
Eupolis. Kock (1880–88:1.258–369).
Euripides: *Electra*. Diggle (1981–94:2.59–113). *Translation*: Coleridge (1938).
Eustathius of Antioch: Commentary on the Hexaemeron. Migne (1857–87:18.708–93).
Eustathius of Thessalonica: Commentary on the Iliad. van der Valk (1971–87).
Eustathius of Thessalonica: Commentary on the Odyssey. Stallbaum (1970 [1825–26]).
Eutecnius: *Paraphrasis in Oppiani cynegetica*. Tüselmann (1900).
Fair Tale of the Donkey the Wolf and the Fox. Pochert (1991).
Falieros: *Enypnion*. van Gemert (1980).
Falieros: Story and Dream. van Gemert (1980).
Farmer's Law. Zepos and Zepos (1962 [1931]:2.65–71). *Translation*: Ashburner (1912).
Father Wine. Eideneier (1988a).
Florios and Platziaflora. Ortolá Salas (1998).
Flower of Virtue (Vienna ms.) Kakoulidi (1971).
Fortounatos. Vincent (1980).
Gabalas: *Letters*. Reinsch (1974).
Galen: De Usu Partium. Helmreich (1968 [1907–9]).
Geoponicon. Landos (1991 [1643]).
George Monachus: Chronicon. de Boor (1978).
George Monachus: Chronicon Breve. Migne (1857–87:110.41–1260).
George Monachus, Continuator. Bekker (1838:763–924).
Glycas: Annales. Bekker (1836).
Glycas: Prison Verses. Tsolakis (1959).
Gregoras. Schopen and Bekker (1829–55).
Gregory Antiochus: Epitaphia. Sideras (1990:53–201).
HDMS. Manuscript held at the Center for the Compilation of the *Historical Dictionary of Modern Greek,* Academy of Athens.
Hermoniacus. Legrand (1880–1913:5).
Herodas: Mimiambi. Cunningham (1971).
Herodotus. Legrand (1963–70). *Translation*: Godley (1920).
Hesychius. Latte (1953–66).
Hippiatrica: Excerpta Lugdunensia. Oder and Hoppe (1971 [1927]:2.272–313).
Hippocrates: Epidemiae. Littré (1961–73 [1839–61]:2.598–716, 3.24–148, 5.72–468).
Hippolytus: Fragmenta in Proverbia. Achelis (1897:169–75).
Homer: Iliad. Allen (1931). *Translation*: Murray (1924).
Homer: Odyssey. von der Mühll (1962). *Translation*: Murray (1919).
Imperios and Margarona. Kriaras (1955:215–49).
Isocrates: *Panegyricus*. Brémond and Mathieu (1929–62:15–64). *Translation*: Norlin (1980).
John Chrysostom: In Herodem et Infantes. Migne (1857–87:66.699–702).
John Damascene: *Sacra parallela*. Migne (1857–87:95–96).
John the Faster: *Penitential*. Migne (1857–87:88.1890–1918). *Translation*: Boswell (1982).
Julian: *Against the Galilaeans*. Neumann (1880:163–233).

Justin Martyr: Dialogue with Trypho. Goodspeed (1915:90–265). *Translation*: Roberts and Donaldson (1885–96:1.194–270).
Katzourbos. Politis (1964).
King Rodolino. Aposkiti (1987).
Koroneos: Bua. Sathas (1982 [1867]:1–153).
Leontius of Neapolis: Life of John the Almsgiver. Festugière (1974:343–409).
Leontius of Neapolis: Life of St. Symeon the Fool. Festugière (1974:1–222). *Translation:* Krueger (1996).
Leo the Deacon. Hase (1828).
Lexica Segueriana: Collectio verborum utilium. Bachmann (1828:3–422).
Lexica Segueriana: Glossae rhetoricae. Bekker (1814:195–318).
Lexicon Artis Grammaticae. Bachmann (1828:425–50).
Lexicon in orationes Gregorii Nazianzeni. Latte and Erbse (1965:170–88).
Life of Aesop G. Papathomopoulos (1990a).
Life of Aesop W. Papathomopoulos (1999a).
Life of Aesop (Vernacular). Papathomopoulos (1999b).
Loukanis. Loukanis (1979 [1526]).
Lydus: *De Mensibus*. Wünsch (1967 [1898]).
Manasses: Compendium Chronicum. Bekker (1837).
Mass of the Beardless Man. Eideneier (1977).
Matthew of Myrae: History of Wallachia. Legrand (1880–1913:2.231–333).
Meletius: De natura hominis. Cramer (1963 [1836]:3.5–157).
Mesarites: Description of the Church of the Apostles. Downey (1957).
Metrical Dictionaries. Miller (1874).
Michael of Ephesus: In librum de animalium incessu commentarium. Hayduck (1904:135–70).
Mirror of Women. Krumbacher (1905).
Morezinos: *Bed of Solomon*. Kakoulidi (1970). [unsighted]
Mytilenaeus: Poems. Kurtz (1903).
New Testament. Aland et al. (1968). *Translation*: King James Version.
Nicholas I: Miscellaneous Writings. Westerink (1981).
Nilus of Ancyra: *Commentary on the Song of Songs*. Guérard (1994).
Nonnus: Dionysiaca. Keydell (1959).
Oikonomu-Agorastu. Oikonomu-Agorastu (1982).
On Exile. Mavromatis (1995).
Oneirocriticon of Achmet. Drexl (1925). *Translation:* Oberhelman (1991).
Oppian: *Cynegetica*. Mair (1928:2–198).
Oribasius: Medical Compilations. Raeder (1928–33).
Origen: Against Celsus. Borret (1967–69). *Translation:* Roberts and Donaldson (1885–96:4.395–669).
Origen: Scholia in Canticum Canticorum. Migne (1857–87:17.253–88).
Origen: Selecta in Ezechielem (fragmenta e catenis). Migne (1857–87:13.768–825).
Pachymeres: *History*. Failler and Laurent (1984).
Palatine Anthology. Beckby (1965–68).
Palladius: *Historia Lausiaca*. Bartelink (1974).
Palladius: On the Races of India and the Brahmans. Berghoff (1967).
Panoria. Hortatzis (1975).
Pantechnes. Miller (1872).

Paraphrase of Nicetas Choniates. Bekker (1835).
Parastaseis. Cameron and Herrin (1984). *Translation:* ibid.
Paschal Chronicle. Dindorf (1832).
Pastor Fide (Cretan). Joannou (1962).
Patria Constantinopoleos: Preger (1901–7:2.135–283).
Philes: Exposition on the Elephant. Dübner and Lehrs (1862).
Philes: On the Features of Animals. Dübner and Lehrs (1862).
Philes: Poems. Miller (1967 [1855–57]).
Phocas: De Velitatione. Dagron and Mihăescu (1986).
Phocas: Praecepta Militaria. McGeer (1995:12–59). *Translation:* ibid.
Photius: *Amphilochia*. Laourdas and Westerink (1983–88).
Photius: Lexicon. Porson (1822).
Phrynichus: Preparatio sophistica. de Borries (1911).
Physiologus. Sbordone (1936).
Physiologus (Vernacular). Gidel and Legrand (1873).
Pindar: *Nemean*. Maehler (1971:122–62). *Translation*: Svarlien (2002).
Pisides: De Expeditione Persica. Pertusi (1959:84–136).
Plato: Laws. Burnet (1900–1907:5). *Translation*: Bury (1967–68).
Plato: Phaedo. Burnet (1900–1907:1). *Translation*: Fowler (1966).
Plato: Phaedrus. Burnet (1900–1907:2).
Pliny: Natural History. Rackham (1983). *Translation:* ibid.
Plutarch: De Sollertia Animalium. Hubert (1959 [1954]:11–75).
Plutarch: Quaestiones conviviales. Hubert (1971 [1938]:1–335).
Prochiron. Zepos and Zepos (1962 [1931]:2.107–228).
Prodromus: *Battle of Cats and Mice*. Hunger (1968).
Prodromus: For a Live Fox. Miller (1967 [1875–81]:2.531–33).
Prodromus: *Studies on the Mouse*. Papathomopoulos (1990b:217–39).
Prodromus: *To the Sebastocratorissa*. Papadimitriu (1903). [unsighted]
Psellus: *Opuscula logica*. Duffy (1992).
Psellus: Oratoria minora. Littlewood (1985).
Psellus: Poems. Westerink (1992).
Pseudo-Codinus. Verpeaux (1966).
Pseudo-Georgillas: Fall of Constantinople. Legrand (1880–1913:1.169–202).
Pseudo-Maurice: Strategicon. Mihăescu (1970).
Pseudo-Sphrantzes. Grecu (1966).
Pseudo-Zonaras. Tittmann (1808).
Ptocholeon. Kechagioglou (1978).
Ptochoprodromos. Eideneier (1991).
Raid on Paros. Kriaras (1938).
Remedies. Legrand (1880–1913:2.17–27).
Rime of Imperios. Legrand (1880–1913:1.281–322).
Rod of the Archpriests. Momferratos (1889). [unsighted]
Sachlikis: Counsels 1. Wagner (1874:62–78).
Sachlikis: Counsels 2. Wagner (1874:79–105).
Sachlikis: Strange Narrative. Papadimitriu (1896), Xanthoudidis (1980 [1909]).
Scholia et glossae in Oppiani halieutica. Bussemaker (1849:260–364).
Scholia in Acharnenses. Wilson (1975:1–150).

Scholia in Aelium Aristidem. Dindorf (1964 [1829]).
Scholia in Iliadem e cod. Genevensi gr 44. Nicole (1966 [1891]).
Scholia in Lucianum. Rabe (1971 [1906]).
Scholia in Nubes (scholia anonyma recentiora). Koster (1974:199–465).
Scholia in Plutum. Dübner (1877:323–87).
Scholia in Plutum, recensio 1. Massa Positano (1960).
Scholia in Ranas. Dübner (1877:315–22).
Scholia vetera in Iliadem. Erbse (1969–88).
Scholia vetera in Prometheum vinctum. Herington (1972).
Secundus: Sententiae. Papathomopoulos (1990b:92–114).
Septuagint. Rahlfs (1971 [1935]). *Translation*: King James Version.
Sklentzas. Kakoulidi (1967).
Socrates Scholasticus: *Historia ecclesiastica*. Bright (1893).
Sopater: Διαίρεσις Ζητημάτων. Walz (1968 [1833–35]:8.2–385).
Sophocles: Ajax. Dain and Mazon (1967–68:2.10–59). *Translation*: Jebb (1893).
Sosanna. Legrand (1880–1913:2.48–50).
Soummakis: *Pastor Fide*. Soummakis (1658). [unsighted]
Spaneas (Mavrofrydis). Mavrofrydis (1866:1–16).
Spaneas (Vatican). Lambros (1917).
Staphidas. Legrand (1880–1913:2.1–17).
Stavrinos the Vestiary. Legrand (1877:16–127). [unsighted]
Strabo. Meineke (1969 [1877]).
Suda. Adler (1928–935).
Synadinos. Odorico et al. (1996).
Synopsis Basilicorum. Zepos and Zepos (1962 [1931]:5).
Synopsis Minor. Zepos and Zepos (1962 [1931]:6.319–547).
Theodosius the Deacon. Criscuolo (1979).
Theophanes Continuator. Bekker (1838:1–481).
Theophanes the Confessor. de Boor (1883). *Translation*: Mango and Scott (1997).
Theophilus Protospatharius: On the Construction of the Human Body. Greenhill (1842).
Theophylact of Ochrid: On the Errors of the Latins. Gautier (1980:245–85).
Theophylact of Simocatta. de Boor (1972 [1887]).
Theseid. Anonymous (1529). [unsighted]
Timaeus the Sophist. Dübner (1839:971–1008).
Thomas Magister: Ecloga nominum et verborum Atticorum. Ritschl (1970 [1832]).
Timarion. Romano (1974). *Translation:* Baldwin (1984).
Timothy of Gaza. Haupt (1869). *Translation:* Bodenheimer and Rabinowitz (1949).
Trebellius Pollio: Vita Divi Claudii. Magie (1932:3.152–91). *Translation:* ibid.
Trivolis: Tagiapièra. Irmscher (1956:33–61).
Troika. Praechter (1895).
Tzetzes: Chiliades. Kiessling (1963 [1826]).
Tzetzes: Epistulae. Leone (1972).
Varoukhas. Bakker and van Gemert (1987).
Vernacular Oracles. Trapp (1964).

Vita of St. Stephen the Younger. Auzépy (1997).
Vita of the Esteemed Donkey. Pochert (1991).
Vulgar Bird Lore. Hercher (1971 [1866]:2.517–73).
War of Troy. Papathomopoulos and Jeffreys (1996).
Xenophon: *De Re Equestri*. Marchant (1900–1920:5). *Translation*: Marchant and Bowersock (1968:7).
Xenophon: *Hiero*. Marchant (1900–1920:5). *Translation*: Marchant and Bowersock (1968:7).

References

Abun-Nasr, J. M. 1975. *A History of the Maghrib*. 2d ed. Cambridge, U.K.: Cambridge University Press.
Academy of Athens. 1933–1984. *Ἱστορικὸν λεξικὸν τῆς νέας ἑλληνικῆς τῆς τε κοινῶς ὁμιλουμένης καὶ τῶν ἰδιωμάτων*. 4 vols. Athens: Ἑστία.
Achelis, H. 1897. *Hippolyts kleinere exegetische und homiletische Schriften*. (Die griechischen christlichen Schriftsteller 1.2.) Leipzig: Hinrichs.
Adler, A. 1928–1935. *Suidae lexicon*. 4 vols. (Lexicographi Graeci 1.1–1.4.) Leipzig: Teubner.
Aerts, W. 1986. "Leontios of Neapolis and Cypriot Dialect Genesis." In T. Papadopoullou and V. Englezaki, eds., *Πρακτικὰ τοῦ δευτέρου διεθνοῦς κυπριολογικοῦ συνεδρίου* (*Λευκωσία, 20–25 Ἀπριλίου 1982*), 2: 379–89. Nicosia: Ἑταιρεία Κυπριακῶν Σπουδῶν.
Agapitos, P. A., and O. L. Smith. 1994. "Scribes and Manuscripts of Byzantine Vernacular Romance: Palaeographical Facts and Editorial Implications". *Ελληνικά* 44: 61–80.
Aland, K., et al. 1968. *The Greek New Testament*. 2d ed. Stuttgart: Württemberg Bible Society.
Alderson, A. D., and İz, F. 1984. *The Oxford Turkish–English Dictionary*. 3d ed. Oxford: Clarendon Press.
Alexiou, M. 1986. "The Poverty of Écriture and the Craft of Writing: Towards a Reappraisal of the Prodromic Poems". *Byzantine and Modern Greek Studies* 10: 1–40.
——. 1999. "Ploys of Performance: Games and Play in the Ptochoprodromic Poems." *Dumbarton Oaks Papers* 53: 91–109.
Alexiou, S. 1954. "Φιλολογικαὶ παρατηρήσεις εἰς κρητικὰ κείμενα." *Κρητικὰ Χρονικά* 8: 238–72.
——. 1979. *Μπεργαδῆς, Ἀπόκοπος—Ἡ βοσκοποῦλα*. Athens: Ἑρμῆς.
——. 1980. *Ἐρωτόκριτος*. (Φιλολογικὴ βιβλιοθήκη 3.) Athens: Ἑρμῆς.
——. 1985. *Βασίλειος Διγενὴς Ἀκρίτης*. (Φιλολογικὴ βιβλιοθήκη 5.) Athens: Ἑρμῆς.
——. 1993. "*Digenes Akrites*: Escorial or Grottaferrata? An Overview." In R. Beaton and D. Ricks, eds., *Digenes Akrites: New Approaches to Byzantine Heroic Poetry,* 15–25. (Centre for Hellenic Studies, King's College London Publications 2.) London: Variorum.
Allen, T. W. 1912. *Homeri Opera*. 5 vols. Oxford: Clarendon Press.
——. 1931. *Homeri Ilias*. Oxford: Clarendon Press.
Amantos, K. 1951. "Ἰατροσοφικὸς κῶδιξ." *Ἀθηνᾶ* 43: 148–70.

Andersen, H. C. 1974. *The Complete Fairy Tales and Stories*. Translated by E. C. Haugaard. London: Victor Gollancz.

Andriotis, N. A. 1955. "Τὰ σύνθετα τοῦ γλωσσικοῦ ἰδιώματος τῆς Ἴμβρου." *Ἀρχεῖον τοῦ Θρακικοῦ Λαογραφικοῦ καὶ Γλωσσικοῦ Θησαυροῦ* 20: 225–70.

——. 1974. *Lexikon der Archaismen in neugriechischen Dialekten*. (Schriften der Balkankommisssion Lingustische Abteilung 22.) Vienna: Österreichische Akademie der Wissenschaften.

——. 1983. *Ἐτυμολογικὸ λεξικὸ τῆς κοινῆς νεοελληνικῆς*. 3d ed. Thessalonica: Aristotle University.

Angold, M. 1989. "Greeks and Latins After 1204: The Perspective of Exile." In B. Arbel, B. Hamilton, and D. Jacoby, eds., *Latins and Greeks in the Eastern Mediterranean after 1204*, 63–86. London: Frank Cass.

Anonymous. 1529. *Θησέος καὶ γάμοι τῆς Ἐμήλιας*. Venice: da Sabio.

——. 1999 [1880–1900?]. *Cinderella, or The Little Glass Slipper, and other stories*. Text available from Project Gutenberg, http://promo.net/pg, Etext #1599. Accessed September 2, 2002.

Aposkiti, M. 1987. *Ροδολίνος*. Athens: Στιγμή.

Aposkiti-Stammler, H. 1974. Nathaniel-Neilos Bertos, Vindobonensis hist. gr. 91, Nr. 59. Ph.D. diss., Ludwig-Maximilians-Universität, Munich.

Ashburner, W. 1912. "The Farmer's Law II." *Journal of Hellenic Studies* 32: 68–95.

Atanasova, T., et al. 1980. *Българско–Английски Речник*. 2d ed. Sofia: Наука и Изкуство.

Auzépy, M.-F. 1997. *La vie d'Étienne le jeune par Étienne le diacre*. (Birmingham Byzantine and Ottoman Monographs 3.) Aldershot (Hampshire): Variorum.

Babiniotis, G. D. 1998. *Λεξικό της νέας ελληνικής γλώσσας*. Athens: Κέντρο Λεξικολογίας.

Bachmann, L. 1828. *Anecdota Graeca*. Vol. 1. Leipzig: Hinrichs.

Bakker, W. F., and A. F. van Gemert. 1987. *Μανόλης Βαρούχας, Νοταριακὲς πράξεις: Μοναστηράκι Ἀμαρίου (1597–1613)*. Rethymnon: University of Crete.

——. 1988. *Ἱστορία τοῦ Βελισαρίου*. (Βυζαντινὴ καὶ νεοελληνικὴ βιβλιοθήκη 6.) Athens: Μορφωτικὸ Ἵδρυμα Ἐθνικῆς Τραπέζης.

Baldwin, B. 1984. *Timarion*. Detroit: Wayne State University Press.

Bănescu, M. 1935. "Un poème grec vulgaire du Moyen-Age: Ὁ κάτης καὶ οἱ ποντικοί." In *Εἰς μνήμην Σπυρίδωνος Λάμπρου*, 393–97. Athens: Self-published.

Bantaş, A. 1995 [1993]. *NTC's Romanian and English Dictionary*. Lincolnwood Ill.: NTC Publishing Group.

Bartelink, G. J. M. 1974. *Palladio. La storia Lausiaca*. Verona: Fondazione Lorenzo Valla.

Bäuml, F. H. 1984. "Medieval Texts and the Two Theories of Oral-Formulaic Composition: A Proposal for a Third Theory." *New Literary History* 16: 31–49.

Beaton, R. 1989. *The Medieval Greek Romance*. 1st ed. Cambridge, U.K.: Cambridge University Press.

——. 1990. "Orality and the Reception of Byzantine Vernacular Literature." *Byzantine and Modern Greek Studies* 14: 174–84.

——. 1993. "An Epic in the Making? The Early Versions of Digenes Akrites." In R. Beaton and D. Ricks, eds., *Digenes Akrites: New Approaches to Byzantine Heroic Poetry*, 55–72. Brookfield, Vt.: Variorum.

——. 1996. *The Medieval Greek Romance.* 2d ed. London: Routledge.

Beaton, R., and D. Ricks, eds. 1993. *Digenes Akrites: New Approaches to Byzantine Heroic Poetry*. Brookfield, Vt.: Variorum.

Beck, A. L. 1965. *Aristotle: Historia animalium.* 2 vols. (Loeb Classical Library.) Cambridge, Mass.: Harvard University Press.

Beck, H.-G. 1971. *Geschichte der byzantinischen Volksliteratur*. Munich: Beck.

——. 1978. *Das byzantinische Jahrtausend*. Munich: Beck.

Beckby, H. 1965–1968. *Anthologia Graeca.* 2d ed. 4 vols. Munich: Heimeran.

Bedini, S. A. 2000 [1997]. *The Pope's Elephant.* New York: Penguin.

Bekker, I. 1814. *Anecdota Graeca.* Vol. 1. Berlin: Nauck.

——. 1835. *Nicetae Choniatae historia.* (Corpus scriptorum historiae Byzantinae.) Bonn: Weber.

——. 1836. *Michaelis Glycae annales.* (Corpus scriptorum historiae Byzantinae.) Bonn: Weber.

——. 1837. *Constantini Manassis breviarium historiae metricum.* (Corpus scriptorum historiae Byzantinae 28.) Bonn: Weber.

——. 1838. *Theophanes Continuatus, Ioannes Cameniata, Symeon Magister, Georgius Monachus.* (Corpus scriptorum historiae Byzantinae 45.) Bonn: Weber.

——. 1838–1839. *Georgius Cedrenus Ioannis Scylitzae ope.* 2 vols. (Corpus scriptorum historiae Byzantinae.) Bonn: Weber.

——. 1853. *Michaelis Attaliotae historia.* (Corpus scriptorum historiae Byzantinae 48.) Bonn: Weber.

——. 1960 [1831]. *Aristotelis opera.* Vol. 2. Berlin: de Gruyter.

Berghoff, W. 1967. *Palladius. De gentibus Indiae et Bragmanibus.* Meisenheim am Glan: Hain.

Bergson, L. 1965. *Der griechische Alexanderroman. Rezension* β. Stockholm: Almqvist and Wiksell.

Berthelot, M., and C. É. Ruelle. 1888. *Collection des anciens alchémistes grecs.* 2 vols. Paris: Steinheil.

Best, T. W. 1983. *Reynard the Fox.* Boston: Twayne.

Betts, G. 1995. *Three Medieval Greek Romances.* (Garland Library of Medieval Literature 98.) New York: Garland.

Bodenheimer, F. S., and A. Rabinowitz. 1949. *Timotheus of Gaza on Animals.* (Collection de Travaux de l'Académie Internationale d'Histoire des Sciences 3.) Leiden: E. J. Brill.

Boerio, G. 1960 [1867]. *Dizionario del dialetto veneziano.* 3d ed. Turin: Bottega d'Erasmo.

Borret, M. 1967–1969. *Origène: Contre Celse.* 4 vols. (Sources chrétiennes 132, 136, 147, 150.) Paris: Cerf.

Boswell, J. 1982. *Christianity, Social Tolerance, and Homosexuality.* Chicago: University of Chicago Press.

——. 1994. *Same Sex Unions in Pre-Modern Europe.* New York: Villard.

Bouboulidis, P. K. 1964. "Ἀνέκδοτοι παραλλαγαὶ δημωδῶν μεσαιωνικῶν κειμένων Α΄: Ὁ κῶδιξ Κωνσταντινουπόλεως 35." *Ἀθηνᾶ* 67: 107–45.

——. 1967. "Διήγησις τῆς φουμιστῆς Βενετίας." *Ἀθηνᾶ* 69: 181–190.
Bounialis, M. T. 1995 [1681]. *Ὁ κρητικὸς πόλεμος*. Edited by S. Alexiou and M. Aposkiti. Athens: Στιγμή.
Bowman, S. B. 1985. *The Jews of Byzantium: 1204–1453*. University: University of Alabama Press.
Brémond, É., and G. Mathieu. 1929–1962. *Isocrate, Discours*. 5 vols. Paris: Belles Lettres.
Bright, W. 1893. *Socrates' Ecclesiastical History*. 2d ed. Oxford: Clarendon Press.
Browning, R. 1978. "The Language of Byzantine Literature." In S. J. Vryonis, ed., *The Past in Medieval and Modern Greece,* 103–33. (Byzantina kai Metabyzantina 1.) Malibu: Undena.
——. 1980. *The Byzantine Empire*. London: Weidenfeld and Nicolson.
——. 1983. *Medieval and Modern Greek*. 2d ed. Cambridge, U.K.: Cambridge University Press.
Burnet, J. 1900–1907. *Platonis opera*. 5 vols. Oxford: Clarendon Press.
Bury, R. G. 1967–1968. *Plato in Twelve Volumes*. Vols. 10–11. (Loeb Classical Library.) Cambridge, Mass.: Harvard University Press.
Bussemaker, U. C. 1849. *Scholia et paraphrases in Nicandrum et Oppianum in Scholia in Theocritum*. Paris: Didot.
Butcher, S. H., and W. Rennie. 1903–1931. *Demosthenis Orationes*. 3 vols. Oxford: Clarendon Press.
Byzantius, S. D. 1874. *Λεξικὸν τῆς καθ' ἡμᾶς ἑλληνικῆς διαλέκτου μεθερμηνευμένης εἰς τὸ ἀρχαῖον ἑλληνικὸν καὶ τὸ γαλλικόν*. 3d ed. Athens: Κορομηλᾶς.
Cameron, A., and J. Herrin. 1984. *Constantinople in the Early Eighth Century: The* Parastaseis Syntomoi Chronikai. (Columbia Studies in the Classical Tradition 10.) Leiden: E. J. Brill.
Caracausi, G. 1990. *Lessico Greco della Sicilia e dell'Italia Meridionale (secoli 10–14)*. (Lessici Siciliani 6.) Palermo: Centro di Studi Filologici e Linguistici Siciliani.
Carrington, R. 1959. *Elephants: A Short Account of their Natural History, Evolution, and Influence on Mankind*. New York: Basic Books.
Chakalov, G., I. Ljakov, and Z. Stankov. 1961. *Българско–Английски Речник*. Sofia: Наука и Изкуство.
Chaucer, G. 1975. *The Portable Chaucer*. Translated by T. Morrison. New York: Viking Press.
Cherry, J. 1992. *Medieval Craftsmen: Goldsmiths*. Toronto: University of Toronto Press.
Christodoulou, M. N. 1983. "Κυπριακαὶ κανονικαὶ διατάξεις." *Ἐπετηρὶς τοῦ Κέντρου Ἐπιστημονικῶν Ἐρευνῶν* 12: 329–490.
Christofilopoulou, A. A. 1949. "Ἡ σύγκλητος εἰς τὸ βυζαντινὸν κράτος." *Ἐπετηρὶς τοῦ Ἀρχείου τῆς Ἱστορίας τοῦ Ἑλληνικοῦ Δικαίου* 2.
Christovasilis, C. 1988. *Διηγήματα τῆς στάνης*. (Ἡ πεζογραφική μας παράδοση A.22.) Athens: Νεφέλη.
Clanchy, M. T. 1979. *From Memory to Written Record: England 1066–1307*. London: Arnold.
Coleridge, E. P. 1938. "Electra." In W. J. Oates and E. O'Neill Jr., eds., *The Complete Greek Drama*. 2 vols. New York. Random House.

Copeman, W. S. C. 1964. *A Short History of the Gout and the Rheumatic Diseases.* Berkeley: University of California Press.
Cortelazzo, M. 1970. *L'Influsso linguistico greco a Venezia.* (Linguistica 2.) Bologna: Prof. Riccardo Pàtron.
Costakis, T. 1986. *Λεξικό της τσακωνικής διαλέκτου.* 3 vols. Athens: Academy of Athens.
Coulon, V., and van Daele, M. 1923–1930. *Aristophane.* 5 vols. Paris: Les Belles Lettres.
Cramer, J. A. 1963 [1836]. *Anedcota Graeca e codicis manuscriptis bibliothecarum Oxonensium.* 4 vols. Amsterdam: Adolf M. Hakkert.
Crane, G., ed. 2002. Perseus Digital Library. http://www.perseus.tufts.edu. Accessed September 2, 2002.
Criscuolo, H. 1979. *Theodosii diaconi de Creta capta.* Leipzig: Teubner.
Cunningham, I. C. 1971. *Herodas. Mimiambi.* Oxford: Clarendon Press.
Cupane, C. 1974. "'Ἔρως–βασιλεύς': La figura di Eros nel romanzo bizantino d'amore." *Atti del Accademia di Arti di Palermo, serie 4* 33(2): 243–97.
——. 1994–1995. "Δεῦτε, προσκαρτερήσατε μικρόν, ὦ νέοι πάντες. Note sulla ricezione primaria e sul pubblico della letteratura greca medievale." *Δίπτυχον* 6: 147–68.
Cutler, A. 1985. "The Elephants in the Great Palace Mosaic." *Bulletin de l'Association internationale pour l'étude de la mosaïque ancienne* 10: 125–38.
Dagron, G. 1978. *Vie et miracles de sainte Thècle.* (Subsidia hagiographica 62.) Brussels: Societé des Bollandistes.
Dagron, G., and H. Mihăescu. 1986. *Le traité sur la guèrilla de l'empereur Nicéphore Phocas (963–969).* Paris: Editions du Centre National de la Recherche Scientifique.
Dain, A., and P. Mazon. 1967–1968. *Sophocle.* Rev. ed. 3 vols. Paris: Les Belles Lettres.
Dalla Croce, G. C. 1988. *Ὁ Μπερτόλδος καὶ ὁ Μπερτολδίνος.* Edited by A. Angelou. (Νέα ἑλληνικὴ βιβλιοθήκη ΔΠ 49.) Athens: Ἑρμῆς.
Dankoff, R. 1991. *The Intimate Life of an Ottoman Statesman, Melek Ahmed Pasha (1588–1662), as Portrayed in Evliya Çelebi's* Book of Travels (Seyahat-Name). Albany: State University of New York Press.
Darkó, E. 1922–1927. *Laonici Chalcocandylae historiarum demonstrationes.* 2 vols. Budapest: Academia Litterarum Hungarica.
Dawkins, R. M. 1916. *Modern Greek in Asia Minor.* Cambridge, U.K.: Cambridge University Press.
——. 1932. *Recital Concerning the Sweet Land of Cyprus entitled "Chronicle."* 2 vols. Oxford: Clarendon Press.
de Boor, C. 1883. *Theophanis chronographia.* Leipzig: Teubner.
——. 1972 [1887]. *Theophylacti Simocattae historiae.* Stuttgart: Teubner.
——. 1978. *Georgii monachi chronicon.* 2 vols. Stuttgart: Teubner.
de Borries, J. 1911. *Phrynichi sophistae praeparatio sophistica.* Leipzig: Teubner.
December, J. 1993. "Characteristics of Oral Culture in Discourse on the Net." Paper presented at the Twelfth Annual Penn State Conference on Rhetoric and Composition, University Park, Pennsylvania, July 8, 1993. http://www.december.com/john/papers/pscrc93.txt. Accessed September 2, 2002.

Decharme, P. 1873. "Extraits d'un lexique manuscript latin–Grec ancien et Grec moderne." *Annuaire de l'Association pour l'encouragement des études grecques en France* 7: 100–113.

della Porta, G. 2001 [1658]. *Natural Magick (Magiae naturalis)*. Anonymous translation. http://members.tscnet.com/pages/omard1/jportat2.html. Accessed September 2, 2002.

de Stefani, A. 1965 [1909–1920]. *Etymologicum Gudianum, fasc. 1 & 2*. 2 vols. Amsterdam: Hakkert.

Diggle, J. 1981–1994. *Euripidis fabulae*. 3 vols. Oxford: Clarendon Press.

Dimaras, C. T. 1972. *A History of Modern Greek Literature*. Translated by M. P. Gianos. Albany: State University of New York Press.

Dimitrakos, D. 1936–1950. *Μέγα λεξικὸν τῆς ἑλληνικῆς γλώσσης*. 15 vols. Athens: Δημητράκος.

Dindorf, L. 1832. *Chronicon paschale*. 2 vols. (Corpus scriptorum historiae Byzantinae 16–17.) Bonn: Weber.

Dindorf, W. 1964 [1829]. *Aristides*. Vol. 3. Hildesheim: Georg Olms.

Dittenberger, W. 1915–1924. *Sylloge Inscriptionum Graecorum*. 3d ed. 4 vols. Leipzig: S. Hirzel.

Dölger, F. 1962a. "Παιδιόφραστος—πεζόφραστος." *Zeitschrift für Balkanologie* 1: 6–8.

——. 1962b. "Note." *Byzantinische Zeitschrift* 55: 350.

——. 1964. *Byzanz und die europäische Staatenwelt*. 2d ed. Darmstadt: Wissenschaftliche Buchgesellschaft.

Downey, G. 1957. "Nikolaos Mesarites: Description of the Church of the Holy Apostles at Constantinople." *Transactions of the American Philosophical Society* N.S. 47: 855–925.

Drexl, F. 1925. *Achmetis Oneirocriticon*. Leipzig: Teubner.

Drossaart Lulofs, H. J. 1965. *Aristotelis de generatione animalium*. Oxford: Clarendon Press.

Drvodelić, M. 1953. *Hrvatsko-Engleski Rječnik*. Zagreb: Školska Knjiga.

Dübner, F. 1839. *Platonis opera quae feruntur omnia*. Zurich: Meyer und Zeller.

——. 1877. *Scholia Graeca in Aristophanem*. Paris: Didot.

Dübner, F., and F. S. Lehrs. 1862. "Manuelis Philae versus iambici de proprietate animalium." In C. F. Ameis, et al., eds., *Poetae bucolici et didacti*. Paris: Didot.

Du Cange, C. F. 1954 [1678]. *Glossarium mediae et infimae latinitatis*. 5 vols. Graz: Akademische Druck- und Verlaganstalt.

——. 1958 [1688]. *Glossarium ad scriptores mediae et infimae Graecitatis*. Graz: Akademische Druck- und Verlaganstalt.

Duffy, J. M. 1992. *Michaelis Pselli philosophica minora*. Leipzig: Teubner.

Duggan, J. J. 1973. *The Song of Roland: Formulaic Style and Poetic Craft*. Berkeley: University of California Press.

Egea, J. M. 1998. *Historia Extraordinaria de Beltandro y Crisanza*. (Biblioteca Neogriega 1.) Granada: Athos–Pergamos.

Eideneier, H. 1964. "Zu den Ptochoprodromika." *Byzantinische Zeitschrift* 57: 329–37.

——. 1976. "Review of Tsiouni, V. Παιδιόφραστος διήγησις τῶν ζώων τῶν τετραπόδων." *Ἑλληνικά* 29: 453–60.

——. 1977. *Spanos: Eine byzantinische Satire in der Form einer Parodie.* (Supplementa Byzantina Texte und Untersuchungen 5.) Berlin: de Gruyter.

——. 1979. "Ein byzantinisches Kalendergedicht in der Volkssprache." *Ἑλληνικά* 31: 368–419.

——. 1982. "Zum Stil der byzantinischen Tierdichtung." *Jahrbuch Österreichischer Byzantinistik* 32: 301–06.

——. 1982–1983. "Leser oder Hörerkreis? Zur byzantinischen Dichtung in der Volkssprache." *Ελληνικά* 34: 119–50.

——. 1983. "Zur mündlichen Überlieferung byzantinischen Dichtung in der Volkssprache." *Homonoia* 5: 218–41.

——. 1985. "Ο προφορικός χαρακτήρας της νεοελληνικής λογοτεχνίας." *Δωδώνη* 14: 39–51.

——. 1987. "Μεσαιωνική ποίηση καὶ οἱ ἀπολήξεις της σὲ νεώτερα κυπριακὰ τραγούδια." In T. Papadopoulos and G. K. Ioannidis, eds., *Πρακτικὰ τοῦ δευτέρου διεθνοῦς κυπριολογικοῦ συνεδρίου* (*Λευκωσία, 20–25 Ἀπριλίου 1982*), 3: 415–23. Nicosia: Ἑταιρεία Κυπριακῶν Σπουδῶν.

——. 1988a. *Krasopateras.* (Neograeca Medii Aevi 3.) Cologne: Romiosini.

——. 1988b. "Review of Tsavare, I. *Ὁ Πουλολόγος.*" *Südost-Forschungen* 47: 481–83.

——. 1991. *Ptochoprodromos.* (Neograeca Medii Aevi 5.) Cologne: Romiosini.

——. 1993. "Lexikalisches zur byzantinischen Tierdichtung." In H. Hockwerda, E. R. Smits, and M. M. Woesthuis, eds., *Polyphonia Byzantina: Studies in Honour of Willem J. Aerts,* 275–81. (Mediaevalia Groningana Fasciculus 13.) Groningen: Egbert Forsten.

——. 1995. "Wie schreit der griechische Esel?" In A. D. Lazaridis, V. Barras, and T. Birchler, eds., *Βουκόλεια: Mélanges offerts à Bertrand Bouvier,* 175–79. Paris: Edition des Belles-Lettres.

Eideneier, H., U. Moennig, and N. Toufexis, eds. 2001. *Θεωρία και πράξη των εκδόσεων της υστεροβυζαντινής αναγεννησιακής και μεταβυζαντινής δημώδους γραμματείας: Πρακτικά του διεθνούς συνεδρίου Neograeca Medii Aevi 4a.* Iraklio: Πανεπιστημειακές Εκδόσεις Κρήτης.

el-Fers, M. 1993. *Mevlânâ.* (Passatempo Biografie.) Amsterdam: Jan Mets.

Erbse, H. 1969–1988. *Scholia Graeca in Homeri Iliadem (scholia vetera).* 7 vols. Berlin: de Gruyter.

Failler, A., and V. Laurent. 1984. *Georges Pachymérès. Relations historiques.* 2 vols. (Corpus fontium historiae Byzantinae 24.1–2, Series Parisiensis.) Paris: Les Belles Lettres.

Festugière, A. J. 1974. *Léontios de Néapolis: Vie de Syméon le Fou et Vie de Jean de Chypre.* (Institut Français d'Archéologie de Beyrouth Bibliothèque Archéologique et Historique 95.) Paris: Librairie Orientaliste Paul Geuthner.

Fiennes, R. 1976. *The Order of Wolves.* Indianapolis: Bobbs-Merrill.

Fletcher, R. 1976. "The Epic of Digenis Akritas and the Akritic Songs: A Short Guide to Bibliography." *Mantatoforos* 8: 8–12.

Fowler, H. N. 1966. *Plato in Twelve Volumes.* Vol. 1. (Loeb Classical Library.) Cambridge, Mass.: Harvard University Press.

Frantzolis, K. G. 1995 [1988]. *Ὁσίου Ἐφραίμ τοῦ Σύρου ἔργα*. 7 vols. Thessalonica: Τό Περιβόλι τῆς Παναγίας.

Frisk, H. 1970. *Griechisches etymologisches Wörterbuch*. 2 vols. Heidelberg: Carl Winter.

Gaisford, T. 1842. *Georgii Choerobosci epimerismi in Psalmos*. Oxford: Clarendon Press.

——. 1967 [1848]. *Etymologicum magnum*. Amsterdam: Adolf M. Hakkert.

Garantoudis, E. 1993. "Προβλήματα περιγραφής και ανάλυσης των πρωτονεοελληνικών δεκαπεντασύλλαβων: η μετρική αποκατάσταση των δημωδών κειμένων." In N. Panagiotakis, ed., *Αρχές της νεοελληνικής λογοτεχνίας*, 1: 118–227. Venice: Biblioteca dell'Istituto Ellenico di Studi Bizantini e Postbizantini di Venezia.

Gardthausen, V. 1913. *Griechische Palaeographie*. 2 vols. Leipzig: Veit und Comp.

Gaselee, S. 1969 [1917]. *Achilles Tatius*. (Loeb Classical Library.) Cambridge, Mass.: Harvard University Press.

Gautier, P. 1980. *Théophylacte d'Achrida: Discours, traités, poésies*. (Corpus Fontium Historiae Byzantinae 16/1.) Thessalonica: Association de Recherches Byzantines.

Giangoullis, K. 1988–1990. *Ετυμολογικό και ερμηνευτικό λεξικό της κυπριακής διαλέκτου*. 3 vols. (Βιβλιοθήκη κυπρίων λαϊκών ποιητών 51.) Nicosia: Self-published.

Giannakopoulos, G., and E. Siarenos. 1978. *Ἄριστον ἑλληνο-ἀγγλικὸν λεξικόν*. 2 vols. Athens: Michigan Press.

Gidel, A. C. 1866. *Études sur la littérature grecque moderne: Imitations en grec de nos romans de chevalerie dépuis le XII*[e] *siècle*. Paris: Auguste Durand et Pedone Lauriel.

Gidel, A. C., and É. Legrand. 1873. "Étude sur un poëme grec inédit intitulé Ὁ Φυσιολόγος." *Annuaire de l'Association pour l'encouragement des études grecques en France* 7: 225–86.

Giet, S. 1968. *Basile de Césarée. Homélies sur l'Hexaéméron*. 2d ed. (Sources chrétiennes 26bis.) Paris: Cerf.

Godley, A. D. 1920. *Herodotus*. (Loeb Classical Library.) Cambridge, Mass.: Harvard University Press.

Goodspeed, E. J. 1915. *Die ältesten Apologeten*. Göttingen: Vandenhoeck und Ruprecht.

Grecu, V. 1958. *Istoria turco-bizantina* (1341–1462). Bucharest: Editura Academiei Republicii Populaire Romîne.

——. 1966. *Georgios Sphrantzes Memorii* 1401–1477. Bucharest: Academie Republicii Socialiste Românii.

Greenfield, R. P. H. 1988. *Traditions of Belief in Late Byzantine Demonology*. Amsterdam: Adolf M. Hakkert.

Greenhill, G. A. 1842. *Theophili Protospatharii de corporis humani fabrica libri v*. Oxford: Oxford University Press.

Grujić, B. 1977. *Rečnik Englesko–Srpskohrvatski Srpskohrvatski–Engleski*. Belgrade–Zagreb: Obod–Cetinje.

Grumel, V. 1958. *La Chronologie*. (Bibliothèque Byzantine 1.) Paris: Presses Universitaires de France.

Guérard, M.-G. 1994. *Nil d'Ancyre. Commentaire sur le Cantique des cantiques.* (Sources chrétiennes 403.) Paris: Cerf.

Haist, M. 1999. "The Lion, Bloodline, and Kingship." In D. Hassig, ed., *The Mark of the Beast: The Medieval Bestiary in Art, Life and Literature,* 3–21. (Garland Medieval Casebooks 22.) New York: Garland.

Halecki, O. 1930. *Un empereur de Byzance à Rome; Vingt ans de travail pour l'union des églises et pour la défense de l'Empire d'Orient, 1355–1375.* Warsaw: Nakładem Towarzystwa Naukowego Warszawskiego.

Halo, T. 2000. *Not Even My Name.* New York: Picador.

Handrinos, G., and A. Dimitropoulos. 1999. *Ἁρπακτικά πουλιά τῆς Ἑλλάδας.* Athens: Efstathadis.

Hase, K. B. 1828. *Leonis diaconi Caloënsis historiae libri decem.* (Corpus scriptorum historiae Byzantinae 5.) Bonn: Weber.

Hatzidakis, G. N. 1977. *Γλωσσολογικαὶ ἔρευναι.* 2 vols. (Κέντρον συντάξεως τοῦ Ἱστορικοῦ Λεξικοῦ, Λεξικογραφικὸν Δελτίον Παράρτημα 2.) Athens: Academy of Athens.

——. 1989–1990 [1905–1907]. *Μεσαιωνικὰ καὶ νέα ἑλληνικά.* 2 vols. Amsterdam: Adolf M. Hakkert.

Hatzigiakoumis, M. K. 1977. *Τὰ μεσαιωνικὰ δημώδη κείμενα: Συμβολὴ στὴ μελέτη καὶ στὴν ἔκδοσή τους.* Athens: Self-published.

Hatzioannou, K. P. 1934–1937. "Κυπριακὰ τραγούδια." *Λαογραφία* 11: 605–33.

Haupt, M. 1869. "Excerpta ex Timothei Gazaei libris de animalibus." *Hermes* 3: 1–30, 174.

Hausrath, A., and H. Hunger. 1959. *Corpus fabularum Aesopicarum.* 2d ed. Leipzig: Teubner.

Hayduck, M. 1904. *Michaelis Ephesii in libros de partibus animalium, de animalium motione, de animalium incessu commentaria.* (Commentaria in Aristotelem Graeca 5.) Berlin: Reimer.

Helmreich, G. 1968 [1907–1909]. *Galeni de usu partium libri xvii.* Amsterdam: Adolf M. Hakkert.

Henderson, J. 1992. *Acharnians.* Newburyport, Mass.: Focus Classical Library.

Heptner, V. H., and A. A. Sludskii. 1992. *Mammals of the Soviet Union. Vol. 3, Carnivores (Feloidea).* Translation edited by R. S. Hoffmann. Washington: Smithsonian Institute and the National Science Foundation.

Herbermann, C. G., et al., eds. 2000. The Catholic Encyclopaedia. http://newadvent.org/cathen. Accessed September 2, 2002.

Hercher, R. 1971 [1866]. *Claudii Aeliani de natura animalium libri xvii, varia historia, epistolae, fragmenta.* 2 vols. Graz: Akademische Druck und Verlaganstalt.

Herington, C. J. 1972. *The Older Scholia on the Prometheus Bound.* Leiden: E. J. Brill.

Herrin, J. 1999. *A Medieval Miscellany.* London: Weidenfeld and Nicolson.

Herzfeld, M. 1986 [1982]. *Ours Once More: Folklore, Ideology, and the Making of Modern Greece.* New York: Pella.

Hesseling, D. C. 1919. "L'Achilléïde Byzantine." *Verhandelingen der Koninklijke Akademie van Wetenschappen te Amsterdam, Afdeeling Letterkunde* N.S. 19.3.

——. 1924. "Note critiques sur deux poèmes grecs du Moyen Age." *Byzantion* 1: 305–16.
Hesseling, D. C., and H. Pernot. 1910. "Poèmes prodromiques en grec vulgaire." *Verhandelingen der Koninklijke Akademie van Wetenschappen te Amsterdam, Afdeeling Letterkunde* N.S. 11.1.
Hioutas, P. 1978. *Κυπριακή λαογραφία τῶν ζώων*. Nicosia: Κέντρον Ἐπιστημονικῶν Ἐρευνῶν.
Holton, D. 1974. *The Tale of Alexander: The Rhymed Version*. (Βυζαντινὴ καὶ νεοελληνικὴ βιβλιοθήκη 1.) Thessalonica: Self-published.
Horrocks, G. 1997. *Greek: A History of the Language and Its Speakers*. London: Longman.
Hortatzis, G. 1975. *Πανώρια*. Edited by E. Kriaras. (Βυζαντινὴ καὶ νεοελληνικὴ βιβλιοθήκη 2.) Athens: Self-published.
Hubert, C. 1959 [1954]. *Plutarchi moralia*. Vol. 6.1. Leipzig: Teubner.
——. 1971 [1938]. *Plutarchi moralia*. Vol. 4. Leipzig: Teubner.
Hunger, H. 1958. *Byzantinische Geisteswelt*. Baden-Baden: Holle.
——. 1968. *Der byzantinische Katz-Mäuse-Krieg*. (Byzantina Vindobonensia 3.) Vienna, Cologne, Graz: Böhlau.
——. 1978. *Die hochsprachliche profane Literatur der Byzantiner*. Munich: Beck.
Hunger, H., and K. Vogel. 1963. *Ein byzantinisches Rechenbuch des 15. Jahrhunderts*. (Österreichische Akademie der Wissenschaften, philosophosche-historische Klasse, Denkschriften 78 II.) Vienna: Österreichische Akademie der Wissenschaften.
Hutter, I. (ed.) 1977–1997. *Corpus der Byzantinischen Miniaturenhandschriften*. 5 vols. Stuttgart: Hiersemann.
Inalcik, H. 1973. *The Ottoman Empire: The Classical Age 1300–1600*. Translated by N. Itzkowitz and C. Imber. London: Weidenfeld and Nicolson.
Irmscher, J. 1956. *Τριβώλης, Ἰάκωβος: Ποιήματα*. (Berliner Byzantinische Arbeiten 1.) Berlin: Akademie-Verlag.
Irving, T. B. 1980. *Kalilah and Dimnah: An English Version of Bidpai's Fables Based Upon Ancient Arabic and Spanish Manuscripts*. Newark, Del.: Juan de la Cuesta.
Jacoby, D. 1989. "From Byzantium to Latin Romania: Continuity and Change." In B. Arbel, B. Hamilton, and D. Jacoby, eds., *Latins and Greeks in the Eastern Mediterranean after 1204,* 1–44. London: Frank Cass.
Jannaris, A. N. 1897. *An Historical Greek Grammar*. London: Macmillan.
Jeanselme, E. 1920. "La goutte à Byzance." *Société française d'histoire de la médécine* 14: 137–64.
Jebb, R. 1893. *The Ajax of Sophocles*. Cambridge, U.K.: Cambridge University Press.
Jeffreys, E. M. 1975. "Constantine Hermoniakos and Byzantine Education." *Δωδώνη* 4: 81–109.
——. 1993. "The Grottaferrata Version of Digenes Akrites: A Reassessment." In R. Beaton and D. Ricks, eds., *Digenes Akrites: New Approaches to Byzantine Heroic Poetry,* 26–37. (Centre for Hellenic Studies, King's College London Publications 2.) London: Variorum.
——. 1997. *Digenes Akrites*. Oxford: Oxford University Press.

Jeffreys, E. M., and M. J. Jeffreys. 1971. "Imberios and Margarona: The Manuscripts, Sources and Edition of a Byzantine Verse Romance." *Byzantion* 41: 122–60.

——. 1979. "The Traditional Style of Early Demotic Greek Verse." *Byzantine and Modern Greek Studies* 5: 115–39.

——. 1983. "The Style of Byzantine Popular Poetry: Recent Work." In C. Mango and O. Pritsak, eds., *Okeanos: Essays Presented to Ihor Ševčenko on His Sixtieth Birthday by His Colleagues and Students,* 309–43. (Harvard Ukranian Studies 7.) Cambridge, Mass.: Harvard University Press.

——. 1986. "The Oral Background of Byzantine Popular Poetry." *Oral Tradition* 1(3): 504–47.

Jeffreys, M. J. 1973. "Formulas in the Chronicle of the Morea". *Dumbarton Oaks Papers* 27: 164–95.

——. 1974. "The Nature and Origins of the Political Verse." *Dumbarton Oaks Papers* 28: 141–95.

——. 1996. "Editorial Politics and the Mediaeval Greek War of Troy." *Parergon* 13(2): 37–50.

Jirousek, C. A. 1995. "More Than Oriental Splendor: European and Ottoman Headgear, 1380–1580." *Dress (New York)* 22: 22–33.

Joannou, P. 1962. *Ὁ πιστικὸς βοσκός: Der Treue Schäfer.* (Berliner Byzantinistische Arbeiten 27.) Berlin: Akademie-Verlag.

Johnson-Davies, D. 1994. *The Island of Animals.* Austin: University of Texas Press.

Joseph, B. D. 1983. *The Synchrony and Diachrony of the Balkan Infinitive.* Cambridge, U.K.: Cambridge University Press.

——. 1994. "Borrowing at the Popular Level: Balkan Interjectional Particles of Turkish and Greek Origin." In *Septième Congres International d'Études Sud-Est Européenes: Rapports,* 507–20. Athens: Greek National Committee for Southeast European Studies.

Kahane, H., and R. Kahane. 1966. "Byzantinoromanica." In P. Wirth, ed., *Polychronion: Festschrift Franz Dölger zum 75. Geburtstag,* 304–17. Heidelberg: Carl Winter.

Kaibel, G. 1965–1966 [1887–1890]. *Athenaei Naucratitae deipnosophistarum libri xv.* 3 vols. Leipzig: Stuttgart.

Kaimakis, D. 1976. *Die Kyraniden.* Meisenheim am Glan: Hain.

Kakoulidi, E. D. 1964. *Νεοελληνικὰ θρησκευτικὰ ἀλφαβητάρια.* (Ἐπιστημονικὴ Ἐπετηρὶς Φιλοσοφικῆς Σχολῆς Παράρτημα 9.) Thessalonica: Aristotle University.

——. 1967. "Ποιήματα τοῦ Ἀνδρέα Σκλέντζα." *Ἑλληνικά* 20: 107–45.

——. 1970. "Ὁ Ἰωάννης Μορεζῆνος καὶ τὸ ἔργο του." *Κρητικὰ Χρονικά* 22: 7–78, 388–506.

——. 1971. "Fior di Virtù—Ἄνθος χαρίτων." *Ἑλληνικά* 24: 267–311.

Kakoulidi-Panou, E. D. 1980. "«Ὁ γεννηθεῖς νεώτερος ἐν καιρῷ ζωδίου»: Ἕνα ἀνέκδοτο ἀστρολογικὸ κείμενο τοῦ 16ου αἰώνα." *Δωδώνη* 9: 75–86.

Karaiskakis, S. 1934–1937. "Das Lehrgedicht von Markos Depharanas." *Λαογραφία* 11: 1–66.

Karanastassis, T. A. 1991. "«Ἔδωκας, ἡγούμενε, τῶν καλογήρων διακόνημα. . .»" *Το Παραμιλητό* 10: 145–53.

Karanastassis, T. Forthcoming. *Λεξικολογικά στην Παιδιόφραστον διήγησιν των ζώων των τετραπόδων.*
Karapotosoglou, K. 1979. "Ἡ ἐτυμολογία τῆς λέξεως γάιδαρος." *Κυπριακαὶ Σπουδαί* 43: 95–116.
Kazazis, I. N., and T. A. Karanastassis. 2001. *Επιτομή του λεξικού της μεσαιωνικής ελληνικής δημώδους γραμματείας (1100–1669) του Εμμανουήλ Κριαρά.* Volume 1. Thessalonica: Κέντρο Ελληνικής Γλώσσας.
Kazhdan, A. 1984. *Studies on Byzantine Literature of the Eleventh and Twelfth Centuries.* Cambridge, U.K.: Cambridge University Press.
——, ed. 1991. *The Oxford Dictionary of Byzantium.* 3 vols. New York: Oxford University Press.
Kazhdan, A., and G. Constable. 1982. *People and Power in Byzantium.* Washington, D.C.: Dumbarton Oaks Center for Byzantine Studies.
Kechagioglou, G. 1978. *Κριτικὴ ἔκδοση τῆς Ἱστορίας Πτωχολέοντος.* (Ἐπιστημονικὴ Ἐπετηρὶς Φιλοσοφικῆς Σχολῆς Παράρτημα 22.) Thessalonica: Aristotle University.
——. 1982. *Ἀπόκοπος. Ἀπολώνιος. Ἱστορία τῆς Σωσάννης.* (Λαϊκὰ λογοτεχνικὰ ἔντυπα 1.) Athens: Ἑρμῆς.
——. 1993. "*Digenes Akrites* in Prose: The Andros Version in the Context of Modern Greek Literature." In R. Beaton and D. Ricks, eds., *Digenes Akrites: New Approaches to Byzantine Heroic Poetry,* 116–30. (Centre for Hellenic Studies, King's College London Publications 2.) London: Variorum.
Keydell, R. 1959. *Nonni Panopolitani Dionysiaca.* 2 vols. Weidmann: Berlin.
Kieffer, J. D., and T. X. Bianchi. 1835–1837. *Dictionnaire turc–français.* Paris: Imprimerie Royale.
Kiessling, T. 1963 [1826]. *Ioannis Tzetzae historiarum variarum Chiliades.* Hildesheim: Georg Olms.
Knös, B. 1962. *L'Histoire de la littérature néo-grecque: La période jusqu'en 1821.* (Studia Graeca Upsaliensia 1.) Stockholm: Almqvist and Wiksell.
Kock, T. 1880–1888. *Comicorum Atticorum fragmenta.* 3 vols. Leipzig: Teubner.
Koder, J. 1969. *Hymnes: Symeon le nouveau théologien.* 2 vols. (Sources chrétiennes 156, 174.) Paris: Cerf.
——. 1972. "Der Fünfzehnsilber am kaiserlichen Hof um das Jahr 900." *Byzantinoslavica* 33: 214–19.
Kolbaba, T. M. 2000. *The Byzantine Lists: Errors of the Latins.* (Illinois Medieval Studies.) Urbana: University of Illinois Press.
Kolias, T. G. 1988. *Byzantinische Waffen.* (Byzantina Vindobonensia 17.) Vienna: Österreichische Akademie der Wissenschaften.
Koneski, B. 1961–1966. *Речник на Македонскиот Јазик со српскохрватски толкувања.* 3 vols. Skopje: Институт за Македонски Јазик.
Kornaros, V. 1984. *Erotocritos.* Translated by T. Stephanides. Athens: Papazissis.
Koster, W. J. W. 1974. *Prolegomena de comoedia. Scholia in Acharnenses, Equites, Nubes.* (Scholia in Aristophanem 1.3.2.) Groningen: Bouma.
Kostomiris, G. A. 1892. *Ἀετίου λόγος δωδέκατος.* Paris: Klincksieck.
Koukoules, P. 1911–1912. "Παρατηρήσεις εἰς τὰ Carmina Graeca medii aevi." *Λαογραφία* 3: 358–81.
——. 1915. "Προδρόμεια λαογραφικὰ ζητήματα." *Λαογραφία* 5: 309–32.

——. 1932. "Κυνηγετικὰ ἐκ τῆς ἐποχῆς τῶν Κομνηνῶν καὶ τῶν Παλαιολόγων." *Ἐπετηρὶς Ἑταιρείας Βυζαντινῶν Σπουδῶν* 9: 3–33.
——. 1936. "Μορφολογικὰ καὶ γραμματολογικὰ ζητήματα." *Glotta* 25: 159–66.
——. 1947–1955. *Βυζαντινῶν βίος καὶ πολιτισμός*. 6 vols. Athens: Institut Français d'Athènes.
Koutrakou, N. A. 1991. "Βυζαντινὴ πολιτικὴ ἰδεολογία καὶ προπαγάνδα: Μετασχηματισμοί, θέσεις καὶ ἀντιθέσεις. Τὸ παράδειγμα τοῦ Λέοντος Ε΄ Ἀρμενίου (813–820)." *Ἵστωρ* 3: 85–91.
Koutsompogeras, X. P. 1979. *Ἀνθολογία ἑλληνικῆς ποιήσεως*. Athens: Ἐκδοτικὴ Ἑστία.
Krawczynski, S. 1960. *Ὁ Πουλολόγος*. (Berliner Byzantinische Arbeiten 22.) Berlin: Akademie-Verlag.
Kriaras, E. 1937. "Βασιλεύει ὁ ἥλιος." *Ἀθηνᾶ* 47: 79–93.
——. 1938. "Λεηλασία τῆς Παροικίας τῆς Πάρου (κρητικὸν ποίημα τοῦ 17ου αἰῶνος)." *Ἀθηνᾶ* 48: 119–62.
——. 1955. *Βυζαντινὰ ἱπποτικὰ μυθιστορήματα*. (Βασικὴ βιβλιοθήκη Ἀετοῦ 2.) Athens: Ἀετός.
——. 1968–1997. *Λεξικό της μεσαιωνικής ελληνικής δημώδους γραμματείας*. 14 vols. (ongoing). Thessalonica: Self-published.
Kroll, W. 1926. *Historia Alexandri Magni*. Vol. 1. Berlin: Weidmann.
Krueger, D. 1996. *Symeon the Holy Fool: Leontius'* Life *and the Late Antique City*. Berkeley: University of California Press.
Krumbacher, K. 1897. *Geschichte der byzantinischen Literatur von Justinian bis zum Ende des oströmischen Reiches*. 2d ed. 2 vols. Munich: Beck.
——. 1905. "Ein vulgärgriechischer Weiberspiegel." *Sitzungsberichten der philosophischen-philologischen und der historischen Klasse der Königlichen Bayerischen Akademie der Wissenschaften* 3: 335–433.
——. 1969 [1894]. *Mittelgriechische Sprichwörter*. Hildesheim: Georg Olms.
Kumbaracılar, İ. 1979. *Serpuşlar*. Istanbul: Türkiye Turing be Otomobil Kurumu Yanını.
Kurtz, E. 1903. *Die Gedichte des Christophoros Mitylenaios*. Leipzig: Neumann.
Laiou, A. E. 1977. *Peasant Society in the Late Byzantine Empire: A Social and Demographic Study*. Princeton: Princeton University Press.
Lambros, S. P. 1879–1880. *Μιχαὴλ Ἀκομινάτου τοῦ Χωνιάτου τὰ σωζόμενα*. Athens: City of Athens.
——. 1880. *Collection de romans grecs*. Paris: Maisonneuve.
——. 1885. *Excerptorum Constantini de natura animalium libri duo*. (Commentaria in Aristotelem Graeca supplementum 1.1.) Berlin: Reimer.
——. 1906. "Λόγος παρηγορητικὸς περὶ Δυστυχίας καὶ Εὐτυχίας κατὰ τὸν κώδικα τῆς Λειψίας." *Νέος Ἑλληνομνήμων* 3: 402–32d.
——. 1908. "Ἡ ἑλληνικὴ ὡς ἐπίσημος γλῶσσα τῶν σουλτάνων." *Νέος Ἑλληνομνήμων* 5: 40–78
——. 1917. "Ὁ Σπανέας τοῦ Βατικανοῦ Παλατινοῦ κώδικος 367." *Νέος Ἑλληνομνήμων* 14: 353–380.
——. 1979 [1902]. *Ecthesis chronica and Chronicon Athenarum*. New York: AMS Press.
Lampe, G. W. H. 1961. *A Patristic Greek Lexicon*. Oxford: Clarendon Press.

Landos, A. 1991 [1643]. *Γεωπονικόν*. Edited by D. D. Kostoula. Athens: Τῆνος.
Laourdas, B., and L. G. Westerink. 1983–1988. *Photii patriarchae Constantinopolitani epistulae et amphilochia*. 6 vols. Leipzig: Teubner.
Latte, K. 1953–1966. *Hesychii Alexandrini lexicon*. 2 vols. Copenhagen: Munksgaard.
Latte, K., and Erbse, H. 1965. *Lexica Graeca minora*. Hildesheim: Georg Olms.
Leclerc, L. 1883. "Traité des simples par Ibn el-Beïthar." *Notices et extraits des manuscrits de la Bibliothèque Nationale* 26.
Legrand, É. 1875. *Les Oracles de Léon le Sage, La Bataille de Varna, La Prise de Constantinople*. (Collection de Monuments pour servir à l'étude de la language néo-hellénique N.S. 5.) Paris: Maisonneuve.
——. 1877. *Recueil de poëmes historiques en grec vulgaire relatifs à la Turquie et aux principautés danubiennes*. Paris: Ernest Leroux.
——. 1880–1913. *Bibliothéque grecque vulgaire*. 10 vols. Paris: Maisonneuve.
——. 1891. "Poésies inédites de Théodore Prodrome." *Revue d'Études Grecques* 4: 70–73.
Legrand, P.-E. 1963–1970. *Hérodote. Histoires*. 9 vols. Paris: Les Belles Lettres.
Leib, B. 1937–1945. *Anna Comnène. Alexiade*. 3 vols. Paris: Les Belles Lettres.
Lemerle, P., A. Guillou, and N. Svoronos. 1970–1982. *Actes de Lavra*. 4 vols. (Archives de l'Athos 5, 8, 10, 11.) Paris: P. Lethielleux.
Leone, P. A. M. 1972. *Ioannis Tzetzae Epistulae*. Leipzig: Teubner.
Leviţchi, L. 1960. *Dicţionar Romîn–Englez*. Bucharest: Editura Sţinţifică.
Lewis, C. T., and C. Short. 1879. *A Latin Dictionary*. Oxford: Clarendon Press.
Liddell, H. G., R. Scott, and H. S. Jones. 1940. *A Greek–English Lexicon*. Oxford: Clarendon Press.
Lindenburg, M. A. 1978 [1961]. "Βασιλεύω dit du Soleil." In *Actes du XII*[e] *Congrès International D'Études Byzantines, 2*: 385–89. Nendeln, Lichtenstein: Kraus.
Lioudaki, M. 1971 [1936]. *Μαντινάδες: Λαογραφικὰ Κρήτης*. 2d ed. Athens: Γνώσεις.
Littlewood, A. R. 1985. *Michaelis Pselli oratoria minora*. Leipzig: Teubner.
Littré, É. 1961–1973 [1839–1861]. *Oeuvres complètes d'Hippocrate*. Amsterdam: Adolf M. Hakkert.
Loernetz, R.-J. 1956–1960. *Démétrius Cydonès, Correspondance*. 2 vols. (Studi e Testi 186, 208.) Vatican City: Bibliotheca Apostolica Vaticana.
Lolos, A., and V. L. Konstantinopoulos. 1983. *Pseudo-Kallisthenes: Zwei mittelgriechische Prosa-Fassungen des Alexanderromans*. 2 vols. (Beiträge zur Klassischen Philologie 141, 150.) Königstein: Anton Hain.
Longfellow, H. W. 1934. *The Poetical Works of Longfellow*. London: Oxford University Press.
Lord, A. 1960. *The Singer of Tales*. Cambridge, Mass.: Harvard University Press.
Loukanis, N. 1979 [1526]. *Ὁμήρου Ἰλιάς*. Athens: Gennadius Library, American School of Classical Studies.
Loukopoulos, D. 1940. *Νεοελληνικὴ μυθολογία: Ζῶα–φυτά*. (Σύλλογος πρὸς διάδοσιν ὠφελίμων βιβλίων 76.) Athens: I. N. Σιδέρης.
Lurier, H. E. 1964. *Crusaders as Conquerors: The Chronicle of Morea*. New York: Columbia University Press.

Mackridge, P. 1993. "An Editorial Problem in Medieval Texts: The Position of the Object Clitic Pronoun in the Escorial *Digenes Akrites*." In N. Panagiotakis, ed., *Αρχές της νεοελληνικής λογοτεχνίας*, 2.325–42. Venice: Biblioteca dell'Istituto Ellenico di Studi Bizantini e Postbizantini di Venezia.

Maehler, H. 1971. *Pindari carmina cum fragmentis*. 5th ed. Vol. 1. Leipzig: Teubner.

Magie, D. 1932. *The Scriptores Historiae Augustae*. 3 vols. (Loeb Classical Library.) London: Heinemann.

Mair, A. W. 1928. *Oppian, Colluthus, Tryphiodorus*. (Loeb Classical Library.) Cambridge, Mass.: Harvard University Press.

Makris, G. 1993. "Zum literarischen Genus des Pulologos." In N. Panagiotakis, ed., *Αρχές της νεοελληνικής λογοτεχνίας*, 1: 391–412. Venice: Biblioteca dell'Istituto Ellenico di Studi Bizantini e Postbizantini di Venezia.

Makriyannis, I. 1907. *Ἀπομνημονεύματα*. Edited by I. Vlahoyannis. Athens: Σ. Κ. Βλαστός.

——. 1966. *The Memoirs of General Makriyannis*. Translated by H. A. Lidderdale. London: Oxford University Press.

Mango, C., and R. Scott. 1997. *The Chronicle of Theophanes Confessor*. Oxford: Clarendon Press.

Manousakas, M. I. 1995. *Λεονάρδου Ντελλαπόρτα ποιήματα*. Athens: Academy of Athens.

Marchant, E. C. 1900–1920. *Xenophontis opera omnia*. 5 vols. Oxford: Clarendon Press.

Marchant, E. C., and G. W. Bowersock. 1968. *Xenophon*. 7 vols. (Loeb Classical Library.) Cambridge, Mass.: Harvard University Press.

Massa Positano, L. 1960. *Joannes Tzetzae comentarii in Aristophanem*. (Scholia in Aristophanem 4.1.) Groningen: Bouma.

Matranga, P. 1971 [1850]. *Anecdota Graeca*. Hildesheim: Georg Olms.

Mavrofrydis, D. I. 1866. *Ἐκλογὴ μνημείων τῆς νεωτέρας ἑλληνικῆς γλώσσης*. Vol. I. Athens.

Mavrogordato, J. 1956. *Digenes Akrites*. Oxford: Clarendon Press.

Mavromatis, G. K. 1995. *Τὰ «περὶ τῆς ξενιτείας» ποιήματα*. Iraklio: City of Iraklio–Βικελαία Βιβλιοθήκη.

May, P., and G. H. Kerridge. 1967. "Harvest Pruning of Sultana Vines." *Vitis* 6: 390–93.

Mayer, L. A. 1952. *Mamluk Costume*. Geneva: Albert Kundig.

McGeer, E. 1995. *Sowing the Dragon's Teeth: Byzantine Warfare in the Tenth Century*. Washington, D.C.: Dumbarton Oaks Research Library and Collection.

Meineke, A. 1969 [1877]. *Strabonis geographica*. 3 vols. Graz: Akademische Druck- und Verlagsanstalt.

Meursius, J. 1614. *Glossarium graeco-barbarum*. 2d ed. Leiden: Elzevir.

Meyendorff, J. 1960. "Projets de Concile Oecuménique en 1367: Un dialogue inédit entre Jean Cantacuzène et le Légat Paul." *Dumbarton Oaks Papers* 14: 147–77.

Michailidis, D. 1970. "Φιλολογικὲς παρατηρήσεις σὲ παλαιότερα κείμενα. 1. Παιδιόφραστος–πεζόφραστος." *Ἑλληνικά* 23: 331–34.

Migne, J.–P., ed. 1857–1887. *Patrologia Graeca*. 161 vols. Paris: J. P. Migne.

Mihăescu, H. 1970. *Mauricius. Arta militară.* (Scriptores Byzantini 6.) Bucharest: Academie Republicii Socialiste România.

Mihevc-Gabrovec, E. 1973. "L'Infinitif temporel en grec du Moyen-Age et en Slovène." *Linguistica (Ljubljana)* 13: 219–28.

Miliarakis, A. 1881. *Βασίλειος Διγενὴς Ἀκρίτας: Ἐποποιΐα βυζαντινὴ τῆς 10ης ἑκατονταετηρίδος κατὰ τὸ ἐν Ἄνδρῳ ἀνευρεθὲν χειρόγραφον.* Athens: Ἑλληνικὴ Ἀνεξαρτησία.

Miller, E. 1967 [1855–1857]. *Manuelis Philes carmina.* 2 vols. Amsterdam: Adolf M. Hakkert

——. 1872. "Description d'une chasse à l'once par un écrivain byzantin du XIIe siècle de notre ère." *Annuaire de l'Association pour l'encouragement des études grecques en France* 6: 28–52.

——. 1874. "Lexiques grecs inédits." *Annuaire de l'Association pour l'encouragement des études grecques en France* 8: 222–84.

——. ed. 1967 [1875–1881]. *Recueil des historiens des Croisades: Historiens grecs.* 2 vols. Westmead, Farnborough, U.K.: Gregg International.

Minotos, D. A. 1953. "Ζακυνθιναὶ μυθικαὶ διηγήσεις περὶ Μεγάλου Ἀλεξάνδρου." *Μακεδονικά* 2: 687–96.

Mitsakis, K. 1967. *Der byzantinische Alexanderroman nach dem Codex Vindob. Theol. Gr. 244.* (Miscellanea Byzantina Monacensia 7.) Munich: Institüt für Byzantinistik und Neugriechische Philologie der Universität München.

——. 1976. "Review of Tsiouni, V. Παιδιόφραστος διήγησις τῶν ζώων τῶν τετραπόδων." *Balkan Studies* 17: 408–10.

Mohay, A. 1974–1975. "Schriftlichkeit und Mündlichkeit in der byzantinischen Literatur." *Acta Classica (Debrecen)* 10–11: 175–81.

Momferratos, A. 1889. "Εὑρετήριον καὶ πρόλογος τῆς Βακτηρίας τῶν ἀρχιερέων." *Δελτίον τῆς Ἱστορικῆς καὶ Ἐθνολογικῆς Ἑταιρείας τῆς Ἑλλάδος* 3: 129–218.

Momsen, T. 1990 [1903]. *Codex Theodosianus.* 2 vols. Hildesheim: Weidmann.

Mondésert, C. 1949. *Clément d'Alexandrie: Le protreptique.* 2d ed. Paris: Cerf.

Montselese, T. 1995 [1646]. *Τραγωδία ὀνομαζομένη Εὐγένα.* Edited by M. Vitti and G. Spadaro. Athens: Ὀδυσσέας.

Moravcsik, G. 1935. *Görög költemény a Várnai csatáról.* Budapest: K. M. egyetemi nyomda könyvesbolta.

——. 1956. *Byzantinoturcica.* 2d ed. 2 vols. (Berliner Byzantinische Arbeiten 10–11.) Berlin: Akademie-Verlag.

Moutsos, D. 1970. "Two Derivatives of a Common Source in Medieval and Modern Greek: ζαβός and ζερβός." *Neo-Hellenika* 1: 183–90.

Müller, K. 1855. *Geographi Graeci minores.* Paris: Didot.

Murray, A. T. 1919. *Homer. The Odyssey with an English Translation.* (Loeb Classical Library.) Cambridge, Mass.: Harvard University Press.

——. 1924. *Homer. The Iliad with an English Translation.* (Loeb Classical Library.) Cambridge, Mass.: Harvard University Press.

Murray, G. 1955. *Aeschyli tragoediae.* 2d ed. Oxford: Clarendon Press.

Neumann, C. J. 1880. *Juliani imperatoris librorum contra Christianos quae supersunt.* Leipzig: Teubner.

Newmark, L. 1998. *Oxford Albanian–English Dictionary.* Oxford: Oxford University Press.

Nicholas, N. 1999. "A Conundrum of Cats: Pards and Their Relatives in Byzantium." *Greek, Roman and Byzantine Studies* 40: 253–98.

Nicol, D. M. 1993. *The Last Centuries of Byzantium*. 2d ed. Cambridge, U.K.: Cambridge University Press.

——. 1996. *The Reluctant Emperor*. Cambridge: Cambridge University Press.

Nicole, J. 1966 [1891]. *Les scolies genevoises de l'Iliade*. Hildesheim: Georg Olms.

Nørgaard, L., and O. L. Smith. 1975. *A Byzantine Iliad*. (Opuscula Graecolatina 5.) Copenhagen: Museum Tusculanum.

Norlin, G. 1980. *Isocrates*. 3 vols. (Loeb Classical Library.) Cambridge, Mass.: Harvard University Press.

Norwich, J. J. 1995. *Byzantium: The Decline and Fall*. London: Penguin.

Oberhelman, S. M. 1991. *The Oneirocriticon of Achmet*. Lubbock: Texas Tech University Press.

Oder, E., and K. Hoppe. 1971 [1927]. *Corpus Hippiatricorum Graecorum*. 2 vols. Stuttgart: Teubner.

Odorico, P., S. Asdrachas, T. Karanastassis, K. Kostis, and S. Petmézas. 1996. *Conseils et mémoires de Synadinos, prêtre de Serrès en Macédoine (XVIIe siècle)*. Paris: Editions de l'Association "Pierre Belon."

Oikonomidès, N. 1984. *Actes de Docheiariou*. (Archives de l'Athos 13.) Paris: P. Lethielleux.

Oikonomu-Agorastu, I. 1982. *Kritische Erstausgabe des Rezeptbuchs des Cod. Par. gr. 2316, f. 348^v^–74^v^. Inaugural-Dissertation zur Erlangung des Doktorgrades der philosophischen Fakultät der Universität zu Köln*. Thessalonica: Self-published.

Oldfather, W. A. 1995–1996 [1925–1928]. *Epictetus*. (Loeb Classical Library.) Cambridge, Mass.: Harvard University Press.

Oliveri, A. 1935. *Aëtii Amideni libri medicinales i–iv*. (Corpus medicorum Graecorum, vol. 8.1.) Leipzig: Teubner.

——. 1950. *Aëtii Amideni libri medicinales v–viii*. (Corpus medicorum Graecorum, vol. 8.2.) Berlin: Akademie-Verlag

Omont, H. 1888–1898. *Inventaire sommaire des manuscripts grecs de la Bibliothèque nationale et des autres bibliothèques de Paris et des départements*. 3 vols. Paris: Ernest Leroux.

O'Neill, E. Jr. 1938. "Plutus." In W. J. Oates and E. O'Neill Jr., eds., *The Complete Greek Drama*, 2.1063–1115. New York. Random House.

Országh, L. 1953. *Magyar–Angol Szótár*. Budapest: Akadémiai Kiadò.

Ortolá Salas, F. J. 1998. *Florio y Platzia Flora: Una novela bizantina de época paleóloga*. (Nueva Roma 6.) Madrid: Consejo Superior de Investigaciones Cientificas, Universidad de Cádiz.

Ostrogorsky, G. 1968. *History of the Byzantine State*. 2d ed. New Brunswick, N.J.: Rutgers University Press.

Pallis, A. 1951. *In the Days of the Janissaries*. London: Hutchinson.

Panagiotakis, N. M. 1975. "Παιδιόφραστος." In *Φίλτρα: Τιμητικός τόμος Σ. Γ. Καψωμένου*, 275–90. Thessalonica: Self-published.

Papadimitriu, S. D. 1896. *Стефань Сахликись и его стихотворенiе* Ἀφήγησις παράξενος. Odessa: Экономическая.

——. 1903. "Ὁ Πρόδρομος τοῦ Μαρκιανοῦ κώδικος XI 22." *Византийский Временник* (St. Petersburg) 10: 102–63.

Papadopoulos, A. A. 1926. "Ἐξορκισμοὶ καὶ Ἐξορκισταί." *Ἐπετηρὶς Ἑταιρείας Βυζαντινῶν Σπουδῶν* 3: 225–234.

——. 1950. "Φρασεολογικά." *Λεξικογραφικὸν Δελτίον* 5: 3–52.

——. 1953. "Φρασεολογικά." *Λεξικογραφικὸν Δελτίον* 6: 3–88.

——. 1961. *Ἱστορικὸν λεξικὸν τῆς ποντικῆς διαλέκτου*. 2 vols. Athens: Μυρτίδης.

Papaharalambous, G. H. 1945–1946. "Ἀπὸ τὴν Παιδιόφραστο διήγησιν τετραπόδων ζώων." *Κυπριακὰ Γράμματα* 10: 262–66.

Papathanasopoulos, T. 1998. *Περίστα Ναυπακτίας: Ιστορικά–Λαογραφικά*. Athens: Μελέαγρος.

Papathomopoulos, M. 1990a. *Ὁ Βίος τοῦ Αἰσώπου. Ἡ παραλλαγὴ G*. Ioannina: University of Ioannina.

——. 1990b. *Varia Philologica et Papyrologica*. Vol. 1. Ioannina: University of Ioannina.

——. 1999a. *Ὁ Βίος τοῦ Αἰσώπου: Ἡ παραλλαγή W*. Athens: Παπαδήμας.

——. 1999b. *Πέντε δημώδεις μεταφράσεις τοῦ Βίου τοῦ Αἰσώπου*. Athens: Παπαδήμας.

——. 2002. *Παιδιόφραστος διήγησις τῶν ζώων τῶν τετραπόδων*. Thessalonica: Ζῆτρος.

Papathomopoulos, M., and E. M. Jeffreys. 1996. *Ο Πόλεμος της Τρωάδος*. (Βυζαντινή και νεοελληνική βιβλιοθήκη 7.) Athens: Μορφωτικό Ίδρυμα Εθνικής Τραπέζης.

Parnell, T., et al. 1872. *The Minor Poems of Homer: The Battle of the Frogs and Mice; Hymns and Epigrams*. New York: Denham & Co.

Paschalis, D. 1926. "Οἱ δέκα λόγοι τοῦ Διγενοῦς Ἀκρίτου." *Λαογραφία* 9: 305–440.

Passas, I., ed. 1961. *Νεώτερο ἐγκυκλοπαιδικὸ λεξικὸ Ἡλίου*. 18 vols. Athens: Ἥλιος.

Peck, A. L. 1942. *Aristotle: Generation of Animals*. (Loeb Classical Library.) Cambridge, Mass.: Harvard University Press.

Perry, B. E. 1952. *Aesopica*. Urbana: University of Illinois Press.

——. 1965. *Babrius and Phaedrus*. (Loeb Classical Library.) Cambridge, Mass.: Harvard University Press,

Pertusi, A. 1959. *Giorgio di Pisidia. Poemi. I: Panegirici epici*. (Studia patristica et byzantina 7.) Ettal: Buch-Kunstverlag.

Philippides, M. 1990. *Byzantium, Europe, and the Early Ottoman Sultans 1373–1513: An Anonymous Greek Chronicle of the Seventeenth Century (Codex Barberinus Graecus 111)*. (Byzantine and Ottoman Studies 4.) New Rochelle, N.Y.: Aristide D. Caratzas.

Pichard, M. 1956. *Le roman de Callimaque et de Chrysorrhoé*. Paris: Les Belles-Lettres.

Pignani, A. 1983. *Niceforo Basilace: Progimnasmi e monodie*. (Byzantina et Neo-Hellenica Neapolitana 10.) Naples: Bibliopolis.

Pochert, C. 1991. *Die Reimbildung in der spät- und postbyzantinischen Volksliteratur*. (Neograeca Medii Aevi 4.) Cologne: Romiosini.

Politis, L. 1964. *Κατζοῦρμπος*. (Κρητικὸν Θέατρον 1.) Iraklio: Ἑταιρεία Κρητικῶν Ἱστορικῶν Μελετῶν.

——. 1966–1967. *Ποιητικὴ ἀνθολογία*. 6 vols. Athens: Γαλαξίας.

——. 1973. *A History of Modern Greek Literature*. Translated by R. Liddell. Oxford: Clarendon Press.

Politis, N. 1902. *Παροιμίαι*. 6 vols. (Μελέται περὶ τοῦ βίου καὶ τῆς γλώσσης τοῦ ἑλληνικοῦ λαοῦ.) Athens: Π. Δ. Σακελλαρίου.

——. 1914. *Ἐκλογαὶ ἀπὸ τὰ τραγούδια τοῦ ἑλληνικοῦ λαοῦ*. Athens: Ἑστία.

Porson, R. 1822. *Φωτίου τοῦ πατριάρχου λέξεων συναγωγή*. 2 vols. Cambridge, U.K.: Cambridge University Press.

Preger, T. 1901–1907. *Scriptores originum Constantinopolitanarum*. 2 vols. Leipzig: Teubner.

Psichari, J. 1886–1889. *Essais de grammaire historique néogrecque*. 2 vols. Paris: Ernest Leroux.

Psychoundakis, G. 1955. *The Cretan Runner: His Story of the German Occupation*. Translated by P. Leigh Fermor. London: J. Murray.

——. 1979. *Ὁμήρου Ὀδύσσεια*. Athens: Self-published.

Praechter, K. 1895. "Das griechische Original der rumänischen Troïka." *Byzantinische Zeitschrift* 4: 519–46.

Rabe, H. 1971 [1906]. *Scholia in Lucianum*. Stuttgart: Teubner.

Rackham, H. 1983. *Pliny: Natural History*. 10 vols. (Loeb Classical Library.) London: Heinemann.

Raeder, J. 1928–1933. *Oribasii collectionum medicarum reliquae*. 4 vols. Leipzig: Teubner.

Rahlfs, A. 1971 [1935]. *Septuaginta*. 2 vols. Stuttgart: Württembergische Bibelanstalt.

Rallis, G. A., and M. Potlis. 1852–1859. *Σύνταγμα τῶν θείων καὶ ἱερῶν κανόνων*. 6 vols. Athens: Γ. Χαρτοφύλαξ.

Rapp, C. 1997. "Ritual Brotherhood in Byzantium." *Traditio* 52: 285–326.

Reichmann, S. 1963. *Das byzantinische Alexandergedicht nach dem Codex Marcianus 408 herausgegeben*. (Beiträge zur klassichen Philologie 13.) Meisenheim am Glan: Hain.

Reinsch, D. R. 1974. *Die Briefe des Matthaios von Ephesos im Codex Vindobonensis Theol. Gr. 174*. Berlin: Mielke.

——. 1983. *Critobuli Imbriotae historiae*. (Corpus Fontium Historiae Byzantinae Series Berolinensis 22.) Berlin: de Gruyter.

——. 1998. "Kodikologisch–Prosopographisches zum Codex Seragliensis graecus 35." In I. Vassis, G. S. Henrich, and D. R. Reinsch, eds., *Lesarten: Festschrift für Athanasios Kambylis zum 70. Geburtstag,* 248–58. Berlin: de Gruyter.

Reiske, J. J. 1829. *Constantini Porphyrogeniti imperatoris de cerimoniis aulae Byzantinae libri duo*. Vol. 1. (Corpus scriptorum historiae Byzantinae.) Bonn: Weber.

Renehan, R. 1969. *Greek Textual Criticism: A Reader*. Cambridge, Mass.: Harvard University Press.

Reuss, J. 1966. *Johannes-Kommentare aus der griechischen Kirche*. (Texte und Untersuchungen 89.) Berlin: Akademie-Verlag.

Richard, J. 1989. "The Establishment of the Latin Church in the Empire of Constantinople (1204–27)." In B. Arbel, B. Hamilton, and D. Jacoby, eds., *Latins and Greeks in the Eastern Mediterranean After 1204,* 45–62. London: Frank Cass.

Ricks, D. 1990. *Byzantine Heroic Poetry*. Bristol: Bristol Classical Press.
Ritschl, F. 1970 [1832]. *Thomae Magistri sive Theoduli monachi ecloga vocum Atticarum*. Hildesheim: Georg Olms.
Roberts, A., and J. Donaldson. 1885–1896. *The Ante-Nicene Fathers*. 10 vols. Edinburgh: T and T Clark.
Robinson, P. M. W. 1996. "Computer-Assisted Stemmatic Analysis and 'Best-Text' Historical Editing." In P. Van Reenen and M. Van Mulken, eds., *Studies in Stemmatology,* 71–103. Amsterdam: John Benjamins.
——. 1997. "New Directions in Critical Editing." In K. Sutherland, ed., *Electronic Text: Investigations in Method and Theory,* 146–71. Oxford: Clarendon Press.
Rodley, N. 2001. *Report of the Special Rapporteur Submitted Pursuant to Commission on Human Rights Resolution 2000/43: Visit to Brazil. Individual Cases: State of Minas Gerais*. Report to the United Nations Commission on Human Rights, April 11, 2001. E/CN.4/2001/66/Add.1. http://www.global.org.br/english/state_of_minas_gerais.htm. Accessed September 2, 2002.
Rolfe, J. C. 1958. *Ammianus Marcellinus*. (Loeb Classical Library.) 3 vols. Cambridge, Mass.: Harvard University Press.
Romano, R. 1974. *Timarione*. (Byzantina et Neo-Hellenica Neapolitana 2.) Naples: Università di Napoli, Cattedra di filologia bizantina.
Rowland, B. 1973. *Animals with Human Faces: A Guide to Animal Symbolism*. Knoxville: University of Tennessee Press.
Runciman, S. 1970. *The Last Byzantine Renaissance*. Cambridge, U.K.: Cambridge University Press.
Rydén, L. 1970. *Bemerkungen zum Leben des Heiligen Narren Symeon von Leontios von Neapolis*. Uppsala: Almqvist und Wiksell.
Ryder, M. L. 1964. "Parchment: Its History, Manufacture and Composition." *Journal of the Society of Archivists* (London) 2: 391–99.
Sadie, S., ed. 2001. *The New Grove Dictionary of Music and Musicians*. 29 vols. London: Macmillan.
Sakellariou, A. A. 1890–1891: *Τὰ κυπριακά*. 2 vols. Athens: Π. Δ. Σακελλάριος.
Sampson, A. 1972. "Τὸ γλωσσικὸν ἰδίωμα Σκοπέλου καὶ Γλώσσης." *Ἀρχεῖον Θεσσαλικῶν Μελετῶν* 1: 94–123.
Šandrovskaja, V. S. 1956a. "Византийская басня «Рассказ о четвероногих (XIV в.)»" *Византийский Временник* (Moscow) 9: 211–49.
——. 1956b. "Византийская басня «Рассказ о четвероногих (XIV в.)» Художвенные особенности и язык памятника." *Византийский Временник* (Moscow) 10: 181–94.
——. 1960. "Die byzantinischen Fabeln in den leningrader Handschriftensammlungen." In J. Irmscher, ed., *Probleme der neugriechischen Literatur,* 3: 10–20. (Berliner Byzantinische Arbeiten 16.) Berlin: Akademie-Verlag.
Sarantakos, N. 1997.*Το αλφαβητάρι των ιδιωματικών εκφράσεων*. Athens: Δίαυλος.
Sathas, C. 1972 [1872–1894]. *Bibliotheca Graeca medii aevi*. 7 vols. New York: Georg Olms.
——. 1982 [1867]. *Ἑλληνικὰ ἀνέκδοτα*. Vol. 1. (Βιβλιοθήκη ἱστορικῶν μελετῶν 172.) Athens: Διονύσιος Νότης Καραβίας.

Savvidis, G. 1993. "Πότε άραγες αρχίζει η νεότερη ελληνική λογοτεχνία." In N. Panagiotakis, ed., *Αρχές της νεοελληνικής λογοτεχνίας,* 1: 37–41. Venice: Biblioteca dell'Istituto Ellenico di Studi Bizantini e Postbizantini di Venezia.

Sbordone, F. 1936. *Physiologus*. Rome: Dante Aligheri-Albrighi, Segati.

Scarce, J. 1987. *Women's Costume of the Near and Middle East*. London: Unwin Hyman.

Scheltema, H. J., D. Holwerda, and N. van der Wal. 1953–1988. *Basilicorum libri LX, Series A*. 8 vols. Groningen: Bouma's Boekhus/Wolters–Noordhoff.

Schenkl, H. 1965 [1916]. *Epicteti dissertationes ab Arriano digestae*. Stuttgart: Teubner.

Schirò, G. 1975. *Cronaca dei Tocco di Cefalonia*. (Corpus Fontium Historiae Byzantinae 10.) Rome: Accademia Nazionale dei Lincei.

Schmitt, J. 1904. *The Chronicle of Morea*. London: Methuen.

Schofield, A. F. 1921. *Claudius Aelian: On Animals*. 3 vols. (Loeb Classical Library.) Cambridge, Mass.: Harvard University Press.

Schopen, L. 1835. *Ioannis Cantacuzeni eximperatoris historiarum libri iv*. 3 vols. (Corpus scriptorum historiae Byzantinae 2–4.) Bonn: Weber.

Schopen, L., and I. Bekker. 1829–1855. *Nicephori Gregorae historiae byzantinae*. 3 vols. (Corpus scriptorum historiae Byzantinae 6–8.) Bonn: Weber.

Schreiner, P. 1991. *Texte zur spätbyzantinischen Finanz- und Wirtschaftsgeschichte in Handschriften der Biblioteca Vaticana*. (Studi e Testi 344.) Vatican City: Biblioteca Apostolica Vaticana.

Schwartz, E. 1914–1940. *Acta Conciliorum Oecumenicorum*. 3 vols. Berlin: de Gruyter.

Scullard, H. H. 1974. *The Elephant in the Greek and Roman World*. Cambridge: Thames and Hudson.

Seal, J. 1995. *A Fez of the Heart*. San Diego: Harcourt Brace.

Seferis, G. 1995. *Collected Poems*. Translated by E. Keeley and P. Sherrard. Princeton: Princeton University Press.

Ševčenko, I. 1960. "Alexios Makrembolites and his 'Dialogue Between the Rich and the Poor.'" *Zbornik Radova Vizantološkog Instituta* 6: 187–228.

——. 1961. "The Decline of Byzantium Seen through the Eyes of Its Intellectuals." *Dumbarton Oaks Papers* 15: 169–86.

——. 1974. "Society and Intellectual Life in the Fourteenth Century." In *Actes du XIVe Congrès international des études byzantines, Bucarest 1971,* 1: 69–92.

Sevin, N. 1973. *On Üç Asırlık: Türk Kiyâfet Târihine Bir Bakış*. Istanbul: Millî Eğitim Basımevi.

Shakespeare, W. 1977. *Ὁ Ἄμλετ*. Translated by K. Theotokis. Athens: Ἑταιρεία Σπουδῶν Νεοελληνικοῦ Πολιτισμοῦ καὶ Γενικῆς Παιδείας.

Sharf, A. 1995a. "Jews, Armenians and the Patriarch Athanasius I." In A. Sharf, *Jews and Other Minorities in Byzantium,* 269–86. Tel Aviv: Bar-Ilan University Press.

——. 1995b. "Jews in Byzantium." In A. Sharf, *Jews and Other Minorities in Byzantium,* 52–79. Tel Aviv: Bar-Ilan University Press.

Siapkara-Pitsillidou, T. 1976. *Ὁ πετραρχισμὸς στὴν Κύπρο: Ρίμες ἀγάπης*. Athens: Self-published.

Sideras, A. 1990. *25 Unedierte byzantinische Grabreden*. (Κλασσικὰ γράμματα 5.) Thessalonica: Παρατηρητής.

Simon, T., ed. 1998. *Poetry Under Oath: From the Testimony of William Jefferson Clinton and Monica S. Lewinsky*. New York: Workman.

Smith, O. L. 1999. *The Byzantine Achilleid: The Naples Version*. (Wiener Byzantinische Studien 21.) Vienna: Österreichische Akademie der Wissenschaften.

Smyth, H. W. 1926. *Aeschylus*. 2 vols. (Loeb Classical Library.) Cambridge, Mass.: Harvard University Press.

Sofianos, D. Z. 1996. "Παιδιόφραστος διήγησις τῶν ζώων τῶν τετραπόδων: Εἶναι ὁ πρόλογός της (στ. 1–9) νόθος καὶ ὀβελιστέος;" *Μεσαιωνικὰ καὶ Νέα Ἑλληνικά* 5: 381–386.

Sofos, A. M. 1987. *Τα λαογραφικά της Κάσου*. Athens: Self-published.

Somavera, A. 1977 [1709]. *Tesoro della lingua greca-volgare et italiana*. Rome: Forni.

Sophocles, E. A. 1900. *Greek Lexicon of the Roman and Byzantine Periods*. New York: Scribner.

Soulis, G. C. 1961. "The Gypsies in the Byzantine Empire and the Balkans in the Late Middle Ages." *Dumbarton Oaks Papers* 15: 141–65.

Soummakis, M. 1658. *Παστὼρ φίδος, ἤγουν Ποιμὴν πιστός*. Venice.

Spadaro, G. 1987. "Edizioni critiche di testi medievali in lingua demotica: Difficoltà e prospettive." In H. Eideneier, ed., *Neograeca Medii Aevi: Text und Ausgabe. Akten zum Sumposion Köln 1986,* 327–56. Cologne: Romiosini.

Stallbaum, G. 1970 [1825–1826]. *Eustathii archiepiscopi Thessalonicensis comentarii ad Homeri Odysseam*. 2 vols. Hildesheim: Georg Olms.

Stamatakos, I. D. 1971. *Λεξικόν τῆς νέας ἑλληνικῆς γλώσσης*. 3 vols. Athens: Ὁ Φοῖνιξ.

Stefanov, K. 1914. *Пъленъ Българо–Английски Рѣчникъ*. Sofia: Ив. Х. Николовъ.

Steiner, A. 1989. "Semantische Entwicklungen im Mittelgriechiscen anhand ausgewählter Beispiele." *Byzantion* 59: 244–57.

Stevanović, M., et al. 1967–1971. *Речник Српскохрватскога књижовног Језика*. Novi Sad: Матица Српска.

Sturz, F. W. 1973 [1818]. *Etymologicum Graecae linguae Gudianum et alia grammaticorum scripta e codicibus manuscriptis nunc primum edita*. Hildesheim: Georg Olms.

Svarlien, D. A. 2002. *Pindar: Odes*. Available at Perseus Project, http://www.perseus.tufts.edu. Accessed September 2, 2002.

Terry, P. 1983. *Renard the Fox*. Boston: Northeastern University Press.

Thavoris, A. 1969. "Ἡ ἐτυμολογία τῆς λέξεως: Τὸ θρασίμι." *Ἑλληνικά* 22: 448–54.

Thesaurus Linguae Graecae. 2002. http://www.tlg.uci.edu. Accessed September 2, 2002.

Thomson, H. M. 1944. *New Turkish–English Dictionary*. New York: Frederick Ungar.

Tiftixoglu, V. 1974. "Digenes, das «Sophrosyne»-Gedicht des Meleteniotes und der byzantinische Fünfzehnsilber". *Byzantinische Zeitschrift* 67: 1–63.

Tittmann, J. A. H. 1808. *Iohannis Zonarae lexicon ex tribus codicibus manuscriptis*. 2 vols. Leipzig: Crusius.

Toufexis, N. 2001. "Η αντιγραφή μεσαιωνικών δημωδών κειμένων του 15. αι. Ο ρόλος του κωδικογράφου." To be included in the proceedings of the Neograeca Medii Aevi 5 conference.

Trapp, E. 1964. "Vulgärorakel aus Wiener Handschriften." In J. Koder and E. Trapp, eds., *Ἀκροθινία sodalium Seminarii Byzantini Vindobonensis,* 83–120. Vienna: Institut für Byzantinistik der Universität Wien.

——. 1971. *Digenes Akrites: Synoptische Ausgabe der ältesten Versionen.* (Wiener Byzantinischen Studien 8.) Vienna: Österreichische Akademie der Wissenschaften.

——. 1976. "Review of Tsiouni, V. Παιδιόφραστος διήγησις τῶν ζώων τῶν τετραπόδων." *Byzantinische Zeitschrift* 69: 444–46.

——. ed. 1976–1995. *Prosopographisches Lexikon der Palaiologenzeit.* 12 vols. Vienna: Österreichische Akademie der Wissenschaften.

——. ed. 1994–1999. *Lexikon zur byzantinischen Gräzitat.* 3 fascicles (ongoing). (Veroffentlichungen der Kommission für Byzantinistik 6.) Vienna: Österreichische Akademie der Wissenschaften.

Treu, M. 1880. *Excerpta anonymi Byzantini.* Gymnasiums-Programm Ohlau.

Triandafyllidis, M. 1963 [1909]. "Die Lehnwörter der mittelgriechischen Vulgärliteratur." In M. Triandafyllidis, *Ἅπαντα,* 1: 299–494. Thessalonica: Aristotle University.

Triandafyllidis Institute. 1998. *Λεξικό της κοινής νεοελληνικής.* Thessalonica: Aristotle University.

Trumpf, J. 1974. *Anonymi Byzantini vita Alexandri regis Macedonum.* Stuttgart: Teubner.

Trypanis, C. A. 1981. *Greek Poetry: From Homer to Seferis.* London: Faber and Faber.

Tsavare, I. 1987. *Ὁ Πουλολόγος.* (Βυζαντινὴ καὶ νεοελληνικὴ βιβλιοθήκη 5.) Athens: Μορφωτικὸ Ἵδρυμα Ἐθνικῆς Τραπέζης.

——. 1993. "Το στέμμα και το κείμενο του *Πουλολόγου:* Μέθοδος και προκατάληψη." In N. Panagiotakis, ed., *Αρχές της νεοελληνικής λογοτεχνίας,* 1: 358–67. Venice: Biblioteca dell'Istituto Ellenico di Studi Bizantini e Postbizantini di Venezia.

Tsiforos, N. 1987. *Σταυροφορίες.* Athens: Ἑρμῆς.

Tsiouni, V. 1972. *Παιδιόφραστος διήγησις τῶν ζώων τῶν τετραπόδων: Critical Edition.* (Miscellanea Byzantina Monacensia 15.) Munich: Institüt für Byzantinistik und Neugriechische Philologie der Universität München.

Tsolakis, E. T. 1959. *Μιχαὴλ Γλυκᾶ στίχοι οὓς ἔγραψε καθ' ὃν κατεσχέθη καιρόν.* (Ἐπιστημονικὴ Ἐπετηρὶς Φιλοσοφικῆς Σχολῆς Παράρτημα ἀρ. 3.) Thessalonica: Aristotle University.

——. 1962. "Παρατηρήσεις στοὺς πρώτους στίχους τῆς «Διηγήσεως παιδιοφράστου τῶν τετραπόδων ζῴων.»" *Ἑλληνικά* 17: 318–34.

Turnbull-Kemp, P. 1967. *The Leopard.* London: Bailey Bros. and Swinfen.

Tüselmann, O. 1900. "Die Paraphrase des Euteknios zu Oppians Kynegetika." *Abhandlungen der königlichen Gesellschaft der Wissenschaften zu Göttingen, Philologische-Historische Klasse* N.S. 4.1.8–43.

Usmanov, L. 1999. *The Chechen Nation: A Portrait of Ethnical Features.* http://www.amina.com/article/chech_nati.html. Accessed September 2, 2002.

Valetas, G. 1947. *Ἀνθολογία τῆς δημοτικῆς πεζογραφίας.* 3 vols. Athens: Πέτρος Ρῖνος.

van der Valk, M. 1971–1987. *Eustathii archiepiscopis Thessalonicensis comentarii ad Homeri Iliadem pertinentes.* 4 vols. Leiden: E. J. Brill.

van Deun, P. 1993. *Hagiographica Cypria. Sancti Barnabae laudatio auctore Alexandro monacho.* (Corpus Christianorum. Series Graeca 26.) Turnhout: Brepols.

van Gemert, A. F. 1980. *Μαρίνου Φαλιέρου ἐρωτικὰ ὄνειρα.* (Βυζαντινὴ καὶ Νεοελληνικὴ Βιβλιοθήκη 4.) Thessalonica. Self-published.

van Gemert, A. F., and W. Bakker. 1987. "Die Belisariada: Mündliche Sage oder gelehrte Geschichte als Quelle des Verfassers." In H. Eideneier, ed., *Neograeca Medii Aevi: Text und Ausgabe. Akten zum Sumposion Köln 1986,* 327–56. Cologne: Romiosini.

Vasiliou, P. 1996. "Κριτικές Παρατηρήσεις στην «Παιδιόφραστο Διήγηση.»" *Ελληνικά* 46: 59–82.

Veloudis, G. 1977. *Ἡ φυλλάδα τοῦ Μεγαλέξαντρου: Διήγησις Ἀλεξάνδρου τοῦ Μακεδόνος.* Athens: Ἑρμῆς.

Verpeaux, J. 1966. *Pseudo-Kodinos. Traité des offices.* Paris: Centre National de la Réchérche Scientifique.

Vince, J. H., and A. T. Murray. 1935–1939. *Demosthenes.* 2 vols. (Loeb Classical Library.) Cambridge, Mass.: Harvard University Press.

Vincent, A. 1980. *Φορτουνάτος.* (Κρητικὸν θέατρον 2.) Iraklio: Ἑταιρεία Κρητικῶν Ἱστορικῶν Μελετῶν.

Vitti, M. 1978. *Ἱστορία τῆς νεοελληνικῆς λογοτεχνίας.* Athens: Ὀδυσσέας.

Vogel, F., and K. T. Fischer. 1888–1906. *Diodori bibliotheca historica.* 5 vols. Leipzig: Teubner.

Volan, A. 2000. "Last Judgments and Last Emperors: Byzantine Imperial Ideology and Eschatology in the Church of Agios Pavlos, Crete." Talk given at the Twenty-Sixth Annual Byzantine Studies Conference, October 26–29, 2000, Harvard University. (See also Byzantine Studies Conference 2000, *Abstracts of Papers* 26: 89–90.)

von der Mühll, P. 1962. *Homeri Odyssea.* Basel: Helbing und Lichtenhahn.

von Hammer, J. 1968 [1834]. *Narrative of Travels in Europe, Asia and Africa in the Seventeenth Century by Evliyá Efendí.* 2 vols. New York: Johnson Reprint Corporation.

Vryonis, S. 1971. *The Decline of Medieval Hellenism in Asia Minor and the Process of Islamization from the Eleventh Through the Fifteenth Century.* Berkeley: University of California Press.

Wagner, W. 1874. *Carmina Graeca Medii Aevi.* Leipzig: Teubner.

Walz, C. 1968 [1833–1835]. *Rhetores Graeci.* 3 vols. Stuttgart: Cotta.

Wattenbach, W. 1958 [1896]. *Das Schriftwesen im Mittelalter.* Graz: Akademische Druck- und Verlaganstalt.

Weigel, K. 1804. *Deutsch-Neugriechisches Wörterbuch.* Leipzig: Schwickert.

Wellmann, M. 1930. *Der Physiologus: Eine religiongeschichtlich–naturwissenschaftliche Untersuchung.* Leipzig: Dieterich.

Westerink, L. G. 1981. *Nicholas I, Patriarch of Constantinople, Miscellaneous Writings.* (Corpus Fontium Historiae Byzantinae Series Washingtonensis 20.) Washignton, D.C.: Dumbarton Oaks.

——. 1992. *Michaelis Pselli poemata.* Stuttgart, Leipzig: Teubner.

White, T. H. 1954. *The Book of Beasts: Being a Translation from a Latin Bestiary of the Twelfth Century.* London: Jonathan Cape.

Wilson, N. G. 1975. *Prolegomena de comoedia: Scholia in Acharnenses, Equites, Nubes*. Groningen: Bouma.

——. 1996. *Scholars of Byzantium*. 2d ed. London: Duckworth.

Winkler, J. J. 1989. "Leucippe and Clitophron." In B. P. Reardon, ed., *Collected Ancient Greek Novels,* 170–284. Berkeley: University of California Press.

Winterwerb, H. 1992. *Porikologos*. (Neograeca Medii Aevi 7.) Cologne: Romiosini.

Wratislaw, A. H. 1862. *Adventures of Baron Wenceslas Wratislaw of Mitrowitz*. London: Bell and Daldy.

Wrogemann, N. 1975. *Cheetah Under the Sun*. Johannesburg: McGraw-Hill.

Wünsch, R. 1967 [1898]. *Ioannis Lydi liber de mensibus*. Stuttgart: Teubner.

Xanthoudidis, S. 1911–1912. "Ἀντιπαρατηρήσεις εἰς τὰ τοῦ Wagner Carmina Graeca medii aevi." *Λαογραφία* 3: 614–21.

——. 1914. "Λέξεις Ἐρωτοκρίτου." *Ἀθηνᾶ* 26: 126–85.

——. 1927–28. "Διορθώσεις καὶ ἑρμηνεῖαι εἰς Διήγησιν παιδιόφραστον περὶ τῶν τετραπόδων ζῴων." *Byzantinisch-Neugriechische Jahrbücher* 5–6: 348–70.

——. 1980 [1909]. "Διορθώσεις εἰς τὰ ποιήματα Στεφάνου Σαχλίκη." In N. Panagiotakis and T. Detorakis, eds., *Μελετήματα Στεφάνου Ξανθουδίδου,* 153–79. Iraklio: City of Iraklio.

Zachariadou, E. 1989. "Holy War in the Aegean During the Fourteenth Century." In B. Arbel, B. Hamilton, and D. Jacoby, eds., *Latins and Greeks in the Eastern Mediterranean After 1204,* 212–25. London: Frank Cass.

Zampelios, S. 1859–1860. "Κόποι καὶ διατριβή." *Πανδώρα* 10: 370–75, 390–95, 414–18.

Zepos, I., and P. Zepos, eds. 1962 [1931]. *Jus Graecoromanum*. 8 vols. Aalen: Scientia.

Zervos, S. 1901. *Gynaekologie des Aëtios*. Leipzig: Fock.

——. 1909. "Ἀετίου Ἀμιδηνοῦ λόγος δέκατος πέμπτος." *Ἀθηνᾶ* 21: 7–138.

Ziolkowski, J. M. 1993. *Talking Animals: Medieval Latin Beast Poetry, 750–1150*. Philadelphia: University of Pennsylvania Press.

Zoras, G. T. 1954. *Ἄγνωστα κείμενα καὶ νέαι παραλλαγαὶ δημωδῶν ἔργων*. Athens: Σπουδαστήριον Βυζαντινῆς καὶ Νεοελληνικῆς Φιλολογίας τοῦ Πανεπιστημείου Ἀθηνῶν.

——. 1956. *Βυζαντινὴ ποίηση*. (Βασικὴ βιβλιοθήκη 1.) Athens: Ἀετός.

——. 1958. *Χρονικὸν περὶ τῶν τούρκων σουλτάνων*. Athens: University of Athens.

INDEX